INTERNAT
(20

FAULT LINES
ON THE FACE
OF CHINA

50

REASONS

WHY CHINA
MAY NEVER
BE GREAT

BY

DAVID   KARL
MARRIOTT & LACROIX

A LACROIX & MARRIOTT PROJECT

COPYRIGHT STATEMENT

CONTENTS

FOREWORD

This book is entitled 'Fault Lines On The Face Of China: 50 Reasons Why China May Never Be Great' and is the sum total of over 20 years of residency and work experience in China by its authors.

Before a single word was written, we had to consider those people who we knew would be deeply disturbed by the tone of our work - our Chinese friends and associates. We will lose some of them forever, since to them it will be unforgivable for Western guests enjoying the 'freedoms' of China, not available to its own citizens, to have betrayed their trust.

Certainly, we knew this book would initiate the classic 'hurt feelings of the Chinese people' response from most loyal citizens of China and even from those who will never actually read a single word of it. Lack of knowledge is not a barrier in a country where unified, mass condemnation of anti-Chinese 'imperialist propaganda' is the norm.

Negative sounding commentary is actively ferreted out within the People's Republic of China. Once identified, correctly or not, it is vilified, now most commonly on the internet where blogging is the 'anti-freedom of speech' weapon of choice.

Perhaps it is a little self-serving to appear to be in the throes of a heartfelt apology in the first few paragraphs when what follows is sheer negativity. But then many times during our stay in China we have given and received a large quantity of shallow head bowing.

The Chinese people cherish the past like a soul-searching beacon, and are blinded by the very light that they think is showing them the true path. China will learn little about the future from the aberrant past its citizens cling to like children who hope to never grow up.

'Fault Lines' demonstrates that as a society the Chinese are presently stumbling towards a precipice of profound calamity for the country of China, and because of globalization perhaps the rest of the world as well.

This book is *not* entitled '*Beauty Spots* on the Face of China: 50 Reasons Why China *Will* Be a Great Country' simply because, as writers of fact, we see, feel and understand the reality of today's China. Besides, the government of China, the Party, has been writing about the 'beauty' of China since 1949, circumventing the country's obvious faults and replacing them with cosmetic communist charms.

This book is also *not* entitled '*Analyzing* the Face of China: 50 Reasons Why China *May* or *May Not* Be Great' which would indicate a more balanced approach. However, the reader will not find the concept of balance within our '50 Fault Lines' simply because of the real lack of equilibrium inside China. With the present state of emergency in which we feel the nation exists, there is little time to waste.

The truth should not be balanced – it is or is not. Truth is the perfect fulcrum. All 50 fault lines we have identified on the face of China

5

are present now, currently festering and should not be hidden, soft-focused or balanced for warm hearted international public consumption.

In various stages of decay, all 50 fault lines are interconnected in a maze of history, tradition, communism, corruption, and ignorance. In fact, we were able to produce more than 75 fault lines deeply affecting China today. After careful consolidation, we have chosen the fifty that are most radically threatening China's hopes to be a viable world leader.

How important is it for books to be written that will encourage China's people to question, debate, and eventually come face to face with their country's inadequacies? Indeed, before they self-destruct trying to turn a growing mirage of false beliefs into the reality of a nation that can only be lost?

As Western writers lacking in Chinese cultural heritage and ethnicity, we did question our right to proceed. In the end, we felt the writing of warnings can only come from thinkers of a younger civilization, who frankly are more experienced in the theories of a multitude of themes that reflect on the building of a modern society.

As writers we indeed do find China perplexing, often feeling the undercurrent of hatred by the nation for anything Western. But as travelers of faraway lands, coming to this truly wonderful kingdom and searching for the nirvana of a logical future, we love it.

The adventure we sought, the clear vision we assumed would emanate from such a historic land, is now jaded by its present consumerist passions. We have long struggled, almost like missionaries, waiting for a profound decree from this new church of power called China.

We have watched as China's people are goaded by communist barkers to spend their lives and the money drained from their hard work, on shiny objects, trinkets, and the fakery sold along with attendant government corruption.

We are tired of the thinly veiled opinions of Western economic or 'cultural' experts, as well as those offered by Sinologists fresh from some ABC University or democratically elected government leaders on publicly funded trade tours. The new-market capitalists from Western democracies fall easy prey to Communist Party leaders offering warm handshakes and reflected 'teflon' smiles.

We are also tired of Western print journalists, erstwhile T.V. announcers, and practitioners of 'fair play journalism' breaking news stories that in the end must be balanced, even if the truth is clearly filled with inescapable horror.

With the recent economic downturn affecting powerful countries worldwide, China will surely feel the brunt of economic loss. Its young people, born since China's economic opening in 1978, have not suffered or experienced the trials of country-building that occurred from 1949 to 1977. Their experience is solely based on the rapid economic rise fed by masses of foreign investment and a sense of solipsism created and fuelled by the one-child policy. It is a profound change from the Mao era, when

6

everything was viewed in terms of communist goals and any expression of individual will was treated with distrust.

Protected from cradle to office, the young movers and shakers of New China can only expectantly visualize their upward mobility. Should the ground fall away beneath their feet, they will have absolutely no foundation in their personal history to prevent freefall.

This book is not a condemnation of China's hopeful future, but of its decaying present. Each of the 50 fault lines is meant to create essential discussion points, not only for Chinese nationals but for all of the world's people.

Today, as in the past, life for the Chinese citizen is directed by semantics issued by the Communist Party. A citizen should help his country 'rise peacefully,' he should 'act harmoniously' and he should promote 'socialism with Chinese characteristics.' In fact it is hard to imagine China without this continuous barrage of pseudo-positive political verbiage, which deflects its ability to deal with the negatives that must naturally occur in every society.

Even so, the Party has yet to initiate any catchphrase, buzzwords or mantra for what a Great China should represent to the world. It is a remarkable lack of political foresight and universal humanist ideology.

Perhaps in the smoke-filled boardrooms of China's corporate and government offices there will be discussions set around producing the super-semantics that will be unleashed on the world's populace in the future, words that will entail energy, creativity and the humanism required to lead the Chinese people and the nation into greatness.

The real truth behind the sound of the future will be much, much harder for the Party to provide.

Visions of horror, with names such as holocausts, the apocalypse and Armageddon are all well-known Western concepts of failed civilizations wreaking the last vengeance of mankind upon itself. In the near future however, Armageddon may well be Asian, and fully 'Made in China.'

Readers of 'Fault Lines on the Face of China: 50 Reasons Why China May Never Be Great' will feel the authors may have already defined the future of the Middle Kingdom as 'Armageddon with Chinese characteristics.'

For this we will not apologize.

David Marriott and Karl Lacroix
June 30th, 2010
2010china50@gmail.com

Reason 1
The Domestic Imperialists

A young Tibetan man stands outside a monastery in his homeland. He looks up at the clear blue sky around him, and then down to the white snow sparkling on the ground. His eyes are dazzled by its purity. His ears fill with the sound of the goats being shepherded along the road by a passing herdsman. In the distance, the Himalayas provide the perfect framing for this picture of serenity.

His mind calm, the young man steps over the threshold into the darkness of the monastery. Momentarily blinded, his eyes slowly adjust, while his mind is full of the brightness of the possibilities the monastery holds for him.

He is 18 years old, and he wishes to become a monk. He has come here to learn his faith. To embrace it as his father did, just like his grandfather and all the men in his family for hundreds of years.

The womb of the monastery is quiet. He walks in, coming to a larger room, his feeling of comfort and safety growing secure. Beyond the room he can hear the echoes of the monks' chanted prayers.

As his eyes adjust further to the gloom, he sees other artifacts of his intended religion – the bell, the traditional walking staff the monks use, and other symbols of their simple traditional life. He studies them closely.

Still, even though elated, he is disappointed because these are only symbols of tradition. They are not the real artifacts of tradition. Even the monastery where he will study is a reproduction of the original centuries-old building which was destroyed by the Han soldiers who came and stayed in 1950.

The icons that surround him are reproductions too. The originals were also destroyed – but not before all the gold, silver and jewels in them had been stolen by Han soldiers and citizens.

The holy books of his religion are modern copies too, since the priceless collections of woodblocks with which they used to be lovingly printed were burned by the Han years ago. Collections of blocks and books dating back two thousand years were destroyed overnight.

And then something else troubles the young man – the terms in which he is thinking these thoughts. In his minds the words of the Tibetan language flash, but they are interspersed with Putonghua, the Han language.

His own ancient language, suppressed until recently, is, now, being taught in some schools. But to learn it is impractical for the others of his generation who choose a secular life, since there is no future without Putonghua.

His mind is always full of the stories his father and grandfather told him, and of the thousands of years of glorious history before the Han.

9

His grandfather tells him that before this Han 'liberation' Tibet had more than six thousand monasteries. Six thousand monasteries full of monks and nuns, and the spirit of Tibetan culture.

After two waves of destruction, the first when the Han armies arrived and the second during the Cultural Revolution, when the Red Guards unleashed their destructive passions, there were just eight monasteries left. Among those destroyed was Samye, Tibet's first monastery, dating back to the seventh century. Gone. Forever.

Sometimes he thinks of what the Samye monastery must have looked like on that day in the hours before the hands of man destroyed what the spirit of man had created.

He tries not to remember the tales of the thousands of monks and nuns tortured and killed, the hundreds of thousands forcibly disrobed, defrocked of both their religion and their dignity.

And he knows that even today everything he does, says – everything he thinks, almost – is watched and judged and allowed – or not by the Han colonizers.

His language. His history. His religion. His freedom of thought. All lie just beneath the surface of his skin, hidden from the Han. On this first day of his initiation into monkhood, the hope of allowing his own culture to grow stronger, beneath his skin, not visible to the Han, makes him proud - makes him Tibetan.

He would have become a monk several years ago, but now the Han make it difficult for anyone under the age of 18 to join a monastery.

His culture must remain under his skin, since, officially, everything he sees around him belongs to the Han - everything - the monasteries, the land, the mountains, the sky, the air. [1]

As if China did not possess enough of Tibet, the Chinese government declared in May 2007 that all religious artifacts in all places of worship in Tibet belonged to the Chinese state.[2]

His thoughts are familiar to most Western people who understand hopes and dreams of freedom. But Han control of his country within the Chinese government makes his freedom an impossible dream.

The People's Liberation Army invaded Tibet in 1950. Though they called it a 'peaceful liberation,' it was in fact invasion – a land grab, an occupation, an act of war. No matter what the semantics of it, the result was clear. The free government of Tibet became defunct.

The Chinese knew that in a world weary of war no other powerful nation would come to the aid of Tibet. None did. Since that invasion, China has ruled Tibet with an iron hand.

In 2006, China completed building a direct rail link to Lhasa, the capital of Tibet. Though China has explained this as a way to bring economic growth to the county, in truth it is a chain to bind Tibet ever more firmly to China.

In the cities of Tibet today there are growing numbers of Han Chinese. Beijing is secretive about revealing precise population figures, and does not include the many Han staying 'temporarily' in Tibet, nor the large number of Han soldiers. Though official figures put the Han population in the capital, Lhasa, at around 25%, many observers say the real figure is more than 50%.

Tibetan frustration with Han control came to a head in 2008, in the run-up to the Olympic Games. Riots rocked the country and hundreds were arrested. China's reaction was swift, pouring armed police into the country, cutting off all access to the outside world, and imposing a curfew.[3]

A Tibetan filmmaker, Dhondup Wangchen, made a documentary interviewing Tibetans about their attitude to the Olympics. He was arrested in March 2008, but managed to escape the following July. He said that he had been severely beaten by police, and deprived of food and sleep. He was soon re-arrested, and in June 2009 was charged with 'inciting separatism.' The authorities would not allow his family-appointed lawyers to represent him, and he was sentenced to six years in prison.[4]

The severe security clampdown on Tibet was still in place two years later. In April 2010, an earthquake hit Qinghai Province, long viewed as part of Tibet and heavily influenced by Tibetan culture. Monks in the region were allowed to offer assistance to the victims of the earthquake. This represented a relaxation on the strict control of the movement of monks in the region, yet the thaw did not last long. Just days after the quake hit, China arrested a prominent Tibetan intellectual, Tagyal, also known by his pen name of Zhogs Dung. Tagyal had signed a letter, along with seven others, that suggested relief donations given to government agencies might end up stolen through corruption. Soon after this the monks were ordered to return to their monasteries.[5]

Other reports from the region suggested the real death toll was more than 10,000, rather than the official 2,000, and that the ferocity of the quake had been misreported as 7.1 rather than 6.9 on the Richter scale. This was done, it was claimed, to cover the fact that many recently-built schools, which by law should have been able to withstand a force 7.0 quake, collapsed.[6]

Hundreds of miles north a young Muslim girl in Xinjiang Province also considers her life and her future. She sees very clearly that every inch of her life, too, is controlled by Han colonizers.

Even their name for her country, 'Xinjiang' means 'New Frontier,' neatly encapsulating just how the Han view her homeland. Territory. Possession. Exploitation.

She is a Uighur, one of eight million in the region, but the area has traditionally also been home to many other cultures, such as Kazakhs, Kyrgyz, and Tajiks, each bringing their own customs and ways of life to the area, working together and respecting each other.

But now this multiculturalism is controlled, organized and governed from Beijing. The Uighur culture and its people are being swallowed up by the dominant Han culture. Government-pushed Han

11

businesses expand as human rights abuses disguised as anti-terrorist acts cause Uighurs to be fearful in their own homeland.

What stories does her father tell her? Tales similar to those told in Tibet.

One is of a 1997 massacre in the wake of Han authorities banning a 'meshrep,' a peaceful gathering of citizens who, in this case, hoped to tackle drug abuse and alcoholism. Han authorities even banned a Uighur football league that had been set up, and destroyed sports facilities.

Her father tells her his memories of the march that took place in Gulja (known in Putonghua as Yining), protesting this repression of culture and heritage. Now, fixed in her mind forever, are the details of the brutal crackdown that followed the killing of hundreds, maybe thousands, in the following days.[7] The Chinese authorities described the Uighur actions as 'terrorism.'

"It was our Tian'anmen," her father and others have said. "But the world took no notice."

Just who are the Han?

While it is common to use the phrase 'Chinese people,' this obscures the fact that China is home to 55 other ethnic minorities, each with their own history, culture, and social traditions. These range from large groups such as the Hui, with around eight million people to the Hezhen, with fewer than 5,000 people.[8]

However, more than 90% of today's Chinese people are of Han ethnicity, which has been converted into a nationality. While they claim ancestry going back to the mythical 'Yellow Emperor' of approximately 5000 years ago, Han ancestry can be dated with more historical certainty to the Han Dynasty (206BC to 220AD), from which they take their name.[9]

This was the dynasty that replaced the better-known Qin Dynasty, with its famous terracotta warriors of Xi'an, often on the itinerary of visiting foreigners.

These dynasties were located in what is today's northern China, and from there the Han spread, pressing further and further south. Their history is not one of consistent domination – for example, they were subject peoples in the Yuan (1279 to 1368) and Qing Dynasties (1644 to 1911).

Han identity has not always been a fixed matter, as at different points in history different minority groups have been categorized and de-categorized as Han. However, Han history is, nonetheless, one of constant expansion, geographical in that they controlled ever larger areas of land and through culture in the dominance of 'their' language, Putonghua or standard Mandarin which is the major uniting communication factor in China today.

Thus the term 'A Chinese person' lacks precision between political and ethnic understanding. For both Tibetan and Uighur people, the term 'Chinese' is not a cultural or ethnic description, but is a political application. For Han people, 'Chinese' is a cultural and ethnic description jointly, certifying a more 'qualified' position within society.

While the political sensitivity of Tibet does get a reasonable amount of world attention – most recently from a number of Hollywood film stars – China's oppressive activities garner much less press in Xinjiang.

Xinjiang, China's vast western colony is three times the size of France and the source of considerable mineral wealth. As with Tibet, China claims that Xinjiang is an 'inalienable' and 'historic' part of its territory.

Deeply religious and with all the historical overtones that implies, the Muslims of Xinjiang feel and sense that they are separate - different, with little prior history linked to China.

While Tibet and China have a long and complex relationship, there has often been a sense of continuance to it – for example, in the year 696 a Tibetan army came within 200 miles of Chang'an, the capital of that time, and in 763 the Tibetans successfully captured it.

At this time, Chang'an was one of the world's great cities, with about a million people living within the city walls and another million around them. Indeed, around this time China paid huge sums of money to Tibet to stave off further attack.

It was under the Qing Dynasty, who were of Manchu ethnicity (from what was beyond China's territory at the time but is now in the north of the nation) that Chinese territory expanded dramatically in the 18th Century. It was only in the 1750s that China was able to exert consistent direct control over Tibet for the first time.

And when the Qing Dynasty collapsed in 1911, so too did China's control over the nation. At that time, Tibet reasserted its nationhood and regained its independence as a country.

China's claim to Xinjiang also represents a very one-sided interpretation of history. Once again, it was the Qing who solidified control over the region. Up until the territorial expansions of the 1750s, China's relationship with the Xinjiang region, the precise borders of the area having changed many times in history, was flexible. Present-day Beijing's declarations such as "Since the Western Han Dynasty (206 BC - 2 AD), it has been an inseparable part of the unitary multi-ethnic Chinese nation" are flatly untrue.[10]

Indeed, over history the identity of the Uighur nationality has itself been difficult to determine. The term was most generally used to describe the people who lived in the Tarim Basin in Xinjiang, but as Islam spread into the area the term 'Uighur' faded from use, not coming back into widespread use until the 20th century.[11]

But no matter how you define the native people of Xinjiang – or the country of East Turkestan as it was called in its brief period of freedom between the collapse of the Qing Dynasty and the rise of the People's Republic of China – it is very clear that the people who have

13

traditionally lived there are very different to the Han. In terms of culture, language and even physical appearance they have little in common.

That culture is under profound attack from Han colonizers in the region, both by direct repression, and by indirect oppression in the form of the heavy influx of Han Chinese migrating to the region.

As with Tibet, China is consolidating its control over the region by connecting Xinjiang with an ever-developing infrastructure of new highways and rail lines into the region.[12]

In 1949, Han Chinese made up 5% of the Xinjiang region. By 1959 they made up 15%. By the year 2000, the area had nearly 40% Han, with 45% Uighur and the rest made up of other ethnic minorities.[13] Out of a total population of 19.25 million, said Chinese media, nearly 8.3 million were Han.[14]

These figures, however, are based on China's 2000 census. China today is secretive about current population figures. But in April 2005, for example, Beijing said 500 of 700 new government jobs in southern Xinjiang would be reserved for Han Chinese, and in September 2005 that year the Xinjiang Daily said that nearly a thousand additional Han cadres were being sent to areas where 'ethnic unrest' had occurred.

Beijing claimed the Han population of Xinjiang was still 40% in 2005, but this figure excluded the tens of thousands of long-term 'temporary' workers as well as PLA soldiers.[15] By now, it is certain that the Uighurs are a minority in their own nation.

This massive influx of settlers has energized Xinjiang's traditionally poor economy, allowing primarily the Han to enrich themselves. The Uighurs, like the other ethnic minorities, remain very much marginalized. In the major cities, traditional dwellings are destroyed to be replaced with modern shopping centers offering pricey consumer goods to the new Han settlers. New Chinese businesses in the area get help in the form of subsidies to compete with Uighur firms.

China regularly uses the excuse of post 9/11 'terrorism' to justify its harsh crackdowns, openly using PLA soldiers and the People's Armed Police Force to patrol villages and cities alike.[16]

The result of this is to leave Uighurs wary of speaking to foreigners, knowing it invites trouble from the Han security services.

Uighurs who occupy a prominent place in the community through social activities, religion or business do so at great risk. Rebiya Kadeer, for example, was a successful businesswoman and, because of that, was invited to join China's National People's Congress. The NPC body includes members from all of China's ethnic minorities, who are often required to wear the traditional clothes of their cultures for a display of unity in front of press cameras.

When Kadeer began to talk about human rights issues, she was jailed on charges of 'leaking state secrets.' Released after the sixth year of her eight year sentence on 'medical parole' she immigrated to the US. 'Medical parole' is the excuse Chinese authorities give when they release prisoners of conscience in response to international pressure. It is a formula that helps preserve the all-important concept of 'face.'

Before she left China, she was warned that if she engaged with members of the Uighur community or spoke out about humanitarian concerns, her business would be attacked and her children victimized.

Unrepentant, she continued to speak out and, in November 2006, says Amnesty International, "three of her sons were made to pay heavy fines on politically motivated charges. One of them received a prison sentence of seven years after he was reported to have been severely beaten, with risk of further torture or ill-treatment."[17]

In April 2007 another of her sons was jailed for nine years for 'secessionist activities.'

When George W. Bush met Kadeer in June 2007, China voiced its "strong discontent with and opposition to" this meeting with the "Chinese criminal."

Foreign Ministry spokesman Jiang Yu said "The U.S. .... wantonly interfere[s] in China's internal affairs, and China is strongly discontented with and opposed to it."[18]

Bush described the jailing of Kadeer's sons as "retaliation for her human rights activities."

When Kadeer was nominated for the Nobel Peace Prize, China described her as a "separatist monster" and an unfit mother to her children. She was additionally accused of trying to overthrow the government.[19]

Official Chinese vilification of Kadeer reached a new level of frenzy in 2009, in response to continued unrest in Xinjiang. The background to this unrest - the most serious in many years - took place far in the south of China. There, in the city of Shaoguan in Guangdong Province, a man whose job application to the Xuri Toy Factory had been rejected sought revenge on the firm by posting an online claim that six Xinjiang natives working at the factory had raped a Han woman.[20]

The rumor spread fast and led to attacks on Xinjiang natives in the city, two of whom were killed. Local police seemed uninterested in investigating the murders. This led to protests in Xinjiang, which soon boiled over into violent clashes. Violence between Xinjiang and Han left 200 dead and thousands injured.[21]

State media blamed Kadeer for inciting these riots - even though she lives in exile in America - and then, in the best traditions of a show trial, used members of her family still resident in China to condemn her. State media claimed that her daughter, Roxingul, wrote, "The riot was 100 percent caused by separatists in and outside China, including those controlled by my mother."[22]

China later announced it would demolish buildings belonging to the Kadeer family, including the trade center where she first rose to prominence.[23]

While foreign media were allowed into Xinjiang to cover the riots, domestic media were not. And, as always, communication methods such as Twitter and online communication were shut down. China's parade of 'openness' was for international consumption only.

In November 2009, China announced it had executed nine people for their part in the riots. Eight of them were Uighurs and the ninth was Han.[24] Four more people, assumed to be Uighurs based on their names, were sentenced to death in January 2010. An additional five people received the death penalty the following May.[25]

In April 2010, the top official in the region, Wang Lequan, was replaced. While no reason was given for this change, it seems likely that Wang, who had run the region since 1994, was removed for allowing the riots to become so serious.[26]

Other Uighurs have been executed on charges of 'splittism,' such as Ismail Semed, who was executed after a confession was coerced from him. "His trial did not meet minimum requirement of fairness and due process" said Nicholas Bequelin of Human Rights Watch.[27]

Also in 2007, Chinese authorities repeatedly denied Canada access to a Canadian citizen, Huseyin Celil, jailed for 'terrorist activities.'

"The case of Huseyin Celil is an internal affair and Canada has no right to interfere" said Foreign Ministry spokesman Liu Jianchao. "We hope Canada can take the right position on this case."[28]

Celil was jailed for life.

Canadian Foreign Minister Peter MacKay said that Canada "remains gravely concerned about allegations that Mr. Celil has been mistreated while in Chinese custody and possibly subjected to torture."[29]

Repression in Xinjiang had grown more intense in the run-up to the 2008 Beijing Olympic Games. The Chinese media ran numerous stories about terrorist threats to the games, using them to justify harsh repression in the region. Just four days before the games began media reported a major 'terrorist attack' which killed 16 policemen in the city of Kashgar. "Xinhua News Agency said the terrorists, identified as two Uygur men aged 28 and 33, hacked the injured policemen with knives, too. Fourteen policemen died on the spot and two on their way to hospital, and 16 were injured. No civilians were killed or injured, however. The two attackers have been arrested" said China Daily.[30]

But in September 2008 the New York Times ran a story casting doubt on this, citing the testimony and photographs of foreign tourists who witness the event. These tourists described a fight between Chinese paramilitaries and other uniformed men. They also said there was no explosion, though Chinese media had reported one.

The Times also mentioned a story in the North American edition of a Hong Kong newspaper, the Ming Pao, which quoted police official in Xinjiang talking of uniformed attackers. Subsequently Xinjiang police refused to talk about this.[31]

16

The Han sense of nationalistic fervor has also reached out to claim other areas that were historically independent.

Inner Mongolia, torn from its natural and cultural motherland, Mongolia, from 1949 onwards, is also experiencing ethnic dilution as Han business entrepreneurs come to the cities while others come to convert the historically open grassland, famous for the Mongol horse riders, into more lucrative farms.

The region's most revered son is the great Genghis Khan, who began to create the empire his grandson, Kublai Khan, would forge into the largest land empire the world has ever seen. It was Kublai who founded the Yuan Dynasty in China (1279 to 1368), after defeating the Han Chinese Southern Song Dynasty.

Genghis Khan's armies captured Beijing in May 1215, slaughtering so many that, according to one witness, even a year later the ground was still greasy with human fat.

When Genghis Khan died in 1227, the final resting place of his body remained a secret. Signs of digging were hidden, and guards were placed at a suitable distance from the grave. As grass and trees slowly covered the area, it became impossible to tell the great warrior's resting place.

Even so, the general area of his burial, on Burkhan Khaldun, the sacred mountain of the Mongols, is known to within a few square kilometers. There is a belief that his tomb contains stupendous riches, but the Mongols say it will never be found. [32]

Given the essentially nomadic nature of the Mongols, it is culturally appropriate that Genghis was at first memorialized with portable mausoleums made from the tent-palaces in which he had lived. Special attendants, known as Darkhad (sometimes spelled Darkhat), attended these mausoleums, passing on the duty from parents to children.

These mausoleums were protected by the later Qing Dynasty, but after the Qing fell a long period of turmoil saw the memorials moving into China proper.

After the founding of the People's Republic of China, Chinese control was slowly exerted over Inner Mongolia, though Outer Mongolia remained free of Communist control. Between 1954 and 1956, the Communist government replaced the portable mausoleums with a fixed building, and about 500 of the Darkhad attendants were dismissed, leaving only seven or eight. This mausoleum was destroyed along with countless other historical artifacts within it by the Red Guards during the Cultural Revolution. It was later rebuilt, with the destroyed relics replaced by replicas.[33]

But the rebuilt version is itself now being marginalized by the Genghis Khan theme park, which is being built on land appropriated from the Darkhads. They have been poorly compensated for the loss of their land, and they say tourists are often diverted to the new theme park without seeing the mausoleum, which lies in a separate enclosure that is obscured by the theme park.

The theme park is owned, operated and managed by a Han business group.

And today Genghis is a 'Chinese' hero, says the government, further robbing Mongolia of its true cultural heritage.[34]

Within China, its many ethnic minorities are also seeing the erosion of their cultures, as well as suffering overwhelming poverty, lack of education and poor medical care.

It was not until 2004 that China's government took specific notice of these highly marginalized groups, saying that "The state has, for the first time, listed poverty relief for ethnic minorities with relatively small populations as a focus of the state's development-oriented poverty reduction program."[35]

By 2007, poverty continued to be endemic among these minorities, with a fifth of them still living in absolute poverty.[36]

The Dongxiang minority, who live in mountainous Gansu Province, are also among China's poorest people. On average, people there have 1.1 years of schooling. They are so isolated that they have only the vaguest idea of the outside world. "I know what China is" said one native, Tie Yongxiang, when asked about the country in which he lived. "It is a country run by people who are supposed to be helping us."

Mr. Tie frequently has to beg to get enough food to live.[37]

While possessing a high degree of sensitivity to their own culture, and perceived insults to that culture, the Han people as an ethnic group show little true interest in other cultures.

In Tibet, in Xinjiang, and all across China's minority areas, Han citizens bring their culture with them. Local cultures simply cannot survive the onslaught.

Ethnic cultures in modern day China have become nothing more than tourist attractions for Han tourists on holiday. Tour buses filled with eager city travelers descend on ethnic villages, historical locations and religious centers, degrading ethnic culture into nothing more than a photo-opportunity.

The lesson learned by other cultures in developed countries is that ethnic diversity is the base of greatness. Rampant, uncaring economic progress often means the death of minor ethnic cultures. That process is now effectively taking place within China.

For some cultures, the only evidence of their existence will be that found in family photo-albums full of holiday snaps, kept on the bookshelves of wealthy Han tourists.

Reason 2
The Five Armies of Instability

In his 2007 New Year speech, China's president, Hu Jintao, called for peaceful development and social harmony. He said "2007 is an important year in building a socialist harmonious society under the guidance of the scientific development concept."[38] The Chinese People's Political Consultative Conference, at the end of its annual meeting in 2007, also called for social harmony.[39]

Harmony remains the much-repeated watchword today. The topic of the 2009 Beijing forum (a high-level government talking shop), for example, was 'The Harmony of Civilization and Prosperity for All - Looking Beyond the Crisis to a Harmonious Future.'

The ultimate political equation for China's communist leaders is a two-way equation – 'harmony equals social stability' and 'social stability equals harmony.' The real equation – which they will not tell the citizens of China – is that 'harmony plus social stability equals continued communist control.' China's Communist Party leaders, in short, are obsessed with 'harmony' and every major issue in modern Chinese society is approached through this theme.

The reason for this is in fact very simple. 'Harmony' is a codeword that means 'power' and 'control.' Harmony, for the Party, means that the people of China should subjugate the individual problems of their own lives and trust to communist leadership. Rather than provide a meaningful response to the various problems facing China today, the Party is solely focused on maintaining power.

Anything that questions the Party's right to power becomes a threat to 'harmony' and thus peace and happiness in China are explicitly linked to a lack of political freedom. Thus, in the minds of many Chinese people, not expressing any interest in the political future of China becomes a sign of patriotism and good citizenship.

The harmony-peace-stability equation is far too simplistic to guarantee more than a temporary peace. Even though the Communist Party has done a highly effective job in creating a country in which individuals are afraid to speak out, it faces a number of problems so huge, and yet so unique, that armies of citizens will be formed, each developed from a specific social condition.

In this book, we discuss Five Armies of Instability, each army of which is capable in itself of creating disturbances and imbalance negative enough to destabilize even the most totalitarian government's 'harmonious' controls. These five armies are not staffed with military experts or legionnaires, but are made up of citizens who have a particular disabling burden the government has thrust upon them intentionally or through neglect.

19

Already, the forces of these armies are reluctantly growing in number and in most cases are blindly unobserved by the government. These are not dissidents, not revolutionaries per se. These are the human result of tampering with nature or the inattention of those in power to reach out with a helping hand.

The Five Armies

The 1st Army – The Poor.
(See also - Reason 11 - Crossing the Line for a Penny)

Location: Primarily China's rural areas, but recently the poor have filtered throughout the entire economic landscape, especially to the cities where the scraps from the tables of the middle class are plentiful.

Gender: Male and female equally.

Strength: 55 million (Chinese estimate) to 150 million citizens (World Bank estimate) all based on earnings of US$1 per day or less.

Education Level: Low. Limited educational facilities in poor areas plus high education fees where schools are available makes study for advancement impossible for most.

Historical Precedent: Absolutely. Poverty has frequently been a driver of change in dynastic China.

Threat Level: Critical. When people perceive they have little left to lose, they revolt.

Political Objective: Fathers want reasonable jobs, mothers want a place to live and children want hope. All they get from the government is dreams couched in political rhetoric which simply instills a sense of hatred for politics and politicians.

The face China presents to the world is one of a prosperous and rising economy. Modern China's image is one of soaring new skyscrapers and multi-billion dollar civil engineering projects on a scale unmatched elsewhere in the world. But there is another face of China that is kept out of sight – the nation's millions of poor. In 2007, China had more than 20 million people who lived on less than US$88 per year, and another 35 million earning less than US$126 a year. And according to the World Bank, 150 million Chinese people earn less than a dollar a day. The 2009 World Bank report also indicated that poverty relief was becoming harder in China.[40]

Historically, widespread levels of poverty have often caused revolution in China. The first emperor of the Ming Dynasty (1368-1644), Zhu Yuanzhang, began life as a peasant. He later took shelter in a Buddhist monastery. This had to close due to lack of funds, whereupon he became a beggar. At this time, China was ruled by the Mongol Yuan Dynasty, and rebellions and protests were becoming widespread. Zhu Yuanzhang took control of one group of rebels, and from that position went on to conquer the nation.

In practical terms, China's government today offers very little to its poorest citizens. While espousing 'harmony' and 'stability' in the countryside it does nothing concrete to ease the plight of these citizens, many of whom belong to China's ethnic minorities. In 2006 in China there were 80,000 protests in the countryside areas. But these 80,000 protests are a fractional indication of the chaos the 1st Army of Instability is capable of if left behind by China's economic success. China's countryside could be roiled by demonstrations and protests as the poorest members of society realize they can throw off the Party control that has locked them in perpetual misery.

Solution: Rather than view the problem of the poor as a statistical matter, China must view it as a humanitarian matter. The poor are not helped by being placed on the 'positive' side of an artificially low poverty line. Treating the poor with basic human dignity would alleviate the anger this army feels. The government is unlikely to offer the poor any remedy soon regardless of how big its foreign reserves grow.

The 2nd Army – The Only Children.

(See also - Reason 14 - The Glass Children)

Location: The result of the one-child policy forms overwhelming numbers within China's economic centers – they are primarily privileged city dwellers. They share little relationship with people in the countryside.

Gender: Male and female, and almost exclusively Han Chinese.

Strength: 100 million and growing, due to enforcement of the one-child policy. They are in fact the ultimate 'me' generation.

Educational Level: With the highest level of education ever seen in the history of China, they have excellent communication skills not only in Chinese but in English. In addition, 2nd Army women will form a second front politicized by feminist thinking, possibly directing this army's democratic motivation.

Historical Precedent: None. This army represents a social phenomenon unseen in any other society in world history, a completely artificially manufactured group of humanity.

Threat Level: Severe politically, since members also come from within the Party, and will suffer the worse casualties should conflict break out relative to change of government. Physically - powder puffs.

Political Objective: Their weakness is that they will wish to continue to be rich even as the government falls, trying desperately to maintain their lifestyles, all the while assuming that they should be the next leaders of China. Their trained intellects will allow them to reach a level of cooperation with each other that will be essential to the survival of the country.

China's one-child policy has created a huge generation of single children, numbering over 100 million. They tend to be more city-based than countryside-based since it is in the cities that the policy was first implemented and has been most rigorously enforced.

This 2nd Army of Instability will eventually be motivated by a new Chinese concept of freedom. In money terms alone they will always be among China's elite, and they will expect intellectual freedoms above and beyond what the government is willing to give them.

They face a different burden – the psychological warping created by the excessively cosseted upbringing many of them have had, combined with a selfish outlook and lack of interpersonal skills generated by growing up without brothers or sisters.

Emotionally, the 2nd Army of Instability also has vast reserve forces, the 400 million brothers and sisters (imagined ghosts) they should have had but who were denied birth by the authoritarian policies of the Party.

The members of this army, by their nature, tend to be isolationist. China's single children are not gregarious. However, these 100 million only-children will be forged into an army when they reject the theories that denied them the possibility of a well-adjusted life and happy family structure, all by a government that forced their parents to take part in the biggest social engineering experiment the world has ever seen.

Solution: Most difficult, since the government intellectualizes through education, thus forcing them to maintain their economic expansion. Since nothing like this army has been seen in history, there are no previous solutions available. Coping with the psychological problems of 100 million people would be an exceedingly difficult matter for a country with a well-developed body of psychologists. In China, where mental health continues to be a taboo topic, a meaningful solution to the problems of this army may well be impossible.

The 3rd Army -The Migrant Workers.
(See also - Reason 26-The Migrant School of Revolution)

Location: Originally from China's countryside, now laboring in its cities, it is their distance from their families and homes that makes them most dangerous in the fact that they are building a glorious society for others.

Gender: Mostly large groups of males, sometimes thousands of miles away from their families.

Strength: 200 million, and rising by 13 million per year.

Educational Level: Basically uneducated, but full of experience and able to deconstruct (re-destroy on purpose) what they have built in the way of infrastructure.

Historical Precedent: Not in China. The social mobility that has allowed the members of this army to seek work in the country's cities has only become feasible in recent years. For much of China's modern history, as well as its longer history, social movement was strictly controlled. However, the members of this army are roughly akin to the US labor movement of the early 20th century.

Threat Level: Front-line troops. The segments of this army are already involved in confrontations with local governments. Their power lies in the interconnectivity from one building site to another, from one city to another. They will be the first to die.

Political Objective: A place in the New China that they have built. They want to bring their families to the city, and they want an honest day's pay – on time – for an honest day's work.

Modern China is being built and serviced by legions of migrant workers, mostly men, who travel from the impoverished countryside areas to the cities in search of better wages. While there is a seemingly endless supply of unskilled jobs available, the migrants who do them face unscrupulous bosses, excessive working hours, minimal safety measures, low quality housing and extremely limited job benefits. On top of this they face high levels of discrimination from urban residents who feel countryside people are beneath them.

The 3rd Army of Instability, though drawn from the countryside, differs from the 1st Army of Instability. The troops of the 3rd Army have worked in China's rich and successful cities. They are the people who have built the infrastructure that has allowed China's economy to succeed, yet they have been denied the fruits of that success.

Solution: Possible. Eventually China's need for migrant workers will diminish as it completes its necessary urban construction and moves towards developed-country status. The anger of the 3rd Army can be minimized if the government takes steps now to prepare for this eventuality. By ensuring decent accommodation and good social services for the members of this army, as well as other avenues of employment, the needs of this army might be answered. Perhaps the last city the migrant workers could build would be one for themselves.

The 4th Army - The Criminals.

(See also - Reason 29 - Blue China Crime, Reason 34 - White China Crime, and Reason 39 - Red China Crime)

Location: Nationwide and in every segment of society, but primarily located in China's cities – where the money is.

Gender: Almost exclusively male, but can be supported by female office staff, girlfriends, and family members, especially for White and Red China Crime. This group is divided into three sections -- Blue China Crime, which involves theft and bodily harm, White China Crime, which involves economic theft and corruption, and Red China Crime, which involves political graft and corruption.

Strength: Unknown – but having a disproportionate value of strength because of the fear they generate, certainly in the case of the Blue China Crime group.

Educational Level: Dependent on 'color.' A greater amount of money stolen or graft can often reflect a higher educational level of the individual concerned.

Historical Precedent: None to this extent. The variety of opportunity created by the clash of capitalism and socialism has opened the door for extensive crime beyond anything seen before.

Threat Level: Extremely critical. The 4th Army is busy destroying the public's faith in the Party's ability to control the criminal element in society since Deng Xiaoping opened up China in 1979. Elements of this army are reducing public trust right across the board.

Political Objective: None. Completely selfish motivation leaves no time for political theories.

Crime is rampant in China today. But in its bid to promote 'harmony' and 'stability,' China's government downplays the extent of the problem, making it hard to put a precise number on the size of this army.

In 2006 4.65 million criminal cases were investigated. Within the Party, around 40,000 cases of corruption are investigated annually, and in 2006 nearly 100,000 members were disciplined for this and other misdemeanors. Most of these were at lower levels. While corruption is endemic in the Party, those at higher levels are generally immune from prosecution.

The number of people involved in financial corruption is also unclear, but the fact that banking fraud reached nearly US$100 billion in 2005 indicates the extent of the problem. To these areas of criminality must be added the growing number of violent and petty crimes perpetrated by those at the bottom of society who have been shut out of China's economic rise but see clearly the good things it has brought to other citizens.

Crime has always been part of human society. But the sheer scale and extent of crime in China makes it a new phenomenon, and the level of institutionalized corruption within the government is on a scale unmatched anywhere else on the planet.

The 4th Army of Instability differs profoundly from the other armies in that its members, in general, wish to remain low-profile. Though within the Party there are extensive corruption rings, in general the members of this army operate as a family/friends unit or in small groups. Nonetheless, these people still count as an army in terms of the effect they are having on China.

The sheer scale of money being stolen by government members – both directly from government coffers and via extortion to citizens denied the right to protest by China's weak legal code – drags down the whole nation's success and stokes resentment among the population at large.

Solution: Possible, but unlikely. While Blue China Crime can be solved by an increase in the competence of China's police force, the solution to White China Crime and Red China Crime relies on democracy.

Democracy allows the public to hold government members accountable, thus eroding the power of Red China Criminals and reducing their ability to protect White China Criminals. However, since the Party will never allow the public to hold accountability over any but its most minor members, the likelihood of stopping the 4th Army is slim.

The 5th Army - The Single Man.
(See also - Reason 43, Can You Trust Men to Hold Up Half the Sky?)

Location: Nationwide, but concentrated in the countryside areas, where the pressure to have male children is strongest.

Gender: 100% Male

Strength: 30 million to 43 million and growing, relative to the number of ultrasound scanners often in illegal operation.

Educational Level: Not to be confused with single-child family males, these men have low education and generally work as laborers.

Historical Precedent: None. A super-aberration caused by traditional gender beliefs, and enhanced by the government's one-child policy.

Threat Level: A silent minority with incredible destructive power, waiting for a catalyst to express their anger, first against women they cannot have, and then against the government officials who restrict their movement.

Political Motivation: None. However, they will have one unifying factor – the desire to express anger which they will exercise in groups, in similar nature to the 'gang' structure operating in the West.

The Chinese cultural preference for male children, combined with the one-child policy and easy access to fetal gender scanning and abortion-on-demand has led to a growing gender imbalance in China, smaller in the cities but large (and growing rapidly) in the countryside areas, where traditions remain at their strongest. So many more boys than girls are being born that it is currently estimated one of out every ten male children today will not be able to marry.

Solution: Impossible. In the case of the 5th Army of Instability, it is already too late. Even if China were able to equalize gender birth rates today – something that is simply not possible -- the unbalanced number of male children born in previous decades will not be able to find wives. They will move through the demographic pyramid of China always alone, unable to marry or settle down. As they seek an outlet for their frustration, rape, prostitution and the kidnapping of women will increase.

These armies represent a colossal problem beyond the ability of Beijing to handle. Yet Beijing is giving very little thought to the looming catastrophe that they clearly indicate. The Party, in its obsessive quest for 'harmony' and 'stability' has kept a very tight lid on these problems, either downplaying them or refusing to acknowledge them.

That just increases the pressure. While the strength of the Party – backed by the huge force of the People's Liberation Army and the People's Armed Police – is currently able sit on it to keep the lid firmly jammed on, it will not be able to do so indefinitely.

When the pressure does finally escape, the explosive force on China will be profound.

Reason 3
Children – The Endangered Species

As writers living in China we have become constant surveyors. Asking questions is easy since most Chinese are eager to explain their life, culture and feelings.

One question we pose to almost everyone we meet socially is, "Who loves their children more - Chinese parents or Western parents?" The response invariably comes quickly with the firm belief that the answer is irrefutable. Chinese parents!

Sometimes we paste a forlorn look on our faces, if only to gauge the sensitivity of our subject under question. Quickly they offer, "Well, I am sure you love your children in a different way…culturally speaking."

Of course it is true that Chinese families love their child (most often a single child, as allowed by the one-child policy) a great deal and expend great effort and finance to prove that. Chinese parents are often overwhelmed, complying with the demands made by their pint sized Emperors and Empresses.

But it seems that China loves its children only one child at a time, because nationally there are thousands of youngsters suffering horrible deaths and injuries every year.

According to state figures released by the Chinese Disease Prevention and Control Center in 2007, 35,000 children are injured or killed in traffic accidents every year and altogether 70,000 children are killed in accidents.

That's a shocking figure. But is it accurate? In 2003, the National Women and Children's Working Committee of the State Council (one of China's highest political bodies) said that 100,000 children were killed every year, and 400,000 disabled.

But the very next year, the Chinese media reported that 200,000 children were killed every year. And all these figures only include children under 14 years old.[41] And in 2008, media were saying the annual number of children killed in road accidents was 16,000, not 35,000 as stated in 2007.[42]

Yet, according to Professor Zhang Ling'en, vice-chairman of the Chinese Emergency Medicine Society's pediatric division, "All the injuries and deaths could be prevented if proper measures are taken."[43]

In 2007, three *years* after Professor Zhang made that comment, a spokesman for the Chinese Center for Disease control said the same thing -- "Most road accidents involving children are preventable."[44] More astonishingly still, this comment came at the end of the *first* comprehensive look at children involved in traffic accidents ever carried out in China, which was only completed in April 2007.

But it is not just on China's roads that little seems to be done about the endless number of young victims.

Just like in any country, children in China are full of high spirits. And surely the hundreds of youngsters at Tutang Middle School in eastern China in November 2006 were full of laughter and joy when their classes ended, all the more so since they had been cooped up in school until 8.30pm on a Saturday. But as they swarmed down the stairs in their hurry to get out of the school, students began to fall over each other.

Their exodus became a stampede in which five girls and a boy were crushed to death, and 11 more were seriously injured. Perhaps the outcome would have been different if there was someone supervising the students, as the school rules required. But unfortunately most of the teachers were on the first floor grading papers.[45]

And no lessons seemed to be learned from the tragedy, since a very similar event took place in 2009. Eight students were killed and 26 seriously injured in a stampede at Yucai High School, in Hunan Province. It began when about 400 students were released from their evening study session at 9.10 p.m. Due to heavy rain they all dashed for the same entrance near to the dorms. One student, running up the narrow, damp stairs, slipped and fell, leading to many others falling and being crushed.

But the rain was not the only reason the students had to hurry; twenty minutes after the study session ended the dorm lights would be turned out.[46]

Recent years have seen a boom in child trafficking across many developing countries. China suffers too.

There are two main reasons for this; poverty and tradition. Poverty drives poor countryside parents to migrate to the cities for work, thus leaving their young children vulnerable to other groups out to make money by seizing them to work as beggars, thieves, sex slaves or to be sold to would-be parents.

Tradition leads to a trap for children because tradition says it is vital for a married couple to have a child, and preferably a male one. This makes couples who cannot have children – or who do not want the risk of having a female child – ready to buy a male baby. In just one city, Kunming, in one year, 200 children were kidnapped.

It is surprising where this figure of 200 comes from. It was given by a man called Wang Xingpu in 2004. Was he a social worker? A police detective? A concerned government official? No. He was a migrant working within the city. He had two sons and a daughter, but the boys were stolen from his home. It was while trying to find his sons that he met many other parents in the same situation, and compiled his list of 200 children, all between one and six years old, who had been kidnapped from the area.[47]

Between 2002 and 2003, police freed more than 42,000 kidnapped women and children. More up to date figures are not available, since, as Wang Xingpu found out, China does not keep nationwide data.

Indeed, such is China's attitude to this problem "that some local government officials don't consider buying children to be a crime," as one reporter for China Daily wrote.[48]

Baby girls are bought and paid for as potential future brides. In China today there is a growing shortage of girls, as testing to determine the gender of a fetus and abortion on demand allows parents to strive for a male child. That's why some people resort to buying baby girls. In 2003, police managed to break up one baby smuggling ring. They found 28 newborn girls hidden on a bus in southern China's Guangxi Province.

The babies were jammed into plastic bags with their arms and legs tied, as if they were livestock, not precious human beings.

This particular gang had stolen about 200 babies, very few of whom were recovered, leaving their parents to a life of heartache and pain. Police broke up another gang in 2004 that was responsible for stealing 76 babies.[49]

Youngsters also are kidnapped to be trained to work as pickpockets or beggars. The charity Save the Children estimated that 'tens of thousands' of children are stolen from China's poor western regions for this purpose.[50]

In 2005 China's courts sentenced a gang that had stolen 56 children, all under the age of five. This gang would either break into people's homes, stealing the babies from the parents at knifepoint, or would grab the children when parents were distracted in public venues such as parks and supermarkets. Only 25 of the stolen children were rescued.[51]

Most of the victims were children of migrant workers. As we've said in reason two, China's migrant workers have a grinding and unforgiving life. With so many migrant workers attracted to the cities in hope of earning a decent wage, China today has an estimated 23 million children who are left behind, to be cared for perhaps by a single parent, or grandparents – or more often no-one at all.[52]

It was only in 2008 that China implemented the 'National Plan of Action to Combat Human Trafficking.' Yuan Xiaoyin, an official at the Ministry of Public Security, said "Twenty-six ministries will discuss details of the plan and how to carry it out in a coordinated way." Given the labyrinthine nature of bureaucracy in China, it might be wondered whether so many different ministries getting involved in the plan is a step forward or backwards.[53]

In 2009, police solved more than 4,000 cases of trafficking of women and children, making 6,200 arrests and catching 1,000 gangs involved in the practice. But many children remain lost. Cheng Zhu, whose own daughter was kidnapped in 2005, now spends his days searching for her and almost 3,000 other lost children. Cheng set up the 'Parents of Lost Children League' in 2009. Like so many parents in his situation, he has very limited resources to rely on, and operates the league on a shoestring budget.[54]

Media announced in 2009 that a DNA bank was being set up to more effectively allow identification of recovered stolen children. Reports also stated that the true figure for kidnapped children could still be as high as 20,000 per year. Shockingly, there is still no official figure for just how many children are kidnapped each year.[55]

But there is another group of children in China who also face a questionable future – the children of China's convicts. According to China's Ministry of Justice, there are about 600,000 children under 18 in this group. There is no government department to look after them. The luckier children are passed around between relatives who have little interest in them, but many are simply abandoned altogether to become street urchins. Nearly all of them live below the poverty line, and face contempt and abuse.

Yang Mei, a social worker at Dalian Children's Village, one of China's very few facilities for such dispossessed children, says "Chinese people have some traditional ideas, in that if your father commits crimes, your son will be a criminal too." Even more tragically, this home is always short of funds, and China's government makes it almost impossible for its kind-hearted operators to get international funds.[56] They have to use their own earnings and life's savings instead. Possibly this goes to explain media reports in late 2007 that said the staff at the village had used a large proportion of donations to pay off their own expenses. Or maybe the truth is that corruption is simply endemic in every area of life in China.[57]

Perhaps, with the pressures of school life and negative social attitudes, it is no surprise that suicide is a major problem among young people. A survey of more than 140,000 high school students found that 20% had considered suicide and 6.5% had made concrete plans to kill themselves. The report found that about 50% of young people felt lonely and 40% had persistent sleeping problems.

The researchers who ran the survey said this was because of a cultural unwillingness to talk about feelings and the lack of ways to explore self-identity. When children were asked to describe their ideal world, they drew pictures of themselves without the restrictive school uniforms and regulation haircuts they have to wear, and free of the control of parents and teachers.[58]

A similar survey in 2008, in the southern city of Shenzhen, found that 12.1 percent of teenage students in the city had thought about committing suicide, 6.6 percent of them had made plans for suicide and 2.2 percent of them had tried to commit suicide in the year leading up to the survey. "As far as I know, the psychological problems are equally common in other cities," said Zhou Li, a director with the Shenzhen Disease Control and Prevention Center.[59] Her words were borne out by another 2008 survey, in another city in the same province, which found that 17% of junior high school girls had contemplated suicide.[60]

Tragically, it is not only the surroundings and social pressures that can pose such a danger to children in China today. Those who you would expect to care most of all – the teachers – can be a threat as well.

A primary school teacher in Qinghai Province was jailed in December 2006 for 18 years for raping a ten-year old pupil. The teacher, Yang Changzhong, 48, had instructed the girl to bring her homework to his office, where he then assaulted her. Shockingly, it came out at his trial that he had performed obscene acts on ten other girls between the ages of six and nine in the school.[61]

It is a combination of the cultural tradition of obeying the teacher combined with a lack of sexual awareness that leads to such terrible events. According to the Shanghai Star, 'One eight-year-old girl told her parents that her teacher liked to put her on his legs and caress her body. She asked her parents if that meant the teacher liked her.'[62]

Speaking in November 2009, Zhang Wenzhuan, vice-director of the Beijing Youth Legal Aid and Research Center, said that molestation by teachers is a national problem in China. Zhang's organization is the only legal aid center for minors in the whole of Beijing.[63]

One survey found that 52% of children had never been told about sexual assault.[64] Because sex education is such a low priority, teenage abortions are also on the rise, with thousands of girls needing abortions in Beijing alone.[65] We will return to the topic of sexual abuse in Reason 49, 'Daughters, Wives and Mothers in Fear.'

Teachers who are motivated to devise their own disciplinary techniques also pose a threat to schoolchildren in China.

In October 2006, in the northwestern province of Shaanxi, a teacher found that two girls in his class had a hair curler and letter among their belongings. As a punishment for this, he forced them to drink a bottle of 'baijiu,' a very strong spirit alcohol around 40% to 50% proof. A boy who attempted to speak up for them was beaten by this same teacher. The girls ended up in hospital.[66]

At the Guilin Dance Vocational School, located in the southern Chinese province of Guizhou, 22 youngsters were given 'work experience' in September 2006 as bar girls in the city of Hangzhou, hundreds of miles away from their homes. The girls, aged 15 or 16, were expected to persuade customers to buy drinks – and were often fondled by those same customers. The girls were told to say they were 18 and were instructed to tell their families 'happy news.' These children were, of course, poor. They were 'paid' 100 yuan a night (about US$13), but half of this went to an agent and 25 yuan of it went to the school. [67]

Student Zhang Jixin, 14, died in 2009 after being made to stand outside his dormitory building all night, in sub-freezing temperatures, as a punishment by a teacher. Another teacher at the school, located in Shandong Province, said that the student "died comfortably… without any pain on his face." The teacher who set the punishment had "temporarily left his job because of the pressure mounting on him" said media. Local police said the death was accidental. "We tend to believe Zhang's death was caused primarily by unknown health problems. But there's still a possibility that the freezing contributed to his death" they said.[68]

Another brutal form of punishment took place in October 2009. A schoolteacher named Sun Qiqi punished 63 'disobedient' children, all aged between three and five, by pricking them with a hypodermic needle. She was later jailed for three years.[69]

One teacher perpetrated an even more horrific crime back in September 2006. Li Hengyi, 28, savagely kicked and punched one of his pupils, 11-year-old Zhang Yaoyi, and then picked up her motionless body and threw it out of the fourth floor window. It turned out he had a history of beating his pupils dating back many years. He had also been previously diagnosed as mentally ill, and because of this he did not face criminal punishment for the murder.[70]

In the words of Zhang Yaoyi's distraught mother, "Why did the school hire a mental patient to serve as a teacher? Who will give my daughter a fair judgment?"

In the early and middle years of this decade, there suddenly appeared a number of newspaper reports about school invasions and slayings. Does this mean such events did not happen before, or that they were just censored as is common in China? As a news phenomenon, it seemed to feed on itself with a rash of such incidents in rapid succession.

The killings seemed to begin in earnest one morning in August 2004, when children at a Beijing kindergarten were happily playing in the schoolyard. Their happiness did not last long as the school gatekeeper, Xu Heping, began attacking them with a knife. Xu had locked an exit door, giving the students no way to escape. When the schoolteachers heard their terrified screams of horror they ran out and bravely tackled Xu. But by the time they had disarmed him, one child was dead and 15 were injured, along with three teachers. The youngest child was two and the oldest was six. Police investigations revealed that Xu had been diagnosed with mental illness.[71]

In September 2004, a man armed with a knife broke into a daycare center in the city of Suzhou, and slashed 28 children. The only reason not one child was killed was that the police responded quickly. When they got to the school, they found that the 41-year-old perpetrator was about to ignite gasoline and explosives.[72]

No word of the damage done to the minds of the students.

Within ten days of this, a bus driver called Jia Qingyou knifed 25 kids and kidnapped a nine-year-old girl at the No. 1 Experimental Primary School in northern Shandong Province. Again, no-one died, and the police successfully rescued the girl. However, the other boys and girls were hospitalized for wounds to their arms and faces.

What had led Jia to such a brutal attack? He had argued with a local resident named Shen, and was seeking revenge. But, being unable to find Shen, he took out his anger on the innocent and unsuspecting children.[73]

In October 2004, four children were stabbed to death and another 12 injured at a primary school in Hunan Province. What made this even more appalling was that the killer was a teacher at the school. No reason was given in the media for this attack.

In that same month a career criminal, Fu Hegong, broke into another Beijing kindergarten looking for something to steal. He was discovered by a teacher on duty, whom he raped and murdered, before killing a five-year-old boy who also saw him and stuffing the body in a washing machine. At his trial, in which he was sentenced to death, he expressed sorrow for his mother but none for the families of his victims.[74]

And then in the very next month, November 2004, another attack happened. A man wielding a knife broke into a dormitory in the city of Ruzhou, in Henan Province, and murdered another eight children. The killer escaped after the murders, but was apprehended the next day when his mother alerted the police. The killer, a 21-year-old named Yan Yanming, was executed two months later, at which time the brief coverage in the Chinese media gave the number of murder victims, all aged 16 and 17, as a total of nine.[75]

The murders continued in 2005. In October that year, a 33-year-old man, Liu Shibing, launched an assault on a school in eastern Anhui Province, using guns he had made himself. He injured 16 children and apparently was jealous because he was childless himself.[76] Locals claimed he'd said, "I have no children and I [will] kill other people's children." Yet this, and the fact that he had suffered from mental illness, seems to have alerted no-one to just how potentially dangerous he was.

In May 2006, a 19-year-old man called Bai Ningyang broke into a classroom on the second floor of a kindergarten in the city of Gongyi in Henan Province. He locked the door and then emptied two canisters of gasoline that he was carrying around the classroom before setting it on fire. Two children, both aged five, died and 13 more were injured. Reports said that before Bai locked the doors he sent one pupil out of the room because he knew the child's parents.

Locals also said that the reason Bai launched the attack was that he had been romantically rejected by the class teacher.[77] Other reports, however, said Bai had quarreled with a villager who stopped him using a newly paved road, and that his anger over this had led to his arson.

Just a few days later in the same province Yang Xinglong, a farmer, killed a neighbor after an argument and then broke into the local primary school. There, armed with a knife, he held 19 youngsters captive and murdered one before being subdued after a police sharpshooter wounded him.[78]

In December 2006, a 33-year-old attacked a group of primary school students in the city of Urumqi as they waited to cross a road to get to school. One student died on the spot and another died later in hospital, and three other children and a teacher were injured. The killer, Abuduhalik Mijiti, was arrested soon after.[79]

We spoke to a senior member of Shanghai's Education Board in November 2006. She told us she was well aware of the problem, but that the city was taking no preventative measures since they were sure it would not happen again. But with our experience of copycat killings in the West, we knew it was only a matter of time before it did happen again. We suggested that the government could post a soldier from China's People's Liberation Army outside each school. With the huge manpower of China's army this would surely pose little logistical problem, and would certainly make the seemingly endless parade of the jealous, angry or mentally unstable think twice before murdering children. But the member of the education board was unwilling to bring our suggestion to her superiors.

In 2007 truck driver named Luo drove his truck into a crowd of school students in Guangdong Province, killing five and injuring 20. He had become enraged when police told him he would have to pay a thousand yuan fine after they had confiscated his motorbike, which bore false license plates.[80]

The killings continue today. In March 2010, Zheng Minsheng, a former community doctor, waited by the gate of Nanping Elementary School in Fujian Province, and stabbed eight children to death, seriously injuring five others. "I have no hatred toward the students I stabbed. I chose them only because they were weak and vulnerable. I wanted to have a big influence among the public" said Zheng, who was executed the following April.[81]

The very day that Zheng was executed (just over a month later, leading one to wonder if the authorities had even bothered try to assess his mental state for insight into dealing with such events), another attack took place at a primary school in Guangdong Province. Chen Kangbing, 33, joined an open class held to demonstrate educational techniques to local teachers. Chen injured 15 students and a teacher with a knife. Police said Chen, himself a teacher from a different school, was undergoing a psychiatric test. He had been on leave since early 2006.[82]

The day after this, yet another murder attempt took place when 47-year-old Xu Yuyuan entered a kindergarten in Jiangsu Province and stabbed 29 children, leaving five in critical condition.[83]

A further attack took place just a few days later, in early May, when a man broke into a school in Shandong Province, attacked five children with a hammer and then killed himself. In response, Zhou Yongkang, one of the most senior politicians in China, said "We must take fast action to strengthen security for schools and kindergartens to create a harmonious environment for children to study and grow up." Given how many years these attacks have been occurring, one can only wonder at Zhou's definition of 'fast action.'[84]

34

Just over a week later, yet another killing occurred, in north-western China. A man named Wu Huanming hacked to death seven children, a teacher and her mother, and wounded 20 more.[85]

China's response to this was to remove news of the incident from the internet and ban extensive coverage in state media.[86]

In the mind of China's government, if the people cannot hear the screams of children being hacked to death, then such incidents simply have not happened.

But children do not die quietly like good citizens, following government policy, maintaining 'harmony' even in death. And hopefully parents are parents before they are good communists.

This fear of abuse and death felt by children at school is uniquely Chinese. So is the press censorship policy that tries to deny such events take place at all.

Sadly, empty desks at schools across China where once happy children sat waiting to learn is now not unique, but commonplace.

Today, the words 'China' and 'children' are in grave conflict.

Reason 4
Degrees of Unhappiness

From primary school your whole life became a prison of endless study. You got up at 6am every day to be at school by 8am, studied until 5 or 6pm and then went home to do more homework. There was no time for sport, so you are not physically strong, and the thousands of hours of reading have left you with poor eyesight. At school, developing close friendships just didn't happen. The weekend required getting up at 8am for piano lessons and then extra tuition. Tired was a way of life.

At high school the burdens simply got worse, with endless hours of politics classes in which you were told what to think, told how much the Party had done for its citizens. Romance was a constant daydream often shattered by teachers who made sure dreams never superseded reality.

And always your parents were in the background, saying study, study, study -- always pushing you to use every moment of free time to cram your mind full of knowledge to regurgitate by rote on the college entrance exam, the single greatest test of your young life.

The months before the big exam were hell. Sleep was a luxury. Headaches, indigestion and backache from poor posture were constant, combined with a distant memory of smiling and laughing.

Four days of the test created pressure almost too much to bear. And then you hear the tales of others your age, in the same city, in nearby schools, those students who succumbed and committed suicide.

This is the life that young students in China must live to progress successfully. Forced by parents and teachers to submit to astonishing pressures, seemingly inputting levels of education beyond what normal children can accept, they become abnormal, seeking high grades like robots for the single purpose of gaining entrance into an elite university.

Yes, you have passed – with a great score. Now, the theory is, any university in the country will accept you. Almost democratically you are able to choose any major, whereas those peers who scored below you will only be offered the seats in majors the universities must fill due to a lack of popularity. Those with scores even lower, so low they miss the cut, must resit the exam or fade away to spend their life in menial jobs.

Hopefully your parents will understand your desire to study the environment, and not force you into finance, accounting, economics, computing or the dreaded international trade. Today, in China, study, study, study is replaced with business, business, and even more business after high school. Most parents think that's the way to go. Some parents know it.

Now comes the biggest question of all. Will your university allow you to think?

One of the reasons behind the system of pressure is the extraordinary change higher education in China has seen in recent decades. China's universities were shut down in the Cultural Revolution (1966-1976). In the years since they reopened, 36 million students have been admitted. Expansion in Chinese higher education has taken place at a truly astonishing rate. In 1999, the country's colleges admitted 1.08 million students. By 2002, that number was up to 2.75 million. In 2008 media reported that at least 5.59 million students would graduate that year – a rise of 13% on 2007.[87] In 2009 it was reported that the following year would likely see 6.3 million new graduates, on top of a projected one million still unemployed graduates from 2009.[88]

But government funding has not kept pace with this expansion. Ke Bingsheng, president of the China Agricultural University, said that "The money allocated to higher education decreased proportionally from 80 to 40 percent in the last 10 years." Much of that missing allocation went to primary and middle school students, said Ke. He also said that the overall amount spent on each university student has fallen by 20 percent since 1999.[89]

This perhaps explains why a survey conducted in 2009 found that "Most Chinese college graduates … were not well prepared for the workplace, lacking in professional skills."[90]

The massive university expansion has increased the pressure on students to stand out in the crowd once they have graduated, and the only way they can do that is by attending a renowned university. In China, it is where you study, and not what or how well you study/think, that guarantees success.

Even at the 'top' universities, students more often face three or four years of inflexible education, disrespectful treatment and personal frustration than a voyage of intellectual discovery.

No matter what course a student signs up for – or, more often, is coerced into attending, either by parents or the system itself – he or she must also take a number of mandatory courses that have nothing to do with the major.

The most burdensome of these are political indoctrination courses, such as 'Mao Zedong Theory,' 'Deng Xiaoping Theory,' and, naturally, copious quantities of Marxism, all designed to espouse political theories that almost no-one – even the tutors – believes in. Political indoctrinization courses continue right up to PhD level, and a large amount of political hagiography must be memorized and repeated by rote. There is extremely little room for any creative thinking or disagreement in these courses; a student who has the temerity to argue against the political effectiveness of Mao, for example, will simply fail the course – no matter how cogently he or she argues – and without passing the course, they student cannot complete the degree.

Many universities also teach courses such as 'A History of the Chinese Revolution' – which, naturally, is biased towards the accounts of modern Chinese history offered up by political leaders and 'Moral Education,' designed to produce a state-sanctioned view of what is right.

Professor Sun Guangwen, a member of Shandong University, in the north of China, speaking in 2006, said "The content of those courses inculcate students with something useless, something that is even anti-scientific. They are taught for the purpose of promoting some communist ideology, leading people to believe that the CCP is mighty, glorious and correct, and that Mao Zedong is great" [sic].

"Many of these thoughts are false. For example, there are other courses that teach some of Deng Xiaoping's theories and Jiang Zemin's theory of the Three Representatives. I have written articles on such courses, and all of the courses should be stopped. Why inculcate college students with something not only useless, but also harmful, such as the concept of class struggle?" said the professor.

"The statements on history are somehow twisted. To inculcate students with these unreal and false thoughts in their education, I think is a very big problem" he said.[91]

Physical education is mandatory. While it is arguable that this is a good thing – especially given the increasing unhealthiness of China's young people today - a low score in physical education can decrease a student's overall grade average.

Today's students must also take a two-week military training course provided by the People's Liberation Army. According to China's Ministry of Education, "the evaluation of the military skill training and the examination results of the military knowledge will be put into each student's personal records." Such training is sometimes conducted in the summer heat, occasionally causing previously sheltered students to faint.

All undergraduates in China are also obliged to learn English. If they do not pass the College English Test, they are not allowed to graduate. The struggle of some to master a foreign language sometimes results in cheating.

For the vast majority of students the first year of undergraduate life – and very often the second – consists of a generalized and wide-ranging education that all undergraduates take in common. It is not until the later years of the course that students begin to focus on the core topics they have signed up to learn.

The Chinese cultural attitude to teachers, based on Confucian thinking, is also a direct barrier to creative thinking.

Mr. Liu: "For as long as I can remember, my parents have always told me 'obey the teacher.' For them the teacher is always right, and it is a sign of great rudeness for a student to question the teacher."

Ms. Sun: "In all the time I was at middle and high school I can only remember one student ever standing up to question the teacher. Everyone said he was a troublemaker, but in my heart I admired him. No one else ever dared question what they were told. And that's still true at my university."

This subservient attitude towards the educational process presents a great problem for China. Speaking at the Chinese-Foreign University Presidents Forum in Shanghai in 2006, Richard Levin, President of Yale University, said that "One thing that tops the innovation agenda for the nation in the next 15 years is critical thinking." Levin said that China's universities needed to encourage students to be more active and to challenge professors through debate and disagreement.[92]

Yet China is taking no steps to ensure this happens. Teaching is done in the form of lectures, but small-group seminars – the ideal training-ground for creative debate – are almost unheard of.

The quality of China's academic staff is rarely rigorously monitored. According to Chen Jun, the president of Nanjing University, "many professors tend to get relaxed or devote most of their time and efforts to their own commercial projects because mediocre performance is enough to ensure they pass the regular evaluation."

Plagiarism remains a big problem, and not just among students. For example, in 2009 Zhejiang University sacked Associate Professor He Haibo for plagiarizing four papers on traditional Chinese medicine that had been published in international journals.[93] And in 2010, Xi'an Jiaotong University sacked Professor Li Liansheng for plagiarizing work on energy and power.

Remarkably, it took the university two years to act from when Li's colleagues first raised the issue. "The university even questioned our motives," said one of the academics who blew the whistle, Chen Yongjiang. "Some university leaders told us that we could share some awards with Li, if we kept quiet about the scandal. It was such a humiliation."[94]

But such behavior is just part of campus life, said Chang Jiwen, a social law professor at the Chinese Academy of Social Sciences. "Professors conduct academic plagiarism and parents bribe to make sure their children achieve. What do you expect students to learn under that kind of environment?" he said.[95]

In every area of the university experience, students receive little respect from the university authorities.

Dormitory life, for example, is just one more challenge students must overcome. There is no private accommodation for undergraduates in China, who must live in dorms of four to six people. Most universities will not let students hire their own off-campus accommodation.

The attitude that university authorities have towards their students is made clear by the experience of one group of students at the Shanghai Institute of Foreign Trade. Dormitories here, like nearly all in China, lack heating or cooling facilities. And Shanghai is bitterly cold in winter. The group of students asked permission to install a heater, which they offered to pay for. The university rejected their claim, with university vice-president, Yu Guanghong, saying "Heating devices are always banned in universities dorms due to the possible dangers they may bring." Chinese media reported that even the city's elementary schools lacked heating facilities, and quoted one primary school deputy headmaster as saying students should be trained to endure unfavorable environments from childhood.[96]

Most universities switch off power to the dorms at 11pm or certainly by midnight, attempting to help students sleep, and reduce 'other activities.' One group of students did protest about the cessation of power supplies – but only during the World Cup. Nine thousand students rioted at Sichuan University, in central China, demanding power was provided at night so that they could watch the games. The angry students threw bottles and even basins out of dorm windows, and set fire to mopeds. The university agreed to the demands to provide power at night.[97]

Students feel more inclined to resist authoritarian school leaders when their future is concerned.

A riot took place at Shengda College, affiliated to the most prestigious university in Henan province, Zhengzhou University, when students found that their degree certificates would not be issued in the name of Zhengzhou University as they had been promised, but would rather bear the much less impressive name of Shengda.

Yet Shengda officials had used the weight of Zhengzhou University's name to attract students who had not gained high scores in the all-important college entrance exam – and charged five times the fee Zhengzhou University itself levied.

When the students found their degree certificate, reading 'Zhengzhou University Shengda Economic, Trade and Management College,' was not quite as prestigious as the one they'd been promised they were enraged. A certificate that said 'Zhengzhou University' alone would have been far more valuable in the hunt for a job. The students rioted, smashing and burning cars, destroying a statue of the college's founder and calling for the resignations of officials.

The state response was swift and predictable. Police closed down the campus and severely restricted entry and exit. All news of the event was suppressed in the Chinese media.[98]

The authoritarian treatment of students extends into every area of their life. Sex, for Chinese students, is also a subject for control by university regulations. Shanghai University, for example, expelled a student because he allowed his girlfriend to spend the night in his dorm room.

The student, Zhu Bin, explained that his girlfriend had come to see him from another university but had missed the last bus home. "I originally intended to arrange for her to spend the night in a nearby internet café, but it was too dangerous for a girl to stay overnight with male strangers about" he said, so he took her back to his dorm. He planned to allow her to have his bed while he slept in a chair but, suffering from a fever, he lay down beside her. The next morning a dorm mate informed on Zhu, and teachers discovered him and his girlfriend on the bed.

In insisting 'nothing happened' Zhu perhaps legitimized the belief that sex is indeed shameful. And certainly Zhu's mother said "I know that my son did something wrong, but things are not the way teachers think… the school should give him an opportunity to reform."[99]

When the Family Planning Commission of China's southern Guangdong Province wanted to install condom machines in eight provincial universities in 2004, some reacted strongly. Kong Xiaoming, publicity chief of the Guangdong University of Foreign Studies, said "We firmly oppose to condom vending machines on our campus. On campus, this very move is definitely prohibited, and we would never allow students to have sex experience while in college" [sic].[100]

Also in 2004, Beijing University – one of China's most prestigious institutions – rejected plans to hand out condoms on World AIDS Day, saying that it was "inappropriate to hand out free condoms openly on campus."[101]

Though China's commitment to expanding higher education seems impressive, it has been carried out in the classic command-economy style of totalitarianism. China's leaders pour money into science and engineering courses, and neglect most of the liberal arts – except those connected to finance and economics.

Yet while this will obviously help create an unbalanced society, there seems little complaint among the students themselves. The primary reason for this is that these areas are seen as the fast-track towards a big salary. Success, in modern China, is most often valued not in terms of personal happiness, but in terms of cash.

This desire for financial success is borne out by a 2006 survey which found that young Chinese students were much more ambitious than those in other countries. While 71.7% of American students said they would be happy with "an average living" only 45.8% of Chinese said the same, the lowest percentage of any group in the study, which also included Korean and Japanese students.[102]

But achieving this success is not easy. By 2007, Beijing alone had 200,000 university graduates, but only 87,000 graduate jobs available. Nationwide, of China's 4.13 million 2006 students, about 30% did not find a job upon graduation, according to the Ministry of Labor and Social Security. That's 1.2 *million* students unable to find jobs in one year. Add to that jobseeking students from previous years and the prospect of another 4.95 million students in 2007 joining the post-education job search stream and you have a mega-problem that may result in students regarding higher education as having no more value than gambling.

Chinese media reported on some of the problems fresh graduates met in the search for work. One student found his interview was held in a restaurant, because, he said "The company was trying to test if I could drink liquor and tactfully talk the customers into reaching a deal with me." Student Wang failed the 'interview' because, he said "I didn't do well enough at the dinner table -- I wasn't prepared for that and I never learned to drink."

According to Zheng Gongcheng, a professor at China's Renmin University and a deputy to the National People's Congress, highly-educated students are often underused. "Some Chinese banks, for example, hire master degree holders to work as tellers. It's a waste of human resources and disrupts the order of the job market -- where can they put people with lower degrees then?" said the professor. [103]

Money is also at the heart of the Chinese university experience in another way – fees. In 1989, the fee for a single semester was 100 yuan (US$12). Today, the fee is around 5,000 yuan (US$641) per semester.[104]

In 2005 the government stipulated that no university should charge tuition fees of more than 6,000 yuan.[105] That same year, one single college, the Xi'an Academy of Fine Arts in Northwest China's Shaanxi Province, overcharged more than five and a half million yuan by arbitrarily raising the standard tuition fee to 15,000 yuan (US$1,860).

The South China University of Technology in Guangdong Province overcharged 2.18 million yuan, the Nanjing Audit University, 1.64 million yuan, and Henan Normal University, 1.17 million yuan.[106]

And China's universities find plenty of other ways to raise money. Accommodation costs are added to the tuition fee, and these are, on average, 1200 yuan a year. For today's Chinese student, everything must be paid for.

Chinese media report the true cost of attending university is around 10,000 yuan a year. But many students we talked to said costs were higher than that. Some students at Shanghai International Studies University's new suburban campus in Songjiang, on the edge of the city, for example, have been obliged to pay an extra 10,000 yuan a year in 'construction costs' to pay for building the new campus. But since this money is – allegedly – paid to the construction firms, it does not count as a fee levied by the university.

And other media reports suggest that when China's university fees are compared to average incomes, Chinese university fees are the highest in the world.[107]

China's government has announced steep increases in the financial aid it provides to students. In 2006, China's student assistance program disbursed 1.6 billion yuan. In 2007, it was predicted to give out 15.7 billion yuan, rising to 30.8 billion yuan in 2008.[108]

Thirty billion yuan is the same amount of money wasted annually in inefficient home decoration materials.[109] It's 10% of what Beijing said it would spend on the two weeks of the 2008 Olympic Games.[110]

It's a tenth of annual costs for operating official vehicles nationwide every year – and nearly 70% of that vast sum of cash (300 billion yuan!) "is swallowed up by individuals … for private purposes and … unnecessary reimbursements for repairs and fuel expenses," said state media.[111]

And in September 2009, China's Ministry of Education announced that it was cancelling its payment of postgraduate grants at 36 universities in Beijing, and that it would also cancel paying grants across the whole nation. This termination of government support was "designed to enhance the quality of postgraduate education and encourage competition among students," media reported.[112]

The persistent treatment of Chinese university students as children in adult form, and the failure to encourage independence of thought, word and deed, comes at an incredible cost. China's halls of higher education are failing to generate the kind of citizens the nation will need if it is ever to become great. In the meantime, thousands of potentially brilliant minds are withering away in the exercise of theory rather than the education of practical solutions.

Students are a country's future. By devaluing them, China devalues itself.

Reason 5
There are no Bill Clintons in China

Politicians who have to appeal to the electorate need to develop star power. Think of Bill Clinton. Think of Tony Blair. Think of Nicolas Sarkozy, or Junichiro Koizumi. Think of Barack Obama. Politicians from democracies can be incredibly sexy.

These leaders won power by taking their case to the people – by showing the people they had a vision and understood the needs of the country. These leaders earned power. Some of them became mired in scandal, yet they never quite lost their star quality, or their sex appeal.

But China's politicians have never earned power in this fashion. They have never had to answer to the people they ostensibly serve. Ever since 1949, when 'New China' was founded, the Communist Party has used violence, fear and intimidation to keep its grip on power, rather than take its case to the citizens of the nation. There's no point in being sexy if you're a Chinese politician.

The one group of people China's politicians do have to answer to, however, is senior politicians – those that can hurt you if they want to. Political success in China comes from working your way up through the Party structure, most often by a process of cronyism famously known as 'guanxi' (in this case, 'connections') combined with total devotion to the goals of the Party.

Today's budding politician passes through the Party School and must spend many years carefully paying lip service to Marxism, Socialism, Mao Zedong Thought, Deng Xiaoping Theory, and, more recently, Jiang Zemin's 'Three Represents Theory,' and be ready to develop his own theory, usually involving three or four tongue-twisting concepts. Hu Jintao's addition to the canon is 'The Four Steadfasts.'[113]

Politicians also have to abide by other 'codes' of dress and demeanor. They should always appear in the same formal dark-colored suits and single solid-color ties, coiffed hair dyed jet-black to ensure not a single strand of gray can indicate the slightest hint of age. Demeanor should include looking generally distant, dour and unsmiling. They should always try to look regal in the presence of other national leaders, giving the impression that they are a touch more 'special' than the leaders of the nations they are standing next to. In our research, we were very hard pressed to find a single photograph of a single Chinese politician looking down the cleavage of a starlet, quite common with Western politicians over their political lifetime. Of course cigars are out of the question.

Those leaders tipped for the highest levels of power must also demonstrate their governmental suitability by exercising Party policy running various provinces in China. For today's president, Hu Jintao, the exercise was Tibet. Hu was initially identified by Deng Xiaoping as a suitable successor to Jiang Zemin, also handpicked by Deng.

Hu really earned his ticket to the top by his time running Tibet, which he ruled with particular harshness from 1988 to 1992. According to the Free Tibet campaign, "Hu's appointment as Party Secretary in Tibet marked the beginning of the end of what had been a relatively liberal decade in the region and the inception of policies which brought a halt to the religious and cultural revival witnessed during that time, leading to much more systematic methods of control being imposed on the Tibetan people."[114]

Hu's strict implementation of hard-line Party policies in Tibet ensured he rose smoothly to the top position. Allegiance to Party dogma always trumps allegiance to basic human rights, and success in Chinese politics is a matter of blending in rather than standing out. Almost as tough as becoming President of China is, once you are president, being able to choose the man who will follow you, and have it stick. The man long-thought to be most likely to succeed Hu as president, Li Keqiang, is currently running the northern Liaoning Province, though in more recent years another contender has stood out, Xi Jinping. Xi became vice-president of China in March 2008, making it likely that in the next leadership shuffle he would become president, with Li serving as prime minister.

Hu Jintao, even more than China's previous presidents, has, in practical terms, made his name by not standing out. His official biography notes that "Hu once said a good leader must have firm beliefs and lofty pursuits, do solid work, seek no fame or gain, do away with a bureaucratic air and share the feelings of the masses."

The same biography also mentions that "When he worked in the Communist Youth League Central Committee, he occasionally danced solo at parties. He also plays table tennis fairly well." By dancing solo, Hu perpetuates the lack of sexiness endemic among Chinese leaders.

The Communist Party of China is therefore driven by internal consensus and strict adherence to the rules. In 2007 China appointed its first non-Communist member to the State Council, its highest political body, in more than thirty years. Wan Gang, a member of the Public Interest Party, became the nation's Minister of Science and Technology.[115] The Public Interest Party is one of China's eight officially allowed non-Communist political parties. Given their almost complete lack of meaningful political power (for how do you gain power without the vote?), it is very clear that the only way to take an active role in running China is via the Communist Party.

While the media had a field day with this earth-shattering news about Wan Gang, a non-Communist taking a government role, no-one in the Chinese media asked the question 'What took so long?'

China's rigidly controlled media also serves to intensify this lack of color in Chinese political life. All news reporting is based on the seniority of politicians within the Party structure, rather than the interest or utility of what they are doing or saying. Rather than gave any insight into the personality of a politician, the media simply reflects the power structure within the Party. China-watchers often base their assessment of who is rising and who is falling with the Party's top echelons via their position in news reporting.

Under this system, Chinese politicians become merely like chess pieces on a board. They are simply ciphers reflecting a power-struggle, rather than living, breathing people.

There are no paparazzi in China. You will never see motorcycles with photographers chasing motorcades hoping to catch some starlet in a tryst with a senior political leader.

In fact there are dangers in standing out amid this parade of grayness. In 1995, Shanghai was given a new mayor, Xu Kuangdi. He came from an academic rather than a political background, and did not even join the Party until 1983, when he was 46.[116] He was "the first and only academician mayor in the Chinese mainland," reported state media proudly at the time.[117] Xu was an extremely successful mayor, significantly boosting Shanghai's international profile, both economically and socially.

Outgoing and personable, he received a lot more coverage in international media than other Chinese politicians, gaining such comments as "In fact, Xu Kuangdi sounds more like pragmatic American mayors such as New York's Rudy Giuliani or Los Angeles' Dick Riordan than an aloof, preprogrammed robot out of Mao's Little Red Book."[118] In 2001, despite his strong success in the role, he was suddenly demoted, removed and replaced, most likely as a result of "rivalry between [then] President Jiang Zemin and [then] Premier Zhu Rongji -- and that between Xu and the Shanghai Party Secretary, Huang Ju."[119]

The strength and color Xu brought to the job meant nothing compared to factional rivalry among his superiors. Amid the rumors swirling in the wake of his demotion, many speculated it was partly because he had been such a high-profile mayor that he was demoted. Xu became president of the Chinese Academy of Engineering and vice-chairman of the 10th National Committee of the Chinese People's Political Consultative Conference, essentially a powerless rubber-stamp body.

China does not have any sexy or charismatic political figures like JFK or Churchill in its recent past. While both these magnetic politicians had flaws, they also had many powerful qualities which enabled them to shape their nations for the better. But even the powerful leader of 'New China,' Mao Zedong, could only bring misery and suffering, balanced by few positive characteristics. There are no Lincolns or Washingtons in Chinese history, no Benjamin Disraelis or Horatio Nelsons. Even regally, there is no Queen Elizabeth the First or Queen Victoria. There is no Uncle Sam, or John Bull. No St. Nicholas. No Harry Potter and certainly no Mickey Mouse.

There is Confucius, who is didactic, remote and controlling. There is Sun Tzu, a military expert, if you're a young boy fascinated with the tactics of war.

And of course there is Lei Feng.

More modern Chinese leaders, perhaps aware of the limited affection they inspired in the people, created a myth to push their goals. This myth was Lei Feng, a soldier in the People's Liberation Army. He was killed in an accident in 1962, at the age of 22. After his death, his diaries were 'discovered' in which he had lavished extraordinary praise on Mao Zedong.

In return for the praise Lei Feng gave to Mao Zedong, Mao deified Lei in a speech. People were urged to 'Learn from Lei Feng' in doing good deeds to honor Mao and strengthen China. Lei Feng's devotion to Mao was spun as devotion to the country.

But as historian Jung Chang points out, "Apart from symbolizing total loyalty to Mao, soldier Lei Feng exemplified another point: the idea that hate was good, which was drilled into the population, especially the young. Lei Feng had supposedly written 'Like spring, I treat my comrades warmly… And to my enemies, I am cruel and ruthless like harsh winter.' Hatred was dressed up as something necessary if one loved the people."[120]

Lei Feng also supposedly wrote:
• A man's life is limited, but serving the people has no end. I will devote the limited life to the boundless work of serving the people.
• At work, one must look up to the comrades with the greatest enthusiasm; in life, one should look up to the comrades with the lowest living standards.
• Each person will die. Some die as light as the goose's feather; others die with the weight of Mount Taishan.
• If you were a drop of water, did you moisten an inch of soil? If you were a ray of sunlight, did you illuminate some darkness? If you were a grain, did you breed a useful life? If you were the smallest screw, would you persist on the post of your life?[121]

Lei Feng is still a part of China's cultural landscape. Even today he is part of the national 'story,' which is taught to all schoolchildren. "To the Chinese, the young soldier whose life was cut short at the tender age of 22 has remained alive, and his patriotism, compassion and self-sacrifice have become a part of the moral standards for the 1.3 billion population" wrote state media in 2003.[122]

March 5th is Lei Feng day, when students are sent into the community to do good deeds. Shanghai media reported in 2006 that "Residents of one seniors' home in the city were besieged by visitors on Lei Feng Day. According to a nurse surnamed Wu, the home received seven groups of people who paid a visit to show their care for seniors on March 5. An 80-year-old man who was good at singing had to sing his favorite song seven times to express his gratitude. "We really appreciate

48

their visits," Wu said. "But the seniors want to be visited regularly, not on a single day."[123]

In 2006, China tried to re-invent this manufactured icon, making him more 'relevant' for modern society. Announcing the publication of a new book, "Lei Feng: 1940-1962," Chinese media said "With over 300 rarely-seen photographs of Lei Feng, the book depicts Lei as a fun-loving young man who was hip in his time. … Many Chinese know Lei for his 10 diaries that display his loyalty to the Party, the army and to the Mao Zedong Thought, the mainstream ideology of China at that time. But not many know that Lei also loved singing and dancing, as the book reveals."

"The book describes Lei as having long hair, which was forbidden in the army, and wearing fashionable sweaters, a leather jacket and wristwatch, all considered luxury items of the day."[124] One wonders how Lei Feng had time to complete his ten diaries, since he was so busy in his short life offering his time and energies in a charitable way.

Lei Feng also became the hero of a computer game in 2006, in which the player had to do as many good deeds as possible to proceed to a higher level. "For beginners, sewing and mending socks is the only way to increase experience and to upgrade," said one sixth-grade pupil. And the top prize in the game? The chance to 'meet' Mao Zedong and win a copy of his writings.[125]

In 2007 a law was even proposed to 'protect' Lei Feng, along with other Chinese heroes. It was suggested China's heroes should be divided into five categories -- Historical Heroes, National Heroes, Revolutionary Leaders, Revolutionary Martyrs, and Model Heroes—and that their reputations should be protected by law.

According to Wang Fengming, a Beijing lawyer, "Chinese heroes are the spiritual support for the whole Chinese nationality." Wang said that when a living person's rights are infringed, that person or their relatives can resort to legal means.

"But once the reputation of heroes is infringed upon, the influence is much larger [so] that compensation and public apology are not enough to make up spiritual hurt, as the damage is upon Chinese people's pride," Chinese media quoted Wang as saying.[126]

Lei Feng was still being relentlessly pressed as an icon of every noble virtue in 2009, when media excitedly reported on Sun Maofang, a 66-year-old volunteer who had won an award for his work. Rejecting a comparison of himself to Lei, Sun said, "Lei Feng was humble. His humbleness represents the selflessness and modesty of the Chinese way of living. He had such a beautiful mind."[127]

A true 'hero,' of course, does not need to be protected by law. But in a country like China where 'heroes' are fabricated or manipulated to serve political ends, perhaps it is not surprising to find such an attitude, also preventing the public airing of scandals.

The scandals that make political life in other countries so memorable, from the Profumo affair to Monica Lewinsky, are absent from Chinese political life. This does not mean they do not happen, however.

"Having a nubile, young mistress is not only fashionable for China's middle-aged officials partial to a spot of corruption but also a perfect cloak for taking a bribe" explained Chinese media in summer 2007, announcing a new regulation to tackle bribery. Many corrupt officials kept 'clean hands' by funneling bribes through family members or lovers. The new rules meant that "for the first time prosecutors will no longer need to provide evidence of the involvement of a mistress in order to convict an official charged with accepting bribes." Under the new guidelines, Zhao Zhanqi, a transport chief in eastern Zhejiang Province, was sentenced to life in prison. He had taken a bribe of 550,000 yuan through his mistress, Wang Peiying, to award an airport construction contract. As well as this sum, Zhao took a further 5.6 million yuan (US$737,000) via his son.[128]

But mistresses only get reported when the leader in question falls from power. This ensures that most politicians in China are never associated with a 'human' side, but remain remote and unknowable figures. There is no way for the population of China to feel any connection with their leaders, and nor are their leaders individual enough to inspire affection or emulation.

Even Sun Yat-Sen (known as Sun Zhongshan in China), today revered as the 'Father of the Republic' for his role in helping overthrow the Qing Dynasty in 1911, was in fact in the United States when the key events leading to the fall of the dynasty took place. Sun read about this event – known as the Wuchang Rebellion, in which army officers took over a city in Hubei Province and then persuaded other provinces to secede from the empire – in a newspaper. Weeks later, when he returned to China, he was elected as head of the new republic, before he gave it up 45 days later. His worst 'scandal' was marrying Song Qingling, who was 27 years younger.

While future Chinese men and women may endear themselves to the world's populace, the spirit of that endearment will most likely come from Chinese admiration of Western leaders and heroes. For a young person in China to proclaim that his hero is Mao Zedong would surely remove him or her from any popularity race fashioned by young Chinese citizens today.

The authors have yet to find a single child in China who has ever been told, as American children are often encouraged, 'You too can grow up to be president of your country.'

Reason 6
Dry Cleaning the News

In early summer 2007 a man walked into the offices of the Chengdu Evening News, a newspaper located in the central Chinese city of Chendgu. He gave the text of an advertisement he wished to place to the young female clerk on duty.

The words of that advertisement were 'Paying tribute to the strong mothers of the June 4th victims.'

The clerk at first accepted the ad. But then, a couple of days later she rang the man back to check up on what the date, June 4th, referred to. The man told her that it was the anniversary of a mining disaster. Satisfied, the clerk allowed the ad to be printed.

In fact, the advertisement referred to June 4th 1989, the Tiananmen Square Massacre. The Chinese government's denial of this event had been so successful, sanitizing the educational system so well, that the young clerk had never heard of it.

The Communist Party is extremely sensitive about any mention of the Tiananmen Massacre in public life. Open discussion of the event is dangerous, so much so that many young people the same age as the clerk often express disbelief if you tell them what really happened on that evening of July 4th in Tiananmen Square. The news is so effectively dry-cleaned that young people who do have some knowledge of the event support what the government did to end it.

The fact that clerk at the Chengdu Evening News knew almost nothing about the Tiananmen Square Massacre is simply part of a wider picture in which the Chinese media is so tightly and so effectively controlled that hundreds of millions of Chinese citizens not only do not know the truth of their own country's past, but also have a warped view of the world that lies beyond China.

The man who placed the advertisement in the Chengdu Evening News also tried to place it in two other city newspapers. But the clerks at those papers were suspicious and phoned older superiors who instructed them not to accept it. No media sources were able to find out if the man who placed the ad was arrested. After the Chengdu Evening Post ran the advertisement, the deputy editor in chief of the paper was sacked, as were two other members of the editorial office.[129]

As well as showing the almost pathological fear the Communist Party has of discussing the truth of modern Chinese history, this incident is just one part of a much wider web of lies, half-truths and misinformation that lie at the heart of today's Chinese media.

The sheer size of the Chinese media makes it highly effective in propagating the Party agenda. As of 2006, China had 9,468 different periodicals published nationwide, printing 2.8 billion copies daily, weekly and monthly, and 1,938 different newspapers, printing 42 billion copies annually.[130]

One of the reasons China has so many newspapers is that the government used to force people to subscribe to them. This practice began to be phased out only in 2003, when more than 670 newspapers were closed down because they had "no social or economic benefits and to relieve financial burdens on farmers and grass-roots enterprises." The total cost of the newspapers to subscribers had been 1.8 billion yuan (US\$217 million at 2003 prices) and axing them saved the printing of 1.54 billion copies.[131]

For example, Zhu Yulong, the Party Secretary of an impoverished village in east Sichuan Province, said his office had to subscribe to multiple copies of 20 newspapers and magazines every year at a total cost of 150,000 yuan (US\$18,122) a year.

Yet the entire budget his office had for administrative expenses was just 30,000 yuan (US\$3,625). "I get a headache every year when the media sales reps call on me" he said. "How can I cough up this money? If I say 'no' to one of them, he may dog me down the road as they all represent various government agencies."[132]

One magazine that was closed in Shanghai was Fire Shanghai, published by the Shanghai Fire Control Bureau. Under the old rules, one large property management agency in the city had been forced by the bureau to buy 20 subscriptions to the monthly magazine. A manager at the property firm said "The magazine provides some helpful information on fire-prevention work. However, 19 copies of the magazine were wasted every month since nobody really reads them. If we could choose, we would only subscribe to one."[133]

After forced subscriptions were terminated, state media also reported that the newspaper publishing business had become "sensitive to the market" – code for the fact that even for the Party being profitable was now more important than spreading the gospel of socialism.[134]

According to Yu Guoming, a media professor at the People's University of China, this press reform would "help the media to better supervise the government and safeguard social justice, which is also the reform aim of the Chinese government."[135]

But Yu's comments are essentially meaningless, as, ironically, other reports in the media made very clear. Describing related media reform in 2004, an official from the country's General Administration of Press and Publication said that "No matter how reforms are carried out, Party governance over the press, cadres, the guiding role of the mass media and assets must not be changed."

In all Beijing's claims to be 'reforming' the media, one thing remained very clear – that the Party would retain absolute control over what the media published.

Controlling China's huge number of newspapers and magazines is a vast bureaucratic task, costing millions of dollars and tens of millions of man hours. The country has a rigorous system of control with the government at the top dictating what can and cannot be said down through successively lower levels to the journalists themselves, who, because the system is so inflexible yet effective, routinely practice self-censorship.

China's television media is also rigidly controlled. China Central Television regurgitates the official government stance, with its nightly news show watched by around 140 million people. The format is unchanging, leading with political news covering the activities of China's leaders in order of their importance. The anchors of the show are extremely formal, seldom offering the banter common among newsreaders in free societies.

The format of this news show is so inflexible that the program kept the same team of six news anchors for nearly a decade. In late 2006, two new readers, Li Zeming and Kang Hui, presented the show – unannounced in advance – and brought with them a more relaxed manner. Though the news they read was exactly the same as before, their warmer manner excited much online comment.

The fact that this change in staff was not announced beforehand is also indicative of the State's attitude towards the people, who are viewed as passive receptacles of whatever the Party deems fit for them. Just one example: when China put its first man in space in 2003, something that would be a cause for national celebration in most countries, the launch was not shown live. A second launch, in 2005, was shown live but was only announced one day before, and the precise time of the launch was released just minutes before it took place.

Those who step outside the lines of what the Party deems is suitable news face immediate and heavy-handed punishment. China has more print journalists in jail than any other country in the world, and current Chinese president Hu Jintao is imposing even more strict controls on the Chinese media than his predecessor Jiang Zemin.

One of the few relatively bold newspapers in China, 'Freezing Point,' was shut down in 2006 after publishing an article suggesting Chinese school text books were not teaching the whole truth about China's past. The writer, Yuan Weishi, was not recklessly attacking the inflated claims such textbooks make about the Communist Party's 'achievements' -- but rather the way China's last dynasty, the Qing Dynasty, was portrayed.

Qin Gang, the spokesman for China's Ministry of Foreign Affairs, said Yuan's article had hurt the feelings of the Chinese people. While Beijing is extremely quick to attack any perceived omissions in Japan's history text books, it takes a very different line about China's own past, which is often carefully reconstructed to eliminate 'negatives.'

'Freezing Point' was later allowed to re-open, but without its pioneering and brave editors Li Datong and Lu Yuegang.

"What do the people want?" the editors later wrote in a public letter of protest over being sacked. "Press freedom, and the freedom of speech granted to them by the constitution; information that is valuable about the environment they live in, the investigation and uncovering of injustice, support for socially vulnerable groups against the powerful, and the sort of profound reflection needed to ensure the survival of the people," reported Radio Free Asia.

Radio Free Asia also quoted Pu Zhiqiang, another outspoken Chinese lawyer active in the struggle for human rights. "I think this is a question of the propaganda department being in breach of China's constitution," he said. "Clause 35 of the constitution of the People's Republic of China protects freedom of speech and freedom of the press, and this action is definitely in contravention of that clause."[136]

"Party governance over the press" dictated that Chinese media were forbidden from covering any aspect of the 'Freezing Point' shutdown.

Li and Lu were demoted to the News Research Institute. This, Li told the Committee to Protect Journalists, a press freedom body, was "a place for children and the elderly."[137] Even so, these two brave men escaped incarceration or worse, the fate of many journalists who try to do their jobs properly.

An example is reporter Lan Chengzhang, investigating an illegal coal mine in China's northern Shanxi Province in early 2007, who was so badly beaten by men at the mine that he subsequently died from his injuries. Local officials said that since he did not have the correct permits he was not a legitimate journalist, and then allegations were made that Lan had attempted to bribe the mine owner in return for not writing unfavorable articles. Subsequently, the owner of the mine, Hou Zhenrun, was sentenced to life in prison, and others involved in the beating received sentences of between five and 15 years. Hou was also ordered to pay Lan's family compensation of around US$50,000.[138]

In late 2005, an editor in the eastern city of Taizhou, Wu Xianghu, wrote an article critical of fees being levied by the police to register electric bikes. Li Xiaoguo, head of the Jiaojiang Traffic Police Detachment under Taizhou Public Security Bureau, reacted negatively to the article and went to Wu's office, demanding the article be retracted and Wu punished. Li then attacked Wu, after which he called for *thirty* more policemen. Together they dragged Wu from his fifth floor office into a police wagon.

While Chinese media did report the basic facts of the case as well as that Li Xiaoguo was subsequently fired, they did not report that Wu, who had undergone a liver transplant two years before, later died from his injuries.[139]

Zhao Yan, employed as a researcher for the New York Times, was jailed for three years after being tried for 'revealing state secrets.' His crime? That he had supplied 'secrets' to help the New York Times correctly predict that former Chinese president Jiang Zemin would retire in September 2004.

At his trial, however, Zhao was acquitted of leaking state secrets, in part because the Times said he had not provided the information in question. Still, he was sentenced to three years in jail for fraud in August 2006, having already spent two years in prison awaiting trial. The fraud charges, said Chinese media, were derived from Zhao's previous job on a Beijing newspaper during which he was alleged to have extorted a bribe from a man in return for political favors.[140]

In China, for journalists, once you are arrested, you must be guilty of something. Subsequently, Chinese media made no mention of the Jiang Zemin report in the New York Times, since they had satisfied their hunger to find guilt. Zhao was freed in September 2007, having served the full three years of his sentence with no reduction (taking into account his two years under arrest before sentencing).[141]

In 2006, Ching Cheong, a Chinese reporter working for the Singapore-based Straits Times, was jailed for five years for spying after having been arrested on the charge in April 2005. At his trial, it was claimed that he had accepted money from Taiwan to buy political and military information in China. He, his wife and his employer rejected the allegation, and international outcry followed his jailing.[142] He was freed on parole in February 2008, though by that time he had already spent almost three years in jail. At the same time that Ching was freed, China jailed Lu Gengsong for four years for 'inciting subversion of state power.' His subversion of truth? Writing about the extensive corruption within China.[143]

According to Reporters without Borders, a media freedom advocacy group, China had 31 journalists in jail at the beginning of 2007. "Media editors receive regularly a list of banned subjects. These might be demonstrations by peasants, the unemployed or Tibetans. Nothing escapes the censors, who cultivate a climate of fear within editorial offices" says the group.

"In the run-up to a series of anniversaries, including the 30th since the death of Mao Zedong and the 40th since the Cultural Revolution, the General Administration of Press and Publication issued a warning in July: 'News publication has an important role in ideological education and our country's security depends on strict control of news production'" it said.[144] "Strict control of news production" as if the news was produced in a factory that can shape its size, color, content and packaging, like a consumer product for the masses who, offered no alternative, gobble up what is offered and ask for more.

In 2009, the group reported on the ongoing use of repression and censorship, documenting heightened control of the internet in the months before the 60th anniversary celebrations of the founding of the People's Republic of China, along with physical attacks on foreign journalists in China and cyber-attacks made on reporters worldwide. It also called for the release of the increased number of journalists and bloggers who had been jailed in the run-up to the Olympic Games of 2008, and who still remained in prison.[145] Reporters without Borders also placed China 168th out of 175 countries in the world in terms of lack of press freedom, a position it still occupied in 2010.

In 2006 China released new regulations banning overseas news agencies from releasing any news in China, and stating that only the government-controlled Xinhua News Agency was allowed to do so. "Foreign news agencies shall be subject to approval by Xinhua News Agency for releasing their news and information in China and shall have entities designated by Xinhua News Agency [to] act as their agents" said state media.

"Foreign news agencies shall not directly solicit subscription of their news and information services in China. To subscribe to news and information services of foreign news agencies, a user in China shall sign a subscription agreement with a designated entity and shall not, by any means, directly subscribe to, translate, edit or publish the news and information released by a foreign news agency" said the rules.[146]

Foreign Ministry spokesman Qin Gang said that "the measures are aimed at standardizing the foreign media's distribution of news and information and regulating domestic users' subscription of news and information from the foreign media, promoting the sound and orderly dissemination of news and information, and protecting the legitimate rights and interests of foreign media and domestic users."

Qin also mouthed the common official lie that "China is an open society."[147]

China has also tried to control foreign coverage of the country in other ways. In 2007 China's State Environment Protection Agency tried to suppress a World Bank report into deaths caused by pollution in the nation. Though the report had been produced in conjunction with Chinese government agencies, Beijing did not like the results – suggesting the death toll was 750,000 people a year -- and the draft formal report was published without this statistic.

Zhou Jian, Vice Minister of China's State Environment Protection Administration, said "I think the World Bank report lacks a precise scientific foundation, regardless of how many people it says die in China because of pollution."[148]

However, the World Bank said the final version of the report had yet to be decided and that earlier version "did not include some of the issues that are still under discussion."[149]

While most Chinese citizens know that their media is controlled by the government, few fully appreciate just how tight this control is. And the sheer love of reading that is apparent in China means that the government-sanctioned version of the 'truth' colors people's world view. The fact that more than 40 billion copies of newspapers are printed annually shows how influential the news media is.

56

Chinese people love to read books. Go into any city bookstore at the weekend and you will see large crowds of people selecting, reading and buying books.

Unfortunately the book market is very tightly controlled, just like the newspaper market. Books that deal with recent history are under particularly close monitoring. In early 2007, China's General Administration of Press and Publications banned eight books including 'Past Stories of Peking Opera Stars' by Zhang Yihe and 'This is How it Goes@SARS.com' by Hu Fayin.

Zhang's earlier books have also been banned since they refer to political campaigns that the Party now wishes to airbrush from history, though Zhang said she had not been told why her latest book had been banned. Hu's book was, perhaps, a more obvious target for a ban given that any mention of the respiratory disease SARS, an outbreak of which was covered up by Beijing in 2003, remains extremely sensitive.[150]

Even though the Party's covering-up of SARS led to the disease spreading abroad unchecked and thus caused wholly preventable deaths around the world, the government learned nothing – or simply did not care. In 2008, government officials covered up news of tainted milk. This milk had been adulterated with the chemical melamine, in a bid to make its protein levels appear higher than they were during testing. Melamine, which is used to make plastics, caused kidney stones. At least four children died and more than 50,000 were hospitalized. News of the adulterated milk broke in late July 2008. That news was suppressed because the government did not want anything to tarnish the Beijing Olympic Games of August 2008. As with SARS, suffering and death meant nothing to the government when set against image.[151] Months after the event, in December 2008, Beijing admitted that the 'true' number of victims was closer to 300,000.[152]

In recent years, the internet has seen an astonishing spread in China. While this is in part fuelled by citizens' search for less stale, controlled news than the government supplies, it is still the case the majority of Chinese people rely on state-controlled online media rather than searching further afield for alternative voices.

In English-language Chinese media, negative stories (more in line with the facts) are mainly directed at international readers to create the illusion of an open media.

What may be reported in English may not be reported in Chinese, but the government's support of English language within China's schools may yet be creating legions of young citizens searching for an alternate opinion within the English-language media.

As China's presence in the international media market place becomes an everyday occurrence, the government attempts to extend its domestic media policy onto the world stage. Politically directed photo-opportunities and press releases concerning China's economic achievements still mixed with China's view of itself as a victim due the world's sympathy have become all part of a grand policy of "strict control of news production."

Now China even criticizes world media's reporting of national and international events it deems somehow negative to the motherland's feelings.

When George W. Bush unveiled a memorial to the estimated 100 million victims of communism in June 2007, Qin Gang responded with the hectoring, lecturing tone that is increasingly common from China. "Some US political forces still cling to their 'Cold War' mentality and, out of political necessity, seek to provoke conflicts between different ideologies and social systems."

"The Chinese side calls on the US side to reject its 'Cold War' mentality, seek to reform its mistaken actions [and] stop interfering in the affairs of other nations."[153]

Are not all deaths and victims of political systems or wars equally memorable? Not in the eyes of China, for whom pushing the Party message comes before the facts.

It takes great energy for the government to maintain its paper curtain, which, with today's electronic media becomes thinner and thinner, sometimes almost the point of translucence, allowing the citizens of China to 'see through' the face of their own state press into the open windows of the international media.

Unfortunately for the Chinese people, the decades of receiving only manufactured news will for some time prevent them from understanding that the 'negative' world media will not harm China, but will enhance its opportunities to find international solutions and solve universal problems.

Reason 7
Better than Cheap – It's Fake

China is the kingdom of fake.

Some methods of cheating are simple and obvious, such as that used by the Shanghai Opera Bakery Co, who simply changed the production date labels on their products so that they could sell stale goods to customers.[154]

Some are far more elaborate. The Shanghai Henghe Real Estate Co., for example, faked an entire English town. Thames Town, an hour's drive from downtown Shanghai, has 'English' style fake Georgian and Victorian housing and even a statue of Winston Churchill.

It also has a pub and chip shop, which have been directly copied from two businesses owned by Gail Caddy in Lyme Regis, in Dorset, England. Ms. Caddy said she felt cheated by having her businesses ripped off without permission or even acknowledgement.[155]

Between a loaf of bread and an entire town, the range of products copied, faked, and eventually sold is overwhelming. In early 2010, Chinese government officials announced that through the first 11 months of 2009 they had dealt with more than 200,000 cases of counterfeit and sub-standard goods.[156]

An inspection launched across nine provinces in China found 775 bogus military vehicles and more than a thousand stolen or faked military license plates. Criminal gangs faked military certificates and seals to produce the bogus vehicles, which they then sold for many thousands of dollars profit.[157]

Owning a 'military' vehicle in China makes one immune from police enforcement of the traffic rules. Drivers of these vehicles can run red lights and use bus-only lanes, and since they effectively outrank the police they will not be pulled over.

Such vehicles are equipped with a horn that makes a different sound than a regular vehicle horn, and it's common in any big Chinese city to hear this horn and then see the impatient driver barging ordinary citizens aside.[158]

In just a few months in Shanghai in 2007 the local army garrison seized 303 vehicles with fake military plates as well as 11 more with genuine plates stolen from military vehicles. Again, people were using these plates to enjoy priority from police on busy roads as well as free parking and exemption from bridge and road tolls.[159]

In Shanghai, the trade in fake tires is big business. Employees in underground workshops gather dumped used tires and cut new grooves into them, making them resemble new products. Each worker can make 30 to 40 such tires a day, and these are then sold on for 25 yuan (US$3) each. A genuine new tire costs 300 to 400 yuan.

The fakes are prone to explode at high speeds.[160]

In eastern Zhejiang Province, a factory manager, Ying Fuming, was arrested after it was found his factory made 'edible' lard from animal swill, sewage and even recycled industrial oil. The Fanchang Grease Factory, in the city of Taizhou, produced six tons of lard a day, and sometimes ten tons. It sold its lard to hotels and restaurants across the country at prices 50% lower than average.

When it was raided, inspectors found 33,760 kilograms of raw materials, such as grease rendered from sewage. It turned out the factory had already been ordered to close some time previously, but though it shut down in the daytime it continued to operate at night.[161]

In the first six months of 2009, officials seized 2.4 billion fake cigarettes, said China's State Tobacco Monopoly Administration. But perhaps this was in fact good news, since 8.3 billion fake cigarettes had been impounded the year before.[162]

China's food industry is beset by counterfeits, low quality products, and foodstuffs made with inedible chemical products.

In 2004, Shanghai-based producers manufactured tofu (bean curd) out of gypsum, paint and starch. They bribed local trade police with about US$1000 a year to make sure they would not be inspected.[163]

In March the same year, a Shanghai businessman, Zhang Wenrong, spent six months investigating local food products. He uncovered a wide range of faked and dangerous foodstuffs, including fish preserved in formalin (a mixture of formaldehyde and water frequently used as an antiseptic and disinfectant, as well as to preserve tissue for medical inspection), bamboo shoots kept fresh with industrial sulfur, cuttlefish dyed with ink, and moldy oranges made to look shiny with an application of paraffin (wax).[164]

A survey held in 2009 found that an astonishing 70% of cooked food products sold in markets and stores in Guangzhou, the capital city of Guangdong Province, failed to meet basic health standards. Another 2009 survey found that 52% of all bottled water used in dispensers in Liaoning province also did not meet health standards.[165]

At least 13 babies died horribly in 2004 in eastern China's Anhui Province as a result of being fed fake milk powder. Though it looked like milk when prepared, it contained so little nutrition that the babies simply starved to death. As many as 200 babies developed 'big head disease' in which the head swells as the body wastes away, with frantic mothers not understanding what was happening to their children.

Perhaps as an afterthought officials held a very public ceremony to destroy more than 4,000 boxes of fake milk powder, which did nothing to make mothers forget about how such a thing could have happened in the first place.

China's Premier Wen Jiabao ordered a thorough investigation.

60

The belated response to these deaths led to the seizure of more than 2,000 kilograms of substandard powder in the western city of Xi'an, and 21,912 bags of pre-prepared milk in the eastern city of Fuyang.

A follow-up survey in southern Guangdong Province found that 32% of milk sold in major supermarket chains did not meet national standards. Nationwide, 45 different brands of bogus milk powder were seized and 141 factories making it were raided.[166]

In October 2006 manufacturers of 'mooncakes' – a traditional pastry eaten during China's 'mid-autumn festival' – had to be reminded that they were not allowed to buy up old mooncakes and reprocess them into new cakes, as was a common practice.[167]

2005 saw a crackdown on the number of fake books reaching the market. These were different to merely pirated books, which are simply illegal copies of legitimate publications.

One such book, 'No Excuse' purported to offer the latest in Western management techniques and came with glowing reviews from the international press. The truth was that the book was a fake, with made up contents, bogus reviews and a fabricated 'Western' name for the author. It was a best seller for several months and sold two million copies.

A survey early that year found that there were 106 fake books on Western-style management in the market.

For those readers who can read Chinese, there are several additional Harry Potter stories that await your critical eye, such as a bogus version of 'Order of the Phoenix' released in advance of the real thing, and an entirely new book called 'Harry Potter and the Leopard Walk up to Dragon.'[168] Other fake Harry Potter novels were Harry Potter and the Water-Repelling Pearl, Harry Potter and the Golden Armor, Harry Potter and the Golden Turtle, Harry Potter and the Crystal Vase, and Harry Potter and the Porcelain Doll.[169]

Many of these books are published by official publishing houses, keen to cash in on the popularity for Western books in the Chinese market, but equally keen to avoid the expense of providing payment to the genuine authors and original publishing houses.

Popular Chinese authors are also used to this phenomenon, with one writer, Ye Yonglie, having found an additional 40 books purporting to be written by him since 1994, a physically daunting amount of writing that even his fans grew suspicious of.[170]

The traditional pirating of books (straightforward copying) is common too. In the first four months of 2007, authorities closed down 13,000 shops and 364 printing factories for illegal operations, and fined another 17,000 shops and 1,825 factories for various violations.[171]

Even the 2010 Expo, held in Shanghai, had to cope with claims of counterfeiting. One of the promotional songs for the Expo, '2010, Waiting for You' seemed to copy freely from a 1997 song by a Japanese artist, Mayo Okamoto. The song was hurriedly withdrawn when this similarity was exposed. But other accusations soon followed - it was alleged that the Chinese pavilion at the Expo seemed to resemble the Canadian Pavilion at the Montreal Expo of 1967. And even the main mascot of the Expo, called Haibo, was said to bear more than a passing resemblance to Gumby, the American cartoon character created in the early 1950s.[172]

People author their own real-life stories in an attempt to 'fake' themselves.

Another well-known figure in China, Zhou Yiming, was the youngest member of Fortune magazine's list of China's 400 richest people in 2005. He was arrested in 2006 because he had faked reports about his financial strength claiming the group he was chairman of was worth around US$150 million. In fact it was US$35 million in debt. He used these fake reports to borrow nearly US$50 million. With this, he took a stake in another firm, which he then drove into the ground by siphoning off nearly US$70 million of its capital.[173]

Dozens of students were cheated in 2006 by a man named Sun, who faked university enrollment letters. He sold these for up to 90,000 yuan to students desperate to join a university. When they tried to enroll with the letters they were, of course, rejected. Sun had made the scam seem genuine by claiming to be a city mayor with influence over the enrollment process. Given the endemic corruption among officials in China, it is no wonder the unfortunate students paid up.[174]

Big-city transport operators are also regularly cheated by passengers who drop fake coins or tokens into fare boxes. Even when drivers suspect fake coins, they do not stop the passenger and argue, since doing so delays the bus, whereupon the police will fine the driver.[175]

Fake cash is big business in China. Workers at a factory in southern Guangdong Province found they had been paid in counterfeit notes in 2007. Many workers who complained about this to factory bosses were laid off.[176] Counterfeit notes are so common that one bride and groom set up a money-scanner at their wedding reception to check the authenticity of the traditional wedding gift of money that they were given by guests.[177]

China's Public Security Bureau used to have a specialist department for counterfeit currency. It was disbanded in 2005. In 2009 the nation's Ministry of Public Security announced that it had seized 684 million yuan (about US$100 million) in fake notes in the first eight months of the year.[178]

In 2006, the Wanshunhua Feed Co in the northern city of Changchun sold 28,000 tons of rice for human consumption when it was fit only for animal consumption. Some of the rice was 17 years old. The company had paid US$110 per ton for the rice and sold it on at twice that price.[179]

Also in 2006, officials seized one *million* towels from nine factories in northern Hebei Province which had been dyed with cancer-causing chemicals such as benzene derivatives. The towels were being sold nationwide.[180]

In the same year, more than 300 people were poisoned when they ate pork laced with a chemical called clenbuterol, which local farmers had illegally fed to their pigs. Though the drug was banned in the 1990s, farmers use it because it can make the animals grow faster.

They usually stop feeding it to the pigs a few weeks before slaughter so that it is hard to pick up in tests. Even so, most pigs are not tested, say local food authorities, since the 30 yuan (US$3.8) it costs to test a pig is deemed too expensive.[181]

And in 2008, around US$30 million worth of fake agricultural materials such as pesticides and fertilizers were impounded. [182]

It is not that the Chinese people are dismissive of their own safety. A survey in 2007 revealed that nearly 65% of people in China were concerned by food safety issues. The figure had been 7% higher the year before, media reported, yet another 2007 survey said nearly 85% of rural citizens felt food safety was a major concern.[183]

Money is consistently the driving force behind sometimes surprisingly inventive ways to cheat the public.

Even those in uniform cannot be trusted. Many small business owners in Shanghai were cheated in 2007 by fake fire safety officers, who would trick them out of money by imposing fines for breaches of fire safety rules or charging for 'fire safety certificates' – fake, of course.[184]

Ticket counterfeiting is also rife in China, especially rail tickets which are at a premium during China's travel-intensive national holidays. In 2007, police in Guangzhou arrested a gang that had nearly US$100,000 worth of fake railway tickets to sell.[185] Thousands more travelers during the three annual 'golden week' holidays are not so lucky, unknowingly buying fake tickets due to a lack of supply of the real thing. In 2008, 2,309 scalpers were arrested and nearly 80,000 fake tickets seized. By 2009, provincial police were offering rewards of up to US$70,000 for tip-offs on scalpers.[186]

China is the world's biggest producer of sex toys, having 70% of the global market by 2004. But the country's sex shops routinely sell shoddy and substandard sex toys. The shops bargain on the fact that customers will be too embarrassed to complain when they find out they have brought low quality goods. One sex toy was on sale for US$60, yet only US$5 was spent on making it to keep costs down. A 2003 survey found that 30% of condoms on sale were not safe.[187]

Durex executives also had a rude shock in 2006 when they found fake condoms bearing the Durex logo and design on the production lines of a factory they were assessing as a potential partner.[188]

Chinese citizens suffering from the scandalous use of illegal additives in food, poorly processed food and mislabeled food may suffer further problems by not being able to get real medical care.

According to Dr. Yu Baofa, a doctor from eastern Shandong Province, China has become "an international medical joke." In the last ten years, the country has given 168,740 permits for new drugs. "It's impossible for China to invent more than 16,000 new drugs in one year" said Dr. Yu. "Even in the US, only several dozen drugs are approved each year. And everybody knows that China's medical technology is still backward."

One of the main reasons behind this vast number of new drugs was rampant corruption in China's State Food and Drugs Administration. This body was headed by Zheng Xiaoyu until 2005, when he was removed from his post. More than a year later, in December 2006, he was accused of taking bribes.[189]

"Under Zheng's protection many medical enterprises got permits in a very short time due to 'special ties' with medical officials. And such 'special ties' mean consumers have to pay 50% more for new drugs" said Dr. Yu.[190]

Zheng was lionized for his 'iron hand' in promoting good drug manufacturing processes. He was cited as a 'model worker' and an 'outstanding entrepreneur.'

Zheng created the 'Good Medicine Product' standard. With GMP certification, he was able to funnel enormous amounts of cash to his own personal use. The GMP, said an anonymous drug producer, was impossible to obtain without cash.[191]

Hypocritically, Zheng commented in 2004 that overuse of antibiotics "has become a key threat to Chinese people's health."[192] He had also said that he, like much of the nation, was worried about food safety.[193]

After the extent of Zheng's corruption became clear, the government announced it would review all of the nearly 170,000 permits the SFDA had given out. Just one firm, the Kongliyuan Group in southern Hainan Province, was alleged to have bribed Zheng in return for permits for nearly 300 medicines, most of them highly lucrative antibiotics.[194]

Due to Zheng's financial greed, numerous fake and substandard medicines reached the market, damaging people's health and in some cases killing them.

China's Ministry of Supervision seemed more concerned with the fact that the SFDA "tarnished the image of the Party and the government" than it was about the threat to public health.[195]

In May 2007, Zheng Xiaoyu was sentenced to death. He was executed in July that year.

The tide of simple medical remedies to complex chemical medical treatments that are faked both for Chinese consumption and exported for world-wide use is now gaining international attention.

A factory in Zhejiang Province, eastern China, made huge numbers of fake 'Band-Aid' bandages, in non-sterile and likely contaminated surroundings. When authorities raided the factory (after the copyright holder, Johnson and Johnson, had complained) they found 33,000 boxes of fake bandages worth more than US$100,000, plus a further 11,000 empty boxes and three million labels.

The factory had been operating for five months before it was raided, flooding the market with a huge number of fakes that may have increased rather than reduced the infections which the genuine product was designed to protect against.[196]

In 2007, 17 members of a gang producing fake rabies medicine were arrested. The fake product, made from starch and water, cost less than one yuan to make but was sold for 130 yuan per dose. When arresting the gang, police also found more than 20,000 bottles of fake cardiovascular drugs.[197]

In 2009, 149 people were detained in connection with a counterfeiting operation in which more than ten tons of fake medicine was seized. More that 17,000 people had bought fake drugs from the gang, which also fielded a team of bogus doctors and pharmacists to promote the drugs at hospitals and drugstores. The fakes cost 30 to 40 yuan to produce and were sold for up to 1,000 yuan.[198]

Among the most widely-faked medicines are Viagra and Cialis. A 2004 survey across several major cities found that 98.5% of sex shops sold fake Viagra.

In 2006 Wang Weiping was jailed for ten years and fined two million yuan (US$260,000) after his firm made a total of 381,000 fake Viagra pills and 1.4 million counterfeit Cialis tablets, worth a street price of US$29 million.[199]

Just how big is the fake erectile dysfunction drug business? Another gang in Bengbu, a city in eastern Anhui Province, was found to have made sixty (60!) tons of fake Viagra.[200] And in 2005 a fake Viagra ring was busted in the city of Zhengzhou in central China. The gang involved was accused of making nearly ten million fake tablets.[201]

In 2004 Chinese authorities had found Pfizer's (the maker of Viagra) patent for the drug invalid in China, and did not grant the company patent protection until 2006.[202]

In 2007, Chinese courts ruled against Pfizer, in their suit to use the Chinese name 'Wei Ge' (meaning 'Mighty Brother') for Viagra because a Chinese firm was using it, in spite of the fact that it is recognized as a trademark in other Asian countries and has been linked to Viagra in China for a decade.[203] Even today, it is still easy to buy fake Viagra clearly stamped with the Pfizer name, at small drugstores, beauty salons and online.

In 2006 a fake version of the antibiotic armillarisin killed 11 people. The drug contained a chemical called diglycol, which damages the kidneys, nervous system and liver. The maker of the chemical, a firm in northern China's Heilongjiang Province, had been sold one ton of diglycol labeled as propylene glycol, the correct ingredient for the antibiotic.

Once again, the government launched another review of chemical plants only after the damage had been done.[204]

Later in 2006, a drug called clindamycin, made by a firm in eastern China, killed six people and caused severe adverse reactions in 80 more patients.

The SFDA posted a note of these adverse reactions on its website on July 27th that year. It was not until seven days later that an 'emergency report' banning the drug was issued.[205]

A crackdown in 2006 discovered 16 bogus military medical institutions advertising and promoting fake drugs. In China, military institutions are not allowed to advertise any pharmaceutical products, but unscrupulous civilian companies use military names and titles in a bid to confuse the public. Such advertising poses "a serious threat to public health and to the image of the People's Liberation Army," said the Health Department of the PLA.

One such fake, a non-effective 'PLA' drug alleged to cure heart disease, sold for almost US$100 per treatment course. Reports detailed the drug cost only US$1.25 to make, without indicating the cost in terms of human suffering.[206]

The SFDA announced that for the whole of 2007 (the most recent figures we could find), it dealt with 329,613 cases of unlicensed drugs and medical products. Among the notable cases that media mentioned was that of a company selling a fake anti-impotence medicine. This firm ran an ad, allegedly voiced by David Beckham (speaking fluent Mandarin Chinese), in which he said "Want to know how I can keep being strong and running on the field? USA Selikon capsules give me big help. It is also the secret weapon with which I satisfy Victoria."[207]

Within its borders China's citizens are becoming fearfully aware of the dangers inherent in an unsupervised, uncontrolled and seemingly uncaring food and pharmaceutical industry.

These same fears are now being exported to the wider world.

In 2006, diethylene glycol had killed 100 people in Panama after it had been mixed with cough medicine. The cheap chemical was falsely labeled as highly pure glycerin.[208] It came from the Taixing Glycerin Factory in eastern China's Jiangsu province.

The SFDA denied it had any responsibility for overseeing the glycerin factory, since the factory was classified as a food producer, not a drug producer, leaving any claimants searching for another official department to assume responsibility.[209]

In 2007, 6000 tubes of toothpaste in Panama were found to contain the same chemical, diethylene glycol that had killed 100 people before. The toothpaste appeared to have been made in China.

China's reaction was not to apologize or offer immediate investigations, but was to accuse critics of seeking pretexts to erect trade barriers.

"Toothpaste is not something you'd swallow, but spit out, and so it's totally different from something you would eat," reasoned a company manager from Jiangsu Province, a suspected source of the toothpaste, to Reuters news agency.[210] A senior manager at another toothpaste firm said he had never seen any official guidelines on chemical use in toothpaste.

Managers at two firms under investigation for manufacturing the toothpaste denied wrongdoing. "We didn't do this; we didn't make the bad stuff" a manager called Shi Lei told The New York Times. But she did say that diethylene glycol was regularly used in toothpaste in China.

However, speaking later to China Daily, Ms. Shi denied she had talked to The New York Times at all. "I got a call from someone asking about the toothpaste, but they said they were from a client company," she said. Even though her name was given on the firm's site as the contact person, she claimed her only connection with it was helping it publish business information on a trade website.[211]

Hu Keyu, a manager at a company which had sold the toothpaste on to Panama, said that if diethylene glycol were poisonous, "all Chinese people would have been poisoned."

More chillingly Mr. Hu observed, "You know, if you're in the export market, the margins are so small, so people use the substitute. Even one percent or half a percent price difference can matter to people here."[212]

Here. China. Apparently profit seems more important to Chinese interests than people's health overseas.

Ironically, the explosion of concern for the quality of the food and medical products China is exporting came about in 2007, which saw numerous family pets die in the US as a result of eating pet food from China made with melamine, a chemical used to give the food a false appearance of high protein content.

Melamine on its own is not usually highly toxic in smaller amounts, and other investigations suggested that it might have been another chemical added to the pet food, cyanuric acid, that led to the deaths. Again, cyanuric acid, though normally used in swimming pool hygiene, is not especially poisonous. However, scientists found that the two chemicals, when mixed, formed crystals that could have led to the kidney failure which killed the pets.[213]

And despite this scandal, melamine was still being added to milk, for human consumption, in 2008. At the time, media stated it caused the death of four children and the hospitalization of more than 50,000 others, their parents frantic with worry that the children might develop kidney stones.[214]

But in 2009, media gave different figures, saying 'at least' six children had died and a truly astonishing 294,000 infants suffered from kidney stones and urinary problems.[215] The company involved, Sanlu, went into bankruptcy but announced a compensation package ranging from around US$30,000 for bereaved parents to US$4,300 for severely sickened children. Many parents wanted to appeal this offer and file lawsuits. China's Supreme Court ordered lower level courts around the nation to accept such cases. Only one court in the whole country did so, a court in Hebei, where Sanlu was located. And even this court only accepted two cases.

All other appeal cases have failed.[216] Furthermore, one of the legal firms that did extensive work representing victims of the tainted milk was later shut down by the authorities.[217]

While there may be little hope for the parents of children harmed by the Sanlu scandal, the future seems brighter for officials involved. Bao Junkai, who was a deputy director general in China's quality control ministry, was given a severe reprimand and a demotion due to his slack control over quality supervision in Hebei Province. A year later, he was promoted to a higher position in a different province. And Liu Daqun, who had been demoted from his job in Hebei's agricultural department, went on to become mayor and deputy party secretary of Xingtai, a city in the province.[218]

A mere 6% of imported Chinese food products were considered pollution-free in 2005, with just 1% being labeled as 'green,' according to the US Department of Agriculture.

China is the world's leading exporter of fruit and vegetables, and huge amounts of other commodities. Various countries have begun to ban entire categories of Chinese products. For example, the EU blocked shrimp imports due to overuse of antibiotics, and South Korea banned imports of kimchi, a dish made from cabbage, after finding it tainted with parasite eggs and lead.[219]

Hong Kong (regarded as an international market) banned sales of Mandarin fish from mainland China after finding it tainted with cancer-causing green malachite dye, and Japan ordered its quarantine inspectors to ensure the county's importers checked the purity of beer sourced from China after fears it was tainted with large amounts of formaldehyde.[220]

China's response to most of these bans was to accuse the countries involved of protectionism. When Japan banned spinach tainted with pesticide and poultry infected with bird flu, China said "The Japanese Government is using food security as an excuse to erect barriers to Chinese exports. Japan's commitment to public health has been turned into trade protectionism" and that the "prohibition on all Chinese fowl and eggs has seriously damaged the interests of China's fowl industry."[221]

When several US states banned catfish imported from China in 2007 due to containing a category of antibiotics known as fluoroquinolones, which are banned in any amount in the US, China said that the US should follow WTO rules about safeguarding food supplies and not manipulate them to protect domestic producers.[222]

Yet inspectors from the US Food and Drug Administration inspect only a tiny proportion of the shipments pouring into the US from China. Even so, the US rejects around 200 Chinese shipments a month, far more than from any other country, due to excessive amounts of pesticides, antibiotics, other chemicals or mislabeling. Italy was the next highest at 35. China's food supply chains are so haphazard that it can be impossible to tell the original source of many foodstuffs.[223]

Frighteningly, in 2006, less than 2% of the almost 200,000 shipments China sent to the US were inspected, due to lack of manpower, time constraints and sheer volume.

In spring 2007, America employed 1750 inspectors. The cost of training and maintaining the high standard required to ensure public safety is prohibitive.

"For the life of me, I cannot understand why terrorists have not attacked our food supply, because it is so easy to do," said Tommy G. Thompson, former secretary of health and human services, told The New York Times. "The word is out" William Hubbard, a former deputy commissioner for the US Food and Drug Administration, also told the paper. "If you send a problem shipment to the United States it is going to get in, and you won't get caught."[224]

In the month of April 2007, a total of 257 food shipments were rejected, of which 137 of them were considered in 'filthy' condition, testing positive for salmonella and banned ingredients. One year later, April 2008, and the tide of sub-standard goods was still flowing. Just some of the problems identified by inspectors in that month were frozen shrimp containing veterinary drug residues, fish fillets containing salmonella, celery containing pesticides, dried orange peel containing chloroflurocarbons, poisonous grape seed extract, and goods from cod and noodles to beancurd and kumquat described as 'filthy.'[225]

US companies are so dependent on Chinese imports that it is very hard to do without them, and shipments are rapidly increasing.

Foodstuffs are becoming as important as other basic commodities such as oil and coal. For example, China now controls 80% of the global market for ascorbic acid, a key component of processed foods.[226]

The European Union cited China as a major violator of health and safety, saying it was responsible for nearly half of all unsafe products reported. Toys were top of the list of 440 unsafe products, followed by white goods, automobiles and lighting.[227]

It is China's willingness to export fake pharmaceuticals and medicines that causes fear around the world. Medical researcher Gao Jingde began to study this issue in 2004 after suffering side-effects from liver medicine he took, and later found to contain fake ingredients. Over the following four years he made 289 reports of fake medicine. But authorities seemed unconcerned, handing out trivial fines.

Gao was beaten badly in September 2008 by four men outside a hospital he had exposed for selling fake drugs. Gao said that the police were ignoring the case, and that he believed the hospital had hired the men to beat him up.

According to Gao, two-thirds of Chinese medicine stores sell fake goods.[228] In 2009, for example, fake diabetes medicine led to the hospitalization of nine people and the death of two.[229] And also in 2009, a woman, A Jiao, announced her intention to sue a clinic that had sold her what she alleged were fake sleeping pills. How did she know they were fake? She had taken a large amount of them in a suicide bid, but nothing had happened.[230]

In 2006, Peter Mandelson, the then EU trade commissioner, said that fake birth control pills and HIV retroviral pills made in China had been found by customs inspectors.[231]

Chinese-made fake Tamiflu, a drug that may help prevent the spread of bird flu, was also seized by US customs inspectors. Previously, in August 2006, more than 400 kilograms of the fake drug were seized by Shanghai officials, and later in that year co-operation between Chinese and US law enforcement agencies led to the seizure of more counterfeits of the drug.[232]

How does it come about that anyone can manufacture a fake drug that they must know can lead to the possible death of the person who takes it? It is beyond human belief that China can make fake Tamiflu, a drug that may prevent a global bird flu pandemic; that it makes fake birth control pills, thus leading to needless abortions or unwanted children; that it can make fake HIV drugs, thus allowing AIDS to ravage a sufferer's body.

China has made great claims about its relationship with the countries of Africa.

According to China's President Hu Jintao, China wishes "to support African countries in their economic and social development, help African countries build the ability to develop on their own and push forward the Sino-African cooperation." [233]

"In the long course of history, the Chinese and African peoples, with an unyielding and tenacious spirit, created splendid and distinctive ancient civilizations. In the modern era, our peoples launched unremitting and heroic struggle against subjugation, and have written a glorious chapter in the course of pursuing freedom and liberation, upholding human dignity, and striving for economic development and national rejuvenation," he says.[234]

Wen Jiabao, China's Premier, adds, "The Chinese government, guided by the principle of sincerity, friendship, equality, mutual benefit and common development, is committed to building a new type of strategic partnership with Africa....To accomplish this we will ... enhance political equality and mutual trust, promote win-win economic cooperation, cultural exchanges and maintain close cooperation in international affairs."[235]

Words do not cure disease or provide medical relief, and apparently neither do some of the drugs sent to Africa from China.

China is home to the sweet wormwood plant, which is a source of the chemical artesunate, used to make artemisinin, a potent defense against malaria.

Malaria kills one person every 30 seconds, and up to three million people a year. Ninety percent of the deaths are in Africa. Most of the victims are children.

Yet Africa, the continent that needs the drug most, is being flooded with fake versions of it. Fakes made in China that either contain too little artesunate or none at all.

In June 2009 the Nigerian government seized a major shipment of fake malaria drugs that it alleged came from China. Had they made it to market, more than 600,000 adults might have been harmed. The fake drugs contained just a single active ingredient. In November 2009, Nigeria moved to arraign two men, Ukogu Donatus and Nnaji Chukwudi, for importing the drugs from China.[236]

Many of these copies are highly detailed, even down to fake security holograms. And they are cheap – around forty US cents, as opposed to US$2.20 for the real thing.

"Most of these find their way into the hands of poor people, they don't have any choice. They buy these drugs with the little money they have and they die," says Kevin Palmer, a World Health Organization official working in malaria prevention.

"People die. We have plenty of instances when people have taken these fake drugs and then they are dead. It's murder."[237]

Reason 8
The Godless

In the summer of 2007 Chinese media announced that the nation had printed 43 million copies of the Bible in the previous 25 years. Media also pointed out that "there are more than 16 million Protestant Christians in China [no mention of Catholics], with 55,000 churches and meeting points, as well as more than 36,000 pastoral personnel."

"There are also over 100,000 voluntary church workers helping to fulfill the ministries. The 18 seminaries and Bible schools are churning out some 500 students. In 2005 alone, about 26,000 church volunteers were trained at provincial levels," said the same report. [238]

Another report in 2007 quoted Deng Fucun, Vice president of the Three-Self Patriotic Movement Committee of the Protestant Churches of China, as saying "The Communist Party of China has established favorable conditions and a sound environment for the five major religions to co-exist in harmony."

These religions are Buddhism, Taoism, Islam, Catholicism and Protestantism.

Vice president of the China Islamic Association, Ding Wenfang, adds that Islam "advocates happiness in two worlds (this world and the hereafter), which means enjoying the harmonious co-existence of society and people" said Chinese media.

Huang Xinyang, vice president of the China Taoist Association, says that Taoists have always believed in "living always with love and kindness, and all living creatures are equal."

And Shi Yongxin, the head Buddhist abbot at the Shaolin Temple, said "The goal of building a harmonious society proposed by the CPC is also the goal of religious people." [239]

In the official version, life in China today is one of religious freedom and harmony. Though the Communist Party is officially atheist, it is keen to suggest it respects and encourages religious freedom.

Article 36 of China's Constitution, adopted in 1982, says "Citizens of the People's Republic of China enjoy freedom of religious belief.... No State organ, public organization or individual may compel citizens to believe in, or not to believe in, any religion; nor may they discriminate against citizens who believe in, or do not believe in, any religion."

The constitution goes on to say that "the State protects normal religious activities" but that "No one may make use of religion to engage in activities that disrupt public order, impair the health of citizens or interfere with the educational system of the State."

The 'protection' of the Protestant church is overseen by two bodies, the China Christian Council and the 'Three-Self Patriotic

Movement,' both government-controlled bodies. The China Christian Council says that "The fundamental content of Reconstruction of Theological Thinking is to elaborate the basic Christian belief and ethical norms in the integration with the national situation and culture in China. The purpose of it is to enable us to evangelize in a more procreate way in the land of China, help believers seek for their faith healthily, and help our churches to be adaptable to the society" [sic].[240]

In the eyes of the Party, Christianity must thus be 'reconstructed' so that it fits in with "the national situation and culture in China." Christianity with Marxist and socialist characteristics becomes an all-encompassing Party ideology.

The 'Three-Self Patriotic Movement' refers to the three ideas of self-governance, self support and self propagation, and is based on a late nineteenth century formula drawn up to guide the development of Christianity in China, and surprisingly co-opted by the Communist Party. All religious organizations must register with these bodies, whose officials then exert direct control over the activities of the church in question.

The Catholic Church is overseen by the Chinese Patriotic Catholic Association, also a government-run body. This body oversees the appointment of bishops in China, and it also enforces approval of Chinese state polices such as contraception and abortion. These are in direct disagreement with Vatican doctrine, and indeed are a contentious issue disputed by each Pope.

Thus, while religious belief is indeed permitted in China, it is under the strict and absolute control of the Party. China's Christians are only allowed to meet in state-approved churches in which their actions can be monitored, their numbers counted and attendees noted.

According to the US Commission on International Religious Freedom in 2007, "The Chinese government continues to engage in systematic and egregious violations of freedom of religion or belief. Religious communities are growing rapidly in China and the freedom to participate in officially sanctioned religious activity increased in many areas of the country over the past year."

Nonetheless, said the Commission, "All religious groups in China face some restrictions, monitoring, and surveillance, however, and religious freedom conditions deteriorated for communities not affiliated with one of the seven government-approved religious organizations, those considered by the government to be "cults," and those closely associated with ethnic minority groups. Religious communities particularly targeted include Uighur Muslims, Tibetan Buddhists, "underground" Roman Catholics, "house church" Protestants [i.e. churches not under direct government control], and various spiritual movements such as Falun Gong."

"There continue to be reports that prominent religious leaders and laypersons alike are confined, tortured, "disappeared," imprisoned, or subjected to other forms of ill treatment on account of their religion or

74

belief. Moreover, legal reforms, which were issued with the promise of increased religious freedom protections, have not halted abuses and are used in some cases to justify arrests and other restrictions."[241]

For example, China jailed two ministers who were operating outside the officially-approved Protestant church in July 2007. The men, Zhang Geming and Sun Jingwen, were caught distributing bibles and were charged with using an "evil cult to obstruct the law." They were punished via an extrajudicial process that meant they were not granted a formal trial, and were sentenced to a year in a labor camp.[242]

China's constitution says that "The people's courts carry out a public trial system. Cases should be tried publicly, except those involving state secrets or individual privacy and involving minors, which according to law shall not be heard publicly."[243] Clearly this did not happen in the case of Zhang and Sun. China's constitution is, in effect, unsupported by the concept of the rule of law. Likewise, in September 2008, Pastor Zhang Zhongxin faced a closed-door trial in which authorities evaluated a two-year labor camp sentence that had been imposed on him previously. His *crimes* were training missionaries and evangelizing Christianity. Authorities claimed this 'endangered state security' as a pretext for refusing to let his attorneys or family meet him.[244]

In 2006 China arrested two leaders of an unregistered Catholic church, accusing them of having illegally left China by using other people's identities. According to the Hong Kong-based Information Centre for Human Rights and Democracy, China seldom grants visas to members of underground churches to stop them having contact with clergy outside China. One of the two men arrested, Shao Zhumin, had been sentenced to six years in prison in 1999 for illegally printing bibles, but was released early, in 2003.[245]

Also in 2006 China executed the leader of an underground church, Xu Shuangfu, and 11 of his deputies. Xu was the founder of the 'Three Grades of Servants' church, an illegal underground church that once claimed to have a million followers. Xu was convicted of murder, but church members said Xu's conviction was wholly based on confessions that had been gathered via the torture of other church members. Li Heping, Xu's lawyer, said that no physical evidence had been submitted at the trial. According to the letter of Chinese law, a confession alone cannot be used to secure a conviction. But once again, it seems, Chinese law was ignored.[246]

In that same year, Chinese police arrested a journalist, Zan Aizong, who had written online about the forced demolition of a church and a crackdown on a group of Christians. Up to 3,000 local Christians had protested when the demolition began. Zan was charged with "spreading rumors harmful to society" and placed in administrative detention for a week. When he was released, he was fired from his job as a provincial bureau chief of his newspaper. He said it would be very hard for him to find another job in journalism.[247]

China's constitution says "Citizens of the People's Republic of China have the right to criticize and make suggestions to any state organ or functionary. Citizens have the right to make to relevant state organs complaints and charges against, or exposures of, violation of the law or dereliction of duty by any state organ or functionary."[248] The words of the constitution are so often not translated into real life freedoms.

In 1996, government authorities demolished a shrine in the village of Donglu in northern China's Hebei Province after many thousands of unregistered Catholic Church followers believed they had seen a vision of the Virgin Mary there. Authorities then arrested Su Zhimin, the bishop of the followers' underground church. After his release, he went into hiding for a year and a half, before being arrested again in October 1997. Since that time, he has not been seen and his whereabouts are unknown.

According to Human Rights Watch, Chinese authorities also destroyed the grave of Bishop Fan Xueyan, who had been Bishop Su's predecessor, to prevent Catholic followers from paying their respects.[249]

"We desperately need to know if Bishop Su is dead or alive. I have heard if the bishop were still alive he would not be in good health because of multiple ailments" said Joseph Kung, to a US Congressional Hearing in December 2006.

Kung heads the Cardinal Kung foundation, an organization named after Cardinal Ignatius Kung, another religious leader sentenced to life imprisonment by the communists in 1960 for refusing to join the government-run Chinese Patriotic Catholic Association. He was not released until 1985, and even then was placed under house arrest until 1987. He then went to the US, where he lived until his death in 1990.[250]

Joseph Kung also told a Congressional Commission in 2004 that "Bishop Su …had been arrested at least five times, and spent approximately 28 years in prison thus far. He was beaten in prison so savagely that he suffered extensive loss of hearing. He met with Congressman Christopher Smith in January 1994 and was arrested and detained for nine days immediately after the departure of Congressman Smith."

"Bishop Su was seen only once when he was accidentally discovered on November 15, 2003 while he was hospitalized in a Baoding hospital. Once the Chinese government realized that Bishop Su was discovered, he was taken away immediately without a trace," said Mr. Kung.[251]

The Cardinal Kung foundation says "Currently, every one of the approximately 45 bishops of the underground Roman Catholic Church is either in jail, under house arrest, under strict surveillance, or in hiding."

And according to the 2005 Annual Report of the United States' Congressional Executive Commission on China, "Despite assurances of its desire to establish diplomatic relations with the Holy See, the Chinese government has not altered its long-standing position that, as a precondition to negotiations, the Holy See must renounce a papal role in the selection of bishops and break relations with Taiwan."

The 2006 report from the same body noted that "Government repression of unregistered Catholic clerics increased in the past year. Based on NGO reports, officials in Hebei and Zhejiang provinces detained a total of 38 unregistered clerics in 13 incidents in the last year, while in the previous year officials detained 11 clerics in five incidents. The government targets Catholic bishops who lead large unregistered communities for the most severe punishment. Bishop Jia Zhiguo, the unregistered bishop of Zhengding diocese in Hebei province, has spent most of the past year in detention. Bishop Jia has been detained at least eight times since 2004."

"The government severely represses Islamic practice in the Xinjiang Uighur Autonomous Region (XUAR), especially among the Uighur ethnic group... The government's religious repression in the XUAR is part of a broader policy aimed at diluting expressions of Uighur identity and tightening government control in the region. The government continues to imprison Uighurs who engage in peaceful expressions of dissent and other non-violent activities. Writer Nurmemet Yasin and historian Tohti Tunyaz remain in prison for writing a short story and conducting research on the XUAR" said the congressional report.[252] The 2007 report said that "Government harassment, repression, and persecution of religious and spiritual adherents has increased." It also reported increased controls in Xinjiang, where "Religious repression ... accompanies a broader crackdown in the region aimed at diluting expressions of Uighur identity."[253]

In 2008, even religious music came under attack from China's authorities. The world-renowned Academy of Ancient Music was due to give a public performance of Handel's 'Messiah' at the Beijing Music Festival in October that year. But shortly before the performance was due, officials insisted it be made 'invitation only.' This effectively banned members of the general public from attending. At the same festival, the Rome Orchestra was due to give a performance of Mozart's 'Requiem.' However, orchestra manager Stefano Palamidessi was told he had to drop this from a planned open-air performance. This performance had been planned to take place in Dujiangyan, a city devastated by the May 2008 earthquake. It was intended to raise money for victims of that quake.[254]

China's domestic religions – Taoism and Buddhism -- have offered a very different perspective on life than Western religions, and therefore receive a higher level of tolerance from the Party. While Western religions support theories of individual belief in an ultimately powerful deity, often in confrontation with totalitarianism active within non-democratic countries, China's main religions conform to the existing civic structure which says "No one may make use of religion to engage in activities that disrupt public order."

Though there are many different sects of Taoist belief, all share the core principle of 'wu wei' or 'non-action.' While the religion does teach ethical ideas such as its 'Three Treasures' of kindness, simplicity and modesty, the religion's overall focus is one of self-cultivation and non-involvement with the world.

Buddhism, like Taoism, is an extremely diverse religion, but at its core, too, is a philosophy of 'turning away' from involvement with the world.

The government has paid particular attention to those of a religious belief espoused by leaders such as the Dalai Lama.

In 1995, the Dalai Lama named a six-year old Tibetan boy, Gedhun Choekyi Nyima, as the Eleventh Panchen Lama, the second highest religious position in Tibet. He was then arrested by Chinese authorities, who installed their own choice, a boy called Gyaincain Norbu. Gedhun Choekyi Nyima has not been seen since. Most Tibetans reject the choice that China has imposed upon them.[255] There is a constant theme behind the façade of religious freedom as described by the Communist Party. That is containerized faith which is then carefully sanitized so it can be fed back to believers in a form devoid of any revolutionary fervor.

Another strand of Chinese belief well-exposed in Western media is Falun Gong, which at this date is still totally outlawed. Part cult, part religion, part exercise, the Falun Gong followers fatally attracted attention to themselves when using an internationally recognized method of religious protest -- the non-violent demonstration.

The crackdown on Falun Gong began in 1999 when members of the group gathered near Zhongnanhai, the Beijing residence compound of many of China's top leaders, to protest about perceived unfair treatment. This unified display of political protest outside Party control terrified China's leaders. Within weeks, China banned the movement with extreme prejudice.

Amnesty International reported soon after that "Tens of thousands of Falun Gong practitioners have been arbitrarily detained by police, some of them repeatedly for short periods, and put under pressure to renounce their beliefs. Many of them are reported to have been tortured or ill-treated in detention. Some practitioners have been detained in psychiatric hospitals. Those who have spoken out publicly about the persecution of practitioners since the ban have suffered harsh reprisals."[256]

In March 2007, Amnesty said "Overseas Falun Gong organizations have recorded the deaths in custody of over 2,000 Falun Gong practitioners since the crackdown began. It has recently been alleged that many Falun Gong detainees who died in custody had been used to provide organs for transplant through 'organ harvesting.' Amnesty International is investigating these reports, but is not yet able to verify them."[257] But in 2010 Amnesty was still issuing reports of the torture and abuse of Falun Gong practitioners.

Lawyers who represent Falun Gong detainees are also regularly harassed. For example, lawyer Wang Hongyang was arrested July 2009. Twenty police broke into his home, without a warrant, in defiance of Chinese law. Police also refused to let him meet with his lawyers, again in contravention of Chinese law. He was beaten in jail, leading to a broken ankle. He was not allowed to receive treatment for this for two weeks, by which time he had developed serious infection. In December that year he was sentenced to seven years in prison.[258] The city of Beijing alone revoked the licenses of 24 other lawyers who had been active in human rights work in general in 2009.[259]

Repression showed no sign of easing up in 2010, with continued harassment of lawyers. Gao Zhisheng, a prominent human rights lawyer, was taken into custody by police in February 2009. He was detained for more than a year, being released in March 2010. But just one month later, he disappeared again.

A legal colleague of Gao's, Li Heping, said that Gao had gone visit his father-in-law in Xinjiang region, and was arrested there. Police put him on a plane to Beijing, but from that point on he was not seen again. "Friends and colleagues fear that he could have been taken back into police custody" said Li.[260]

Responding to US concern in June 2007 about this constant repression, China said the "ban of the anti-social cult Falun Gong is legitimate, a reflection of public opinion and it shows that the government is protecting citizens' rights."[261] China further accused America of "distorting the truth for political reasons" and called on the US to refrain from interfering in China's internal affairs via religious issues (just ten days after China had offered its support to the government of Pakistan for its crackdown on a pro-Taliban mosque. "As a friendly neighbor of Pakistan, China backs Pakistan's measures to safeguard social stability and economic development" said Foreign Ministry spokesman Qin Gang.[262])

Confucianism, relative to the high level of government acceptance, can be added to the major Chinese belief systems. Although it is not exactly a religion in the same sense as Taoism and Buddhism, it has been a key factor in shaping the ethical outlook of the Chinese people. While Confucian belief does emphasize the concept of 'ren,' or 'humanity,' it tends to do so within a very formalized social structure. For Confucianism, the most important thing is a well-ordered society in which every person knows their place.

Confucianism, Taoism and Buddhism were ruthlessly suppressed for much of 'New China's' history. Today, however, the Communist Party has begun to embrace Confucius once more, using the philosopher to support its own target of 'harmony,' a sort of Confucius dressed in Marxist clothes. It's almost as if Confucius was a communist from the very beginning – a red Jesus.

Buddhism too is gaining in popularity, and today the bulk of China's 100 million religious believers are Buddhists, says Chinese media.

A visit to any Buddhist temple will reveal numerous worshippers, both young and old, bowing before statues of the Buddha – something that was unthinkable just a few years ago. Most are doing so to seek good luck, success, personal wealth or a happy marriage. Buddhist temples invariably have an object – an urn, a statue, a fountain – onto or into which people throw coins. If the coin lands on a certain part of the object, this is held to endow the thrower with great financial blessings.

At the core of traditional Chinese belief, then, is the idea of self – either a philosophical extinction of self, as in the case of classic Taoism and Buddhism – or a purely mercenary sense of self, asking the deity in question to provide the blessings of fame and fortune. Self, but not individualism.

What is noticeably absent is the Judeo-Christian ethic of doing good, of helping the less fortunate. In Chinese belief, both ancient and modern, wealth is a sign of heavenly blessings. Even Deng Xiaoping said 'To get rich is glorious.' Rather than wealth being seen as a mandate to help the poor, it is viewed as approbation from heaven. The wealthy man is the righteous man, often above reproach, as is demonstrated by the way some wealth-seekers in China disregard public welfare, environmental concerns, and often basic human morality. 'Glorious' in China has nothing to do with graceful.

One of China's most revered writers, the early twentieth century author Lu Xun, said that "…in China, although we pride ourselves on our virtue, in actual fact we are only too deficient in mutual love and aid. Even moral concepts like 'filial piety' and 'chastity' are simply means to take advantage of the young and weak, while others look on and do nothing. In such a society, the old folk are not the only ones who find it hard to live – even the emancipated young can barely keep alive."[263]

Lu Xun also said of Confucius: "Admittedly, Confucius devised outstanding methods of governing the state, but these were thought up to rule people for the sake of those in authority; there was nothing of any value to the people… We cannot say he had nothing to do with the people, but I fear the politest thing we can say is he has absolutely no feeling for them."[264]

Lin Yutang, another renowned twentieth century writer, identified Chinese indifference as "the fatal disease of the body politic."

"The Chinese people take to indifference as Englishmen take to umbrellas, because the political weather always looks a little ominous for the individual who ventures a little too far out alone. In other words, indifference has a distinct 'survival value' in China," he wrote in 1935.

"Chinese youths are as public-spirited as foreign youths, and Chinese hot-heads show as much desire to 'meddle with public affairs' as those in any other country. But somewhere between their twenty-fifth and thirtieth years they all become wise and acquire this indifference which contributes a lot to their mellowness and culture," Lin wrote.

The reason for this indifference, says Lin, is that personal rights are not guaranteed. "One can be public-spirited when there is a guarantee for personal rights, and one's only look out is the libel law. When these rights are not protected, however, our instinct of self-preservation tells us that indifference is our best constitutional guarantee for personal liberty."[265]

While both Lu Xun and Lin Yutang hail from other eras, their words gave a prescience and immediacy for today's China. Would they be happy they had so accurately described the Chinese people of so many decades later? Or would they reflect negatively on the fact that today in China people are mostly empty, devoid of faith in government, country or Marxist theory?

Religion is comfort. That so many lives in China are devoid of comfort only increases the vacuum for the religions of the world to flow into. Although the Party has yet not imagined such a theoretical catastrophe, communism is not one of those religions.

The Largest Box of Toy Soldiers in the World

China is highly secretive about the detailed structure of the People's Liberation Army (PLA). From the location of many bases to the true amount of financial expenditure, the Party keeps most information about its armed forces firmly hidden from the public eye, as is typical of all armed forces around the world. But by building a 2.3 million strong modern armed force, China has created fear and uncertainty around the world, as well as demands that the nation 'detail' its military intentions.

In an attempt to give the illusion that China is open and honest about its military activities, some information is being made public.

"The Army has no independent leading body, and the leadership of it is exercised by the four general headquarters/departments. A military area command exercises direct leadership over the Army units under it. The Army has 18 combined corps, which are mobile combat troops," China said.[266]

The PLA has ten ranks -- general, lieutenant general and major general; senior colonel, colonel, lieutenant colonel and major; captain, first lieutenant and second lieutenant. China only instituted military ranks in the PLA in 1955, a system which it then abandoned in 1965. It was not until 1988 that the army again began to use a rank system.

In 2007, state media gave equally vague insight into the command structure of the PLA, announcing that President Hu Jintao had promoted three senior military officers to the rank of general, bringing the total number of China's generals to 167.[267]

Between 2003 and 2005, the PLA reduced its troop numbers by 200,000. Over 60,000 military personnel have been removed from the headquarters provincial command areas alone. This was the third round of cuts in recent decades, following a reduction of 500,000 troops in 1997 and an astonishing one million troops in 1987. In spite of these huge reductions, the PLA is still vast, with 2.3 million troops.

"More than 3,000 departments of and over 400 units directly affiliated to the headquarters at and above the regimental level have been cut. A considerable number of agricultural and sideline production units, cultural and sports units, military representative offices at railway stations and material supply organs have been closed. The PLA has also closed 15 educational institutions and 31 training organizations" said the 2006 White Paper.

The White Paper did offer more insight into the structure of the People's Armed Police Force (the PAPF), which may best be described as a full-time version of America's National Guard. "The PAPF has a total force of 660,000... [it] consists mainly of the internal security force." It also networks its troops with several other departmental groups, including the PAPF Gold Mine Force, the PAPF Forest Force, the PAPF Water and Electricity Supply Forces, and the PAPF Communications Force. In addition, border security, firefighting and security guard forces are also components of the PAPF.

"The PAPF General Headquarters is the leading and commanding organ that directs and administers the internal security force and ... provides guidance to other forces subordinate to the PAPF. Every day, more than 260,000 PAPF servicemen are on guard duty. ... The PAPF annually handles an average of over 100 cases of attempted attacks against guarded targets and escape attempts by detained suspects and imprisoned criminals."

According to the white paper "the PAPF effectively safeguards the fundamental interests of the people, social stability and the dignity of the law."[268] And, of course, it offers its total allegiance to the CPC.

The PAPF is much more in the public eye than the PLA. Even so, while remaining tight-lipped about the structure of the PLA, Chinese media is keen to at least offer insight into what daily life in the army is like. But the view is often of a homey, socialized group of 'cub scouts' barracked for camaraderie rather than combat.

"The Chinese army started its IT revolution in the 1990s" said media in 2007. "Digital technology allows commanders to electronically monitor the borders right around the clock even while cooks in the barracks are rustling up some tasty grub using a recipe from an e-Book consulted on a screen in the kitchen."

"With regiments...far from towns, soldiers used to have to travel a long way just to buy a tube of toothpaste. But in January 2007, an online shopping site appeared on the district's military LAN -- and now a soldier staring out at the hillside in a remote border post can simply click on a website to whistle up his favorite brand of rice cakes" said reports.[269]

But perhaps worried that too much hi-tech would corrupt the troops, state media also announced that "the tradition virtues of frugality, discipline and readiness to serve the people remain unchanged among the troops." One can almost see young lads vying for the hard-to-acquire 'frugality' merit badge.

To remind new recruits of the importance of these virtues, members of the PLA are shown the 'classic' Chinese film romantically called 'Guards Under Neon Light.' This film, made some forty years ago, details the virtues of the PLA's Eighth Company while stationed on Shanghai's famous Nanjing road. The film shows how the "soldiers who patrolled on a dazzling road of Shanghai...resisted various lures of the booming city and remained frugal, well-disciplined and ready to serve people."

According to Zhang Daoguang, who commands the Eighth Company today, "we have been screening the film 'Guards Under Neon Light' to new recruits, asking them to carry on the company's traditional virtues."

Zhang says that today's soldiers are also "required to save every cent of money, every piece of paper, every grain of rice, every drop of water and every kilowatt of electricity."[270]

Photographs of PLA life often appear in local press. One picture of the troops engaged in the recent 'Peace 2007' military games showed hundreds of soldiers lined up in a row in front of a troop train washing their clothes in individual wash bowls. While washing clothes together may be a unifying tradition for the Chinese troops, one wonders where all these wet clothes could be hung to dry.

Another picture showed troops training in the sun on a beach, their backs bare, sheets of skin being burned off - red skin the color of fire. It is quite popular to show photographs of martial arts experts demonstrating the quality of their technique.

The following year China held 'Warrior 2008,' another round of war games to which international military observers were invited. This event, involving 5000 troops, 'showed China's sincere hope of strengthening friendly exchanges and cooperation with foreign military forces' China Daily quoted Geng Yansheng, deputy head of the foreign affairs office of the Ministry of National Defense, as saying.[271]

China also showed concern over its soldiers' psychological wellbeing as well as their moral uprightness, by introducing mental health tests for new recruits for the first time in 2007. The tests, said China's Liberation Army Daily "aim to find out whether the applicants are suited to a military career."

"With China increasingly aware of the importance of good mental health among its armed forces, the PLA headquarters issued a set of new recruitment rules last year, requiring that China's military colleges carry out drug and psychological tests when recruiting would-be military officials," said media, noting that "Tests have been a part of PLA recruitment since 2006."[272]

In 2007, Shi Baohua, deputy chief of the Personnel Department of the PLA's General Political Department, announced that "The military will establish a new personnel training and educating system, which combines basic and continuing education, academic and military education, and domestic and overseas training."

"The Chinese military officers of the future will be brighter tacticians, better educated and adept at commanding the highest tech weaponry under an innovative training plan to build a better armed forces in the information age" said media, explaining the reasoning behind the new training plan.[273]

China's Air Force also announced it had recruited more than 1,400 pilot students in the first seven months of 2007 – 1,300 of them straight from middle school. Since 1987, the Air Force has recruited more than 25,000 students from middle school.[274]

It was only in 2006 that the PLA began to use civilians in support roles. Traditionally, all jobs had been done by serving soldiers. The change meant that "active-duty officers, who are limited in number, [could] mainly take up command and combat posts." Since the change, 20,000 non-military staff had been recruited with an additional 6,000 in 2007.[275]

China opened one of its major military training exercises to media inspection in 2006, touting this as a great step forward in "China's military forces striving to enhance their transparency," said Chen Hu, a military expert.

The exercise in question was the 'Friendship-2006' China-Pakistan joint anti-terrorism exercise, running from December 11 to 18. Surprisingly, China allowed publication of failure, as if failure indicated openness and honesty. Some of the mistakes offered for press release:

- The division commander put off launching an offensive three times, to the point where the first echelon assault units stayed at the enemy's forward position for upwards of 50 minutes.
- The division requested firepower support, but did not provide specific times and targets.
- A new missile was launched at five targets, but only hit two.
- Individual units failed to set up radio stations, but rather used walkie-talkies and military mobile phones to communicate.[276]

How open can these reports really be in a nation that controls it media every bit as rigidly as it controls its army? The international media, apparently, were not invited.

International observers were, however, invited to an exhibition of the PLA's weaponry and technology as part of its 80th anniversary celebrations in 2007.

Argentinean Colonel Rolando Moyano said "We have learned a lot about advanced commanding theories there, and have got along with the Chinese teachers quite well," reported state media.

Another visitor, Captain S.A. Zakai from Nigeria, said "What impresses me most is the Chinese military's love for the people and the people's love for the military."

Major-General Luo Yuan said "The invitation to military attaches to the exhibition shows that Chinese military is (getting) more and more in line with international practice, more confident and transparent."

"China attaches great importance to military exchanges. Just as the New Concept of Security indicates, China seeks mutual trust, mutual benefit, equality and coordination. The Chinese military has always sought development that would benefit all, instead of zero-sum games," he said.

Captain Shahid Baig, of Pakistan's air force, however, seemed only interested in the PLA's new uniforms. "I think the new uniforms are very fashionable, modern and special, very different from many other countries" [277]

"Brand new ceremonial and casual uniforms -- and new battle fatigues -- were unveiled in Hong Kong on July 1, the 10th anniversary of Hong Kong's return to China, unleashing a loud hurrah from the mainland's enlisted men" reported breathless state media.

86

"When compared with military uniforms from other countries our uniforms appear baggy and dull. Men have new uniforms that highlight shoulder breadth and look taller and stronger" said Wu Yu, a senior engineer with China's Quartermaster Equipment Institute.

Surprisingly, Wu Yu, a woman in a man's world, said the "Women [have] uniforms featuring contracted waists [that] are much sassier." Will recruitment posters picture women in military uniform echoing the oft-used America slogan "Be all you can be – Be sassy"?

General Liao Xilong, chief of the PLA General Logistics Department, notes that "Despite the changes, the uniforms retain 'key PLA elements and icons' [essential visual representations while serving] under the command of the Communist Party of China, serving the people and performing bravely and skillfully in battles" reported media. [278]

The new uniforms were predicted to cost six billion yuan (US$789 million) said General Liao. "The expenditure is necessary, because uniforms serve as the name card of a country, revealing the discipline and bearing of armed forces."[279]

"My impression is that the top leaders of the military really want to make the rank-and-filers look smart and feel comfortable. They are very open-minded," said Yang Tingxin, president of the Quartermaster Equipment Institute.

General Liao also announced that in addition to making sure its soldiers were smart and sassy, the government's defense department was paying attention to their diet by increasing each soldier's daily food subsidy by 10% -- from 10 yuan to 11 yuan. The one yuan increase represents 13 US cents, bringing the Chinese soldier's daily food subsidy to a total of US$1.45.

The increase will "help offset the impact of price hikes and improve food for soldiers, as military training demands a lot of energy and a strong body" the general said. "The Chinese central government and the top military authority wanted soldiers to see the effects of the country's booming economy and improved living standards in their plates" he added.[280]

As part of its ongoing PR offensive, Chinese media noted that "more and more foreigners want to know more about the Chinese army." Reports described "the most frequently asked questions by foreign generals and senior officers." Among those questions released by the media were:-

• Is the United States China's biggest enemy?
• Who is your imaginary enemy in training?
• How does the Chinese army promote political education?
• Where do military officers' wives and families live when visiting their husbands?
• How many days of holiday can officers have?
• Why do you raise pigs and plant vegetables in camp?

Media said "that officers and soldiers always answer these questions frankly and this has helped promote the exchanges between the Chinese and foreign army. The openness and transparency also demonstrate the image of Chinese army as mighty, just, civilized and peaceful, which is conducive to increasing the friendship between the Chinese army and armed forces of other countries, as well as the exchanges and cooperation."[281]

More salient questions we suggest might lead to more interesting answers are:-

• What if the Party rejects invading Taiwan but the PLA wishes to 'march on'?
• What is an acceptable civilian/military death ratio should the PLA invade Taiwan?
• What is an acceptable economic loss for the nation should Taiwan attack Chinese infrastructure such as the Three Gorges Dam or coastal cities?
• Do you agree with General Zhu Chenghu's belief that is it acceptable to use nuclear weapons against the US if it supports Taiwan should the PLA invade?
• Should the army use force against its own people protesting for freer government and a freer society?
• How do you think PLA soldiers felt after shooting unarmed students at Tiananmen Square in 1989?

The PLA celebrated its 80th anniversary in other intriguing ways. One of these was by re-opening a memorial to the 'Nanchang Uprising.' This insurrection, which took place in 1927, saw around 20,000 soldiers break away (and basically mutiny) from the Nationalist army, and led to the foundation of the People's Liberation Army. The memorial had been closed for a year to undergo a renovation costing around US$20 million.[282]

Today, of course, such actions of mutiny would be excoriated by the Chinese government as 'splittism' and 'terrorism.'

Another 'celebration' of the anniversary was organized not by the PLA, but surprisingly by China Unicom, one of the nation's two major telecommunications firms. The company announced a new service to let users download film clips onto their mobiles of the PLA's military activities.

"I believe [the service] will be popular since we have so many military fans in China. We have more than 300,000 pictures of weapons and military figures in our database along with clips of hundreds of movies" said Yu Peng, a senior company official. "It's not just about making money. By doing it, we are celebrating the PLA's 80th anniversary," he said. The service costs 10 yuan a month, or about US$1.3.

"In the process, [we are] providing more healthy content through mobile phones" said Yu.[283]

A more truthful 'healthy' view of the PLA might be to reflect that since 1949 over 300,000 members of the army have died on active service.[284] This is according to government figures which are, naturally, much lower than outside independent estimates. According to Beijing, for example, the official death toll in the Korean War was around 140,000 deaths. But the historian Jung Chang, citing an unofficial statement by Deng Xiaoping, puts the number at 400,000.[285]

When a soldier dies for his country it should mean something, serve a purpose, or gain freedoms. What do China's 300,000 military deaths mean? What purpose have they served? What freedoms have they gained?

China still vilifies Japan for its military past. But it can be suggested that Japan's recent military history since 1945 is far more successful than China's. In the same decades that China has lost at the very least 300,000 soldiers, Japan has had no military casualties at all.

None.

Zero.

The Builders of Myth, the Tellers of Tales

Joseph Goebbels, Nazi Germany's propaganda master, is reputed to have said "If you tell a lie big enough and keep repeating it, people will eventually come to believe it. The lie can be maintained only for such time as the State can shield the people from the political, economic and/or military consequences of the lie. It thus becomes vitally important for the State to use all of its powers to repress dissent, for the truth is the mortal enemy of the lie, and thus by extension, the truth is the greatest enemy of the State."

His words have been put so deeply to work by China's communist leaders that the country today is, in effect, a kingdom of lies. Virtually every official news release and every official statement is a mix of half-truths and whole lies, ranging from subtle distortions of the truth to claims so outrageously improbable that one is almost moved to smile – until one remembers the suffering that the lie has been designed to hide.

The invented and mythic past of the Party leads to hypocritical statements today, such as that of Foreign Ministry spokesman Qin Gang, who announced in mid 2007 a donation of new historical records to the Nanjing Massacre Museum. Qin referred to efforts by some Japanese politicians to downplay the massacre as "attempts to obliterate or conceal the historic facts including the Nanjing Massacre [that] would bring them international condemnation." He added that "those who tried to blot out the memory of the massacre have an unethical approach to history and lack courage" and said that "China hoped Japan would adopt a responsible attitude in handling historical issues including the Nanjing Massacre and the issue of comfort women."[286]

Can one imagine a Japanese Foreign Ministry Spokesman saying "Japan hoped China would adopt a responsible attitude in handling historical issues including the Tiananmen Square Massacre"? Hypocrisy is a two-way street.

The Party has an irresponsible approach to history as part of its modus operandi, consistently fabricating stories to glorify its own actions, often at the expense of others. The true 'Long March,' for example, bears little resemblance to the internationally famous version the Party gives of it, and the many mistakes of Mao Zedong, which led to the death of tens of millions, are airbrushed out of the official record, at least within Chinese history books.

The government claims that "China has never launched pre-emptive strikes against any country. It is not part of its defensive ministry strategy."[287] This statement, made in blustering denial of Pentagon worries concerning China's huge military spending, is simply a lie. China's invasion of South Korea in the 1950s was clearly a pre-emptive strike, and its attack on Vietnam in 1979 was wholly unprovoked.

With its upbringing of historical falsehoods, it is perhaps no wonder that myths and lies are virtual 'truth' for the government of China today.

The 'truest' lies start at the top. Chinese Vice-Premier, Wu Yi, meeting US Treasury Secretary Henry Paulson in mid-2007, said that China was still a poor nation and thus no economic threat to anyone else. "Who could China threaten? We don't have the ability. We do not and will never be a threat to anyone," she said. Ms. Wu offered the fact that China has 23 million people living in poverty as 'evidence' to back up her claim. Wu also referred to Paulson's visit to China's poor Qinghai Province, saying she was happy he had seen the levels of poverty there.[288]

While millions in China do lack the most basic amenities of life, the country as a whole is far from poor. At the time Wu made these claims, her own government was hoarding a US$1.33 *trillion* foreign currency reserve, a fast-growing cash mountain almost beyond imagination, and clearly not available to Qinghai's poor. By late 2008 that cash mountain had swelled to US$1.8 trillion.[289]

Though quick to deny it could be a threat in any possible way, China is always ready to claim other nations pose a grave threat. According to a statement issued by the Taiwan Work Office of the Central Committee of the Communist Party of China and the Taiwan Affairs Office of the State Council, Taiwan's 2007 bid to join the UN "proved that [Taiwan president] Chen Shui-bian is an out-and-out schemer and saboteur who would not hesitate to sacrifice peace and stability across the Taiwan Straits and in the Asia-Pacific."[290]

China has repeatedly threatened Taiwan with war and maintains a massive and growing military presence on its side of the Taiwan Straits.

China also sought to demonstrate that America was a threat in its 2006 annual report on human rights in the US. A "Pentagon research team monitors more than 5,000 jihadist Web sites, focusing daily on the 25 to 100 most hostile and active" noted the report, which went on to say "In May 2006 human rights group Amnesty International condemned the detention of some 14,000 prisoners in Iraq without charge or trial."

China spends vast resources not just monitoring extremist websites but monitoring almost every single action its citizens take online – as well as blocking numerous sites, among them that of the very Amnesty International that it uses to criticize America.[291]

"The Chinese document also slams the United States for its lack of proper guarantee for people's economic, social and cultural rights" said related reports in China's state media, noting that "ethnic minorities are at the bottom of American society." As we have detailed elsewhere in this book, the Chinese government regularly abuses the "economic, social and cultural rights" of its people in the most serious fashion, and the country's own ethnic minorities are among its poorest citizens.[292]

Later in 2007, a delegation from the China Society for Human Rights Studies visited New York City. During this visit, the head of the Chinese delegation, Dong Yunhu, said "The Chinese government has made tremendous efforts to promote the country's democracy and legal construction and safeguard citizens' political rights, and remarkable progress has been made in this regard," media reported.

"In recent years, China has attached greater importance to the fostering of human rights in the country and has already enacted a series of important laws including the Supervision Law and the Property Law, which are instrumental in strengthening supervision and control over public power and safeguarding people's political rights," Dong said.[293]

Most fairy-tales begin with "Once upon a time…" But in China, fairy tales begin with "China attaches great importance to…" This is the formulaic rhetoric China uses to spin the lie that it is doing something about a problem.

In spite of "attaching great importance" to safeguarding people's rights, other media reports in 2007 made it clear just how sharply Beijing cuts personal freedoms. Hui Liangyu, a Chinese vice-premier, addressing members of the Chinese Catholic Patriotic Association (the state-controlled portion of the Catholic church) on the 50th anniversary of association's foundation, said that the association had "achieved a lot in training … maintaining the lawful rights of the Catholics," clearly defining the government's sense of religious freedom.

Hui urged the association "to unite the masses of religious people, upgrade their working capacity, and contribute more to the building of 'socialism with Chinese characteristics,'" it was reported in Chinese media. It is very clear that the 'rights' of people are only respected in so far as they meet with Party goals.[294] What child will spring forth from the religious rights of the people and the political goals of the Party?

The effectiveness of the Party's lies is shown by a survey published by the Chinese Academy of Social Sciences (CASS) at the end of 2006. According to this survey, covering more than 7,000 households, "some 74.9% of China's urban and rural residents consider China 'very harmonious' or 'relatively harmonious,' and around 75.8% regard the present stage of Chinese society as 'relatively stable' or 'very stable.'"

China currently suffers over 80,000 social protests or riots against perceived injustice every year.

The survey also found that "about 83.4% of those polled 'relatively agree' or 'very much agree' to the question that 'some problems emerging in China's current social development are only temporary ones'… about 91.6% 'relatively agree' or 'very much agree' to the judgment that the 'Party and the government is capable of governing the country well.'" In China, the Party knows where you live and what you say, which can be reflected in any public survey undertaken in China.[295]

In 2007, a report from the Party's central organization department "showcased… endeavors to build a permanent in-house democracy mechanism," said media, reporting that between 2003 and 2006 about 15,000 members of the Party "ascended to leading positions through open elections."

However, careful reading of the report exposes the lie. "More than 390 [of the 15,000] were prefectural-level cadres and about 3,800 worked at leading positions at county level," said media – meaning that the vast majority of those 'leading' positions were below county level and thus of no importance whatsoever.

"Experts point out that developing democracy within the Party is an important part of political restructuring and building of political civilization in China" said media, giving a typical Chinese-style statement that sounds reasonable – after all, developing democracy is unquestionably good – but says nothing at all about how that democracy will be created, or how that democracy will be placed in the hands of the people.[296]

In the summer of 2007, a string of scandals involving sub-quality food, real or otherwise, resulted in a spate of government demands and pronouncements. Government departments such as the Party's publicity department, China's State Administration of Radio, Film and Television and the General Administration of Press and Publications issued statements that reminded state media and provincial-level publicity departments in charge of local media to "brush up on journalistic ethics" and "maintain the image and social credibility of the Chinese media."

"Authenticity is the lifeblood of journalism while fabricated reporting is its arch-enemy" said one such statement.[297]

Do the words "authenticity" which is the "lifeblood of journalism," actually have veracity when placed into action in China?

In June 2006 Chinese media released glowing reports about the positive situation in Tibet. "A news conference held by the State Council Information Office announced that, in 2006, the per capita GDP in China's Tibet Autonomous Region reached 10,396 yuan – exceeding 10,000 for the first time."

"Qiangba Puncog, chairman of the Tibet Autonomous Regional Government, said that fifty years after the peaceful liberation of Tibet - under the loving care of the Central Committee, the energetic support of the people throughout the country, and through the arduous efforts of people of all nationalities in Tibet - the economy and society is developing comprehensively. Now it has entered a new stage of advancement and is making great leaps in development, and building a comfortable and well-off society."[298]

While the Han Chinese colonizers who live in Tibet are making plenty of money from their stranglehold on the country, the average Tibetan is doing far less well. Most Tibetans are excluded from any other job but farming, and among farmers in the region the average GDP is 2,435 yuan – less than a quarter of the 'true' figure Chinese media announced.

94

And the Tibetans have little choice in the matter. "The minority nationalities cannot be separated from the Han, and the Han cannot be separated from the minorities" said Chinese Vice-Premier Hui Liangyu in summer 2007, reminding all China's oppressed non-Han citizens that they would never be free.[299]

China applies its culture of myths and lies not just to territories it has colonized, such as its 'autonomous' regions Tibet, Inner Mongolia and Xinjiang, but to those it seeks to colonize, such as the vast areas of maritime territory it claims sole right to.

On 25th May 2007, media reports announced "conducive" talks between China and Japan concerning territory in the East China Sea which both countries laid claim to. The territory in question lies midway between China and Japan, and is the site of several large gas fields. Japan had proposed a median line giving each nation roughly half of the disputed area. China's proposed line pushed significantly past the median line suggested by Japan, putting the gas fields in their entirety on the Chinese side, leaving Japan with nothing.

The Chinese side was represented by Hu Zhengyue, Director of the Asian Affairs Department of China's Foreign Ministry. He said the talks were a "new beginning" and said China was ready to make joint efforts with Japan to push forward consultation.[300] In another article published on the same day, Feng Zhikai, a senior researcher at China's Institute of Japanese Studies, said that "It is fair to say China's emphasis on cooperation in energy development has been a prominent feature in the development of bilateral relations."[301]

The very next day Chinese media issued another report, this time quoting Jiang Yu, a Foreign Ministry spokeswoman. Jiang said "that China wanted to promote the negotiation process and achieve a joint development plan at an early date, and reiterated China's opposition to a demarcation line proposed by Japan," adding that "China has not and will never accept the median line and will not accept the median line as the basis for discussing joint development."[302]

Jiang Yu's words made it clear China had no intention whatsoever of backing down from its greedy and rapacious desire to exploit the gas fields to their utmost, sharing them with no-one.

This strategy of appearing conciliatory while having no true intention of changing can be seen in other areas of contemporary Chinese life. One manifestation of this is the 'apologizing' official.

The governor of China's northern Shanxi Province, You Youjun, made an almost unheard-of public apology for the high number of coal mine deaths that had become a regular fact of life in the province. "It's remarkable progress in China's politics to see leaders actually say they're sorry" noted media.

Governor Yu's apology certainly seemed sincere, especially since, as reported, Shanxi had in fact managed to reduce the coal mine death toll from 185 deaths per million tons of coal in 2000 to 85 deaths per million tons of coal in 2005. Yu's apology sparked other officials to do the same.

"Within months of Yu's statement, a vice premier, an education minister, the state environmental chief, [and] vice mayor of Sanya all came forward with confessions of failure and promises to do better" noted state media. "Some officials seem to be trying to head off greater trouble by seeking forgiveness from the public. They seem to feel if they look solemn enough and say sorry with enough conviction perhaps they'll be forgiven when they should be punished. A few ... have even been accused of crying crocodile tears." [303]

However, the government almost seemed convinced by the tears. At the end of May 2007, China's Central Commission for Discipline Inspection (CCDI), its government corruption watchdog, urged officials "who have traded power for money to confess their crimes before the end of June in return for leniency."

In the following month 1,790 officials did just that, between them owning up to crimes involving 77.89 million yuan (US$10.2 million). Gan Yisheng, a spokesman for the CDDI, did not give details of what punishments these officials would face. He did, however, say that "CCDI regulations have clearly stated government will show leniency to those who confess their wrongdoings by themselves within 30 days."[304]

Apologies apparently not required.

The easy-going attitude towards law-breaking officials is also – perhaps inadvertently – revealed in other media reports. After police boarded a ship floating off the coast of Guangdong Province, they found it loaded with more than 5,000 rare wild animals destined for the province's dinner tables. The ship had apparently been abandoned by its crew and its lack of registry made it hard for police to track down the smugglers. "Of the major illegal international businesses plaguing the area, animal smuggling is second only to drug smuggling in terms of scale" said media.

"To serve as a positive example, almost all of Guangdong's high-ranking government officials have refused to eat wild animals" said Li Tao, director of the information center at the Guangdong Wild Animals and Plants Protection Center.[305]

'Almost all' officials - not all officials, and no penalties were mentioned should an official break his promise.

The Chinese government is brilliant at semantics after the fact, making high-minded statements such as "The local government held an emergency meeting on Friday, ordering educational authorities to strengthen psychological guidance for all students and guard against accidents on campus caused by psychological problems."

This particular statement was reported by media after five fifth-grade primary school girls attempted to commit suicide, when one of them (who media gave an alias, Wang Xiao) had rejected advances from a boy in her class. This led to extensive class gossip, making Wang feel "uncomfortable," and caused her to react in a youthful, impetuous and very emotional way. She decided to kill herself "in order to safeguard her reputation" said media, explaining that four of her closest friends joined her in the attempt. They drank wine and beer together and then tried to drown themselves. Two of the girls, including Wang, subsequently succeeded and died.[306]

China simply does not have the necessary number of psychologists to deal with this problem. The truth is that the two girls' only memorial was a high-sounding yet wholly empty government statement.

The government is not above 'going Hollywood' when necessary.

This was what the government officials did in China's northwestern Gansu Province, by building a two kilometer wall along a major road. What was the purpose of the wall? To hide poverty-stricken dwellings "from sight of drivers and other passers-by" said media. "It's nicer to look at, so people won't see how shabby our homes are from the road," said villager Zhang Ping, who said she "had no money to renovate the house or build a new one, so the local government tried to disguise the scene with a wall of cement."

The wall has made lives even more difficult for the villagers. One, Zhang Tianzhi, had had to close his roadside shop after the wall was finished. "Building walls is to beautify the villages," said the vice-governor of the county.[307] In China, the way to deal with poverty is to hide the poor from sight rather than help them.

China's embracing of myths is also energized by its quest for historical glory. A skull unearthed from an archeological site in China was found to have a smooth, apparently man-made hole in it. Tests revealed the skull was 5,000 years old. "After years of study and research, experts and scholars presume that the defect was caused by an artificial craniotomy" said media.

"The ['patient'] did not die immediately after the craniotomy, but had survived for at least more than two years. This shows that Chinese neurosurgery technique was quite advanced at that time." [308] Medical reports into the patient's psychological wellbeing were not available, nor details of why the doctor put a hole in his skull.

Perhaps China's attitude to its past – and its present – is best summed up by Ai Weiwei, one of the nation's leading architects. Ai helped design the remarkable 'bird's nest' stadium built for the 2008 Olympics. He feels that the Olympics are a "pretend smile."

"Can a nation be celebrated and be so proud with this ignoring of its past?" he asked. "Can you have the self-confidence to clearly examine yourself, rather than to give this pretend smile on your face... It's this kind of fake smile which is disgusting" he told Reuters news agency. Ai spoke from direct experience on China's shameful but often hidden past, since his father, once a leading poet, was branded "an enemy of the state and a rightist" and send to a labor camp.

"I spent five years with him at a labor camp where he cleaned toilets" Ai said, adding that China today was trying to hide an endless parade of faults. "There are too many things. The whole political structure, the condition of civil rights... corruption, pollution, education, you name it."[309] Bravely, Ai made his statements while still in China.

He paid the inevitable price for his commitment to truth in 2009, when he was beaten by police in Sichuan Province, in an attempt to prevent him giving evidence at the trial of a dissident. He was injured badly enough to require specialist cranial surgery.[310]

Police in China's southwest Guangxi Zhuang region arrested a judge, Li Chaoyang, on suspicion of bribery in March 23rd 2007. By April 2nd, he was dead.

Relatives said "there were wounds on his body, [and] a gash across his lip and he was missing one of his front teeth" reported media. However, an official investigation "found that Li was mentally unstable and would not stop shouting and refused to return to his cell after an exercise period.... Investigators say Li attempted to escape many times and detention center officials say were forced to shackle him."

"On March 28, Li again attempted to escape but tripped and fell, hitting his face on a piece of angle iron, severely cutting his upper lip cut and knocking out one of his front teeth. He was taken to hospital for treatment and had a six-cm-long cut on his lip sutured," said reports.

What was the conclusion of the investigation? Li died of "Adult Sudden Death Syndrome." "This" said forensic scientists at the Guilin Medical Sciences College Hospital, "might have been sparked by an unstable state of mind, and abnormal sleeping and eating habits."[311]

Adult Sudden Death Syndrome?

State-of-the-art myths and tales are a refined science in China.

Reason 11
Crossing the Line for a Penny

Two Chinese men, workers in China's poor northern area, stretch out their right hands to receive their pay, the palms of each hand clearly telling the history for generations of their own and similar families of friends, neighbors and relatives.

Neither hand has felt the luxury of milled soap, or the touch of a doctor's care, or the weight of a good book, or the handshake from knowing leaders to the south in Beijing.

The finger tips of each hand long for the first touch of fine material of a quality suit, the unknown feel of fine porcelain gracing the pleasures of culinary delights, or the even the true sensation of their own skin long ago covered by layers of dirt, the ravages of sunburn, scars from work injury and quite likely disease that will never be treated.

These hands have never held a TV remote control, or danced over a computer keyboard and certainly never gripped the steering wheel of an automobile.

Today the two men, each with a family waiting at home, are to receive their yearly wages. One of these workers will receive enough money to be considered a 'low income' earner, while the other will receive just one coin less, and be subjected to another year of 'absolute poverty,' as determined by the same knowing leaders to the south in Beijing.

The paymaster counts out one yuan coins, placing them carefully on top of the thin stack of paper money held in the first worker's hand. The paymaster counts slowly, almost tantalizingly -- 783, 784, 785 yuan -- and then stops.

Into the second outstretched hand he again counts carefully -- 783, 784, 785 -- and then counts out one more coin that falls amongst the rest, bringing the total to 786 yuan.

The man holding 786 yuan is a new 'low income' earner by virtue of that single coin, while the man holding only one coin less, 785 yuan, is now statistically determined by the government in Beijing as being in 'absolute poverty.'

The hand holding 785 yuan is one coin short of crossing the line.[312]

The nomenclature of the government that graces the man with the extra coin effectively removes him as an important but negative statistic. Having crossed the line, he is regarded as another government accomplishment. He is another 'success story' in the fight against poverty.

Is it better to receive the one coin extra to cross the line so that your family can now be called a 'low income family' and thus be forgotten, or is it better to received one coin less and be constantly in the government's eye and be registered as a problem worthy of attention?

Historically, one of the major catalysts for revolution and the overthrow of dynasties in China has been a large gap between rich and poor. Hence our identifying the poor as China's 1st Army of Instability. The 1st Army will be those millions of people within China who are constrained to march on in poverty.

But defining the precise number of millions suffering poverty is not easy. China's definition of absolute poverty is earning up to 785 yuan a year. Those who earn between 786 and 1067 yuan a year are defined as 'low income' earners. They are recognized as 'needy' but not 'poor.'[313] In 2008 China began mulling raising the poverty line to 1300 yuan. Media said this was "a manifestation of the people-first governing concept that the new leadership is advocating." Yet no decision to raise the line was made, and more focus seemed to be placed on the fact that redefining the line would double the number of people defined as poor.[314]

However, the World Bank defines 'poverty' as living on less than US$1 (about 7.6 yuan) a day. This figure is generally accepted as an international measure of poverty. The bank's 2009 report pointed out that China's figure for poverty "is particularly stringent, and is the lowest amongst a sample of 75 countries. The official poverty line seems low not only compared to international standards, but also relative to the rapid rise in mean incomes and growing aspirations within China."[315]

If we use the World Bank figure – which equates to about 2800 yuan a year – the picture in China is very different, the World Bank figure representing a sum more than three times *higher* than the sum used by China for its definition of 'absolute poverty.'

China is still home to 18% of the world's poor, according to the World Bank, and around 150 million of its people are living on less than a dollar a day.[316]

Add to this a further 800 million farmers who have a per capita disposable annual income of US$405 – just US$40 higher than what the World Bank defines as 'poor' -- and a very different picture emerges than the one which China has painted for the world.[317]

Regardless, the poverty line has famously been crossed by millions in China's cities. China's new middle class is fast growing rich, and taking advantage of the trappings of modern life that come with new wealth.

China has the world's fastest-growing economy, but many millions in China's countryside have been left behind, forming the ranks of the 1st Army of Instability.

Aside from an accounting of the amount of money that determines poverty, there is of course the true human accounting of those who are living the life of poverty.

In 1978, before China reformed its economic policies, the country had 250 million people who lacked adequate food and clothing. By the end of 2005, that number had dropped to 23.6 million.[318]

By 2007 that figure had dropped a little further, to 21.48 million. In addition to these people, defined as living in 'absolute poverty' there were another 35.5 million in the 'low-income' category, said Zhang Baowen, vice-minister of agriculture.[319]

Still within the timeline of China's modern history, between 1959 and 1962, around 30 million people died from famine. Though the Chinese government claims this was a 'natural disaster' it was in fact directly caused by the catastrophic policies of Mao Zedong.

While great claims can be made for the reduction of poverty, equal blame should be applied to those in power who at that time exacerbated the poverty in China beyond all natural factors.

By the end of the 1970s, about 30% of the entire population lived under the poverty line, but by 1985 only 9.2% were still poor, based on the Chinese standards mentioned above.

Again, using a different pencil to do the accounting for a definition of poverty, a different picture is drawn. Using the WHO standard, at the end of the 1970s 60% of the population lived in poverty, a proportion which had dropped to 40% by 1985.

It is easy to be impressed with the drop of poverty accomplished no matter which accounting method is used. However, even under the best circumstances, there are still 23 million living in absolute poverty - and maybe many more, since one report in Chinese media in late 2009 stated that 40 million people in the nation were living in absolute poverty.[320]

That's equal to two-thirds of the population of Canada or one-third of the population of the UK. It's more than the entire population of Australia – or the State of Florida.

That's twenty-three million citizens who cannot even afford an extra change of clothes or nutritious daily food. Or afford school fees for their children. Or a simple visit to a doctor.

After 1985 the poverty reduction program began to falter. According to the United Nations' Development Program (UNDP), poverty within China began to increase again, rising from 86 million in 1988 to 103 million in 1989. The roller coaster ride continued from 1992, when the numbers of poor again began to drop, but this time more slowly than in the earlier period.[321]

In 2001, a UNDP survey compared China with a group of other countries that had a similar per capita income in terms of PPP, or 'purchasing power parity.' This is a method of equalizing the purchasing power of the different currencies compared.

The results showed that China had a greater percentage of people under the US$1 a day line than the other countries. China had more than twice the rate of poverty of Indonesia, even though Indonesia had a 28% *lower* per-capita PPP income. The same survey also found that between 1996 and 1999 poverty in China remained totally unchanged, even though the economy overall grew at 7% per year in this period.[322]

Urban poverty has also had the opportunity to begin to grow. Currently 13 million urban workers become unemployed each year, and, according to Tian Chengping, Minister of Labor and Social Security, there will soon be 24 million job seekers but only 11 million job openings.

And He Ping, president of China's National Institute for Social Insurance, says that in 2004 only 443,000 of the country's 120 million migrant workers received unemployment allowances. Though employers are meant to provide unemployment insurance for their workers, most refuse to do so in order to maximize their profits.

Local governments often turn a blind eye to this because they want rapid economic growth above all else. Meeting or exceeding economic growth estimates for the year can mean extra bonuses for officials, and even promotion.

By the end of 2005, only 100 million of China's 760 million workers were covered by unemployment insurance.[323]

Just how serious is China about poverty reduction? In 2005, the central government assigned about US$1.7 billion for poverty reduction.[324] In the same year, it said it spent more than US$30 billion on its armed forces. The Rand Corporation, a US-based nonprofit think-tank, estimated the true figure was closer to US$70 billion per year.[325]

Clearly, no matter which way you measure poverty, it is hard to get a precise picture of just how difficult life is for the hundreds of millions in China's rural areas. Examining other areas of life in China brings into focus just how hard the situation is.

For example, in China's western regions, home to about 400 million people, 20% of the population cannot afford hospital fees and more than a third cannot afford high school fees. Sending a child to college took 74% of an average family's entire income. Again – 74%! Illiteracy, another side-effect of poverty, was at 28%.[326]

Poverty is at its most extreme for China's ethnic minorities, who account for almost 50% of China's officially-labeled 'poor.' For example, among the Suli ethnic minority in southwest China's Yunnan Province, more than 90% of villagers live in poverty.

Poverty among minorities is on the increase, climbing by 1.8% between 2004 and 2005,[327] and among China's poorest 10% of the population, income dropped between 2001 and 2003.[328]

It is figures like these, and not quibbling over daily income to the last yuan, which give the true picture of China's poverty. Whether it is the UN's US$1 a day or China's 785 yuan a year, the definition of poverty in human terms means not being able to experience the real life that other citizens of your own country are enjoying to the fullest – and often to excess.

Excess and poverty define income disparity, which is measured by the Gini Coefficient. In this index, 0 represents perfect equality (everyone having the same amount of income) and 1 represents complete inequality (one person having all the income and no one else having any.)

102

In 1981, China's Gini Coefficient was 0.28, said the World Bank.[329] In 2007, said China Daily, it had risen to 0.496. In Beijing, one of China's richest cities, the average annual income is US$2,263. But in poor Qinghai Province, in China's west, rural incomes are, on average, just US$277 – again, well below the global poverty line.

China's Gini Coefficient is not only larger than other developing countries, such as India (0.33), but also highly developed ones, such as the US (0.41).[330] Taiwan's Gini Coefficient was 0.35 in 2001 and has been falling since then.[331]

In China today, the richest 10% of families in China possess more than 40% of total household wealth, while the poorest 10% only have 2%. Per capita GDP of China's wealthiest province is more than 1000% greater than that of the poorest province.[332]

China lacks a national minimum wage. Instead, regional governments set a figure they think is appropriate. A nationwide study of minimum wages in 2004 found that it was set at 545 yuan (US$67) per month in Beijing, yet the average monthly living cost in the city was 1,017 yuan (US$127). In Shanghai at that time, the minimum wage was 635 yuan, just 25% of the city's average income. By 2007, the nation's highest minimum monthly wage was in Shenzhen, at 810 yuan, and the lowest was in Jiangxi Province, at just 270 yuan.[333] Shanghai raised its minimum wage to 960 yuan a month in early 2008, followed by Shenzhen some months later to 1000 yuan a month in downtown areas only.[334] Yet Chinese media also said in 2008 that someone in Shanghai earning less than 2000 yuan a month "would have a tough time making both ends meet."[335]

According to international guidelines, the minimum wage should be 40% to 60% of the average wage. While in Shanghai the 2008 minimum wage is within these guidelines, at 48% of average wage, in some provinces, the minimum wage has not risen at all in real terms in a decade.[336] And by 2006 China had not established an urban poverty standard nor conducted national research into urban poverty.[337]

Slum areas are encroaching within China's big cities. In Beijing, the government announced that for the Olympic project it would demolish many of these areas, home to the city's poorest residents (usually migrant workers) without saying what would happen to those living there.[338]

The reason behind the Gini Coefficient is to provide a warning system. The fact that the internationally-accepted danger point is 0.4 makes it clear why the government of China is alarmed. It is worried not because of poverty per se, but because poverty represents another direct threat to its control, just as the emperors of the past feared the poor.

The Communist Party's history is most well-known by the Communists themselves, and it is a repetition of this history that they fear the most. It was among those poor sections of society that Mao Zedong found the converts with whom he went on to build 'New' China. Using the poor and dispossessed, those who had nothing more to lose, he managed to overthrow the existing order.

Though our worker who, by virtue of one single yuan is classified as 'low income,' is better off in minuscule financial terms than his 'poor' compatriot, life remains extremely precarious. A single unforeseen bill, for hospital treatment or one of the random fees so often levied by China's schools and colleges can push him back into the absolute poverty bracket.

And because China's poverty reduction efforts tend to focus on areas more than individuals, those who experience such one-off income shocks are often overlooked. Among China's poorest people, 70% have experienced such sudden demands on their income. The key problem for people affected by this kind of poverty is that income shock happens randomly across the whole of society. That means that poverty is spread randomly, too, rather than clustered in 'poor' areas which can receive concentrated government action, as was the case in the past. Today's individual poor simply slip under the radar and are forgotten. [339]

These millions of 'low income' individuals exist in something like a state of limbo. Hovering just above absolute poverty, they face a daily struggle to keep their sanity and their bodies functioning for the next day of work.

We have seen these members of the 1st Army clustered around the single television in their village, which is often perched on the shelf of a store owner's establishment. They watch in disbelief at the flickering pictures from Shanghai or Beijing, and they see the glittering towers of modernity. Programs, commercials and reports show cars, restaurants and the happy and content life of the upwardly mobile new middle classes.

They do not see their own life. They see the good life.

One day, when they finally realize this good life is not on another planet, but is in their own country, and that the pictures on the screen represent now, not some promised future, they will begin to march, the first of the armies that spell a colossal threat to China.

104

Reason 12
The Conformists

How many red lights did you run last month? Last week? Yesterday?

If you were a driver in China, it would not be unusual for you to jump three or four red lights a day.

In China, everyday rules are there to be ignored. Bicycles and mopeds ride on the pavement. Pedestrians jaywalk, even on the highways. Subway passengers push on to carriages before those inside get off. Queues deteriorate into melees of pushing and shoving as more and more people simply jump to the front. Customers negotiate purchases without receipts, meaning neither party pays tax and street-corner touts hand out fliers for all manner of illegal services from satellite dishes to fake diplomas.

Ignoring the rules is so pervasive that it has simply become a part of life. It is accepted and even tolerated, and hardly ever directly challenged by the police or other authorities. In many ways China is a freer country than you might have imagined. Not all Chinese people, of course, ignore the rules, but quite often the option is there should the inspiration hit you.

The authors, in all their time in China, have never seen a traffic cop stop a car or a highway patrol pull over a car for running a red light and its driver given a ticket. You would expect to see at least one driver pulled over in our almost 20 years in China, but we never have. Not once.

We often see police cars parked near a junction, officers either inside talking or smoking, while scores of cars jump red lights in full view. In summer perhaps their excuse is that the air conditioning inside the car is running so cold that the windows are too misted over for the officers to be able to see the traffic violations.

But we do quite often see China's police harassing roadside vendors, who are normally among China's poorest citizens, and just trying to make a living. It seems that the less the connection you have with the city you are in, the more attention you will draw from the police and the more severe their application of the rules will be. Countryside folk beware.

Is that because, in modern China the richer you are, the more easily you can break the rules?

Not surprisingly, because people have no respect for the rules, they also have little respect for the sometime guardians of the rules. While those from the countryside have few rights and face the risk of being thrown out of the city if they are not subservient and obedient to the police, no such concerns hold back city dwellers, whether they be compliant tax-payers or not.

Every roadside altercation in China, from a minor dispute between two pedestrians to a collision between two cars, results in a crowd of eager watchers and usually the intervention of a policeman. As the policeman tries to sort out the arguments, those involved shout and even curse the police officer, at times jabbing an angry finger to dent the shirt on his chest. In a nation like America, even a raised voice to a law enforcement officer would bring the threat of arrest. In China, on-the-job abuse is apparently part of the job description.

In 2007, Chinese media reported that "officers who died in the line of duty [in 2006] were younger than those in 2005. According to the ministry, the average age of officers who died last year was about 40 years old, four years younger than the average in the previous year."[340]

In China, only the small rules are ignored, and ignoring them is quite socially acceptable. Small indiscretions such as hanging out washing in contravention of local ordinances of dropping fake coins into fare boxes on public transport are not a problem, as is continuing construction work beyond permitted hours. And when you make good use of China's lack of convertible instruments, who is to know how much cash you have been given in your hand - certainly not the taxman.

For China today, ignoring the rules is a rule for life itself.

Ignoring the rules is, often, a socially trivial matter, certainly when it is accepted by the masses. But *breaking* the rules is a very different matter from ignoring the rules. Breaking the rules takes bravery. It requires great courage to stand up in China today and say "Stop. This is wrong. I protest." And doing that, in China, is dangerous.

The lack of those citizens with the courage to stand up and say 'I protest' is today the weakest link in the connection between China and greatness. Those few who do stand up suffer perils beyond imagination.

Consider Dr. Jiang Yanyong. He was the man who blew the whistle on the government's cover-up of an outbreak of Severe Acute Respiratory Syndrome (SARS) in 2003. His bravery forced the government to admit the truth, that indeed the disease was out of control and killing many patients. At that time, Dr. Jiang was hailed as a national hero. He later used this influence to urge the government to admit it had been wrong to use the army to end the Tiananmen Square protests in 1989, where he himself had played a role in attending to wounded victims of that massacre. For this, he was detained by security services for several months, and after release was placed under constant surveillance. He was barred from speaking to the media.

In 2007, Dr. Jiang was awarded the Heinz R. Pagels Human Rights of Scientists Award by the New York Academy of Sciences in recognition of his work. Effectively, even without a word from Beijing, he was banned from traveling to the US to collect it simply by that powerful entity, his work unit, which refused him the right to file travel papers.[341]

Another whistleblower, Wu Lihong, also faced persecution when he tried to deal with companies that were dumping pollution in China's

106

Lake Tai, located in the east of the country. Rather like Dr. Jiang, Wu was at one time lionized in the media, being nominated as one of China's top ten environmentalists in 2005 by official environmental authorities in his home province of Jiangsu.

But when he tried to use his fame to continue his good work, he soon drew a very different response from the authorities. In April 2007, he was arrested and charged with having tried to blackmail firms that were continuing to pollute the lake. "Prosecutors said Wu's diary detailed a list of blackmail targets and showed amounts of money he had planned to extort from each factory or enterprise involved in pollution," reported Chinese media.

After a trial lasting less than a day, he was sentenced to three years in jail and ordered to repay 55,000 yuan that he was alleged to have extorted. He was also fined 3,000 yuan.

Chinese media, naturally, did not report that his wife and friends said the charges were untrue and had been "concocted by local officials embarrassed by Wu's whistle-blowing." Nor did Chinese media report that Wu said he had been beaten in custody, and that the arrest had come as Wu was about to travel to Beijing in hopes of presenting in detail the results of his research to the central government.[342]

And in 2008, activist Huang Qi was arrested. His crime? Assisting parents whose children had died in the May 2008 earthquake in Sichuan Province with their attempts to complain about the shoddy construction of the school buildings which had collapsed. He was not even allowed to see his lawyer until three months after his arrest.[343] Likewise, teacher Liu Shaokun was arrested and sent to labor camp for a year for the 'crime' of posting images of the collapsed schools online.[344]

Mysterious misadventure often befalls whistleblowers before they can travel the bureaucratic distance between local governments and the authorities in Beijing.

Wu Lihong's wife, Xu Jiehua, continued fighting for the environment even after her husband had been arrested. She sued China's State Environmental Protection Agency (SEPA) after it named the couple's home city of Yixing as a 'model city.'

"The pollution here is very heavy and there are lots of complaints from residents" she told Reuters News Agency. "We do not think the city is qualified to be a model city for good environment." Courts refused to accept Xu's case, but she told Reuters she would not give up until SEPA withdrew the award.[345]

Family members who take up the original point of protest may well be subjected to similar mysterious misfortunes, the least of which is to be placed under 24-hour house arrest.

Even internationally, China fears raised voices. The nation banned an AIDS meeting that had been planned to help AIDS suffers in the country stand up for their legal rights, rights which are frequently ignored. The meeting, set for mid-2007, would have assembled experts from all over the world.[346]

Zhou Huanxi, a woman who worked for a pharmaceutical firm in Hangzhou for 17 years, also found out the reaction that awaits whistleblowers. She reported to authorities that her firm was using fake or unauthorized ingredients in a medicine it made for pregnant women. "Rather than act on her complaint, she said, local authorities leveled charges against her," reported the Los Angeles Times. She was jailed for three years.

The Los Angeles Times also reported on the pervasive nature of bribery in China – and how while those who took bribes were sometimes punished those who gave them seldom were. "Those who take bribes face criminal charges for taking a cent more than US$665" said the paper. "Those who give bribes can hand out as much as US$1,300 before facing prosecution."[347]

Blowing the whistle also led to harassment for a group of more than 1,000 farmers in China's northeastern Shandong Province. The farmers had been deprived of their livelihoods beginning in 1993 when local authorities started to squeeze them off their land, hoping to take it over in order to set up a development zone. By 1997 the authorities had taken over all the farmers' land, and in 2003 tried to force the villagers to relocate entirely. When the villagers attempted to protest this forced expulsion they were arrested.

Yet even by 2007, said media, more than 13 hectares of the land that had been seized remained unused. Villagers said that the authorities would rather leave the land idle than let them farm it again.[348]

Big-city dwellers are equally powerless in the face of officials who break the rules. Shanghai, under then mayor Chen Liangyu, spent billions of dollars on prestige projects that brought very little benefit to the people. The New York Times reported that "In recent years, as rumors of high-level corruption spread, Mr. Chen's government could not convene without large security deployments worthy of a visit by a foreign head of state, because of the persistent turn out of demonstrators."[349]

But these citizens' protests, brave as they were, achieved precisely nothing. Mr. Chen lost his job in 2007 not as a result of public anger, but as a result of political jockeying at the highest levels of government.

Despite the fact that the government sometimes persecutes whistleblowers, in 2007 Beijing tried to encourage its civil servants to voluntarily report bosses who were wasting money on constructing lavish government buildings, a pervasive practice in the country. This came after scandals such as that in Puyang County in central China's Henan Province. "Despite Puyang being one of the poorest counties in China, the Puyang county government spent 32.84 million yuan (US$4.21 million) on a new office building … The county's labor and social security bureau was found to have misappropriated 7.7 million yuan of pension funds and living subsidies for laid-off workers from a fertilizer factory to build the bureau's office building and training center," said media.[350] At the beginning of June, 20 officials were punished for ordering the construction of extravagant office buildings.[351]

Given the dangers of retaliation and abuse that whistleblowers face, it surely seems unlikely that many officials will be willing to step forward and implicate profligate Party bosses in the future.

The danger of speaking out in public about perceived injustices perhaps explains the growing popularity of internet 'arrest orders' in China. This social phenomenon began in early 2006 when videos of animal cruelty appeared online, showing a woman wearing high-heels stamping on a kitten. The anger that this caused led to an online search for her, and in a matter of days she was found. Her name, address, ID number and even her car number plate were all posted online. She was fired from her job, as was the person who made the film.

In the wake of this 'success' online vigilante action boomed as people sought to track down those who had upset perceived social order. Professor Liu Xin, who teaches Administrative Law at the China University of Political Science and Law, said "Online arrest orders can contribute to improving social morality."

But are those who post 'arrest orders' really online heroes, or are they faceless cowards? No one has yet called for the arrest of the perpetrators of the Tiananmen Square Massacre.

Professor Xu Xiang, who teaches sociology at Nanjing University, said "Most of the time these online arrest orders are a kind of internet violence or torture fuelled by private feuds and have nothing to do with improving social morality."[352]

'Internet arrest orders' in fact crystallize Chinese society's attitude to 'the rules.' The arrest orders are based on the principle of 'safety in numbers.' By getting thousands or even hundreds of thousands of people mutually outraged over a single incident, no one individual needs to stand out. Likewise, when it comes to ignoring the rules, the socially acceptable 'everyone does it' principle again leads to safety in numbers.

Ignoring minor rules only allows the excess steam to vent from a pressure-cooker nation where rule by law has no power. And a society that unquestioningly accepts such conditions its leaders place on it cannot develop. It is only by questing, standing up to and possibly breaking the rules that a society can change and become better. Perhaps even great.

China has taken as its political force the theories of foreigners, primarily those of Lenin and Marx. Beijing is quick to over-interpret such theories for its benefit. These foreign 'heroes' become examples, even idols. There are no idols of 'Socialism with Chinese Characteristics,' only followers like Mao and Deng.

China has its dissidents, who have a similar problem. They do not have a tradition of dissent and struggle in which to orient themselves, at least not a Chinese one. Their idols and role-models are also foreigners, such as Lech Walesa, Aleksandr Solzhenitsyn, and Vaclav Havel. And the great American dreamer of freedom, Martin Luther King garners great respect. Theatrical 'Bravehearts' of the silver screen are seen in heroic lights.

Brave Chinese dissidents are very much a minority, and they are almost totally ignored by Chinese society. There are no parades calling for the freeing of China's prisoners of conscience. How can there be? Most Chinese people are not allowed to know such prisoners exist, and of those who do know, many simply do not care enough to raise their voice, possibly to suffer a similar fate.

Think of William Wilberforce, who did so much to end slavery at the beginning of the 19th Century. Think of Emmeline Pankhurst, who fought to get women the vote in the early 20th century. Think of Rachel Carson, whose 1962 book 'Silent Spring' sparked off the global environmental movement.

These are people who did not just ignore the rules. They broke them, and allowed their countries to grow positively and dynamically freer. It is not that such people do not exist in China, it is that they will not raise their head above the parapet. Today, Chinese culture and society stresses conformity and consensus above all else. There is conformity in ignoring the rules, and conformity in refusing to break them.

When Chinese people feel fear, the fear that comes when they see their country is not changing, not developing its political liberties, then and only then will the charge be led over the parapets and into the firing line.

Reason 13

Culture's Price Point

You cannot see the Great Wall from space. Yang Liwei, China's first man in orbit said he was unable to see the Wall while circling the globe in October 2003.[353]

But in today's China it's getting even harder to see it from the ground. Briton William Lindesay has been researching the Great Wall since 1997, and in 2007 he held an exhibition of photographs, matching location for location, showing how the Great Wall had changed in the last one hundred years.

The older photos show a Great Wall that is very different to the one that the world knows today. This photographic Great Wall is topped with turrets and towers, its walkways strong and secure, its ramparts standing proud. Today's real-life Great Wall is a crumbling shadow of this, with decayed sections of walkway and very few other features except rubble where so much beauty and strength once stood.

A century-old picture of a section of the Great Wall known as the Sister Towers shows two mighty stone guard towers built into a hillside dotted with trees and shrubs. Strong and imposing, they overlook a broad river. They are a sign of strength, confidence and glory, a symbol that all China could be proud of.

But the photo Lindesay took showing the condition of the towers today is deeply shocking. All that remains is a few layers of base stones of one of the towers. The other is wholly gone – a phantom. The two photographic images placed side by side play tricks with your mind. First the shock, then comes the wonder, then comes sadness as you realize that in this case 'gone' means forever.

Even the river has gone, sucked up by China's overuse of water and neglect, both based on the fallacy that economic development should take precedence over historical preservation. The hillside shows a few straggly trees and an expanse of bare soil and rock.

Lindesay spoke to a local dweller, 82-year-old Lu Wencai. "The Towers aren't here anymore, they're gone" said Lu. Lu told Lindesay that the towers were first damaged by Japanese bombers in the Second World War. But, says Lu, the real damage came in the 1970s when the People's Liberation Army built a railway into the area. They dismantled the towers and used their stones to build temporary shelters. Once the soldiers had gone the locals used the bricks themselves.[354]

Lu's story can be found repeated all along the Great Wall as decades of neglect and active abuse have destroyed one of the greatest feats of construction completed by mankind.

Often China cries 'We are the victim of foreign intervention,' which in many cases has caused big difficulties for the country. However, the destruction of the Great Wall and the present lack of attention it receives is entirely caused by the neglect of the Chinese people. It is as if the words 'Chinese' and 'culture' are at war with each other.

"The last century couldn't have been much worse," Lindesay told Reuters. "Even into the 1990s I have seen farmers with hoes dismantling towers, putting the bricks in their baskets to carry downhill to build pig sties and outhouses and toilets."[355]

"The greatest danger to the Wall is the burgeoning tourism industry" says Lindesay. "Badaling, which in turn-of-the-century photographs shows itself to be a prime wall section with magnificent vistas was, on account of its proximity and accessibility to Beijing, earmarked for mass tourist development back in the 1950s. Tackily restored, accessed by an expressway and with cable cars, kitsch and karaoke to boot, 'Badalingisation' robs the Wall of its greatness."[356]

Chinese media reported in 2004 that "that only one third of the 6,350 kilometers of wall now exists and the length is still shortening." In one example of the destruction, in China's northern Hebei Province, "A survey team was stunned when they saw a 14-meter-long breach at the 600-year-old Hongyukou section of the Great Wall. The blocks removed from the Great Wall rampart had been set aside and on both sides of the breach" said Chinese media, adding that the extensive sections of the wall on both sides of the breach had been defaced by concrete.[357]

A firm in Inner Mongolia demolished a section of wall built in the Warring States period (475-221 BC) in 1999 to make way for a road they were constructing. The firm was fined about US$10,000 US dollars. "Such a joke-like, meager fine is in effect a green light for demolition" said Wall expert Dong Yaohui. Dong, vice-president of the China Great Wall Society, walked the entire length of the Wall, west-east, between 1984 and 1985, and was likely the first person to do so since New China was founded.[358]

Perhaps the low penalty is why a different firm in Inner Mongolia excavated earth from a 2,200 year old section of the wall to use as landfill for a factory they were building in 2006. The damaged section was 98 meters long, 5.8 meters wide and 3.4 meters high, said Zhang Haibing, head of the cultural relics protection in Inner Mongolia.

"It's just a pile of earth," said Hao Zengjun defensively. He was a village head who guided and helped the workers to take earth from the wall, even though he knew it was protected. Yet this 'pile of earth' represents the very heart of China's culture, and an achievement many centuries old that should be honored, not defaced.

Heritage authorities also announced an investigation in 2007 into coal mining companies on the border of Shanxi Province and Inner Mongolia which had smashed holed in a section of Ming Dynasty (1368-1644) wall so that their trucks could avoid paying road tolls.[359]

In the same year, media reported that sections of the wall in the nation's northwestern Gansu Province would likely have disappeared entirely within 20 years due to erosion from sandstorms. These sandstorms are a direct result of environmental degradation caused since the 1950s. Forty kilometers of the wall, dating back to 200BC, have already disappeared in the last 20 years.[360]

China did pass various laws regarding the Great Wall in 2002 (Revisions to the Law on Protection of Cultural Relics) and 2003 (Administrative Regulations on Protection of the Great Wall.) But, as so often in China, these laws were vague and failed to specify which government departments were responsible for what, who would enforce the rules and what the penalties would be, and how it would be policed.[361] One wonders why, with all the PLA soldiers available to the country, there is no national guard for the Great Wall.

In spite of the continuation of the gravest destruction, China did not pass its first meaningful law protecting the Great Wall until the very end of 2006. This law banned graffiti and, incredibly, driving motor vehicles on the wall. It also forbids taking soil or bricks from the Great Wall, planting trees, carving on the wall or building anything that does not protect it. It specifies that those who break the law can be fined between 10,000 and 50,000 yuan (US$1,275 to US$6,377). Companies that break the law can be fined 50,000 yuan to 500,000 yuan (US$6,377 to US$63,775). But no harsher punishments, such as jail time, were mentioned.[362]

China's attitude to the Great Wall is the most visible manifestation of a process that might be called 'cultural genocide' as the nation, in pursuit of economic growth, destroys its cultural heritage.

China has a long history of cultural self-mutilation. Many of China's most impressive cultural artifacts were destroyed in the Cultural Revolution (1966-1976) and the decades leading up to it. This period of turmoil, launched by Mao Zedong in an attempt to consolidate his grip on power, resulted in the wholesale destruction of thousands of years of priceless heritage – destruction mostly by the people, who wholeheartedly joined Mao's quest to obliterate China's past. Incredible as it may seem that an entire nation could so easily be persuaded to vandalize some of the greatest treasures of cultural history, precisely the same thing is happening today. And almost no-one is protesting.

But one part of China's cultural history does get a lot of attention – the Yuanmingyuan, or 'Garden of Perfection and Delight.' This garden, painstakingly built by six generations of Qing Dynasty emperors, was burned and looted by British and French forces in 1860 as a 'lesson' to China.

Since that time, it has remained a ruin. But in 2004 a meeting was held to discuss whether it should be restored. The consensus was that it should not be restored.

"The ruins are the most concrete evidence of Western atrocities and should be reserved as the scene of a crime. The lonely, desolated site is a silent accusation of the aggressive acts of foreign invaders, serving as an ideal place for a 'patriotic education'" said Ye Yanfang, a researcher at the Chinese Academy of Sciences.

Another commentator said "Without rehabilitation, the Yuanmingyuan displays explicitly the crimes committed by the Western allied forces. As time goes by the new Yuanmingyuan may obliterate the painful history in the minds of Chinese people."[363]

In 2008, a different approach was mooted, when a Chinese firm wanted to build a US$2.8 billion replica of the original garden in Zhejiang Province in eastern China. But Zong Tianliang, a spokesman for the Yuanmingyuan, said that the ruins represented a historical event which should not be copied. And internationally noted architectural expert Ruan Yisan said "The replica is unnecessary because the Yuanmingyuan was destroyed by the Allied Forces and the present-day ruins serve as a testimony to that period of humiliating history."[364]

The victim mentality runs deep in modern China's psyche.

But as so often, China is as much the victim of its own people as of external powers. Many cultural relics did in fact survive the looting by the British and French, but they were lost over the succeeding decades as the Chinese people themselves slowly stole objects from the garden. And, in the Cultural Revolution, there was extreme destruction as 800 meters of garden wall were knocked down, 1,000 ancient trees cut down, and numerous other objects looted or destroyed.

Who is calling for a memorial to the destruction China has visited upon itself? No-one. For China, as a victim, the aggressor must always be someone beyond its borders.

The traditional style of housing in Beijing, the hutong, is disappearing fast. Hutongs are grey-brick single-story courtyard houses with elegant tiled roofs. Beijing had than 3,600 hutongs in the 1980s, 458 of which dated back to the Ming Dynasty (1368-1644). Forty percent of these were destroyed in the 1980s alone to make way for urban roads and skyscrapers. Today, nearly 70% of the city's original hutongs have been destroyed or mutilated. Of this 70%, 15% have been totally demolished and replaced by modern buildings and the rest have suffered serious damage.

"Many people worry that Beijing has lost something of its essence as an old capital city," said Chinese media. And though laws do exist to protect this cultural heritage, they are frequently flouted.[365]

Perhaps the Chinese people gained their first inspiration from Mao Zedong, who ordered the destruction of the ancient city wall surrounding Beijing, thus giving the first indication to modern China of how it should think of its cultural heritage.

"There has been some enforcement of rules protecting preservation zones, but not always" Hu Zhaonian, an official with a

Beijing architectural preservation society told the Christian Science Monitor. "There are a lot of 'interesting' relationships between the authorities and property developers."[366]

In February 2007 authorities in one district of the Beijing ordered 80 families to vacate their homes in a hutong called the Dongsi Baitiao (literally, 'Eighth hutong in the Baitiao area'). The hutong dates back centuries, to the Ming Dynasty. The families living there were given a deadline of May, 2007 to leave.

In addition to the hutong's long history, one of China's most famous cultural figures, the Peking Opera star Mei Langfang, once lived there. Mei Langfang's memory was also being desecrated in another part of the city as officials announced they would demolish the ancient Guanghe Theater, where Mei began his career as a ten-year-old boy. This theater also dated back to the Ming Dynasty, but with dwindling audiences it fell into disrepair and, in 2000, was declared unsafe by the Beijing Architecture Design and Research Institute. Ma Dekai, a Beijing city planner, said in 2007 that the old theater would be replaced by "a modern, professional venue like those on Broadway in the United States, where regular shows are offered all year round, and high-end performance can also take place."[367]

The Dongsi Baitiao hutong, despite being in one of the city's 25 listed preservation areas, had also been slated for demolition to make way for a new commercial building. In the face of protests, demolition plans were suspended after one courtyard had been bulldozed – but were not cancelled.

A district official said the redevelopment project had not been terminated, and that "the demolition office will continue negotiating with local residents over the amount of compensation they will receive." Residents were upset that the compensation they were offered was less than half the going rate for a downtown apartment.

Here we see Chinese government officials and Chinese citizens debating economics rather than the destruction of culture, and it is this negatively unified approach to culture that is obliterating China's architectural culture at a horrifying rate.

Many residents of these houses are keen to move out, since they are cramped and often unsanitary. Yet while it seems there is no money available to both rehouse those living in poor conditions and renovate the hutongs, thus maintaining China's cultural heritage, billions of dollars were made available for prestige projects surrounding the 2008 Olympics.[368]

In similar situations in Europe, mews housing, now extremely popular and expensive, is sometimes converted from former stables. With the right attitude, historical buildings can easily be renovated and used to help communities prosper.

Shanghai, too, was once full of its own traditional style of housing, the shikumen, or 'stone-gate house.' These stone and brick houses were each uniquely distinguished by the stone lintel around the main entrance. Though they did combine Western and Chinese architectural thinking, they were nonetheless a distinctly Chinese hybrid. In 1949, when 'New China' was founded, the city had 3,000 shikumen lanes. By 2004, more than two thirds of them had been pulled down, said Lin Weihang, a researcher into historic architecture at the city's Tongji University. "At such speed, the remaining old lanes will die out within the next decade," he said.[369]

Ruan Yisan, the internationally acclaimed expert on traditional Chinese architecture, and also a member of Tongji University, said in 2006 that a city the size of Shanghai should have around 50,000 protected buildings. Astoundingly, Shanghai has declared only 632 protected buildings. And while Shanghai authorities did state the entire city's garden villas, mansions, apartments and residential lanes should be protected, they again did not specify any legal penalties, meaning the regulation was essentially worthless.[370]

Ruan was still fighting to preserve the city's heritage in 2009. Shanghai Daily reported that "he has petitioned, successfully, to save Nie's Garden, an 8,000-square-meter, 1920s private estate in Yangpu District, and the 100-year-old Shanghai Rowing Club on the Bund."[371]

But other fights to save the city's heritage seemed less successful. The city was one of the last places in the world to accept Jews fleeing Nazi Germany, and as a result has a rich seam of Jewish architectural history. In 1943, the Japanese, then in charge of the city, confined the Jews to a limited zone of the city. One popular venue here was the White Horse Inn, where musicians who had fled the Nazis often performed and traditional food was served.

In 2006 Professor Ruan oversaw city plans for turning this area into a protected heritage zone; yet the essential meaninglessness of such law was shown by the fact that the White Horse Inn was listed for demolition despite being in the zone. Shanghai officials decided that widening a road was more important than preserving the city's heritage, and the inn was duly demolished, along with several other notable buildings in the zone. And despite Shanghai Daily claiming Ruan had saved the rowing club, it was subsequently torn down - ironically, as part of a development project to restore the 'original' look of the location.

"Normal people all want these buildings knocked down, the government wants to knock them down, the developers want to knock them down. It's only us conservationists who want to keep them," said Ruan.[372]

As a result of the lack of planning and cultural appreciation for its architectural heritage, Shanghai has allowed the construction of more than 4,000 high-rise buildings basically anywhere that space could be made. From the air, Shanghai appears as if the economic gods have sprinkled the city haphazardly with skyscrapers.

A US$170 million redevelopment, aimed at saving some of the city's shikumen from being replaced by identikit office blocks, reopened as a 20,000 square meter upscale bar and entertainment area.[373] Known as Xintiandi (meaning 'new heaven and earth') it used to be a residential area and home to many Shanghai families. The original inhabitants were moved elsewhere, most often into far-flung suburban areas.

While the carefully-preserved buildings do indeed reflect the Shikumen style, with the residents effectively removed the original community spirit is lost. Replacing the residents are upscale boutiques, wine bars, restaurants and clubs, making a Disneyfied temple to capitalism.

In one of the many ironies visible in China today, it is in the very same area that the Communist Party, dedicated to ending the gap between rich and poor, held its first Congress in 1921. One wonders if the 12 delegates who attended the first Congress understood that the politics they were creating for the nation would lead to such revision and destruction of China's cultural heritage.

China's wholesale redevelopment of its cities has led to "a thousand cities having the same appearance" said Qiu Baoxing, China's vice-minister of construction in 2007. He sharply criticized the "blind pursuit of large, new and exotic" and said that China was facing a third round of destruction since 1949, the first two being the 'Great Leap Forward' of the late 1950s, and the 'Cultural Revolution' (1966-76).

Tong Mingkang, deputy director of the State Administration of Cultural Heritage, echoed Qiu's words, attacking local governments for their "reckless decision" to demolish valuable historical sites which were in poor repair and replace them with fake cultural relics. "It is like tearing up an invaluable painting and replacing it with a cheap print" said Tong, perhaps reflecting on developments like Xintiandi, which because of its economic success, is now being duplicated in cities throughout China.[374]

Speaking in December 2007, Shan Jixiang, director of the State Administration of Cultural Heritage, said "In Zhengzhou, which ... has more than 2,700 years of history, 30 percent of local developers begin construction before we are even aware of their projects and all of a sudden, nothing's left."

"Our generation may well have destroyed and depleted the majority of mankind's most precious relics," said Shan in a truly shocking statement.[375]

The destruction of its own culture often suggests to younger people that foreign cultures have more value. Such culturally poor sensitivities filter down to other elements of social thinking. A survey of more than 3,000 students carried out by the sociology department of Shanghai's prestigious Fudan University found that 93% of them rated the English language as very important, but only 87% said the same of Chinese language.

"Obviously, English has gained a landslide victory over Chinese" said the director of the survey, Yu Hai. "The impact is so strong that Chinese, and even Chinese culture, seems to be marginalized." The same survey found that only 52% of students could name all of China's major four historical inventions of paper, printing, the compass and gunpowder. Additionally, 41% could not name any traditional Chinese festivals beyond the major national holidays.[376]

The relationship between architectural 'presence' and less physical cultural sensitivities is deep and meaningful. Without its architectural culture demonstrating China's unique and glorious past, young Chinese people find their cultural perspectives drifting.

With Chinese festivals becoming less popular, Western ones are being increasingly accepted. Both Valentine's Day and Christmas are popular in China's big cities. In Shanghai, Christmas decorations throughout commercial districts are now the norm, along with a the strains of 'Rudolf the Rednose Reindeer,' 'Santa Claus is Coming to Town,' and 'White Christmas,' all of which can be heard over muzak systems citywide.

In 2006 an online petition called for a boycott of Christmas. Sina, one of the biggest Chinese websites, held a survey on the issue, which drew more than 40,000 replies. The results indicated that 53% of respondents agreed Christmas should be boycotted, while 30% said celebrating it was a matter of personal choice.[377]

In China, a 'ripped-off' Christmas proves destructive in two ways. First, Christmas celebrated by young people diminishes traditional Chinese festivals, of vital importance to perpetuating Chinese culture, and second the false hysteria with which Chinese people celebrate Christmas diminishes a cultural and often religious celebration to a meaningless party atmosphere where young people celebrate the event by going to discos.

While it may be convenient to blame overseas interests for the erosion of Chinese culture, the truth is that the biggest "tramplers" of China's heritage and traditions are the Chinese themselves.

Rui Chenggang, an anchor for CCTV, China's state broadcaster, wrote in his blog that a branch of Starbucks located in Beijing's Forbidden City "undermined the Forbidden City's solemnity and trampled on Chinese culture."

In spite of the fact the branch had been operating since 2000, Rui's words sparked a storm of debate with more than half a million netizens backing his call to have the branch removed. In July 2007 the branch was closed.

Yet the reason Starbucks opened a branch in the Forbidden City in the first place was that managers of the complex invited the corporation to do so since they desperately needed money to maintain the facility.

Feng Cheng'en, a museum spokesman, said "The outlet has not done any damage, and blends in well with the surroundings... We allowed it because we wanted to have more international standard service provided." Feng also said that the rent Starbucks paid is used for conservation – a source of revenue that the Forbidden City will now lose.

Perhaps if the people of China really were concerned about "the Forbidden City's solemnity" they would be better off making sure it was fully funded by the government.[378]

118

When the authors have discussed such issues of cultural preservation with locals, we ask "Who does China's culture belong to?" the common reply is that Chinese culture belongs to Chinese people. We offer them a different view by saying "Doesn't Chinese culture belong to the world? Should not all the world's people enjoy your 5,000 years of history and cultural achievement?" They pause, they reflect, and usually they agree.

Our next question is not always met so positively. "Then why are you destroying it if it does not just belong to you?"

Reason 14

The Glass Children

The Glass Children of China now number over 100,000,000 according to figures provided by government authorities in Beijing. They are the children that have been allowed to be born to couples since the 1979 implementation of the 'One-Child Policy,' which constitutes the largest birth control restriction in the history of mankind.[379]

They are 'glass' children because they are easy to see through or perhaps see 'into,' seeming to have a similar set of physical and psychological problems. The Glass Children of the one-child policy are also very fragile.

These 'Little Emperors' and 'Little Empresses' are only-children and are the object of their parents' love as well as that of four grandparents. Such children are often known as 'one mouth, six pocket' children.[380] Even though boys tend to be spoiled more than girls, both boys and girls suffer from an excess of love and an upbringing that would be considered astonishingly cosseted by any world standard.

According to Chinese media reports, they are 'described by critics as spoiled, self-centered and in need of discipline.'[381] Their built-in fragility is quickly exposed should a parent ever actually say 'No.'

The average urban Chinese family spends more on its single child than on the parents and grandparents combined, with over half the family income being used in this way.[382]

A survey in Tianjin, one of China's major cities, found that more than one in three children under school age in the city suffers from psychological problems. Thirty-one percent of children aged two to four years old had behavioral problems such as being reserved or, at the other extreme, exhibiting aggressive behavior such as bullying, fighting and unruliness. They suffered from hypochondria, often feeling scared, and having low self-esteem.

Among children aged five to six years of age, 37.3% had abnormal psychological problems, and 24% were overactive or absent-minded. Liu Xunian, an official with the city's health service, said this was caused by the problems of being over-indulged by parents.[383]

A typical Glass Child's psychological health is often under attack from a lack of sleep. In China's cities, 71.4% of school children get less than the government-recommended 10 hours of sleep a day. This "could result in health problems among school children and trigger a wide range of behavioral and psychological problems" says Shen Xiaoming, director of the Shanghai education commission.[384]

Those Glass Children born since the early 80s are now of legal marriage age in China (20 for women, 22 for men), and now adult psychological problems are beginning to surface.

Only-children are more likely to divorce than those with brothers or sisters. A 2006 survey showed a divorce rate of 24.5% among couples when both partners were only-children, but 11.7% for couples who had brothers or sisters.

The survey also showed how the excessively close parent-child relationships could turn negative, by indicating that 87% of only children felt they had to get married to please their parents. Compounding the problem, nearly 60% of single children said their parents contributed to a subsequent divorce, and 55% said their parents, unable to let go, interfered in their marriages.

It is not surprising, then, that 92% of only-children want to live away from their parents when they get married.

A survey in 2004 also found that 60% of these couples did not know how to be good parents.[385] The cycle of the love-hate relationship was revealed by a survey in 2005 that found that 50% of only-children wanted to hand their own offspring back to the parents they so wanted to live away from.[386]

Another survey revealed that 80% of young couples still ate meals prepared by their parents, and that 30% had their laundry done by their parents.[387]

And a survey in 2010 found that among this group, "52.6 percent said they are under great pressure" which they attributed "to issues such as buying a home, raising children and supporting their parents."[388]

Tan Jianfeng, a psychological expert, said that China had around 16 million patients with psychological problems, one third of who witnessed the first symptoms during their childhood or puberty. It is estimated that psychological problems exist in some 20% to 30% of the population, but that most sufferers are children.[389]

According to Liao Yi, vice-director of the Guangdong Comparative Education Research Association, only children are often self-centered and disrespectful. "As long as they are happy, they don't care about how others feel," said Liao in 2009. "They do not like helping others, being part of a team or showing respect to teachers."[390]

Even though through their young years to adulthood these 100 million children have such similar and easily-identifiable psychological problems, they have few resources to call upon.

China has only 17,000 professionally registered psychiatrists, according to the Chinese Psychiatrist Association. That is 113,000 psychiatrists short of what is needed to meet rising demands.[391] Another estimate puts the figure at an astonishing 2.4 psychologists per million people.[392] Most Western countries have a 10-times better ratio.[393]

According to one of these psychologists, Zhang Dasheng, a director of a psychological counseling center, parents over-protect their married children instead of teaching them how to cooperate. Children who have never been taught independence tend to feel disappointed when, as adults, their new spouse does not provide such a doting level of care, says Zhang.[394]

Single children have little ability to solve problems and conflicts in their marriage, and often seek divorce as a remedy to trivial arguments, says He Liyin, vice president of the Beijing Marriage and Family Studies Association.[395]

Yuan Xin, a psychology professor at Nankai University in northern China, says that only-children tend to be more self-centered, and have less concern for others. He says that they have limited ability to take care of themselves and do not follow traditional family ideas of mutual respect and care. [396]

These psychological abilities shown in home life are often taken to the workplace, where the concept of 'me' can be more important than the needs of the group, the result being that single children face increasing work discrimination.

Only-children, employers feel, tend to be unable to cope with the rigors of learning a new job. They are also prone to repeated job-hopping as they seek to avoid difficulties rather than embrace them.

"Only-children are prone to be effeminate and overconfident," one worker told China Daily. "Sixty per cent of staff who are only children will hop from job to job. My company attaches more importance to strong will and vitality to conquer hardships."[397]

Another survey of 7,000 young people aged from 15 to 25 found that 60% of them suffered from loneliness. Fifty-eight percent admitted to being selfish and willful, and 66% were sad to have no brothers or sisters.

Yet the 2005 survey found that 14% were glad to be single children. In the words of one only-child, Wu Ye, who was born in 1982 and works in Beijing, "I do not want another child to share the love and care from my parents. I want my parents to love me as the only one, forever."

In an example of the psychological twists possible within the minds of only-children, Ms. Wu also says that she does not want a child herself because "I will love him/her so much. I am afraid such love will weaken my care for myself, which I cannot accept. I do not want a child."[398]

As a warning to the financial health of commercial enterprises everywhere, single kids also tend to be very bad at managing money. "The one-child generation has no idea of thrift," says Xing Yuan, a sociology professor at Shanxi University. According to the professor, university graduates tended to squander their salaries and then depend on their parents.[399]

For all the psychological deficiencies of the children of the one-child policy, they are the most well-educated group of Chinese people in the country's history.

These 90 million plus loners form the 2nd Army of Instability. From their university-educated ranks will come the officers, the captains, and the generals – giving leadership not in the traditional sense of the military, but offering leadership as individuals asking psychological questions.

The 2nd Army's intellectuals are already asking the simple yet dangerous questions such as 'Who am I?'

In China, control of the family has been at the center of society for nearly all of recorded history. As far back as the semi-mythical Xia Dynasty (c.2100BC-1800BC) soldiers who disobeyed orders would be killed along with their sons. This practice continued in the more historically verifiable Shang Dynasty (1700BC-1027BC).

In the Warring States Period (475-211BC) this system was expanded by Shang Yang, who founded a school of political thought known as 'Legalism.' Unlike Confucianism, which stresses rulers should rule through benevolence, Legalism advocated the absolute imposition of strict state law. Shang Yang sought to end feudalism, which arranged power in a chain of devolution to big land owners, and concentrate it in the hands of a single ruler.

To do this he created the system known as 'lianzuo.' In this, five or ten households would be grouped together, and each member of the group would be expected to monitor the others. If a member of one family committed a crime, others in the group would be punished.

This practice was again copied in the military, where soldiers were divided into groups of five, with all being punished if one transgressed.

Shang Yang's reforms allowed the State of Qin (globally famed for its Terracotta Warriors) to take absolute power and unite China for the first time, thus putting in place the dynastic system that lasted 2,000 years.[400]

His 'command and control' attitudes towards the family and personal freedom were always a part of that system, and soon spread beyond his initial reforms. Marriage became a social tool used to benefit families, and one person's honor or dishonor belonged to the whole family. That is why throughout much of Chinese history whole-family punishments were common, though execution tended to be reserved for the most serious crimes.

When a woman married she 'belonged' to her husband's family, and would therefore only be punished for the crimes of his family, not her birth family. In the Ming Dynasty (1368-1644) the practice of punishing a whole family was extended, with even the unfortunate students of one scholar, Fang Xiaoru, being executed when he angered the emperor.

In the last years of China's last dynasty, the Qing (1644-1911), the 'lianzuo' system was abolished. Yet, after the fall of the Qing, one of the political parties that succeeded it, the Kuomintang, re-instituted the system, grouping units of ten families together and obliging each member to take responsibility for the other.

When the Communists took over in 1949, they used a different tack, trying to redesign the family structure altogether. In the first of the Party's misdirected social policies, in 1954, the government began to implement collectivization, in which land was farmed collectively but families kept titles to their own land. However, in 1955 the government abolished family ownership, and even insisted on people taking their meals communally.

But the old traditions were still under the surface, and the Communists took up the historical practice of persecuting people for their family connections, especially during the disastrous 'Cultural Revolution' (1966-1976), where family members turned on each other in an effort to receive political favor from the Party.

The residue of the 'Cultural Revolution' still exists in Chinese society today, with parents and grandparents passing on deep psychological problems resulting from this persecution which they are unwilling to face.

After 1979 the life of Chinese families took a different direction as the one-child policy began to be implemented across the country. This was a sharp reversal from the ten years of the Cultural Revolution, during which birth control had been denounced as 'anti-Marxist heresy' as the Party extolled the virtue of motherhood by encouraging large families.[401]

The one-child policy was implemented in the cities at first, and then, more gradually, across the country. China's ethnic minorities have been generally exempt from the policy.

Countryside couples whose first child is a girl are allowed to have a second child, and married couples who are both only children are allowed two children themselves.[402]

The policy is often ignored in the countryside, where the traditions of having large families and male children are still observed, even though the third and fourth children are often kept hidden from census-takers.

In the countryside, though, forced abortions are not uncommon, with horror stories of unwilling women being forced to terminate pregnancies or undergo compulsory sterilization.

Amnesty International, for example, reported on a sterilization campaign run by authorities in Guangdong Province, which aimed to sterilize about 10,000 women - some against their will. "The authorities started the campaign to sterilize people who already have at least one child on 7 April" said Amnesty. "Four days later, the authorities said they had already met 50 per cent of their target. A local doctor told the media his team was scheduled to work from 8am until 4am the following day."[403]

However, many local officials ignore those who flout the rules, well aware that for rural farmers having several children is their only possibility of support in old age. Those children who are simply hidden from officials may be safe for now, but as they grow older they cannot be registered for school or medical care, and do not even have legal rights to their name.

Those who have grown rich in China's booming economy, however, have been able to more openly get round the law by simply paying the fines levied (which can be up to US$130,000) for having more than one child.

The punishments levied for breaking the one-child policy vary wildly because the fine is vaguely based on 'the social cost of raising the child.' This, given the vast social disparities we have mentioned elsewhere in this book, makes it an extremely imprecise measure. One couple in the rich southern city of Shenzhen were fined 780,000 yuan (US$94,250) when the mother had twin boys in 2003, after having had a son in 1997.

Their house was sealed up 'according to the law,' reports revealed, and a strip of white paper bearing the stamp of a local court pasted across the front door. Reports also noted that punishments for breaking the one-child rule can also include the power to the relevant couple's house being turned off.

Authorities are also allowed to cut off power to the homes of offenders' relatives.[404] The ancient policy of 'lianzuo' is clearly alive and well in 'New' China.

However, other rules say the punishment fee is three times local average wage, a figure that was raised to six times average wage in 2007 in some parts of China in an attempt to crack down on flouting of the rules.[405]

In a recent attempt to deal with this, authorities in eastern China announced a 'name and shame' policy to denounce those who had more than one child.

Zhang Wenbiao, a family planning official in one such province, said that "The public is very much aware that some celebrities simply pay money to have two or more children. This kind of behavior must be stopped."

Statistics show that in the face of government policies, about 60% of Chinese people would like to have more than one child.[406]

In 2006, Shanghai's government announced it would give a cash grant of 4,600 yuan (US$575) to retired couples who had no children. This was "not to encourage couples not to have children, but to reward those who have made a contribution to the country's family planning" said Lu Guanghua, a family planning official.

Families whose first child was physically handicapped in an accident before the age of 16 but who did not have a second child (as Chinese law allows) were also eligible for the bonus.

Couples who had adopted a child, however, were not eligible. Perhaps offering a home to a homeless child does not 'contribute to the country.'[407]

Yet in 2009, Shanghai announced that married couples without siblings were being encouraged to have two children. This policy was meant to counterbalance the city's rapidly aging population. The simpler solution - to make it easier for young people elsewhere in the country to move to the city - did not seem to have occurred to officials.[408]

This policy to reward childless couples is also being used in the countryside, where those over 60 who have only one child will get a bonus. But they can only get 600 yuan (US$72) a year. According to Chi Fulin, vice chairman of the Chinese Research Society for Economic Reform, this is a move that greatly helps reduce rural poverty.[409]

Given that nearly 80% of China's hundreds of millions of rural residents have no welfare care, and depend on their savings and their children to look after them, 600 yuan "is only a small amount per person per year" concedes Wei Jianmin, an official from the Development Research Centre of the State Council.[410]

China has also begun to crack down on Party officials who flout the law. In 2007, for example, Qin Huaiwen, an official in northern Shaanxi Province, was fired and thrown out of the Party for having three daughters with his wife, and a son and a daughter with his mistress. He was only discovered when his mistress began to complain of insufficient child support.

He was also charged with adultery.[411]

This was a much milder punishment than received by farmers in several counties in China's southwestern Guangxi Province. In May 2007 family planning officials launched a strict crackdown on family planning transgressions.

Pregnant women were forced to undergo abortions, and women were made to take health check-ups.[412]

According to one local, Lu Wenhua, fines of around US$1300 were levied on families that had too many children, with some reports saying the fines levied ran from US$780 to US$7800.[413] The average income of local residents, said Lu, was about US$130.[414] The family planning teams were dressed in military uniforms and carried sledgehammers.

The result was a major riot, involving up to 20,000 people hurling rocks, breaking windows and setting fires. Some reports said up to five people were killed, though government officials denied this.

Another villager, identified only by the surname Wu, said "The family planning officials were just like the Japanese invaders during the war. They took everything away, and destroyed or tore down the houses if people could not pay the fines. In some families, even the gates and bowls were taken away, leaving them with an empty house."[415]

It is brutal measures like these that drive ordinary Chinese citizens to take big risks with their health. According to China's vice-minister of health, Jiang Zuojun, "Some women, who dare not apply for financial aid with childbirth for fear of being punished for having more than one child, choose to have their babies delivered at home or in low-cost, but substandard private clinics."[416]

In the countryside, where it is much more common to have an illegal child, the maternal death rate during childbearing was 65.4 deaths for every 100,000 mothers in 2003, much higher than in China's cities, where it was 27.6 per 100,000.[417] In the US, the rate in 2003 was 9.3 maternal deaths per 100,000 births.[418]

In addition, rural children were between three and six times more likely to die before the age of five than city children, media said in 2010. In 2007 (the most recent figures available), 229,200 rural children died in the first month of life.[419]

Women also put themselves at risk by taking fertility drugs to boost the chance of giving birth to twins or triplets, since having multiple births is not punishable under the rules of the one-child policy. Fertility drugs are available without question in pharmacies, and many women taken them with little understanding of the risks. Overuse of such drugs can lead to ovarian or breast cancer.

China keeps no official figures on multiple births, but based on figures from hospitals in the southern city of Nanjing, the rate might well have doubled in the last decade.[420]

Richer couples also attempt to have children overseas, securing a foreign passport for the new child and thus exempting it from Chinese family planning rules.[421] The increasing numbers of rich people having large families is causing growing resentment in China. A survey released in early 2007 found that 60% of people felt it was unfair that the rich and famous were able to have more children than generally allowed.[422]

Others bribe officials to gain fake certificates saying their first child is mentally or physically disabled, thus giving them the right to have a second child.[423]

In addition to the draconian measures mentioned above, the country also uses more subtle means. China's marriage age is 22 for men and 20 for women. It is set higher than in many countries purposely to increase the age at which women have their first and only child, which usually is a traditional prerequisite immediately after marriage.

According to Zhang Weiqing, director of the National Population and Family Planning Commission, "Early marriages are still prevalent in some parts of the country, especially in rural areas, which goes against the family planning policy."[424]

Li Yunli, a senior official with the Beijing Municipal Population and Family Planning Committee, said in late 2006, "Beijing's current family planning policy will not change."

Referring to requests for those individuals with university degrees to be allowed a second child, Li said, "Those people are actually not necessarily well-rounded in other areas since personality quality is a complicated issue and certainly not guaranteed by higher education. For

128

example, their babies might not be as physically strong as those in rural areas."

Li also said that since urban residents enjoy much better social security benefits than people in the countryside, countryside people get preferential treatment when it comes to having a second child.[425]

In Li's view, the 'rewards' of a rural life are an additional child -- whether or not medical care, schools and finances are available to provide a healthy existence for that child.

The concept of birth control around the world can take many forms, most directly by abortion, and indirectly by condoms or pills. Or, as in the case of China, birth control can be imposed by government edict.

China's government champions that its family planning policies have been successful, and frequently offers the fact that birth of 400 million children have been prevented as a great success story.[426]

Seen in a different light than the one shone from Communist doctrine, these 400 million could have been family members, siblings - brothers and sisters - unborn souls who may have provided normalcy, trust, happiness, and the continuation of family blood for those 90 million who were allowed to have life.

There is a psychological difference between choosing not to have a child and being ordered not to have a child. In some societies the spirit of the aborted child is often considered to have a soul. If this thought can be transferred to those who are not permitted to be born, then their spirits will prove to be a powerful force.

The Glass Children may eventually take the view that their parents were tricked, fooled and finally coerced into limitations on a scale never experienced by any non-warring society. The 2nd Army, with 400 million forbidden souls in tow, will then seek 'lianzuo' in reverse, asking for justice both for their parents and the liberation of the Chinese family.

Reason 15
The Value of our Death

Liao Shide started a new job in a gold mill in the Guangxi Zhang region of southern China in 1997.

The dust in the mill was so thick that workers could not see each other even when they were standing a few feet apart. In such mills, the dust particulates are so fine that if you try to brush it away from your face, it smears. As it enters your nostrils and mouth, finding its way deep inside your lungs, it transforms healthy tissue into diseased flesh.

After only five years in these conditions, Mr. Liao developed the serious lung disease that would kill him. Unable to work, he had to retire. But retirement in his case was no more than a long, agonizing process of dying, made all the quicker by being unable to earn the almost 3000 yuan (US$390) he needed every month for proper medical care.

He died in 2005. Then, he was the twelfth man to die in his village after working in the gold mill. The count continues.

Fu Huimei, a 16-year-old girl, got a cleaning job in an electronics factory in Guangdong Province in southern China in 2005. The young migrant worker from Jiangxi Province was overjoyed to receive employment in the heart of the economic boom that is driving modern China.

Her joy lasted fewer than ten days. The colorless liquid chemical that the factory gave her to use was so toxic that on the tenth day she needed to be hospitalized.

The chemical had damaged her skin, liver and kidneys. Working its way through her body, she died in agony. The chemical that had killed her was called trichloroethylene. Used as a solvent, it kills when workers inhale excessive amounts deep into their lungs. A job as simple as removing grease from metalwork had taken the life of another migrant worker who, at 16 years old, would never live out the dreams she must have had on her first day of work.[427]

In China, 200 million people are at risk from occupational diseases and work-related accidents, according to the country's Ministry of Health. Nationwide, more than 16 *million* companies offer potential hazards from dangerous or poisonous production methods, said the ministry.[428]

A report drawn up by the ministry said that "the incidence of occupational disease in China will continue to increase in the next 10 to 15 years before real work safety measures can begin to take effect."

Meanwhile, migrant workers such as Mr. Liao and Miss Fu who cannot wait the ten or fifteen years will have to ignore their own health and safety in order to earn a wage.

Ministry of Health figures also suggest that around 90% of the patients suffering from occupational diseases are migrant workers.[429]

There are about 120 million people who have given up work as farmers to seek better-paid employment in the big cites. Less than 10% of them have health or accident insurance, and few have formal contracts with their employers that may allow them recourse should they be injured on the job.[430]

One of the most common occupational diseases is called pneumoconiosis. It is a lung disease caused by inhalation of fine particles of dust, usually as a result of mining and construction activities.

Since the 1950s, when monitoring began, more than 580,000 cases of lung disease have been reported, and 140,000 people had died by 2004.

Other media reports indicate that China currently has around 150,000 pneumoconiosis patients alone, not counting other respiratory diseases and infections acquired through the workplace.[431]

Conveniently excluding Tibet and Shaanxi, a major coal-mining province, which would balloon the figures, there were 11,000 new cases of occupational disease in 2006, said an official with the Ministry of Health.

More than 90% of these were pneumoconiosis cases, and 621 of these cases occurred in workers under the age of 18. The official said the total number of workers contracting occupational diseases had risen past the 2004 figure to 677,000.

The official also said that coal mining caused 41% of workplace illnesses in 2006, with non-ferrous metal mining accounting for 13% and construction for 6.5%.[432]

In 2009, media reports stated that the total number of sufferers from workplace related diseases had risen to 700,000. Huang Zhendong, director of the Internal and Judicial Affairs Committee of the National People's Congress said that, "The rate of occupational disease has been on the rise since 2005… Workers face many troubles in receiving compensation when they find they have contracted an occupational disease."[433]

One example of the difficulty workers face is the case of Zhang Haichao. In 2004, he began working in a brick factory. By 2007 he was experiencing chest pain, and he suspected he had developed pneumoconiosis. To qualify for free treatment, he needed assessment from a government-designated clinic.

He thus went to the Zhengzhou Occupational Disease Prevention and Treatment Center. They gave him an x-ray and insisted he had tuberculosis. He did not accept this, and visited several large hospitals where he was diagnosed as having pneumoconiosis. But Zhang struggled to get official recognition of this. In the end, he asked doctors at the No. 1 Hospital affiliated with Zhengzhou University to open up his chest to provide conclusive proof of his malady. This, and the ensuing media coverage, was enough for him to get official recognition. But this process had taken almost three years, until mid-2009.

"If the diagnosis had been made earlier, my condition, pneumoconiosis at almost terminal stage, would not be that serious" said Zhang. "My biggest wish now is for the government to continue safeguarding rights for more migrant workers in all corners of the country, because not everyone in need is as lucky as me to be reported by the media," he said.[434]

Astonishingly, provincial authorities later punished the hospital that had performed the operation on Zhang because it was not authorized for occupational disease diagnosis.[435]

Another hurdle such workers face is that they cannot get state-provided healthcare if they do not have a contract. But many companies refuse to give contracts to workers, despite this being wholly illegal, to avoid any compensation claims.

"More than 100 migrant workers who have been diagnosed as suffering from pneumoconiosis because they worked as dynamiters for more than a decade cannot be certified as having the disease by the occupational disease prevention hospital in Shenzhen. The hospital refused to diagnose and certify their occupational disease because they don't have a labor contract with their employers or relevant documents from their employers," noted Chinese media in December 2009.[436]

While the government seems to bandy about imprecise figures and totals, for the relatives of migrants injured and killed in boomtown China the misery is 100%.

In 2006, 320 people were killed in the workplace in China every day. That's around 110,000 people per year, said the head of China's State Administration of Work Safety, Li Yizhong (apparently forgetting some 6,800 victims indicated by the mathematically correct figure).

Li said that he does not expect this situation to improve significantly over the next ten to twenty years. His words were seemingly borne out when, in 2008, media reported in the whole of 2007, the number of people killed in workplace accidents was 101,480. At that time, Li seemed to retreat on his earlier stance, saying "The production safety situation is improving nationwide," though he did acknowledge "relevant agencies still shoulder arduous tasks in the coming year." Li also said that the total number of workplace accidents was 506,376.[437]

In 2008, the number of accidents was 413,700, with 91,172 deaths; for 2009, the number of deaths was given as 83,196. These are improvements, certainly, yet still represent an almost unimaginable level of suffering.[438]

Mining is the single most deadly industry. In addition to the huge number of disease victims it causes, thousands die in China's mines every year, due to fires, floods, cave-ins and gas build-up. Though the number of deaths has dropped sharply, it is still a staggering toll – 3,786 in 2007,

3,215 in 2009 and 2,631 in 2009. And alongside the decreasing death rates, serious accidents were on the rise, increasing by 35% in 2008 over 2007.[439]

Many of these deaths are due to managerial indifference to safety rules or lack of safety equipment.[440] And labor rights groups say the true figure is several times higher than this, due to extensive cover-ups of accidents. [441]

Corruption plays the biggest role of all. No matter how often the central government tries to tackle the huge death toll in China's mines, it makes almost no headway. Coal, the fuel of the economic engine, is a major money-spinner, and in today's China money is more important than life.

For example, in the Xinjing Coal Mine in northern Shanxi Province, a single accident left a large group of miners trapped underground.

The mine's first response was to claim that just five miners were trapped. Then, as news of the disaster spread, mine managers admitted there were 44 miners trapped. Later, this number rose to 57.

It also became clear that the mine was producing as much coal in a single month as it was licensed to produce in an entire year.

As the scale of the disaster unfolded, the mine manager in charge of safety fled. Other managers were arrested to stop them fleeing. At the same time, yet other mine managers transported the families of the trapped miners out of the province to prevent them from speaking to the press.

Silencing family members proves to be a continuously effective measure since it can be illegal for reporters in one province to write stories about events happening in other provinces, thereby leaving the families no way to expose their suffering.[442]

Some of the miners who escaped the disaster had an even more shocking tale to tell. They said that six days before it had happened, there had been flooding in the mine. A team leader told managers that mining should stop since it was clearly too dangerous. One manager slapped this leader in the face and forced the miners to continue.[443]

The mining team are contracted to be paid 34 yuan (about US$5) per ton of coal mined. The mine owner then resells each ton for six times as much. A clause within the contracts signed by the miners states the mine owner will not be responsible for any accidents which happen to the miners while underground. While such contracts are illegal under business law, they are still widely used all over China.

Conveniently for the mine owner, his brother was a senior local government official, and was in charge of local coal production.[444]

Rescue work carried on for several days, but without hope for the anxious and distraught family members. In total, 56 miners died.

The head of the township where the mine was located, Liu Yongxin, was arrested for abuse of power, corruption and bribery.

In his first trial he was sentenced to one year in prison with a reprieve (sentence suspended) of a year and half. A superior court, saying this was too lenient, later increased the sentence to 12 years.

More judicial reconsidering followed as press reports slowly exposed the corruption of both mine owners and civic officials involved.

The local Party secretary, Chang Rui, was sentenced to two years in prison, later increased to three. Another local official, Chen Xiqing, was sentenced to one and a half years in prison, later increased to two and a half years.[445]

China frequently launches showy crackdowns, announced with glowing headlines in the media, to try to reduce the endless cycle of corruption and death.

In 2005, it announced a campaign to close 7,000 small mines. This was slightly under a third of the total number of mines operating at the time, approximately 24,000.[446] But the central government soon had to back down on this plan due to extensive opposition around the country.

Officials admitted that by January 2006 nearly 60% of the 5000 mines they had ordered to close had refused.[447]

Once again, in April 2006, front page news declared all mines with a capacity of less than 30,000 tons a year would be closed by the end of 2007. Reports in early 2008 said that in total 11,155 smaller mines had been shut since 2005. Yet in July 2008, Zhao Tiechui, head of the State Administration of Coal Mine Safety, said that "The large number of small coal mines remains a threat to production safety." Statistics given indicated that China still had more than 14,000 small mines at that time. [448]

However, other reports indicated clues that the plan to close smaller mines was more to do with profit than humanitarian concerns. The government of Shandong Province announced it wanted to close down its smaller mines and focus on super-mines with an output of a million tons per year, citing efficiency and costs as the top concern.[449]

Officials also acknowledge that plans to shut down the small mines 'run into considerable resistance from owners and from local officials who often have a lucrative stake in them.'[450]

Li Yinzhong, a minister at the State Administration of Work Safety, said that officials charged with improving mine safety in fact took bribes to protect mines or illegally owned shares in them. "Some government officials colluded with mine owners," said Li. "Also, some local governments developed countermeasures against policies from higher levels and acted as protectors of illegal activities."[451]

Another big crackdown on mining was announced to the usual fanfare in March 2007. This time, the governor of Shanxi Province announced success in reducing coal mine deaths in his province.

Just a few weeks after this announcement, an explosion at the Pudeng Mine, in the governor's province of Shanxi, killed 28 miners.

The owner cheated inspection officials by showing them the only section of the mine that did follow safety rules.[452] This contradicted earlier reports that said the mine had been ordered to close outright but that its owners had disobeyed.[453] Media announced in 2008 that the general manager of this mine, Zhang Xiaodong, was sentenced to life in prison.[454]

Once again work safety minister Li Yinzhong repeated his formulaic response that the rules so often ignored by mine owners obsessed with profits should be more strictly enforced, without offering a single new measure to counteract the growing death rate.

Wang Jianjun was another Shanxi mine owner who also disobeyed orders to close his mine, with the help of corrupt local officials. In March 2007 an explosion in his mine trapped 21 miners underground.

Instead of calling the emergency services, Wang tried to cover up the accident. He cut the cables of the pit shaft, forcibly sent the victims' families out of the province and ordered other workers not to talk to the media or even strangers.

All 21 trapped miners died.

In a ground-breaking move, the Chinese court jailed Wang for life. Historically, this made him the first mine owner in the history of Chinese mining to receive such a sentence. 'It's a good signal to society. Harsh punishment to clean up such chaos highlights the Party and government's efforts to improve work safety,' said Li Yinzhong, conveniently forgetting that the punishment occurred after the deaths of 21 men.

The central government also announced a new crackdown to close 4000 unsafe mines in the aftermath of Wang's trial.[455]

The death toll continued throughout 2008 and 2009. In 2008, 30 miners were killed in a mine in Yuxian county, Hebei Province in July, 37 were killed in a gas blast in a mine in Zhengzhou, Henan Province in September, and 35 more the month after, again in Hebei Province. And 277 people were killed in September in Xiangfen country, Shanxi Province, when a retaining pond at an unlicensed iron ore mine collapsed.

The disaster at the Yuxian mine was notable because of the attempts made to cover it up. Mine bosses relocated bodies, destroyed other evidence, and paid local journalists 2.6 million yuan (US$380,000) to withhold reports on the accident.

But it was not just the mine owners who wanted to hide the truth. The accident took place in the run-up to the 2008 Olympics, a time when China placed a premium on a positive national image. This was why Li Junqi, then director of the Hebei Bureau of the Farmers' Daily newspaper, was able to extort 200,000 yuan from the local government in return for keeping quiet about the accident. The ruse worked, for a time, but after 85 days the truth came out. This led to the prosecution of 48 local officials, and, in 2010, Li Junqi was sentenced to 16 years in jail.[456]

In 2009, 18 were killed in Hunan Province in April, and 108 in Heilongjiang Province in November. Thirty-eight miners died in a mine flood in Xiangning, Shanxi Province, in April 2010, plus another ten in the same month in Xinjiang. And these are just a tiny fraction of the virtually ceaseless parade of deaths and injuries in the industry.[457]

Other industries also cover up workplace accidents.

In March 2007 the contractor building a new subway in Beijing covered up an accident which killed six people. When the accident happened, managers ordered all workers to stay on site and not to contact the media. They even confiscated workers' mobile phones for that purpose. It was not until a full eight hours after the accident that authorities learned about it.[458]

In 2010, a steel plant in north China tried to cover up a gas leak accident. At first they said a dozen workers had been poisoned. The day after, they admitted seven of these workers had died. Eventually they had to admit to the true figure - 21 deaths.[459]

In April 2007, a ladle containing molten steel sheared off its support gantry at the Qinghe Special Steel Corporation in northeastern Liaoning Province, unleashing a wave of 1,500-degree-Celcius molten steel that that engulfed 32 workers changing for a shift in a nearby room.

So little identifiable recognizable remains of the workers were left that officials said they would have to use DNA analysis for identification. The families of the victims each received US$26,000.[460]

It is difficult to find any reports of minor accidents happening in the steel industry before these major accidents. But then, suddenly, the papers started to report a series of smaller accidents.

In that same month a spill of molten steel killed a workshop head in Chongqing, a city in central China.[461] And then another report followed of six more who were injured in the next month. These workers were injured by a spill of molten steel from a cracked furnace in Shaanxi Province, just after the furnace had been 'fixed.'[462] ' A spill in December 2008 killed four and critically injured four others, and a spill in January 2009 killed four more.[463]

Rather like the sudden outbreaks of school slayings discussed elsewhere in this book, it often seems that incidents only get reported when they catch the public imagination. A major industrial accident unavoidably grabs headlines, after which the media report on several similar events.

One wonders how many thousands of accidents occurred before reports of this major accident.

Even in modern industries that you would think are reasonably clean, sickness and injury are common. China's booming use of mobile phones is also helping boost workplace illness. According to the Center for Research on Multinational Corporations, companies in China that supply major global firms such as Nokia, Motorola and Sony Ericsson do not provide adequate safety measures for their workers.

At one factory in Shenzhen, across the border from Hong Kong, nine workers were hospitalized at the end of 2006 after coming into unprotected contact with toxic chemicals. One woman had to undergo an abortion.

This Chinese firm supplied Motorola, a spokesman for whom said that the company had strict regulations for their plants and those of their suppliers, but not for sub-suppliers such as the Shenzhen firm. Motorola said it would act to prevent similar episodes.[464]

In the same month, the media reported the plight of women working in two battery factories in Guangdong Province, in south China. The manufacturing process used cadmium, a highly toxic metal that can harm lungs and kidneys. A Guangdong hospital found that 177 workers at the factories had abnormally high levels of cadmium in their blood. Some had suffered from severe aches and pains, headaches and hair loss.

The factory offered compensation to those women who quit their jobs of between 3,000 yuan (US$370) to 20,000 yuan (US$2,470). The compensation came too late for the three women who worked at the factories who died.

A large group of women sued for higher compensation, based on the long-term effects they would undoubtedly suffer. However, Chinese law does not cover compensation for future illness, so their case was dismissed.

"We were all frightened to death and most of us chose to quit," said one of the victims, Liu Hongmei. But with few skills and few employment alternatives, risking their health became second choice to earning a living. "The so-called compensation was inadequate and we regret quitting our jobs," Liu said.

The women therefore sued to get their jobs back, but the court refused to accept the case.[465]

Factory managers and local government officials even attempted to intimidate these workers in their quest for justice. In September 2006, management from both factories issued a joint statement with the local government announcing that the matter had been handed over to the police who were looking into public order offences and illegal petitioning.

In addition, company bosses also threatened workers with prosecution if they petitioned the central government.[466] In China, workers who should have the power in a nation that claims to follow socialist ideals must instead accede to the power of profit.

In December 2006 a major political body – the National Committee of the People's Political Consultative Conference – decided that workers at foreign-funded companies needed more protection. They said that low wages and a lack of safety measures were behind the growing number of disputes in such firms.

Their response to this was to call for an increase of the insertion of Communist Party organizations within such firms. Early in December 2006 employees set up a Communist Party branch in Walmart's China Headquarters.

The real intention behind this is something very different.

In China, all trade unions are outlawed except those who are in the All-China Federation of Trade Unions, which is directly controlled by the Communist Party. Because of this it does not, in the view of the International Confederation of Trade Unions, (a worldwide body representing free trade unions) stand for the true voice of Chinese workers.[467]

For example, both the factories in the cadmium poisoning case mentioned above have branches of the All-China Federation of Trade Unions. But they are staffed by the same management who are clearly trying to intimidate the workers into silence.

Expanding Party and Union presence inside foreign-funded firms is more to do with control than care. Indeed, workers in foreign funded firms feel freer to complain about their working environment than those in local firms do.

They know that without direct Party oversight they do not run as much risk of being branded 'troublemakers.' As we have identified in other chapters in this book, standing up for your rights in China often leads to harassment, house arrest and even imprisonment.

China did not begin to consider criminalizing accident cover-ups until April 2006.[468] And it did not formally announce that officials who try to cover up workplace accidents could face criminal charges for abuse of power or dereliction of duty until almost a year later.[469]

The new rules stated that managers would face criminal charges in the following situations:

- Giving false information or covering up accidents
- Falsifying or destroying accident scenes
- Concealing or transferring personal property
- Refusing to cooperate with investigators
- Committing perjury or asking others to do so
- Escaping to avoid punishment

These crimes could also be punished by fines based on yearly income. The new rules also said that individuals responsible for industrial accidents would be fined at least 60% of their annual salary.[470]

Amazingly, the new rules did not contain one single statement that would indicate management would face criminal charges for not providing safety equipment, material for worker education or other training that would help workers who are constantly exposed to danger.

It was not until 2009 that China implemented legislation obliging companies to monitor workplace hazards.[471]

Ironically, while attention at home to 320 people dead a day stirs not one change to regulations concerning safety, Chinese politicians instantly demand actions, solutions and apologies when problems involve their citizens overseas.

In April 2007, in Milan, Italy, police gave a Chinese woman a parking ticket since she was unloading goods from her car in a restricted area. They also tried to confiscate her car documentation. The woman, Bu

Luowei, says that the policeman turned his back on her and began insulting Chinese people with his colleague. Police say Bu pushed them, and have charged her with insulting a civil servant and injuring police officers.

Whoever is telling the truth, what happened next is not in doubt. Hundreds of Chinese staged a protest, and fighting broke out when Italian riot police were called in to stop the unscheduled gathering. More than ten Chinese were hurt along with seven police officers.

In the days following this event, China protested. "We hope the Italian side deals fairly with the issue and seriously considers the justified demands of local Chinese nationals and takes real measures to protect their legitimate rights and interests," a statement on the Foreign Ministry's website said.[472]

The Chinese government demanded a meeting with Milan mayor Letizia Moratti, and China's Premier, Wen Jiabao, demanded a report on the riot.

China's ambassador to Italy, Dong Jinyi, said that Italy ought to "seek a fair resolution to the incident, give serious consideration to the reasonable demands of overseas Chinese and protect their legitimate rights so as to avoid a negative impact on bilateral ties."[473]

Or consider the case of Zhao Yan, the 37-year-old Chinese businesswoman who was beaten by a Homeland Security officer in the US as she returned from a visit to the Niagara Falls. The arresting officer, Robert Rhodes, believed that Zhao was involved in drug smuggling. He ordered her into the inspection station, but she ran away. He chased her, tackled her to the ground and sprayed pepper spray in her face.

Zhao denied that she ran, saying instead that two others near her ran but she "was wondering what kind of help the police might need and approached the glass door [of the inspection station]."[474]

The event caused a firestorm of protest in China. China's foreign minister, Li Zhaoxing, telephoned Colin Powell, at the time the US Secretary of State, expressing "China's strong demand that the US side do serious and thorough investigation on Zhao Yan's suffrage in terms of human rights in the United States, during her stay there, and punish hard the wrongdoers concerned." [sic]

Chinese media also said that "There has been a long list of US law-enforcing departments' brutal execution, willfully trampling upon human rights. Some of them.... despise law and human rights are obviously affected and driven by US hegemony mentality and arrogance...Justice and truth must be upheld and those who trample upon law and human rights must be punished. Zhao Yan's tragedy reminds the US government of self-warning and self-discipline in human rights issue, and also tells the world that the United States has no right at all to criticize other countries."[475] [sic]

The homeland security secretary, Tom Ridge, had to express his apologies,[476] and a Chinese-American trade group also lodged a protest.[477]

Zhao Yan sued the US government for US$10 million.

The officer was removed from duty shortly after the incident. At his trial, two fellow officers, though critical of the level of force he had used, said that Zhao was indeed resisting arrest. Rhodes was duly acquitted.[478]

For China, a relatively trivial incident overseas in which no one died and no one was seriously hurt creates a diplomatic storm and nationalistic breast-beating because it plays well in the international press – China cares for its citizens.

Yet the more than 300 deaths every day from workplace accidents within China, plus the thousands of serious injuries and poisonings every year indicate a little less care on the domestic front.

Reason 16

Mt. Rubbish

Rubbish is the prime residue of the middle class. Products themselves have a predetermined lifespan before they are used up by consumers. Before that, products have packaging. And it is the excessive packaging that is causing the greatest amount of rubbish and is the evidence of China's burgeoning middle class.

Paper wrapping, cellophane windows on cardboard boxes, plastic drink bottles, cartons for high-tech products, and, in China particularly, Styrofoam lunchboxes each with the obligatory disposable wooden chopsticks form a mountain of rubbish the size of which cannot be imagined.

In the year 2000, China produced 100 million tons of rubbish.[479] By 2004, this had risen to 190 million tons in its urban areas alone. By 2020, it is predicted that the nation will produce 400 million tons annually, according to a 2007 state report, 'The Status and Trend of Solid Waste in China.'

The quantity, in millions of tons, cannot possibly be understood. So, to put it another way, in 2020 it is predicted that China will produce as much rubbish as all other countries in the world did in 1997. China's mountain of waste must of course be added to the rest of the world's rubbish, exacerbating its global impact.

Currently, 70% of China's urban waste is buried in landfills, with the remaining 30% being used to make fertilizer. Many landfills are reaching capacity, and it is estimated they will be full in 13 years. But given how rapidly China has broken other predictions (such as in the production of CO2 emissions) it seems likely this limit will be reached well before then. Already, 50,000 hectares of land throughout China is unusable due to buried waste. Methane generated by dumped waste has caused explosions in more than 20 cities.

The report said that the average urban resident generated 440 kilograms of waste a year, and that 60% of all China's rubbish was generated by just over 50 of its consumer-packed cities. China's apparently lax attitude to the problem was indicated by the fact that the same report also said that there was no data on garbage generation in rural areas.[480]

While China's richer cities can afford to build high-tech rubbish treatment plants, this is not an option for the many less wealthy cities in the nation. And even in the wealthier cities, there is strong opposition to paying rubbish disposal fees. In Shanghai, for example, a 2004 survey found that most people over 35 found it hard to accept the fees being levied for waste collection. Even those under 35 who were more accepting of fees only wanted to pay between three yuan (US$0.36) and 10 yuan

(US$1.2) a month per household. The trouble is, the city government factors the price out at between 10 and 20 yuan a month for efficient waste collection.

In 1999 Beijing city government asked residents to pay three yuan a month to help pay for rubbish disposal. By 2004, only 20% of residents were doing so.[481] In that same year, the city generated 4.91 million tons of garbage. Nearly a million tons of this was "dumped directly on local lands" said media, with the rest being "disposed in environmentally sound landfill sites."[482] By 2010, Beijing was producing 18,000 tons of rubbish per day - that's 6.57 million tons a year.

The 'environmentally sound' status of these landfill sites, however, was questioned by a 2005 report by the World Bank, which said "Landfills need urgent attention to improve overall operating conditions. They need to be sloped to minimize leachate, developed in stages, and operated according to international standards for sanitary landfills. ...Most landfills do not meet national standards"

The report also said that "Significant improvements have been made in the waste management sector over the last ten years. ... Even though the pace of China's solid waste improvement is significant, China has been unable to keep up with the growing demand for waste service coverage, environmental requirements for safe disposal systems, and rationalization of cost-effectiveness in service delivery. China's waste management practices now have global impacts. The Ministry of Construction's goal of increasing the rate of waste incineration to 30% (up from the current 1%) would likely at least double the global ambient levels of dioxin"

"Dioxin," notes the report, "is a highly toxic persistent organic pollutant; total global loading is a concern locally and globally."[483]

Chinese media reports in 2009 backed up the findings of the World Bank report, stating that almost half of China's rubbish dumps did not meet the country's environmental standards.[484]

Even by 2007, fees for rubbish collection were not being levied in all of China's cities, though the government promised to implement them by the end of the year. While "many cities already collect such fees," said media, "their methods are all different and there have been complaints that the funds have not been used properly."[485]

In 2008 Beijing followed Shanghai in announcing plans to boost the amount of rubbish that was recycled.

"But as I see it little has changed," wrote commentator Huang Qing. "Most people still get rid of garbage the way they did before the announcement was made. In our neighborhood, for example, there are two rubbish containers for every building, one for recycling and the other for solid waste. However, I still see people dump things without proper sorting, place all trash in the same plastic bag and throw it at will in either container.

144

"I have tried to sort out waste that could be recycled and placed solid waste and recycling in two different containers meant for them. However, the garbage pickup next day disappoints me. Every morning the waste collection service worker empties both containers into just one cart," Huang wrote. "Then on my way to office, I also pass by a waste collection station. There I see workers stop their carts and dump waste onto trucks. There is no differentiating, solid waste or recycling, all is treated as waste, full stop. I know these truck-loads of waste will then be transported to landfills or incineration stations to be buried or burned. For most residents, so long as garbage is out of sight, it is out of mind."[486]

Chen Deming, vice chairman of the National Development and Reform Commission, said in 2007 that "garbage can no longer simply be buried. Some garbage can be recycled… but these projects require financial aid" media reported. But reports did not indicate where such financial aid would come from.[487]

A growing proportion of this mountain of rubbish is made up of electronic goods. "Hand phones, computers, and video and audio equipment are already a substantial component of the waste stream as consumers upgrade to newer versions," says the World Bank report.[488]

Chinese media reported in 2005 that the nation was, collectively, throwing away 70 million mobile phones per year. "They throw away their mobiles before they no longer work, simply because 'don't like it any more,' 'no camera,' 'no MP3,' 'looks a little bit old,' and 'no longer presentable'" said reports [sic]. "This unique phenomenon is called 'China-style extravagance.' However, the resources waste and environmental problem it brought about are worrying."[489]

In the 2005 report, media also said that 50% of China's mobile users – then numbering 300 million – changed their handset within one or two years, and nearly 20% changed in less than one year. The number of mobile users by the end of 2006 jumped, incredibly, to 461 million who bought 120 million new sets in that year alone. By 2010, China had 700 million mobile phone users.

Xie Linzhen, deputy chief of the China Mobile Communications Association, said in 2007 that "Chinese phone users on average buy new mobile phones every 21 months."[490] With every new phone purchased, there is an old phone to be disposed of.

Naturally, with each mobile phone that is purchased, there is the presentation packaging which must also be disposed of.

One especially notable way in which presentation packaging in over-used is in the mooncake industry. Mooncakes are a type of traditional Chinese sweet cake popularly given as gifts during the Mid-Autumn Festival. "Under international norms, the cost of packaging should not exceed 15% of the total value of the product" noted Chinese media in late 2004. "In the case of some mooncakes, packaging accounts for a staggering 70% or more of the total."

One particular brand of mooncakes has a printed glossy cardboard exterior cover. Inside that box is a three-tiered plastic box with a handle. Inside of each tier lie the mooncakes, each in a plastic tray. That plastic tray and the mooncake is covered by clear cellophane packaging. With the fading desire of young people to consume mooncakes, but the tradition of giving the gift remaining strong, the actual presentation packaging means more than the cake inside.

"China currently has no laws or regulations to govern this area" said the same report, which also noted that "Environmental campaigners highlighted the fact that excessive packaging accounts for 20% of the daily rubbish collected in Chongqing," a major city in central China.[491] Other reports in 2005 said that fully 600,000 tons of Beijing's annual total of three million tons of rubbish comprised wholly unnecessary packaging.[492]

By 2005, China's domestic packaging market was worth US$50 billion, and was growing at an astonishing 20% a year, said the China Packaging Federation.

The World Packaging Conference, held in Beijing in 2006, drew attention to 'green packaging,' "a new but highly significant concept for China." Vice-Premier Zeng Peiyan told the conference that China was working to develop 'green packaging' as part of its efforts to build an environment-friendly society. But he made no mention of formal laws to regulate the industry.[493]

And again, in 2006, reports once more noted "The moon cake box, for example, has become heavily decorative and consumes a large amount of paper materials, posing a threat to our forests."[494]

It was not until late 2008 that China even began considering creating laws to control packaging. Media announced that draft regulation would ban products with more than three layers of packaging, or where packaging took up more than 45% of the total product volume. But as so often in China, no timetable was given beyond the fact that the draft would be submitted to China's State Council 'soon.' Figures released at this time stated that China threw away US$40 *billion* worth of packaging every year. [495]

Styrofoam (that is, foam polystyrene) is an especially serious problem for China. First introduced in the early 1980s, it became rapidly popular for the ubiquitous white, rectangular lidded lunchbox. "It was common for people to toss the containers after using them, resulting in white disposable tableware littered everywhere, many piling up along the railways and floating in the river," said Chinese media. "Such unpleasant terms as 'the white Great Wall' and 'white blanket' are often used to describe the messy scenes throughout cities."

In the early 1990s, China's State Environmental Protection Administration 'advocated' recycling when dealing with plastic waste. But without the force of law, such advocacy did little. "In 1999, the former State Economic and Trade Commission, China's top economic supervisor, declared that the production and use of disposable styrofoam tableware would be no longer tolerated" said Chinese media, adding that in the early years of the new century, many of China's big cities began to pass local restrictions of the use of styrofoam.

In Shanghai, for example, in May 2000, Xia Bojin, director of Shanghai Municipal Food Office, announced "Styrofoam lunch boxes will be banned in downtown main restaurants and snack stores by the end of this year." [496] But a survey in 2005 found that on average 70% of disposable boxes were still made of Styrofoam, rising up to 95% in supposedly 'green' Shanghai. So while the city did make big strides in collecting Styrofoam, Xia Bojin's claims of a ban on the substance came to nothing.

Collecting discarded polystyrene packaging only hides the environmental problem from sight. It does not eliminate it. According to the Polystyrene Foodservice Packaging Group, "Presently, polystyrene food service packaging is generally not recycled because it is not economically sustainable."[497]

Chinese people, it seems, sadly have little interest in using environmentally-friendly alternatives. In China's southern Guangdong Province, for example, there were 16 firms producing eco-friendly containers in 2000. By 2005, 11 of them had closed down, unable to make a profit even in a market as vast as China.

And while media stated that in 2006, sales of environmentally-friendly tableware reached two-fifths of that of Styrofoam, it also had to admit that much of what was being labeled as 'environmentally-friendly' was in fact nothing of the kind. Many of the products in fact contained "more water or oil-resistant substances, the latter of which are not easily degradable under natural conditions" said media. "If discarded everywhere, the so-called biodegradable tableware can also cause white pollution," said Tang Saizhen, a degradable plastics expert with the China Light Industry Information Center.[498]

Beijing began a large-scale push to boost recycling in 2008. Ten thousand special recycling bins were distributed, serving 160,000 city residents. Officials went from door to door explaining how to use these bins. But despite residents saying they were keen to take part in the project, their enthusiasm did not last long. One resident, Zhang Rui, said she and her husband were simply 'too busy' to sort out waste. "We know how important garbage sorting is, but to be honest I don't think our efforts in our little apartment have much impact on the city's waste situation," she said.

Other residents, such as Liu Guichun, 75, began to question the entire plan after seeing city garbage collectors toss bags of sorted and unsorted waste into the same collection vehicle, thus rendering the whole process futile. Media also noted that the city's former efforts to promote recycling had been basically worthless since they only dealt with residents sorting out waste, but did not provide effective transport for the trash.

Even so, Beijing plans to extend the plan in 2011 to half the city's permanent residents, though Deng Jun, deputy director of the Solid Waste Administration, says there is still a lack of funds to build facilities to deal with sorted waste. [499]

Likewise, official attempts to encourage the Chinese people to reduce their use of plastic bags have largely failed. China uses a billion plastic bags every single day, using nearly half a million tons of oil a year. Attempting to tackle this problem, China's government banned retailers from giving out free plastic bags from June, 2008, in an attempt to make shoppers use them more carefully. It also banned ultra-thin plastic bags outright.

At the end of that month, media noted "Judging from reports from across the country, there is no way to not consider the outcome embarrassing. Major shopping venues have indeed stopped offering free disposable plastic shopping bags. But even in Beijing, people continue to get free plastic bags, most of which are subject to an outright ban according to new standards, from street vendors and grocery stores and stalls. The situation is worse in many other places. Besides the weakness of the order itself, which allows too much room for maneuver, a more important cause seems to be poor awareness at the individual and household levels."[500]

One such 'weakness' in the order is the fact that meat, seafood and bakery counters are still allowed to offer free plastic bags. "Many consumers would tear one or two more bags than they needed, fold and hide them in shopping trolleys" said media.[501]

The environmental NGO, Global Village, carried out a survey to mark the one-year anniversary of the plastic bag ban. They found that 96% of open food markets in Beijing were still offering illegal ultra-thin plastic bags. And for bags that were legal, 85% were not charging, again in defiance of the law.[502]

When Wal-Mart began offering biodegradable plastic bags in August 2008 as part of a joint plan to promote the Olympic Games and the environment, the move was not a success. The biodegradable bags, with cost 0.69 yuan rather than 0.1-0.3 yuan for a plastic bag, were deemed too expensive by shoppers. 'Officials said there had not been a significant drop in the use of ordinary plastic bags since the nation ordered a halt of free bags in supermarkets and stores,' said reports.[503]

Astonishingly, the one ray of light in this dark tale is coming under attack, not support, from the Chinese government. Recycling.

Today, China has around ten million junk collectors, who are, in truth, the only 'green' recyclers in the nation. They traverse the streets of China's cities, often on tricycles ringing handbells. They collect bottles, glass, paper, cardboard, pots and pans, old electrical goods, clothing – in short, anything that has even the smallest cash value based on its recyclability. They are, in effect, recycling 'road warriors.'

In May 2007 a new law came into force. The Regulation on Recycling Resources stipulated "that scrap collectors should not only obtain a business license, but also register with their local commerce bureaus." The reason these millions of people work as junk collectors is, of course, that they have only received the most basic (if any) education. Most of them are among the poorest levels of society. How can such disadvantaged people as these recycling road warriors be expected to enter into and negotiate the complex labyrinth of Chinese bureaucracy?

Furthermore, to get a business license one needs a fixed address, something many of the collectors simply do not have. Their very poverty dooms them to an itinerant life, which disqualifies them from obtaining the business license they will now need. They eat and sleep with their bounty collected during the day, lest it be stolen by someone else.

"If they're driven out of business by strict enforcement of the regulation many scrap collectors would be left with nothing to do as most are from the countryside and have had little education or skills training" noted media.[504] Collecting recyclable material on the roads and streets of China is not a career choice. It is, however, a logical choice brought about by desperation. The Chinese government, by restricting them, is pushing them down rather than helping them up, seemingly not realizing that the road warriors are the first soldiers of the Green Army.

As if the mountain of trash China was building was not big enough, the nation has been importing vast quantities of discarded goods, mostly used electronic items, for recycling. "China has become a major dumping ground for electronic waste and risks becoming the world's high-tech waste bin, posing hazards for people and the environment, Greenpeace warned" said media in 2005. "Although China has banned electronic waste from being imported, companies still export the waste there illegally."[505]

In 2007, media reported that Britain was exporting about two million tons of waste, much of it plastic, to China every year. Though China has banned the import of wastes that could not be used as raw materials or cleanly recycled, many Chinese firms flout the law. "Driven by profits, some dealers smuggle or associate with overseas organizations and illegally bring foreign garbage to China, endangering public health and the environment," said an unnamed official with the State Environmental Protection Administration.[506]

The seemingly unstoppable growth of Mt. Rubbish is a profound problem not only for China but for all humanity. Yet despite the epic proportions of trash China is producing, awareness of the problem remains tiny in the country.

It is a common sight in China to see someone throw an ice cream wrapper, cigarette box or drink bottle to the street, often within a few feet of a rubbish receptacle. The authors often tap the offending citizen on the shoulder, point to the garbage, and say "Keep China beautiful." The individual in question often will look aghast that he or she has been exposed as a litterbug.

In China, shame works.

Reason 17
Faux Pop-Culture

Mando-pop (Mandarin pop music) is characterized by softness. No hard edges are exposed where young people might cut themselves some independent thinking. No difficult subject matter interferes with the music mesmerizing young minds.

The typical male mando-pop star is a designed metrosexual. Reasonably good looking, his hair, never long, is designed to gently fracture his face, the eyes possibly kohl shadowed. It is permissible to unbutton the shirt exposing an oiled or sparkled hairless chest. Wiry thin, dressed in dark tones or blinding bright colors, the male mando-pop star whispers his song, never yelling, at least until the penultimate moment when all the girls will have their hearts stolen as the music in its crescendo closing requires our star to give it all he has.

In the audience hearts and glow sticks are all a flutter. One, possibly two well-mannered girls jump up on stage with bouquets of flowers. Our male star offers his cheek which the two girls shyly kiss, to the orgasmic cheer of the audience. Glow sticks flutter double time.

For the typical mando-pop female star, perfect in her makeup, dress and hair must be wistful, wishful and virginal. No sex allowed. That is reserved for Japanese, Korean, and Taiwanese pop stars. If she can produce a tear, not during the song but when her adoring fans shriek her name through their glow sticks, a tear that she wipes away ever so gently with a single finger, then her concert will be considered a smash.

The songs are soft, breathy love ballads, almost spoken, and with the one essential quality that guarantees their success – they can be sung by anyone.

It is in the Karaoke TV parlors that a mando-pop's star quality is manufactured. Hundreds of thousands of locations throughout China require the latest superstar efforts to be available for local singing fans, 15 to 25 years old, to duplicate the sounds of their favorites. If you can sell your songs to the KTV palaces, you are ensured stardom.

The kids can't sing rock 'n roll, so don't bother making it. It's just too Western for sensitive Chinese ears. And rock n' roll just might tell the kids something they do not even want to hear.

Hip-hop is extremely popular, not because of the music but because of the costume. Loose-fitting baggy pants and sloppy shirts combined with the rhythmic shuffle are easily imitated – to a degree. It's a common sight in China's big cities to see younger males emulating the African-American hip-hop style, but without the philosophy. Very few Chinese people emulating the style of black music understand that it essentially has its roots in poverty and arises out of the habit of older brothers handing down clothes to younger brothers. The bigger and baggier the clothes fit the stronger the elder brother in question. A problem for China's 'bros' is that they do not have any elder brothers due to the one-child policy.

Aside from the look of hip-hop, the meaning behind the words is completely lost, totally transparent and devoid of any similarity in social experience. From being a black child in North America, possibly without two parents and a home, limited job potential and drug wars in the streets, to China's pampered single children with every opportunity in the world to progress is a stretch that tests the imagination. While Chinese seek exactness and perfection in foreign societies relative to the understanding of Chinese culture, they torture and twist other cultures' self-expression to the point of ludicrousness.

While young Chinese people are fascinated with overseas culture, that culture is most often presented to them in a highly controlled fashion – Western Culture with Chinese Characteristics. It is a simplified, sanitized version of Western culture, with anything thought-provoking or challenging scrubbed out.

Cinema, one of the most visible manifestations of culture, is especially highly controlled in China, where only 20 newly-released American films are theoretically allowed to enter each year. Naturally, of course, the illegal DVD market allows every single American film (and all other films) to be viewed by Chinese film fans, uncensored.

The films that China's censors allow into the cinemas, often censored, are mostly big-budget Hollywood crowd-pleasers. And they're wildly popular. Each of the 'Pirates of the Caribbean' films made millions in China's cinemas, with the third film in the series taking more than US$10 million in its first week after being released in China in June 2007. 'Spider-Man 3,' released the month before, took just under US$10 million in its first week. Box-office receipts are of course minuscule compared to world-wide rankings.

By contrast, Disney's film 'The Secret of the Magic Gourd,' released in June 2007 with the government's blessing, made just over US$1 million in its first week. This film was made in Hong Kong, and is based on a modern Chinese story, written by Zhang Tianyi in 1958, about a boy who owns a magic gourd. It is 'one of the most popular contemporary Chinese children's books,' says Chinese media, yet it proved not too popular with film-goers.[507]

Harry Potter is far more profitable. The first film in the series took US$7.4 million, the second took US$6.2 million, and the third took US$ 4.9 million. 'Harry Potter and the Goblet of Fire,' however, the fourth installment, was one of 2005's biggest hits in China, taking US$11.5 million that year. And the only two films which took more money were 'King Kong' and 'The Da Vinci Code.'[508]

As an aside, fake copies of the Harry Potter novels abound, providing additional profits for underground markets.

152

Vivian Wu, a Chinese actress, says "If Chinese cinemas are occupied by foreign big-budget films, no one will dare to invest in Chinese films." Wu said she "wonder[ed] why Chinese don't watch home grown movies. It's unreasonable that almost all screens in all cinemas show 'Spider-Man 3.'" She was referring to cinemas such as the Shanghai Wanyu cinema, which devoted all six of its screens to the film. "Most people like Hollywood blockbusters, so we decided to show Spider-Man 3 on our screens all the time" said the manager of that cinema, adding he was under "financial pressure" to do so.[509]

Yet the situation is not quite so simple as the blanket colonization of China by 'cultural imperialism' from Hollywood. China's censors make sure that the films the Chinese public get to see push the Party line, or the Party's view of what a film should be.

Tom Cruise's 'Mission Impossible 3,' for example, was held up by the censors due to the fact that it showed scenes of Shanghai residences with washing hanging out on their balconies. This, an everyday sight in the city, was deemed as pejorative to the international image of Shanghai, and was cut from the film. The 2002 James Bond film, 'Die Another Day,' was rejected in its entirety, since it showed North Korea, a close ally of China, in an unfavorable light.[510]

'Pirates of the Caribbean 3' also endured the censor's knife. "Chinese movie star Chow Yun-Fat's role in [the film] has been slashed in half by censors in China for vilifying and defacing the Chinese" explained state media. "The captain starred by Chow is bald, his face is heavily scarred, he also wears long beard and long nails, whose image is still in line with Hollywood's old tradition of demonizing the Chinese" [sic].[511] China also refused to let Jackie Chan's 'Rush Hour 3' be screened. Variety Magazine's Asia website said the decision was "likely to further stir speculation that problem issue is a scene featuring a Chinese organized crime family …The issue of organized crime is extremely politically sensitive in China these days, as greater economic openness has been accompanied by the emergence of Triad-style gangsters in the big cities."[512]

Ang Lee's film 'Brokeback Mountain' was banned in China due to its homosexual theme. Despite the fact that homosexual love is a key element of some of China's greatest literature, such as the Qing Dynasty novel 'A Dream of Red Mansions,' even traditional Chinese attitudes of tolerance are erased by the Party machine. Yet Chinese media had the hypocrisy to announce that "Ang Lee is the pride of Chinese people all over the world, and he is the glory of Chinese cinematic talent."[513]

The film 'Memoirs of a Geisha,' in which Chinese actress Zhang Ziyi played a Japanese woman, was banned because "many people still angry about Japan's World War II military atrocities in China regarded the participation of Chinese actresses as an insult to national pride."[514] Again, China's victim mentality shapes its attitude to culture.

So too does the Communist Party's need to mythologize its own past. When Ang Li's film 'Lust, Caution,' based on a novella by the famed Shanghai writer Eileen Chang, was shown in China it was heavily censored. The sex scenes, naturally, disappeared. But sections of dialog were altered, too. In the original version of the film, the heroine, a member of the Chinese resistance, says to her lover, a collaborator with the invading Japanese, "Kuai zou!" – "Go quickly!" – to warn him of an imminent assassination attempt. But the censors toned this down to the far more neutral "Zou ba?" – "Shall we go?" Such is the mythology the Communist Party has constructed around its own past that even fictional heroines have to toe the party line.

Such is the reputation of China's censors that Warner Bros did not even submit the Batman film 'The Dark Knight' to them for consideration when it was released in 2008. While Warners did not give a reason for their decision, it seems likely based on the kind of bans China had imposed before that the parts of the film shot in Hong Kong, showing a Chinese money-launderer working for criminals, were what they feared would cause offense.[515]

And even when a film is cleared to be shown, it faces other hurdles. 'The Da Vinci Code,' for example, was pulled from China's cinemas.

The reason for this, said media, was to make way for a film festival celebrating the 85th anniversary of the founding of the Chinese Communist Party. One of the films shown was 'The Backbone,' which "depicts how the leaders, including Mao Zedong, led the nation in developing modern industry, agriculture, science, technology and education [and] tells how the New China reclaimed control of its customs, which had been held by 'imperialist powers,' such as the United States and Great Britain since 1861. ..It also describes how John Leighton Stewart, the U.S. ambassador to the then ruling Kuomintang government in the first half of the 20th Century, 'fled' from China before the communists seized power in 1949."

One assumes that Chinese censors thought a cinematic portrayal of Americans on the run would draw in the crowds. In fact, the cinemas were quite full – because state employees were ordered to buy tickets.

Other media gave different reasons for the Da Vinci Code being pulled. "...Authorities acted on a warning from Chinese Catholics that the film threatened social stability... protests by China's official Catholic Patriotic Association and a small-scale demonstration involving a few dozen Catholics in Hebei Province were cited as evidence that the film was becoming a political risk" wrote Joseph Kahn in The New York Times.[516] The Chinese government's obsession over controlling the religious activities of its people ensures that any hint of religious stress leads to a swift response.

The 2009 film 'Avatar' also ran into trouble. The Chinese government's response to the film - an immediate hit when released in

China - was to order 1,600 cinemas across the nation to stop showing it. Many of the 'messages' of the film were deeply unpalatable to the Communist Party. For example, the film shows a scene where colonizing humans cut down a massive tree in which natives of an alien planet live. To Beijing, this was an uncomfortable reminder of the many thousands of Chinese citizens who have been thrown out of their homes by greedy property developers. More broadly, the overall action of the film, showing an insurrection against cruel and ignorant invaders that scared leaders, who feared the general public rising up against them more than anything else.

The cinemas were ordered to show a film about Confucius instead, perhaps suggesting official resentment at the popularity of Western entertainment over China's staid homegrown efforts. This effort was not a success, and there was such demand to see the film that the censors backtracked a little to allow more cinemas to show it.[517]

In addition to the Chinese government's attempts to dictate what foreign culture is and how it is presented in the nation's cinemas, domestic films are also rigidly controlled.

Chinese director Jia Zhangke, who won the Golden Lion Award for Best Film at the Venice Film Festival for his film 'Still Life,' said that "Cinema managers always say the market and audience decide what they show, but it's not true. The truth is cinema managers speculate on which films might be profitable and which are not. They make feature lists based on their assumptions and let audiences follow, which results in domestic small-budget films always being shown at the worst times."

Jia's words are partially accurate. Because ticket prices in Chinese cinemas run from 40 to 120 yuan (meaning only the wealthier middle classes can afford to go) cinema managers have to rely on showing the most popular films only. Smaller, domestic films simply cannot attract an audience when ticket prices are so high.

But the greater reason for the lack of domestic films in the cinemas is that China's censors exert extremely rigid control over what can be shown.

"All those working with China's movie industry should stick to the correct political direction all the time and incessantly drive up their sense of social responsibility to further the prosperity of China's movie industry," said Chinese president Hu Jintao in late 2005.[518]

Films that are remotely political are banned, as are most films dealing with social issues. Sexual content is banned, as are most forms of violence beyond traditional Chinese martial arts. And since China does not have a film rating system, all films shown must be suitable for all age groups.

That's why though China made 260 films in 2005 – a number that put it third in the world, behind America and India – only 90 of them were shown in the nation's cinemas. [519]

But again Beijing's efforts to shape Western culture to its own political agenda and to control Chinese culture, at least in the cinemas, are undermined by the extremely widespread DVD piracy in the nation. This ensures that people can see the latest films within days of their release, and if that is not possible counterfeit copies of movies depicting violence, pornography and other sadistic material are readily available at local DVD dealers, unrestricted even to children.

The most popular among those pirated DVDs are international films. Hollywood of course tops the list, but Korean and Japanese films are also very popular. The sad fact is that Chinese films enjoy little popularity, TV soap operas being a notable exception.

China's government censors have total success controlling TV and print media, which together enjoy a far larger audience than cinema.

The huge success of the US TV show 'American Idol' led Chinese TV to invent its own version of the show, which it called 'Super Girl' (or, to give it its full name, 'Mongolian Cow Sour Yogurt Super Girl Contest.') Aired in 2005, this proved extremely popular, with more than 400 million people watching the final episode. The show, in all practical terms, copied the American production.

However, in 2007, the State Administration of Radio, Film and Television (SARFT) issued "a list of rules to uphold high moral standards on a sequel." These rules said that the show "should include only 'healthy and ethically inspiring' songs and try to avoid 'gossip' about the contestants and scenes of fans screaming and wailing, or losing contestants in tears." In other words less emotionally American.

The censors also ordered the title of the show to be changed, banning use of the word 'super' along with 'girl' (it became 'Happy Boys' Voice' instead), restricted its running time to six weeks, and "decreed their hairstyles, clothes, fashion accessories, language and manners should be in line with the mainstream values." There was to be "No weirdness, no vulgarity, no low taste," and contestants from outside China were banned.[520] Once again, Chinese culture was copying the West, yet Party bosses were dictating that culture should be a pale shadow of 'Chinese characteristics.'

Satellite TV is banned across China – at least for the average Chinese citizen. International visitors at three-star hotels and above can have access to international TV, as can those living in accommodation designated for expatriates in China. And even here, China is clamping down. At the beginning of 2007, SARFT announced that hotels for international guests would only be allowed to show 31 selected international channels. Hotels would have to apply for an annual license to show these channels, it said.

The Party's interference into culture also extends into the virtual world. Online role-playing fantasy games are extremely popular in China and one of the most popular is called 'World of Warcraft,' which was unveiled by the California-based Blizzard Entertainment in 2004. It has more than 3.5 million players in China.

156

But when an upgraded version of the game was released in China in 2007 (half a year after it had been released in the US) fans were angry to find that key visual elements of the game had been changed. Figures that were once represented as skeletons now had flesh, and bones that signaled dead characters had become gravestones instead.

Chinese media quoted an official with 'The9,' the company that runs the Chinese version of the game, as saying the changes were made according to "China's particular situation and relevant regulations" and "to promote a healthy and harmonious online environment." Other company officials said the change was merely "operational strategy."[521]

China's Ministry of Culture says that "all foreign online games must accept content examination by the ministry before they enter the Chinese market." It failed to mention whether foreign game online game companies have access to appeal changes made within the game structure.

One game that fell afoul of the Ministry's interpretation of culture was the Swedish-made 'Hearts of Iron.' This was banned for "distorting history and damaging China's sovereignty and territorial integrity," said the Ministry. "'Manchuria,' 'West Xinjiang,' and 'Tibet' appeared as independent sovereign countries in the maps of the game. In addition, it even included China's Taiwan province as the territory of Japan at the beginning of the game," -- a case of fantasy being too historically correct for ministry officials.

The Ministry also said that "Internet bars that provide downloads of the game or fail to stop those Internet surfers who download, install or play the game, will be fined or even ordered to stop business." Sino-spite designed to hurt profit margins.

China has also banned a number of other games for "for smearing the image of China and the Chinese army."[522]

While Chinese people today are consumed by Western culture, the culture they actually receive is thus very carefully controlled. Chinese society appropriates Western culture without actually understanding what it means, sometimes producing a Western culture with Chinese characteristics/Chinese culture with Western characteristics hybrid.

Sadly, it is not only Chinese understanding of Western culture that is weak. It is now becoming true that Chinese people's understanding of Chinese culture is also weakening. Young people tend to follow their peers in the chase to be popular. What is popular now in China has virtually nothing to do with Chinese history, traditions or culture. The result is a pseudo-culture environment leading eventually to a huge generation gap between children and their parents larger than anything that has ever existed in the West.

Perhaps it's not surprising that, in a country where traditional cultural self-expression is ailing, present day cultural heroes are too.

A survey conducted by the Chinese Medical Doctor Association in 2007 found that one-third of people in the public eye, such as recreation and sports stars and famous actors, had sleeping problems and "poorer immunity capabilities than ordinary people." Out of 186 stars surveyed, 46.5% had abnormal heart beats, 43.5% had excessive blood fat and more than 37% were overweight.

Around 33% of the men had prostate problems, and more than 45% of the women had mammary problems.[523] Apparently the pressure of competition also forced them into excessive smoking, overuse of alcohol and attendant dietary problems. No mention was made of recreational drug problems.

A nation's heroes normally receive the best medical care, the best living circumstances, and achieve a level of personal satisfaction that should alleviate the suffering of these problems.

Great countries produce great culture. To coin a phrase, perhaps China needs a new cultural revolution.

Reason **18**

The Mirror of Japan - The War of Apology

She sits waiting in her wheelchair, provided for her even though she does not require it. At home she walks freely to do her household chores. Some of her elderly friends need a wheelchair, yet cannot afford one. Her brand-new wheelchair has been provided by the government of China, to literally and figuratively push her around.

At 86 years of age does she have any choice? She waits outside a courtroom, somewhere in Tokyo, feeling she is a long way from home, as she was in those early years of her youth, when she provided 'comfort' for the Japanese soldiers.

Now, occasionally, some official looms in front of her, asking her "Are you okay?" "Are you comfortable?" or "Can I get you anything?"

She wonders why no-one ever asked these questions of her just after the war, when she desperately needed help. They never asked these questions during the big famine, or the Cultural Revolution, or indeed after she retired at 50. It has taken them 36 years since her retirement to ask these questions.

When the men ask her, she feels they are sincere. But when the women ask her, she can see in their eyes always the same look, that look that says "How could you allow those men between your legs - to take advantage of you - to put their seed in you?" And they have that look that says "I would have killed myself. You should have done the same."

These modern women always have the look that makes her feel maybe she should have killed herself. "What if we had all committed suicide in those times?" she thinks. "And the next woman, and the next, and the next…"

Soon, they will take her into the court, where she must tell them from her memories what the Chinese people expect to hear. That she suffered, that she felt shame, that she had lost her innocence forever. They will ask her how many men lay between her legs in those days.

Why should she remember this total? She will say a few hundred, perhaps even a few thousand, but in her mind she wishes she could tell the truth to the court. She wishes she could just say 'more than one' because after the first one, for her, nothing else mattered.

They will not ask her what she felt as she looked into the faces of the Japanese soldiers. Some were grown men, real soldiers, hard bodies, hard faces, scars. All were efficient in the release of their passion. But later on more and more were just boys. These boys seemed more afraid of her as a woman - to be inside her - than they were of dying. She wonders whether, if she ever met one of those soldiers again, he would recognize her, her old, beautiful face full of creases of experience and a touch of sadness.

She will not tell the court the mental game she played with each man who lay between her legs. She imagined that when each man came into to her, they were practicing their death. The expression at the height of their sexual pleasure often an imitation of the expression they would use when they were killed, victims of their own country's aggression.

Some of the men held their breath when they came inside her, their face contorted, twisted. "Yes" she thought, "You will die well when the bullet strikes your brain." Some of the younger boys would scream out their pleasure – or was it their death? Their grimy faces were torn between pain and pleasure. Those who did yell out, she thought, would die the most glorious death. Some, of course, she thought, needed more practice. They hadn't yet quite fashioned the best face of death when taking pleasure from her.

Some never got the chance to practice with her again, as the real stage of war forced them to play out their deaths earlier than they ever could have imagined. When she did not see them again, she knew that justice had been served – hopefully by the brave hands of her Chinese compatriots fighting for their freedom.

Today she is well looked after. She has an attendant to push the wheelchair, good food, air travel, a nice hotel room. She has been brought to Japan to talk. All she should do – all she must do – is tell China what it wants to hear. She must tell the court how she, as a Chinese woman, was shamed by the Japanese.

Once again, she must become a 'comfort woman,' this time offering comfort to her own government, to the Party. She is a mirror in which China can see itself in the war of apology.

There is no way that the government of China or the lawyers assigned to the case can win. But they have not told her that. Like those before her, and those after her, she is a symbol of a wishful policy of retribution.

In 1972 China and Japan issued the 'Joint Communiqué of the Government of Japan and the Government of the People's Republic of China.' This document, signed in Beijing by both countries, normalized relations between the two countries.

"The Japanese side is keenly conscious of the responsibility for the serious damage that Japan caused in the past to the Chinese people through war, and deeply reproaches itself" said the statement, prior to listing nine provisions.

The fifth of these provisions stated, "The Government of the People's Republic of China declares that in the interest of the friendship between the Chinese and the Japanese peoples, it renounces its demand for war reparation from Japan."[524]

Yet despite the signing of this document, for China, the 'Chinese People's War of Resistance against Japanese Aggression,' as the China-

Japan war of 1937 to 1945 is called in China, has never truly come to an emotional closure. When China looks in the mirror of Japan, it sees an enemy, a country with which it is still fighting a war of apology.

And the one constant refrain of this emotional war is that Japan must 'truthfully face up to history.' The youth of Japan are declared ignorant about the need for reflection, and the youth of China therefore reflect only hatred.

How deep that hatred goes was made clear in an editorial in People's Daily in June 2007. Li Xuejiang, the newspaper's chief resident reporter in the US, wrote that "The massacre of the Jews by the German Nazis during WWII was a trampling upon the human justice, and the issue about 'sex slaves' is an identical one and has no reason whatsoever to make it fade or weaken," [sic].[525]

To equate one of the greatest tragedies in all human history – the Holocaust – with sex slavery, which, though a grave crime, is one that has been committed in almost every war ever fought – is simply obscene, and a deep insult to all Jewish people as well as many other nationals who suffered the horrors of the gas.

In making a link between the Japanese nation of today with Nazi Germany of the past, China simply distorts history and keeps hatred alive.

The Song Dynasty historian Sima Guang (960-1279) wrote the 'Zi Zhi Tong Jian,' or 'The Mirror to Aid Government.' The point of this work, as its name suggests, was to help governors rule more effectively by having a clear understanding of history and avoiding the faults of the past.

The Ming Dynasty (1368-1644) prince Zhu Shunshi, fleeing China at the collapse of the dynasty, took these ideas to Japan, where they began to spread among the population.

Giving a speech in September 2005 to mark the 60th anniversary of Japan's surrender at the end of World War Two, Chinese President Hu Jintao said that "the Chinese people thoroughly foiled the attempt of Japanese militarists to destroy China, putting a clear end to the record of humiliation suffered by China as a victim of repeated foreign aggression in modern times, and safeguarding the achievements it made in the course of its development."

Hu also said that "After the end of the war, many Japanese from all walks of life faced squarely the historical fact that Japanese militarists had launched the war of aggression against foreign countries and strongly denounced the atrocities Japanese aggressors had committed in China. Many Japanese soldiers who participated in the war of aggression repented of their crimes of war with all sincerity and henceforth they have done a lot to promote the friendship between Japan and China. Their conscience and courage are highly commendable."[526]

Reasonable words. The words of a powerful leader reflecting on his country's past with emotion, but objectively. Words that historian Sima Guang would approve of.

But the words do not stop there. Hu goes on to say that there are "...forces in Japan that have categorically denied the aggressive nature of the war Japan launched against China and the crimes it committed, and have tried their best to whitewash its militarist aggression and call back the spirit of those Class A war criminals who have been condemned by history."

"Such actions have not only breached the Japanese Government's commitment regarding historical issues, but also shaken the political foundation of the Sino-Japanese relations, thus badly hurting the feelings of the Chinese and other Asian peoples concerned," said Hu.

It is true that there are those in Japan who downplay or even extol its wartime past. Yet these are a minority voice, and a regrettable but unavoidable side-effect of living in a democratic nation.

When citizens are allowed to voice their opinions freely, some of those opinions will be objectionable. But, short of direct hate speech, such freedoms must be honored. This is something China, in its War of Apology, and without democracy, simply cannot understand.

"The past, if not forgotten, can serve as a guide for the future," said Hu Jintao. "By emphasizing the need to always remember the past, we do not mean to continue the hatred. Instead, we want to draw lessons from history and be forward-looking. Only by remembering the past and drawing lessons from it can one avoid the repetition of historical tragedies."

It is disingenuous for a Chinese president to extol 'remembering the past.' In China, after all, those who want to talk about the truth of such events of Chinese history as the Tiananmen Square Massacre are silenced – and often imprisoned – by the State.

Hu's lecturing of Tokyo is therefore somewhat surprising. "We hope that the Japanese Government and its leaders will, with a highly responsible attitude toward history, the people and the future, and proceeding from the overall interest of the Sino-Japanese friendship, regional stability and development of Asia, handle historical issues in a serious and prudent manner and translate the apologies and remorse they have expressed for that war of aggression into concrete actions" he said.

But in what must rank as one of the most breathtakingly false, mendacious and hypocritical statements ever issued by any world leader, Hu said "History has eloquently proved that only when it adheres to the leadership of the CPC and the socialist road with Chinese characteristics can the Chinese nation create a brighter future." [527]

Exhaustive and meticulous research by Professor R. J. Rummel, Professor Emeritus of Political Science, University of Hawaii, suggests that between its founding in 1949 and 1987, the government of the People's Republic of China was responsible for the death of more than 75 million of its own citizens.[528]

75 *million*!

This is the leadership that, says Hu, history 'eloquently' proves leads to a 'brighter future.'

China's media is obsessed with extracting an endless parade of apologies from Japan (though senior government officials have already made around 40 apologies since the signing of the 1972 communiqué), and it is this government-induced attitude that promotes the continuous claims for compensation from those remaining Chinese citizens directly harmed by the war, who are mobile enough to be wheelchaired in front of Japanese judges.

A number of lawsuits have been pursued against the Japanese government in connection to wartime 'Comfort Women,' the women and girls forced into prostitution. Lawsuits have also been brought for forced slavery in the war, when Chinese citizens were made to work for Japanese companies.

The claims for these cases have been denied by the courts, because of the either the 1972 Joint Communiqué, or because the 20-year period for demanding compensation has expired, or because the government of Japan today says it is not responsible for the acts of Japan's wartime government, which operated under a different constitution. [529]

Similarly, responding to claims for compensation related to a massacre of 3,000 men, women and children by Japanese soldiers in the Chinese village of Pingdingshan in 1932, Japan's Supreme Court said that Japan's government could not be sued for acts that took place before it passed its State Compensation Law in 1947. In so ruling, the Supreme Court confirmed the prior rulings of the Tokyo District Court and the Tokyo High Court.[530]

Japan's Supreme Court has also said that the 1972 treaty between China and Japan absolves Japan from paying further war reparations, though some critics say the treaty applied at a national, not personal level.[531]

In Japan, unlike China, the rule of law takes precedence over political posturing and policy instilled with patriotic fervor.

The Chinese government and media's consistent portrayal of Japan as a strongly militaristic and wholly unrepentant nation has had profound effects on modern Chinese society.

In September 2003, there was an eruption of anti-Japanese feeling when a group of Japanese visitors to the southern city of Zhuhai hired a number of Chinese prostitutes. The Chinese media reported that hundreds of thousands of outraged online commentators labeled this as "the shame of the nation."

The assistant manager of the hotel where the Japanese guests stayed was later sentenced to life in prison, as was another person involved. *Life.* Twelve more got terms of between two and 15 years, and 15 high-ranking local officials were punished. [532]

Less dramatically-from the same mirror's reflection in 2003, Sino-Japanese company - Hangzhou Futong Showa Optical Communication Co

163

Ltd., ran into trouble when it planned to float on China's stock market. The reason was that 'Showa' is the name for the reign period of the Japanese Emperor, Hirohito, the emperor of the war years.

Hundreds of angry Chinese citizens protested to the China Securities Regulatory Commission and the Shanghai Stock Exchange. The company had to change its name.[533]

When chemical weapons left over from the war were uncovered in the northern Chinese province of Heilongjiang, for example, in 2004, this was taken as 'evidence' of Japan's continuing activities to harm China. "Indignant Chinese citizens have urged the Japanese Government to take a proper attitude toward history" explained the Chinese media.

And Liu Chunfeng, a university student in the region, said that "Although the Japanese side refuses to look squarely at history, their chemical weapons have injured innocent Chinese people time and again. They should apologize to us!"[534]

2004 also saw the Asian Cup Final between Japan and China, held in Beijing.

In the run-up to the match, Chinese media criticized Japan, saying "In the eyes of some Japanese politicians and media, however, it is also more of a political event than a match. They have collaborated to equate some Chinese fans' booing of the Japanese team in earlier matches to mean all Chinese supporters are hostile towards the visitors."[535]

Chinese media also noted that "the Japanese brochures for the event contained a map of Asia on which China's mainland and the Taiwan island are marked in different colors... and the Chinese organizing committee of the Asian Cup complained to Japan as soon as the error was noticed."

"Officials from the Chinese Foreign Ministry also complained to the Japanese embassy to China, urging Japan to correct the mistake and to eliminate 'negative influences,'" said the media.[536]

When the match began and the Japanese national anthem was played, it was effectively drowned out by the booing of the Chinese fans in the stadium.

When Japan won the game 3-1, the Chinese fans erupted in fury. A bus carrying Japanese officials was pelted with bottles and stones by angry Chinese fans. Two thousand Japanese fans, who had to be heavily protected during the match itself, were obliged to remain in the stadium for nearly three hours after the match since it was simply too dangerous for them to leave until riot police had removed the enraged Chinese fans outside.

The Japanese embassy in Beijing, as well as the Japanese ambassador's house, also required heavy police security.[537]

Chinese media made very little mention of the rioting, saying that the fans were simply "agitated" and that "the situation at that time was chaotic."[538]

164

Similar events took place in 2008, during the East Asian Cup. Chinese fans booed and jeered the Japanese team (playing against North Korea) at a match in the central Chinese city of Chongqing. Angry Chinese spectators also burned Japanese flags. Later in the competition China was beaten 1-0 by Japan, leading angry Chinese fans to call for the head of the Chinese Football Association, Xie Yalong, to be sacked. Xie himself had stirred the nationalistic fervor of the fans pre-match, referring to Japan's heavy bombing of the city during World War Two and saying, "Never lose to the Japanese team in Chongqing."[539]

Japan's bid to join the United Nations Security Council in 2005 sparked huge protest in China. One Chinese website collected 16 million signatures protesting Japan's bid, while another found 99% of young Chinese people opposed to it.

There were protests across many Chinese cities. In Guangzhou, in south China, more than 10,000 people signed a 10-metre banner bearing an anti-Japanese slogan, and in Chongqing, in central China, protestors paraded a banner reading "Smash Japan's vain hope to be a permanent member."[540]

Chinese media even drew attention Japan's use of 'expo diplomacy' -- its intent to use the World Expo of 2005, which was being held in the country's Aichi Prefecture, as a chance for Japanese leaders to press their case to visiting world politicians.

"For leaders of developing countries that are in tough financial circumstances, Japan has created an 'expo honored guest' system, and will pay for their lodging and transportation" said Chinese media. "Thanks to these efforts, heads of state from almost 29 participating African countries will visit Japan…. Africa holds the key to realize Japan's permanent UNSC membership because of the large number of countries on the continent."[541]

Such tactics, of course, are precisely what China itself uses when it comes to the 'Taiwan Kowtow,' more of which will undoubtedly be seen when Shanghai holds the World Expo in 2010.

Also in 2005, a group of Chinese citizens held a rally to protest Japan's claim to the Senkaku Islands in the East China Sea. China, which knows them as the Diaoyu Islands, insists it has total ownership rights. Shouting "Down with the Japanese imperialists!" the Chinese protestors held banners displaying the Chinese character for 'Shame.'[542]

In 2007, there was online anger over China's State Forestry Administration's suggestion that an endangered species of crane known as the 'Dandinghe' could serve as the avian symbol of China. The bird is a common symbol in Chinese, Japanese and Korean tradition, but, unfortunately for its future notoriety, it is also known as the 'Japanese crane.' The fact that the crane also has China as its natural habitat is not enough for it to gain patriotic respect.

"It is definitely unacceptable" said a wildlife photographer, Zhu Chenzhou. "Although [the] dandinghe is considered a symbol of longevity, it's not reasonable to pick a 'Japanese' bird as the icon of the country."[543]

Against this background of anti-Japan sentiment, one factor stands out more than anything else: the Yasukuni Shrine. This Tokyo shrine honors all Japan's war dead since its construction in 1869. Currently, around 2.5 million war dead are honored there.

Among these are 14 major war criminals from the Second World War, and it is the presence of these that enrages China.

Responding to former Japanese Prime Minister Junichiro Koizumi's visit to the shrine in 2006, Chinese media said, "He could be forever spurned by Asian people, and be firmly nailed to the pole of historical shame."[544]

Japan, says the Chinese press, has "repeatedly failed the trust of the Chinese people" and "tramples the conscience of mankind."

Yet many Japanese people are equally angry about high-level political visits to the shrine, among both the general public and officially elected members of government, and protest against them, voicing their anger against Koizumi's visits.

The Japanese people have moved on from the war years to successfully grasp the full meaning of democracy in action. The Chinese people however would have to reflect very seriously on the dangers of protesting against the actions of their own government leaders.

A second major event in Sino-Japan relations is the Nanjing Massacre. The Japanese army captured this southeastern city in late 1937, and, in a six-week period, murdered thousands of Chinese soldiers and civilians.

From 1949, when 'New China' was founded until the early 1980s, there was no active study of the Nanjing event within China, and certainly it was not promoted as the massacre it was. Save for one passing reference in the 1960s, it was not mentioned in Chinese school textbooks until the 1980s.

There is even no record of Mao Zedong having ever spoken of it publicly. Indeed, even after Mao's death in 1976 and up to the early 1990s, historians were banned from holding conferences to discuss it.[545]

Today, it is much more clearly in the public eye, fostered by government policy that on one hand declares 'harmony' and on the other hand inspires hate.

China's government puts the number of dead 300,000. A tribunal set up by the Allies at the end of the war put the figure at around 140,000. Both numbers are horrific totals of man's inhumanity to man, but Beijing reacts with fury should anyone suggest fewer than 300,000 were killed, indicating that even after death one can be subjected to government policies.

In constantly highlighting Japan's 'mistakes' and in calling for endless apologies, Beijing suggests that the country has never apologized at

166

all, leading many Chinese people to believe that Japan has never attempted the slightest apology for victimizing Chinese as well as many other Asian peoples.

Speaking just two weeks before Hu Jintao's anniversary speech of September 2005, then-Prime Minister of Japan Junichiro Koizumi said "In the past, Japan, through its colonial rule and aggression, caused tremendous damage and suffering to the people of many countries, particularly to those of Asian nations."

"Sincerely facing these facts of history, I once again express my feelings of deep remorse and heartfelt apology, and also express the feelings of mourning for all victims, both at home and abroad, in the war," said Koizumi. "I am determined not to allow the lessons of that horrible war to erode, and to contribute to the peace and prosperity of the world without ever again waging a war."

Koizumi also said "Through squarely facing the past and rightly recognizing the history, I intend to build a future-oriented cooperative relationship based on mutual understanding and trust with Asian countries."[546]

That is as full an apology as any country's modern day leader could offer another nation's people.

Previous Japanese Prime Ministers, such as Keizo Obuchi and Tomiichi Murayama, also made apologies.

It is true the visits to the Yasukuni shrine are offensive to some. It is true that Japan's downplaying of its appalling military history is objectionable. And it is undeniable that the small but vocal number of ultra-right activists are every bit as repellent as Germany's neo-Nazis.

These views may be offensive, but they have killed no-one. Since the end of the Second World War, Japan has been a remarkably peaceful and secure nation.

Not all of China's media coverage is so strongly anti-Japanese. One Chinese report in early 2007 reported a survey by the Japanese newspaper Asahi Shimbun that found 85% of 3000 Japanese respondents believed "it is necessary to reflect on history."

The report quoted Japanese historian Hosaka Masayasu's dictum that "to be truly patriotic, one should not evade history" and spoke of the importance of using history as a mirror.[547]

The real reason for China's inability to forgive is best perhaps illustrated by the Communist Party's desire to forget battles which it did not fight.

Speaking in 2005, Hu Jintao recalled the CPC's eminent role during the war, saying that "the CPC is the pillar for the whole nation to unite and fight against the Japanese aggression. The heroic stories and lofty style of the CPC-led armed forces during the war are a valuable spiritual wealth for the country to strengthen its defense and build the Army." [548]

"The CPC upheld the line of all-round resistance, formulated correct strategies and policies, implemented the line and policies of mobilizing and relying on the people, put forward the general strategic principle of a protracted war and a complete set of strategies and tactics for the people's war, created large numbers of battlefields in the enemy's rear, and became the core of resistance against Japanese aggression. Its admirable patriotism and formidable spirit of fearing no death made the CPC the hope of the Chinese people for national salvation and the vanguard of the nation in seizing victory in the war of resistance" he said. [549]

For most independent historians, this statement is simply untrue. It was in fact the Nationalist armies who did the bulk of the fighting against Japan. They fought 22 major engagements, most of which involved more than 100,000 men on each side.

Zhou Enlai, China's Prime Minister between 1949 and 1976, wrote in a secret CCP report to Stalin that in the first three years of the war against Japan, one million Chinese soldiers had been killed - but only 3% of these casualties, said the report, were suffered by the Communists. [550]

The Communists preferred to mount only limited hit and run guerrilla raids against the Japanese, so that they could preserve their fighting effectiveness to attack the Nationalists after the Japanese had been defeated. True to this goal, they began fighting the Nationalists just weeks after Japan had surrendered. Nine months after the Japanese surrender full-scale civil war broke out in China.

The failings of the CPC are not open to inspection, like the failings of other governments in other powerful nations. To replace this inspection process, China showers blame on what it views at excesses from outside its borders, such as Western cultural influence, 'splittists' and 'terrorists' who cause supposed 'disharmony' and the few nationalist Japanese who are able to incite the anger of the Chinese government.

Hatred should be based on facts, not half-truths, rumors and misinterpretations of historical conflict, now only teachable by history books written by the citizens of each country, each book containing prejudices the other country will never accept. Teaching children how they should act in future may be more valid than teaching them how they should be guided by historical mythology.

Gao Feng, a 23-year-old visitor to a museum near Beijing's Marco Polo Bridge, the site of an incident in 1937 that led to the beginning of the Sino-Japanese war, said "I have always hated the Japanese... I don't know why, but from the bottom of my heart, I don't like them." [551]

Another visitor to the museum, Li Jie, a 25-year-old student, said, "It gives me great pain to come here. It is very tolerant of Premier Wen [Jiabao] to go to Japan, considering our history and how much we suffered." [552]

168

These words offer 'comfort' to the Communist Party. Just like the elderly women paraded in Tokyo to fight a case they cannot possibly win, today's Chinese government feeds the public with the anger and hatred which it stirs up in pieces small enough not to disturb the economic flow of money from Japan.

Grace in defeat such as that displayed by present day Japan, should be followed by grace in victory, as yet not exercised by China today.

Perhaps one day, someone in the Chinese government will be brave enough to smash the mirror of Japan, and erect China's own mirror, to see the country's own face, the Party's crimes against its people, the horrors against its citizens, and the subjugation of the spirit of the motherland itself.

The Mothers of Tiananmen Square wait at home in Beijing, sometimes under house arrest, especially around the time of the June 4th anniversary. When Tiananmen occurred they were 40 to 50 years old, worried mothers concerned for their children's new found voice.

Many of their sons and daughters who were at Tiananmen on June 4th never came home. Inquiries by the mothers to this day have never been answered by the government responsible. Not once.

Perhaps those mothers, now at least 60 years of age, must wait a further 26 years until they will be offered a wheelchair to be paraded in court by a Chinese government that finally realizes one's own history must first be reflected upon before they can judge the misdeeds of others.

Reason **19**

Hegemony with Chinese Characteristics

In China, the 'kowtow' has long been the traditional form of obeisance on meeting the emperor. The ceremony involves crouching on one's hands and knees and knocking the head against the floor, and a full performance of the ritual requires the giver to fall to his knees three times, each time knocking his head to the ground thrice.

The origins of the kowtow go back as far as Chinese history itself, but it was in the Zhou Dynasty (1027-221BC) that a set of complex rules developed around the ceremony. In the Han Dynasty (221BC-220AD) the process became more widespread. Rather than just being performed in front of the emperor, as in the Zhou Dynasty, it became a central part of official life. Lower officials would kowtow to higher officials all the way up the command chain.

The ceremony expanded into daily life, with pupils kowtowing to masters, and younger people kowtowing to older relatives.[553]

The idea of paying homage to those higher in rank or more powerful also influenced China's foreign relations.

As the minor states of the Chinese nation unified and grew powerful during the Sui (580-618AD) and Tang (618-907AD) Dynasties, the kingdoms on China's borders began to be influenced by Chinese culture and customs.

Though these nations remained independent, they were expected to send regular tribute to China.

While there were rewarded with trading rights in return, the essential meaning of the tribute was very clear – it was an acknowledgement of Chinese superiority.

The kowtow was used extensively by the Qing Dynasty (1644-1911) again as a tool of control. The Qing Dynasty rulers were Manchu people, not Han, and the kowtow was used to underline their superiority.

Indeed, it was not until 1689, when China signed the Treaty of Nerchinsk, that China accepted the principle of diplomatic equality with another nation, in this case Russia. Before this treaty, all other nations had been viewed as inferiors.

In 1792, England sent an ambassador to the Qing court, George Macartney, to try to secure increased trade with China. Macartney refused to perform the kowtow, although other methods of recognition were proposed.

Historians are divided whether Macartney's failure to kowtow lay behind the failure of his mission.

The emperor, Qianlong, refused all of Britain's requests, and, regarding the gifts Macartney had brought with him, said in a written reply to the king of England, "As your ambassador can see for himself, we possess all things. I set no value on objects strange or ingenious, and have no use for your country's manufactures."[554]

Another ambassador, William Amherst, traveled to the Qing court in 1816 and again refused to kowtow. His mission was also unsuccessful.

The concessions England could not gain through diplomacy she later took by brute force – one result of which was the establishment of Hong Kong.

Holland also sent ambassadors to the Qing court, seeking trade concessions. Aware of the failure of Macartney's mission, they hoped to gain an advantage over the British by following Chinese protocol to the letter. During the 37 days they stayed in Beijing they performed the kowtow 30 times – including kowtowing to a banner bearing the emperor's name as well as in front of a bunch of grapes he had sent them.

Their mission failed also.[555]

Kowtowing to your immediate superior and those above theoretically ended when the Qing Dynasty fell in 1911. Occasionally you will see staff members at various hotels genuflect with less formality and depth, indicating a sense of the past still lives in China.

The idea that China is still the center of the world has reappeared in subtle ways, although perhaps subtlety is not the correct term to use when considering China's approach to Taiwan – which is unification by any means, with force if necessary.

Today China has reached back into its traditions to create the 'Taiwan kowtow,' a kowtow with politics added to it, easily the one overriding political idea that consumes Chinese political cadres, as well as the public.

For example, in May 2007, Sheng Huaren, vice chairman of China's parliament, the National People's Congress, met the Speaker of Australia's House of Representatives, David Hawker.

Sheng reiterated the fundamental principle of "peaceful reunification and one country, two systems," and zero tolerance towards "Taiwan's independence," said the Chinese media.

Mr. Hawker told the Chinese delegation that both the Australian government and the parliament would stick to the one-China policy and allow no changes to it. [556]

In March that year Australian Prime Minister John Howard told visiting Chinese Vice-Premier Zeng Peiyan that his country sticks to the one-China policy and will not support any talks or deeds of de jure Taiwan independence, said the Chinese press. [557]

Perhaps Mr. Hawker and Mr. Howard, in their eagerness to perform the kowtow in its new guise in order to achieve economic advantages for their country, have forgotten that the Australian parliament is a democratic body made up of freely elected and free thinking individuals who may not always share the same views as the Communist Party of China.

Zeng Peiyan's early 2007 trip then took him to New Zealand, Vanuatu and Papua New Guinea.

Helen Clark, New Zealand's Prime Minister, reiterated her country's one-China policy.[558]

Vanuatu's Prime Minister, Ham Lini, said in an exchange of messages with China's Prime Minister at that time that his country would adhere to the one-China policy.[559]

Papua New Guinea's Prime Minister, Michael Somare, said Taiwan is an inalienable part of China and his government sticks firmly to the one-China policy.[560]

Vice-Premier Zeng Peiyan scored four for four on kowtows during his trip.

Just to be sure, in May 2007, China's Foreign Minister Yang Jiechi visited New Zealand and gained an added kowtow from New Zealand's foreign minister, Winston Peters, who said the country would not change its stance on the one-China policy.[561]

A few days after this, Yang met senior EU leaders such as foreign policy and security chief Javier Solana, and European Commissioner for External Relations and European Neighborhood Policy Benita Ferrero-Waldner. "The EU officials" said the Chinese media, "reaffirmed that Europe will continue to abide by the one-China policy."[562]

In April 2007, Chinese Vice President Zeng Qinghong met Germany's Defense Minister, Franz Josef Jung, in Beijing. Jung said Germany would adhere to the one-China policy.[563]

Perhaps Defense Minister Jung forgot that Germany's reunification was accomplished by democracy, something at this point that only Taiwan has accomplished.

Again that month, Chinese Vice-Premier Hui Liangyu met the Dutch Foreign Minister, Maxime Verhagen, in The Hague. During the meeting, Verhagen reiterated the Dutch government's continued adherence to the one-China policy.[564]

In May 2007 Wu Bangguo, one of China's most senior leaders, was in Warsaw, Poland, to discuss relations between the two countries and to collect the prerequisite Taiwan kowtow, meeting the speaker of the Polish parliament's lower house, Ludwik Dorn

Dorn said that Poland's position on the issues of Taiwan and Tibet will never change and that the Polish government and its people firmly oppose any secessionist activities in any forms.[565]

A remarkable statement from a leader in a nation that suffered so much at the hands of so many totalitarian occupiers throughout its history. Poland only found its freedom through the democratic Solidarity movement which allowed it to break away from a communist regime and form a free nation – similar to some of Taiwan's democratic intentions.

Foreign Minister Yang Jiechi was again busy in this month, visiting his Canadian counterpart Peter Mackay. Foreign Minister Mackay said that the Canadian government would stick to the one-China policy and would not develop official ties with Taiwan.[566]

While mouthing the required Party line kept his guests happy, perhaps Foreign Minister Mackay's political party also gained votes from the vast number of Chinese who have made Canada their new home – unless of course some of their reasons for moving to Canada were to escape Chinese communism.

Yang moved on to Azerbaijan the following month, where his Azerbaijani counterpart, Araz Azimov, said Azerbaijan would unswervingly adhere to the one-China policy.[567] The kowtow is probably common sense for Azerbaijan, a country that is geographically much nearer to China.

Soon after his election, French Prime Minister Nicolas Sarkozy spoke with Chinese President Hu Jintao. Sarkozy said that Taiwan is an indispensable part of China, and France would firmly adhere to the one-China policy.[568]

France's famous national motto is 'Liberté, Égalité, Fraternité – 'Liberty, Equality, Fraternity.'

But not, alas for Taiwan.

It appears that every single country's leaders, freely elected or not, must mouth the golden words of the new Taiwan kowtow.

In the first half of 2007 alone:

Madagascar's President Marc Ravalomanana said his country would stick to the one-China policy.[569]

Barbados's Prime Minister, Owen Arthur, said his country had been steadfast in following the one-China policy.[570]

Slovakia's Prime Minister, Robert Fico, reiterated Slovakia's firm adherence to the one-China policy.[571]

Maltese Foreign Minister, Michael Frendo, said Malta firmly sticks to the one-China policy.[572]

Greek Foreign Minister Theodora Bakoyianni, perhaps forgetting Greece is the birthplace of democracy, said that her government would unswervingly adhere to the one-China policy in the future.[573]

Sri Lankan President Mahinda Rajapaksa said that, "There can be no change and there will be no change in this. We will always remain firm in our acceptance and support of the one-China Policy." [574]

Cote d'Ivoire Minister of Foreign Affairs Youssouf Bakayoko said his country firmly adheres to the one-China policy.[575]

Zambian President Levy Patrick Mwanawasa said the Zambian government will adhere unswervingly to the one-China policy and supports China's cause of national unification.[576]

President Runaldo Ronald Venetiaan of Suriname reiterated the Suriname government's adherence to the one-China policy. He said

Suriname supports China's efforts to fully realize reunification of the country.[577]

Tonga. Estonia. Kenya. Latvia. Mozambique. Samoa. Nepal. Ukraine. Brunei. Seychelles Islands. Venezuela. Albania. The Philippines. Colombia. Laos. Spain. Czechoslovakia. Hungary.

They all took the pledge in the first half of 2007. And carried on taking it, through 2008 and 2009 and, presumably, for just as long as China requires. When the EU announced its new president, Herman van Rompuy, in November 2009, Chinese media was quick to say "the 62-year-old EU president is clearly supportive of the one-China policy and does not back any separatist activities against China"; when Barack Obama visited China that same month, media noted that he "reaffirmed America's commitment to the one-China policy."[578] And, prior to Hu Jintao's visit to Washington in April 2010, Hu extracted the pledge from Obama once again.[579]

One can well imagine today's high ranking politicos, right hand on their heart, head tilted upwards towards the emblematic red flag of China, eyes watering sympathetically as they symbolically bang their heads on the floor as if they were magically transported back in time to stand before the ancient emperors.

Sadly, even the distressed African country of Sudan signed up for the program. Its Chief of Joint Staff of the Sudanese armed forces, Haj Ahmed El Gaili, said that the Sudanese government and people will continue to support China's reunification cause.[580]

The Sudanese people, it might be thought, in the middle of a brutal civil war that has killed 200,000 and created a million refugees, perhaps have other life and death situations to surmount than the one-China policy.

China's view that the obligatory Taiwan kowtow has any basis for consideration within the war-ravaged Sudanese countryside is an example of the self-importance 'We the Chinese People' exemplifies. Assuming every Sudanese citizen personally took the oath, would that effectively bring Taiwan back to China? Would it allow the Sudanese to live in peace and rebuild their country?

China is more than happy to trade with Sudan, and the world's other oppressive dictatorships – such as Myanmar, Zimbabwe and North Korea -- as long as they perform the ritual Taiwan kowtow and provide access to their natural resources.

Attempting to make sure no nation anywhere in the world speaks up for Taiwan, Beijing offers lavish aid to smaller nations, in a direct attempt to make them say the magic words.

Taiwan also tries to win friends around the world and offers generous aid to countries willing to recognize it. But as Taiwan's unofficial envoy to the UN, James Wu, says, Taiwan cannot match Beijing's resources – for example the US$600 million in aid it offered the country of Senegal, conditional on that country switching allegiance.

Wu says Taiwan's use of aid is different to China's, since all such aid must be approved by a democratically-elected parliament and is open to scrutiny by a free media.[581]

Worldwide, only 23 nations recognize Taiwan.[582]

In the Caribbean, various islands recognize Taiwan's claim to freedom. Beijing is trying to purchase their allegiance with money. Beijing offered the tiny island of Dominica US$112 million, a huge sum of money for an island of just 80,000 people, prior to its 2005 elections if it would agree to sign up to the one-China policy.

China's interference with another country's free elections based on its own self-serving need to add another country to the one-China line up would be considered an affront, and illegal in most developed and democratic countries around the world.

And certainly in China, whose response to such internal interference would be loud and vociferous. "We the Chinese people are deeply offended," some high-ranking Chinese official would be certain to say.

Money talks, and ties with Taiwan were broken after the Dominican election.

Beijing is also putting intense pressure on Haiti, one of the world's poorest countries, to switch allegiance, and threatens to veto UN forces being sent to the violence-torn nation, indicating that China feels its own internal political concerns are of more importance than life and death situations for citizens in other countries.[583]

This is not the first time China has used its UN muscle to effect internal political change in other countries.

China vetoed the UN sending peacekeepers to Guatemala in January 1997 because of Guatemala's ties to Taiwan.[584]

In 1999, China vetoed an extension of a peacekeeping force in Macedonia, outraged because the country had established ties with Taiwan.

Alexander Dimitrov, Macedonia's Foreign Minister at the time, said that his government had not expected China to block the extension, since UN troops were proving extremely helpful in providing stability, a key concern given the continuing unrest and violence in nearby Kosovo.

"Macedonia has a legitimate right to establish relations with any country," said Dimitrov.[585]

Not in the eyes of China's policy makers.

Global organizations also are viewed in the light of the 'one-China' policy, with China often deflecting the worldwide mandate of the particular organization in question for its own self-serving interests and the domination of Taiwan.

Every year, countries who are members of the World Health Organization (WHO) are deflected from their duties in order to prevent Taiwan's attempt to join as a full member because China insists Taiwan is merely a province and has no independent international standing.

In addition to angrily protesting at Taiwan's wish to join the WHO Beijing also views its own membership of global organizations as a vindication of the one-China policy.

For example, when the World Organization for Animal Health (also known by its French initials, OIE) agreed to let China join as a member state in 2007, China's Foreign Ministry reported that "this shows that the international community at large supports the one-China policy." [586]

What the Chinese media did not report was that China had previously been invited to join the OIE in 1993. At that time, China refused to take up the seat it had been offered because Taiwan was a member also.

China only agreed to fill its seat in 2007 once the OIE demoted Taiwan's status to a non-sovereign state and changed its membership name to 'Chinese Taipei,' completing a semantic kowtow.

The OIE defines health standards for trade in meat and farm animals. It has been involved in the 'mad cow disease' crisis and, more recently, the H5N1 bird flu outbreaks. The OIE clearly has a vital role to play in world health and animal wellbeing, yet such issues took second place to Beijing playing politics.

Recently, China has begun to externalize its internal political affairs by exporting the Taiwan situation to its own overseas citizens and quasi-political organizations located around the world.

In May 2007, Jia Qinglin, Chairman of the National Committee of the Chinese People's Political Consultative Conference, talking to delegates of the China Overseas Friendship Association, said that 'compatriots' from home and abroad should stand firmly against Taiwan independence.

He said the association should unite compatriots from Hong Kong, Macao and Taiwan as well as those in other parts of the world to stand firmly against Taiwan independence.

Jia also said that peace and stability across the [international waters of the] Taiwan Strait is being seriously threatened by that county's "conspiracy of seeking de jure Taiwan independence through so-called constitutional reform," said Chinese media.[587] Of course, people in China have zero access to any form of constitutional reform whatsoever.

Chinese Premier Wen Jiabao, giving a report on the work of the government in March 2007, said that "We will faithfully follow the Party's policy on overseas Chinese affairs and bring into full play the unique role of overseas Chinese nationals, returned overseas Chinese and their relatives in promoting reunification of the motherland and rejuvenation of the Chinese nation."[588]

Chinese State Councilor Tang Jiaxuan, speaking to members of the Chinese American Alliance for China's Peaceful Reunification, visiting Beijing in June 2007, again called for them to "firmly stand against the Taiwan regime's secessionist activities."[589]

A group of Chinese citizens living in Germany held a photography exhibition in May 2007 promoting the cause of reunification. The exhibition, said Chinese media, "is designed to illustrate that the island is an inseparable part of China."

Ye Haijie, chairman of the Council of Overseas Chinese in Germany for the Promotion of China's Peaceful Reunification, said that reunification is of fundamental interest to Chinese all over the world. Wang Fuqing, chairman of the Beijing-run Taiwan Affairs Office, said that the exhibition demonstrated that reunification is the common wish of all Chinese people, both at home and abroad.

Johannes Pflug, a member of the German parliament who attended the exhibition, said that the German government and parliament will always stick to the one-China policy. Again, rather a surprising comment for a politician in a democracy to make.[590]

As a representative of his government, Pflug might do well to remember Germany's previous history where kowtows were fashioned in the form of salutes and verbal affirmations of loyalty and allegiance were shouted above all.

Across the globe, the South and Central American Foundation for the Peaceful Reunification of China also held activities to promote the internal Chinese policy of reunification in May 2007.

Five hundred overseas Chinese attended the meeting held in Caracas, the capital of Venezuela, and reached a unanimous declaration that "2007 is a key year to fight Taiwan's separatist forces and maintain peace across the Taiwan strait."

The declaration also spoke of drawing together the "wisdom and efforts of all Chinese people living in Central and South America towards this cause [of reunification]."

In previous years, meetings have been held in Lima, Sao Paulo, Buenos Aires and Santiago. [591]

In 2008 China even set up a hotline so that people could report websites that 'wrongly' labeled Taiwan a country. "Some websites publish sensitive or confidential geographical information, which might leak State secrets and threaten security," said Min Yiren, Deputy Director of the State Bureau of Surveying and Mapping. "Foreign organizations and individuals engaged in making and publishing online maps will also be stopped" said Min, without saying how this could be achieved, given the global nature of the internet.[592]

A look at the historical results of Chinese interference in the political affairs of other nations is illuminating. Soon after the establishment of the Ming Dynasty in 1368, for example, Tibet refused to offer fealty to the new emperor. China's response was to attack, and in 1379 Tibet was forced into obedience.

Some centuries later, in the Qing Dynasty (1644-1911), a border tribe known as the Zunghar also experience Chinese political meddling. The Zunghar were a branch of the Mongols, whose most famous leader,

Kublai Khan, had himself conquered China and established the Yuan Dynasty (1279-1386).

The leader of the Zunghar people died in 1745, and there was a struggle over the succession as various powerful factions fought to claim the throne. The Chinese emperor Qianlong backed one of these contenders, a man named Amursana, and dispatched two armies to make sure he took the throne.

But after he had been installed as king, Amursana refused to pay the necessary tribute, to kowtow to the Qing, and rejected a summons to attend the Chinese capital.

Qianlong's response was decisive. He sent a large army, and ordered it to show no mercy to the 'rebels.'

No mercy was shown. The Zunghar people were massacred in an act of genocide and disappeared from history.[593]

Almost as a parody, the power of the Chinese emperors has been diluted over the centuries and replaced by another form of emperorism. So much so that even a small island in the Caribbean can, with reasonable safety, watch China huff and puff its one-China policy frustrations from afar.

In true box-office style, 'The Mouse that Roared' was revisited in early 2007, when the Caribbean island of St. Lucia, a nation of 168,000 people living on 616 square kilometers, refused the obligatory kowtow and decided to fully recognize Taiwan as a nation as well as China.

The Party emperors in Beijing were not pleased.

Chinese foreign ministry spokesman Liu Jianchao said that this was a flagrant violation of the declaration of relations between China and St. Lucia. He demanded that St. Lucia correct its "wrongful decision."

In one of the most amazing political statements of 2007, Liu said that St. Lucia's decision was "interference in the internal affairs of China."[594] While aggressively seeking external affirmation of its internal policies around the world, a refusal to adhere prompted a declaration of interference in its internal affairs.

St. Lucia's Foreign Minister Rufus Bousquet said, "We have been very careful about making this decision, and now that we have made it we do not expect the Chinese will love us any more for it. But we expect that they will conduct themselves in a manner that is acceptable to our government."

"St. Lucia did not win its sovereignty from one power [the UK] to be now dictated to by another power as to who its friends should be" said the island's media. The one-China policy should not be forced on St. Lucia "as though we, too, were a colony of China."

Democracy prevails.

Beijing demanded that St. Lucia drop its recognition of Taiwan. Using the dark threatening language of the kind utilized by evil minded foreign ministers of Balkan state governments in the spring of 1914, just before the Great War, Foreign Ministry spokesman Liu Jianchao cautioned the people of St. Lucia in no uncertain terms.

Correct their wrongful decision or, "Otherwise, the government of St. Lucia will be fully responsible for the consequences incurred."

"The consequences incurred"!

One could well imagine retired soldiers on St. Lucia mustering themselves on the beaches to form patrols and issuing binoculars so they could scan the horizon for the first sign of Chinese warships. Others are assigned to crane their necks skywards as they watch for the first signs of attacking aircraft - just like the ones in the Pearl Harbor movie.

At night, the locals would train their flashlights on coastal waters waiting to shout out that they had been the first to see a periscope break the surface of the water. Chinese submarines!

No, it's not Hollywood, but close enough.

Chinese Ambassador to St. Lucia, Gu Huaming lodged 'solemn representations and strong objection' to the government of St. Lucia. Gu announced the suspension of diplomatic relations with St. Lucia and the cessation of fulfilling all agreements between the governments of the two countries, reported Chinese media.[595]

Great nations have no need of such simplified all-or-nothing diplomatic pronouncements.

Surprisingly, China does not realize that in the end pledging allegiance to Taiwan is not about politics. Not for nations of 168,000 people. It's strictly business. It's all about the money.

Tourists are why most Caribbean countries agree to mouth the Taiwan kowtow – that and China's excessive financial largesse.

Chinese tourists are a valuable asset that any country's tourism industry would love to capture. However, the hordes of sunburned tourists from China have not yet appeared on the beaches of the Caribbean. Ironically it is a question of cultural misunderstanding that any Caribbean island thinks that citizens of the People's Republic are similar in nature to Western people.

Describe an idyllic beach scene where nothing is happening but sun, surf and sand and the average Western person sighs and says "Oh, yes...."

Describe local seafood delicacies prepared in the Caribbean way, topped off with rum cocktails, backed by gentle steel drums and the picture is made perfect in the minds of hundreds of thousands of winter-suffering Westerners everywhere.

Describe the same scene to a Chinese person and he/she will probably be aghast. The first thing that will eliminate them as tourists will be the wife or girlfriend's terror of the sun, which would darken their skin, which culturally is a huge negative for those living in China's chic cities.

The tourism budget of an island like St. Lucia pales against the advertising budget of giant international cosmetic companies who do huge business in sales of skin-whiteners to the very same customers that the Caribbean islands would like to tan.

If young Chinese people were to change these traditional negative attitudes about the way of Western relaxation in the sun, the revenue from Caribbean-bound visitors from China would still be several decades away.

It is a wonder that China does not see the affinity the Caribbean islands might have for the democratic country of Taiwan. The geographical concept of the island is a unifier, as is the fact that each and every Caribbean island was once dominated by a 'mother' country – Britain, France, Spain, Holland – much the same as Taiwan is dominated by its motherland, China.

China has clearly decided the 'We the Chinese People' face it offers to the world has been besmirched. It is surprising that a nation the size of St. Lucia has been able to do this so effectively, thus exposing the weakness of China's foreign policy

Perhaps a greater nation than China, instead of cutting off its relationships, would have said, "Fine. We still want to play, let's see what we can do to improve our game."

Face is an opportunity for reflection.

Reason 20

Suicide China

In traditional Chinese culture, suicide was often viewed as a heroic action used either to avoid ignoble capture or to protest the unjust action of rulers.

Xiang Yu, for example, was a general who helped overthrow the cruel Qin Dynasty, known globally for its terracotta warriors, now famous among tourists. Though Xiang is remembered as cruel and at times as arrogant, he is also honored for the manner of his death – suicide.

There are a number of legends about the precise way he died, but the most stirring runs that, when surrounded by the soldiers of an opposing general, he saw an old friend among the enemy troops. "I hear there is a great reward for my head," he is supposed to have said to this friend. "Let me give you this." He then used his own sword to decapitate himself.

While this legend may be romanticized beyond the bounds of physical possibility, it nonetheless shows a 'cultural' attitude towards suicide that has associations of bravery and admiration.

One of the most famous suicides in Chinese history is that of Qu Yuan, a renowned poet of ancient China. He was a minister at the court of the King of Chu, and advised the king how to deal with the neighboring state of Qin, which was then growing powerful.

But the king, prompted by the machinations of other factions at court, rejected Qu Yuan's advice and banished him. The Kingdom of Chu was later swallowed up by the Kingdom of Qin in 278 BC.

Qu Yuan, upon hearing this, committed ritual suicide by wading into the Miluo River, in today's Hunan Province in central China, in protest at the corruption and political blindness that had led to the Kingdom of Chu's downfall.

Even today, more than 2000 years later, Qu Yuan is revered for his patriotism and stand against corruption. His poetry is still very widely known, but perhaps the way his death is commemorated, via the Dragon Boat Festival, is better known to Western readers.

But while Qu Yuan's life and death are still a part of Chinese cultural awareness, suicide today has become something very different – a vast and largely unspoken problem that is very much ignored.

The raw statistics of suicide today are shocking.

Around 250,000 people kill themselves every year, according to statistics from China's Ministry of Health. To put this another way – every two minutes of each hour, 24/7, eight Chinese people kill themselves. The figure of 250,000 is those whose deaths are reported as suicide. It does not include the suicide deaths that are hushed up or attributed to other causes.[596]

A further two *million* people attempt suicide annually.[597] Furthermore these two million attempts were just the ones that ended up in hospital, indicating a far higher true total.

Even more shocking, of these two million, "less than one percent receive psychiatric assessment and guidance during the emergency treatment" said Chinese media.

One report in 2010 suggested that China had 173 *million* adults with some form of psychiatric problem, and that 91% of these have never received any help.[598]

The suicide death toll among today's Chinese citizens is beyond the ability of government officials to calculate accurately. According to the Beijing Suicide Research and Prevention Center, which was set up in 2003 by the Society of Neurology and Psychiatry of the Chinese Medical Association and Beijing's Huilongguan Hospital, the figure is 23 suicides per 100,000 people. Based on an official population of 1.3 billion, that's almost 300,000 suicides a year.

Suicide is the number one killer of Chinese people between the ages of 15 and 34. Surprising, when you consider the burgeoning economy and new-found 'freedoms' offered by the state that pronounces stability and harmony as its watchwords. In a country where young people have everything to live for, they are ending their lives at a rate that surely must make government leaders question the speed of change that is overtaking the Chinese people in the name of progress.

The suicide rate among women is 25% higher than among men, and rural suicide rates are *three* times higher than urban rates.

The Beijing center also says that 16 million people suffer from severe psychosis, with 63 million suffering other mental disorders. But, says Professor Zou Yizhuang of Huilongguan Hospital, altogether China could have up to 90 million people suffering from mental problems – not including children and the elderly, which is surprising given that previous totals indicate that children sometimes use suicide as the only way out of stressful situations.

A survey of 2,700 citizens in Shanghai in 2008 found that almost 60% said someone close to them suffered from emotional or psychological stress. The Shanghai Medical Center said that the prevalence of depression had *quadrupled* from a decade ago.[599]

And help is not on the way. Using figures from 2004, the center said that China had just over 16,000 psychiatrists – a ratio of psychiatrists to population just 5%-10% of that of industrially developed countries.

In fact, 90% of cases of clinical depression are never treated, due to "low awareness, stigma and non-insurance." Half of schizophrenia cases are never treated.[600]

This acute shortage of mental health assistance was illustrated in a particularly bloody fashion in late 2009. In November that year, 21-year-old Chen Wenfa, apparently aware of his deteriorating mental health,

184

sought help at Kunming Psychiatric Hospital. He was diagnosed with acute schizophrenia.

But instead of being hospitalized, he left the facility. He then killed six members of his family - his parents, grandmother, uncle, uncle's wife, and his cousin.

That very same month, in China's Inner Mongolia region, a poor villager named Wen Tiequan committed suicide after he had stabbed six people. He too had mental problems, but was simply too poor to afford treatment.[601]

One reason often given for this lack of medical care is that China only began to offer psychiatric care in its hospitals in the 1980s. Another reason is that even though suicide as a political statement is traditionally understood in China, suicide arising out of mental stress is still viewed as shameful. Culturally, there is great reluctance in China to talk about 'difficult' feelings and personal mental turmoil.

It was not until 1992 that China opened its first dedicated psychiatric treatment ward in a general hospital, at Tongji Hospital in Shanghai. This was able to provide less extreme refuge for patients with psychiatric problems than the numerous mental health asylums, sometimes used by political leaders wanting to hide away 'political enemies.' Even so, facilities such as the Tongji Hospital Center remain very limited.

Government rules have stated that by 2005, 70% of municipalities should have at least one general hospital providing psychiatric services. But in the countryside, where the problems are worse, these rules stated that 50% of country hospitals should have one such general hospital – by 2010.[602]

In 2005 Professor Cong Zhong at Peking University's Centre of Clinical Psychology said that there was little investment from the government and hospitals in mental health service. Professor Cong also said this underinvestment was putting young people off becoming psychiatrists.[603]

City-based suicide tends to be a reaction to stress. For example, in just May 2007 alone, five university students in Beijing killed themselves.

This prompted what Chinese media reported as a "psychological raid" which would be used to tackle students' mental health problems, as launched by the city's Renmin University.

Some, such as Lin Yonghe, a professor at Beijing Technology and Business University, supported the idea, saying "Suicide is a long process full of huge psychological conflicts, and signs of those conflicts will reveal themselves." But others, such as Ma Shaohua, a teacher at Renmin University itself, were less sure, saying "It delivers a negative message, including distrust."

Indecision leads to inaction, as we have seen previously, and it is indecision that allows the continuation of the lonely deaths of thousands and thousands of suicides every year. Teachers often display a negative attitude towards psychological openness, leaving students with no outlet except the path they have already chosen – death.

According to Fei Lipeng, then-director of the Beijing Suicide Research and Prevention Center, "Many students are on the brink of a suicide attempt, but they do not want help from their teachers or university counseling centers because they fear the information will be leaked to the school authority, which will bring them more troubles."

In 2006, Beijing had 108 psychologists for its 700,000 university students.[604] That's one psychologist per 6,481 often troubled, confused and sometimes suicidal students.

2008 set a record for student suicides - 63 deaths from 38 universities. Current director of the Beijing Suicide Research and Prevention Center Yang Fude said that for today's highly pressurized students "Suicide seems to be a way of escaping the fear."[605]

In 2009, suicide became the leading cause for student deaths, as well as for all people aged 15 to 34. Among this latter group, the death rate was 22.2 per 100,000 people - a figure barely different from that given in previous years.[606]

Columnist Qin Zhongwei, writing in China Daily in 2010, wondered if the high number of student suicides was linked to the one-child generation. "I don't want to discuss the reasons that made these students give up on living in this world. Life is full of obstacles" he wrote. "But I do believe that our post-80 generation, which is termed by some media as the 'Me Generation,' should have second thoughts before doing anything rash. The suicide stories just tell the cold truth that the parents' love and devotion was in vain."[607]

The causes of suicide in rural areas tend to arise out of different factors, most commonly poverty and domestic abuse, with women suffering by far the most.

According to Xu Rong, who works with the Cultural Development Centre for Rural Women, "Most suicides in rural areas start with small quarrels between couples...Some of them are accidental; some are actually rooted in unhappy marriages."

In China's countryside, there is great pressure on young women to conform to society's expectations of traditional marriage, meaning many arranged marriages.

Many marriages are not based on love, and, says Xu Rong, "Rural men tend to be reluctant to express their love or care for their spouses, who have more romantic emotions."[608]

One of the problems that Xu Rong's organization faces is that it remains very small scale. She says that when the project began she faced criticism because people felt suicide was a "private issue." Even though the project soon began to achieve good results, it only served six villages in three rural counties.[609]

Many women face greater problems than lack of love. One rural woman, reported the Washington Post in 2007, said that her husband beat her frequently. "I can't remember how many times he beat me," said Ms. Wang, a 45-year-old. "Every day I was angry and unhappy. I felt life was meaningless.... You can see the scars on my hands, where he beat me with a stick."[610]

Wang attempted suicide three times. The most common way for rural women to commit or attempt suicide is by drinking pesticide.

Acknowledging this problem, Liu Denggao, a vice-director at the Ministry of Agriculture, said his ministry would restrict production of the most poisonous insecticides, change the color and smell of poisons, package chemicals in small amounts, and educate the public about appropriate uses and storage of pesticides. He was speaking as a workshop on a National Suicide Prevention Plan for China in 2003.[611]

However, lethal pesticides today are freely available off the shelf, are inappropriately stored in home environments, and this inexpensive answer to a moment's anger or feeling of depression too readily is the answer taken.

Speaking in 2004, Han Jinzhi, chief nurse of Haixing County Hospital in Hebei Province, said that the most frequently used poisons include omethoate, methamidophos, DDT and herbicide, all containing lethal chemicals.

Poisonous pesticides in China cost as little as 7 yuan (85 US cents) a bottle, said media, and still could be easily obtained.

And in 2006, Xu Rong said it was still too easy for women to obtain pesticides, three years after the Ministry of Agriculture had said it would address the problem.[612]

The needs of an intended suicide victim are not culturally exclusive. The desire to take your own life is normally preceded by a desire to reach out, to find somebody to listen to your problems – perhaps a warm arm to reach around your shoulder to try to alleviate the pain you feel. The Chinese, unfortunately, can call on few such resources to help them, even if they openly did so.

Outreach groups in the countryside are desperately underfunded, and China's few telephone hotlines are overwhelmed.

Michael Philips, executive director of the Beijing Suicide Research and Prevention Centre, says that the hotline they run is so busy that nine of out ten callers cannot get through. "It's very dangerous because they may be at high risk of committing suicide," he said.[613]

The hotline department costs 25,000 to 30,000 yuan (about 3,600 US dollars) in telephone charges per month, but with salaries taken into account, the true cost is around one million yuan (about 120,000 US dollars) annually. Most of this is paid for solely by the hospital where the Beijing Suicide Research and Prevention Center is located.[614]

One of the other problems the hotline faces is that many of the callers who do get through want to talk sex rather than suicide. One of the counselors who works at the center, Wang Cuiling, said that "such callers keep describing the details of their sexual experiences rather than responding our questions. Or they talk to us with very heavy breath, trying to sound horny."

And even in 2010, eight years after the center opened, the center still faces a shortage of volunteers to answer the calls, meaning that those who do work there have to take 16 hour shifts.[615]

A hotline set up in Shanghai in has 2005 similar problems. "It is clear that having only one line will not be able to satisfy demand" said an official involved with the hotline.[616]

According to a paper written by Professor Kwok-kan Tam of the Chinese University of Hong Kong, "The traditional Chinese regarded the self as primarily a role-self, expressed in familial and social relationships... In this relationship a person is not an independent individual, for he has little individual identity or individuality, and lives mainly to fulfill dutifully the various roles expected of him. Individuality is only allowed within the limits of roles. Self-awareness in traditional Chinese culture, if there is any, is therefore presented mainly as role-awareness, and identity crisis is seldom conceived as a problem of self-identity in the traditional Chinese consciousness."

Professor Tam's theory helps explain the underlying malaise of today's Chinese society. Even though the Communist Party set out to destroy culture, tradition and even history, large areas of the countryside remain deeply traditional, and the Confucian attitudes that Professor Tam discusses are still present. Rural women lack any outlet for their mental stresses, and too often see suicide as the only answer in a cultural system that allows them no other options.

But in China's cities the traditional influences of Confucian culture are much less strong. Speaking of the modern Chinese psyche, Professor Tam writes "the lack of a cultural heritage ... leaves the modern Chinese in much puzzle about the new selfhood and identity. Individualism becomes synonymous with selfishness, the self is subordinated under the collective self (or 'gigantic self'), and personal-identity is displaced by national identity."

In addition, Professor Tam says "When Descartes says 'I think, therefore I am,' the 'I' is a mind, which can be considered separately from the body. But in cultures other than that of the West, such as the Chinese, the 'self' is both body and mind. The notion of self is culture-specific, and there lacks a universal definition that can be accepted by all cultures."

The older fabric of society – the family – has been erased by the terrors of the Cultural Revolution, in which family member informed on family member, and the destruction of the extended family as a result of the one-child policy. This leaves people today with few avenues for self-expression. And in any case, given a cultural attitude that does indeed equate individualism with selfishness, the very idea of discussing mental health issues is frowned upon.

Professor Tam suggests that it "is both the traditional Confucian discourse and the Communist discourse that have discouraged the construction of a self-identity by asking seriously the question: 'Who am I?'"[617]

As we have already argued, the idea of self in China has been replaced by uni-national thinking, and this has forged inflexibility in the soul of the modern Chinese citizen. For today's urban Chinese, self-identity is expressed merely in terms of money. The more cash you have, the more of a person you are and the larger your reflection in society.

This, of course, is an immensely destructive attitude, and the crushing pressure it creates for success is what lies under the spiraling suicide rates and the young and educated.

In such a society, what hope is there for the soul of China? What are its citizens supposed to represent? How should they construct their soul to cope?

Tens of thousands of young men and women every year cannot cope. They take the only way out that they can clearly understand and perform as a function of self. Suicide.

Early in 2007, a young woman was preparing to kill herself in the central city of Chongqing. As she stood, ready to jump off a six-storey building, a crowd gathered below.

Some yelled for her to jump, and some phoned friends to "come and enjoy the spectacle." Others were upset she had not jumped before the emergency services arrived to try and talk her down. One young man sat in the window of an opposite building playing his guitar to entertain the crowds. When the emergency services persuaded the woman to give up the attempt, the crowd below booed.[618] The unfolding of tragedy before the eyes of many Chinese citizens is today viewed with a sense of pleasure.

In 2009, a man named Chen Fuchao attempted suicide by leaping from Haizhu Bridge in Guangzhou, a venue had already seen 12 suicide attempts in the preceeding two months. Unable to bring himself to jump, Chen stood on the side of the bridge, holding up traffic for five hours. At that point a man named Lai Jiansheng broke through the cordon police had set up, ran towards Chen - and pushed him off. "I pushed him off because jumpers like Chen are very selfish. Their action violates a lot of public interests," media quoted Lai as saying, before he was taken away by police.[619]

For China's government, 'harmony' is today's mantra, repeated ad infinitum. In the headlong rush for economic expansion, the identity of the Chinese self is lost. The ancient harmony that was the Chinese soul has been displaced by financial yearnings, desires for a wealthy future, and the building of worlds based on the new Chinese 'I.'

Reason 21

Boxing in Ideas for Mr. Marx

In the late 1950s, China's military had developed a number of basic computer networks. Each network was made up of a number of workstations. Each of these stations could communicate with each other. But they could not communicate with other networks. Furthermore, each network had been built for different purposes and by different people. Each had its own set of operating rules.

In the early 1960s, one brilliant, forward-thinking Chinese scientist working in a military research program realized that what was needed was one computer workstation that could communicate with any other network, and one set of operating instructions for all machines.

The scientist began to work on a set of theories to enable this change to take place. Others on his visionary team helped design and implement the necessary protocols.

As they did so, they realized another benefit of their dream; it could be expanded to link together the country's universities, research institutions and libraries, and it could allow cheap and efficient communication for ordinary people. In a country as vast as China, this would have been a great advantage.

But China's military and political leaders had a different agenda. They saw that this system would make China's secrets invulnerable to the outside world, even nuclear attack. If one research base and its computer network were destroyed, other machines linked to it in other places would be able to take over. Top research scientists from the country's leading universities were drafted to help create this defendable system.

Several noted scientists protested about this squandering of the network's wider benefits. They wanted to open up the new system to more academic collaboration. They wanted the entire technological community to be able to take a role in creating this new system, because they knew that in this way many new advantages would be found.

China's military leaders firmly disagreed. They had no interest in opening up the possible benefits of the new system to the people. For them, all that mattered was the tactical advantage such a network would give them. Dissenting scientists were dismissed from the program and relocated. Some were even jailed.

The new system of networked workstations never left the research base. China's military kept the secrets in the box.

Around the same time, China's computer manufacturers, under direct state control as is all industry in the country, were directed to focus their efforts on the military benefits alone.

Because of this, even though computers were not user-friendly, it did not matter, as only specially trained operatives needed to use them.

And since Chinese society valued conformity above all things, there was no possibility for any young and talented student to drop out, create a start-up business at home, and invent a more easily usable system.

Though computers slowly began to permeate wider society, few were networked.

Since Chinese computer scientists remained under strict military control, no-one invented programs that would allow easy browsing of the data in the now-huge Chinese defense department computer network.

The world, of course, knew practically nothing of the system the Chinese had invented. Rumors filtered out of some great connective system whereby a computer in New York might easily communicate with a computer in London.

Occasionally, an arrest was made of a particular scientist or military specialist, who tried to reveal the secrets. But the Chinese Communist Party had a death-grip on the system.

As news leaked out into the West, the press had a field day with speculation, rumor and conjecture.

It even earned itself a nickname – they called it 'the Internet.'

Fantasy? Absolutely, but entirely plausible if you consider the present day nature of the policies and actions of the political regime which desperately wants to put the World Wide Web back in the box.

Imagine, if the above story was true...

No World Wide Web. No Internet Explorer or Firefox, Yahoo, EBay, Google, YouTube, or Facebook.

Probably the boys at Microsoft would find something else to do. And imagine what kind of poor country cousin the NASDAQ stock exchange would be.

Had China 'discovered' computers and networking in the way that America did in the 1950s, 1960s, and into the 1970s, the internet as we know it today would never have been born. The world would have been a totally different place. There would be no hi-tech 'connected' economy, no 'wired generation.'

Guessing alternative history or the future is an unprovable science, but presently it is very clear that China's government desires to use the net as a tool of control, not as a tool of freedom.

In 2007, Hu Jintao, China's president, ordered officials to ensure the internet was "ethically inspiring." He said he wanted the Communist Party to help "purify the internet environment," and said that "whether we can cope with the internet is a matter that affects the development of socialist culture, the security of information, and the stability of the state."

China's top political body, the Politburo, added "development and administration of internet culture must stick to the direction of advanced socialist culture, adhere to correct propaganda guidance."

It was vital, they said, to "consolidate the guiding status of Marxism in the ideological sphere." [620] Perhaps the Communist Party wishes that Karl Marx had invented the internet.

But control, not 'guidance' is what lies at the heart of the internet for China's government. Whereas in the West the great achievement of the internet is that it allows each user to create their own individual world, for China its purpose is to spread government propaganda and to consolidate control over society and individual freedom.

China's army of wired citizens is so huge that any figure we can give on it will certainly be exceeded within weeks. By the middle of 2007, it was around 150 million internet users and around 60 million blogs, and by the end of 2007 there were around 210 million users. By late 2008 the number had jumped to 275 million users, giving China the planet's largest internet population. [621] By 2010 it had hit 400 million. [622]

But those in the countryside had not joined the wired world. Xinhua reported that, "The rural countryside is home to 57 percent of China's population, but has only 12 percent of its Internet users." [623]

According to one domestic survey in 2007, 70 percent of Chinese netizens suffer from psychological problems, experiencing, "amnesia, anxiety and scatterbrained problems, however, 90 percent of them never resort to psychological doctors, the survey showed" noted media. [624]

Internet addiction has become so common in China that a number of internet addiction camps have been set up to wean people away from the online world. One such addict, 15-year-old Deng Senshan, was sent to an addiction camp in the province of Guangzhou.

Staff at the camp beat Deng to death. [625]

A few weeks after this, another young student, Pu Liang, was beaten so badly at a different net addiction camp that he ended up in intensive care in hospital. Luckier than Deng Senshan, he recovered.

Three months later, China's Ministry of Health banned the use of physical punishment in such camps. [626]

One of the strongest expressions of individual freedom that the internet facilitates is blogging. Blogging allows everyone a voice, and while the sheer number of blogs means each voice might not always be heard, the voices in most societies shout freely.

The Chinese government is terrified of what blogging represents. A society in which every voice is free to speak is the antithesis of the goals of today's Chinese government.

Beijing would be happy to be able to be able to design a Marxist-style box to control China's burgeoning blogosphere. In 2006 the government looked into the feasibility of requiring all bloggers to register with their real names.

Due to the complexity of such a registration system it has not, at the time of writing, been implemented. But "a real name system will be an unavoidable choice if China wants to standardize and develop its blog industry," says Huang Chengqing, head of the Internet Society of China. [627]

And in 2010, Beijing announced that it wanted to implement a real-name system for anyone posting comments online. China was "embarking on a crusade against online anonymity and trying to put a stop to the many discussions on sensitive political and social subjects that are taking place on the Internet" said reporters without borders.[628]

The true meanings of the words 'standardize and develop' can more accurately be described as to 'shackle and restrict' to the point of total control of those who "anonymously disseminate irresponsible and untrue information via the internet, bringing about very bad influences not only to individuals but to society as a whole."

In Chinese terms, 'irresponsible and untrue' information is anything which does not agree with the government line.

Shi Tao, for example, was jailed for ten years in 2005 for 'leaking state secrets.' His crime? Using the energy of the internet, which allowed his words to reach the outside world, he wrote an email summarizing the press restrictions that were imposed around the time of the 15th anniversary of the Tiananmen Square Massacre in 1989. The information he used was merely that which the authorities had distributed to many journalists in China.

To Beijing, equal to keeping things inside the box is the fear of what happens when the truth escapes outside the box. Shi Tao was arrested after Yahoo acceded to Beijing's request for information about his online activities.

His lawyer, Guo Guoding, pointed out that the police seizure of Shi Tao's computer had been illegal, and thus his arrest had been illegal too.

In response to this, Guo's license to practice law was cancelled for one year by the Shanghai Law Department, meaning he was no longer able to represent Shi Tao. Guo was subsequently put under house arrest.

The hearing into Shi Tao's case was held in secret. His family was not allowed to attend. The 'trial' lasted just two hours. Afterwards Shi Tao was allowed to spend ten minutes with his family.[629] Mr. Shi was honored by the World Association of Newspapers as its 2007 'Golden Pen of Freedom' Laureate. (The 2008 winner was Li Changqing, who was jailed for three years for writing on a US-based Chinese language website about an outbreak of Dengue fever, news of which the government had banned from domestic media).[630]

A human rights lawyer, Yang Maodong (also known by his pseudonym Guo Feixiong) was arrested in September 2006 for 'illegal business activities.' His real crime, however, was that he wrote news reports about matters the Chinese government preferred to be kept hidden from the public eye. He told his lawyer he had been tortured in prison with electric shocks to his genitals. He subsequently tried to commit suicide.[631] In November 2007, he was sentenced to five years in prison.[632]

Blogger and filmmaker Hao Wu was held for five months after being arrested in February 2006 when he was making a film about an

194

underground Protestant church. He was never allowed to see a lawyer, or have visits from relatives. According to security officials, he had 'breached national security.'

According to Reporters without Borders (www.rsf.org), worldwide there are 61 people in jail for posting 'subversive' comment on a blog or website. Fifty-two of them are in China, giving the country five or six times the total number of imprisoned voices in the rest of the globe.[633] "China is by far the world's biggest prison for bloggers and cyber-dissidents" says the organization.[634]

The Reporters without Borders 2007 China report says that "... self-censorship is obviously in full force. Just five years ago, many people thought Chinese society and politics would be revolutionized by the Internet, a supposedly uncontrollable medium. Now, with China enjoying increasing geopolitical influence, people are wondering the opposite, whether perhaps China's Internet model, based on censorship and surveillance, may one day be imposed on the rest of the world."

The organization also says that "China keeps a tight grip on what is written and downloaded by users and spends an enormous amount on Internet surveillance equipment and hires armies of informants and cyber-police."

"It also has the political weight to force the companies in the sector - such as Yahoo!, Google, Microsoft and Cisco Systems - to do what it wants them to, and all have agreed to censor their search-engines to filter out websites overcritical of the authorities. This makes the regime's job very much easier because these firms are the main entry-points to the Internet. If a website is not listed by these search-engines, material posted on them has about as much chance of being found as a message in a bottle thrown into the sea." [635]

The situation did not improve in 2008, said RSF in their annual report for that year. "Many observers had expected more tolerance to be shown to the press along with greater freedom of expression, as the authorities had pledged. But the government and in particular the political police and the propaganda department did everything possible to prevent the liberal press, Internet-users and dissidents from expressing themselves," said the organization.[636]

In 2010, RSF noted that "China is the world's biggest prison for journalists, bloggers and cyber-dissidents. Most of the around one hundred prisoners have been sentenced to long jail sentences for 'subversion' or 'divulging state secrets' and are held in harsh conditions, with journalists often being put to forced labour. The local authorities, fearful of bad publicity from reports on corruption and nepotism, continue to arrest journalists."[637]

In a further bid to stop the free flow of information, China has also been trying to find a reliable way to establish a real-name system for all mobile phone users since 2005. While many other nations also require mobile phone users to register, in those nations using a phone is unlikely to lead to attention from the police, as it certainly would in China if the user looked at or shared 'sensitive' information. In early 2010, Chinese industry experts said they expected such a system to come into use by the end of the year.[638]

Another great assistance to the Chinese government in its quest to silence freely-expressed opinions is, sadly, the Chinese people themselves.

In China, the compulsion to conform creates a 'herd mentality' which dominates to such an overwhelming extent that those who do try to speak out with a different voice are routinely attacked or ostracized. This is masked as citizen action taken in order to subjugate those individuals who step outside preconceived notions of morality.

A case in point was the widespread online outrage in the 'Bronze Mustache' affair. This occurred when a man going by the online name of 'Freezing Blade' posted an online denunciation of a student, 'Bronze Mustache,' whom he accused of having an affair with his wife, 'Quiet Moon,' in April 2006.

The denunciation caught fire, and within days a mob of online activists had gathered online to track down the unfortunate student. Soon, all his personal details were posted online. He was forced to leave university and even his home was besieged by mobs.

There were thousands of online posts, many calling for such medieval punishments as 'Bronze Mustache' to be beheaded and 'Quiet Moon' to be drowned. China's largest bulletin board, Tianya.com, saw a 10% surge in daily traffic. What should have been a personal matter for the three people to resolve became a nationwide crusade.

Another case of online vigilantism concerned a young Chinese woman, Grace Wang, who was a student at Duke University, in America. During the Tibetan riots of 2008 (see Reason 1) pro-Tibet and pro-China groups faced off on the Duke campus. Wang, who had friends in both camps, attempted to mediate. Offering a calm, logical and sensible approach, she urged leaders from each side to tone down the rhetoric and talk.

Her commendable attempt backfired. The next day, her image was posted on a China-based online forum with the phrase 'Traitor to your country' scrawled on it. Along with this, her full name (in Chinese) was given, along with her ID number, her home address in China, and even directions to her parents' apartment. The apartment was vandalized (with possessions being stolen and feces thrown on the doorstep) and her parents had to flee. Wang herself received vitriolic email messages, such as "If you return to China, your dead corpse will be chopped into 10,000 pieces." She was even struck off the alumni list from her high school.[639]

In an interview with National Public Radio, Wang said that "… if the government is not inciting this, they have acquiescence to this. Chinese parties, official TV website, cctv.com, they called me as the 'ugliest overseas Chinese ever.'"[640]

This phenomenon of online activism has become known as the 'human flesh search engine,' via which netizens, even free of government encouragement seek to impose a definition of right and wrong on other people.[641]

A clear example of this was the 'Chinabounder' case, which again exposed contemporary Chinese society's inability to deal with the freedoms that blogging offers.

The Chinabounder blog detailed the sex life and social opinions of a Western expatriate character living in Shanghai. Within a few weeks of the blog being posted on an American blog site, it was attracting vitriolic and abusive comments from Chinese readers.

The blog really caught fire when Zhang Jiehai, a professor of psychology and member of the Shanghai Academy of Sciences, wrote a long and impassioned denunciation of the blog and its writer.

"Today, with tremendous anger, I will tell you the story of an immoral foreigner and I call upon all Chinese compatriots to get together and kick this immoral foreigner out of China" he began, going on to give a recap of some of the things Chinabounder had written about. "But what makes it intolerable for me" Zhang wrote, "is that this piece of garbage deliberately hurt the feelings of the Chinese nation… and he openly spoke to divide China."

"This undisguised disclosure of the mind is too shocking!" wrote Zhang. "I am a researcher in psychology. There is only one reason why this piece of garbage would meticulously and laboriously write out his bedtime dalliances, and that is because he is a pervert."[642]

Zhang Jiehai also sent out a clarion call to the men of China. "I also have something to tell the Chinese men: Please think about how these foreign trash have dallied with your sisters and made fun of your impotence. Do you want to say that this is no big deal? Do you still want to treat the foreigners as important? Do you still quiver when you see foreigners? Please straighten out your backbones.

Zhang's angry protest sparked a manhunt akin to that which befell 'Bronze Mustache.' The 'Chinabounder' story leaped into the national press and then the international press, being picked up by the BBC, CNN, Time Magazine and newspapers in every continent in the world.

'Chinabounder' was in fact created and written by David Marriott, and in the latter stages, augmented by Karl Lacroix.

What was so interesting – and frightening -- about the reaction to the blog was that it laid bare some of the attitudes beneath the surface of the skin of modern Chinese society.

There were thousands of comments, both on the blog itself and through email, expressing extreme hatred and threats of violence, offering sickening sexual violence and mutilation not just to 'Chinabounder' but also to his father, mother, and any other relatives that he might have.

When the story hit its fever pitch in China, both writers of this book were acutely aware of the risks we faced. One of the blogs that sprang up in response to the 'Chinabounder' affair, the 'Who Is Chinabounder?' was a site completely devoted to exposing the author.

Perhaps the author of that blog about a blog was unaware that he was relying on the very freedom that blogging allows to try to curtail the freedom of someone else.

At that time we were traveling internationally, and were somewhat apprehensive about being able to return to China, where we had established homes. Indeed we had to pause for reflection entering customs and immigration about a week later. Would we be stopped at the border? Fortunately we returned through Hong Kong into Shenzhen without incident.

Nonetheless, if we had been exposed, physical attack was possible, and political trouble was certain. We prepared for this eventuality by shredding large amounts of the research we had done on China, and by destroying the hard drives of the computers we had used to write the blog. That way, if the 'knock on the door' did come, there would be little evidence to be found, save for the guilty expressions on our faces.

We both prepared 'grab bags' of our most vital possessions so that we could leave our homes in the city within moments, and we took other steps to preserve our anonymity. We also decided to shut down the blog for a few months, and gradually the fickle attention of the Chinese public moved elsewhere.

Next in line was Meng Guangmei, a Taiwanese model, who was at the center of the 'toiletgate' scandal. She had a successful career in China, but when she returned to Taiwan to talk about it she sparked controversy by mentioning the poor quality of toilets in China. She also mentioned she received a low salary for her TV work and that Chinese state TV broadcast old-fashioned songs. Most incendiary of all, she suggested that the since the Nanjing Massacre was a historical event, it should not be used as the basis of current relations between China and Japan.

Online opinion in China was outraged.

In a survey held by Sina, a major Chinese website, perhaps adding fuel to the fire, 52% of respondents said they no longer had a good opinion of Meng, and 42% said she deserved criticism. Apparently, no one agreed with her.

A reader's comment on the China Daily bulletin board in response to its coverage of the incident said "There is no reason for anyone to come here and throw insults at us, unless they feel they are better, or are jealous of us." Given how strictly China Daily monitors the comments on its site, these words can be taken as having official approbation. [643]

A report on the event carried by Danwei, the influential website on daily life in China, mentioned online comments suggesting that since

Meng worked in China she had no right to say anything negative about the country.[644]

A key element in the negative commentary about the 'Chinabounder' affair --- apart from the numerous wild threats of castration and mutilation (and that was just in English – in the Chinese language the abuse was much worse) -- was for 'Chinabounder' to be thrown out of the country (preferably in a box.)

'China, love it or leave it' has a familiar ring to it. Different culture, but it hearkens back to another era. Once upon a time, in America, the spirit of the Stars and Stripes required that you had to adhere to the voices tuned to nationalism.

Thankfully, America has left that attitude in the past.

In China, however, the attitude is still very common, and underlies the assumption of the 'uni-nation' – the idea that the Chinese nation is the only nation, that Chinese ideas are the only ideas, and that the Chinese voice is the only voice.

Utilizing all the negativity towards 'Chinabounder' Zhang Jiehai was able to publish a book about the affair, called 'I'm Angry.'

In the end, what was written as 'Chinabounder' means absolutely nothing. What is important is the fact that we tried to say something outside the norm, beyond what Chinese people expected Western people to comment on with reference to China. In China it is not only what you say, it is also why you say it, who says it, and the medium in which you say it. To that end, 'Chinabounder' was successful.

In announcing that the 'medium is the message' Canadian Marshall McLuhan meant that the method of communication could have a more important effect than the communication itself.

He did not mean that the 'message' was less important than the 'media' carrying it, or that the content was unimportant. What he meant was that new inventions could change the world in unforeseen and non-obvious ways, and that this was their true, abiding message. It was the nature of the medium that changed society over the longer term, rather than the messages carried on it. Those messages could be individually important, but the more profound effect came from elsewhere. The medium itself could change the way society operated.

Based on McLuhan's ideas, the true visionary is one who is aware of the possibilities of these unforeseen advantages and is ready to encourage them or respond to them. In China, a lack of fear also helps.

That being the case how would McLuhan address China's issues? Perhaps he would suggest that the Chinese, on the whole, have singularly failed to 'get' the point of blogging. Chinese society is simply not open to the possibilities blogging offers, and the ways in which this new medium might transform society. In approaching the new media with old ideas, contemporary Chinese society misses the message.

China's 'Operation Golden Shield' is a vast program employing between 30,000 and 70,000 operatives (estimates vary widely, but new

199

recruits are added daily) whose sole purpose is to monitor and guide internet usage. One of the negative offshoots of this project is how eagerly Western corporations such as Cisco, Microsoft, Yahoo and Google collude with China to provide the hardware and software that the government fashions into the shackles which imprison the country's internet users.

Google at last began to live up to its motto of 'Don't Be Evil' in early 2010, when it announced it would no longer work with Beijing to censor search results in China. The company withdrew its servers to Hong Kong, which falls outside the Mainland's rigid censorship, a move that was in part prompted by China-based hacking into the accounts of human rights activists in the country. But money talks loudest, and Google snuggled up to the goverment again in mid 2010.

Another part of the 'Golden Shield' program collects as much information as possible on China's citizens, even if they are not part of China's online population. This has been a remarkably effective part of the program. Since its launch in 2003, it has collected data on 1.25 billion of China's 1.3 billion people.[645]

China has a vast army of 'virtual cops,' government spies who monitor, in real time, what people are doing online. If a user reads something that does not meet with official approval, he or she is blocked.

More seriously, should a user post commentary that is viewed as being out of the boundaries or the 'box' of uni-national thinking, the posts are wiped. Should the user's post receive interaction from others, there is the terrifying possibility of the 'virtual cops' becoming real police knocking on your door.

The 'virtual cops' were first used in the southern city of Shenzhen in 2006. A cartoon icon representative of a policeman was placed on large websites, linked to local police stations.

"The simple appearance of these floating icons will remind people these websites are under surveillance," said Lu Benfu, an internet expert with the Chinese Academy of Sciences.[646]

The 'virtual cops' (housed in high-security buildings along with their own command structure) were then deployed in the city of Guangzhou, before being expanded to nine cities, with large units established in Beijing and Shanghai. Currently, the government plans to expand the surveillance system to 100 cities nationwide.[647]

Much like rapid-deployment anti-terrorist squads, the electronic suppression of information counter to government policies is extremely effective.

For example, when the media freedom organization Reporters without Borders set up a Chinese language website, it took China's net police less than eight hours to find it and block it to Chinese surfers. When the group moved their site to another host, it was again shut down.[648]

China amazingly denies it actually censors anything. For instance, China's representative at a meeting of the Internet Governance Forum claimed that, "In China, we don't have software blocking Internet sites. Sometimes we have trouble accessing them. But that's a different problem."[649]

This is factually untrue. China now has the ability to block access to foreign websites at will. For instance, during the APEC (Asia-Pacific Economic Cooperation) meetings of 2001, sites such as CNN and the BBC, long blocked in China, were opened up. China was keen to show the visiting dignitaries how open its society was. But when those same international leaders had left, access to these sites was immediately blocked.[650]

It was obvious that exactly the same thing would happen in the 2008 Olympics. China created the appearance of an open society for the two weeks of the games. But once they were over, the gates were slammed shut and the restrictions were reimposed. This pattern will likely be repeated during the forthcoming 2010 World Expo, to be held in Shanghai.

China's educational facilities add an additional layer of control. Universities choose members of the student body to 'monitor' the university's internet chat rooms. These monitors act secretly, pretending to be simply taking part in conversation, yet their real purpose is to steer student postings in a healthy 'Marxist' direction.

For example, one of these monitors spoke of her belief that, "We don't really control things, but we really don't want bad or wrong things to appear on the web sites…. As I'm a student cadre, I need to play a pioneer role among other students, to express my opinion, to make stronger my belief in communism."

Another 22-year-old student said, "Our job consists of guidance, not control."[651]

The restriction of sexual expression, long ago left unfettered by developed economies, is only beginning to gain steam in China.

Online restrictions are gaining energy, with China launching a 'People's War' on sexual freedom in one of a series of attempts to influence sexual morality.

In the first month after the campaign began in early April 2007, authorities blocked 4,800 websites and 160,000 pieces of online information. [652] The war was still underway in 2010, with media announcing 5,394 people had been arrested the year before in connection with online pornography.[653]

The 'People's War' gave rise to a number of alarming statements. Wu Heping, a spokesman for China's Ministry of Public Security, said that "In recent years from the cases we have discovered, the proportion of young people guilty of cheating, rape or robbery who are given to using the Internet or have been corrupted by online filth, is very high…Our preliminary figures for arrested youth criminals is that almost 80 percent of them have been seduced by the Internet."[654]

What mode of questioning or analysis of how this information was compiled has not been revealed. Far from seeing that an interest in sex is a normal and healthy part of growing up, China's puritanical streak equates sexual images with crime.

Zhang Hui, a deputy public security minister, said that "The inflow of pornographic materials from abroad and lax domestic control are to blame for the existing problems in China's cyberspace."[655]

How nude images of Western women translate into cheating, rape and robbery has again not been indicated.

Twenty-eight year old Chen Hui ran a porn-based website in China that drew 600,000 registered users. That's over half a million citizens freely exercising their desire to view the images provided. What might be seen as a measure of popularity, or perhaps a vote for freedom, resulted in a life sentence in prison for the entrepreneurial Chen.[656]

In the eyes of the Chinese legal system, running a porn website is punishable as seriously as murder.

Reason 22

Once the Masters of Invention

Once, China was the cradle of invention. Home to writers and thinkers, scientists and explorers, the Han civilization created a dazzling array of inventions, many of which exerted the most profound influence first on China and then on the entire world.

Four of these inventions, in particular, have so shaped society that history would be totally different without them. Gunpowder, the compass, printing and paper-making -- each has completely changed human life.

Printing was invented in the early Song Dynasty (960-1279). Song society used the invention not only to print vast numbers of books (running into many millions of copies) but also to print paper money, perhaps the most revolutionary tool of economics.

Song society was diverse and creative, with a passion and curiosity for every area of life. The Song investigated and wrote books about "anything and everything" and "Scientific treatises appeared on mushrooms, bamboos, peonies, fruit trees, birds, crabs, citrus fruits... Medicine, geography, maths, astronomy – there were treatises on them all," says historian John Man. [657]

The compass, also created in the Song Dynasty (though Chinese awareness of the properties of magnetism date even further back), enabled China to later develop into a maritime power. And gunpowder, in addition to allowing the most beautiful firework displays, revolutionized warfare in the hands of Western powers.

In addition to the 'big four' China also created a dazzling array of other inventions, from cast iron (known in the 6th century BC and refined by the invention of the blast furnace around 2000 years ago) and the seismograph (invented around 100AD) to the wheelbarrow (100AD or earlier) and logical solutions such as a refined horse collar (around 300BC) that allowed the animal to breathe more freely. In its long history, China has created numerous inventions to improve human technology and daily life.

In the Ming Dynasty (1368-1644) China became a major seafaring power. Under the command of admiral Zheng He, China launched seven voyages between 1405 and 1433. One of the most remarkable vessels in the fleet had nine masts and weighed 1500 tons. It was 138 meters from stern to bow and was 56 meters wide at the widest point. At this time, most European shipbuilders could only make ships with a maximum length of 60 meters.[658]

From a historical tradition of great inventiveness and a spirit of creativity, China then slowly descended into a nation where innovation was devalued and often neglected. This process began in the Qing Dynasty (1644-1911), whose rulers were essentially conservative, inward-looking and complacent, all conditions that led to the domination of China by Western powers territorially and intellectually.

The clash of the history of Eastern inventiveness and the newness of Western technology caused a brief spurt of intellectual fearlessness in the early years of the 20th Century, when China briefly became a republic in 1911. The Japanese invasion and the subsequent advent of World War Two ended the attempts of China to rediscover its traditions of creativity and invention.

Once the Communist Party came to power 1949, all thoughts of ingenuity were effectively removed. Conformity became the new passion, since conformity meant survival. In the first rush of controlling China, its leaders were more concerned with food, expulsion of foreign ideas and the institution of basic industrial production, hardly the atmosphere required to germinate world-changing inventions.

With the population of China now desperate to follow every behest of the Party, education became a production line for a nation of followers, not leaders. With the citizens of China pacified, Chinese leaders found themselves trapped in a no-win situation. They knew that to retain the support of the people – even if often grudging support – they would have to ensure China's economy began to grow.

They hoped money, beyond anything else, would keep the population acquiescent to the controls of personal freedom that the Party exerts and needs. After the death of Mao Zedong, Deng Xiaoping's opening-up policy revolutionized the way China thought and acted.

With the doors wide open, China today is the economic engine of the world, and it bases its ability to do this on its vast population of people willing to do poorly paid and monotonous jobs.

In addition to the influx of foreign direct investment designed to incorporate China's masses into a functioning production house for export products, modern technology has come from the developed nations eager to capture market share. The rush to increase production levels has redirected bright minds into the development of positive statistics rather than the development of new science.

While rapidly becoming an economic giant, China is also very keen to move from the status of a 'developing country' to a 'developed country,' but the only way it can do that is by beginning to create its own technology. China must begin to harvest the minds that have lain dormant for so long. Not an easy task.

This need to rediscover the talent for invention that China has lost lies behind the National Scientific and Technological (S&T) Awards program, which was launched in 1999. Its purpose was to identify and honor annual advances in these fields. Three prizes were on offer -- the National Award for Natural Science, the National Award for Science and

Technology Progress, and, the top prize, the National Award for Technological Invention.

Between 1999 and 2005, the top prize was only awarded twice, in 2002 and 2003. In other years no invention was deemed creative enough to win. And it was not until 2006 that all three prizes were given in the same year for the first time.[659]

"According to the awards organizers," said Chinese media, "only internationally acknowledged inventions that exert a tremendous impact on scientific subject can receive the first prize... In the past few years, the state laid stress on tracking scientific frontline rather than develop things of its own and so the nation's invention competence is rather low."[660]

This clearly shows the current official view of scientific creativity and innovation in China. Rather than simply award the most promising scientific achievement in a given year, bestowing encouragement, the prize judges are setting a certain barrier that must be passed. China's search for scientific excellence is purely utilitarian, rather than a celebration of achievement.

The lack of respect accorded to scientists in China is also clearly shown by media announcements in 2006 of China's "new four great inventions," chosen by unidentified "experts," and is basically a copy-cat attempt to recreate the aura behind China's original four great inventions. Instead of praise and encouragement the inventors were offered condescension.

The first of these newly-announced inventions was a computer math model created in 1978 by Wu Wenjun. But following a technical analysis of his invention, the media then surprisingly offered a criticism, that Wu's method had "not come up with any major fruits... a mathematic method ought to be of practical use."

The second invention was the development of a hybrid rice strain by Yuan Longping, in 1970, but again Yuan's invention was criticized as an "innovation on the shoulders of forerunners, because foreign scientists had conducted researches of hybrid wheat before."

The third invention, the 1965 synthesization of bovine insulin (the first time a protein had been synthesized by mankind) by a team of scientists was criticized as being less impressive because "Other countries have carried out similar researches and synthesized a lot of living materials... China has lost the lead in this regard."

And the final invention, a geological theory of oil formation by Li Siguang (1889-1971), was downplayed because it "contributes much less to utilization of oil" since most oil fields are sea-based but his theory applied to land-based fields. [661] Surprising, since other nations value any attempt to squeeze oil from their land.

In 2007 media announced a slightly different line-up for China's four great modern inventions. While the hybrid rice and the creation of the insulin protein were still cited, they were now joined by a treatment for malaria and a method of photocomposition for Chinese character typesetting, albeit without the attendant 2006 media criticism.[662]

China's attitude towards scientific innovation continues to be one of diffidence and confusion, and perhaps false modesty. The media response indicates a certain level of patronizing embarrassment.

The media's use of the terms 'four great inventions' locks in the public's view the idea that new Chinese inventions must be equal to or greater than the four original inventions, which are classics of all time. While China was silent in the creative fields for most of its subsequent history since the creation of those four great inventions, other civilizations, mostly from the West, have developed thousands of ideas. Those lost years and the lost minds that China suffered by internalizing its sense of self are forever gone. Public criticism by the media is not the way to rediscover that lost talent.

The situation is compounded by the fact that today China seems more focused on 're-economizing' the wheel than discovering something new. For several years China was the world's biggest producer of DVDs (90% of world total), but many of these machines were produced without paying royalties to the consortium that had developed the DVD standard. This led the consortium to threaten to take legal action against China.

Before finally negotiating a lesser royalty, China began to develop its own version of the DVD, which it called the enhanced versatile disc or EVD, announced to much press fanfare in 2003. But almost immediately the new standard was bogged down in legal squabbles among the development partners, and it made very little impact on the market. In 2006 China announced it planned to end DVD production in 2008 in favor of EVD, but since Japanese manufactures have already surpassed EVD's abilities with Blu-ray and HD-DVD discs, EVD seems unlikely to succeed.[663]

Likewise, China also tried to push its own version of W-LAN (Wireless Local Area Network) technology, which it called WAPI (W-LAN Authentication and Privacy Infrastructure), as an alternative to the widely-used US wireless standard, called 802.11. China said that the 802.11 standard lacked security. The government sought to force all equipment sold in China to use the home-grown WAPI standard. Not only would this be a big boost to Chinese manufacturers, it would also ensure that the Chinese government, the proprietary holder of WAPI, would be able to spy on all network communications using it.

"If the Chinese WLAN standard had been implemented, sales of 802.11-based WLAN equipment would not have been permitted in China after June 1. To license WAPI, foreign vendors would have been forced to share their technology with Chinese companies" said a technology commentator."[664] In the face of international protests – and many vendors announcing that they simply would not sell to China under these conditions – China dropped plans to enforce use of WAPI in the nation.

However, China still tried to get WAPI adopted as a global standard by the International Standards Organization (the ISO). The ISO held an international meeting to decide between WAPI and 802.11, attended by *thirty* national bodies. After the vote was counted, only eight of the international rated organizations supported China's WAPI.

The Chinese delegation walked out of the meeting, held in Prague, in protest.

Despite the international nature of the vote, members of the Chinese consortium said that result was "unacceptable" to China, and Chinese media said the vote should be overturned due to the "unethical activities" by the Institute of Electrical and Electronics Engineers (a voting member of the ISO), which "included organizing a conspiracy against the China-developed WAPI, insulting China and other national bodies, and intimidation and threats." Chinese media did not elaborate on the nature of the "intimidation and threats."[665]

"The monopoly force from the American standard maker IEEE poisoned the voting process and created an unfair atmosphere at the Prague meeting" reported Chinese media, quoting a member of the Chinese delegation. "In appeals made to the ISO in late April, China asked the organization to delay analysis of the voting result and IEEE to apologize for its amoral behavior" said the report.[666]

The Chinese delegation single-handedly created the concept that identifying bad science equals having a bad attitude, thus inventing the concept of techno-spite, which can be defined as the act of being accusative or spiteful when the technology your company or country has spent millions developing is not accepted by consumers or chosen as an international standard by other countries.

And despite appearing to back down on its WAPI standard, China began to take active standards to push it at home, banning imports of iPhones with Wi-Fi in a direct bid to leave market share for the home-grown system. According to telecommunications expert Kan Kaili, speaking in 2010, "In order to promote this so-called national innovation [WAPI], China disabled Wi-Fi and sacrificed the interests of millions of cell phone users. Users can't freely and conveniently access the mobile Web. If they want to, they must take the risk buying a smuggled phone on the gray market."[667]

Any great nation needs to rely on creativity and innovation in order to leave its mark on history as well as to drive its economy. For China's economic miracle to continue, it is imperative to re-discover its native sense of inventiveness, the same inventiveness that created China itself.

This is one of the reasons China implemented its National Scientific and Technological Awards program, however critically. It is also why China's leaders have begun tinkering, in an extremely limited fashion, with educational reform.

However, the country's leaders know that a truly creative and free-thinking population will also be much more likely to demand innovation in politics as well as industry, meaning the Party remains wary of too much reform. Democracy is a great energizer of invention, but is a step too far for the present government.

Instead, the Party has sought to channel national innovation into paths that will bolster its own hold on power. Rather than allow any form of 'blue skies' thinking (that is, free and undirected scientific enquiry), the Party directs innovation and a huge amount of finance into politically impressive projects such as its space program. Whereas in the United States, cash and ingenuity results in creativity (as in the case of Microsoft, for example), in China the government's money directs all things, which usually dampens the sparks of innovation.

And the Party's insistence on having communist cells in as many organizations as possible means that scientists and state companies have little choice but to obey the wishes of their political masters.

China's space program put the nation's first man in space in 2003 (more than forty years after the Russians did it) and in 2005 Hu Shixiang, deputy chief commander of the space program, said China would put a man on the moon and build a space station within ten to 15 years.[668] Chinese astronauts completed the nation's first spacewalk in 2008.[669]

Projects such as this contribute very little to the sum total of human wellbeing, and they certainly do not make the life of the average Chinese citizen any better – indeed, the life of the average Chinese citizen becomes worse given that billions of dollars poured into space projects becomes unavailable to provide the schools, hospitals and social welfare that rural China so desperately needs. This money also siphons off research funding for scientists who are working on projects of real benefit.

The space program unites the Chinese people with a feeling of pride, and it is this pride the Party uses to leverage its grip on power. Yet national self-esteem is only one aspect of China's rush into space. China's wish to put a man on the moon has perhaps more to do with Chinese desires for military expansion into space.

Since 'New China' was founded in 1949, it has really only made one innovation that we feel can be described as having global importance – and even that hearkens back to the past.

On January 11, 2007, China, which has a long history of rocketry, destroyed one of its own space satellites with a ground-launched rocket. This was something that no country had tried since the last anti-satellite test by the US in 1985. China's successful test created a large amount of additional space debris – between 500 and 800 pieces more than 10cm (4 inches) wide, said experts – which greatly increased the possibility of debris colliding in space with other satellites or even the space shuttle, effectively destroying their functions.[670]

"Orbital debris, large or small, poses a risk not only to human activities in space but also to people on Earth should the detritus eventually fall from the sky. And collisions with floating rubbish can be disastrous to spacecraft and satellites," said Liu Jing, one of China's own researchers with the country's Space Environment Prediction Centre in 2003, offering a premonition of things to come.[671]

The act sparked widespread international concern. Did this outcome even occur to Chinese politicians and/or generals before they launched their rocket? Did they give any consideration to what the global effect of their destructive act might be?

Inevitably, extensive worry about the weaponization of space followed China's home-run launch strike. "We are concerned about it firstly from the point of view of peaceful use of space and secondly from the safety perspective," said Japan's Chief Cabinet Secretary, Yasuhisa Shiozaki. Japan, keenly aware of China's rising space capabilities, now is edging ever closer to full cooperation with America in its concept of the 'Star Wars' anti-missile shield.

US State Department spokesman Tom Casey said "We certainly are concerned by any effort, by any nation that would be geared towards developing weapons or other military activities in space.... I think you've seen comments from the Japanese Government as well as from Australian Prime Minister Downer and I think several other governments as well raising these same issues."

"We certainly don't want to see a situation in which even tests of this kind that produce extensive amounts of space debris have the potential for disturbing or accidentally disrupting communications satellites or other kinds of space vehicles that are out there. So certainly this is an issue that I think is of general concern not only to us but to the broader international community and we'll be looking to get some more information from the Chinese about it" he said.

"My understanding is the last time the United States tested or attempted any kind of test of this kind of device or an anti-satellite related device was in 1985" said Casey. "I think you need to look at the development of space in those past 22 years. The extent to which countries not only the United States, but countries throughout the world are dependent on space based technologies, weather satellites, communications satellites and other devices to be able to conduct modern life as we know it. And so the consequences of any kind of activity like this are significantly greater now than they were at that time."[672]

China refused to confirm it had conducted the test until January 23. During the two weeks of enforced silence when China made no comment to the international press Liu Jianchao, a spokesman for China's Foreign Ministry, told Reuters that "I can't say anything about the reports. I really don't know; I've only seen the foreign reports." [673]

Wang Baofu, a research fellow and deputy director of the Strategic Studies Institute of the Chinese National Defense University, wrote an opinion piece shortly afterwards that was clearly inspired by the anti-satellite test but which did not directly mention it. Wang said that

"China, with a certain spaceflight capability, has kept to its principled stance of opposing the weaponization of space" and sought to blame the United States for the "unilateral hues of its outer space policy."[674] Even from success, the Chinese sought to exercise their sense of techno-spite.

The real reason for China's 'innovative' test, however, was a none-too-subtle reminder to the US that, if China decided to invade Taiwan, it could hamper a US response by damaging or possibly destroying its military satellite network.

And in the wider analysis, the test was not only a demonstration of China's might to its own people, but also a clear signal that if it cannot gain acceptance of its economical, social and political goals through creativity and innovation, China will resort unilaterally to pure force.

Sadly, the vast majority of Chinese people quickly smile, registering self-satisfaction when the space race and the new arms-in-space race is brought up in general conversation. For them, the allocation of billions of dollars of research funds to vanity projects, when domestic matters require creative solutions to real problems, is totally acceptable.

It's Hollywood they want and Hollywood they pay for, backed by a government willing to provide the big show.

Reason 23

Graying Reds

China's constant talk of a 'peaceful rise' and of 'peaceful development' is an attempt to create an image of a young and dynamic new economy. The astonishing growth of the country's economy in recent years can make it appear like a strong economic youngster growing into a powerful and confident world of developed countries.

Yet real Chinese society is gray, both in age and numbers. According to the World Health Organization, an 'aging society' is either one in which 10% of the population is over 60 years old or (in another measure) 7% of the population is over 65.

Nationwide, by the end of 2008, China had 149 million people over the age of 60, accounting for 11% of the entire population. The number of elderly people is rising fast, at 3% a year overall,[675] with the number of those over 80 rising by 5% a year.[676]

By 2025, there will be 280 million people in China over the age of 60.[677] By 2045, that number will have risen to 400 million.[678]

The average age in China, which was around 30 in 2000, will rise to 39 by 2025.[679] By 2040 the average age will be 44, meaning the country will age faster in a generation than Europe has in a century.[680] To put it another way, by 2050 average age will be three years higher than average *lifespan* was in 1950.[681]

Shanghai – so often touted as a lean, young and fit powerhouse -- became China's first city with an ageing society in 1979, when it recorded 1.15 million people aged above 60, accounting for 10.2% of the total population.

At the same time, its population over 65 years old reached 7.2% of the total. By 2001, 18.6% of the population was over 65.[682] By the end of 2006, 20.2% of Shanghai's population was over 60, and was predicted to rise to 23% by 2010.[683]

There was even sharper growth among the very old, with the number of people over 80 increasing 6.9% compared to the year before, and the number over 100 rising by 13.3% in the same period. By 2020, experts say, up to 33% of the city's population will be over 60.

In total, in 2006, Shanghai had 13.68 million people over 60. It had just 60,000 hospital beds for the elderly.[684]

Currently Shanghai has a higher percentage of elderly people than anywhere else in China. But already all China's major cities have more than 10% of their population over 60 years old. [685]

China's dilemma is that it will grow old before it grows rich. As the number of elderly continues to rise and China's use of the one-child policy prevents an increase in younger people to support them, the situation will get exponentially worse.

In 1990, the ratio of working people to retirees was 10:1. In 2003, it had dropped to 3:1. By 2020 it will be 2.5:1, [686] and by 2040 there will be only two working people to support each elderly person.[687]

By 2050, by some estimates the average lifespan will be an incredible 85 years.[688] This means many one of the one-child workers of the future will have to devote even more resources to supporting two retired parents and four retired grandparents. This is a situation which is already being observed today, but the acceleration of medical needs and increased lifespan will make this situation more critical.[689]

Shanghai did not open its first private nursing home until 1998.[690] Currently, China has 10 nursing home beds per 1,000 elderly people, compared to a developed country average of 50 to 70 beds. Though China announced it would add 3 million beds nationwide by 2010, this is still far short of the number required now, in excess of 7 million.

Of the millions of people who retire in China every year, just 15% have pensions. But there is not even enough money to pay these people, since by the end of 2005, according to China's Ministry of Labor and Social Security, the country's pension fund had a deficit of US$100 billion. By 2006, the shortfall was given as US$300 billion.[691]

Shanghai was able to pay for all its pension obligations in 1998. However, in 1999 it racked up a 0.7 billion yuan deficit, which then reached 2 billion yuan (US$250 million) by 2000, and a four billion yuan deficit was posted by 2001. After that, the city began to use its previous budgets savings to pay its pension bills, reports said. [692]

About 65% of the elderly population in rural areas receives no benefits from China's social welfare system. That's a total of 85 million people who do not receive pensions and lack adequate medical care. As Li Bengong, an official with China's National Committee on Aging notes with some understatement, "Welfare services can not match the rise in demand." [693]

Another estimate says that 90% of China's 900 million rural population falls through the safety net. Their situation is exacerbated by the fact that one of China's most ancient traditions, respect and care for the elderly, is crumbling.

A nationwide survey of more than 10,000 farmers over 60 years old found that 94% of them were relying on their children to support them in their old age. Yet the survey found that among farming parents, half of their young offspring were apathetic towards them.

The survey was privately financed by Zhai Yuhe. Though he is a member of the government, there was no public money available for his survey.

Among the over-60 farmers, 45% were not living with their children, and 5% did not know where their next meal was coming from.

Sixty-nine percent had just one set of clothes and 67% could not afford medicine. A startling 85% still had to work in the fields.[694]

One man who fell through the safety net was Li Zhaokun. In November 2006 he started a forest fire hoping to get arrested and taken to prison. He wanted to go to prison since it guaranteed food and shelter. A lifelong vagrant, Li had no official documents and did not even know where he had been born.

Because money for the homeless is provided by local governments, they reserve it for local citizens only. Itinerants like Li get nothing – except a warning to move on. Even after he started the fire, in the southern city of Guangzhou, a local official said, "He needs to find out where he's from. The local government in his hometown should take care of his needs and probably send him to a senior citizens center," apparently oblivious to the fact Li had long lost the proof of his origins.[695]

One method the government has suggested to improve the lot of senior citizens is via the State Administration of Radio, Film and Television offering cash bonuses of between 300,000 and 800,000 yuan to producers who makes shows highlighting filial piety. In this way, the government feels, it can enhance 'social stability and harmony,' yet it does nothing in practical terms.[696]

By 2040, when China's aged population will be at its peak, the country's social security budget will have a shortfall of US$128 billion annually, says Li Bengong at the National Committee on Aging.[697]

The World Bank estimates China's pension debt obligation is currently US$1.5 trillion. And of today's workers who do pay into a pension scheme (just 25% of the working population), most of their money is 'borrowed' from present pension budgets by local officials who are obligated to pay legacy pensions for workers from the pre-reform era.

This means that present day workers' pension accounts contain no actual money, but just IOUs to be paid by workers sometime in the future.[698] Most citizens have little idea that the money, which is supposed to go into their individual account, is used in this way.[699]

Given Li's estimate that medical resources used by the elderly are three to five times higher than other groups,[700] and given such estimates as Deutsche Bank's prediction that by 2050 every 100 workers will need to support 79 retirees, these IOUs simply cannot be repaid.[701]

Misuse and abused of pension funds is endemic throughout the system. A national audit in 2006 found that US$3.85 billion had been misused, much of it for "overseas investment, commercial loans to companies, construction of government buildings and other purposes," said China's National Audit Office.

After an audit in 2007 it was announced by local officials that 3.7 billion yuan (US$480 million) was misused from the Shanghai pension fund alone. This led to the sacking of Chen Liangyu, the city's Party leader. His sacking was considered more to do with a power-struggle between

Beijing and Shanghai politicians rather than any true concern for the welfare of the people.[702]

Abuse is also rife in other systems to help the poor and elderly.

A number of cities in the wealthy eastern province of Zhejiang have recently begun to build retirement homes. For example, the city of Shaoxing spent 100 million yuan to build a 258-apartment complex, with a 6,000 square meter activities center, a shopping and entertainment complex, a canteen, a gym and abundant green space.

Following Shaoxing, local governments in the cities of Yuyao, Shengzhou, Jiaxing and Xiaoshan followed suit.

The coastal city of Ningbo rented the apartments it built for its elderly out to contractors at 2,200 yuan per square meter, one third of the going rate of local commercial housing.

The contractors re-rented the apartments to retired government officials, doctors, and parents of businessmen. Some of the present residents are not even from Ningbo, but from Shanghai or elsewhere in the province. Retired government officials apparently sold their own homes in the city to move into the retirement homes, where government continues to subsidize the annual cost of the operation of the center. [703]

China's government has plenty of bland pronouncements to make about its attitude towards the elderly. "The State values and cherishes senior citizens for their knowledge, experience and skills, and respects them for their good ethical values. It thus makes vigorous efforts to create good conditions for senior citizens to bring into full play their expertise and capability, and gives them encouragement and support to integrate into society and continue to make contributions to the social development of China" said a recent white paper on the elderly from the Information Office of China's State Council.

But apart from mentioning current facts and figures – such as that the nation had only 20,000 professional nurses for the aged by the end of 2005, the 7,500 word document (released at the end of 2006) had almost nothing concrete to say about what needs to be done in the future.[704]

As with so many of the vast problems facing China, public awareness of the situation is limited. According to a global survey of retirement attitudes across 12 countries by the insurance firm AXA, 39% of workers in China felt that retirement would mean improved living standards – a figure far higher than in any other country in the international survey. In Germany, for example, just 4% of current workers felt retirement would lead to an improvement in living standards. Chinese people are also more convinced their own retirement income will be adequate for their senior years than those in any other nation.

Working people in China begin saving for their retirement later than in any other nation, starting at the age of 37, compared to 28 in the UK and 30 in the US. And when it comes to the percentage of workers who have begun to prepare for their retirement, the figure in China is among the lowest in the world, at 31%, compared to 85% for the US and 74% for the UK.

Around 55% of current workers say the present social security system is only in 'some trouble,' with 12% choosing the more realistic answer that 'it is in crisis.' Fully 16% believe it is 'not in trouble at all.' Also, 87% of workers today believe the official pension system will still exist when they are 75. Again, China leads the world in positive feelings about this belief.[705]

China's retirement age is lower than that of most other countries. Under current law, the male retirement age is a mandatory 60 and the female retirement age is set at 55 for officials and 50 for other workers.

This discrimination against women is exacerbated by the fact that Chinese regulations say a worker can draw 90% of their final salary as pension only if they have worked for more than 35 years. That means a regular woman worker would had to have begun her formal career at the age of 15 to gain this level of pension. A man would have needed to start at the age of 25.

However, many enterprises encourage their workers to retire early, meaning the current average age of retirement in China is 50.2 years old.[706] About one-third of all workers retire early.[707]

Yet the obvious solution to the looming pensions catastrophe, to raise the retirement age, is a step the government seems unwilling to take. Such a move, reported China Daily, would be "likely to add more pressure on an already tight job market," revealing the fact that by keeping the retirement age low, the government can open up more jobs for young workers.

Keeping up the appearance of a healthy local economy and at the same time pandering to the younger population, who are much more able to voice their discontent than the elderly, some employees in state-owned enterprises have been allowed to retire in the 40s without reduced pension.[708] This allows local officials to claim new employment for young workers.[709]

One employee, Zhou Xianghua, taking exception to the fact that as a woman she had to retire at 55, took her employer to court when it insisted she stop working. Zhou said that being obliged to retire at a younger age than a man amounted to sexual discrimination. She lost her case because the court said it was not its responsibility to judge whether the regulations run contrary to China's constitution.[710]

China's growing numbers of elderly also face other attendant problems. Loneliness is very widespread, with a 2005 survey by China's Ministry of Civil Affairs showing that 25.8% of those over 60 are childless or live without their kids.[711] In China's new mega-cities this percentage is even higher. In 2004, more than 30% of the over 65s in China's urban centers lived apart from their children, a figure that it is estimated will rise to 80% by 2010, says Zhao Baohua, an official in China's National Office on Aging.[712]

In 2006, 30% of the over 65s nationwide had no spouse. Seventy percent of people in this group were women. But while China's traditions of filial obedience have been forgotten, its prescriptions on how parents 'ought' to behave have not. Elderly people who have been widowed do not often remarry, in part because Confucian culture frowns on remarriage (especially for women) and in part because their children will not allow it.[713]

Some experts in China say suicide is spreading among the elderly. Li Qiurong, for example, a 70-year-old farmer in China's eastern Jiangxi Province, committed suicide by drinking pesticide after she broke her leg and was unable to care for herself. Though her five sons had all built houses for themselves, they chose to leave her to live alone in a hut.[714]

In the cruelest of twists, China's modern society now makes dying a prospect even more expensive than living.

In Shanghai in 2007 grave prices ran from 10,000 yuan (US$1250) to 40,000 yuan (US$5000). But in the most popular cemeteries, prices were higher, with the cheapest grave, of 1.5 square meters, costing nearly 20,000 yuan (US$2500) and the most expensive, at 7.5 square meters, more than 120,000 yuan (US$15,000.)[715]

Funeral home owners maximize their profits with mark-ups of up to 20 times the original price, counting on the fact the bereaved will not argue with them.[716] Tombs were even seen as an investment at one point, with pyramid selling schemes for grave sites.[717]

Since the mid 1990s, burial plots have become around 14 times more expensive. Draft regulations issued in 2007 sought to rein in burial ground speculation by allowing only those who could show a death certificate to buy a plot.[718] This, of course, will make it impossible for people to choose their own last resting place.

In New China, with about 8.5 million deaths a year,[719] there is ample opportunity for unscrupulous individuals, whether they are government officials or private citizens, to ensure that those who came into the world with nothing leave the world with nothing.

Why am I Speaking English?

Between the years 1978 and 2007 China allowed 1,200,000 of its young citizens to study abroad. More than 880,000 of those citizens never came home.[720]

They never returned to 'the motherland,' and have never returned to be Chinese. Three out of four of those more than one million minds, full of new information, education and ideas, nation-building qualities, are still keeping the company of Western economies and living a Western lifestyle.[721]

When they leave, they all sound the same. They all say 'Yes,' they will come home to help the motherland generate its economy, to become strong. They say they will return to support their parents, to build a family. They say that China is where their heart is. Their eager faces often show incredulity in front of immigration officials when they are asked 'Do you intend to return home?' – a question often asked by officials of developed nations to developing country citizens searching for entry visas into the promised lands.

"Return home? Of course I'm going to return home, I'm Chinese" they exclaim indignantly. Visa finally in hand, they strike out tearfully from the arms of their parents, from their friends, from their country, vowing to return like 'New China' citizens, having absorbed Western education for the betterment of the motherland.

In the earlier years of this exodus, the most popular study designations were the US, Canada, Australia and the United Kingdom. But more recently many other countries have joined the list. New Zealand. Ireland. France. Germany. Italy. Spain. Austria. Even Russia and the Ukraine.[722]

It seems that almost any country educationally is preferable to departing Chinese youth than China.

Some countries, seeing the opportunities available to milk the education drive of the Chinese, stumble over each other with the grandeur of their offers, often hastily formulating overseas education plans for the eager mainland students. Brochures are designed and printed containing photographs of 'Chinese' people enjoying leisure time activities and group social events. Claims of long-term educational history by second and third rate colleges tempt anyone wishing to read these brochures – though they hardly ever do, believing almost any educational facility in the West is good.

Among all the facts we have listed in this book, perhaps the most embarrassing one for China is that hundreds of thousands of young people do not wish to continue the revolutionary fight, coming home to develop their minds and ideas in China.

Somewhere between their youthful fervor for their motherland and their exposure to Western culture, lifestyle and liberties, they turn a corner. They are mentally redirected. They become international.

The response of China's government to this overwhelming vote of no confidence has been to announce, in 2007, that overseas students who choose to return would have the right to "live and work freely" within China, as well as the right "to work without residency restrictions, personnel quotas and pay limits."

The above measures, which would be regarded as basic human rights in most nations around the world, were heralded as "special privileges."

China's government also announced that returning graduates were expected "to introduce more advanced foreign technologies and to fund and establish more high-tech enterprises," without due consideration and concern as to where these students would gather such advanced foreign technology. Some questions are best not asked.[723]

Now, as recently generated by the Chinese government, the words "overseas Chinese" seek to reclaim citizens who remain in foreign lands in the work of the motherland and the Party.

Difficult to find is evidence that the government has asked the hard question – "Why - why do so many students not return?" White papers, blue papers, and news reports seemingly do not exist that contain the answers to such a great educational diaspora.

We asked the question.

Mr. Wen: "I never planned to stay overseas, but when I finished my degree I was offered an internship, so I took it. When I returned home at the end of it I was shocked at how different I felt about my home city. All I could see was the noise, the dirt, the pollution. I couldn't wait to get back to Australia."

Ms. Zhou: "Here in America I am judged on my talent. But back in China your success depends on knowing the right people, having the right connections. I don't want to be judged by my connections. I want to be judged by my skills."

Ms. Hao: "It's simple. Freedom. Living overseas, I can speak my mind. Abroad, I can talk and think freely. Back home I am only allowed to say the 'right' things."

Mr. Zheng: [laughing] "No residency restrictions? What the Chinese government offers as a 'gift' is simply a way of life for me now. They just don't understand what people want."

Mr. Li: "Well, I do want to go back to China. I miss my country. But when I was a child I was lonely. Like most people my age, I had no brothers or sisters. And school was just too full of pressure ever to make meaningful friendships. The reason I cannot go back to China is that I want to have several children, and I am not allowed to do that in China. And even if I had kids here and then moved back, they would have to go

218

through the same tough education system I went through. I can't let that happen to my kids, so I can't go home."

Ms. Liao: "Respect. I do not feel I am respected in China."

Mr. Peng: "I do not want to live in a country run by a government I do not believe in, that my friends do not believe in, that my family does not believe in. No one I know has any respect for communism or Marxism, and I do not want to live in a society where I have to pretend to believe something I know to be a lie."

Mr. Chen: "I'm just not interested in all that government stuff. I don't feel it's my duty to 'introduce advanced foreign technologies' just because the Party says so."

China's Hebei University, located in the north of China, conducted a survey in 2006, investigating the hopes and plans of undergraduates. It found that 64.5% of students listed a successful career and satisfying life as their top priority, and 10.6% chose a happy family. A further 14.7% chose 'self-actualization.'

Just 1% chose the option 'to struggle for the cause of communism.'[724]

To decode the words of the option 'to struggle for the cause of communism' one could say 'to struggle for the cause of the Party.' Just 1% of educated minds choose to continue the revolution's fight against imperialism and capitalism, and joyfully embrace Marxism, even with 'Chinese characteristics.'

While nearly 900,000 students not returning home is shocking, there is more. So far, there have not been any surveys of students who want to go overseas, and are mentally prepared to go, but cannot do so due to academic failure, lack of parental support, or inability to obtain a visa. The failure-to-success ratio must be very high, with each of the failures now discontent, certainly unhappy, and quite possibly angry with their future lot in life, which will not include a Western lifestyle, high-paying positions or the prestige of being 'out.'

The many tens of thousands of international students are far from a homogenous mass, and there are various reasons why students leave China. Some are surprisingly simplistic, indicating the basic yearnings of any young person.

There are several conditions affecting the thinking of students before the expensive journey overseas begins:-

1. The student who is compelled to follow parental directives and who seeks 'space' overseas.

Western teachers often tell us their conversations with their students run like this:

Q: "What will you study overseas?"

A: "Accountancy / business / international trade."

Q: "Is that what you really want to do in life?"

A: "No."

Q: "Then why are you going to study it?"

219

A: "My parents said I must."

China is sacrificing an entire generation of musicians, writers, painters, historians, psychologists and other 'creative' professions as parents force their children into perceived high-earning careers in finance, banking, accounting and computing. And China's one-child policy has led to the expectations of an entire family being placed on the shoulders of a single son or daughter. For some students, these expectations are simply too much.

Ms. Wang: "I learned to be free studying in Australia. If I went back to China I'd have to give that up. My parents would expect me to live at home and would control my social life. They'd pressure me to get married, have a child."

2. The student who must follow an educational path as set down by China's less flexible education system.

The degree a student studies is rarely a matter of choice, but is more often dictated by the universities, who offer students courses based on their school results rather than personal wishes or aptitude.

According to Xue Ying, president of a Beijing-based education research institute, 40% of university students are unhappy with their present majors, and 65% would switch to another major if they were allowed. [725]

Mr. Gu: "I always wanted to study French. My college entrance test was good enough for me to enter [a prestigious university] but only to study engineering. I could have gone to [a less prestigious university] to do French, but I knew that doing so would make it hard for me to get a job, because employers really only care what university you went to, not what you studied there. So now I'm an engineer, and that's what I have to study abroad."

3. The student who is sent overseas because of the parents' social/community standing.

Ms. Hu: "My father occupies a high position in local government. As his daughter, it was expected that I would go overseas to study, to give him 'face.' But when I got there I really struggled. I didn't like it at all. I feel it was all a waste of time."

Mr. Xie: "It's better that I stay overseas, because that's what my parents want me to do. It makes my father proud to say his son is outside of China, in the West. Strange."

4. The student who wants to follow a love interest.

"My girlfriend/boyfriend is studying, living and enjoying Western life in Melbourne/London/Toronto. That's why I'm going there."

5. The student who wishes to emigrate.

The view of many young Chinese people is that the educational process is also a holiday, as would be working for a few years – not realizing of course that any extended stay in a country changes you.

But when asked if they were given the option to create the perfect life overseas, including a great home, a high salary, and a happy family, in any country they wished to, but would never be able to return home to China – ever – 99.9% said they would not go.

6. The student who is tired of working and thinks education will improve/change his/her life.

A surprising number of gainfully employed professionals quit premium jobs simply to improve an education they feel they lack, not being fully aware that removing themselves from working life for one or two years can cause them grave difficulties in re-entering the job market.

Mr. Lu: "After graduating I joined a local firm in my home city. But after a few years I felt I was not being promoted fast enough. Education is the key to a good career, and overseas study would make me more valuable. So I quit my job to focus on English. I'm living at home so I don't need to pay rent. When I pass my English exams I'll be able to study abroad."

Mr. Wang: "I was a supervisor in my company, but I quit to get the education of a leader."

Ms. Qiao: "Things will not change so much in the two years I'll be away. Study in England will let me earn more money than other people."

7. The student who wants to be a student forever.

Yes, China has lots of those too.

8. The student who is only following fashion/trends for overseas education.

It is extremely difficult for young people not to get caught up in the frenzy of overseas education when their peers are all heading abroad. The desire not to be left behind creates an exodus mentality.

9. The student who has been extended beyond their intellectual motivation by family pressure.

More than 90% of Shanghai parents expect their children to earn at least a bachelor degree.[726] This parental pressure to succeed often pushes students down an academic path they do not want to take.

Ms. Zhao: "My aunt works as an accountant and she told my parents it was a good career. That's why my mum and dad sent me overseas to study. First of all I went to a university in England but I found it too hard and at the end of my first year I could not pass all my exams. That meant I had to work all summer to take them again."

Mr. Xu: "I didn't do very well in my Chinese college entrance exam, so I couldn't get into a good enough university. That's why my parents have sent me to Australia instead."

10. Because of previous family history, the student follows previous educational path of other family members.

Mr. Bao: "My dad did an MBA in the United States and then came back to China to set up his own company. Now he wants me to go to America to study business so I can take over his firm when he retires. But I don't really like business, and we argue a lot about it."

11. The student who has designed his/her goals with

logistical thought and progress in mind.

Ms. Yang: "I made my life study plan when I was still at high school. I studied International Business at a Chinese university that had a program in conjunction with a British University. After completing that degree I worked for three years and saved as much as I could so that I could study overseas to get an international perspective."

"Currently I am applying to go to America to do an MBA. It's very expensive and I don't have enough money to pay for it all by myself. I'll have to borrow from my parents, which I feel quite guilty about, so I am also hoping I can get a scholarship.

"After I graduate? I hope I can work in the US for a few years but then I want to come home to China. I'll always be Chinese and by working in China I hope I can make my country stronger too." Rare.

Yet though there are many different reasons for going overseas, there is one factor that unites nearly all of China's international students. That factor is their sheer unpreparedness for how international education will change them.

One theme that ran through the words of the many conversations we heard was the way in which international education pushed students to think in far more creative and free ways than they had ever experienced at home.

Again and again we heard about sharp contrasts between the Chinese way of learning, which focuses on by-rote memorization and obedient acceptance of what the teacher says, and Western styles, which emphasize individuality and questioning.

A 2007 study of the experience of Chinese students in the UK, conducted by Professor Greg Philo, found the same thing. Philo quotes one graduate student as saying "When I study in China, I have a textbook. The teacher gives lessons according to this textbook. In classes we listen to the teacher carefully and then we take notes and recite what the teacher taught and we pass the exam."

Philo quotes other students as saying "We can follow but not create. The style of education in China does not encourage creativity" and "The British academic attitude respects data – in China people use their position as experts to speak and people will think they are right, but without having offered any proof."

We found that students who studied in America, Australia and Canada made similar comments.

Ms. Liu: "I'll never forget a lecture I had in my first term. The tutor was discussing a point about international law, and asked me what I thought. That had never happened in China. I was nervous to speak out, but I did. And what really impressed me was how the tutor listened to my comment and then incorporated it into his lecture. I saw that education was really a two-way process."

Mr. Jiang: "In China we are used to just copying from textbooks or the internet. But in Australia that was not allowed. We had to do a lot more reading and then come up with our own answers. I found it really tough, and I spent nearly all of my time reading. It was extremely hard work, but it made me creative. Now, when I look at my friends in China who never went abroad, I can't help feeling how different they are to me."

It is not only the different academic styles that come as a profound shock to Chinese students. Very few of them have a realistic understanding of what life outside China is like in terms of culture and society.

Professor Philo's study found that most students based their image of the country on images drawn from the novels of Charles Dickens and Jane Austen, or the fictional detective Sherlock Holmes.[727]

Again and again, we heard the same cultural stereotypes when it came to study in the UK. "All British men are gentlemen" was the single most common reply when we asked about impressions of England.

We found conceptions of life in other countries were equally shallow. Australia was frequently connected with kangaroos, koalas and social welfare, Canada with fresh environment and cleanliness, and the US with good economy and Hollywood.

Not surprisingly, when asked what city they will go to, or what institute of learning they will apply to, younger students often said "I don't know," "I can't remember the name" and "My parents know."

Chinese media reports in 2007 also indicated the apparently arbitrary decision-making process that lies behind students' educational strategy, saying that "Spain, Italy and Austria became more popular for overseas study in 2006. They became new hot spots among Chinese students from their presence at the International Education Exhibition in 2006." This suggests that Chinese students actively accept what is stylishly marketed to them.[728]

As is the case the world over, students expect they will be financed for studies by their parents. Every student is convinced that their education will allow them a fast-track career and high salary which will enable them to repay their parents' investment. Parents blow off vast amounts of money that was saved in harder times and cannot be regenerated.

What is entirely different is that China's only-children are also expected to provide for parents and grandparents, which makes the repayments of vast amounts of money spent on airfares, school fees, Western lifestyle and the attendant expenses unlikely. If, as an adult, that same student also wishes to maintain his or her own home and spouse and child, the situation becomes virtually impossible. Superb jobs with gargantuan salaries are still a rare commodity in any of today's world economies.

And if Chinese nationals return home after completing their studies, they face other problems. 'Sea turtles,' as these students are known (a pun on the words 'hai gui,' or 'overseas returnee,' which sound the same as the word for 'sea turtle) face growing difficulty in getting jobs. This is due "to several major factors: too many students concentrated in too few academic areas, such as IT and MBA programs; lack of work experience; and high salary expectations."[729]

Mr. Sheng: "I took an MBA course in the UK. It was at a well-known university, and it was very expensive. But I was sure it would help me get a good job. I thought I should earn around 15,000 yuan a month, and I put that on my CV. I didn't get a single reply to my first round of applications. I dropped my demand to 10,000 yuan… and lower and lower over the next few months."

"Eventually I had to settle for my current job, which pays 4000 yuan a month. That's better that a lot of 'sea turtles' get, I know, but I'm asking myself if it was worth paying all that money for my MBA. And how will I ever be able to repay my parents?"

As with all things, there is a 'heart,' a 'hub,' a center around which overseas education revolves, to which all Chinese citizens must apply themselves. The 'heart' is the English language.

Nearly 80% of Chinese students – from primary age to undergraduates – listed learning English as their top priority. [730] One survey, said Chinese media, suggested that 56% of students not studying English majors spent 'a large portion' of their time on English, and another 19% spent almost *all* their time studying the language. All Chinese university students – no matter what they are studying – must pass English exams otherwise they cannot graduate. For many students, cramming to pass these exams is the single biggest burden on their time.

According to China International Business magazine, English is a 'status symbol' and can even be a factor in marriage. "A man without a grasp of English is nearly paralyzed" a young Chinese woman told the magazine, describing her requirements for a potential husband. "It is obvious that a young man without a fair command of English won't be able to climb up the social ladder."[731]

Nationwide, around 300 million people in China are studying English, 100 million of whom are students. Experts say that in coming years the number of people learning English in China will exceed the *global* number of people whose mother language is English.[732]

English can be viewed as a 'virus' in terms of the effect it is having on China. The combination of the internet and widespread ability to read English has created a democracy of communication in China. Government censorship of English-based websites is much less severe than Chinese-based websites – a 'one internet, two systems' culture. Yet China does not have a democracy in thought, since its government restricts the combination of free thinking and free expression among its people.

While the Party is remarkably efficient at controlling how people think and speak using the Chinese language, when it comes to English their control is severely limited. Knowledge of English allows Chinese citizens to escape the straitjacket of government control.

224

"Why am I speaking English?" they ask. The question is asked by those who have no direction or purpose regarding the communication ability that English has given them. This has created a 'cultural purgatory' in China, a vast army of potential radicals stuck between a state-controlled Chinese identity and the possibility of personal freedom conferred by a democratic language.

Drifting between their Chineseness and a new-found internationalism some will be forever lost. Others will lock in to the reality that English may yet turn out to be the greatest revolutionary tool ever seen in Chinese history.

Overseas education may well be a training-ground for the new bilingual Chinese revolutionaries - if they ever decide to come back.

The Silence of Chinese Conservation

The natural world, in traditional Han Chinese belief, has always been something to be controlled. In dynastic China, the emperor was seen as the 'Son of Heaven.' Chosen by heaven, it was his duty to ensure the well-being of the people of China – or the 'Middle Kingdom,' as the Chinese themselves refer to the country. With heaven above, man in the center, and earth below, the Han Chinese believed in a well-ordered world. Man was the master of the earth. Nature was his to control.

When that world went wrong, dynasties often fell. Disorder in nature was frequently seen as a sign that heaven had withdrawn its favor from a particular emperor, and even the entire dynasty. Natural disasters such as the flooding of the Yellow River (which has brought so much misery to China over the centuries), could therefore catalyze political and social change.

Mindful of this, conscientious emperors expended great energy and finance on controlling nature, seeking to reduce these natural disasters.

Though the emperors have gone, the attitude remains. In today's China, nature is still something to be controlled. It exists to do man's bidding.

The impact of this attitude on the environment is very clear.

Han Chinese civilization began in the Yellow River valley in today's northern China. The river has been central to the cultural psyche of the Han, and its frequent catastrophic floods throughout history have given the river an alternative name – 'China's Sorrow.'

Yet today, perhaps China should be known as the 'Yellow River's Sorrow,' for the river has been subject to a level of environmental abuse that is beyond anything experienced anywhere in the world.

The river is 5,400 miles long and is a water source for more than 150 million people. Yet it is so polluted that 66% of its water is undrinkable. More than four billion tons of waste water was dumped in the river in 2005 (88 million tons more than the year before), 73% of which came from factories.[733]

A single city along the banks of the river shows why the situation is so negative. Wuhai, a city of under 500,000 people located on the river, had just four factories in 1998.[734] Today, it has 400. None were built with environmental safeguards in place, and nowadays they often ignore government requirements to clean up by operating at night. In that way, they avoid environmental inspections.

Just one single province – Gansu – dumps more than 200 million tons of sewage into the river each year, with almost 70% receiving no treatment.[735] Today, 30% of the Yellow River's fish species are extinct.[736] According to Li Guoying, director of the Yellow River Conservancy

Committee, 60% of the water in the Yellow River is used by society, compared to an internationally recognized limit of 40%.[737]

The Tibetan glaciers which supply the Yellow River are melting at a rate of 7% a year.[738] And since China as a whole is home to 50% of Asia's total glaciers and 15% of the ice fields in the world, the ramifications for global health are profound. Shockingly, Chinese experts predict that 64% of the country's glaciers may be gone by the end of the 2050s, and that nearly all ice will be gone by 2100.[739]

In just one county in this area, more than 3,000 of lakes out of a total of 4,077 have disappeared in the past 15 years.[740]

China's other major river, the Yangtze, is the third longest on the planet. It is approximately 6,300 km long and accounts for more than a third of China's total freshwater supplies. It discharges more than a million *million* cubic meters of water into the sea annually.[741] A river so huge, it might be thought, would be almost impossible to pollute heavily.

Yet according to the 2007 health report on this river (which, despite being billed as 'annual' by the Chinese government is the first of its kind) it is under major pressure. Around 10% of the Yangtze is in 'critical condition,' and 30% of its major tributaries are seriously polluted. According to Yang Guishan, a researcher at a department of the Chinese Academy of Sciences, the nation's leading intellectual body, this impact is 'largely irreversible.'[742] In 2006, the Yangtze fell to its lowest level since records began in 1877.[743]

Every species that lives in the river is in decline, most dramatically the white-flag dolphin, or 'Baiji,' one of only five species of freshwater dolphin in the world.

A six week search for the white-flag along the river did not find a single dolphin, leading some researchers to conclude it is in fact extinct.[744] If so, it will be the first time mankind has driven a cetacean to extinction.

As a species, the Baiji is over 20 million years old.

Another rare species that is facing extinction is the Yangtze finless porpoise. Its numbers are in steep decline. There are now between 1,200 and 1,400 porpoises left, about half the 1991 total.[745]

In 2006, more than 26 *billion* tons of wastewater was pumped into the river. In the 1950s, fishermen caught about 500,000 tons of river products. Today, they catch just 100,000 tons. And fishermen say that "even if they catch some fish from the polluted river, they dare not eat them."[746]

The Yangtze absorbs more than 40% percent of the country's waste water, 80% percent of it untreated. But, shockingly, a professor at the China University of Geosciences says that, "Many officials think the pollution is nothing [serious] for the Yangtze."[747]

Currently, China's State Environmental Protection Agency, (SEPA) will only charge polluters a maximum fine of 200,000 yuan (about US$25,000). 'But all a factory has to do is stop treating wastewater for

228

about five days to save 40,000 yuan a day to pay the fine,' one report in the official media pointed out.[748]

Massive engineering projects on the river, such as the Three Gorges dam, also create serious problems. The reservoir behind this dam is heavily polluted with fertilizers, pesticides and sewage from the numerous tour boats on it. Though China's government allocated four billion yuan (around US$500 million at 2007 rates) to environmental care, given the endemic corruption that has dogged construction of the dam (just like every other large scale project in China) it is legitimate to question just how much of this money was used for the intended purpose.[749]

Since 1949, lakes in the lower and middle areas of the river shrunk from 18,000 square kilometers to 7,000 square kilometers. Across the entire nation, wetlands have shrunk by nearly two-thirds in the same period.[750]

China's second largest lake, Dongting Lake, connected to the Yangtze, is also under extraordinary stress. In 1949 the lake was 4,350 square kilometers. Today, due to silting and land reclamation, it is 2,625 square kilometers.[751]

The lake is suffering from serious pollution, in large part from the more than 100 paper mills along its shores. Of these, only two meet pollution discharge requirements. The rest were at long last closed in 2007.[752] But given that it is very common for such closure orders to be ignored, or only obeyed while the latest government minister is in town, it is hard to be hopeful about this development.

The situation is depressingly similar in China's lesser known rivers. In the Honghe River in southwest China, water sources that 150,000 people rely on were found to be so heavily contaminated with lead and other heavy metals that water supplies had to be suspended.[753]

Another 80,000 people went without safe water for a month in the town of Yixing in eastern Jiangsu Province because of polluted tap water supplies in early 2007. Yixing has 1,685 chemical factories, and it was these which poisoned the water. "We know the water is toxic because fish died when we put them in the water for just three minutes" said a local. He also said that the local government leader "only told us to stop drinking it after the media exposed the contamination."[754]

Nationwide, only 8.8% of tap water in rural areas meets bacteria standards, and about 230 million people have unclean supplies. More than 60% have no access to tap water at all.[755] In early 2008, media reported that in just one province in China, Sichuan, 17 *million* people were living without access to safe water.[756]

In December 2006 more than 450,000 kilograms of fish were killed after a city in central Henan Province released water contaminated with sewage and industrial waste. The poison tide swept into neighboring Anhui Province, devastating aquatic life in the Tuohe and Xinbian rivers.[757] A similar disaster had already happened in 2004, when a chemical fertilizer plant in Sichuan polluted the Tuojiang River in Southwest China in 2004, killing more than 500,000 kilograms of fish and leaving more than a million local residents unable to use the water for nearly a month.[758]

At the end of 2005 the release of 100 tons of benzene into the Songhua River in northeastern China not only poisoned supplies for those living along its banks but also poisoned the water for those downstream in Russia. Again, in the typically secretive way in which China deals with such problems, officials lied about the very existence of a problem for ten days, putting hundreds of thousands at severe risk.[759]

And even when authorities do try to impose a clean-up, they seem to have little success. A chemical plant located in the central Chinese city of Xiangfan was fined around US$30,000 after it had dumped toxic waste into a tributary of the Yangtze River. Previously authorities had ordered the factory, along with 13 others, to close. Factory bosses simply ignored the order and went on tipping poison into the river.[760]

Nationwide, about 70% of China's rivers are polluted, and 96% of rural villages do not have adequate sewage plants.[761] At the end of 2005, 40% of cities had no wastewater treatment plants. And even in those cities that did have such plants, often they were underused or left idle since the cities authorities were unwilling to pay the cost of running them.[762]

Nor is the problem confined to rivers alone. Groundwater supplies in a staggering 90% of Chinese cities are polluted, and 400 of China's 600 cities face water shortages.[763]

Though in absolute terms China's fresh water supplies rank sixth in the world, in per-capita terms the country has only a quarter of the world average. The bulk of China's water supplies are sucked up by its agricultural sector, which is responsible for more than two-thirds of total water consumption. Yet 55% of the water used in agriculture is wasted through leaking pipes, over-watering and spillage, twice the level of developed countries.[764]

China's coastal areas are also facing extreme stress. About 140,000 square kilometers of China's shorelines are polluted, and in 2005 31.7 *billion* tons of wastewater was dumped into the sea, containing more than 25 million tons of pollutants.[765] In 2006, China dumped 500,000 tons of ammonia-nitrogen and 300,000 tons of phosphate into the ocean.[766]

In 2009 China released its first ever joint inspection of its coastal areas. This report, compiled by nine government agencies, found that the marine environment was continuing to deteriorate fast. The report said that most local governments remained focused on growth at all costs. Projects were being started before passing environmental impact tests, as required by law, and from poor Guangxi Zhuang region to rich Jiangsu Province, pollutant discharges were rising fast.[767]

China released its first national pollution survey in 2010. This had taken two years to prepare, and gave the total amount of wastewater produced in 2007 (the most recent figures available) as 209 billion tons. The amount of waste gas the same year was 63.7 trillion cubic meters.[768]

230

The estuary of the Yellow River, just like that of the Yangtze, has been declared a 'dead zone' by the United Nations Environmental Program. This means that algal blooms, caused by pollutants in the water, have grown to such an extent that they absorb all the oxygen. All other marine life dies. In June 2006, a 1,000 square kilometer bloom killed 12 million fish in the Yangtze estuary.[769]

Somewhat surprisingly, however, the Chinese media reported in mid-2006, just a few months before UN's announcement, that the Yellow River estuary was 'the cleanest in years,' even though in 2005 that same media had printed reports that more than 70% of the river was polluted.[770]

China did introduce new regulations to tackle water pollution at the start of 2010. These regulations were based on 'chemical oxygen demand,' or COD. COD is a measure of the amount of oxygen used up by pollutants reacting in the water. A high COD reduces overall oxygen in the water, taking an obvious toll on aquatic life. Under the regulations, city governments will be fined 100,000 yuan for every milligram rise in COD in local waterways.

The first fines - a total of 500,000 yuan (US$74,000)- were levied on two cities in northern China's Shaanxi Province, Xi'an and Xianyang, in March 2010. However, according to Li Xiaolian, deputy chief of the provincial environmental department, "The penalty is not a huge amount for the two cities, which rank as the first and third biggest economies in Shaanxi." Li suggested that "It's a loss of face for the local government and will prompt them to do a better job." But given the fact that allowing pollution to rise is generally profitable for local governments, one must ask how much credence can be placed in Li's hope.[771]

The 2010 national pollution survey found that COD in 2007 was twice the official estimate given at the time.[772]

It's safe to say that the idea of "harmoniously coexisting with nature," which China introduced in 2003 as a "new concept" is not working.[773]

In fact, the measures China has taken to help the environment can do more harm than good. On the surface of it, China's tree-planting campaign has been a success, with 50 billion trees planted in the last 25 years. More than 550 million people were involved in planting this huge number of trees. However, according to Friends of Nature, a Chinese non-governmental environmental group, more than two-thirds of these trees are conifers, rising to 95% in some provinces.

Such forests, unlike mixed woodland, are of extremely limited benefit to the environment, since almost nothing else can live in them. They are, however, a lucrative source of profit.

And when single species is planted in such high densities, it becomes very vulnerable to disease. More than 400 million conifers have died in recent years, leading to about 90 billion yuan in direct economic losses. In areas where this planting has been rapid, there have been dramatic rises in soil erosion. Furthermore, the government has privatized

231

168 million hectares of forest, a move that Friends of Nature says will speed up the extinction of natural forests.[774]

Roughly 6,000 of China's plant species are threatened, and 104 species are in danger of extinction.[775]

Sometimes China even gets paid for harming the environment.

The country is the world's biggest producer of HCFC-22, a refrigerant used in air-conditioners that is a major cause of global warming. While China is perfectly capable of using more modern, safer refrigerants (and indeed does so for European markets) it continues to use HCFC-22 in the equipment it manufactures for other countries. This is because making the chemical creates a waste gas, and manufacturers can claim hundreds of millions of dollars from a UN agency for incinerating this gas.[776]

China's construction boom is also another major cause of environmental pollution.

According to Qiu Baoxing, deputy minister of construction, though 95% of new designs proposed in 2006 claimed they would meet environmental standards for new construction, fewer than half of those completed lived up to that promise. Construction related activity is a major polluter in China, and the industry accounts for 27% of China's energy usage, a figure that is rising by 1% a year.[777] Much of this building activity is totally unnecessary. Provincial governments regularly design excessively lavish buildings – for both official and private use. This often leads to stern warnings from the central government.[778]

One city government caused environmental damage by cutting down 200 hectares of trees in a *preservation zone* to build a complex of lavish villas, tennis courts and swimming pools. Nearby locals said that most of the villas were empty, though at least half had owners. And of these owners, 75% were government employees.[779] Nationwide, 183 of China's roughly 660 cities plan to embark on major building sprees.[780]

It is because of factors like these that in terms of ecological care, China ranks 100th out of 118 countries assessed, according to the 2007 China Modernization Report. This was the same position it held in 2004, the last time the report was issued.[781]

Even the successes China has in tackling some of the worst polluters in the country seem to make little difference. China closed down 3,176 firms for breaking environmental rules in 2006 and settled with 13,000. Despite this China failed to meet its pollution control targets for 2006, a year which saw 600,000 complaints about pollution made to the government.[782]

One reason that the national government has such limited success in controlling pollution is that local governments do everything they can to keep the inspectors out.

For example, many local governments set up industrial parks which banned other government departments from conducting any inspections whatsoever without direct approval. This is why most of the

232

hundred firms in one such industrial park in Henan Province did not install any pollution control equipment at all, and instead just dumped untreated waste into a local river.

Similar parks can be found in Anhui, Gansu and Zhejiang Provinces. All across China county governments collude with polluters to keep the money flowing into their pockets and the poison flowing into the environment.[783]

Central authorities are hampered by provincial governments which often fake their pollution control statistics. According to China Daily, only six provinces out of China's 31 met their pollution control targets in 2006. But even this mediocre accomplishment should be taken with caution since, according to Zhou Shengxian, the Director of China's State Environmental Protection Agency, some local governments simply fabricate their figures.[784]

A report aired by China Central Television, China's national broadcaster, said that smelting factories in one north China town had remained open for years, even though they did not meet environmental standards.

Local government measures to control the pollution had been exposed as "mere shows to fool higher authorities and central governments." That's why the number of factories failing to meet standards *increased* despite these 'clampdowns.'[785]

In May 2007, the State Council, China's leading political body, issued a new regulation forbidding foreign organizations and individuals in China conducting any hydrological activities. The regulations, which came into force on June 1st 2007, said that water assessment information could only be released to the public by relevant government departments or government authorized hydrological organizations.

The government claimed that this regulation was designed to "regulate the quality of foreign involvement in hydrological activities." It follows a regulation previously issued restricting land surveys.

The government claims these activities are a potential risk to national security. However, the truth is that China simply wishes to hide the extent of its environmental degradation.[786]

A regulation banning land surveys came into force on March 1st 2007, stating that "those who intend to engage in surveying and mapping must obtain approval from the central government and be supervised by local governments."

On March 5th 2007, four Japanese scholars were arrested for "illegal mapping and surveying activities" in China's Xinjiang region. The four, who had been doing research for Japan's Research Institute for Humanity and Nature, were fined 20,000 yuan (US$2590). Their activities, said Li Quanzhan, director of the region's Bureau of Surveying and Mapping, were "disrespectful to Chinese laws and their actions will not help research cooperation between the two countries." Li also said their equipment and results had been confiscated.[787]

233

The gravest threat of all facing not only China's environment but the entire world ecology is the nation's astonishingly large consumption of coal.

In 2003 it burned a billion tons of coal per year. Today, it burns two billion tons per year.[788] And it is very inefficient at mining this coal, for in addition to the enormous cost in human suffering created by China's coal industry, it takes from five to 20 tons to produce one ton of usable coal, compared to 1.2 to 1.3 in developed countries.

Since 1970, China's largest coal producing province, Shanxi, has produced eight billion tons of coal. But to do so, it used about 20 billion tons of mineral resources. At the same time, six billion cubic meters of coal-bed gas is wasted annually, 50% of the total gas transferred from west to east China. Furthermore, 1.2 billion tons of water is wasted every year.[789]

Five of China's cities are among the top ten most polluted in the world due to coal emissions. Acid rain, primarily caused by coal burning, falls on 30% to 40% of China, and a similar percentage of China's citizens breathe coal-polluted air.[790]

One especially serious health worry is a disease called fluorosis, caused by the fluoride that is released when coal is burned. Fluorosis weakens the bones and can lead to paralysis.

In one province of China, Guizhou, where coal is widely used for indoor heating, an almost unbelievable 97% of the population has in some degree been affected by this illness.

Nationwide, 42 million have fluorosis and 100 million are at risk.[791]

And this is a situation that will only get worse, for China is engaged in a power-station building spree beyond anything the world has ever seen.

In just one year, 2006, China built 100 gigawatts in new electricity generating capacity. That's significantly more than the entire power generating capacity of the entire United Kingdom.[792]

To achieve this, China is building at least one new power station every three days. The true figure is more than this, since, as the central government admits, provincial governments build their own stations without permission.[793] This has been a frequent problem in China in recent years.[794]

According to the International Energy Agency's chief economist, Fatih Birol, in the next eight years alone China will add as much generating capacity as exists in all 25 current members of the European Union. Ninety percent of these new plants will be coal-fired, says Mr. Birol.[795]

China is investing in green energy, it is true. In 2010, China said it drew 8% of its energy needs from renewables. The nation aims to derive 15% of its energy needs from non-fossil fuels by 2020, and it is pouring investment into the sector. But some question the feasibility of these plans. Lin Boqiang, a professor at Xiamen University, says that for the foreseeable future, "Coal and oil will still remain the mainstream energy in the country."[796]

Between 2003 and 2005 China invested one trillion yuan in new power capacity. In 2004 the central government authorized 60 gigawatts of new capacity, but 120 gigawatts of other projects were built without approval. Most of this failed to meet environmental regulations.[797]

China's power sector is responsible for 80% of nitrous oxide emissions, 44% of sulfur dioxide emissions, and 26% of carbon dioxide emissions.[798]

Carbon dioxide emissions are the major culprit behind global warming.

In 2004, the International Energy Agency suggested China would become the world's biggest emitter of CO2, by 2025. But in fact some experts were predicting even then that China would overtake the U.S. in 2007. Many say that it did.[799]

One reason that estimates of China's CO2 pollution change so drastically is that China offers extremely limited information in this regard. In the words of China's own National Coordination Committee on Climate Change, "We don't have estimates of CO2 for such a recent date." The same committee estimates that China's plan to report its CO2 emissions will not be ready for two or three years.[800]

China is polluting the world in pursuit of economic growth. Rather than learn from the mistakes of Western economies, it duplicates them.

Yet, at a major UN climate change conference in May 2007, China wanted to impose its interpretation of the problem on the Western world, demanding that delegates formally recognize that Western countries were responsible for 95% of emissions up to 1950 and 77% from then until 2000.

At this same conference, China rejected language that would have required the entire world to deal with climate change, once again putting the focus on the developed world.[801]

A German delegate, Michael Mueller, said that the Chinese negotiators had been "masters of deception and the art of interpretation."[802] By the end of the conference, however, many delegates felt China had become more reasonable.

Reports in early 2007 speculating that China would soon be the world's biggest greenhouse gas emitter were angrily rejected by a senior government official. Dismissing these claims as "utter nonsense," Gao Guangsheng, head of China's Office of the National Coordination Committee for Climate Change, said that, "The allegation is nonsense since it lacks evidence and statistics" – before conceding (apparently unaware of the irony of the statement) that China had published no statistics about its energy consumption since 2003. These speculations were later confirmed. Today, most scientists agree that China in the leader in global CO2 emissions.[803]

Independent estimates about China's CO2 output are derived from the figures China does make public, such as the 9.3% rise in fuel use in 2006.[804] In 2008 scientists at the University of Berkeley announced research that revised estimates for China's CO2 emissions. Whereas CO2 level had been expected to rise by 2.5% to 5% per year, the figure was re-estimated at 11% per year.[805]

Gao also said that the most recent calculation of China's CO2 emissions was made in 1994, before summing up the country's attitude to the problem of climate change. Such claims, he said, were "irresponsible and might be used to impose pressure on the Chinese government."[806]

Organizations such as Greenpeace and other environmental concern groups around the world are important pressure groups at this time because internally, in China, there is no adequate pressure on the government from citizens.

China justifies its CO2 emissions in part by pointing out its per-capita emissions are much lower than those of the US. This is true, but if you ask the average Chinese citizen what they want in life and the answer is always the same; they want a high-consumption Western-style life.

Yet this is impossible, as the leaders in Beijing clearly realize. Xu Dingming, a senior official in China's economic planning ministry, said that if China's per capita energy consumption matched America's, the country would need 4.5 billion tons of oil annually, yet global annual oil supply is only 4 billion tons.[807]

China is setting increasingly tough targets for pollution control. It plans to cut energy used per unit of GDP by 20% by 2010, boost average car fuel efficiency to 40mpg within five years (more stringent than current US standards), to reduce water pollution by 10% by 2020 and increase industrial solid-waste recycling by 60%.[808]

Yet China does not even have a clear picture of where the pollution is coming from, given that it was not until January 2008 that the first national pollution census was announced.[809]

And in 2010, when the census was released, it was also announced that China had missed the target of a 20% reduction in energy use per unit of GDP, achieving 14.38% instead. At the same time, a set of new targets were given - for instance, a plan to shut down outdated power plants. More money (83 billion yuan / US$12.2 billion) was also allocated to pollution control.[810]

But given the many past failures to meet targets, it is surely legitimate to be skeptical about these plans. In the first half of 2006, for example, energy consumption per unit of GDP rose by 0.8%. Likewise, waste-water production rose by 2.4%, to 12 billion tons, also just in the first half of 2006.[811] And China has already rejected replacing coal power stations with nuclear plants, citing the global limitation of uranium as well as disposal of waste products.[812]

Officials are promoting hydropower as the energy of the future, since, they say, 20% of China's total water resources are suitable for hydro energy plans. Last year, the nation added six million KW of hydro capacity, and, nationwide, hydro power accounts for nearly 14% of energy generated.

For economic development within China, coal power is still the king, at nearly 84%.[813]

One of the reasons for China's reliance on coal is that is only has limited oil reserves. In 2006, for example, it had to import nearly 50% of the oil it required, around 145 million tons. However, in 2007, China National Petroleum Corporation announced it had found an oil field with proven reserves of over 400 million tons, and possibly one billion tons.

The news was greeted with jubilation, but little mention was made of what effect this might have on the environment, to say nothing of the effect of extraction on Bohai Bay, at the mouth of the Yellow River, where the field is located.[814]

A few months prior to this find, China also announced it had found vast metal reserves in its Qinghai-Tibet region, comprising 30-40 million tons of copper, 40 million tons of lead and zinc and several billion tons of iron ore.

It also found more than six *hundred* sites for new mines.

Zhuang Yuxun, director of the Department of Geological Investigation of the China Geological Survey, said "We will speed up the surveying process to more accurately locate these minerals... Once mines are developed they will greatly relieve the strain on China's existing resources."[815]

The development of such natural lands will require detailed and precise conservation plans, as yet unenforced in China.

China's commitment to hydro energy is admirable. However, in 2005 the central government had to stop 32 hydroelectric projects because they did not follow relevant environmental regulations.

By the time the government stepped in, 20 billion yuan (about US$2.46 billion at that time) had already been spent. This money was thus totally wasted.[816]

Beijing, host of the 2008 Olympics, is particularly heavily afflicted by pollution. In the winter of 2006/2007, when Beijing fired up its 6,000 coal-fired furnaces, particulate levels rose to *seven* times higher than the safety level.

Sulfur dioxide and carbon monoxide levels also rose to several times above the danger limit.[817]

The city vowed to clean up its air in time for the Olympics, and set a target of 238 'blue sky days' (days with only light pollution) in 2006. Most of these so-called 'blue sky days,' however, were said to be "hazy affairs with heavy pollution."

On December 12th the situation was so bad that the city's Environmental Protection Bureau advised residents "to reduce outside activities" due to the extraordinarily high level of pollution in the atmosphere.

At the time this announcement was made, the city claimed to be just eight days short of hitting its 'blue sky days' target.[818]

Yet, according to a report issued in January 2007, between December 12th, when citizens were advised to stay indoors because of the excessive pollution, and December 24th, the city experienced the eight 'blue sky days' required to meet the annual target. Not only this, but it had a further three such days between December 24th and the end of the year.[819]

International Olympics Committee vice-president Ludmilla Linberg said on a visit to the capital in March 2007, "I can feel [the pollution] in my throat. I think living here is not good for your health."

Local politicians believed all problems would be solved by 2008. "I'm sure the quality of the air will be good enough for athletes - that is very important" said Tu Mingde, assistant to the president of the Beijing organizing committee.[820]

One way in which the city prepared for the games was by using cloud-seeding to force it to rain prior to the opening ceremony, thus hoping to ensure dry skies on the day itself.

As an added bonus, meteorologists said, the rain would help wash the pollution out of the air. "Rainfall is a way to naturally clean the air," said Wang Jianjie, a meteorologist at the Beijing Meteorological Bureau.[821] The World Health Organization says the Air Quality Index safety limit is 50. During the Beijing Games, it was 88. This was spun as a 'success' by Chinese authorities, since China defines an index of 101 as unsafe – more than twice the WHO level![822]

But in the end most of the measures used were far from high-tech. The government simply shut down numerous factories and used severe traffic restrictions to halve the number of cars on the roads. Yet these essentially cosmetic methods did not prove notably effective.

Just six months before the Games began, Olympic officials described Beijing's air quality as "awful."[823] Even two weeks before the games, the New York Times reported that, "Beijing's skies are so murky and polluted that the authorities are considering emergency measures during the Games beyond the traffic restrictions and factory shutdowns."[824]

However, the day before the Games began, Jacques Rogge, head of the International Olympic Committee, announced that Beijing's air quality was indeed safe.[825]

But in mid-2009, the journal Environmental Science and Technology painted a very different picture. Research carried out in a joint program between Oregon State University and Peking University found that the pollution level was double that of the previous games in Athens and three and a half times that of the Games in Sydney. The study found that levels of coarse particle air pollution were higher than the WHO safety limit 81% of the time and that fine particle pollution (the most dangerous type) was at an unacceptable level 100% of the time.

238

These levels were higher than those announced by China during the Games. While there is no evidence that China obfuscated the facts, it is true that China used a different measuring standard than the one that has been used and accepted worldwide for many years.

Staci Simonich, an associate professor of environmental and molecular toxicology at Oregon State University, said that it was unlikely this pollution would have harmed athletes or visitors to the games, since they were only exposed for a short time. She also said "Millions of other people there face this air quality problem their entire lives. It was unlike anything I've ever seen. You could look directly at the sun and not have a problem, due to the thickness of the haze."[826]

Even so, due to the measures the city had taken - combined with favorable weather conditions - the city had its lowest level of August pollution for ten years.

But shortly after the Games were over, Beijing ended all the restrictions it had imposed, thus letting full-strength air pollution roar back into the city.[827]

Currently, China suffers more than 400,000 premature deaths per year from air pollution. Of this, 300,000 die from outdoor pollution and 100,000 from indoor pollution.[828]

Speaking after the discovery of that huge oil field in Bohai Bay, China's Premier, Wen Jiabao, said that, "I was so happy on hearing the news that I couldn't even fall asleep."[829]

If China's government leaders truly comprehended the environmental disaster that awaits China's future, perhaps they would never sleep.

Reason **26**

The Migrant School of Revolution

China is an economic powerhouse – and the foot soldiers of that powerhouse are its vast legions of migrant workers. Drawn from the impoverished countryside, where jobs are scarce and wages low, they come to the nation's booming cities, often raw recruits to be burned up in the furnaces of construction that give dimension to China's rise.

China's migrants have built the factories and office blocks that support the country's rise to economic supremacy. They have built roads, rail, docks and airports that allow it to import and transport the millions of tons of raw ingredients it needs and export the billions of dollars of finished goods it produces. And most of this has been done by sweat and muscle power rather than by hi-tech machinery. Spade and sinew are the most common sights on China's construction projects, often without labor-saving hydraulic equipment.

China's migrants also work in the kitchens of the cities, providing meals for socialites and office workers that they could not themselves afford. They clean the houses of the richer city elite. Migrants are available for any job beneath the social and economic standard of the city's better-educated residents.

China currently has over 200 million migrant workers (225 million according to 2009 figures), 120 million of them working in the country's big cities and the rest in its smaller towns. Official figures suggest that this vast body of people will increase by around 13 million a year as farmers and particularly the sons leave the land in search of a better standard of life.[830]

But though migrant workers can earn more money in a single year of city labor than they could in many years tilling the land, they face a labyrinth of problems and prejudices which stand in the way of their wish to build a better life. Prejudice from city dwellers, who routinely look down on – and even despise – migrant workers. Unjust bosses who either make the workers wait up to a year before paying them, or do not pay them at all.

They suffer from a lack of formal benefits, such as contracts, accident insurance or enforced work safety regulations, not to mention professional safety equipment. Such disregard for the importance of their efforts in the development of China is passed on through their families. Wives find it hard to land jobs, children are denied basic education in formal schools, and medical care is often sub-standard. Secure, private and comfortable housing is a dream that never comes true.

Life has always been hard for countryside dwellers in China – so much so that their way of existence has entered the very language. The

241

English word 'coolie' is taken from the Chinese words 'ku li,' meaning 'bitter strength,' a testament to how many centuries China's poor have labored for China's rich.

Such language and such attitudes reinforce the ostracization of these city-builders to a point where they feel they live in one country while building another.

Their numbers continue to grow, and as they come to the clear realization that they will never share in the good life enjoyed by the millions of city dwellers, China's migrant workers will form the 3rd Army of Instability.

In March 2002, Wu Mingxi, a member of the Chinese People's Political Consultative Conference, said "The government should help create an environment friendly to rural job hunters in cities and see to it that their rights and interests are well protected."[831]

In August that year, China began what it called "a bold reform experiment." The purpose of this experiment was "to abolish all discriminative policies leading to inequality in employment for laborers of urban and rural origins, establish a unified employment system for urban and rural labor, and draw migrant workers into the social security system," according to Wang Aiwen, an official with the Ministry of Labor and Social Security.[832]

Two years after Wang had announced the "bold reform experiment," in the summer of 2004, Chinese Vice-Premier Zeng Peiyan said that more than 360 billion yuan (US$43 billion) in unpaid wages was owed to migrant workers on 124,000 different projects nationwide. [833]

"Some have remained unpaid for up to 10 years," said Zeng. He not so boldly said that migrant workers on central government projects would be paid by the end of that year, but workers on local government projects would be paid by the end of 2005, sixteen months later.

In 2005 a government report said that "A mechanism will be promptly set up to ensure migrant workers in cities get paid on time and in full, and the work of getting their back wages paid to them will be continued." [834]

Yet China's Labor Law, passed in 1995, states that "Wages shall be paid to laborers themselves in the form of currency on a monthly basis." [835] But, as with so many other laws passed by the central government, it failed to give specific details, provide penalties, or in fact state who would make judgments and enforce obedience.[836]

However, riding the sometimes inflated, sometimes deflated hobby horse of government accounting, Zeng later claimed two disparate figures of accomplishment.

In July 2006, he reported that a total of 177 billion yuan, or 95.2% of the arrears reported by construction companies before the end of 2003, had been paid to migrant laborers.[837]

But in 2007, Zeng said the government had helped migrant workers reclaim "most of their back wages amounting to 33 billion

242

(US$4.25 billion), which had accumulated before 2003." Other reports in 2007 indicated that Zeng's earlier figure of 177 billion yuan 'repaid' was in fact general bills, rather than back wages to migrants.[838]

A particularly telling statistic is that whereas in Western nations salary payment makes up around 50% of the total costs of a company, in China wages account for just 10%. Add to this the fact that Chinese firms are much more labor-intensive than Western firms, and it becomes clear just what a raw deal many of China's migrant workers face.[839]

Aside from the negative financial aspects of being a migrant worker, there are the psychological and social aspects that cost migrant workers a sense of livability. Wang Chun'guang, a researcher at the Chinese Academy of Social Sciences, said in 2004 that migrant workers "live in isolation - far from families, no community support, suffering discrimination from urban neighbors and with no relationships. This will probably cause emotional breakdowns."

Chen Bing, a psychiatrist at Beijing's Anding Hospital, said in the same year that "rural migrants are vulnerable to cultural shock, unfair treatment and hard travel to distant cities."[840]

Yet despite these nationwide problems, according to He Luli, vice chairwoman of the Standing Committee of the 10th National People's Congress, "legitimate rights and interests of employees have been basically safeguarded since the introduction of the Labor Law on January 1, 1995" reported Chinese media in 2005.

But Ms. He's assurances that all is 'basically' well do not match up with calls by the All-China Federation of Trade Unions (itself controlled by the government) the year before. The ACFTU called for three new regulations -- that migrant workers should be paid monthly or weekly, that payment could only be delayed with trade union agreement (and then only for two weeks) and that detailed punishments for bosses who withheld payment should be specified – suggesting that the Labor Law was indeed severely lacking force.[841]

And in 2006, the All-China Federation of Trade Unions had to help 2.8 million workers chase unpaid wages, equal to a total of 1.3 billion yuan (US$162.5 million).[842]

Ms. He also said "Social incidents triggered by overdue salaries, especially by employers who escape and hide, are on the rise, seriously undermining social stability."[843]

Apparently Ms. He has correctly labeled one of the reasons that migrant workers will form the 3rd Army of Instability, without fully understanding the depth and breadth of the discontent felt by each and every worker.

In 2007, the government was *still* saying help was on the way. Chinese Premier Wen Jiabao said that the government should establish a social security system specially designed for the migrant workers as soon as possible – four years after the nation's "bold reform experiment" to "draw migrant workers into the social security system" had begun.[844]

A major survey undertaken by China's Ministry of Labor and Social Security, which covered 2.84 million migrant workers across 19,000 enterprises in 40 cities, found that 79.2% of workers listed their greatest concern as income and nearly 40% talked about lack of social insurance. Just over 25% said unpaid wages were a major concern. Of those who had not been paid on time, said the survey (without giving the precise number of unpaid workers) the average amount owed was 2,100 yuan (US$270).

Regardless of the lack of a precise number of unpaid workers, fully one in four migrant workers has not been paid, fears they will not be paid, or has reservations about the truth behind the company that they work for and the ability of the government to enforce the retrieval of the funds should they be withheld.

The survey also found that migrant workers toiled an average of 8.7 hours a day to earn an average monthly income of 1,020 yuan ($131). But 8% of workers put in an 11 hour day, 35% of whom were not paid.[845]

Article 36 of China's 1995 Labor Law says "The State shall practice a working hour system wherein laborers shall work for no more than eight hours a day and no more than 44 hours a week on the average." Such words indicate a labor utopia which is not to this day enjoyed by any migrant.

Just a few days after this report was released, other government departments announced good news. According to the Beijing Labor and Security Bureau, in 2006 they dealt with 1,965 cases of unpaid wages, a 63% drop from 2005. Again, those riding the hobby horse of government statistics ride roughshod over reality. Those almost 2000 cases accounted for more than 40 thousand workers – only in Beijing – who were owed a total of 94.18 million yuan. The Bureau said it fined 41 enterprises involved in pay delays 127,600 yuan – 0.13% of the total unpaid wages.[846]

Also in 2006, Ma Yang, who works at a Beijing organization that assists migrant workers, said "Things have gotten better in recent years, especially in 2006. The number of people seeking help in our office fell remarkably."[847] Such hollow statistical claims are virtually unverifiable.

Again, it was only in 2007 that the government announced that "China will make it mandatory for employers across the country to deposit money into a fund this year to guarantee that migrant workers get their wages." Yet given how little regard employers have paid to legal requirements to date, it is questionable whether the new law will be effective.[848]

Certainly, late payment and non-payment of migrant workers was still routine in 2007. In July 2007 a group of 300 migrant workers, from the central city of Chongqing, went on strike at a project in southern Guangdong Province on which they were working, after having not been paid for four months. Their employer's response was to send gangs of armed thugs to intimidate the striking workers.

"The first batch of about 50 gangsters came with spades in their hands, and the second batch had axes, steel pipes and sabers, and there

244

were more behind them," said one worker, Liu Gangqing. And even when police arrived the thugs carried on beating the migrants.

One victim was beaten so badly that he was admitted to hospital where he was diagnosed as brain dead. He died soon after. A Guangdong government spokesman tried to play down the violence, saying it was a "violent conflict" between 30 migrant workers and company staff.[849]

But Li Zhonggui, who runs a migrant workers' rights protection group in Chongqing, reacted angrily to this assertion. "If it was really group fighting, why were the injured all migrant workers? ... We will take our frustrations to the police and we will not rest until the issue has been addressed."[850]

In December 2006, another migrant worker, Xie Hongsheng, was beaten to death by a gang on a construction site after demanding outstanding wages of 40,000 yuan (US$5,130) owed to a group of migrant workers from northwestern Shaanxi Province including himself and his father. The group had finished constructing an apartment in November but had only been paid 11,000 yuan of the money owed.

Xie's father was also beaten so badly that he suffered a cerebral concussion and fractured bones, and would need several months to recover, said Dr. Gao Lijun at a local hospital.

Also in 2006 a group of 137 construction workers in central Hunan Province had to resort to suing the local court for failing to protect them. The developer they worked for had owed them a total of over 860,000 yuan (US$110,260) of wages in arrears since 2002. Courts had frozen the company's assets until payments were made. But the company sold its assets illegally in 2005.

Only after this had been done was the firm's legal representative, Liao Heping, arrested. And the 100,000 yuan he was obliged to pay went to cover legal fees. The workers sued the court for breach of duty. They lost when Hunan Provincial People's Higher Court ruled that 'market disorder,' rather than the intermediate court, was to blame.

And early in 2006 a group of 18 workers from the southwestern city of Chengdu were not paid after completing a construction project in the western province of Xinjiang. Penniless, they began to walk home to Sichuan, but became lost in Xinjiang's deserts, where one of them died. This death was apparently sufficient to prod authorities into helping, and the Chengdu trade union eventually forced the employer to pay up.[851]

As usual within 'New China' people willing to speak out for the dispossessed and disadvantaged such as the migrant workers are few, and often wisely so.

Wang Yuancheng, who was once a migrant worker himself, became principal of a vocational training school in eastern Shandong Province as well as a member of China's National People's Congress. He said that in the NPC there are four members per million urban citizens, but just one deputy per million rural citizens. Wang said that NPC members like him, drawn from the rural community, often felt reluctant to

245

speak the truth given the large number of provincial governors and mayors also attending NPC meetings.[852]

Such political under-representation ensures China's migrant workers do not have a voice. And the few voices they do have, such as NPC members like Wang, are very much voices in the wilderness. Wang has been pushing for better rights for migrants, such as equal education and employment opportunities as well as affordable health care since 2003.

Yet in 2007 these basic provisions of a just and inclusive society were still not being met. Chinese media reported in summer 2007 that "Chinese employees' legal rights, such as their employment contract, overtime pay and safe working conditions are not adequately protected."

A survey by the Chinese Academy of Sciences in June 2007 found that most migrant workers received no payment for overtime, and that two thirds of them had no opportunity to negotiate wages. It also found that more than 30% of migrant workers injured in industrial accidents received absolutely no compensation.

Another survey by the Academy in 2007, which questioned 5,000 migrant workers in the construction industry, found that 53% of them did not have an official contract, even though Article 16 of the Labor Law, established in 1995, says "Labor contracts shall be concluded if labor relationships are to be established." The survey also found that among those who had signed a contract, only 41% had a copy of it. Furthermore, only 17% understood the legal terminology of their contract.

Only 31% received their wages on time and only 31% had medical insurance. Eighty percent of the workers were married, but only 25% of them lived with their spouse. Feeling disenfranchised, 44% said that urban citizens looked down on them, and a large majority of the workers said they felt alienated from society. Most spent all their time on the work site, with just 3.7% saying they had any form of social life outside it, not surprising since as they work in the city socializing would mean acceptance of the negativity bestowed upon them by city residents.[853]

It was only at the end of June 2007 that China implemented a labor contract law, in response to the scandal that drew worldwide media attention in the preceding weeks in which many hundreds of people forced into *slavery* in brick kilns in Shanxi Province had been freed. [854] Shockingly, media said that up to 1,000 children were among those enslaved. And even when parents of the children knew they were being held as slaves, Shanxi police refused to help. "Boys as young as eight had been taken from bus and train stations and sold for 500 yuan each to kilns where they were beaten, starved and forced to work 14 hours hauling bricks" media reported.[855]

State media also revealed in 2007 that the living standard of migrant workers was just 53.2% that of an average urban resident – and that the gulf was growing. [856] Reports in 2008 indicated that even in Guangdong Province, one of China's wealthiest areas, 22.2% of migrant workers were not able to save any money at all, since their wages were only just enough to cover the most basic costs of living.[857]

The financial crisis of 2008 led to a new problem to be faced by China's migrant workers - factory bosses disappearing overnight as once-lucrative markets dried up. In the city of Shenzhen alone, 370 firms shut down abruptly, leaving nearly 40,000 workers short of 100 million yuan in salary. "The bosses can easily escape overseas and once they are overseas, mostly back to Taiwan or Hong Kong, it's hard to get them back," said one government official. Government estimated that 20 million migrant workers lost their jobs as a result of the crisis.[858]

And the labor law which had been introduced at the end of 2007 immediately ran into problems. Though it stipulated companies had to pay workers one month's salary for each year they had worked if their contracts ended, the relevant government departments that handled claims for breaking this law were rapidly overwhelmed, building up a year-long backlog.[859]

Problems continued in 2009 and 2010. In 2009, for example, 500 migrant workers were left unpaid after completing a construction project in the city of Chongqing. They were reduced to living on plain rice and sleeping on concrete floors in bitter winter conditions.[860] Also in 2009, a large group of migrants staged a rooftop protest on a building in Guangxi Zhuang region, threatening to jump off if they were not paid the wages owed to them.

In 2010, migrant worker Gao Zhiqiang argued with his boss over 70 yuan in unpaid wages. That's just US$10, but for migrants living hand-to-mouth, even small sums make a big difference.

Twenty other migrants protested along with Gao, who then dialed a police hotline for help. After three calls, the police eventually arrived. But since this was a civil dispute, they refused to get involved and left again.

The boss then agreed to pay up, but said the workers had to accompany him to a different location. On the way to this location, a car blocked the migrants' path, and a man got out from it and stabbed Gao. Gao was rushed to hospital, where doctors had to remove a kidney to save his life.

Gao now faces a bill of 40,000 yuan. It is completely beyond his means to pay this.[861]

The low wages that migrant workers receive make it extremely difficult to educate their children. Beijing alone had 400 unlicensed schools, set up by migrants for migrants, since official city schools are just too expensive and often exclude the children of migrant workers because city parents wish to instill what is, in practical terms, cultural apartheid.

Such cultural apartheid can apparently be wiped away, as migrant worker Luo Yang was asked to 'donate' 8,000 yuan every semester to the primary school he wanted to send his child to in the eastern city of

Nanjing where he was working. Average migrant worker salaries in the city are 1,000 yuan a month.

One couple, Zhao Shengjie and Dong Qingyun, set up a school in a suburb of Beijing in 2000 for the children of migrant workers. Soon after, the buildings which housed the school were torn down for a new highway. They moved to a new site, but were soon shut down by Beijing's educational authority.

Shockingly, the authorities seized all the school's tables and chairs. "What about the 400 students? No school would take them," said Zhao. Lessons continued with students sitting on the bare ground for a whole week before the couple found a new place for the school. And even that building, said media, was due to be pulled down for a government construction project

Qin Jijie, another migrant, spent four years building a school in another Beijing suburb. He financed the entire project, with the government contributing nothing. The 37 teachers at the school rely on the tiny fees they charge the parents of the 1,000 children who attend.

"I am so sad to see the children of my fellows play in construction sites, bazaars [shopping areas] and at streets when they should be in the classroom," he said. "Our people left their poor hometown for cities not only to make a living. More importantly we hope our children will have a different life from us, for example, to receive more education. But they are still as far from a good education as they were back home."[862]

Nearly two million children of migrant workers were not able to go to school due to high fees in 2004. Chinese media reported the plight of one 12 year old boy, Chen Qiguo. Chen's father, who was ill in bed, could not afford the 300 yuan (US$36) fees to send his son to school. On the verge of tears, Chen's father said "I'm sorry for my son, I couldn't send him to school."[863]

And in 2010, four thousand children of migrant workers who were receiving education in and around Beijing were put in limbo as the city government demolished five primary schools and seven kindergartens.

One of those schools, Wende Primary School, had a teaching contract lasting until 2013. Based on that, the Principal, Cui Kezhong, refused to vacate the school. Shortly after this, the school office was broken into twice, and much of the teaching equipment was destroyed. In addition student vaccination records went missing.

"I am very worried about the study plans of my children," said Cui. "Some of the lucky ones have been accepted by other schools, but the forgotten majority just wander around in the village or go back to their hometowns with their parents."

One 12-year-old student at Wende School, Ma Lili, said she had no idea where she would be able to continue her studies. She said that she had switched schools five times in the past four years, and that if she did

248

find a new school the tuition fee would be double that of Wende School - a sum she could not afford.

The parent of another student at Wende did have an option to place his son at a different school. But, he said, it was too far away and was too poor. "Four students share a desk. My son couldn't even put his textbook on the desk," he said.

Media also reported that another 30 schools for migrant children around the city would soon be demolished, leaving an additional 20,000 students without education.

The fee that Ma Lili could not afford was just 800 yuan - less than US$120. And the cost of desks for students to be able to study comfortably is low. Yet a nation that apparently cannot afford these basic provisions in 2010 could find a huge sum to spend on the Shanghai Expo - US$4 billion according to official figures, or nearly US$60 billion according to unofficial figures.

The problem of securing good education means that many migrant workers leave their children in their home villages. It is estimated that China has 20 million such children, most of whom are also neglected by the government. In 2007, Gu Xiulian, vice chairwoman of the Standing Committee of China's National People's Congress, said that the central government should improve social welfare for children whose parents have gone to work in the cities and set up a "special working mechanism focusing on care" for these children.

Children in these circumstances find warmth and friendship easy with the spirit of youth. When their youth is gone, and the demands of the market economy require education to learn productive skills, then they also will quickly join the ranks of the 3rd Army of Instability, demanding reasons why. And when no reasons are given, demanding satisfaction.

Migrants and their children also face extensive discrimination from city dwellers. The authors have frequently seen this prejudice in action. Migrants are often easy to spot since not only do they tend to dress in a more traditional fashion than city people but they often tend to have regional accents and are unable to speak city dialects such as those found in Shanghai and Shenzhen. Their difference makes them a target of harassment from city police and other officials who routinely abuse and belittle them. A simple request for help from a migrant worker wishing to understand the use of a subway ticket can result in an abusive tirade from local workers. Abuse is also directed at work-hardened construction crews pushing brick-laden wheelbarrows along city streets to access worksites, by drivers of official vehicles, company cars, taxis and other commercial vehicles.

Two natives from China's Henan Province sued the Public Security Bureau of the southern city of Shenzhen in Guangdong in 2005 after the Bureau put up banners reading "Strike Henan racketeering gangs" thus suggesting Henan people were inherently criminal. Henan people often face discrimination, so much so that some even want to change the birthplace listed on their ID cards in an attempt to avoid prejudice. The two, Li Dongzhao and Ren Chengyu, said they were offended by the banner and which damaged their reputation and caused them mental distress. [864] Li and Ren settled the case in January 2006 after court mediation and an apology from Shenzhen police.[865]

It was not until October 2006 that China's cabinet, the State Council, held its first national conference on issues relating to migrant workers.[866] In 2007, with classic hindsight, the Chinese People's Political Consultative Conference said more attention should be paid to the education of migrant workers' children.[867]

Chinese history repeatedly shows the errors of ignoring the many millions of poor and cheated rural citizens. Mao Zedong knew the power of discontent when he mobilized those at the bottom of society to help him create 'New China.'

What makes China's 200 million migrant workers different to those that Mao roused earlier in the last century is that they are far more mobile. Mao found his discontented army in China's countryside, where, though poor, they had been poor for centuries and thus only saw one side of life. Today's disadvantaged migrant citizens, however, have been to the cities. They have seen the accoutrements of the new China – the exclusive restaurants, the fashion, the cars, the consumer culture, the good life. To them, it is not a distant vision of what seems to be another planet accessed through TV by the elders, children and women left at home on farms and in small villages. To the migrants, it is real and immediate. They can actually reach out and touch the riches that they will never have possession of, rights to or use of.

And so perhaps this is an army that does not need a visionary general, for each and every migrant worker need only look into the eyes of each other to know what they want and fully understands what they will never have.

Cheated of wages, disrespected by the people for whom they labor, unable to afford education for their children and healthcare for even one family member, the time may be coming when they will stop building elite cities and start to take them apart brick by brick.

The Chinese 'Gold' Push

Coming from countries like Canada and Britain, the authors have the ability to appreciate coming second or third, even the necessity of it. There is true glory in silver and bronze.

Not if you are a citizen of China. Unless you achieve gold medal ranking, your accomplishments will disappear along with hundreds of thousands of other second and third place finishers. On Chinese television, if you win on a live broadcast, you are certain to be replayed over and over. If you or your team loses, a terse three sentences on the evening's sports program will be all the glory you will receive.

An example of the obsession with coming first was seen after the 2004 Athens Olympics, when only gold-medal winners from mainland China were allowed the grace of celebrating their achievements in front of politicians and the public in Hong Kong. Silver and bronze medal winners had to be content with the warmth of family congratulations at home, out of the limelight. Only mere fractions of distance and milliseconds of time separate winners from losers. But in China the gulf between winners and loser is physical, spiritual, and huge.

For China, coming first in major international competitions is almost a matter of life and death, and is comparable to a major military campaign. Liu Peng, President of the Chinese Olympic Committee, said in early 2007 that "Battle preparations for the 2008 Olympic Games are in a grave state. To the outside, we must display humble troops and keep a low profile, but inwardly we must plant grand ambition to scale great heights, and there can be absolutely no slackening."[868] Would words of actual war be any less bombastic? Would the call to arms be any less spiritually demanding?

Others recognize the fallacy of the Gold Push. "In China, the concept of athletic spirit is too narrow. The blind pursuit of championships and titles still dominates Chinese sport," said Song Jixin, a sports expert and director of a sports academy in China.[869]

The pursuit of titles is so dominant that it restricts the personal freedom of athletes. In late 2006 Liu Peng announced "In order to prepare for the 2008 Beijing Olympics, our country's athletes, including celebrity athletes, are banned from participating in all kinds of social activities." In typical Chinese fashion, what was meant by "social activities" was not specified. And while media suggested the ruling was primarily aimed at sports stars who gave commercial endorsements to products, the vaguely worded nature of the statement meant it could be used to control athletes in the widest possible range of ways.

For China, its sportsmen and sportswomen are nothing more than winning machines. They are obliged to spend virtually all their time training, with education a distant second. If they win gold at the games, then some measure of financial security for their future is likely. But if they win silver or bronze, or do not win at all, then they will simply be forgotten. When they retire, they will have virtually nothing; and the new ruling means that the one chance to provide for their future while they are still viewed as hopefuls has been taken away from them.

If you are a winning machine, you get the oil, the attention, the maintenance required to live a reasonable life. If you lose you are thrown on the junk pile, like other pieces of redundant technology.

Restricting social activities is anything but new. Tian Liang, an Olympic diving gold medalist, was sacked from the national team in 2005 after he made several television adverts and product endorsements. Having won gold once was not enough – and Tian's attempt to be something other than a medal machine ended in a summary judgment.[870]

The poverty faced by those athletes who do not achieve the highest level of success is shown by the example of Ai Dongmei. Ai was a runner, and won a bronze medal at China's 1997 National Games, a national sporting event held every five years. Training to be a winning machine in China, means receiving only a few hours of schooling each week, and absolutely no schooling prior to and during major sporting events.

Without even basic education after retirement, Ai had a 'pension' of 300 yuan a month (just under US$40), a sum so small that she and her husband took to vending small items on the street so that they would have enough money to live and raise their child.

In 2007, Ai had become so destitute that she announced she was selling her bronze games medal. One of the reasons she had to do this was to raise money to sue her former coach, Wang Dexian, for allegedly embezzling her wages when she was on the team.

State media claimed that "Ai… [does] not represent all the retired athletes, especially the former Olympic champions, who are enjoying entertainment, host or hostess, college students and entrepreneur lives after their sports career" [sic].[871] But this obscures the truth, for while Olympic champions may gain some measure of lifetime success, they are a tiny number of lucky few. For the hundreds of thousands of others who give their entire youth to the glory of China, the future holds little but menial jobs and heartbreak.

The winner-takes-all mentality is apparent in many areas of life in China today, but one of the most obvious is in the field of education. The single most important test in a young person's life is the three-day college entrance exam, taken in the final year of high school. This test is virtually the sole measure by which a student's academic future is decided.

A good result in the test means access to a good university, and attendance at a good university means access to a good job. Judgments of character, intuition, and creativity are not in the least bit measured, perhaps forcing thousands of brilliant minds to a life of routine.

The name of the university that a person attends counts for far more than their actual academic success as a student. The result of this is a truly enormous level of pressure placed on children from a very young age. The shocking truth is that in China today academic slavery is simply a fact of life.

The pressure to attend a prestigious university has naturally led to intense face-saving competition to study overseas, since international universities are seen as more desirable. America's Ivy League is, of course, the 'gold medal' of education.

In 2000, the Chinese Writers' Publishing House published 'Harvard Girl – Liu Yiting.' Liu Yiting was a young woman who had gained admission to Harvard, and the book was an account, written by her parents, of how their guidance had led to her success. A description of the book said it showed:
- How to establish an excellent quality system
- How to train creativity
- How to acquire the learning skills of each course
- How to effectively help children study
- How to form the habit of working out
- How to seize the method and chance of sex education in the family
- How to check the development speed of infants' mind and intelligence

The book sold 1.2 million copies in its first year and has remained popular ever since. Naturally, it has also inspired copycat volumes, such as "Harvard Boy Zhang Zhaomu."[872]

Success sells. Though books on academic achievement sell well, they are vastly outsold by get-rich-quick / be a winner self-help books, which become virtual bibles for millions of young would-be competitors in China's Gold Push.

In China, trying counts for very little. All that matters is success, and the concept of the 'noble failure' is virtually non-existent. The 'success at all costs' attitude is at the root of many other social phenomena observable in China today. It is the reason behind the stock market frenzy, and the reason behind the fact that manufacturers are willing to sell low quality or dangerous goods just so that they can close the deal. It underlies China's conspicuous consumption, and it explains why students are expected to seek financial success over personal satisfaction – and why the student who wants to be an artist or musician faces social derision.

But true greatness lies in understanding that without honoring those who win silver and bronze – and indeed those who do not win at all but have tried their best – then holding the gold medal of victory in your hand will always be a hollow prize.

The defeated should be respected. Without the defeated, there are no victors.

A Traditional Feast of Cruelty

Late in the evening, in the summer time when we have our windows open, we can hear cruelty. In a construction site 500 meters away, the workers keep dogs, most usually one dog kept for a few days only. The animal has been captured from some unsuspecting pet owner, or is perhaps lost but now imprisoned after accepting a kind hand, as pets do.

Usually the size of a large terrier since big dogs are rare in China, it whines and cries for several days until the evening that its time has come. The animal, someone's beloved pet, will never hear its name called again. Instead it starts to feel the swinging bats' sting with ever increasing intensity on every part of its body that it cannot hide.

Unknown to the dog, the longer it whimpers and cries, the more it will be beaten, until the final moment that it is struck directly over the head to be dispatched for consumption. The fear and the agony expressed through its cries make its meat tastier, more succulent — at least in the minds of the workers who tonight will dine on dog.

Claims of cruelty made directly to the workers will result only in their derisive laughter and subsequent expressions of how they love their pet, which inexplicably changes size, shape and color every few days.

"Some of the world's most violent and cruel acts occur every day in towns and cities all over China. The victims of these dire acts are defenseless, unable to speak or to fully express the extent of their suffering... I am of course talking about animal cruelty and the central role China plays in trafficking and trade in animals, both living and dead," wrote James Rose, founder of Corporate Governance Asia, a news, analysis and research website.

"Anyone who has spent time in China will be aware of the common practice of publicly butchering dogs, cats, poultry, fish, or knows restaurants that serve up monkey brains, served in the skull, or bear paws severed from still living bears," Rose wrote.[873]

Chinese media even explained the practice of eating monkey brains in more detail. "A live monkey is fixed in the centre of the dining table. The cook then cuts open the monkey's head and exposes the living, warm brain. Diners then use spoons to eat the brain and the fresh brain is said to be very nutritious."

Cruelty to animals has a long history in China. "Rich people in ancient times used to put live ducks onto hot iron plates and the ducks end up dancing themselves to death. The diners then eat the meat on the ducks' feet because it was said to be much more delicious than the meat of ducks cooked in the ordinary way" said media.

China has many cruelly-prepared dishes. One is called 'the three squeaks.' This dish consists of live baby mice, and its name comes from the fact they squeak first when picked up by the diner's chopsticks, second when dipped in sauce, and third when placed in the mouth and bitten.

Media also noted that while some people were kinder to animals, this could "stem from a fear of being punished if animals are treated badly" because "Buddhism encourages people not to eat animals since … after death, people may become animals themselves." [874] It is fear of religious retribution that may dictate positive treatment of animals rather than the natural expression of kindness itself.

China does have laws to protect its endangered species, though like so many laws in the country they carry little judiciary weight, the result of which leaves rare animals hunted for food in an age of grocery stores and supermarkets.

A nationwide campaign called Spring Thunder in 2003 saw Chinese police inspect nearly 16,000 animal fairs and 67,800 hotels and restaurants across the county. During the inspection, which lasted just nine days, 838,500 endangered animals were confiscated, saved from China's kitchens. About 45,000 of them were wildlife with first-class state protection.[875]

In 2007, demand for wild and exotic animals on the dinner table was still high. Thirteen people were sentenced to up to 14 years in prison after they were found guilty of illegally buying and selling thousands of state-protected wild animals in the largest wild animal trade case the country had seen, said media. One man, Ma Weihu, illegally bought about 900 owls, a Grade-II state protected animal, to sell to restaurants in southern Guangdong Province.[876]

That same year, police were involved in more than 172,000 cases "involving the destruction of wildlife and forest resources, and rescued about 1.5 million wild animals from poachers" said media in July 2008.[877]

Of these cases, 175 involved endangered species. Though this dropped to 87 cases in 2008, the overall trend in recent years has been upwards. "Illegal wildlife trade is alive and dynamic," said Xu Hongfa, director of the World Wildlife Fund's (WWF) East Asia Program. "We have noticed an increasing amount of trade and consumption in wildlife, including bear paws, tortoises, pangolins and monitor lizards," he said.[878]

But even as one branch of China's government was trying to increase the people's respect for rare wildlife, another branch was pandering to the fashion for eating it. China's State Forestry Administration gave permission to one distillery to farm tigers to make a special 'strength-giving' wine with their bones, and allowed another restaurant to serve dishes made of farmed Chinese alligators. Only around 50 tigers exist in China's wilderness, while only 150 wild alligators survive.[879]

By 2010, the number of tigers thought to exist in the wild in China had dropped to just 20. Chinese officials denied this was linked to the legitimization of tiger-based products created by the dozen tiger farms operating in the nation. Yin Hong, deputy director of the State Forestry Administration, said that "disappearing natural habitat and cross-border illegal trade are major causes, rather than the farms."

Ge Rui, Asian Regional Director of the International Fund for Animal Welfare, said "The existence of tiger farms and increasing illegal trade in tiger products is seriously threatening this precious species. In the Year of the Tiger, we should be doing more."

And 2010 being the Year of the Tiger according to the traditional Chinese calendar has only intensified demand for tiger products. The words of doctors such as Yue Debo, who has worked at the China-Japan Friendship Hospital for more than 20 years and says tiger bone wine "..is the same as other medicinal wines - it doesn't have any miraculous effect" do little to change attitudes.

Even China's zoos brought bad news for tigers. Thirteen tigers starved to death at a zoo in Liaoning Province, and their bones were used in medical products, in direct contravention of Chinese law. The zoo in question, Shenyang Forest Wild Animal Zoo, had been making such products since 2005. These products were often given as bribes to visiting officials and inspectors.

The background to this story exerts a grisly fascination as well as insight into how corruption infects so many areas of Chinese life. A decade ago, the zoo was state owned. But then a corrupt official, Mu Suixin, sold and 85% stake in the zoo to a private entrepreneur. This entrepreneur used zoo income to pay his own debts, meaning the zoo could not afford to pay its staff or look after its animals correctly.

That's why *fifty* tigers - as well as many other animals - died at the zoo between the takeover and 2010. The zoo had so little money that its tigers were fed on chicken bones, since meat was too expensive. It was even alleged that zoo staff, angry that their wages had not been paid, purposely let the tigers starve in a bid to exert pressure on the government to step in and pay the missing salary.

Among the other dead animals at the zoo were one red-crowned crane, four stump-tailed macaques, one rhesus monkey and one brown bear, all under state protection. Along with these deaths were four camels, one African lion, one yak, one ostrich, one springbok, one dalmatian, and one Mongolian horse. [880]

Bear bile is also keenly sought after for medicinal purposes in China by practitioners of traditional Chinese medicine. In 2005 media reported that there were about 7,000 bears on more than 200 farms in China. The bears are restrained and catheterized to drain the bile from inside their bodies.

"Bear farmers are exploiting, barbarically treating, and killing China's ... highly endangered species," said Jill Robinson, chief executive of Animals Asia Foundation. "There exists no humane method of bile extraction from bears on farms in China - and there never can be. The government is being deceived by those who are driven by profit alone - and have put economics ahead of ethics," she said.[881]

The government reaction to international outcry over this appalling animal cruelty was to deny there was a problem at all. "Approved bear farms will continue to exist in China for the time being, as painlessly-extracted bile is crucial for medical purposes" said Wang Wei, deputy chief of the Department of Wildlife Conservation under the State Forestry Administration in early 2006. "Before we find good alternatives for bear bile, we do not have a timetable to eliminate the practice."

According to the Animals Asia Foundation, which, along with other animal welfare projects, works to enhance public awareness of cruelty to bears, "Chinese medical practitioners stress that all bear bile products can be easily replaced by herbal or synthetic alternatives, which are cheaper, more readily available and just as effective."[882]

Wang, apparently, disagrees. "Bear bile, considered an indispensable ingredient in traditional Chinese medicine, is used in 123 drugs and has an efficacy not matched by any other substitute," media quoted him as saying. "The cruel farming practice has basically been abolished."

Wang also sounded the common cry of Sino-spite. "Some organizations or individuals are still using old videos or photos of illegal farms to exaggerate the current situation. This distorts the facts and misleads donors into providing money," he said, thus suggesting that those who simply wanted to alleviate the vast suffering of the bears were either dupes or operating out of anti-China sentiment.[883]

A more realistic appraisal of the situation would therefore suggest that the government is not being 'deceived' but that it simply does not care about animal welfare. Certainly, to judge by the 'National Animal Olympics' held in 2006 in Shanghai, the official view of animals is that they are simply a source of profit and entertainment.

"Over 300 animal athletes took part in the opening competitions" at the 'Olympics' said state media. "Among the featured events were boxing bears, a bicycle race involving monkeys, bears and humans and a monkey climbing competition. The competitions will continue over the next two months with events ranging from track and field to soccer. More than 30 species of animals on teams from 26 Chinese provinces and cities will take part."[884]

Nor it is just tigers, bears, and monkeys that are made to perform for the amusement of China's people. Media in 2006 reported, seemingly approvingly, about a man in Henan Province who had taught a myna bird to smoke. Printing a picture of the bird with its owner holding a cigarette to the animal's beak, the caption read, in part, "The owner said the bird regularly likes to smoke after it learned from him. It is now addicted."[885]

While China's laws on endangered species are clearly ineffectual, the country also does not have a single law ruling against animal cruelty. None. "(Animal abuse) cannot be tackled with public opinion or moral pressure, it's time for legislation," said Mang Ping, assistant professor with the Central Socialist Academy, and a long-time advocate for animal rights in China.[886]

It was not until mid-2009 that an animal cruelty law was even proposed. The draft of this law suggested a fine of up to about US$900 and two weeks' detention for animal cruelty. It also proposed banning pet owners from breeding their pets.

This draft, however, is not part of China's current legislative agenda, meaning it will not even be considered until 2013.[887] And even then it might take another decade before such a law could be fully implemented, said Chang Jiwen, a researcher at the Chinese Academy of Social Sciences who is leading a panel of experts on the draft.[888]

Given the apparent almost total disregard for animal welfare in China, combined with the lack of law and the inevitable need for several re-writes should any relevant law be implemented, Mang Ping will likely have to call for action for many years yet.

Kindness to all animals does not indicate a great nation, just a civilized one.

Reason 29
Blue China Crime

The streets of Shanghai are easy. Roadways are filled with private cars (or company cars used privately) in flash colors. Figuratively, you could call it 'fat city,' and judging from the size of its people it's growing literally too.

Still, the women are fine, well-dressed and well-educated. The men are confident, with an air of success about them. In hand the latest mobiles abound, accoutrements of the good life.

Retail stores are full of gorgeous stuff. Gold, platinum, diamonds, and luxury watches sparkle within easy reach. From French lingerie to Italian leather goods you can buy it here in 'Rich City.'

Good jobs fill pockets with cash. Bags of it - all carried on arms by the chic women, under arm in man bags by Chinese metro men.

On the week-ends nobody is home. Almost everyone is out - shopping. Buying more stuff to decorate themselves or their child or their 'house,' which is the word they use instead of 'home' to describe the high-rise apartment they have purchased, usually after just a few years of work.

Let's eat! There are thousands of choices at upscale restaurants and eateries. Don't be shy, dig in – but be sure to leave plates of half eaten exotic dishes. Leaving food so that it can be thrown away is the style of folks in Shanghai, where the sentiment is "We can afford to order whatever food we want…and then look…we are rich enough not to care if we eat it or not."

Cool.

Even cooler if you own a dog and the smaller the quivering, whimpering, excuse for a canine it is, the better to display conspicuous consumption designed to make your neighbor envious, or your grandparents wince.

In the countryside they still eat dogs. (Granny probably cooked up a few in her day). Here in the big town, matrons spend more on their pet dogs than the average Chinese farmer earns per year. And sometimes the unfortunate pooch is better dressed.

Shanghai has it all. And it is all here waiting to be picked up, grabbed, stolen, robbed and burgled. It is easy on the streets of Shanghai.

Now Shanghai is remarkably safe. The Shanghainese are still the 'special ones' of China. They still get the added respect from criminal elements from other parts of China that affords them an additional layer of protection, something the folks in booming cities like Shenzhen across from Hong Kong no longer have.

In Shenzhen if they want your purse but you hang onto it too tightly, they might just cut your arm off.

But even as residents here in Shanghai for over 20 years, the authors have not been touched by it, or even really seen it. Sure, a pick pocketed wallet and a pinched mobile phone, both lost more from carelessness than to an exercise of someone's criminal ability - but real crime? It's best to watch the late night local TV news to see that.

Real crime, the violent multiple murder, gang rapes, smash and grab B&Es and the gun in your face "Give your money, jewelry and the dog" while you walk home from work in the evening light kind of crime, has not yet touched this city of rich folks.

But the bad guys are coming sure enough. And the young ones are in training.

Blue China Crime forms the most fearful element of the 4th Army of Instability. In the end, the White and Red elements of the 4th Army may cause more financial long term harm, but it is the physical nature of the Blue Army that paralyzes most people with fear.

Big city Shanghai, with a population of 18.5 million by the end of 2006, nearly six million of them migrant workers, does have crime – and it's growing, as it is all through China.[889]

The share of crime the Shanghainese people will get has yet to be decided by the criminals. But just how many will be caught, judged and convicted is certainly up to the government and its law enforcement agencies.

In early 2007, three different government agencies released crime statistics for 2006 – the courts, the police, and the Ministry of Public Security. Understanding crime trends and the statistics of law enforcement in China is no easy task.

Here's the count for Blue China Crime:

On January 17th 2007, statistics released by China's Central Committee for Comprehensive Management of Public Security said China's police solved 1.947 million criminal cases in 2006. Police authorities investigated 484,000 'serious' crimes, which were defined as arson, robbery, homicide, rape and kidnapping.

On February 7th 2007, the Ministry of Public Security (MPS) announced their own crime figures at a regular press conference. They said the total number of criminal cases reached 4.65 million.

The 'serious' crime cases within the statistics provided by the MPS broke down into 782 explosion cases, 18,000 murder cases, 502,000 robbery cases, 6,701 arson cases and 32,000 rape cases. That's a total 559,384 'serious' crimes (kidnapping figures were not provided.)

On 13th March 2007, it was the turn of Xiao Yang, president of the Supreme People's Court, to reveal his counts at the Fifth Session of the Tenth National People's Congress.

He said local courts at all levels in China heard 798,572 criminal cases, which included 245,254 'serious' crimes, defined (like above) as explosion, murder, robbery, rape and kidnapping. In the process of trying these, the courts locked away 340,715 criminals.

262

Various percentages of increases and decreases indicating various levels of success were given along with all three statistical reports. However, there are a number of worrying discrepancies in the figures given. Such discrepancies may cause concern for citizens of a city like Shanghai, with their false sense of safety.

The February 7th figures indicate 559,384 'serious' cases were dealt with by police, while the March 13th court-released report indicated 245,254 'serious' crimes were dealt with. This leaves 314,130 cases involving 'serious' crimes, undoubtedly committed by real criminals, still pending.

The January 17th police report indicates 484,000 'serious' crimes were investigated in 2006 (not including kidnapping), which is a shortfall of 75,384 compared with the figure given in the February 7th report.

The above figures do not include gang crime, drug trafficking, prostitution, gambling, embezzlement, and bribery.

Of note also is that while in the January 17th report police say they solved 1.947 million criminal cases in 2006, the February 7th report by the MPS indicated the total number of criminal cases reached 4.653 million.

None of the above totals includes the 292 judges who were found to have abused power for personal interest, and subsequently, 109 were given criminal penalties.

The March 7th court reports mentioned that they had pronounced 1,713 criminal defendants innocent, 'following the principle of meting out penalty to the guilty and setting the innocent free in time in accordance with the law.' [890]

1,713 criminal defendants innocent out of 340,715 convictions! That's 0.5027%.

On January 17th China's Central Committee for Comprehensive Management of Public Security said "the general social security situation is stable."

Bao Suixian, deputy head of the Public Security Management Bureau under the Ministry of Public Security, said "A great number of disputes and unharmonious elements exist in China. In the face of such pressure, it is impossible to rely solely on the 1.8 million-strong police to maintain stability in a country with 1.3 billion people. Police forces need more manpower."[891]

Whatever the true crime figures are, it is certainly true that the number of criminals at large represents a dangerous element disrupting the economic and social stability of the country.

To this must be added a new specter entering the criminal society of China – the youth factor. Disadvantages in the economy are attracting a great number of adolescents to the crime game.

The 7th February report said China's police had arrested 679,000 juvenile criminal suspects in 2006.[892]

Even worse, on May 31st, 2007 an official with the Supreme People's Procuratorate released figures showing China arrested 92,574 underage criminals in 2006, a 33% rise from 2003.

A Procuratorate official also said that between 2000 and 2006, more than 430,000 people under the age of 18 were convicted on criminal charges.

About one in ten of all criminals prosecuted in 2006 was underage, said the Procuratorate, adding that there was a visible increase in gang crimes. "This is a major issue which endangers social stability," said the official. [893]

The lack of a focused understanding by different enforcement agencies and social help societies within China is causing hundreds of thousands of young people to fall through the net of social care, vastly increasing the number of recruits for the 4th Army.

Chinese society at large seems to be confused about what causes juvenile crime. In 2006 they blamed the internet. "In a high proportion of robbery, sexual assault and fraud cases involving young people, the internet is a factor," said Wu Heping, the MPS spokesman.

However, a report by the China National Children's Center in 2006-07 gave other reasons for this huge number of juvenile criminals. The report blamed broken families, a lack of ethical education at school and negative influence by 'bad guys.' The center said that only 16.8% of these children had finished China's nine years of 'compulsory' education.

It also said the average age of young criminals was 15.7 years.[894]

Amazingly, back in 2004, even smoking was blamed for much juvenile crime. More than 95% of juvenile delinquents apparently started their lives of crime because of smoking, explained Chinese media at the time.[895]

China, a country that often professes its modesty, its calmness, has its own demons to slay. Rapidly following the path of developed countries, China's list of serial and mass killers grows ominously.

Recent well-publicized attacks on schoolchildren while at lessons, families, and company employees titillate Chinese news readers at a far too regular rate.

In southwestern Guizhou Province in November 2006, a magistrate, Wen Jiangang, his wife, his son, his sister-in-law, his mother-in-law and even his nursery maid were all murdered. Police rapidly arrested 42-year-old Cao Hui, announcing he had murdered Wen and his family purely for money. Yet other swirling rumors suggested that since Wen had been in charge of closing down illegal mines in the area, it might have been resentful mine owners who arranged his killing.[896]

The same month that Wen was killed also saw the murder of a restaurant owner and three of his relatives in Dongguan city in Guangdong Province.

The month after, December 2006, saw the murder of a family of five in southern Guangdong Province's Foshan city. Among the dead were a seven-year old boy and his mother. The mother, surnamed Cai, was alleged to have had a poor relationship with customers of the restaurant and drugstore the family owned, leading to speculation this might have been a revenge killing. But it later turned out the father had committed the murders, also killing one of his customers thus bringing the total number of dead to six.[897]

Also in December 2006, another magistrate, Chen Yiming, was murdered along with his wife, seven-year-old grandson and housemaid in northwest Gansu Province.[898]

Another family of six was murdered in southern Guangdong Province in May 2007, after burglars forced their way into a home and made the home owner open the safe. After taking the contents of the safe the burglars killed everyone present, including four children, the youngest of whom was four years old.[899]

Between January and July 2008 a 37-year-old named Li Dexin murdered five people and raped eight women in the country's northeastern Liaoning and Jilin provinces.[900]

In July 2008, Yang Jia, a 28-year-old man, murdered six policemen in Shanghai. He was angry that he had been stopped by the police and questioned for riding an unlicensed bicycle in October 2007.[901]

In 2009, a man named Shi killed five members of his girlfriend's family, because they did not approve of his relationship with her. The same year, Li Lei hacked to death his parents, two children, wife and sister, and Liu Aibing killed 13 with guns and arson. In addition Zhang Chengyu killed five women and an eight-year old boy in the city of Changsha, and Li Zhongquan killed four in the city of Wuhan.[902]

In February 2010, Zhu Caifa used a knife and ax to kill seven members of his own family. The same month, Zhang Yimin stole his employer's bus and drove it through the streets of Tianjin, deliberating targeting pedestrians, killing nine. In May that year, Zhou Yezhong, 36, killed eight people, among them his mother, wife and daughter, using a knife to commit the murders.[903]

Not all killings reach the press. In some small villages where nightmares have actually become reality, there are only rumors of what happened.

According to Ministry of Public Security spokesman Yu Xinmin, mass killings in 2006 were 63% lower than in 2005. In the same report, a professor at the Chinese People's Public Security University, Li Meijin, said that "In a big country such as China, 10 mass murders a year is relatively low."[904]

With the acceptance of such figures, does this mean that mass-murder is a tradition in China?

It is the growing number of Blue China Crime footsoldiers that will form the largest element of the 4th Army of Instability. Whether adults now or juveniles doomed to a future life of crime, these are a troop of brigands with allegiance to no one, and will cause fear in the public's mind, especially those citizens who have the compulsion to display riches far in excess of average.

The 4th Army of Instability has as its center the Blue China Crime troops, fired by the furnace of economic disparity, disadvantage and despair which can neither help them catch up nor persuade them to wait for the trickle-down theory to give them the good life.

The Fallibility of Chinese Characters

Mr. Luo: "My grandfather never learned to read or write. My father didn't learn. And I have never learned either. What is the point? I am a farmer. I need to understand plants and animals, not reading or writing."

Ms. Wang. "Most people in my village can't read or write. We've never had a school there, and the nearest school is too far and too expensive for most people. I wanted to go there but my parents didn't think it was worth spending money on me because I was a girl. I want to learn to read, but I do not know who can help me."

The Chinese definition of literacy is the ability to read and write at least 1500 Chinese characters.

In 1949, when 'New China' was founded, the illiteracy rate was more than 80%. By 1992, 22.3% of adults in China were illiterate. Ten years later, that proportion had dropped to 8.72%.

While 8.72% seems relatively small, that translates into a total of 85 million illiterate people in China at the beginning of this century. Twenty million of them were between the age of 15 and 50, with 70% of the total number of illiterate people being women.[905]

In 2002, state media reported that the government had set a target of "wiping out illiteracy among grown-ups" by 2005. Major efforts would be made to promote the literacy drive in poverty-stricken areas, regions inhabited by minorities and among women, said Wang Dai, an education ministry official said in 2002.[906]

Two years later, in 2004, Chinese Education Minister Zhou Ji said China would reduce the youth illiteracy rate in western provinces to below 5% by the end of 2007. Zhou said that China would allocate more funds from the central budget in partial payment for approximately 60% of the local rural educational expenditure and 78% of local teachers' salaries.[907]

Also in 2004 China's Prime Minister, Wen Jiabao, took advantage of China's National Teachers' Day on September 10th to announce that "Education is of fundamental importance to the fulfillment of China's long-range missions."

"Only when education is available to everyone, can social equality be achieved and quality of the citizens improved," he said, pledging his government to ending illiteracy and ensuring education for all children within five years.[908]

China's leaders often take national problems as opportunities to make ineffectual but rhetorically grand statements that are in fact no more than photo-opportunities to maintain the image that the Party is solving the people's problems.

Despite China's huge recent economic expansion and the country's trillion-dollar plus foreign reserves, the total amount of money allocated per year since 2000 to fight and eliminate illiteracy among 85 million people was just eight million yuan (US$1.03 million). Wen Jiabao's 'fundamental importance' of education was worth a paltry 0.07 yuan per person, an amount that would certainly not buy a book of lessons, nor even a pencil or one single sheet of paper to write on.[909]

Small wonder then that by 2007 the number of illiterate people had not dropped -- it had risen. Since official figures were released after China's last census in 2000, giving a base of 85 million illiterate people, China has experienced an increase in illiteracy equal to the entire population of Canada -- 30 million people – becoming unable to read or write. Today, 116 million people are unable to meet China's definition of literacy.

Although not all would do so, each and every citizen of these 116 million people is denied the opportunity to unleash their potential, both for self and country, simply through the malaise of illiteracy.

In order to put the size of these figures into perspective, in the year 2000, 11.3% of all illiterate people on the planet lived in China. Incredibly, by 2005, that total had risen to 15%.

With the limited funds allocated to eradicating illiteracy, and a government unwilling to confront the problem, the pressure becomes critical. Yet government solutions are intensely localized and seldom reflect on the immediacy required to reverse a growing problem.

Behind the massive failure in China's commitment to reducing illiteracy, there is a complex story of missed targets, opportunities and solutions.

With the initial illiteracy reduction campaign focusing on China's poor western areas, at that time home to 50% of China's illiterate people, the government crowed about positive results, indicating that overall illiteracy dropped where their energies had been focused.

However, the government's insistence on regional focus results in only regional patchwork solutions. While these satisfy some basic targets and are used to announce the success of government policies, the lack of attention in maintaining these early victories has led to illiteracy surging in central and eastern provinces.

Why?

Chinese media, quoting Gao Xuegui, Director of the Illiteracy Eradication Office of the Basic Education Department of the Ministry of Education, reported that the reason for the rise in illiteracy was "the changing perception of knowledge in the market economy. Farmers today can earn money by working as laborers, too. So they tend to ignore the nine-year compulsory education despite having access to it."

268

China's get-rich-quick attitude is not confined to its cities alone, and the nation's growing status as the workshop of the world means there are lots of jobs on offer for which education is not a prerequisite. "Why spend nine years in school when you can earn money right now?" some would say. It's a case of young people in particular not even 'dropping in' before they can 'drop out.'

Gao also said that one of the reasons illiteracy had begun to rise again was that many local governments closed down their illiteracy-reduction departments, believing the fight against it has been won. In this case, the photo-opportunities claiming victory in various programs proved too compelling to not be believed.

With the Illiteracy Office still receiving a paltry US$1.03 million a year in 2007, the government was in fact guaranteeing that literacy continued to fall. The actual figure quoted by Gao as needed to do the job was almost US$13 million.[910]

China did, however, find enough money to establish the UNESCO Confucius Prize for Literacy back in 2005, which offered an annual fund of US$150,000 and a US$20,000 top prize.[911] This, declaimed Chinese media, quoting the very same Gao Xuegui who two years later had to beg for enough funding to do his job, "demonstrated its total commitment to eradicating illiteracy."[912]

The funding for the Confucius Prize for Literacy ironically came from the government of China's northeastern Shandong Province, which is today one of the epicenters of illiteracy, with nearly 10 million people unable to meet China's basic educational standards. [913] The high-level UNESCO profile has allowed Shandong's politicians the chance to strut on the world stage, while in fact eradicating illiteracy is losing ground on a daily basis.

Another key problem faced by China's millions of poor and mainly rural residents is an inability to speak Putonghua, or Mandarin Chinese. This has been the official language of the country since 1956, though even today China has about 80 languages and major dialects currently in use. While all of China uses the same set of written characters, its different regions pronounce these characters in very different ways. Traditional Chinese people are loath to change their spoken tongue, but for millions of people the unifying act of being able to write is missing, resulting in the inability of people from one area being able to communicate with people from another area.

A full 40% of Chinese people cannot speak Mandarin and, once again, it is the countryside population rather than the city elite who suffer. The isolating factor of speaking only your own dialect in a country of 1.3 billion people fractures the very nationhood of China.

Ms. Liu: "I had to leave school at 14, since my parents could not afford the fees. To help support my brother at school I traveled south to look for work. But I couldn't understand what the people there said, and they could not understand me, so I had to come back home. Now I work in my home city but I cannot earn enough to support my brother. He might have to stop going to school also."

Yuan Zhongrui, director Ministry of Education's Putonghua Popularization Department, says that "people who cannot speak Putonghua are mainly those with little education, or the illiterate, and most of them are rural residents" Chinese media reported in 2005. [914]

This mosaic of language prevents the government from giving a clear message of unity to all citizens. In addition, the inability to speak a common language, combined with the inability to read and write, dooms China's poor citizens to a life of very few opportunities.

If they chose to leave the impoverished areas in which they live in search of jobs they would basically become foreigners with no way to communicate through language, even though still citizens in their own country.

Should the boom times end and the energy of the peaceful development of China dwindle, the compulsion to learn spoken Mandarin and learn the skill of writing Chinese characters would be even less important, allowing cultural differences of language to increase, further fracturing the Chinese nation.

Illiteracy is a weapon against nationhood.

Reason 31
The Poison Pill of Democracy

Democracy is bitter medicine, and for some political regimes it is difficult to make them take it. As a medicine, democracy protects the individual and grants immunization against party politics. Like all medicines, democracy contains many negative side-effects, yet also provides the individual with a basis in which to survive and grow strong.

Usually, democracy can be delivered into the political system in many different ways – an internal fight for freedom by its citizens, throwing off a colonial harness, or perhaps the result of a large-scale war. Most democracies are not born easily.

A more unique method of injecting democracy into a totalitarian or communist state would be in the form of a 'poison pill.' The system of a country where the individual's civil liberties are restricted may cause government leaders to underestimate the power of the democratic medicine they are about to receive.

Today, there are two doses of democracy available, waiting to be delivered into the system of Chinese politics.

They are Hong Kong and Taiwan.

China obviously views the medicine of democracy as a 'poison pill.' In practical terms, China could long ago have dominated Hong Kong, not waiting for the British to release their hold. And since they have not signed a formal peace agreement with Taiwan, there exists a technical state of war that could be escalated at any time. But China has chosen not to take either of these steps.

Currently, Hong Kong is a limited democracy, and its freedoms are closely monitored and often controlled by Beijing. Since Hong Kong was returned to China in 1997, Beijing has imposed its own interpretation on the city's basic law three times, and critics say the city's media has engaged in self-censorship to please Beijing.[915] The Party resists the pressure of democracy within Hong Kong in a cat-and-mouse game designed to keep the people of Hong Kong waiting. The Party knows that they only have approximately 40 more years to wait until the 50 years timeframe of guaranteed political autonomy for Hong Kong has expired, whereupon a smile will return to the faces of Party bosses as they tell the world 'things change' and end any hint of democracy in the former colony.

If Hong Kong were to achieve full democracy, could a Hong Kong citizen travel to Beijing on June 4th to commemorate the anniversary of the Tiananmen Massacre, exercising his or her democratic freedoms? Could a Hong Kong democratic political activist use his or her freedoms to set up a democratic political party in another major city in China? Or could a Hong Kong journalist ask a party politician a question which may reveal 'state secrets'?

271

Cleary the answer is 'No.' Beijing could not tolerate any of these scenarios. This is why, in the opinion of the authors, Hong Kong will never be granted full democracy by Beijing.

It is surprising that the British, with all their colonial history and all their experience of foreign affairs, did not realize that Hong Kong would never become democratic simply because the medicine of democracy is far too strong for the Communist system to take in and digest.

Once the body ingests the 'poison pill,' democracy will achieve a virus-like replication, city after city, a process that the government will attempt to choke off.

Presently the excuse for the lack of movement towards universal suffrage in Hong Kong is based on an inability of the Hong Kong people to focus on both democracy and the economy at the same time. Beijing will enforce Hong Kong's focus on its economic stability, not the instability of individuals seeking democracy.

Allowing Hong Kong to formalize its democratic notions may cause other major cities in China to demand democracy, but these would remain small-scale calls relative to an entire province demanding true political freedom.

However, should Taiwan be taken back with its political system intact, the situation would be profoundly dangerous for China. Other 'autonomous regions' such as Xinjiang, Tibet and Inner Mongolia would see democracy of Taiwan and demand the same for themselves. China's system of provinces, fractured by democracy, would collapse in on itself, with the Communist Party unable to stop the democratic leaks in the dikes as democracy starts to 'cure' the Party's previous indiscretions.

Taiwan, aside from being the largest democratic poison pill for China, may thus also be viewed as a democratic silver bullet.

But slaying the often-demonized communist Party of China with one 'shot' of democracy is simply not going to happen. The attempt by the Beijing government to force other countries to kowtow, accepting the 'One China Policy,' is mere bluster. China seeks validity for its policy of reunification in order to legitimize any untoward action such as war in the Taiwan straits.

China's present view of former and current democratically-elected leaders of Taiwan gives an indication that Beijing will resist the medicine to the last.

When former Taiwan president Lee Teng-hui spoke of "One nation, two states" in regard to the Taiwan-China situation, Chinese media labeled him as "scum of the nation." He was also "the number one filth of the nation," said Chinese media, "but those who uphold unity and oppose divisiveness will prosper and those who resist this historic trend will perish."[916]

Long after Lee had left power, he was still being vilified by the Chinese media. In 2007 he visited Japan's Yasukuni Shrine, where his only brother is among the 2.5 million dead commemorated. Lee described the trip as a "private, family event," and the Japanese Chief Cabinet Secretary said it would not comment on "the actions of a private individual."

The Taiwanese Foreign Minister said "Mr. Lee is now a civilian. We respect his personal decision, and this has nothing to do with the government."

Beijing, however, had no respect for Mr. Lee. The trip, said Chinese media, was 'evidence' of Lee's "ugly face as a separatist favoring 'Taiwan Independence.'"[917]

When prominent Taiwan businessmen Hsu Wen-lung spoke in favor of pro-independence politicians, Chinese media reacted with fury, using racist jibes to belittle him. "Hsu does not speak Mandarin; instead he likes to talk with others in Taiwan local twang or Japanese" said People's Daily, implying that only the Han language is the language of civilization. The media also sneered at his business success, saying that "In fact, the Taiwan businessmen who support 'Taiwan Independence' often play some hidden tricks in order to make profits from the Chinese Mainland."

People's Daily also quoted an unnamed businessman who said "Making money in the Chinese Mainland, but supporting 'Taiwan Independence,' is just unreasonable."[918]

Previous Taiwan leader Chen Shui-Bian has also received endless amounts of abuse and snide commentary. He is "a troublemaker and saboteur" who has "evil motives."[919]

The former vice-president, Annette Lu, was said to have "exposed her true hideous face of an extremist and incurable Taiwan independence agitator." She was also "the number-one scum of the Chinese nation."[920]

This rhetoric is backed up the direct threat of violence, should the Taiwanese people go too far in determining the course of their own future and embracing the democracy they so actively enjoy.

China fails to understand that Taiwan simply does not view itself as a colony, as is the case with Hong Kong and Macau. Indeed, most Taiwan people identify themselves as 'Taiwanese' rather than purely Chinese.

Speaking of the possibility of Taiwan declaring independence, People's Liberation Army Major General Peng Guangqian said that "If Taiwan separatists want to gamble on it (by pushing for independence), they will pay a heavy price and be defeated with shame."

China says its most important goal is reunification. This matters more than any other single problem, even the huge ones we have discussed in this book. The Party says it is willing to lose WTO membership, international investment and, naturally, the lives of its soldiers, to regain the 'renegade province.' It even said it was willing to lose the Olympic Games, despite the billions of dollars it was spending in preparation for the games at that time.[921]

Even more explicitly, China promulgated the 'Anti-Secession Law' in 2005 which stated that if Taiwan did declare independence then China would 'employ non-peaceful means and other necessary measures to protect China's sovereignty and territorial integrity.'

More worryingly, the law also allowed 'non-peaceful' means if it was determined that 'possibilities for a peaceful reunification should be completely exhausted' – meaning that China could simply decide the possibilities were exhausted and use this as a pretext for 'legal' invasion.[922]

The 'Anti-Secession Law' states 'the Taiwan question is one that is left over from China's civil war of the late 1940s,' showing how Beijing is only able to see this situation in historical terms, with no regard for the present situation. Taiwan's achievement in reaching democracy within 50 years of that date – something China has never had in its oft-touted '5000 years of history' - is simply an irrelevancy to the Communist Party.

How history finally tells the story of Taiwan and China can be logisticized today into seven possibilities:-

1. China launches all-out war and destroys Taiwan. The political fallout of such an action would be extreme. China would be ostracized by the world. There would be severe damage to the country's trade and industry as overseas capital fled the nation. Many countries would reject trade with China, harming its domestic industries, and many countries would refuse to accept Chinese students, thus damaging the country's future in intellectual, academic and creative terms. The Taiwanese military response would inflict major damage on China's infrastructure, and the possible use of nuclear arms could lay waste to the environment for decades. This would also involve other sovereign nations, thus widening the scope of the war. The people of Taiwan would be annihilated.

2. The military nightmare for China would be if Taiwanese forces succeeded in making inroads of victory against the unwieldy, uncoordinated and inexperienced forces of China's People's Liberation Army. In this scenario, joined by other sovereign nations, successful Taiwanese counter-attacks cause other parts of China (beginning with Tibet and Xinjiang) to rise up against the Communists. All-out war convulses China. Years of turmoil continue the country's history of war followed by political effort and again the 'humiliation' of foreign troops trampling on the body of China. However, this time the armies would be from the UN and defeat for China would offer democracy.

3. China fights a limited drawn-out war with a great loss of men and materiel. A complete hardening of attitudes in Taiwan to China and the Communists. The world would be deeply divided into

two camps, pro-Taiwan and pro-China. Those countries positive towards China would flourish in terms of arms and commodity sales. Those supporting Taiwan would have their own political problems at home relative to citizens' civil disobedience / anti-war protests and the wish to stay out of 'someone else's fight.' The world economy would suffer due to constricted shipping lanes. Imports and exports would suffer, and the reduction in Taiwan's IT industry would cause global economic cooling. An eventual UN-brokered peace treaty leaves both countries back at square one.

4.   China decides to drop its claim to Taiwan and allows the island to formally declare independence. Taiwan gains full democracy and global recognition. In China, this is at first perceived as an inherent loss of face. Yet letting Taiwan declare independence gains immense admiration for China from the rest of the world. The global consensus is that a possible war conflict has been avoided and China, as a great nation, has taken the high road. The world economy booms, Taiwan booms, and China and Taiwan enjoy amicable relations. China remains unaffected by democracy and maintains 'socialism with Chinese characteristics.'

5.   A diplomatic agreement is negotiated under which Taiwan comes back as a full province. The island finally succumbs to the overtures from China, either by force or peace, and decides to reestablish itself as a province of China. As an autonomous region, democracy would soon fade as the power of the CPC would slowly change any constitutional measures previously taken by the Taiwanese people. War is averted, economies boom, but Taiwan's experiment in democracy – the first achieved in all of China's history – dies.

6.   Taiwan comes back under the 'One country, two systems' principle. But Taiwan is not a colony such as Macau or Hong Kong, and to subjugate itself under the 'One country two systems' principle is to imitate the state of being colonial. If Taiwan was genuinely allowed to maintain its democracy in the face of the Communist Party's love of interference, it would be dangerous medicine for China. For China, ingesting a wholly democratic 'state' would cause questions from other provinces as to why they could not have similar democratic elements within their local governments. This particular choice, presently not debated in the Chinese press, is perhaps truly the most dangerous of all the choices for China. Taiwan's democracy as medicine may well 'cure' communism in China.

7. Taiwan rejoins under a different political framework. Taiwan believes that the issue of negotiations with China should be based on state-to-state communication. Much the same as the black sheep of the family, the 'renegade' Taiwan people have established their own house, their own family rules, and their own familial processes, in the very neighborhood of the motherland herself. Should China accept Taiwan as an adventuresome child who has struck out on its own to see what it can become as an adult, then Taiwan remains free to succeed or fail at democracy, maintain its Chineseness, and the Party can refuse democratic medication for a little while longer. This new framework would be 'One people, two countries.'

8. A fantasy solution to the problem would be that China forewent its Communist system and began to follow democracy along the lines of the Taiwanese model. In this situation – once the Taiwanese people were convinced it was a genuine change – Taiwan would reunite with a free, democratic and open society.

Fantasies aside, even though maintaining the status quo is in Beijing's interests now, China is clearly preparing for the day when it backs up its aggressive words with action.

Beijing's expenditure on its military is massive. A report, 'The Military Power of the People's Republic of China 2006,' by America's Defense Intelligence Agency, put China's total military-related spending in 2006 between $70 billion and $105 billion, two to three times the budget Beijing officially announced. The DIA also noted that "Consistent with a near-term focus on preparing for Taiwan Strait contingencies, China deploys its most advanced systems to the military regions directly opposite Taiwan."

The report also said that "In September 2005 the PLA held one large-scale, multi-service exercise that dealt explicitly with a Taiwan invasion. China has conducted 11 amphibious exercises featuring a Taiwan scenario in the past 6 years."[923]

The 2007 report said that "China's near-term focus on preparing for military contingencies in the Taiwan Strait, including the possibility of U.S. intervention, appears to be an important driver of its modernization plans. However, analysis of China's military acquisitions and strategic thinking suggests Beijing is also generating capabilities for other regional contingencies, such as conflict over resources or territory."

"The Defense Intelligence Agency (DIA) estimates China's total military related spending for 2007 could be as much as $85 billion to $125 billion" said the report.[924]

China reacted with anger to this report, saying "China is a peace-loving country which sticks to a path of peaceful development and adopts a defensive national defense policy."[925]

The 2009 edition of the annual report stated, "China's armed forces are rapidly developing coercive capabilities for the purpose of deterring Taiwan's pursuit of *de jure* independence. These same capabilities could in the future be used to pressure Taiwan toward a settlement of the cross-Strait dispute on Beijing's terms while simultaneously attempting to deter, delay, or deny any possible U.S. support for the island in case of conflict."

This report estimated that China's military spending in 2008 was between US$105 billion and US$150 billion. China itself claimed its military budget was US$70 billion.[926]

The US report noted that China's military budget in 2005 was ten times that of 1989, and estimated the 2009 budget would be double that of 2005.[927]

China once again claimed it was no threat to anybody. Li Zhaoxing, spokesman for the second session of the 11th National People's Congress said, "China's limited military force is mainly for safeguarding our sovereignty and territory and poses no threat to any other country."[928] And Huang Xueping, deputy director-general of the Information Office of the Ministry of National Defense, said that "China has always advocated developing military cooperation and relationships based on principles of peaceful coexistence, characterized by non-alliance and non-antagonism."[929]

But the Taiwanese people have never been convinced by China's talk of peace.

"Taiwan people will by no means knuckle under China's mounting military threat" said Yu Shyi-kun, chairman of Taiwan's ruling Democratic Progressive Party, in response to a march by around 100,000 Taiwanese protesting China's continual military threats. Protestors shouted slogans such as "Opposing reunification, protecting democracy!'[930] Taiwanese people feel that they have more to lose politically if they rejoin China than they could ever gain economically.[931]

When James Soong, an opposition politician in Taiwan, was invited to China, a live broadcast of a speech he was giving was suddenly cut off when he referred to Taiwan as 'Republic of China,' rather than maintaining the fiction that Taiwan is part of China. The number of journalists allowed to cover him was reduced from 30 to 10. Chinese media also censored remarks that the trip was a "bridge building visit," again because it suggested Taiwan was not a part of China.

It is interesting to note that while Taiwanese people see that China's refusal to let Taiwanese politicians speak freely clearly demonstrates that Beijing would never allow the nation freedom if it did return, it is simply not apparent to policy makers in the Party.

Likewise, when Chinese envoy Chen Yunlin met current Taiwan leader Ma Ying-jeou in November 2008 in the highest ranking political meeting since 1949, Chen refused to address Ma as 'president' – once again denying any measure of respect to the society and culture of the nation. Chen's visit was accompanied by angry protests from many Taiwanese people who viewed it as setting a dangerous precedent in playing along to China's fiction that Taiwan is a 'rogue province' rather than a nation in its own right.[932] Such fervent expression of political belief would certainly be banned if China did regain control over Taiwan.

Taiwan's people are also Hong Kong watchers. They listen to the words of politicians such as Anson Chan, who was the Chief Secretary of Hong Kong during its handover to China in 1997, a position that made her the second most powerful leader in the city. In June 2007, Chan said she lamented the lack of progress in the ten years since handover. "I don't see any reason ... why Hong Kong people are not ready for universal suffrage" she said in an interview with AFP. Chan said that Beijing should view Hong Kong as a testing ground for democracy and stop holding back reform.[933]

A reminder: according to the Sino-British Joint Declaration on the Question of Hong Kong, signed before the takeover, "The Hong Kong Special Administrative Region Government shall maintain the rights and freedoms as provided for by the laws previously in force in Hong Kong, including freedom of the person, of speech, of the press, of assembly, of association, to form and join trade unions, of correspondence, of travel, of movement, of strike, of demonstration, of choice of occupation, of academic research, of belief, inviolability of the home, the freedom to marry and the right to raise a family freely."[934]

But once again, it is as if China does not understand the words to which it is a formal signatory in the UN-registered document. Speaking in 2007, the Chairman of the Standing Committee of the National People's Congress, Wu Bangguo, said that "Hong Kong's high degree of autonomy is not intrinsic, but authorized by the central government."

"It only has as much power as authorized by the central government. There is no so-called residual power," said Wu. Meaning, of course, the Hong Kong people are not vested with the right to democracy.

Beijing tasted a sample of the bitterness of democratic medicine when, in 2003, it tried to impose an 'anti-subversion law' on Hong Kong. Half a million people – 7% of the city's population -- marched in the streets in protest, making it the biggest protest since the Tiananmen Massacre of 1989.[935]

Though Hong Kong basic law said the city government had to control 'sedition, subversion and treason' the new law would have imposed a Beijing-style stranglehold that would have made its media as tame, timid and scared as the mainland's press. The law would also have required organizations banned in the mainland to be banned in Hong Kong, as well as severely restrict academic and worker freedom.

Only 16% of Hong Kong citizens supported this law, the University of Hong Kong found. [936] The city's Legislative Council, normally pliant due to being stuffed with hand-picked pro-Beijing supporters, revolted.

278

The Party simply failed to understand how citizens used to democratic freedoms think, and, in attempting to engineer a result they sought, Beijing in fact achieved the opposite effect.

While often professing that other nations should 'learn from history' the Party seems to be reluctant to learn from its own past actions. In 1996, when Taiwan was electing a new president, Beijing fired missiles into the Taiwan Straits in an attempt to dissuade the Taiwanese people from choosing the pro-independence candidate Lee Teng-hui. This action not only precipitated an international incident, with the US sending two aircraft carriers to monitor the situation, but also had precisely the opposite effect intended, leading the Taiwanese to rally around Mr. Lee and re-elect him resoundingly.

In 2000, when Chen Shui-bian was running for the presidency, Beijing did not go so far as military action, but instead used fiery rhetoric. "The Chinese people are ready to shed blood and sacrifice their lives to defend the unity of their motherland and the dignity of the Chinese nation" said then-Prime Minister of China, Zhu Rongji.[937]

Such threats perhaps lay behind the narrow victory of Chen Shui-bian, the candidate Beijing least wanted to win.

The Communist system is based on rules that resist reform. The democratic system is based on constant analysis, change and redesign – a work in progress. The words of pro-Beijing Hong Kong lawmakers, such as Elsie Leung Oi-sie, deny the flexible nature of democracy. Speaking in June 2007, Chinese media reported, "Leung admitted that more than 150 years of colonial rule had caused some blur of identity on some people, and that some of them had not a clear sense of identity. It takes time to change, Leung said." [sic].[938]

Ms. Leung's words are especially menacing, in that they suggest that Hong Kong people do not know what is good for them. Ms. Leung tries to suggest that as a result of British rule, Hong Kongers do not properly understand their self-identity.

The challenge of democracy makes a clear sense of identity a flexible, movable and changeable process for every citizen.

Ms. Leung fails to understand that, as with many colonial territories that are now sovereign, 150 of more years of colonial rule increases the desire for democracy, clearly making the identity of the former colony's systems definitively democratic. To suggest, as Ms. Leung does, that Hong Kongers do not properly understand their self-identity is to suggest that they would wish to throw off the shackles of colonialism and don the shackles of communism.

The game of indignation that Beijing plays to perfection masks their awareness that to swallow Taiwan, with all its democratic energy, would poison the communist system beyond recovery.

The problem of self-identity is China's alone. China's politicians feel they are the doctor offering a remedy to post-colonial territories such as Hong Kong and non-colonial splinter territories such as Taiwan, when in fact they are the patient whose system is slowly deteriorating beyond recovery.

Reason 32
China Fat

One of the most remarkable changes that has come in the wake of China's reforms over the last 30 years is in the health of its people.

In 1982, just three years after the opening-up policy began, researchers commented that "Chinese food policy planners are doing much better from a dietary point of view than their Western counterparts, while avoiding problems associated with increased obesity and higher incidence of cardiovascular disease."[939]

In 1985, just 0.2% of urban boys between seven and 18 years old were overweight. By 2006 that figure had risen to an astonishing 25%. That's an increase of more than 100 times.[940]

Yet more than 9% of children five years old or less in China's countryside were underweight in 2005, and in the poorest rural areas, 14.4% were underweight. Furthermore, 17% of rural children were growing more slowly than was normal.[941]

Shanghai is China's fattest city, with 15.1% of boys and 9.2% of girls obese (as opposed to merely overweight), compared to an average of 11.9% for boys and 5% for girls nationwide.[942] One of the reasons that boys are fatter than girls is that boys are still viewed as superior to girls, and thus are spoiled much more by parents, grandparents, aunts and uncles. Nationwide, said media in 2008, 8% of urban Chinese children between the ages of 10 and 12 are obese, while another 15% are overweight.[943] And in October 2008 media said that by 2015, 10% of the entire nation would be obese – and by 2020 60% of the population would not be getting enough physical exercise.[944]

In Beijing, more than 50% of middle school and 60% of high school students have abnormally high blood pressure.[945]

A survey of more than 13 million students found that lung capacity – a key measure of overall health – had fallen by more than 300ml since 2000.[946] To put this into context, the average lung capacity of a six-year-old is about 2100ml and for a 14-year-old about 3600ml.[947]

According to China's Ministry of Health, urban Chinese boys at the age of six are 2.5 inches taller and 6.6 pounds heavier than six-year-old urban kids 30 years ago. They are three feet 10.5 inches tall and weigh, on average, 47 pounds. In America, urban six-year-olds average out at the same height and are just three pounds heavier. China is catching up fast.[948]

In China, the saying that 'A fat child is a healthy child' is still widely believed.[949]

Add to that the rapid decrease in physical exercise and increase in sedentary habits such as watching TV and playing computer games, and you have a sure recipe for weight problems.

Play areas for kids are shrinking in China. Due to the frenzied pace of urban development in the country, many outdoor play areas have been lost, some to development and some to the increasing need for car parking sites. According to a 2007 survey of 2,500 students, 53% of children could only play at home and 45% around their residential areas or in parks, since they lacked proper play areas. Nineteen percent rarely did any exercise because of a lack of facilities.[950]

Children's "joints are seizing up, their muscles are becoming flabby and their movements are uncoordinated due to lack of exercise,' says Mao Zhenming, head of the School of Physical Education and Sports Science at Beijing Normal University.

Yang Guiren, director of the Sports, Health and Arts Department of the Ministry of Education, adds that modern lifestyles, heavily reliant on cars, exacerbate the problem. So does the common use of elevators and escalators, and a general lack of physical labor.[951]

And Wang Xiaobo, a researcher at the Tianjin Academy of Sciences, says that "Many Chinese parents don't like their children to play outside out of worries about worsening road traffic and public security." [952]

China's exam-oriented culture is also part of the problem. Many schools cut short their PE classes, or even cancel them entirely, since they are considered a 'waste of time.' Academic performance matters more than physical fitness. [953]

"Although students have been getting bigger in recent years their physical fitness has deteriorated" says Liao Wenke, deputy director of the Department of Physical, Health and Art Education.

"Many parents and teachers are utilitarian and only care about whether their children can get a decent job and earn good money" says Wang Longlong, a PE researcher with China's Ministry of Education. "The current philosophy in many schools of 'exam results override all' has meant that students are concentrating only on their academic scores and not on their health." [954]

Take Zhuzhu, for example, a 12-year-old Beijing girl. She goes to school for nine hours a day from Monday to Friday, giving her a longer working day than her parents. And at the weekend, when mum and dad can lie in bed, Zhuzhu must attend piano lessons in the morning and English and math lessons in the afternoon, on both Saturday and Sunday.

She is allowed to play with her toys for one hour on Saturday and Sunday evenings. "She will have plenty of time to play after she enters university" says her 42-year-old mother, An Hui.

A survey in 2007 by the Chinese Youth and Children Research Center found Zhuzhu's story was typical. The survey of 2,500 children in China's major cities found increasing numbers of children have unhappy and overworked childhoods, spending on average 8.5 hours a day in school and some up to 12 hours a day. About half the parents interviewed said they often stop their child from playing outside as it leads to less study time, and 60% of children said they had no friends to play with.

More than half the children surveyed said the one thing they wanted more than anything else was 'a good night's sleep.'[955]

Nine-year-old Yang Yifan is another case. He gets up at 6:30am on schooldays, returning home at 5:30pm where he has three more hours of tutoring. At the weekends he gets up at 8am for piano lessons and Chinese painting classes. He is allowed time off on Sunday afternoons. He spends this sleeping since he is so tired, and says that even if he did go to see his friends they would be asleep too.[956]

But while many parents know this, they feel they have no choice. Zhuzhu's mother says, "If she gives up now and doesn't study hard, she will regret it as her future will be lost." And Yang Yifan's father, a university professor, says that "I don't know if it makes any sense for us to work [him] so hard, but it seems we have to do it, just like everyone else does. Because if we don't work hard to get him into a better middle school, other kids will [take his place]. Then they will always have an advantage over our son in choosing a better university, a better job and ultimately a better life."

And when children do get time to play, many of them spend it in front of the TV or playing computer games.

A nationwide survey found that 76% of high school students and 83% of university students were near-sighted.[957] Another survey in Shanghai found that 71% of students also had visual problems, a 9.25% rise from the previous survey in 2000.

"The deterioration, in my view, is due to an epidemic obsession with video games and negligence of eye exercises" said Liu Xin, a director of public health in the city.[958]

"Going to class, doing homework, watching TV and surfing the net is my daily life," says Li Xiao, a 16-year-old Beijing boy. "I only do sports during PE lessons. At the moment we have about two PE lessons a week."[959]

Naturally diet plays a major role in this change. International fast-food giants such as KFC, McDonalds and Pizza Hut must take a large share of the blame.

Yet, shockingly, awareness of the dangers of a high-fat diet does not seem widespread.

According to experts at the Healthcare Institute for Primary and Middle School Students in Taiyuan City, capital of north China's Shanxi Province, parents often believe improved living standards automatically lead to a better diet and healthy growth. They thus allow children to eat high-calorie foods, unaware of the health implications.

Beijing parent Gao Guizhen says that, "My son likes KFC and McDonald's very much and I take him there as a reward for getting good exam marks.... It is so popular among the children.... They should be okay." [960]

Nutritional awareness is extremely low in China. Shanghai, the mainland's most advanced city, has just 100 nutritionists, and many of them are not even certified. A nutrition survey in the city found that less than 40% of children drank milk on a daily basis, and that 8% missed breakfast several times a week. More than 10% of young people are too fat or too thin, and suffer from calcium deficiency or anemia.

"Improper eating and living habits can cause health problems" says one city nutritionist, Cai Meiqin. She said that parents needed to set a good example for their children by keeping good eating habits.

Shanghai planned to have nutritionists in all schools by 2009, compared to 30% now.[961]

The boom in Western-style fast food joints is showing no signs of slowing. KFC, for example, considered dropping its franchise fee from eight million yuan (US$1.04 million) to two million yuan to enhance its plan of opening around 400 branches every year to add to its current total of 1,700.[962] McDonalds also expanded its opening of drive-thru restaurants in the country and began opening some of its branches around the clock. The burger giant currently has 770 stores and plans to open 100 more every year. [963]

One survey placed the Chinese among the world's top five fast-food fans, with 30% eating fast food once or twice a month and 21% once or twice a week. Six percent ate fast food every day, and 3% more than once a day.[964]

But fast food alone is not the whole story. If you walk along almost any major road in a Chinese city in the morning you will pass numerous food vendors selling Chinese-style breakfasts, most of which is deep-fried. 'Ci fan gao,' for example, is a type of deep-fried rice, and 'you tiao' are deep-fried breadsticks. These breakfast vendors also sell a wide range of fried pancakes and doughnuts, as well as dumplings filled with fatty pork.

The pace of life is such in most Chinese cities that there is simply no time for the more traditional, and healthy, sit-down alternatives such as 'zhou,' a type of rice porridge. From primary school children to white-collar workers, breakfast is eaten in the street, on the way to school or work.

"The classical Chinese diet - rich in vegetables and carbohydrates with minimal animal-sourced food - no longer exists," said one study released in 2008.[965]

Even among the older generations, one in five adults can be viewed as overweight, and another one in five suffers from high blood pressure or anemia – in the big cities at least. But more than two-thirds of the 30 million residents in China's poverty-stricken rural areas are short of nutrition, according to a 2005 study by the National Development and Reform Commission.

Diabetes is on the rise too, with one in every 20 diabetes sufferers in Beijing aged 13 or younger.

Yet one wonders if the purpose of this survey was humanitarian or financial, given that the study said, "The problematic nutritional intake of the Chinese may hinder the country's economic development in the long run, and it has to be tackled seriously." [966]

In addition to the dietary risks facing China's youth, the country's tobacco-friendly culture also suggests major health consequences in the coming decades.

Currently China has around 350 million smokers – more people than the entire population of the United States, and between them they smoke 1.7 trillion cigarettes a year. That's one third of all cigarettes smoked annually in the entire world.

The majority of smokers believe that smoking does not have much effect on health. Many even believe it is good for them. And it's easy for children to buy cigarettes, even though it is ostensibly against the law. [967]

Sixty percent of men in China smoke, yet only 4% of women. People over the age of 15 are included in these figures, but of the totals there are more than 100 million smokers under the age of 18. In addition, three million people take up smoking every year. In 2005, 700,000 were dying every year from tobacco related diseases. By 2025 it is estimated that number will rise to 2.5 million deaths a year. [968] A report released in October 2008 put the figures in a broader context, saying that 2.2 million people in China suffered from cancer in 2002, of whom 1.6 million died - and that by 2020 four million people would have cancer. [969]

In 2005, smoking related diseases cost China 250 billion yuan (US$32.5 billion), 10 billion yuan more than the pre-tax profits of the smoking industry.

Just over 166 billion yuan of these costs came from treatment for 23 major diseases caused by smoking, with 86.11 billion yuan eaten up by decreased life span, lost work days, the effects of passive smoking, environmental pollution and smoking-related fires.

A 2008 survey found that smoking among schoolchildren was on the rise, showing that in Beijing, 17% of students had tried smoking, compared to 7% in 2005.

And - almost beyond belief - a 2009 survey found that "one-third of doctors in the country do not know smoking causes coronary heart disease, and nearly four in five do not know passive smoking can cause sudden infant death syndrome." Furthermore, the report said, "three in five smokers do not know that smoking causes heart disease, and four in five do not know it could lead to a stroke." [970]

China's tobacco taxes are low, and for many years were half the world average. More recently the government has increased taxes - by 36% in June 2009, for example - yet this has had almost no impact on sales. In many cases, cigarette manufacturers simply absorbed the increase rather than passing it on, even though those firms are government-controlled. [971]

But once again money trumps public health in China. According to the deputy chief of China's State Tobacco Monopoly Administration, Zhang Baozhen, "restraining smoking threatens social stability."

"Smokers rioted when the former Soviet Union collapsed because they could not get any cigarettes," he said, speaking in March 2007. "The principle applies in China as well."

"As a developing country, China still needs the tobacco industry," Zhang said, noting that tobacco industry contributed 80 billion yuan ($10.33 billion) per day in tax to the country in 2006.[972] Annually, that's about 10% of China's total tax take.

The Chinese government's greed to maximize the profit it makes from harming the health of its own people lies behind a rule change announced that same month banning foreign companies from selling tobacco in China. Major companies like Wal-Mart and Carrefour were ordered to end tobacco sales, and even Chinese-international joint ventures were told to stop. The current tobacco licenses these firms hold run until 2008. They will not be renewed.[973]

It seems the only tobacco habit the government wants to kick is the one that allows others to make money.

The research by the international team of scientists with which this chapter begins concludes by saying:-

"There is much to learn from China, a country that is successfully feeding a billion people primarily on plant derived food, and rapidly making the transition from an agrarian to an industrial society, but so far avoiding much of the major diseases affecting Western countries."

Those words were written more than 15 years ago. It is a profound shame that China has almost wholly squandered this advantage. From what could have been a position of great strength, China has allowed cynicism, greed and disregard for the wellbeing of its citizens to unleash grave problems on society.

Arise, ye who refuse to be slaves;
With our very flesh and blood
Let us build our new Great Wall!
The peoples of China are at their most critical time,
Everybody must roar defiance.
Arise! Arise! Arise!
Millions of hearts with one mind,
Brave the enemy's gunfire,
March on!
Brave the enemy's gunfire,
March on! March on! March on, on![974]

The above words, China's National Anthem, were written by the poet and playwright Tian Han, in 1934.

Tian died like so many of China's other citizens during the 'Cultural Revolution' (1966-1976). "In 1968, Tian Han disappeared after endless torture of being criticized and beaten. He never left a word to anybody. Even his bone ashes couldn't be found. Ten years later, [he] was finally exonerated," following the normal in-and-out of favor process, says the state-run China Radio International.[975]

The music to China's National Anthem was written by Nie Er, originally for a film called "Sons and Daughters in a Time of Storm." Nie was perhaps fortunate to have drowned in a swimming accident in Japan in 1935, likely escaping the torture and brutal beating that led to Tian's death.

When the national anthem was written, the target of 'marching on' was clear – the Japanese armies which had invaded China. It was 'fighting' against the Japanese on which the People's Liberation Army hangs it reputation after being formed in 1927.

But today its goal is less clear, less defined, obscured by military inactivity and often politicized by grand-sounding rhetoric.

• "China's military forces will not serve as a tool for strategic expansion. But that does not mean China does not have the right to or should not develop offensive military capabilities. China's military capabilities must be both offensive and defensive." – Rear Admiral Yang Yi, June 2007.[976]

• The armed forces should "make greater contribution to the building of a harmonious socialist society and firmly safeguard the country... They should also improve [their] capability in safeguarding national security, sovereignty and territorial

287

integrity, while strengthening ties with the lower ranks in terms of boosting democracy and giving more care." – The Central Military Commission of the Communist Party of China, December 2006.[977]

• "China is pursuing a self-defensive nuclear strategy. It remains firmly committed to the policy of no first use of nuclear weapons at any time and under any circumstances. China will not engage in any arms race or pose a military threat to any other country." -- National Defense White Paper, December 2006.[978]

• "The first step [for the PLA] is to lay a solid foundation by 2010, the second is to make major progress around 2020, and the third is to basically reach the strategic goal of building informationized armed forces and being capable of winning informationized wars by the mid-21st century... The PLA ensures that it is well prepared for military struggle, with winning local wars under conditions of informationization and enhancing national sovereignty, security, and interests of development as its objective. -- National Defense White Paper, December 2006.[979]

• The new White Paper "fully embodies the basic concept of China's national defense is to maintain peaceful development. It constitutes China's basic national policy to take the road for peaceful development, to build a harmonious society at home and to spur the construction of a harmonious world globally. So China has to implement its national policy of a defensive nature [for its armed forces] -- Chen Zhou, researcher, Warfare Theory and Strategy Research Department, PLA Academy of Military Sciences.

• [The white paper] increases the transparency of China's defense policy and strategic intention. The purpose in increasing such transparency is to build up mutual confidence between nations. The new white paper enunciates in an open way many aspects with regard to the judgment of security environment, security strategic concepts as well as the country's defense policy and military strategy and effectively refutes the allegation about China's military threat." Says Chen Zhou, a researcher in the Warfare Theory and Strategy Research Department at the PLA Academy of Military Sciences.[980]

• "With the rapid development of information technology, the PLA speeded up its modernization with an increased focus on mechanization and informatization. The PLA has announced that it will reach its goal of building 'informationized' armed forces and be capable of winning informationized wars by the mid-21st century. – People's Daily Feature on PLA 80th Anniversary Celebrations.[981]

• "We will continue to make the utmost effort with the highest sincerity in promoting peaceful development of relations across the Taiwan Strait and strive for the prospect of peaceful reunification. ... We will absolutely not allow Taiwan to secede from China under any pretext or in any manner." – Cao Gangchuan, Chinese Defense Minister, August 2007.[982]

You may have noticed many of these claims are made to convince the world that China's goals are peaceful. Yet these have been undermined by the actions of both China's government and the PLA itself. For example, China passed a law in 2005 which said that if "possibilities for a peaceful reunification should be completely exhausted, the state shall employ non-peaceful means and other necessary measures to protect China's sovereignty and territorial integrity."[983]

But how will it be determined that the "possibilities for a peaceful reunification" have been completely exhausted? With such rhetorically flexible words, China gives itself free reign to interpret the law in any way it likes. China's leaders can simply claim they have determined the possibilities are 'exhausted' and thus invade and overrun its theoretical 'breakaway' province.

The same flexibility is worked into many of the other statements of the PLA's mission.

The Central Military Commission's directive that the PLA should be active in "safeguarding national security, sovereignty and territorial integrity" effectively allows it a politically and militarily free hand. In a nation like China, often quick to claim that negatively perceived everyday events are 'an insult to the Chinese people' or anti-China, many matters can become an issue of sovereignty.

For example, at the end of July 2007, during the final of the Asian Men's Basketball Championship which took place in Tokushima, Japan, the national anthem of Taiwan was played. This infuriated China, which requires that Taiwan be represented as 'Chinese Taipei' using an Olympic flag and demands that any music played for the team must be the Olympic theme.

The Chinese Foreign Ministry subsequently gave the Japanese ambassador in Beijing a stern rebuke, and announced that playing the Taiwanese anthem had "seriously violated the spirits enshrined in the three political documents including Sino-Japanese Joint Statement, and relevant rules of the International Olympic Committee (IOC) about Chinese Taipei's taking part in competitions."

"China expresses strong protest and demands the Japanese side to immediately take effective measures to remove the vile influence and avoid similar events from happening again" said the ministry.

If such a minor indiscretion invokes this level of Sino-spite, imagine the consequences of something more serious, such as an inadvertent incursion into national airspace, an accident in the sea-lanes, or over-zealous troop intrusion during military games.

And how should one interpret China's "unconditional" pledge "not to use or threaten to use nuclear weapons against non-nuclear-weapon states" and its "policy of no first use of nuclear weapons at any time and under any circumstances"? Do the words "not to use or threaten to use nuclear weapons against non-nuclear-weapon states" imply that use of nuclear arms against nuclear states is open and available as part of national policy?

Let us here remind ourselves of the words of PLA general Zhu Chenghu who, in mid-2005, said that if America came to the aid of Taiwan in the event China invaded the country, "I think we will have to respond with nuclear weapons." Zhu said that "We . . . will prepare ourselves for the destruction of all of the cities east of Xian. Of course the Americans will have to be prepared that hundreds . . . of cities will be destroyed by the Chinese."[984]

And it is interesting that while Zhu said these remarks were his personal opinion, and while Beijing said they did not reflect official policy, internal criticism of General Zhu was remarkably limited. A senior general in an army in a developed nation that made such inflammatory remarks would face almost certain demotion, perhaps even forced retirement. Yet General Zhu apparently went unpunished, keeping his post as a head of the College of Defense Studies at China's National Defense University, where he was still making policy pronouncements in 2006 and 2007.

Had Zhu inadvertently slipped out the true national policy, reflecting the imminent destruction of Taiwan, perhaps in 2015-2020? It is very clear that retaking Taiwan is one of the PLA's key goals – a goal it may eventually try to fulfill whether or not political leaders give it permission.

From an international perspective the PLA has other less obvious goals. One centers around East Timor. East Timor – correctly known as Timor-Leste – became an independent nation in 2002. China was the first nation to establish ties with Timor-Leste, surprisingly involving itself in the internal politics of another nation -- which of course is forbidden in its own affairs.

Since then China has directed increasingly large amounts of aid to the poor nation. In 2007 China began work on a Presidential Palace, which it was donating and building entirely free of charge, along with a Foreign Ministry building. One should assume the construction includes the installation of electronic bugging devices.

Su Jian, China's ambassador to the nation, said to the New York Times that "The leaders of Timor-Leste regard China like an elder brother and a most reliable friend."[985]

The authors suggest that within the next ten years the world will see military port facilities constructed in Timor-Leste at which China's navy ships will 'train,' marines will be garrisoned, and most certainly a squadron of fighter-bombers will be stationed inland. China's patrol of sea-lanes and the omnipresent 'thumb' of its South China Seas territorial claims will undoubtedly be reasoned by the government to require local protection.

Mongolia's recent military relationship with the United States may yet hold off a future 'reunification' of Inner Mongolia and Outer Mongolia as perceived by the Chinese government and the PLA. At present the Han population vastly outnumbers the Mongol population in Inner Mongolia, but historical references may yet be used to initiate a Chinese move for 'sheng cun kong jian' or 'living space.'

And having already been somewhat victorious in North Korea in the 1950s, should the political situation there deteriorate to the point where China felt a need to 'pacify' the situation, the PLA would have no hesitation in issuing new medals to a new series of Chinese military heroes.

By virtue of its very nature, the game of war is also a guessing game. Undoubtedly Chinese military experts will be readily employed in the future, devising probability factors for conflicts yet unimagined.

All conflicts are prefaced by a plethora of rhetoric, which at present the CPC seems happy to engage in. It is when they stop talking that the trouble begins.

As the lyrics to the National Anthem say, 'The peoples of China are at their most critical time.'

The peoples of the world also, waiting to see where China 'marches on.'

Reason 34
White China Crime

The second element of the 4th Army of Instability's triumvirate of crime is made up of those wearing white shirts and dark ties with direct access to the finances of companies and banks nationwide.

White China Crime rarely involves just a single culprit, simply because it is almost socially acceptable to rip off the hand that feeds you. While they form an element of the 4th Army of Instability, White members rarely have contact with Blue China Crime members by virtue of their social standing.

White China Crime is a rampant force in China, especially in the country's banking sector, because that's where the real money is.

Banking fraud reached US$95 billion in 2005, a 31% increase over 2004.[986]

One major scandal emerged in January 2005 as the head of a branch of the Bank of China in northeastern Heilongjiang Province, Gao Shan, fled overseas after a company in the province, Northeast Expressway, announced that nearly US$35 million it had deposited with the bank was missing. Several other bank officials also fled. Investigations then found that another US$85 million deposited by other firms was missing.[987]

Police later arrested the chairman of Northeast Expressway, Zhang Xiaoguang, on suspicion of fraud.[988] Gao Shan, the bank manager, was finally arrested in February 2007, in Vancouver.[989]

In 2005, the head of China's Construction Bank, Zhang Enzhao, abruptly resigned after being accused of taking four million yuan (US$530,000) in bribes to arrange loans. At the end of 2006, he was sentenced to 15 years in jail.[990]

Also in 2005, regulators punished nearly 800 staff across China's big four banks for making illegal or unauthorized loans worth US$73 billion.[991] Illegal or unauthorized loans yield healthy kickbacks to managers in the form of cars, housing, travel or other non-monetary gifts.

In 2006, the Shanghai Pudong Development Bank announced it had uncovered a fraud case involving nearly UD$50 million in unsecured loans. The borrower, Qu Heping, had used other people's ID cards to secure the loans, with which he then bought high-end apartments.[992] Also in 2006 the Bank of Communications found a fraud case in one of its branches in north China involving US$25 million.[993]

China's National Audit Office found 20 fraud cases in 2008 involving 6 billion yuan (US$878 million), about half of which involved China's top three government-controlled banks, the Industrial and Commercial Bank of China, the Bank of China, and China Construction Bank.[994]

In 2009, police arrested Li Qun, a head of a subsidiary bank of the Agricultural Bank of China for a scam involving 165 million yuan (US$24 million), though much more money seemed to be involved, with media reports noting that "about 300 million yuan had been transferred from accounts associated with Li Qun to eight enterprises." Li perpetrated her scam with forged bank documents.[995]

In their endless pursuit of White China Crime, police also closed down seven illegal underground banks in 2006, with a turnover of 14 billion yuan (US$1.75 billion.) One of these, in Shanghai, was involved in money-laundering five billion yuan (US$630 million), making it the biggest such case ever uncovered in China.[996]

Speaking of these busts, Han Hao, an investigator with the country's Ministry of Public Security, said that "Drug trafficking, smuggling, corruption, graft and other crimes are now closely interlinked and form a serious threat to our nation's political, economic and social security."[997]

Han did not give a precise figure on how much money is being laundered in China. But according to Cai Yilian, an official with the anti money-laundering unit of the People's Bank of China, the country lacks accurate statistics because "anti-money laundering work started very late in China."[998]

One of China's biggest cash thefts (as opposed to corruption via loans and so on) came in 2007, when two employees of a bank in the country's northern Hebei Province stole 51 million yuan in cash (US$6.6 million), 43 million yuan of which they spent on lottery tickets.

The largest banknote in China has a denomination of 100 yuan. Therefore the two erstwhile employees would have had to steal 510,000 notes, stuffed in pockets, lunchboxes and briefcases. The suspects said stealing the money was simple since the bank did not count its cash on a day-to-day basis.[999]

The quest to win the lottery failed - an endeavor in which the two men were no more successful than in their career as bankers.

Fraud is widespread in retail business too. In 1997, a group of businessmen set up a Chinese version of the US supermarket chain PriceSmart, paying the US firm to use its name and image but having little other connection. Perhaps because of its foreign image, viewed as prestigious in China, by 2004 the new venture had 41 stores across the nation.

But expansion had been so fast that the group had heavy debts. So managers cheated, diverting money illegally and faking contracts to gain bank loans. Before the firm collapsed it had up to two billion yuan of debt (US$250 million) but only 600 million yuan of fixed assets. Upon its collapse in 2004, founder Liu Weyi fled overseas and remains at large. His company managers were less lucky, with former Chief Executive Wu Weidong being sentenced to life in prison in early 2007, and seven other executives given sentences of up to 16 years. But there was no word whether the many unpaid suppliers and ordinary members of the public, who lost hundreds or thousands of yuan they had put on to store club cards, would ever be reimbursed.[1000]

In the first 11 months of 2006, police uncovered 58,000 cases of economic fraud throughout all areas of Chinese business, not just the banking sector, and recovered nearly US$2 billion. The real figure of the amount actually stolen is of course unknown, but the number of cases seen was 6% higher than in 2005.[1001]

Big fraud cases that hit the headlines in 2007 and 2008 involved the businessmen Zhang Rongkun and Zhou Zhengyi. Zhang was convicted of giving out bribes to government officials of more than US$4 million, in return for which he won major highway construction contracts. Zhang had also set up an investment firm in 2003 with nearly US$30 million that had been embezzled from the Shanghai social security fund. He was sentenced to 19 years in jail in April 2008. [1002]

Zhou, once one of China's richest men, fell from power in 2003, when he was given three years in jail for stock market manipulation. Soon after his release in 2006, he was again arrested, this time for embezzling almost US$30 million from a company and forging VAT receipts to get bank loans. At the end of 2007, he was sentenced to 16 years in jail. Though this news was reported in the Chinese media, they made no mention of both Zhang and Zhou's extremely close connections to the highest level of political leadership in Shanghai.[1003]

The increase in individual wealth in China has been vast. In 2000, China had just two billionaires. By 2009, it had 79 billionaires. But this goes hand in hand with what has become described as 'The Curse of Forbes' - a reference to the fact that many of those entrepreneurs who appear on Forbes' annual list of wealthiest citizens seem to be arrested or detained soon thereafter for a range of white-collar crimes.[1004]

The love of money does not only drive crime in big business, for in China even small-scale entrepreneurs can take part. Chinese media reported on the problem of fake coins in middle 2007, saying that it had become common for convenience stores to purchase large amounts of fake coins to give out as change.

As elsewhere in China, the crime chain is neatly worked out. Media described how a middleman would buy fake one-yuan coins for around a third of their face value, and then sell them on to stores. Reporters spoke to two employees of one such middleman, one of whom said he was in charge of sales – in this case, posting adverts for the illegal service on walls and lampposts around town, as well as online.

Police raided several illegal-coin factories, including one located under a pigsty, from which they seized eight tons of coins. Though media said the center of production for coins was Henan Province (a province often blamed for crime) they added that in another province, Hubei, police seized nearly 11 million fake coins in the first ten months of 2006.[1005]

Corruption seems to be endemic in all areas of public life.

A police raid on a casino in Lishi city, in northern Shanxi Province, revealed that the owner was a prominent city judge named Feng Jianxiang.

Casinos, like most forms of gambling, are illegal in China. Yet Feng's casino was located just 200 meters from the police bureau, and most of the city's police had gambled there. This was why the raid had to be conducted by police from outside the city. No local police dared intervene or wished to cut off the illegal benefits they received.

The casino had been operating for a year, and fashioned its own system of justice for the benefit of the loan sharks at the casino. Those who couldn't return what they had borrowed from the loan sharks were thrown into underground cells, with Feng's connivance, until they arranged repayment.[1006]

Judicial corruption, another form of White China Crime, is widespread in China. In 2006, five judges in Shenzhen Intermediate People's Court were arrested for soliciting and taking bribes. Also in 2006, three top judges in Fuyang Intermediate People's Court in eastern Anhui Province were charged with taking bribes.

In 2004, 461 judges were charged with corruption. In 2005, the number was 378, and in 2006 it was 292. But even though the number of judges being prosecuted is dropping, China's Chief Justice, Xiao Yang, says he still has ongoing fears about the "grave situation" of judicial corruption. [1007]

In 2008, Huang Songyou, vice-president of China's Supreme People's Court, was removed for corruption, making him the highest-ranking legal official to be fired since 1949.

He was suspected of taking bribes worth 400 million yuan. That's nearly US$60 million.[1008]

In 2009, Wen Qiang, former head of the Judicial Administration Bureau in Chongqing, was arrested. He was alleged to have taken bribes to protect local criminal gangs. Media reports said that, "Investigations showed Wen and his accomplices, mostly former officials of the city's public security bureau, taking part in money laundering, rape, illegally holding firearms, offering loans at high interest rates, forging official and enterprise seals, introducing women to prostitution, and selling official positions during their terms. Their illegal income of over 100 million yuan ($ 14.5 million) has been confiscated."[1009]

Police later held a show of some of the goods seized from this gang. The show was for officials only - public and the media were not invited - but one enterprising reporter bluffed his way in. He reported seeing 65 luxury cars, 85 expensive watches, 29 antiques, 15 items of jewelry, 60kg of drugs and advanced weapons. A civil servant who attended spoke of seeing 20 million yuan, "which had been wrapped in oiled paper by Wen and buried underneath mud of a fish pound near an airport expressway."[1010]

296

A judge's skill may also be measured by his ability to keep himself one step ahead of the laws he has been entrusted with. And when officials step down from their jobs - as Wen Qiang and his cronies found out - then they often lose the protection than makes them virtually invincible.

Over the next few decades, the ranks of White China Crime will swell because it is incredibly easy to join up and 'share' the wealth. All the new recruit will need is a job with position, the ability to play with the figures, and a willingness to recruit others in the grand scheme.

With an uncontrolled booming economy, unfortunately it is fitting that China should have an uncontrolled booming crime industry.

Looking for Mr. Anuode Shiwaxinge

The strict control of language is tantamount to the control of thought and ideas, and consequently freedom. China's government monitors the use of language with great precision, so that leaders' speeches can either be totally obvious and to the point, or worded to imply a variety of meanings. Or they can mean absolutely nothing at all, just like the speeches of any government.

While the government may well have the meaning and use of verbal politics under control, there are 'leaks' within the Chinese language (which is known either as 'Mandarin' or 'Putonghua'), caused by the powerful influence of English.

English usage within another tongue is a problem experienced by many languages in the world. The advent of popular American culture is one of the engines that has pushed English to the front as a lexicon of liberal societies.

Some people, such as media commentator Xue Yong, feel that this is a good thing. Xue says that the use of English can strengthen Chinese words and enhance their creativity, and that the acceptance of foreign words in Chinese "should be taken as a necessary linguistic strategy to embrace new things."

Dong Kun, deputy director of the Institute of Language Studies at the Chinese Academy of Social Sciences, suggests that the absorption of foreign words creates a trend that will inspire and initiate a new direction for the evolution of the Chinese language, and will help make it easier to accept unique English words.

But such voices are in the minority and the real power in China today – the government – is firmly set against such free-thinking innovation.

Liu Bin, a former minister of education, says that "Allowing disorder to exist will greatly undermine the healthy development of our mother language." He talks of the "alarming" and "abusive" use of English abbreviations such as CD or DVD in Chinese-language newspapers and magazines, which, he says, violates China's National Language Law.

This law demands that when foreign words or abbreviations of words are used in a Chinese publication, they must be followed by Chinese-language notation. In actual practice, newspapers and popular magazines eventually drop the foreign word or abbreviation, leaving only Chinese characters.

Liu also claims that "The word-formation function of Chinese is actually strong enough to ensure any English word and abbreviation can be given an accurate Chinese translation." In essence, while that may be true, it consigns English words into phonetic oblivion. Common inanimate objects suffer no indignity in this process, but other cultures' city names, country names and personal names lose their color and uniqueness, and are given the indignity of imperial phoneticism.

Karl Lacroix (French pronunciation) becomes 'Ka er [Karl] La ke lu wa [Lacroix]' and David Marriott (English pronunciation) becomes 'Dai wei [David] Ma li ao de [Marriott].' If you say the name 'David Beckham' many Chinese people won't know who you're talking about. You must say 'Dai wei Bei ke han mu.' And if you want to talk about Arnold Schwarzenegger (Germanic pronunciation), you have to call him 'A nuo de Shi wa xin ge.' The result of this is that the vast majority of Chinese people, even those with good English skills, find themselves restricted in conversation with non-Chinese speakers because they lack the understanding of other tongues due to Chinese government restrictions.

Since Liu, at the time he made his comments, was a member of the Standing Committee of the National People's Congress, the country's top legislature, and also a member of the NPC's Education, Science, Culture and Public Health Committee, he was in a position to help enforce his rigid interpretation of what a language should be.

Some have harsher viewpoints. Professor Hu Shoujin of Shanghai's prestigious Fudan University said that the abusive use of English words poses a grave threat to the purity of the Chinese language. According to Professor Hu, the incorporation of English words into the language has already hurt its internal harmony.

Partly in response to academic attitudes like this, China's State Administration of Radio, Film and Television issued regulations prohibiting news anchors from using foreign words in Chinese-language TV programs, effectively obliterating the native pronunciation of the entire world's languages – except, of course, Chinese.[1011]

The very fact that Chinese is such an ancient language makes some commentators see it almost as an antique. According to Wang Shuda, writing for China Daily, "You cannot learn Chinese without understanding basic background knowledge." That's a fair enough statement in any language. But what does Wang mean by "basic background knowledge"?

"Do you know 'wu xing,' the five important elements: metal, water, wood, fire and earth, the relationships … among them?" Wang asks, suggesting that a cultural understanding of these elements in a Chinese way equals an understanding of Chinese as a language.

"Do you know Chinese classical poems, such as 'tang shi,' the Tang [Dynasty, 618-907] Poems? How many can you recite?" he writes, as if a modern language must first be respected for its roots. His implication is that a student of English could not learn the language without first understanding the sonnets of Shakespeare.[1012]

Linguistic experts say around 1,000 new (foreign) words are being added to the language every year.

300

In many ways the Chinese language, spoken by more than 20% of humanity, has reached a dead end. No new characters can be made. New words have to be coined by combining the present set of characters, which is a problem when using hieroglyphic languages (one character for one word).

While English has been adapted by many other cultures, the Chinese language has never exerted the same influence. Historically, many characters in the Japanese language came from China, but the Japanese written language has gone off in its own direction.

Bill Poser, Adjunct Professor of Linguistics at the University of British Columbia, explains that "Prior to 1446, the Korean language was rarely written at all. The written language used in Korea was Classical Chinese. The combination of the use of a foreign language with the large amount of memorization required to learn thousands of Chinese characters meant that only a small elite were literate, overwhelmingly men from aristocratic families. The great majority of people were illiterate."

"On the relatively rare occasions when Korean was written, it was written using Chinese characters, in part for their sound, in part for their meaning. This too was a complex system poorly suited for mass literacy," he explains.

The Koreans created a new language, called Hangul, in 1446 to eliminate this problem. Hangul "was the first writing system to make it easy for any Korean to read and write his or her native language," writes Poser.[1013]

China commentator Jacob von Bisterfield, also mentioning the Korean example, adds that the Chinese style of writing is "complicated, time-wasting, hard to learn and inflexible as sounds cannot be represented by an individual character."[1014]

The precise number of Chinese characters is hard to estimate, since over China's long history many have dropped out of common use. However, according to the Department of East Asian Languages and Civilizations at Harvard University, an authoritative modern dictionary contains around 56,000 characters. But, says the department, junior and senior high school students in China learn around 3,500 characters.[1015]

Today's Chinese students thus spend dozens of hours in class repetitively practicing their Chinese characters. Those who are successful in the execution of each character perhaps may extend the practice to calligraphy, considered a fine art in China.

Chinese does not easily incorporate new words into its lexicon. The language's ability to cope with the international environment is severely limited by the fact that it has a relatively narrow range of sounds -- 21 'initials' that are used to begin words and 35 'finals' which are used to end them.[1016]

Instead, it tries to strike an uneasy balance between sound and meaning to try to represent the original product name. 'Ke kou Ke le' is as close a phonetic transliteration as possible to 'Coca-Cola,' and the meaning of those characters is 'tasteful and enjoyable.' And the linguistic solution for furniture retailer IKEA, 'Yi Jia,' means 'pleasant home.'

The original names of these brands were invented. Coca-cola is derived from the two of drink's original ingredients, cocaine and Kola nuts. Cocaine was soon removed from the drink, but the name stayed. The name IKEA is derived from the initials of its Swedish founder, Ingvar Kamprad, combined with the initial of the farm he grew up on, Elmtaryd, and the village it was located in, Agunnaryd.[1017]

Other major global brand names have been created in similarly inventive ways. The name of the ice-cream brand Haagen-Dazs – known as 'Ha gen Da si' in Chinese, for example, was invented "to convey an aura of the old-world [i.e. European] traditions and craftsmanship" though the brand is in fact American.[1018]

The problem this creates in China is that when translators want to look up the meaning of a product name they often find no meaning exists, leaving them with the conundrum of translating this lack of meaning into Chinese.

Chinese faces the same problem incorporating most other languages around the world. Though the shortcomings of the Chinese language are clear, the vast majority of people we spoke to felt it was the 'right' of the language to become a truly global tongue. State media point to polls that show nearly 80% of respondents think it is time to 'protect' the Chinese language.

Stuck between a government ideologically bent on enforcing purity and an inherent inability to cope with new words, how will the Chinese language be able to cope with the global environment in the coming decades? Can it respond to the huge advances in science and technology that lie ahead?

In terms of scientific ability, the language is already falling behind. Chinese, says the country's Youth Daily newspaper, has become a 'spectator' in scientific conferences.

"It's not rare for Chinese professors to address their speeches in English instead of Chinese" reported national media. "Chinese was not used in the International Conference on String Theory in Beijing in 2006." The Youth Daily also suggested that since research in the field was led by British and American researchers, the use of English was unavoidable. The paper also added that academics feel it is "hard to reach an academic peak if they don't make English a priority." [1019]

The internet again tests the Chinese government's attitude towards new methods of communication. The internet is leaving TV programs behind as an agent of language change. Because of the interactive nature of the media, it appeals primarily to young people.

Inputting Chinese into a computer is a laborious task, driving many users to innovate. In fact, pin yin, the Romanized version of Chinese, is more likely to be used to input data in the electronic world.

Today's instant messaging program users (for internet or mobile phone) are coining new abbreviations, such as 'PLMM' ('piaoliang meimei,' a beautiful woman) and using old words in new ways – a 'konglong,' or dinosaur, for example, is an ugly person.

Lin Yunfu, an associate professor at Northwest University in the western city of Xi'an, quite liberally says innovations such as this fully reflect the creativity and personality of young people.

The professor suggests the public hold a tolerant attitude towards the use of Internet language. And, he adds, "Since it is used in a very limited scope, Internet language has little negative impact on the Chinese language as a whole."

But Liu Bin, the former education minister, again disagrees. "Some linguists have adopted incorrect attitudes towards the disordered Internet language by calling for toleration and non-interference of the non-standard use of language," he says. "Any responsible linguist should criticize and help rectify the disorder."[1020] Chinese as expressed by the national government is not a democratic language.

Beijing has also found the inventiveness of parents who give their child a unique name, wishing to foster a sense of individuality, has caused logistical difficulties for the uniformity of government computers.

China's government is implementing a names database that will list a set of officially-approved characters from which parents must choose the name of their child. Those rare Chinese characters used for some children's names often cannot be recognized by computers. When the government began to issue new identity cards in 2004, 40,000 Beijing residents were unable to apply due to the complexity of their names, since the characters within their names were not recognized by standardized official computers.[1021]

Even with the complexities and failings of the written Chinese language, it has been extended internationally as rapidly as Chinese's economic growth also extends itself.

This extension is reflected at the highest levels of government. One member of the National People's Congress, Hu Youqing, said that "…promoting the use of Chinese among overseas people has gone beyond purely cultural issues. It can help build up our national strength and should be taken as a way to develop our country's soft power."[1022]

In line with Hu's demands, China has recently been setting up 'Confucius institutes' around the world. These institutes are named after the famous Chinese philosopher, and their aim is to spread Chinese language and culture around the world.

Yet until very recently, Confucianism was shunned by the Party. Confucius was held to be a symbol of feudal China and has been rejected for much of modern China's history. In the Cultural Revolution (1966-1976) rejection was replaced with outright vandalism under the 'anti-Confucius campaign.' This campaign, explains the Association for Asian Research, "was aimed at removing all Confucian influence upon Chinese society through burning books and denunciation of the ancient and deeply ingrained teachings. Countless Buddhist and Taoist scriptures as well as temples were also burned to ashes among other classic books and ancient architectures."[1023]

Today, however, the Party embraces the philosopher. This is because Confucian ideas focus on respect for authority and a society in which people know their place. Confucianism also emphasizes the Party's current watchword, 'harmony.' China's communist leaders, wary of diminishing respect among the Chinese people for their political philosophy, simply wish to replace it with another set of rules – this time something home-grown, unlike communism – which will allow them to maintain their grip on power.

"The Chinese Government" wrote Qin Xiaoying, a researcher at the China Foundation for International and Strategic Studies, has "decided to go all out in establishing Confucius institutes overseas."

Only six institutes existed by the end of 2004. By 2007, that number was up to 150, and the government announced it planned to open 500 such institutes by 2010. In the event, the target was surpassed, with 554 Confucius Institutes or classes established by April 2010.[1024]

Qin says that "the Chinese language popularization drive will inevitably lead to the worldwide spread of Chinese culture, which is part of the intention to begin with. Once the goal is clear, so is the nature and position of the campaign to establish Confucius institutes overseas, namely, to popularize the Chinese language all over the world."[1025]

"This move is to comply with the surging demand for Mandarin learning, as more and more people have realized the important role China has been playing in the world" says Kong Lin, a senior official with the National Office for Teaching Chinese as a Foreign Language, which coordinates the creation of the institutes.

While Beijing announces the Confucius institutes are a way of externalizing Chinese language and cultural ideas, it may well be that these government sponsored and government supported Confucius institutes may become rallying points for other political policies of the Communist Party in the future.

"More and more Confucius institutes will help Chinese language and culture gain popularity in the world" says Kong.[1026] China's rapid extension of 'soft power,' as demanded by Hu Youqing, is a sign of the country's new PR offensive.

The Chinese government places communist cells in nearly every single private business in the nation. This same need to monitor and control surely cannot be absent in this high-speed deployment of the institutes.

It smacks of the old days of the 'Cultural Revolution' to see the once-disgraced yet now ideologically repackaged Confucius rehabilitated to serve the Communist Party.

Reason 36
Hot Borders

In the language of politics, the German word 'lebensraum' (living space) has deep meaning. If you were to translate its feeling and the sense of trepidation it creates in other countries, from the German word to a Chinese equivalent, one would need to also translate the sense of need to expand, a sense of righteousness, and a sense of superiority.

The Chinese equivalent of 'lebensraum' would be 'sheng cun kong jian' - the space in which one lives or exists.

Another term which has a similar resonance in meaning comes from the history books of China. That phrase is 'zi qiang' or self-strengthening.

In the middle of the 19th century, the technical strength of Western nations became a matter of increasing concern to China. One adviser to a senior government official suggested mixing Chinese culture with "methods used by the various nations for the attainment of prosperity and strength," and this was later put into practice in the 'self-strengthening' movement. Strength – but with Chinese characteristics.

At the beginning of the 20th century China created a powerful fighting force known as the Self-Strengthening Army.[1027]

Today, China has chosen 'peaceful rise' or 'peaceful development' as catch-all phraseology to help pacify the fears of the independent nations orbiting the middle kingdom. But the reality of the behemoth that China is becoming both militarily and economically is casting a long shadow over the 14 nations who share a land border, and sometimes a troubled historical relationship.

China presently has a common land border with more nations than any other country in the world.[1028]

They are:

Afghanistan (76 km, population 31.8 million)
Tajikistan (414 km, population 7 million)
Laos (423 km, population 6.5 million)
Bhutan (470 km, population 2.3 million)
Pakistan (523 km, population 164.7 million)
Kyrgyz Republic (858 km, population 5.3 million)
Nepal (1,236 km, population 28.9 million)
Vietnam (1,281 km, population 85.3 million)
North Korea (1,416 km, population 23.3 million)
Kazakhstan (1,533 km, population 15.3 million)
Burma/Myanmar (2,185 km, population 47.4 million)
India (3,380 km, population 1.13 billion)

Russia (3,645 km including a 40km sliver in the northwest, population 141.4 million)
Mongolia (4,677 km, population 3 million)

China also has close proximity by virtue of international waterways to countries such as Japan, Malaysia, Indonesia, Brunei and the Philippines, if one includes the territorial claims of China in the South China Sea, where China's claim line projects down like a giant thumb.

Land and sea borders bring the total number of countries that China must have good neighborly conduct with to 19. Because Taiwan is still in a theoretical state of war, we have not included it in our count.

China's 'neighborly conduct' sometimes has resulted in aggressive expansion, as is quite obvious in its military control of Tibet and Xinjiang, its claim to Taiwan, and its recent regain of control of Hong Kong and Macau.

Current claims of 'peaceful rise' aside, in its short history since 1949, China has fought wars with four of its land-based neighbors – Korea, India, Russia and Vietnam.

In June 1950, North Korea attacked South Korea. A combined UN force of 15 countries led by America came to South Korea's aid, pushed the North Korean armed forces back to the north out of the country and advanced as far as the Yalu River, on North Korea's border with China. The Chinese counter-attacked, fearful that UN forces would push across the river into the motherland, eventually driving the UN allies back to the original North-South border. This much is well known in China. What is less well known, however, is that the Chinese armies then crossed the border, attacking South Korea, and even briefly capturing its capital, Seoul, on 4th January 1951. A million PLA soldiers are estimated to have died.

In October 1962, China attacked India in the Himalayan border areas. Though the agreed line of the border remained unclear, in 1954 and 1956 the Chinese had stated they were satisfied with the situation. However, in the early 1960s there were a number of minor skirmishes in the area, culminating in a full-scale Chinese attack on October 20th 1962. Chinese troops successfully captured most of the disputed border areas and withdrew from others. Both sides suffered heavy losses. A ceasefire was declared in November 1962 with China keeping a portion of the territory it had won.

In 1969 China launched an unprovoked attack on Russia, attempting to seize a small island called Zhenbao in Chinese and Damansky in Russian, which lay on China's northeastern border with Russia. China's initial attack left 32 Russians and up to 100 Chinese dead. Russia responded in force, firing missiles into China, which killed about 800 people. China's militarists anticipated that Russia would launch an invasion. Frantic negotiation by the Chinese government managed to avoid a further showdown.

306

In 1979, China attacked Vietnam. It did this, in the words of then-leader Deng Xiaoping, 'to teach Vietnam a lesson.' Vietnam had attacked Cambodia, where the Khmer Rouge were slaughtering millions, because it feared the conflict would spread across its borders. But the Khmer Rouge, as nominal socialists, were suspected of being heavily funded and supported by China, even though China knew the horrific slaughter they were unleashing. Surprised by the ferocity of the battle-hardened Vietnamese army, China withdrew. China's history books recount a glorious victory.

The echoes of these wars persist today, even though the vast majority of Chinese people know nothing about the truth of them. For example, the average Chinese citizen, assuming he or she has even heard of China's Vietnam War, will confidently tell you it was initiated by Vietnam attacking China first. Undoubtedly, most Chinese citizens know more about America's Vietnam conflict than their own Vietnam War.

The Sino-Indian border dispute has never been formally settled. The region that China invaded in 1962 was known as the North East Frontier Agency and is presently called Arunachal Pradesh (the 24th state of the Indian union.) Though China withdrew voluntarily from this area it maintains its claim of territorial ownership even today.

When Vice-Foreign Minister Wu Dawei visited India in 2005, Chinese media reported that "The visit aims to enhance mutual trust, deepen friendship, expand co-operation and plan the future in the spirit of 'being a good neighbor and a good partner.'"[1029]

"China hopes to see a big South Asian family enjoying peace, prosperity, solidarity and security" Wu said.

However, in 2006 the Chinese ambassador to India, Sun Yuxi, said "In our position, the whole of Arunachal Pradesh is Chinese territory … We are claiming the whole of that. That is our position."

The Indian reply was indignant. "This is an arrogant way of negotiation from China" said Arunachal Pradesh's governor, S. K. Singh. "The Chinese have done this before, it is an odd way." [1030]

China's Foreign Minister Yang Jiechi told his Indian counterpart, Pranab Mukherjee, that the "mere presence" of settled populations in the region did not affect Chinese claims.[1031]

Speaking later in response to this comment, Mukherjee said "The days of Hitler are over. After the Second World War, no country captures the land of another country in the present global context."[1032]

But perhaps in the politically and historically charged context of 'sheng cun kong jian,' other countries apart from India should have concerns for their future.

China also claims the Diaoyu Islands. These islands are located 170 kilometers from Japan, and 186 km from Taiwan. They are tiny – just 7 square kilometers (2.7 square miles) and no one lives on them. China and Japan, instilled with a long history of enmity and conflict, are giving these islands the greatest sense of importance.

"The Diaoyu Islands and surrounding islets have been Chinese territory since ancient times. China has undisputable sovereignty over these islands," said Foreign Ministry spokesman Kong Quan in 2003.[1033]

In 2004, Chinese media said "Tokyo has made no active response to China's workable proposal of 'common exploitation' of the Diaoyu Islands, and has even turned a blind eye to unbridled visits to the islands by Japanese right-wingers and other radical factions."

Conveniently ignored is the fact that Chinese activists visit the islands too. More surprisingly, given Beijing's wish for 'common exploitation,' in 2006 China rejected a proposal from Tokyo to do just that with regard to gas deposits in the area. China ignored the Japanese-suggested median line dividing the disputed territory and extracted gas from beyond the demarcation point.[1034]

Present day negotiations, begun in the summer of 2007, are no more advanced than previous negotiations, both countries drawing lines in the water. By July 2008 Chinese Foreign Ministry spokesman Liu Jianchao was repeating the same inflexible line – "The Diaoyu Islands and adjacent islets belong to the Chinese territory since ancient times."[1035]

This was a note China was still sounding in December 2009, when media announced that 'The Sea Land,' a book written by an author named Shen Fu in 1878, had recently been rediscovered and published for the first time. In the book, Shen writes "about going to Liuqiu (Japan) via Diaoyu Island over 200 years ago, proving Diaoyu Island had been a part of China" said media. This, they claimed, proved that "Shen's journey is in line with *uni possidetis*, a principle in international law which states the one who discovers something first takes it as property."[1036]

China also claims the Spratly Islands (around 100 in total, called the Nansha Islands by China), lying in the South China Sea. Again, they are tiny, with a total area of less than 5 square kilometers. Spread over a large area they contain fantastic reserves of oil and gas. This time, China has more competitors, with claims from Vietnam, Malaysia, the Philippines and Brunei (and Taiwan).

China insists its claim is 'indisputable.' Much of its claim is based on the fact that it has ancient maps from as early as 1279AD indicating the islands' location.

China's 'thumb' in the South China Sea runs all the way down the length of Vietnam, down to the Nantuna Islands off Indonesia, then along the northwestern coast of Malaysia, only a few miles offshore, past Brunei and along almost the full length of the Philippines archipelago, questing by the island of Luzon within sight of its beaches and continuing up to encompass the whole of Taiwan before meandering its way up into Japanese waters.

In 2004, a spokesman for China's Foreign Ministry, Zhang Qiyue, said that the South China Sea had been a "Chinese lake" for "centuries."

All countries with coastal waters have a political right to exercise control 12 miles off shore. However, China's territorial claims are always directed by the rules of the EEZ – Exclusive Economic Zone – which through international law allows economic control up to 200 miles off a country's shore.

China's land-claim philosophy is based on a hop, skip and jump across coral outcroppings, volcanic atolls and scraps of land, some that are only visible at low tide. It is interesting to note that every other country involved in the dispute with China has, quite frankly, made rational land claims, basically indicating ownership of territory within the 200 mile claim of its main land mass.

China's claim line, however, running as far south as the Learmonth Shoal, just off the coast of Malaysia, is more than 900 miles distant from China's southernmost territory, Hainan Island. China's claims even lie inside the legal zones of other nations. Scarborough Shoal, for example, one of the Spratly Islands, is inside the Philippines' EEZ.

China also claims the Nantuna archipelago in the South China Sea. This group of 272 islands lies 240 kilometers off Borneo. John Daly, a scholar at the Middle East Institute, Washington, explains that "In 1993, China presented a map of its 'historic claims' on the Spratlys during a workshop in Surabaya, Indonesia, which included not only the entire South China Sea but a portion of Indonesia's EEZ off the Nantuna Islands."

The Nantuna Islands, of course, lie on top of vast proven oil and gas reserves. [1037]

In 1974 China also took control of the Paracel Islands, located one third of the way between central Vietnam and the northern Philippines, by force. They are still claimed by Taiwan and Vietnam. China currently maintains various units of its armed forces on the islands.

The Chinese government is always quick to eliminate any discussion or negotiation on various areas and territory that it considers its own.

"China has indisputable sovereignty over the Nansha Islands and their adjacent waters and neighboring marine areas," said Qin Gang, a spokesman for China, in June 2007. Any one-sided actions taken by any country in the waters are "illegal and invalid," said Qin.[1038]

China bases its claims on 'proof' such as explorations of the area during the Han Dynasty (206BC-221AD).[1039]

China, bolstered by the domestic imperialist policies of the Han people within the mainland, continues territorial, political and economic claims on other territories even while its own land, air and water problems increase. This is a key concern for the 14 nations ringing China, many of whom have historical land claim disputes that even in the year 2007 seem impossible to solve.

Bhutan: According to the Journal of Bhutan Studies, "In 1954 PRC published A Brief History of China where a considerable portion of Bhutan was included as a pre-historical realm of China. In 1958, another map claimed a large tract of Bhutanese lands.

"The Chinese claim surfaced again in 1960 when it openly declared that Bhutanese, Sikkimese and Ladakhis form a united family in Tibet, that they have always been subject to Tibet and to the great motherland of China, and that they must once again be united and taught the communist doctrine." [1040] The border issue remains unsolved to this day.[1041]

Myanmar (Burma): While there are no current land disputes, politically the governments of the two nations go hand in hand, since the political detention of democratic activists like Aung San Suu Kyi is supported by China. In January 2007 China vetoed a UN resolution that would have called on Myanmar to free its political prisoners and return to democracy. According to Jeremy Woodrum, director of the Washington-based US Campaign for Burma, "Aung San Suu Kyi is much a China prisoner as she is a prisoner of the Burmese regime."[1042]

Kazakhstan: As with many of the new central Asian states, China had border disagreements with Kazakhstan after the nation became independent following the collapse of the USSR in 1991. The two countries disputed 944 square kilometers of territory, finally settling the matter in 1998, with Kazakhstan retaining 57% of the disputed territory and China 43%.[1043]

In 2006, environmentalists in Kazakhstan expressed alarm that China was taking too much water from the Ili and Irtysh rivers, which rise in China and flow into Kazakhstan. "There will be ecological refugees. We'll have a lifeless desert here" said Mels Eleusizov, head of Kazakhstan's 'Tabighat' or 'Nature' movement.[1044]

North Korea: China disputes ownership of several islands in the Yalu River, which borders the two countries, as well as territory around Mount Paektu, also on the border between the two countries. Though China only shares a border with North Korea, it has caused great anger in South Korea by claiming that ancient Korean kingdoms were actually founded by ethnic Chinese. Korean analysts feel this would allow China to redraw its borders in case North Korea collapsed.

Pursuing the same goal, China deleted references in its online history archives to Koguryo, a Korean kingdom which conquered large areas of what is today northern China. These moves breached a commitment both countries had made in 2004 to ease problems over the interpretation of history.[1045]

Kyrgyz Republic: Also a nation that was only created in 1991. In 1999 the country signed a border agreement with China. But when it came to ratification in 2001 many Kyrgyz MPs were unhappy, believing it ceded too much territory – about 125,000 hectares – to China.[1046] These agreements were voted down by the Kyrgyz parliament in 2001 among threats of impeaching Kyrgyzstan's president, Askar Akaev, who had negotiated them – in secret, some said. The border conflicts were finally settled in 2004, with China keeping about 20% of the disputed land.[1047]

Laos: China and Laos signed a border agreement in 1991, thirty years after they established diplomatic relations.[1048] Since then, Chinese economic activity in Laos has surged. "Thousands of Chinese laborers have come across from neighboring Yunnan to grow corn and sugarcane for export back to China" says the Economist magazine.[1049] The small population of Laos is being inundated with Chinese immigrants, and even its traditional agricultural practices are changing. This becomes a de facto Chinese expansion.

Mongolia: Currently China administers the province of Inner Mongolia as an SAR. China directly controlled Outer Mongolia (more often just known as 'Mongolia') until 1921, when it declared independence. It then fell under the control of the USSR. Relations between Mongolia and China were tense up until the mid-1980s, with Mongolia claiming China was planning to annex it. Today diplomatic relations are more amicable, and China is investing heavily in Mongolia. Yet many of the jobs provided by Chinese investment go to Chinese workers, and some Mongolians fear China will end up controlling the country via its economic might.[1050]

Nepal: Diplomatic relations between Nepal and China (PRC) were established in 1955. The border was disputed, but a settlement was reached in 1961. However, in the negotiations for this agreement, China wished to claim all of Mount Everest, saying the entire mountain was in its territory. Nepal argued that the mountain straddled the border, half in each side. Beijing rejected this on the basis that the maps then current used either the English name 'Everest' or the Tibetan name, 'Qomolangma,' but did not show a Nepalese word for it. When Nepal countered with the claim that their word for the mountain was 'Sagarmatha' the Chinese side claimed this name was too recently coined to count.[1051]

Fortunately, today Nepal still has claim to its half of the highest mountain in the world. It is likely that in some dark library some enterprising young Chinese researcher will find a document that will be able to divest Nepal of its natural heritage.

Pakistan: Peaceful relations since settling border disputes in 1963. One of the reasons for the quick settling of disagreements was that

311

Pakistan was keen to cement friendly relations with China as a buttress against India. However, some of the land in Kashmir ceded to China by Pakistan is still claimed by India, which will constrain the three countries to years more strident negotiations.

Russia: All outstanding disputes settled in 2005, after 40 years of negotiation. The final area of disputed land, a group of islands totaling 365 square kilometers, was shared 50/50.[1052] The 3,645 kilometer border with China makes it difficult for Russia to patrol, resulting in thousands of Chinese people crossing over without proper entry procedures to engage in commerce, occasionally outnumbering Russian residents. This inherently increases the possibility of future conflicts.

Tajikistan: China claimed more than 17,000 square kilometers of Tajikistan, but in 2002 agreed to drop this claim in return for control of 618 square kilometers of the Pamir Mountains. [1053] While seemingly a small amount, the 618 square kilometers demonstrates China's prowess as a negotiator, since land which used to belong to Tajikistan now belongs to China.

Vietnam: Final land border disputes settled in 2002.[1054] The two countries remain in dispute about maritime territorial claims. The dispute between China and Vietnam may yet cause the South China Sea to erupt in armed conflict. Both claim rights over the Spratly Islands and the sea area surrounding, which is laden with vast undersea mineral and oil wealth.

The four serious wars that China fought with its neighbors between 1949 and 1979 came at a time when China was surrounded by far fewer independent states than it is now, as well as at a time in which its need for resources was much lower. But today China is sucking in vast quantities of material and energy resources from all around the world and also has a much more pugnacious sense of international self-identity.

This combination gives rise to a number of possible future scenarios:

> • **Scenario One** - Strife in one of China's neighbors spills over into China. China has always been wary of the variety of what have been called 'Color Revolutions' that have taken place among the central Asian states as they threw off the shackles of communism. The Rose Revolution of 2003 in Georgia and the Orange Revolution of 2004 in Ukraine were relatively peaceful, certainly compared to the Tulip Revolution that took place in Kyrgyz Republic in 2005 partly in response to China's land claims.
>
> For example, what if another Color Revolution broke out in one of the 'Stans' and spilled into Chinese territory, possibly with

Chinese casualties? Would China's rulers, using the pretext of protection for the motherland's citizens, invade and try to neutralize a foreign nation's territory and maintain armed forces outside China's own borders? China additionally worries that its citizens today may learn the old methods of revolution and choose a color other than red for revolution themselves.

• **Scenario Two** - China's growing need for resources may be constrained by the unwillingness of its neighbors to sell. For example, China is rapidly increasing its interests in mining Mongolia's mineral wealth. But Mongolia is wary of Chinese economic hegemony. A price dispute develops – or perhaps a transport dispute or perhaps the grading of the minerals proves contentious. Mongolia cuts the contract and decides to sell to Russia instead. While only a trade dispute, Mongolia's sparse population and flat, rolling terrain offers easy domination by military forces. Who would come to Mongolia's aid? The world would protest, certainly. But no-one would come. Remember Tibet?

• **Scenario Three** - Perceived mistreatment of nouveau riche Chinese citizens in one the neighboring countries where China has developed manufacturing businesses could well lead to a forceful response, to 'save lives and property.' China's reaction to minor injustices suffered by its overseas citizens is often greater than its reaction to major injustices received by its citizens at home. It's a question of face. China, in its pursuit of face, could use the wellbeing of its citizens as a pretext for military action and crossing borders.

• **Scenario Four** - Ethnic strife or 'terrorism' in one of China's turbulent neighbors might also lead to a forceful response – especially from Nepal (Maoists) or Burma (junta-led), countries that both border Tibet. Equally, increasingly confident Muslims grouping on China's borders would alarm China with regard to its restive Xinjiang Province. Already disadvantaged and oppressed, the province's Muslim population of Uighurs expresses solidarity with cross-border liberation organizations. China moves across the border to wipe out the heart of the problem.

China is in effect like a youth who has just joined the circus. Hired as a juggler, the ringmaster requires the youthful apprentice to juggle a far greater number of balls - or in this case, countries - than has ever been achieved before.

313

His juggling should be 'measured – peaceful – not aggressive,' causing awe and respect in the audience. The task is formidable. Our juggler is allowed practice. A failure, a dropped ball, merely stops his exercise and he begins again, while the audience applauds his humility.

In the reality that is China, there is no practice time, no appreciative clapping for a nice try. And China feels that its true historical calling is not to be the juggler, but the ringmaster.

China's failure in juggling just one ball – one country, carefully -- could result in catastrophic results for itself, Asia, and possibly the world.

Reason 37
Brand China

Can you name three international Chinese brands within the time it takes to read this chapter? Difficult? Don't worry – we'll give you some hints along the way.

Developing international brands is a matter of great importance to China's government today. Speaking in summer 2007 Chinese Premier Wen Jiabao said that domestic firms should improve the quality of their products and develop world-class brands.[1055]

But the 2007 Global Business Leadership Survey, created by Fortune China and a consulting firm, found that while 83% of respondents saw the importance of developing a global brand name, only 22% demonstrated the necessary skills for operating in the global marketplace. The survey was conducted among senior Chinese business leaders and also revealed that, while 75% of them had traveled overseas, most travel was for a short period of time, and only 45% of the total was business travel.

Surprisingly, only a third of leaders maintained personal networks outside China, indicating an isolationist attitude among Chinese business leaders. "The report indicates that there are capability gaps between business leaders who are effective and capable in the domestic market and those who can operate effectively at a global level," said media.[1056]

According to Professor David Schmittein, deputy Dean of Pennsylvania University's Wharton School, speaking on internationalization by Chinese companies, there are three questions that the would-be global Chinese firm must answer:-

• Why the company wants to build a global brand
• What kind of brand it wishes to build
• What the company offers that makes it unique or distinguishes it from competitors.[1057]

In China today there are few senior business leaders who could substantially answer just one of these questions necessary to define their company's future direction.

So what global brands does China offer today? Business Week magazine offered its list of the top 20. Here are our first five hints. We assume, of course, that you have not yet named three international Chinese brands.

Number 20 – China Overseas Property Inc. A large property developer, with a staff of around 16,000 and total asset value around US$1.8 billion.

Number 19 – China Netcom. A telecommunications firm run directly by the Chinese government.

Number 18 – Gree. The Gree company, says Business Week, is "the world's biggest maker of air-conditioners. It has moved successfully into high-end, digitally controlled units and has expanded overseas production."

Number 17 – Vanke. A real estate firm.

Number 16 – Changyu. "Initially focused on the production of wine and related products, the company has vigorously expanded into areas including the development of health care wines and Chinese herbs, the processing of liquor and alcohol, import and export, packaging, machinery and glass products" says the company website.

Anything familiar yet? While you're trying to think of some Chinese global brands, we'll tell you about one more firm you likely haven't heard of – Hangzhou Zhongce Rubber Co. Ltd.

This firm makes tires. One of its international markets was the United States, where the New Jersey based Foreign Tires Sales Ltd. imported its tires. In May 2006, as the story goes, an ambulance using Zhongce's tires crashed when they blew out. Though no one was hurt in that accident, the head of the US importer, Richard Kuskin, ordered inspections on the tires. His test engineer wondered if Zhongce had omitted to use a gum strip that prevents the tire's steel belts separating from the rubber. But Zhongce assured Kuskin the tires were fine.

Apparently, when the engineer inspected the tires from the ambulance accident he found that the gum strips were missing. But Zhongce again insisted the tires were "not a problem," said Kuskin. So he flew to Hangzhou. And during his talks with the firm, he later related that he found out the company's chief engineer had decided to stop using the gum strip, since he did not know why it was important.

Then reports of more accidents involving vehicles using Zhongce tires occurred, one of them fatal. But the van involved in the fatal accident was equipped with three Zhongce tires and one Michelin tire, of a different size.

Foreign Tire Sales organized a recall of the Zhongce tires, costing an estimated US$90 million, asking Zhongce to bear some of the financial burden of the recall, since they also bore some of the responsibility. But Zhongce still insisted the tires were not defective and displayed the kind of Sino-spite reaction 'big' brands avoid by having their PR departments kick in with the appropriate 'We are sorry' attitude. Not in China.

"A lot of people would do things in order to cut the throat of Chinese manufacturers," said Xu Youming, director of the firm's legal department, reported the New York Times. "I think you should think about the issue thoroughly."[1058] And Zhongce's board chairman, Shen Jinrong, said "We have probed this issue and found that our products meet the U.S. import safety requirements. The real cause of the fatal accident was the misuse of the tires."

In the papers in America, blaming dead consumers for misuse of tires surely caused many American consumers to scrutinize all the more carefully which country made the products they were buying.

Further comment came from Ma Lianqing, head of China's tire quality inspection center. Obviously a man who has never had a public relations course in his life, he said "It is not justified to claim a tire is defective simply by the absence of a gum strip or the thickness of the gum strip." When major manufacturing companies claim that leaving out parts that cost only a few pennies in the product's price structure is acceptable, consumers will have to initiate their own sense of product safety or pressure their government to impose restrictions.

Jim Smith, writing in The Tire Review, said "I doubt Hangzhou Zhongce Rubber Co., with its relationships with so many major tire brands, makes a bad product. I'm equally sure American private branders can vouch for their China-made tires. Mistakes happen, though, just as they do here. If Hangzhou Zhongce is guilty of anything, it is a lack of understanding about how things work here and about preserving valuable customer relationships."

"The Chinese don't like to be embarrassed, but they absolutely hate scrutiny. It's not surprising that Hangzhou Zhongce has dug in its heels. But, with concerns about China-made goods – tainted dog food, toothpaste, exported food, toy trains, and now tires – [they] should be cooperating instead of posturing," he wrote. "To remain a viable exporter, China has to reach Western product safety standards."

However, the problem remains that even with safe products, China's branding relations with overseas consumers needs a few lessons in politeness, respect and the age-old concept that the customer comes first.

Here are five more hints in our company quiz – assuming, of course, that you need them. We suspect you do:-

Number 15 – Air China. A national carrier, also listed in 461st place in the top 500 global brands according to the World Brand Lab.

Number 14 – Wuliangye. A distiller, with a work force of 10,000 and an annual liquor production capacity of 120,000 tons, its premier liquor sells for US$3500 per bottle "and was a great hit in the both the domestic and international markets" says the company. Have you ever tried – or even heard of – their US$3500 liquor?

Number 13 – ZTE. A telecom equipment maker.

Number 12 – Gome. A white goods manufacturer.

Gome provides an example of the frequent boom to bust nature of Chinese business. Its founder, Huang Guangyu, built up the firm from a single street stall in Beijing. By the age of 37, Huang was China's richest man. But in April 2010, he was put on trial for illegal business dealing, insider trading and corporate bribery. He was later sentenced to 14 years in jail.[1059]

Number 11 – Netease. China's biggest online game operator.

Having told you about tires, here's a tale about a car manufacturer with the expectant name of Brilliance Auto. "We hope to build Brilliance Auto into an international competitive automaker over the next five to 10 years" said the firm in 2002.[1060] "The only choice for China's auto sector is to stick to self-development by learning from world advanced technology and conduct R&D by itself," said a company president in 2005, a perfect first step for international branding.[1061]

By 2006, the firm was showing its wares at major auto shows. "Chinese carmakers surprised visitors to this year's Beijing auto show by rolling out the sort of sports cars and concept models that usually bear a foreign nameplate. Domestic auto companies exhibiting at Auto China 2006 in Beijing…were clearly trying to say to the world that they're ready to compete with the sexy, high-tech stuff and will not be satisfied simply turning out boxy family models" said state media in late 2006.[1062]

With such aggressive support from the state, in 2007 the company announced that it was going to sell its flagship model, the Zhonghua Zunchi, in Europe. Wisely, Brilliance Auto changed the rather vegetable-reminiscent name of 'Zunchi' to a more high-tech but equally suggestive BS6.

Brilliance Auto's chairman, Qi Yumin, said "The European market is the touchstone of Chinese cars."[1063] And at the Shanghai Auto Show in early 2007, Liu Zhigang, a company president, told Reuters that Brilliance was "making preparations currently and hope[s] to ship the first batch of BS6s to the United States late this year or in early 2008."[1064]

All great products travel a tortuous route before they are fully accepted into the hearts of consumers as a great brand. Brilliance Auto would find the route very tortuous indeed. When BS6 was safety-tested by ADAC (the Allgemeiner Deutscher Automobil-Club), a reputable German motoring organization, along with the attendant crash-test dummies inside, "the car disintegrated with such potential for injury to occupants that it was only awarded one star - the lowest possible given."

"During the frontal offset crash test, designed to mimic a head-on collision, the pedals intruded 18 inches into the driver's space. Damage to the Brilliance was so substantial the doors had to be cut off to remove the [test] occupants."[1065]

In the light of this disastrous result, European dealerships withdrew from plans to sell the car. Brilliance delisted itself from the NYSE, and of course accused German media of 'viciously playing up' the test results.

Vital for any successful brand is a series of in-house tests, and more. Consumer satisfaction is based on the purchaser knowing that the company he or she is buying from went beyond what is necessary to test the safety and quality of the product the consumer is investing in. It is quite typical of Chinese state companies, departments and organizations to announce the concept of success before the success has actually been achieved.

Duly chastised, Brilliance Auto said it would improve the quality of the car so that it would achieve a three-star safety rating within a year.[1066] We suspect that China's auto industry has a long way to go yet before achieving worldwide status.

Another Chinese model, the Amulet, produced by the Chery company, achieved the indignity of one of the worst results in crash test history when it was tested by Russia's AvtoRevu magazine. AvtoRevu said the car's front door sills "crumpled like newspaper" after a collision at 64 kilometers per hour (40 mph), reported the Wall Street Journal. The damage was so bad that the crash test dummy, totally intertwined in the wreckage, had to be removed piece by piece. "We have never seen such terrible deformation of a car's body," said Yury Vetrov, a reporter for the magazine.

Chery said the test was biased, with a company spokesman claiming 'dirty tricks' by competitors. Yet he gave no details of how the test might have been manipulated, and nor did Chery officials, present at the test itself, make any complaints at the time.[1067]

The next five brands in Business Week's list may prove more recognizable to you.

Number 10 – Lenovo. This computer manufacturer bought IBM's laptop division in 2005, making it the world's third largest computer manufacturer after HP and Dell – very tough competition.

Number 9 – Bank of Communications. One of the four oldest banks in China.

Number 8 – Moutai. Along with Changyu and No.16 and Wuliangye at No.14, this distiller controls 60% of China's drinks market, says Business Week. "With about 4,000 employees, Moutai Distillery Group has been in the wine industry for 2,000 years" the company claims, somewhat improbably. The distillery also says "Moutai, along with Scotch Whisky and Cognac Brandy, is one of the three most famous liquors in the world." So what's your favorite spirit – whisky, brandy or Moutai?

Number 7 – China Merchants Bank. Another large bank, founded in 1987.

Number 6 – Ping An. This insurance firm, says Business Week, has "diversified beyond life insurance into trust services and securities and has strategic tie-ups with Goldman Sachs, Morgan Stanley, and HSBC."

China's attitude to building globally recognized brands seems to be based more on the assumption that China has a right to such kudos than the need to earn it. Unfortunately, China's 'victim mentality' when it comes to its rights in the world is creating real victims.

In the wake of a series of scandals linked to Chinese-made products, China testily complained about "smear attacks" on its goods. "Blowing up, complicating or politicizing a problem are irresponsible actions and do not help in its solution" China's Washington Embassy said in summer 2007, perfecting its 'Sino-spite' vocabulary. "It is even more unacceptable for some to launch groundless smear attacks on China at the excuse of drug and safety problems."[1068]

One of these "safety problems" occurred in 2006 when tainted cough medicine from China led more than 100 deaths in Panama. The medicine had been made with a chemical called diethylene glycol, instead of the correct chemical, glycerine. The products also used the trademark 'glicerine.'

The original source of the diethylene glycol was a factory in China's Jiangsu Province, which has labeled the chemical as 'TD Glycerine.' This product had been sold to a Spanish firm. The Chinese firm said they told the Spanish firm the product should not be used in medicines. But Panamanian businessmen brought the chemical from the Spanish firm, changed its name to 'Pure glycerine' and extended its sell-by date.

Because of this, said Wei Chuanzhong, Vice Minister of the General Administration of Quality Supervision, Inspection and Quarantine, "The Panamanian merchants are mainly responsible because they changed the scope of use and shelf-life of this product."[1069]

China has yet to learn that the word 'sorry' prefaced before such statements goes a lot further in the view of customers and certainly of those whose relatives died after ingesting cough medicine.

The chemical diethylene glycol also led to problems with China-made toothpaste. When the US Food and Drug Administration found levels of this chemical at 4% in imported Chinese toothpaste, they warned people against using it.

China's response? To deny there was a problem. The nation's Ministry of Health asked experts to assess the dangers of the chemical. "The results showed that diethylene glycol is low-toxicity chemical substance. It is discharged immediately after entering human body. There is neither significant accumulation nor evidence that demonstrates that it is carcinogenic, teratogenic, or mutagenic" said state media.[1070]

At no time did state media, the government or the company producing the chemical indicate an understanding that perhaps Chinese testing and Chinese assertion of safety may not be accepted by consumers in other countries.

Li Yuanping, director of China's Supervision, Inspection and Quarantine bureau, said that the eligibility rate of China's food exported to the US has remained stable at 99% within the past two years, and a little higher than the qualifying rate of US food exported to China. He made no mention of the numerous problems with food exports from China reported in the world press beyond blaming "some foreign media for stoking fears about the safety of Chinese food and drugs." Li said the international media had "wantonly" reported on so-called unsafe Chinese food products.

Chinese media reported Li as saying "99% is very high eligibility rate for food. Recently, some media tampered with an unauthorized report on China's lack of food security, but the eligibility rate figures show it as speculation. Nothing has zero risk and not all food can be entirely eligible for the market. Just because one enterprise has a problem, it does not mean China has a problem. If a set of food is ineligible, it does not mean that all Chinese food is ineligible."[1071]

Li Yuanping should be reminded that while 99% satisfactory testing rate looks good, it in fact must be viewed with some caution. Claims by the US Food and Drug administration that over 98% of goods arriving in America from China are not tested casts statistical doubt on the safety of Chinese food products.

In fact, when Li's own Supervision, Inspection and Quarantine Bureau checked a wide range of goods made in China for Chinese consumers in the first half of 2007, they found 19.1% were "laced with toxins or too many additives, without safety protections or lacking required label information."[1072]

Further exacerbating world consumers' fear of tainted Chinese products is that fact that, according to US customs officials, 80% of the fake goods they seized in 2006 came from China.[1073] It's as if Chinese experts and officials are looking at a completely different picture than the picture global consumers see. World consumers tend to want to look at the picture up close, every detail clearly defined, whereas China prefers to look at landscapes and vistas, where detail is not as important as the overall picture.

The last five companies surely must be recognizable to you, but we suspect that you are unable to name one or two of these twenty brands without our hints.

Number 5 – China Life. China's largest life insurance company

Number 4 – China Telecom. A telecommunications firm with a large domestic base.

Number 3 – China Construction Bank.

Number 2 – Bank of China. You've probably heard of the Bank of China. Like Air China, every country has its own 'Bank of…' and the attendant political power.

Number 1 – China Mobile. With more than 200 million customers, says Business Week, it is the world's largest mobile phone operator.[1074] And getting bigger every month.

Did you know any of those names?

While China today faces great problems in creativity and innovation, the seemingly impenetrable barrier to developing global brands comes from the nation's attitude. China's response to problems with its goods is generally bad-tempered and self-serving and dished out with the usual Sino-spite. Whatever the rights and wrongs of any case, China seldom approaches the matter calmly, instead seeking to exonerate itself and blame the bad attitudes of others.

For China, the legitimate worries of consumers all over the world count for little. In a world where international markets are driving the global village concept, China offers no shared sense of working together to solve problems.

We have one more tale for you about 'Brand China' and its attitude to consumers.

A girl in the city of Jiayuguan, in China's northwest Gansu Province, was involved in a traffic accident in 2006, injuring her leg. City doctors advised she be quickly flown to the provincial capital, Lanzhou, for an operation.

When her family tried to take her on board a flight to Lanzhou, the carrier, Hainan Airlines, refused because she was on a stretcher. "China's civil aviation rules say sick and disabled passengers must get approval from carriers before boarding and that carriers have the right to reject them."

And with apparently no time to get approval, Hainan Airlines refused to carry the girl. As most parents would, her distraught father got down on his knees to beg the crew to let her fly. The flight captain refused, supported by his aircrew.

Unfortunately, the girl had to be driven to Lanzhou instead. By the time she got there, it was too late and part of her leg had to be amputated. When her family sued Hainan Airlines, the court turned down her lawsuit because, they said, the carrier had been following industry regulations.[1075]

Even in an emergency situation, with other customers watching, ignoring the pleas of the distressed father, the airline chose the possible headline 'Hainan Airlines causes child to lose leg' rather than the alternate, more brand-positive line, 'Hainan Airlines saves child's leg.'

China must learn that branding is not only about industry regulations. It is also about people.

322

Reason 38
The 'Big' Factor

Every national entity, no matter what the size of land area or number of people, feels its particular national interests are significant, perhaps even unique. Even the smallest countries in the world feel their own problems are big. Certainly no exception, China, since 1949, has discovered its own unique set of big considerations.

China's perception of itself as an emerging and developing nation has inherited many difficulties and paradoxes from its past history. But modern day leaders have in many cases exacerbated some of these 'traditional' problems, leading the country into a maze where they are forever trying to find the way out, often with a limited handful of solutions.

Part of the problem is that China wants development *now*. It wants modernity *now*. And it wants a technologically developed society *now*. But the breakneck speed at which the leaders are driving the country causes them to miss the road signs warning of danger ahead. A few of these warning signs, such as false claims of 'growth' which resulted in great famine of the 1950s, Mao's encouragement of large families, and again Mao's encouragement of students to become Red Guards, heralding the start of the ten-year 'Cultural Revolution,' show a lack of insight into the simple notion of cause and effect in China, which is often followed by big problems.

This book identifies many severe situations and circumstances which are affecting China's greatness. Perhaps the most intrinsic problem is that all manner of things in China seem to be big. This particular chapter of approximately 3,000 words will hardly do justice to the 'big factor' that plagues China.

Developed democracies around the world often decry the concept of 'big government.' Big government is often the first critical element of negativity that people cry when the capitalist system falters in recessions and the occasional economic depression.

Well, they have big government in China. Really, really BIG government!

The membership of the Communist Party of China had blossomed to 73 million by 2008, according to official statistics. Eighty-seven years old on July 1st of 2007, the Party began in 1921 with just 50 members.

"Party organizations cover more new economic organizations, new social organizations, urban neighborhood and townships" said an official with the Organization Department of the CPC Central Committee.

The Communist Party of China, once logistically focused on farmers and the proletariat, now has redirected its gaze to business. The

Party is now focused enough to have established CPC cells in 97.9% of China's more than 98,000 private businesses.[1076]

The feeling in China is that no organization that involves communism can be too big. The Communist Youth League of China (CYLC) was established in 1922 as a mass youth organization, directly under the leadership of the CPC, and is considered to be the CPC's 'assistant and backup.' More than 800,000 young people joined the CYLC every year from 2000 to 2005.

In June of 2008, media announced that the number of members of the Communist Youth League of China had reached 75.4 million at the end of 2007.[1077]

The report additionally stated that the Communist Party of China and the Communist Youth League of China were "the two most attractive political groups for young Chinese."[1078]

Unmentioned within these statistics is the problem that when you have such a large amount of people thinking the same way, solutions often lack imagination, depth and innovation.

Today's problems of economy, society and governance have increased in complexity to a point where volumes could be researched and written about each particular negativity within citizens' lives.

Years ago, the first thing an average Chinese person would think on waking up was where that day's food would come from. Today, that big problem has changed scope to the point of where China will *sell* all the food it grows.

Did you know that China grows....

75% of the world's garlic

50% of world's vegetables

15% of the world's fruit

47% of all apples on the planet

China is the world's largest producer of wheat (96 million tons in 2005) and rice (185 million tons), and the largest producer of beer (24 million tons a year.)[1079]

It's the largest producer and consumer of rape seed oil, growing a third of the world's total,[1080] the biggest producer of cotton,[1081] the biggest producer of milk powder and also sheep milk.[1082]

China has 25% of the world's chickens, 65% of the world's ducks, and 87% of the world's geese – hence the greater likelihood of bird flu coming out of China.[1083]

China is the world's top producer of green beans, broad beans, buckwheat, cabbages, cantaloupes and melons, cauliflowers, chestnuts, chilies and green peppers, cucumbers and gherkins, eggplants, ginger, honey, lettuce, onions, peaches and nectarines, pears, persimmons, plums, pumpkins, squash and gourds, sesame seeds, sweet potatoes, tea, walnuts, and watermelons.

Big is best judged when compared with something else.

In 2005, China produced 5.9 million metric tons of asparagus. The next biggest producer is Peru, with 193,000 tons.

Carrots? 8.3 million tons. In second place is the Russian Federation with 1.7 million tons.

Mushrooms? 1.4 million tons. Number two is the USA at 391,000 tons.

Potatoes? 73 million tons. *73 million!* China is followed by the Russian Federation with rather less at 36 million tons.

Tomatoes? 31.6 million tons, with the USA in number two spot at 12.7 million tons.

How much, precisely, is all the tea in China? 940,500 tons is how much.[1084]

Such large totals are impressive. But China, home to one-fifth of humanity, has just one-tenth of the planet's usable land. The per capita amount of arable land in China is only 0.09 hectares, less than 40% the world average. With a large population base of 1.3 billion, food growth takes precedence over quality of food production

That's why China uses more than 1.2 million tons of pesticide every year. Overuse of pesticides is common in China's rural areas, partly driven by government policies that keep pesticide prices artificially low, thus giving farmers little reason to conserve them. Additionally, farmers do not always read usage instructions or inadvertently use fake goods laced with unverifiable chemicals. Furthermore, it is common for farmers to toss empty pesticide containers into the fields, once again leading to soil pollution.

"You have to work on the manufacturing process, you have to work on educating the farmers, you need legislation in place to regulate accessibility to pesticides, and then of course you have to have monitoring programs in place" said Angelika Tritscher, a scientist with the World Health Organization's International Program on Chemical Safety.[1085]

China's State Environmental Protection Administration says that about 12 million tons of crops are polluted with heavy metal residues every year, causing a loss of more than $2.5 billion.[1086]

China consumes 35% of world fertilizer. While the country produces 30% of the global total, it still imported around 12.5 million tons of it in 2006. Heavy use of fertilizers creates a major source of environmental pollution in rivers, lakes and ocean estuaries.

At least 10 *million* hectares of China's arable land is polluted, one tenth of the country's total. And China's total supply of land is shrinking too. China's National Land Use Program decreed in 1996 that the level of available arable land should not fall below 129.3 million hectares by 2000. But by that year, the amount had dropped to 128.2 million hectares. A new target of 128 million hectares by 2005 was set. It was missed too, with actual land available dropping to 122 million hectares by that deadline. And a survey completed towards the end of 2006 found the total area of farmland had dropped yet more, losing 306,800 hectares in the first ten months of 2006.

Experts say the absolute minimum arable land required for basic food security is 120 million hectares.

The key factor in this loss of land is rampant new construction. Local governments, keen to raise money, frequently expropriate land from farmers, paying them minimal compensation. For corrupt politicians, the lure of big cash outweighs their sense of duty to the country's future.[1087]

And this massive construction spree is behind China's vast production of cement.

The country became the world's biggest cement producer in 2003, producing more than 700 million tons in that year.[1088] By 2006, production figures had increased to around 1.2 billion tons.[1089]

Cement production is extremely energy-intensive. According to the Netherlands Environmental Protection Agency, China has 44% of world cement supply. The agency said cement-making gave rise to 9% of Chinese CO_2 emissions, a figure it put at 550 megatons out of a total of about 6200 megatons of CO_2 produced by China annually. Such figures rank China No.1 in the world in terms of CO_2 emissions.[1090]

As inefficient as China is in the use of its energy, it is even more inefficient in its collection of the sources of that energy.

The collection rate (the extraction of useful minerals) for China's mineral resources is only 60%, compared to up to 80% extracted in developed countries. For mineral intergrowth (where different minerals are found intermixed) the recovery rate is a stunning 30% to 50%, half that of developed countries.[1091]

According to the China Non-Ferrous Metals Industry Association, the country's output of nine nonferrous metals topped the world in 2006. Kang Yi, president of the association, said that combined production of aluminum, copper, lead, zinc, nickel, tin, magnesium, titanium, antimony and mercury was set to reach 22 million tons in 2007.[1092]

Perhaps the biggest concern for the future industrial growth of China is oil, the precious liquid that has the world's great nations prospecting. Ages-old technology causes China's oil refineries to literally leak into the ground the oil so essential to the country's future. Inefficient production methods allow China's oil refineries to yield averages of only 58%, against an average yield of 80% in Asia generally.

Oil exploration, a key element in the acquisition of industrial might, uses obsolete equipment long ago disused by developed countries. This results in average recovery ratios of only 40% in the western region of Xinjiang and, worse, only 20% in northern Shaanxi Province.

China is the world's largest producer and consumer of steel. It exports around 50 million tons of steel a year, and in just the first four months of 2007 accounted for 36% of world production.[1093]

In 2006, the nation produced 9,349,000 tons of aluminum, approaching double the 2003 figure of 5,547,000 tons.[1094] The country is the world's biggest producer for aluminum used in automobiles and airplanes.

China is the planet's biggest user of copper, consuming so much in 2005 and 2006 that it drove global prices steeply upwards – copper futures prices gained more than 50% around the world in 2005.[1095] For the whole of 2006 it imported 2.06 million tons of the metal.[1096]

Sounds impressive, but again such dimensions of such seemingly positive growth have resulted in big problems elsewhere.

China's insatiable demand for metals caused a surge in scrap metal collection – and theft – all across Asia. The International Herald Tribune reported in 2004 that "market forces are cleaning up Asian landscapes that have long been cluttered with Soviet-era junk." While this was clearly a positive effect, some Mongolians said they wished their country could have recycled the scrap instead.

"In Mongolia," said the paper, "fences have disappeared from cemeteries, spigots have been torn from public fountains, and manhole covers have vanished." It quoted one resident of Ulan Bator, Mongolia's capital, as saying "It is irritating when you wake up and discover you can't use the telephone. Someone has stolen the wire in the night."[1097]

On the industrial front, China is the world's largest producer of electrical goods, exporting US$78 billion worth in 2006.[1098] By 2003 it was producing around 70 million DVD players a year, 70% of the global total.[1099] China makes 90% of the world's electric bicycles, producing about three million in 2005, and the country plans to sell 30 million by 2010.[1100]

A single city, Chaozhou, in south China's Guangdong Province, is the world's largest manufacturer of wedding gowns and evening dresses.[1101] Another city, Wenzhou, in eastern Zhejiang Province, made 70% of the world's cigarette lighters in 2004.[1102] China also produces more than half the world's sex toys each year.[1103]

Sounds good. And China leads the world in the production of many other products. However, it still does not make full use of even the best goods it manufactures - such as energy saving light bulbs.

China is the world's biggest producer of them, but only 30% of what it manufactures is sold domestically. If China made nationwide use of the bulbs it was so efficient at manufacturing, it would save 60 billion kilowatts of electricity a year. This, and other energy-saving measures, could reduce China's coal use by 300 million tons a year. But China's National Development and Reform Commission said, in 2006, that the prospects of introducing basic energy efficiency moves to make the savings were "not promising."[1104]

"China has to develop a new approach of industrialization, using energy and other resources more efficiently, even more efficient than achieved by the best practice in the world now" said Zhou Dadi, the chief energy planner at China's Reform and Development Commission in 2007. Yet from so far behind, how soon can China even catch up, let alone overtake other nations?[1105]

Per dollar of GDP, China uses five times more energy than the US average and an astonishing 11.5 times the Japanese average in its industrial production, countries that China wishes to emulate in order to establish its world-leader status.

Let's put that in dollars and cents. As the China Economic Review explains, a single kilogram of coal used as energy to create industrial products in China earns only 36 US cents worth of GDP in China. The same kilogram of coal if used in the Japanese industrial sector would generate US$5.58 worth of GDP.[1106]

One of China's most serious – and, yes, biggest – problems is water, and water in every condition. Too much water - not enough water - and/or polluted water. Amazingly, within 48 hours, two reports issued by the government indicated, at opposite ends of the scale, how big water problems are in China.

First, on July 26th 2007 Xinhua News Agency reported that worsening drought conditions in the country's northeast had left the total number of people having no access to drinking water at 8.68 million. More than 11 million hectares of land were affected, as were 7.6 million head of livestock. Up to 65% of all crops in the area were affected by the lack of rainfall, groundwater and other irrigation sources.

On the very next day, July 27th, Xinhua reported figures from China's Office of State Flood Control and Drought Relief Headquarters which said that up to the 15th of June 2007 flooding had devastated more than one million hectares of land in other parts of the country and affected 22.72 million people, bringing a direct economic loss of 8.92 billion yuan.

The State Flood Control and Drought Relief Headquarters must schizophrenically split their budget down the middle, relative to the amounts of relief required in each type of disaster. They announced they had put 100 million yuan towards this disaster, bringing the total spend on flood relief to 377 million yuan – just 4% of the economic losses caused.[1107]

But even if you have water in China that is no guarantee you can drink it, or that it is serviceable for any use. A survey in 2006 also found that more than half the water samples inspected in nearly 70 locations across north China contained excessive nitrites (a by-product of excessive fertilizer use), a potential cause of diabetes and kidney damage. And less than 9% of water checked at 243 water supply stations passed checks for acceptable bacteria levels in another 2006 survey.[1108]

Yet another 2006 survey of 112 sewage outlets in just one province, Guangdong, found that 75% of them were discharging pollutants above the permitted levels. The province was also responsible for dumping 8.3 billion tons of sewage into the sea, a rise of 60% from five years before.[1109] And in 2008 media reported that one-fifth of the coastal waters around the province were polluted with sewage, with "9,300 sq km of the shore ...polluted to some degree."[1110]

The now-infamous industrial waste that companies deposit into the nation's waterways adds to the pollution level. In not one city in China would it be considered absolutely safe to drink a glass of water from a household tap.

Even the most glorious of all resources is being eroded faster than nature can possibly handle. The Qinghai-Tibet plateau was once home to one of the world's largest alpine wetlands. Yet in recent years, this area – also one of the planet's most important areas in terms of biodiversity – has shrunk by 40% due to human activities. A single lake in this region, the Xingcuo Lake, used to span 469 hectares. Now it covers 10. Desertification is increasing at 12% a year, with another 135,333 hectares under threat of desertification. Laobuza, a Tibetan who was born and grew up in this area said "There are now very few swamps in the reserve. I could ride my horse for 50 kilometers and not find one." [1111]

As in all things Chinese, some authorities view large problems being inconsequential, while other authorities view problems as bigger than they really are, requiring a greater attention to detail than one can possibly imagine.

In southwest Yunnan Province, a 2,800 square meter swathe of mountainside had become an "eyesore for years following quarrying in the area" said Chinese media. A local businessman, surnamed Du, thought he had the ultimate answer when he had the entire mountainside painted green. Out of 'feng shui' consideration, the traditional Chinese belief in 'harmonious' surroundings, media reports suggested it was done for good luck. Other reports, indicating that the government wanted in on the big news, stated that the local forestry bureau had ordered the mountain to be painted green to make it look more environmentally healthy.[1112]

If that's enough to make you want a drink, we have a big one for you. A drinks company, the Guangzhou Pearl River Yunfeng Winery Co. Ltd, was a big taxpayer in Hanzhou City in central Hubei Province, contributing 13 million yuan to government coffers. Yet its local sales remained poor.

So they cut a deal with the government, and political bosses issued a circular ordering its 105 local government departments to consume a total of 2 million yuan (US$250,000) worth of liquor from the firm "as a support to its investment." Hanzhou's police forces, for example, were ordered to drink 25,000 yuan worth of liquor, and its government reception department, 100,000 yuan. Departments who drank up their quota would be rewarded with 10% of its cash value, whereas those that failed would be criticized.[1113]

It's easy to be slightly jovial about some of these matters. Perhaps the largest problem is to find individuals and creative people who are strong enough and willing enough to say "No! That isn't good for our country. That isn't good for our land, our water, or our air."

It may be the greatest thing of all that China needs is a sense of willpower and a different dedication to the future than the one the country currently perceives as being correct. Commerce, industry and technology in lock step with Western economies are simply not progressive enough.

Evidenced by the 2009 collapse of Western corporate led economies, the bigger they are, the further they fall.

Sometimes a small dose of common sense is all that is required, because 'big' is a long way from 'great.'

Reason 39

Red China Crime

Red China Crime is the best game in town – but you have to be a Party member to get a seat at the table.

Forming the last element of the 4th Army of Instability, Red China Crime has been entrenched as the thing to do since even before the Party gained power. Favoritism and nepotism may not appear basically criminal in nature, but down the line the cash goes into someone's pocket.

Today's cadres (political functionaries) and Party officials mouth political perfection while devising new methods and policies, the best of which take tiny, innocuous slices of the pie from millions of unknowing citizens. Red China Crime creates headline stories in major Chinese newspapers and around the world.

It includes theft of public funds, bribery, extortion, prostitution and cronyism, all of which are endemic among Party officials, including spouses, lovers, offspring and relatives. Corruption is simply a way of life for today's government.

China's penal code specifies 55 crimes linked to government positions. Each year nearly 40,000 alleged cases of corruption are investigated.[1114]

In 2006, 97,260 members of the Communist Party were disciplined for corruption, among whom 3,530 cadres were prosecuted, said Gan Yisheng of the CPC Central Commission for Discipline Inspection. Penalties can involve expulsion because of corruption or the milder probation prior to possible expulsion.[1115] In the first six months of 2007, another 24,879 cases involving corrupt government officials were investigated, comprising a total of nearly US$900 million worth of bribes.[1116]

In the whole of 2008, about 150,000 officials were punished nationwide, with 20,000 of these handing over nearly US$24 million in bribes they had taken.[1117] In the first half of 2009, 24,000 cases were investigated and 9,000 officials were found guilty of corruption.[1118]

China's first regulations to specify what punishment corrupt officials would receive went into effect on June 1st 2007.

The new rules say that government officials who are corrupt, or who organize 'superstitious gatherings,' use drugs, engage in the sex trade or otherwise neglect their duties, can be fired or demoted. Officials will also be punished if they use their influence to benefit lovers.[1119]

In a strange twist of Communist logic, the new rules also say the same punishments can be applied to officials who do not support their elderly relatives. Look after your mother and father and the Party will look after you.

Between 1978, when China began to open up to the West, and 2004, the country's Ministry of Commerce said that about 4,000 Party officials suspected of crimes involving US$50 billion of public money had fled overseas, reported Xinhua in 2005. Yet in 2010 - five years later! - the Ministry of Commerce said, citing this exact figure, that "it has never released any data on the country's corrupt officials fleeing abroad ... The ministry has never investigated into the matter of fleeing corrupt officials."[1120]

Recent overtures by China to sign extradition treaties with developed countries have met with resistance because of China's use of the death penalty.

In the years since 2004 the situation has undoubtedly got worse, as even those officially charged with eliminating corruption have themselves been guilty of it.

In April 2007, Zeng Jinchun was charged with taking bribes totaling 30 million yuan (nearly US$4 million) and being unable to account for another 50 million yuan found in his possession. Zeng had been secretary of the Commission for Discipline Inspection in Chenzhou city in China's central Hunan Province.

He was caught after being ratted out by another top official in the city, Li Dalun, who had been arrested for taking bribes of more than US$1.6 million in recent years, and having nearly US$4 million in assets which he could not explain.

Astonishingly, Zeng had been cleared of wrongdoing in *three* prior investigations during 2006.[1121] Yet he was known as 'the greediest person in Chenzhou city,' and when he was caught, locals let off firecrackers to celebrate.

During the same investigation, 150 corrupt officials and business people were revealed to be involved with the Li Dalun city case. As one local official said, "You felt isolated if you weren't involved in bribery." [1122]

The trial of Zeng and Li took place in April 2008. Both officials got the death penalty, with Li's sentence reprieved for two years, meaning that if he showed good behavior in that time his sentence would be changed to life imprisonment.[1123]

The Chinese characteristic of corruption is defined by the number of people involved in the group who engineer the stealing of public funds. The length of time the particular graft syndicate lasts and the amount of money it successfully removes from the public purse has a direct relationship with the number of people involved in the scam.

Red China Crime is endless. In 2007, Hunan Province party boss Zhou Zhengkun was removed from his post as secretary of the Party Committee of the Hunan Provincial State-owned Assets Supervision and Administration Commission for "taking advantage of his posts to seek personal gain."[1124]

Du Xiangcheng, another Party senior discipline official in Hunan, made his name with his 'tough on crime' stance. In 2004, he led an investigation into a corrupt leader who had amassed nearly US$100,000 in bribes. With startling premonition, Du said that officials were "only human and they have desires, so we should all be tested."

Perhaps Du was testing himself when police discovered him with a prostitute from Belarus in a Beijing hotel room in 2005. He was expelled from the party in 2007 – itself an indication of just how slowly the wheels of Party justice can turn. The Party's Central Commission for Discipline Inspection also ordered an investigation into his assets and finances.[1125]

Government posts are popular, even with recent university graduates, who choose them over better-paid private industry jobs. The reason being, of course, that opportunities for 'extras' abound, not to mention warm leather chairs, hour and a half lunches, and an extremely relaxed working attitude.

"The older senior officials who survived wartime were different from the younger [new] officials, who tend to think about themselves and are mainly after power, salary, status, housing and medical care. This thinking triggers jealousy and encourages the buying of official posts to get promoted," said Zhang Quanjing, former head of the Party's Organization Department.[1126]

Of course, those who gain advancement by bribery are then able to regain the outlay by gaining access to peer corruption. Living a life of power and luxury allows their children access to government jobs in the future, emulating them, and thus creating a vicious circle.

The list continues.

One particularly high-ranking official caught was Qiu Xiaohua, who was removed from his post as director of the National Bureau of Statistics in October 2006 after being implicated in a 10 billion yuan (US$1.25 billion) social security fraud. [1127]

Zhang Weihua, the politically-appointed vice director of China's sports lottery, was also accused of abuse of power in 2006. Among his set of crimes, Zhang set up a printing plant which made a profit of 120 million yuan (US$15.7 million) despite never printing a single ticket.[1128]

In 2007, Du Shicheng, a deputy Party secretary in northern Shandong Province, was removed from power for taking millions of yuan in bribes.[1129]

In April 2008, the Party chief of Shanghai, Chen Liangyu, was sentenced to 18 years in jail. He had been removed from power in 2006 after being involved in the misuse of US$400 million of social security funds, making him the most senior figure to fall in a decade.[1130]

Also in 2008, Jiang Renjie, former mayor of Suzhou, was sentenced to death for accepting more than 100 million yuan (US$14.6 million) in bribes.[1131]

In 2009, when police searched the home of Huang Peng, Deputy Director of Guangzhou's Planning, Land and Construction bureau, they found US$330,000. Huang, who was then arrested for corruption, said collecting cash was "only my personal hobby."

Also in 2009, Kang Huijun, the former deputy head of Shanghai's Pudong New Area, was sentenced to life imprisonment. He had been charged with taking more than 5.9 million yuan (US$860,000) in bribes. He had a further 12.11 million yuan whose provenance he could not account for. His wife was sentenced to five years for corruption. Between them, the couple owned more than 30 million yuan of property.[1132]

Another high-ranking scalp in 2009 was Li Tangtang, vice-chairman of China's Ningxia Hui autonomous region. Reports did not go into detail about his crime, beyond saying he was being investigated for a 'serious violation of discipline' relating to corruption. However reports did mention that in 2007, when he was vice-governor of Shaanxi Province, he had received a 'severe inner-Party warning' for trying to manipulate votes to get a higher-ranking job in Shaanxi. Though he failed to do so, the 'warning' did nothing to stop him from getting the prestigious Ningxia post.[1133]

In 2010, Zhao Shiyong, a Party Secretary of Malipo County in Yunnan Province, was sentenced to 18 years in jail. He had taken five million yuan in bribed and amassed property worth more than 10 million yuan. Malipo County was one of the poorest places in the whole province, with an annual per-capita income of 1,879 yuan (US$275) in 2009.[1134]

Red China Crime is also closely allied to Blue China Crime (See Reason 29.) For example, in 2010 state media announced that more than half of the criminal gangs that had been caught in the city of Chongqing in a crackdown the year before had, up to that point, been protected by local officials.[1135]

But maybe the most eloquent testimony to the fast-track to wealth that a good connection to the Communist Party brings is this: 91% of China's 3,220 citizens worth more 100 million yuan are the children of high-ranking officials.[1136]

Any of the above crimes would cause a freely-elected government in a democratic country to fall immediately. But in China, without the aid of independent oversight bodies, the bags of money will continue to walk out of the door.

On the face of it, the 4th Army of Instability's Red China Crime element would seem to be the most evil. But with more than 70 million Party members, and with an enrolment system that sees that number grow by around 2.3 million a year,[1137] the 'face of evil' may become as familiar as the people next door.

Reason 40
Party Capital & Sino-Cash

Perhaps the biggest admission of the failure of Chinese Communism came in 2002, when then-president Jiang Zemin delivered the keynote speech for the 16th Party Congress.

Jiang said that "the CPC should admit into itself advanced elements of other social strata who accept the Party's program and Constitution, work for the realization of the Party's line and program consciously and meet the qualifications of Party membership following a long period of test, in order to increase the influence and rallying force of the Party in society at large," reported media.[1138]

Behind these rather bland, anodyne words lies something truly startling, for the "advanced elements of other social strata" that Jiang was keen to allow into the Party were in fact private businessmen – in other words, capitalists, in this case Chinese citizens with cash.

Chinese media, naturally, presented this as a great advance for the cause of socialism. Hearing the report, said the board director of one business group planning to list on China's stock market, was that the news was similar to "having taken a 'reassurance pill' and all our remaining worries and fears are completely gone. ... Now we want more to make our brand famous worldwide so as to serve our country."

Perhaps the most exclusive working club in the world opens its door and finds a long line of rich citizens salivating to get in. Men with money welcomed by men with power.

In reality, of course, it was nothing less than the acceptance of the fact that Chinese Communism has nothing substantial to offer the people of China and nothing to offer the world that the world has not already seen. The 'reassurance pill' is not that the Party is going to do great things for Chinese businessmen – it is, rather, the hope that the Party will not simply appropriate all private holdings as it has in the past. It was at this same meeting that the Party, for the first time, "introduced the concept of property rights and pledged to formulate legislation protecting private property."

Chinese Premier Wen Jiabao, noted media, "said enhancing legislation to protect private property will help accelerate China's economic development, ease employment pressure, and give greater incentive for people to establish their own businesses."[1139]

But perhaps the real reason behind admitting businessmen into the Party, was less altruistic and more to do with control and greed. In today's China, the Party wishfully attempts to control everything. Rather than persecuting private businessmen as it once did, it now welcomes them with open arms – after all, it is new money that provides the fuel for the economic engine, and new money is the new god in China.

335

A clear example of the change in official attitudes to businessmen is illustrated by the case of Yin Mingshan. Yin, said state media around the time of these changes, is "listed in 'Fortune' magazine as one of the top 50 millionaires in China, is chairman of the Chongqing-based Lifan Hongda Industrial Group and vice-chairman of the General Chamber of Commerce of Chongqing Municipality. He is also a member of the National Committee of the CPPCC."

What media failed to mention was that for much of Yin's life he was ruthlessly persecuted by that same Party. He was expelled from high school in 1960 for making 'rightist' remarks and, three years later, he was jailed. He remained a social outcast, spending many years laboring on a farm until 1979, when the Party informed him his punishment had been a 'mistake.'

He did not receive any apology for the nearly two decades of his life that the Party had wasted. However, when he built his firm into one of the nation's leading motorbike manufacturers, the Party was suddenly keen to hear what he had to say. Money and success mean far more to today's communists than morality, and indeed more than individual freedom itself.

"Experience shows that prosperity is coupled with the activities of private entrepreneurs" noted an article by Zhang Houyi, director of the Research Centre for Private Enterprises with the Chinese Academy of Social Sciences. "Affluent regions such as Beijing, Shanghai and Guangdong have more than 50% of the country's private companies. By comparison, the less well-off inland provinces account for a very low proportion of private firms. But as the economy grows in a more balanced way, there will be more room for the development of private businesses. Now an irresistible force, private entrepreneurs will go on to greater success in the foreseeable future."[1140]

In giving the green light (or should that be a patriotic communist red light?) to the political cachet of money at the 16th Congress in 2002, China perhaps was merely offering one more route for its corrupt officials to enrich themselves. According to Shao Daosheng, a retired special researcher with the CPC Central Commission for Discipline Inspection, "The number of high-level officials being investigated and arrested in the past four years is higher than any other period in the Party's history." Shao, speaking in 2007, explained that "The most striking feature of [recent] corruption cases was Party and government officials colluding with business people to misappropriate billions of yuan," state media reported.[1141]

The government attempted to crack down on the wholesale corruption among its members by banning officials from running companies. "Other blacklisted bribery includes well-paid nominal jobs -- usually for relatives of the officials -- purchases of property or cars at conspicuously lower than the market price and even deliberate losses by businessmen at gambling tables which would somehow find their way into the officials' pockets" said media, explaining that in return for these covert

336

bribes businessmen expected "policy favors, approval of lucrative land deals or the granting of contracts in a closed political system that permits few checks and balances on official power."[1142]

In 2007 media announced – as it had so often announced before – a new 'push' against government corruption. This time, the cosmetic campaign was focused on commercial bribery, which "usually refers to bribes from companies and often involves a firm paying money to government officials for special favors." Media announced that since 2005 China had dealt with 21,889 cases of commercial bribery, involving a total of 5.2 billion yuan (US$676 million.)[1143]

Media reports in the years since businessmen were welcomed into the Party have increasingly focused on the importance of the private sector to China's future growth. And the increasing wealth and ostentatious prominence of private businessmen means that in China today, to be a businessman is cool. This is why the majority of young Chinese people want to study business-related areas, all stating their desire to be the boss.

The new focus on business above all else, however, is leading China in some intriguing directions. In 2006 Xiamen University, in the southern coastal city of Xiamen, announced it was adding a course in golf to its curriculum. This was not as part of a leisure management degree, but rather, said officials, "to improve students' career prospects." Zhu Chongshi, president of the university, said that "students majoring in management, law, economics and software engineering will be required to take a course in golf" and that others could take it as an elective. "It is as beneficial to society as compulsory education… The highest embodiment of the education system is producing socially elite people with the best education" he said.[1144]

Shanghai University of Finance and Economics followed suit. Professor Chen Xiao, a faculty member, said that "Our university is one that produces business talents. Nowadays, businessmen like discussing business on golf courses. We hope our students can master the sport. Other Shanghai universities were in talks with Chen about setting up their own golf courses, said media.[1145] Communists playing golf is a revolution in itself.

While some sectors of society seem to be racing ahead in China's new business-friendly milieu, other sectors lag behind. The concept of personal income tax, almost unheard of in China's more socialist years, still remains hazy despite government efforts to instill its people with suitable respect for this capitalist practice.

New rules coming into force in early 2007 mandated that individuals earning over 120,000 yuan a year (US$15,530) would need to file personal income statements. Yet just a few days before the deadline, tax officials had received only 20% of the number of tax forms they were expecting. Those who had not filed returns faced fines of up to 10,000 yuan, and those who tried to evade paying tax could be jailed and fined five times the amount of tax owed.

The tension at the heart of China's government was shown by the director of the State Administration of Tax's press office, Niu Xinwen. Niu said that the number of tax returns the administration was expecting was a secret. The needs of an open society, as demanded by capitalism, collided with the inherent secrecy and evasiveness of Chinese government.[1146] In today's China the question "Have you paid your taxes, Comrade?" is a lot less dangerous that the question "Are you a capitalist roader?" which was asked by the Red Guards of the Cultural Revolution.

Similar confusion was apparent in that other part of a well-developed capitalist society – charitable donations. Chinese media reported at the end of 2005 that only 1% of Chinese companies made any donations to charity. Around 0.05% of GDP was donated to charity in China, as opposed to 2.17% in the United States.

Yet apparently this was not purely a matter of greed and selfishness. Speakers at the China Charity Conference said that the main reason they did not donate to charity was that the country's tax laws made it almost impossible. "The more you donate, the more you have to pay" said one businessman. "Given the low ratio of tax exemption, enterprises in China lack the economic incentive to donate" said Xu Yonggang, vice chairman of the China Charity Federation. Media also reported that the situation was made worse by the fact that tax exemption was only allowed on donations to seven registered charities. This, of course, is a sign of the obsessive control that Beijing exerts in every area of life. While its tax laws may still be rudimentary, the government nonetheless tries its best to oversee how every dollar is spent.[1147]

Now the doors to capitalists are open, will China develop rules and regulations designed to control the wealth in its citizens' pocket-books as a way of extracting the cash from the capitalists?

The Party's embrace of businessmen is an act of profitable hypocrisy. For most of its history the very idea of entrepreneurship and leading your life for profit was castigated by communist officialdom. Bringing capitalists into the Party is an explicit retreat from the goals of socialism. But the covert and piecemeal way in which the Party is encouraging capitalism means that the tensions between the two systems, already clear, can only grow much worse in the future.

While maintaining lip-service to socialist goals, the government embraces any political strategy that will either enrich its members or cement its grip on power.

The vast majority of Chinese citizens, those that are not Party members, those with limited finances, will just have to fall further behind.

Reason 41
A Nation of Health Terrorists

Wang Bing followed his father into the business just as his father's father had done. The youngest of three brothers, there was little money left for his education.

He took to the tasks of a poultry seller like he was born to it, slicing the throat of his first chicken at the age of 5.

Now 45, with a son of his own, his wife assisting him from 6 a.m. till 6 p.m. unless he runs out of stock, Wang's trade has reached the front pages of the world press. But he is not aware of the explosion of news items internationally about H5N1 – more commonly known as bird flu.

"In my grandfather's time there was no trouble. In my father's time, also no trouble," Wang affirms. "All my birds are healthy." Then he adds, "And if a chicken or duck is sick, I have customers who don't mind - if they get a discount - so I sell it quickly, no problem."

Wang Bing lives half of his life with his ducks, and chickens, and with the occasional pheasant or other exotic if he can get them. There is a customer for every bird, he says.

After his lunch, eaten while standing, his boxed meal perched on the top of poultry cages stuffed with birds, he sleeps. His cot is pushed up next to his stall, other market customers brushing by.

His wife continues to sell stock that is personally chosen by the customers. Once selected, the fowl is tucked under her arm, its neck extended to the quick flash of her blade.

Then quite unceremoniously the struggling bird is dumped into a large black plastic barrel, where it can be heard thumping away the last few seconds of its life in the sticky darkness inside.

The couple is quite lucky to have electricity and cold running water, provided by a garden hose that winds its way from somewhere. But the market roof over their heads does not prevent the extremes of the weather from making their life's calling an arduous test, particularly in the summer. The stench can be overpowering.

The short life experienced by the birds is worse. Cramped up in cages far too small that are stacked up one on top of the other, the fowls at the bottom receive the droppings from above with a wary eye.

"The government tries to change this way, but my customers demand my birds are fresh," Wang says. "I don't believe there's any harm to it." And when told through an interpreter what Western papers are reporting, some predicting pandemics and millions of potential deaths if the H5N1bird flu mutates, enabling the virus to be spread human to human, he replies with a laugh, "Nonsense!"

But it is not nonsense.

A recent study estimates that if H5N1 did mutate into a human-to-human form, the resulting pandemic would kill more than 60 million people, most of them in the developing world.[1148]

H5N1 is a recent mutation of avian flu, which has always been part of the natural world. It is a much more potent form of the disease, and it has a close connection with China. It was first seen in birds in China's southern Guangdong Province, spreading from there to Hong Kong, then across Asia. It is now spreading across the world.[1149]

"Guangdong is the source of multiple H5N1 strains spreading at both regional and international scales," scientists at the University of California said in March 2007.

Scientists think the spread of bird flu is generated by intensive farming of poultry and pigs, and that the infection jumps into humans when poultry, pigs and people live in close contact. This is common in developing countries, but especially so in the intensively farmed areas of east China.

Intensive farming raises other disease risks. In 2009, a report presented to the National People's Congress (China's rubber-stamp parliament) spoke of the "grave hidden peril" of animal disease epidemics due to insufficient monitoring and control of farming. "The problems of excessive veterinary drug residues and banned food additives in livestock products were not fully under control in certain areas" said the report.[1150]

At present H5N1 can infect humans, but only when they come in direct contact with an infected bird. The scenario that terrifies scientists is that H5N1 will mutate into a form that can be passed between humans. If it does that, millions – and maybe hundreds of millions, according to some estimates – will die.

H5N1 "... is probably still originating [in China] and spreading," said Walter Fitch, one of the California scientists. "If you can control the virus at its source, you can control it more efficiently."[1151]

But China is making it extremely difficult to control the virus 'at its source.' Aside from allowing the continuation of the working conditions of poultry sellers, the country is extremely secretive about the spread of the disease within its borders and routinely hampers research efforts aimed at monitoring and control of the disease.

For example, it was only in August 2006 that China revealed its first death from bird flu actually occurred in 2003, rather than in 2005 as the government had previously claimed. It said this was because it had not checked samples from the victim until 2004.

Checking samples usually takes days, or at most weeks. In China, apparently, it improbably took a year – and then another year for the results of those tests to be announced. The announcement only came after Chinese researchers had revealed the 2003 death in the New England Journal of Medicine.[1152]

There were numerous media reports that China was still covering up outbreaks of H5N1 in 2009. Early in that year, dead birds washed up in

Hong Kong, some of them infected with the virus. Hong Kong said there were no poultry farms near where the birds washed up, leading to the suspicion they had come from the Pearl River Delta in China.

Because H5N1 can be passed on by eating infected meat, it is critically important to keep affected birds out of the food chain. Yet rumors in 2009 said that infected birds had been chemically treated to look healthy and sold in markets.[1153]

Outbreaks of bird flu can devastate flocks and thus the economic wellbeing of farmers.

According to reports in 2005, Chinese authorities, in an attempt to protect the country's poultry against the disease, urged farmers to inoculate their flocks with a drug called Amantadine during the 1990s to protect them against the less virulent forms of bird flu.

This drug is designed to protect humans against bird flu, and its use in poultry is banned in international livestock guidelines. China ignored this ban, and "Such misuse could have caused the avian flu virus to evolve into the drug-resistant H5N1 strain. In any event, medics and pharmaceutical experts now agree that Amantadine has become useless in protecting people in case of a worldwide bird flu epidemic." [1154]

Alternative drugs, such as Tamiflu, are harder to produce and may be thus much more expensive. They are also less effective.[1155] Due to China's disregard of the basic principles of health care, the world must now develop new drugs.

China denied that it had ever allowed its farmers to use the drug, saying the claims were not "in accordance with the truth." [1156] Yet given that a handbook issued by the People's Liberation Army Agriculture and Husbandry University gave detailed instructions about using Amantadine in poultry, it is hard to agree with the Chinese government's definition of 'truth.'

Even if Amantadine is taken out of the picture, many suspect that poultry farming practices are behind the disease. For example, China's Qinghai Lake is an area of very intense poultry farming. The waste from these farms – excrement, feathers and soiled litter – is used as fertilizer in local fields or fish food in local farms.

The World Health Organization says that the bird flu virus can live in bird feces for up to 35 days. [1157]

The WHO is leading research into the disease, but has been repeatedly denied samples of avian flu by China. In April 2007 the WHO complained that it had been almost a year since it had received any such samples. This, said experts, slowed down research into controlling the disease.[1158]

China's response to the WHO's complaint was to claim that "the government has always worked closely with the international community as part of the global effort to prevent a bird flu epidemic." [1159]

In April 2010 Juan Lubroth, the U.N. Food and Agriculture Organization's chief veterinary officer, stated that H5N1 remained entrenched in China (as well as Egypt, Indonesia, Bangladesh and Vietnam). He said the "Though public attention shifted to the H1N1 influenza pandemic for most of 2009, H5N1 continues to be a serious menace" and a continuing threat to global animal and human health.[1160]

China has always been reluctant to share health information with international bodies, as for example was the case during an outbreak of SARS (Severe Acute Respiratory Syndrome) in 2003.

The initial outbreak of this disease was hidden from the public, since it came at the time of a big political meeting during which only good news was allowed into the press. And even when the WHO itself was warning people against travel to China, the Chinese government was claiming the disease was under control.[1161]

SARS infected 8,098 people and caused 774 deaths in 26 countries. And for some of those who survived, the cure caused severe bone disease.[1162]

For China, political ideology trumps human health. China consistently uses its power to block Taiwan from joining the WHO, or even taking 'meaningful participation' in the organization. This is because China regards Taiwan as part of its territory, even though the island is, to all intents and purposes, independent.

For Taiwan, which clearly cannot trust China's handling of healthcare issues, this is a humanitarian issue. For Beijing it is a political one. "As part of China, Taiwan is not eligible to join the WHO as a member or quasi-member. Neither is it qualified to join the WHO as an observer," says Beijing, to whom the health concerns of the island's 23 million citizens simply do not matter.[1163]

"No matter how Taiwan authorities change their tricks, their attempt to use the health issue to serve 'Taiwan independence' will never succeed," says Qin Gang, a spokesman for the Chinese foreign ministry.[1164]

And even as China made the WHO's job more difficult, it also asked for more money to help fight avian flu.

Li Jianguo, deputy director-general of the health ministry's centre for public health emergencies, said that, "Although the government has invested a lot of money in the fight against bird flu and pays it great attention, we need more money and technical aid to raise preparedness."[1165]

Beijing's attitude to Taiwan's wish to look after the health of its citizens shows that Li's statements are essentially self-serving.

However, in 2009 the situation did seem to improve somewhat, when Beijing finally dropped its objections to Taiwan joining the WHO. This allowed the nation to send 15 people to a WHO conference in May, though they had to attend under the name 'Chinese Taipei,' the name Beijing insists they use to maintain the fiction Taiwan is part of China. This was the first time Taiwanese representatives had attended such a meeting in nearly 40 years. This softening of Beijing's stance was less to do with any health concerns about avian flu and swine flu, and more to do with a general easing of tensions that occurred after Taiwan's pro-independence political party lost power.

Beijing's attitude to healthcare is mirrored in the population, to whom healthcare concerns seem utterly foreign. Spitting in public is an extremely common phenomenon in China, along with related health dangers such as public urination and ejection of nasal mucus by forcible expelling of breath through the nose.

For example, the Shanghai Patriotic Sanitation Committee monitored spitting at ten public spots in the city. In just one of these spots, it recorded 164 people spitting in half an hour. The city government's response to this was to impose a new regulation. 'Spit sacks' were attached the city' taxis for both passengers and driver to spit into should the need arise (it is very common for taxi drivers to spit out of the window of their vehicles).

After the pilot scheme was introduced, the Sanitation Committee monitored the same public spots again and found 'just' 46 people spitting in half an hour. Spit sacks, the government says, will now be attached to all taxis in the city's fleet.[1166]

Spitting, nose picking and coughing without covering the mouth, even in crowded and congested areas such as public transport, are common among Chinese travelers, according to the Spiritual Civilization Steering Committee of the Communist Party. Nationwide, the government is trying to make people clean up these bad habits.

During the May 2007 holiday, the China National Tourism Administration warned travel agencies and tour guides to correct such bad behavior.[1167]

Hoping to eliminate such behavior in advance of the then-forthcoming 2008 Olympics, the government said it would distributed millions of spit bags in Beijing. "It is unhealthy to swallow spit" says Zhang Huigang, who is in charge of the program to persuade people to behave better. "So we need to help people spit in a civilized way." But as even Zhang realizes, "Raising people's quality and civilization is not something we can do in one or two months, or even one or two years."[1168]

Littering is a common practice in many Chinese cities. Undoubtedly the spit bags will form part of the tide of litter thrown to the ground.

"People have no sense of personal responsibility," one city resident told us. "They only think of themselves. That's why they won't spit in their own community but they will spit in other places. They think that because they don't live there they don't need to look after it."

Though China still has a relatively low number of AIDS sufferers (about one person per 2000), the disease is increasing fast – at 11% a year – due to widespread ignorance of the transmission of HIV.

A survey in one of China's northern provinces found that almost 60% of government officials lacked even a basic knowledge of AIDS. And along with ignorance, fear is widespread. Nationwide, about 50% of the population feel that AIDS patients have no right to work or study.[1169]

One survey among more than 400 homosexual men found that only 15% of them understood that they were at risk of contracting HIV. Another survey of more than 200 men found that only 20% used a condom, and yet another report found that 80% of gay men said they knew nothing about how HIV/AIDS was transmitted.[1170]

Aside from the fact that homosexuality is still seen as shameful in China, many gay men are socially forced into heterosexual marriages making it harder to deal with their sexuality and possibly exposing wives and children to infection.

Up until 2004 homosexuality was classified as a 'psychiatric disorder of sexuality' in China, and it was only after that definition was altered that China attempted to come up with an official figure on homosexuality.[1171]

Ignorance about AIDS is not just confined to the gay community.

China did not issue its first detailed policy guidelines on dealing with HIV/AIDS until the beginning of 2006. This document ignored what role non-governmental organizations were allowed to play. In China, NGOs have always been treated with suspicion. Even when they are engaged in such harmless activities as delivering toys to underprivileged children, NGO workers face arrest.[1172]

At the start of 2007, Beijing had 3,462 registered HIV carriers or AIDS sufferers. Though the city's health bureau says the total number of such patients might be three times higher, Dr. Lu Lianhe, a Beijing AIDS specialist, says even a figure of 12,000 "is the tip of the iceberg."

The measures the government does take to try to control the growing AIDS epidemic do not get very far. When the Beijing municipal government told all local hotels to provide condoms in their rooms, only 60 obeyed, out of 658 starred hotels in the city in 2006.[1173] And though free premarital health checkups are offered, only 30% of couples take them.[1174] Up until October 2003, such tests were mandatory before marriage. Now, they are voluntary.[1175]

One reason for this level of official ignorance about HIV and AIDS is the government's amnesia about one of the worst health scandals in modern history.

Throughout the 1990s, 'bloodheads' traveled through villages in China's interior, mostly in Henan Province, collecting blood from poor peasants in return for payment. Because in traditional Chinese medicine it is viewed as unhealthy to donate blood, and to make it more economical, the 'bloodheads' would extract whole blood from people, extract useful ingredients from it, and then re-inject a similar amount back into the individual.

The blood that was given back to each person came from a common supply of each blood type. This meant that if one person had a blood disease, it would easily be transmitted among hundreds due to the mixing of blood. The blood was not screened for HIV.

The United Nations estimates that 55,000 people in China contracted AIDS in this way. A China AIDS expert, Zhang Ke, estimated the real figure was more than 170,000 among those who had given blood in Henan Province, where most of the 'bloodhead' activity took place.

Frighteningly, another 130,000 were infected while receiving treatment in hospitals. Many of the transfusions they received were unnecessary and only prescribed as a way to boost hospital income.[1176]

This scandal is still almost unheard of in China today, beyond those directly infected and their families and children. No doctors involved have ever been punished, much less any officials.

During the time the blood was being collected, the Party chief of the province was a man named Li Changchun. He is now China's eighth highest leader. His successor, who also helped cover up this scandal, was Li Keqiang. He is tipped to be China's next prime minister.

Reports indicate that in 2007 clandestine blood collection was still underway in China. Several officials were questioned in Guangdong Province about illegal blood collection activities that organized hundreds of people to give blood for money. Given that this process was carried on in a clandestine fashion, it is legitimate to wonder just what level of health checks were used.[1177] In 2008, media announced that during the course of the previous year, 280 illegal blood collections were reported, and an astonishing 4,915 blood banks were shut down for violating collection regulations. The same reports also said that since 2005, a total of 251,000 unlicensed health organizations had been closed.[1178]

One of the few doctors who did speak out about this episode was Doctor Gao Yijie.

Dr. Gao has worked tirelessly to draw attention to the plight of the victims. The government's response to this was to harass her. They tapped her phone. The monitored her movements. They opened her mail. They even confiscated her photographs.

She was banned from leaving China to collect the Global Health Council's Jonathan Mann award in 2001[1179], and banned again in 2003 from collecting the Ramon Magsaysay Award in the Philippines.[1180]

Such treatment is the price health activists such as Dr. Gao must pay for revealing information such as that the average payment to those who gave blood, often with the additional penalty of contracting HIV, was US$5. [1181]

When Dr. Gao was invited to the Vital Voices annual awards in the US in 2007 at the age of 80, she was put under house arrest in Henan, preventing her from traveling to Beijing to apply for a visa to the US.[1182]

The international outcry that followed the 2007 ban forced Henan authorities to lift the house arrest Dr. Gao had been placed under, enabling her to get a visa and travel to the US.

When she returned she was placed under surveillance once more and her phone was cut off.[1183] "I would rather die so I can save the government the money they are spending on spying on me," she told Reuters news agency.[1184]

Dr. Gao was allowed to travel to the United States again in 2009. And there she stayed.

"I am not afraid of adversity, but I have to publish a book to tell our descendants about the truth of what Aids victims have gone through. So I decided to leave. I have since cried many times, sometimes my tears soaked the pillow. I am now in my 80s and my days are numbered" she said at a conference in Washington.

"I am aware that this trip could mean that I will be buried on foreign soil. But to tell the truth about China's Aids epidemic, I have no choice."[1185]

Sadly, her tale is not unusual. Other AIDS activists, such as Wan Yanhai, have also experienced the intimidation and brutality that comes when Chinese citizens attempt to speak out over injustices. Wan, who worked for Aizhixing, an AIDS activist group, disappeared after police arrived at the group's Beijing offices to forcibly shut down a symposium on AIDS that the group was going to hold two days later. Wan had a brief conversation with a colleague in which he said he was being questioned.

Thereafter he disappeared.[1186] He was released three days later, after having been forced to cancel the AIDS seminar, at which he had hoped experts from around the world would attend to offer help to China.[1187]

And in 2010, Wan, just like Dr. Gao, also fled to the United States. "As an organization and personally, the attacks from the government had become very serious. I had concerns about my personal safety and was under a lot of stress," Wan told the Associated Press.[1188]

Hu Jia, an AIDS activist who drew global media attention to the way the authorities had treated Dr. Gao in 2007, bravely did so at a time when he too was under house arrest.

Hu Jia's wife, Zeng Jinyan, was followed by police wherever she went, typical of the harassment of the families of people who anger the authorities. Police would follow her to work or when she went shopping, either walking behind her or blocking her way. Whenever she drove anywhere, one or two police cars followed her, Hu said.[1189]

Hu was jailed for three and a half years in 2008, after a one-day trial, on the charge of 'inciting subversion of state power. In the trial, the fact that he had written articles about the government for a range of overseas websites was cited as 'evidence.' His jailing occurred shortly before the Olympic games, suggesting that the government wanted to silence him in advance.

He spent his 35th birthday in jail, alone. His wife, mother and sister were refused permission to visit him because, said the authorities, they were "too busy to make the necessary arrangements."

Hu is now seriously ill, with suspected liver cancer. Though this would qualify him for parole under Chinese law, prison officials said it was highly unlikely he would be paroled, even if cancer were confirmed. His family is unable to ascertain if Hu does in fact have cancer, since the prison authorities refuse to release his medical files to them.[1190]

The picture for the future looks bleak. Professor Jing Jun, a member of the AIDS Policy Center at China's prestigious Tsinghua University, said, in April 2007, that "I think China is entering a stage of AIDS fatigue. Now officials are questioning how much more should be invested in the field, and some scholars working on AIDS have now transferred to other fields…The government is not investing enough money."

"There was roughly 3 billion yuan (US$388 million) invested last year, which is 20 kilometers (12 miles) of expressway in Beijing," he said.[1191]

Towards the end of 2006, HIV cases jumped 30% in China, according to its health ministry, to a total of more than 180,000 by October that year. It said more than 40,000 of these cases developed into AIDS, and that there were 4,060 deaths. [1192]

Yet, at the end of 2005, the ministry said China had around 650,000 people with HIV, 75,000 of who had full blown AIDS. This, it said, was a more accurate estimate than its 2003 figure of 840,000 HIV/AIDS sufferers and about 84,000 full-blown AIDS patients.[1193]

Syphilis, which virtually disappeared between 1960 and 1980, is becoming a major problem in today's China. In 1993 the country had 0.2 cases per 100,000 people.

By 1999, it had risen to 6.5 cases per 100,000 people. By 2007, it had risen to 24.9 cases per 100,000 in Beijing and an astonishing 55.3 cases per 100,000 in Shanghai.

Syphilis is divided into three categories, primary, secondary and tertiary. The first two categories accounted for 5.7 cases per 100,000 people in 2005. In most developed countries that rate is much lower. For instance, in the US, it is 2.7 per 100,000 people.

Congenital syphilis – which is when a mother passes the disease to a child in her womb – rose from 0.01 cases per 100,000 live births in 1991 to 19.68 per 100,000 in 2005. This form of syphilis can cause stillbirth and a wide range of problems in babies that are born.

China's success is eliminating syphilis in the past means today's population has very little natural resistance to the disease. This, combined with increasingly open-minded attitudes to sex among young people, the huge gap between rich and poor, and the strong gender imbalance (which has caused a huge rise in prostitution) has led to the disease spreading rapidly.[1194]

The situation had become so bad by 2010 that media announced one child with syphilis was being born every *hour* in China. Researchers for the New England Journal of Medicine, which revealed this data, also said that no other nation had ever seen such a sharp rise in the disease since the invention of penicillin.[1195]

Yet rather than recognizing the profound danger the spread of STD represents for China, the government seemed to being doing its best to ensure education about these matters was held back. In July 2009, a new regulation came into effect meaning that websites giving information on sexual health could only be accessed by registered professionals.

Media reported the case of Wu Linfeng, who runs a sexual health website. "Currently my website averages thousands of hits per day, but is not registered with health authorities" he said. "Once the registration is required, I expect considerable viewers will go and we may face closure."[1196]

At the time of writing - mid 2010 - Wu's website did indeed appear to be shut down.

Hepatitis infections are also rising fast. Hepatitis is a viral disease that affects the liver. There are three main types – A, B and C – along with three lesser types, E, F and G. While the body generally heals from hepatitis A naturally, hepatitis B and C can become lifelong problems, even causing death. The A form is usually spread by food, but B and C by blood.

In China, 120 million people carry the hepatitis B virus, with 30 million developing the disease, suffering symptoms such as flu-like conditions, tiredness and muscle pain. In some the disease can worsen and can lead to liver failure and death. In China, about 300,000 people die from such complications every year.[1197]

There is a vaccine that will provide lifelong immunity from hepatitis B, yet according to one survey of 334 doctors not specializing in infectious diseases, four in five did not fully understand how hepatitis B was spread and did not know that it could be effectively prevented.

And only two thirds of doctors who were specialists in such diseases were fully aware of hepatitis treatment procedures. Even so, there is good news to be found. Media reports in November 2009 announced that between 1996 and 2006 hepatitis B infections among children had fallen by 96% due to a robust vaccination program. Vaccination programs for hepatitis A as well as meningitis A and C were also showing success.[1198]

More than half of hepatitis B sufferers say they face discrimination from family, friends, fellow workers and society in general.[1199]

Hepatis B is primarily spread through having sex with an infected person without using a condom, by sharing drugs, needles, or from an infected mother to her baby during birth. It is not spread through food or water, sharing eating utensils, breastfeeding, hugging, kissing, coughing, sneezing or by casual contact.[1200]

In China, hepatitis B carriers can be banned from most jobs – including civil service jobs – making it difficult for them to earn a living.

In April 2003, a university student in east China's Zhejiang Province murdered an official after he was banned from public service even after passing all examinations and interviews because he had the virus for the disease though not the disease itself.[1201]

One survey of 3,500 people in 2007 found that 49% of people would refuse to work with someone carrying hepatitis B and that 55% would refuse to hire such a person.[1202]

More than 41 million people in China have hepatitis C. According to Professor Xu Daozheng, a liver disease expert with Ditan Hospital in Beijing, this is a "quiet epidemic.' Unlike hepatitis B, there is no vaccine for hepatitis C, though recent research indicates one might become available in the next five years.

One of the key dangers of hepatitis C is that sufferers often do not know they have it in the early stages of the disease. In 2004, Professor Xu called for screening for hepatitis C to be included in health checks.[1203]

His call was ignored, and two years later, in 2006, Zhuang Hui, director of the Society of Hepatitis Diseases, repeated the call. In 2005, there were 60,000 new infection cases, compared to 20,000 in 2003. Yet Chinese hospitals still do not run regular hepatitis C checks.[1204]

Part of the reason for this jump in numbers was that a blood drug produced by a Chinese firm actually activated the disease. Around 90,000 doses of the drug were recalled in an investigation linked to Zheng Xiaoyu, the former head of China's State Food and Drug Administration (SFDA).

Zheng, who was removed from that post in June 2005, came under investigation in December 2006 because he "neglected his duty to supervise the drug market, abused the administration's drug approval authority, took bribes and turned a blind eye to malpractices by relatives and subordinate officials."[1205] He was later executed (see Reason 7).

Other diseases, once almost unheard of, are roaring back in the new China. The deadliest diseases in China at present are not AIDS or hepatitis. They are tuberculosis and rabies.

Rabies, like syphilis, was very rare before China embarked on its economic reforms. Under Mao Zedong, dogs were 'a symbol of bourgeois decadence,' but as today's middle class Chinese more and more closely follow Western living standards, dogs have become a popular pet.

However, the dog license fee is high. In the southern city of Guangzhou, for example, a dog license costs 10,000 yuan (around US$1,400) with subsequent annual fees of 6,000 yuan. Many people therefore avoid the proper licensing, and this 'definitely increases the risk of getting rabies,' according to Zhu Xingquan, professor of parasitology at South China Agriculture University.[1206] That's why only 1,000 of Guangzhou's 50,000 dogs had been vaccinated in 2006.[1207]

In Shanghai, it can cost 14,000 yuan per year to keep a dog. That is why most of the city's 400,000 dogs are unregistered. The money is collected by the police - who have never revealed what they do with it.[1208]

Nationwide, China has an estimated 150 million pet dogs. [1209]

Severe restrictions on walking dogs in public areas along with them being banned on public transport also make life difficult for dog owners. They persevere for two reasons – the first being that the sheer expense of owning a dog makes it a status symbol and the second that, in one-child families, the dog is seen as a surrogate for when the child moves out.

Yet rather than make dog ownership easier and therefore simpler to control, delegates at the National People's Congress (a political body sometimes consulted by the leadership) called for increased revenues by proposing further taxes to be levied on owners. [1210]

Despite numerous laws on dog ownership, puppies of unknown health can often be found for sale on the street in urban areas. They are sold without records of veterinary care. [1211]

In 1996 there were only 159 fatalities from rabies. [1212] In 2006, there were 3,215. [1213]

In just the first two months of 2007, 61 people died from rabies in a single province, Hunan, leading to the provincial governor ordering a cull of dogs. [1214]

In Mouding County in Yunnan Province in 2006, more than 50,000 dogs were slaughtered after three people died from rabies. [1215] Only 4,292 of the dogs in the county had been vaccinated for rabies. [1216] In May 2009, 40,000 dogs were killed in Hanzhong, Shaanxi Province, in an anti-rabies campaign. Also in response to rabies, the city of Qinhuangdao, in Hebei Province, implemented a law in September 2009, banning any dogs more than 35cm tall. Any dogs over this height would be shot, the law stated. [1217]

Tuberculosis is also becoming a big killer in China, killing 3,339 people nationwide in 2006, according to China's ministry of health.

Once again, however, there are major discrepancies in China's reports of illness and disease.

Chinese media reports from 2004 also spoke of 130,000 tuberculosis deaths per year, with a further six million people suffering from it, citing Wu Qiqiu from Beijing Tuberculosis and Chest Tumor Institute. [1218]

However, all reports agree that the majority of infections occur in China's rural areas. This is because medical treatment to control the disease before its symptoms become deadly is simply too expensive.

Tuberculosis is spread when sufferers cough, sneeze, speak, kiss, or spit in proximity to others. It can also be spread via unsterilized eating utensils. There can be 40,000 infectious droplets produced by a single sneeze. [1219]

After tuberculosis and rabies, AIDS, hepatitis B and encephalitis B are leading killers. Encephalitis B killed 461 people in 2006, twice as many as it killed in 2005. Gonorrhea and dysentery are also on the rise. In

2006, there were a total of 4,608 million cases of infectious diseases, leading to 10,726 deaths. [1220]

International travel is becoming increasingly popular among China's growing middle class. Some estimates predict 50 million outbound Chinese tourists by 2010 and 100 million by 2020, if not sooner.[1221] Given the apparently limited understanding of personal health concerns, it is legitimate to worry about the wider health concerns that will be engendered by this coming boom. It is a concern that has already been voiced by some Chinese commentators.[1222]

Additionally, the fast-growing number of workers China is sending to Africa will pose even greater challenges for tackling AIDS than China currently faces. The widespread prevalence of the disease in many of the African nations in which China is investing heavily, combined with the limited understanding many Chinese people have of the disease and social attitudes that view prostitution as a normal social activity, raise the specter of workers returning from Africa to pass HIV on.

Aside from the technical, scientific and financial reasons that portend China as the epicenter of pandemics, there are other intangibles that will coddle the next super-virus.

These intangibles, of which there are four, have grown silently and purposefully for thousands of years within the body of China.

- Ignorance
- Selfishness
- Tradition
- Face

Ignorance has a stubborn resistance to education. The depth of ignorance from adults and parents, down to children coughing on each other within schools, is surprising given the evidence available today in many educational reports, television documentaries, newspapers and frankly, common sense. In China even the dangers of the simple act of coughing remains a mystery.

Selfishness as used here is based on a stunning lack of caring for the next man, woman and child and, as we have shown continuously within the pages of this book, selfishness is active in many of the faults that restrict China's ability to be great. As negative as centralized religion can be within many cultures, its total lack of a presence within the Chinese soul may well be the pandemic's secret weapon.

Tradition within China today is a blindness that causes suffering and anguish far greater than comfort and the sense of culture Chinese political leaders use to generate the concept of past glory. Thousands of years of repetitively traditional yet unsanitary health and food handling practices provides a welcome home for bacteria.

Face may well give Chinese people a personal modus operandi for their private life but, in the global village the world has become, face has become superfluous and deadly. Hiding behind what appears to be normal for the individual but is in fact terrifying for societies has already shown China to be lacking in any modern sense of internationalism.

China's actions during the SARS outbreak, its reluctance to share information on current viral infections, and refusing to accept that all the people (Taiwan) of the world need a voice, clearly demonstrates its uni-national attitudes.

China continuously acts as if the Middle Kingdom is alive and well, the center and the 'Emperor' of all countries.

Unfortunately, the next pandemic may well end that shell game forever.

Reason 42

Sino-spite

Spite is a petty emotion, often driven by a sense of trivial revenge and a feeling of being both wronged and powerless.

Sino-spite, however, is an act of Chinese political bluster. It is an expression of self-righteousness and strident belief that, for any given problem, someone else must be the cause, the originator of the trouble. Sino-spite currently shapes China's relations with the world.

For China, the solution to a problem rarely invokes an official apology, and if it does come, it is seldom conciliatory. China never says 'We were wrong,' but instead adopts a more aggressive hectoring and lecturing tone.

Sino-spite exists most frequently on a government level, though sometimes on a corporate level too. In the political and corporate world of Sino-spite, no criticism of China is justified. Ever.

Sino-spite is a way of ignoring China's problems and negating the concerns of other nations. Sino-spite is a black and white world view. There are no shades of gray, no soothing words of understanding as China promises to investigate a problem. In the Sino-spite view of things, the equation is simple: The world is against China. And China's going to let you know it knows it.

For example, in mid-2007, a spokesman for Japan's Foreign Ministry observed that "The Chinese people are experiencing the most rapid... changes in their 2,000 year history." The spokesman, Tomohiko Taniguchi, said that China's rapid economic growth was a potential problem. "The more rapid the growth is, the more dangerous I think it is going to be for nationalism to play a role or change the course of the... nation" he said.

China's reaction was pure Sino-spite. The Chinese Foreign Ministry mischaracterized the nature of Taniguchi's remarks and showed no understanding of or interest in legitimate Japanese concerns. "We are surprised and dissatisfied with the Japanese comment. The comment that China's economic boom leads to nationalism is illogical and should not become a reason to criticize China," the ministry said.[1223]

In response to the seemingly unstoppable flow of bad news from China concerning sub-standard, shoddy or downright dangerous products being exported around the world, the Gibraltar-based Alvito company applied to the EU for the right to use a trademark that said 'Not Made in China.'

Dong Baolin, China's Chief Representative for GATT intellectual property trademark negotiation, said that this trademark "would disgrace China's national prestige and dignity. Any Chinese enterprises, citizens or government has the rights to raise objections to the EU. Such a trade mark that harms Sino-Europe diplomatic ties will not be tolerated," reported Chinese media. But Dong apparently made no remark as to the reasons behind Alvito's application.[1224]

While the existence of a 'Not Made in China' trademark is clearly a cause of concern for the nation, surely a mature response would have been to recognize the legitimate concerns of international consumers? Not from the Sino-spite point of view.

In mid-2007 the giant US toy company Mattel was forced to announce two huge product recalls within a month. The first recall involved more than a million toys that had been made with paint containing high levels of lead that could potentially cause brain damage in young children. The second recall involved an astonishing 18 million toys, nine million of them in the US, which contained small magnets that could easily fall out of the toy, posing a serious danger if swallowed. Both had been made in China.

Mattel's response to the inevitable outcry that followed was prompt. "As a parent of four children myself I know that absolutely nothing is more important than the safety and wellbeing of children" said Bob Eckert, Chairman and CEO, in a video on the company website. "I sincerely apologize for the situation and I promise you we will continue to work hard to enforce the highest levels of quality and safety to uphold your trust in us." Eckert laid out a specific plan detailing what measures Mattel was taking, as well as its plans to ensure future safety.

China's response was rather different. "Some media and irresponsible people take a small problem and make it into a large one," said Wang Xinpei, a spokesman for China's Ministry of Commerce. "The Chinese government steadfastly opposes these actions by irresponsible people."[1225] Wang insisted that most toys were "produced in accordance with importers' designs, techniques and quality criteria" said Chinese media.

This, as it turned out, was true. The problem with the magnets was due to poor design in America, and in September 2007, when it became clear that Mattel's own design was at fault, the company officially apologized to China.[1226]

However, one of the most negative qualities of Sino-spite is that you never take one step back, never take a second look at the developing situation and never redirect your policy once the decision you've been wronged has been made. "Media reports can't see the overall picture" Wang said. "They use individual cases to describe the overall situation, and some even go deliberately over the top in coverage. They are not rational and some are even malicious."[1227]

Wang also adopted a similarly defensive tone earlier in 2007 when the US complained to the WTO about rampant piracy in China which, said the US, cost it billions of dollars a year. "Such a move (the latest at the WTO) will seriously damage cooperative relations in this sector, and will have a negative impact on bilateral trade" he said, adding that the US action "runs against the consensus reached by leaders of the two countries on developing bilateral trade relations." China, he said, expressed "great regret and strong dissatisfaction."[1228]

China also criticized the US in June 2007 when America's Food and Drug Administration (FDA) announced that a Chinese made toothpaste contained a poisonous chemical, diethylene glycol. "Our research shows that toothpaste containing up to 15.6% diethylene glycol... is safe, even after prolonged use" said China's General Administration of Quality Supervision. "Therefore, the FDA warning is unscientific, irresponsible and contradictory" said the Administration. And "experts" from the Chinese Ministry of Health said that the chemical "is a 'low-level' poison that does not accumulate in the body."[1229]

Apparently, it is acceptable to consume poisonous chemicals as long as they do not remain in the body.

In response to the numerous quality scares throughout 2007, the Chinese government held a four-month crackdown on product safety, with a particular focus on toys and foodstuffs. When this concluded in early 2008, it was hailed as a "complete success" by Beijing vice-mayor Lu Hao, speaking of the results in his city.

Pu Changcheng, deputy head of the General Administration of Quality Supervision, Inspection and Quarantine (AQSIQ), said that international worries over the quality of Chinese-made goods were "totally unnecessary."

"We're 100-percent confident about and more than capable of providing safe food for the [Olympic] Games," said Pu. And Li Changjiang, head of AQSIQ, said "All the rectification objectives were achieved according to schedule."[1230]

Sino-spite is even applied to matters outside China's borders. At a Foreign Ministry press conference, spokeswoman Jiang Yu was asked a question about political reform in Myanmar (the former Burma). "China has been insisting the issue should be resolved by the Myanmar government and its people through consultations," she said. "The international community should adopt an active and constructive attitude to help Myanmar promote the process of national reconciliation without damaging the nation's sovereignty and national dignity."[1231] Dignity and national pride come above human suffering. Sino-spite is also self-serving as political policy.

Or take the media reaction to a 'stunt' that was pulled off by "A pair of alien blond youths and a man of Asian race." The three threw a handful of coins into the street and filmed the result.

"They particularly pointed coins scattered on the ground to an old man, who was seen collecting mineral water bottles, and induced him to bend down to pick" said media [sic]. "The mineral water plastic bottle collector referred himself as a retired veteran worker with a retired pension on a monthly basis."

Yet instead of asking why this elderly man had to resort to collecting other people's rubbish, media stuck an outraged pose.

"These aliens do not seem to know China and its people. They play dirty tricks by tossing a few coins for shooting scenes to be telecasted abroad to vilify the Chinese people. How mean and stupid they are indeed!" said media. "The dirty tricks of the handful of aliens cannot distort or tarnish the image of China and the integrity of its people. The sinister aim of these aliens is fully exposed, and people take pride in these honest men in street as well as their noble actions and upright attitude, as they have not let down the motherland and its countrymen."

Once again, Sino-spite led to a total denial of the problem that lay behind the incident. "People are not in abject poverty in today's China" said the report, in complete defiance of the facts.[1232]

In May 2007 the German Bundestag (parliament) passed a resolution condemning China's use of labor camps to, 're-educate' its citizens, and called for a boycott of goods produced in such camps.[1233]

Jiang Yu, the Foreign Ministry spokeswoman, responded by saying "China advocates to hold international dialogue and cooperation on human rights on the basis of equality and mutual respect." Then she said "The German parliament ignores China's achievements in the democratic and legal system construction, but distorts and assaults China's reeducation through labor system, which greatly interferes in China's internal affairs."[1234]

"We are opposed to irresponsible remarks on China's internal affairs by other countries including the German parliament."[1235]

"Irresponsible remarks" and "distorts and assaults" are not words of "mutual respect" but rather the typical voice of Sino-spite in full roar.

This voice also rejects any comment on Chinese affairs from non-political perspectives. In response to the Pope releasing a letter to Chinese Catholics in 2007, Foreign Ministry spokesman Qin Gang said "China has always stood for the improvement of China-Vatican relationship and made positive efforts for that." Then he added "China's stance on improving China-Vatican ties is persistent, that is, Vatican must sever its so-called diplomatic ties with Taiwan and recognize the People's Republic of China as the sole legitimate government representing the whole of China, and shall never interfere in China's internal affairs, including in the name of religion."[1236]

Qin responded with a similar attitude to activities of another religious leader, the Dalai Lama, when he met Australian Prime Minister John Howard. "It is a gross interference in China's internal affairs that Australia, regardless of China's repeated solemn representation, allowed Dalai Lama to visit Australia and arranged his meetings with Australian officials including the Prime Minister. China expresses strong dissatisfaction and firm opposition to that."[1237]

356

And responding to the US Commission on International Religious Freedom's 2007 report, spokeswoman Jiang Yu said "The China section is filled with ignorance and prejudice, distorting and attacking China's religious and nationality policies. China expresses its strong indignation and resolute opposition. It is witnessed by all that the Chinese Government protects its citizens' freedom of religious belief in accordance with law, under which Chinese citizens enjoy extensive human rights and religious freedom."[1238]

In the 'us-versus-them' worldview of Sino-spite, the basic level of care and concern for human suffering is missing. Toys containing poisons that might harm a child? 'Alarmism!' Food that does not meet basic hygiene regulations? 'Scaremongering!' Concern over human rights in China? 'Politicization!' Rejection of China-made technology that does not meet international standards? 'Anti-China prejudice!'

Stiff, inflexible and unyielding, Sino-spite grows out of a government view that is used to demanding, not persuading.

Such demands could be viewed as being the remainder of empire, imperial semantics askew with totalitarian power. No matter who you are, no matter how righteous you think you feel, when there is a hint of being wrong, greatness begins with an apology.

Reason 43

Can You Trust Men to Hold Up Half the Sky?

There are no marches against abortion in China. There are no anti-abortion rallies led by bible thumpers, preaching to audiences of the converted who shake their head disapprovingly at the news of another fetus 'murdered.'

There are no weekend protest rallies at designated abortion centers, its erstwhile members angrily banging on car hoods trying to shock young pregnant women into keeping the baby growing inside them, just as they try to enter 'demon' clinics.

The expression that you 'come into the world alone and you leave the world alone' has a particular extension of meaning in China if you happen to be an unborn fetus. Perhaps you're 'alone from day one of conception' because if one day you feel the suction of an abortion procedure pulling at the beginnings of your newly forming body you'd better hang on tight to the walls of the womb because it's just you against China's one child policy.

There will be no one to help you discuss the moral implications of your situation. No Moral Majority. And forget the misnomer of a Silent Majority even in concept because in China everyone is silent about abortion along with mostly everything else.

Silent or dismissive. According to Shanghai doctors, nearly half of the young women who sought abortions did so alone, aware their parents would not offer understanding. And of those who did tell their parents, more than 70% "were given a severe scolding and criticism instead of support and guidance," said doctors.[1239]

China's abortion epidemic is driven by a number of factors, such as widespread ignorance among young people - who still receive only basic sex education - and by China's one-child policy. But it is also driven by the cultural need in China to have a son rather than a daughter.

This is a "result of the deep-rooted notion in Chinese culture that men are superior to women," said Liu Bohong, vice director of the Women Studies Institute under the All-China Women's Federation. "Discrimination against the female sex remains the primary cause of China's growing gender imbalance," she said.

In any average human population, natural male births tend to outnumber female births by about 105 to 100, though numbers tend to differ slightly among various ethnic groups. In some areas of China, upwards of 138 boys are born for every 100 girls. And in cases where parents ignore the one-child policy, the figures are even more extreme.

The figure rose to 143.22 boys per 100 girls for the second child and 152.88 boys for the third. "Clearly, parents go in for pre-natal sex determination tests during the second and subsequent pregnancies" noted Chinese media in 2008.[1240]

The results of these skewed birth ratios will leave an astounding number of men unable to ever find a woman, make her his wife, have children, establish a home and leave his name behind.

Projections on the size of this aberration of nature vary, from 30 million to 43 million in 2010. Other reports put it in a different way, saying that one out of every ten male children born today in China will never find a woman to marry.[1241]

Even the words 'gender imbalance' are cleansed of the reality of its true descriptive condition. It should be exactly termed the 'abortion based gender imbalance' since nature has nothing to do with this man-generated phenomenon.

Studies have long shown that women have a pacifying effect on men. A man unable to marry will often become restless, violent, aggressive, and will have a destabilizing effect on society.

Unfortunately, when it comes to the reproductive cycle, China's women have borne the brunt of the political whims of the country's politicians, who are, to an overwhelming degree, men. Though birth control was available, between the years 1953, when the first national census was held, and 1964, the population grew from 600 million to 700 million.

During the 'Great Leap Forward' (1958-1961), birth control was abandoned, due to Mao Zedong's belief that the bigger the population was, the stronger the country would be. One popular slogan propagated during this period was 'Strength Lies in Numbers.'

But in 1957, Dr. Ma Yinchu, then president of Beijing University, calculated that if the population continued to rise at the rate it was then increasing then within 50 years China's population would rise to 2.6 billion. He published an article calling for policies to control population growth.

The Communist Party leadership did not agree with him. Dr. Ma was severely criticized and population studies were almost banned. Dr. Ma did not back down, and subsequently had to resign as president of Beijing University. After this he was banished from public life and not rehabilitated until 1979, three years after Mao had died.[1242]

The crackdown on population studies makes it hard to be precise about historical birth rates in China. But according to one source, by the 1960s each woman had an average of 7.5 children.[1243] By 1970 the rate had decreased slightly, but was still running at 5.8 children per woman. And during the early years of the 'Cultural Revolution' (1966-1976) birth control was criticized as 'anti-Marxist heresy.'[1244]

"Until 1970, no national policy on family planning had been formed, so the population basically witnessed a runaway increase," said Yu

Xuejun, head of the Department of Policy and Legislation under the National Population and Family Planning Commission of China.[1245]

On-again off-again birth control policies continued until birth control was once again encouraged in the late 1970s as Deng Xiaoping took power, and in the years following the government stance on this was gradually hardened into the infamous present day one-child policy.

Today's government is always keen to announce that this policy has prevented 400 million births. But the various degrees of human suffering caused by rapidly changing government policy is only alluded to in vague concessions that the country is facing a 'complex situation.'

In 2007, the government said that "the birth rate, which has been kept low for many years, faces a possible rebound; overall population quality is not high; the number of work-age population is huge and the employment situation is more severe; an increasingly aging society puts unprecedented pressure on social security and sustained serious gender imbalance constitutes a hazard to social security."[1246]

This gender imbalance is what will create the 5th Army of Instability for China, an army manned by upwards of 40 million men unable to find a wife. The level of disharmony created by the lack of the ability to enhance their life through marriage and build a family will fester and cause disruption within society.

This demographic time-bomb is locked in for these men's lifetime. Even if the government reversed the birth ratio today, these men would still be unable to become husbands and fathers.

The vast majority of these men unable to find partners will come from the countryside, where the gender imbalance is highest, and where limited educational opportunities will doom them to unskilled labor that will make it even harder to find a wife.

According to Therese Hesketh, a researcher at University College London, the situation will likely only get worse. "Because of migration, we are hearing again and again that women are going to urban areas and staying. In rural areas that will exacerbate the sex ratio very markedly," she said. "In the past, migrants have tended to go back home to permanently settle. But women [now] are finding partners in urban areas and not going back. Men are unable to do that. Urban women will not marry a migrant man; men can't marry up."[1247]

The creation of the 5th Army is based entirely on the concept of female infanticide. The 'death' of millions of female fetuses in the march of time is populating this army with men who quite likely will do incredible harm to the women who have 'survived' and been born. Demand for prostitution will increase, the selling of young female child brides, and violence against women, including rape, will create additional instability beyond natural order due entirely to government policies.

For Chinese people, in the year 2000, the nationwide average of males to females was 110:100. By 2005, it had climbed to 117:100, and in 2007 it was 119:100. And this average itself masks some even sharper statistics. While in Beijing there were 109 males born for every 100 females in the first 11 months of 2006, the figure was 135 in the southern island province of Hainan and upwards of 138 in eastern Jiangxi Province.[1248]

Nor is this a new problem. Modern writer Chen Naishan, for example, in a story set in the last years of imperial China, talks about attitudes to female children in countryside areas circa 1900.

"Families in the countryside were poor, and the killing of baby girls – considered an unnecessary burden – was common. Indeed, since Xiuzhen had an elder brother, she herself had very nearly been killed at birth, and it was only the intervention of her grandmother, who had argued that 'we might as well keep her so she can help in the kitchen and take care of her brothers' that had prevented her being drowned in the water-hole. ... Suddenly, the memory of how her mother had killed her new-born baby sisters in the well, using a broom-stick to pin the struggling infants down, rose before her eyes. The broom-stick was to prevent them floating to the surface... Xiuzhen broke out in a cold sweat."[1249]

Despite China's commitment to 'modernization,' this centuries-old belief that males are better than females has hardly altered at all.

What has changed, however, is that modern medical technology has made it easy for parents to determine the gender of their child at a very early stage, and China's lax abortion laws then allow them to abort unwanted female fetuses.

This puts a different light on China's 'positive' statistic of 400 million births being prevented. Today's gender imbalance makes it very clear that rather than couples choosing not to have children at all, since the early 1970s and the beginning of the one-child policy, hundreds of thousands of couples have in fact conceived, determined the fetus to be female, and then aborted it. Therefore, 400 million births 'prevented' births have been added to by millions of aborted female fetuses. No one has counted these.

Government response to this looming crisis, as with so many of the others that China is facing, has been piecemeal and haphazard. In 2003, for example, media reports stated that the Chinese government had banned gender selection of babies by ultrasound and selective induced abortion. Yet while such procedures were 'banned' they were not criminalized.

In late 2006, press reports stated that "Although it has been a rule within the Chinese medical community to not divulge to pregnant women their embryo's sex, it has not been instituted as a criminal offence."

This report also said that "A draft amendment to the Criminal Law submitted to the Standing Committee of the NPC for review earlier this year would institute penalties of up to three years in jail, probation and fines for those involved in gender identification of embryos for non-medical purposes. But the provision was later removed because lawmakers

362

were divided on the provision. Opponents say it is a woman's right to know her baby's sex."[1250]

Having rejected a countrywide law criminalizing gender-selective abortion, the Communist Party Central Committee and State Council issued a typically passive document that said "People who conduct illegal gender testing of fetuses and sex-selective abortions should face serious punishment."

Chinese press reports said that the document pledged to improve protection of baby girls and said that "people who kill, abandon or injure infant girls or ill-treat their mothers, should be severely punished." 'Should' becomes an inactive legal term in a country where the rule of law is not yet firmly entrenched.

Additionally, the document said that medical institutions that use ultra-sound technology and abortion medicines will be more closely 'supervised,' and it noted that China plans to increase its current per-capita spending on family planning from the 2005 figure of 10 yuan (US$1.28 dollars) to 30 yuan by 2010.[1251]

The Chinese medical industry is riddled with White China Crime (see Number 34). In 2003 the media noted that "many doctors secretly provide such services for extra fees, sometimes as high as 1,000 yuan (about US$120)." The fees levied on abortion services are rising as they would in any demand market.[1252]

But while "many Chinese localities have outlawed fetus gender diagnosis," says Chinese media, there is still no legislation from central government criminalizing the procedure.

Instead, the government launched a "care for girls" campaign nationwide in 2000 to promote the belief that men and women are equal, as well as offering cash incentives to girl-only families in the countryside. But given the steep rise in gender imbalance since 2000, it is clear these policies are not working.

Another gambit the government tried was allowing families in the countryside, where the preference for male children is at its strongest, to have a second child if the first was a female.

But this has simply legitimized the perception that boys are 'better' than girls. The research paper produced by Therese Hesketh, cited above, found that the male-female imbalance was at its highest among second births allowed as a result of this policy. In Anhui Province the average ratio was 190:100, and in Jiangsu Province it was 192:100.[1253]

The moves towards making abortion difficult are cosmetic at best.

Chen Guangcheng was an activist who collected evidence of forced late-term abortions and sterilizations carried out by government officials keen to keep population numbers low in northern China. A self-taught lawyer, he helped locals make legal complaints. He was charged with 'instigating an attack on government offices' in August 2006 and sentenced to four years in jail. Amnesty International described the trial as "grossly unfair."

Chen was beaten in jail by convicts who, according to his wife, said "the Communist Party is going to give us extra points [towards early release] for beating you." Though Chen believed the beating had broken one of his ribs, prison authorities refused to allow him an x-ray – or indeed any medical treatment at all.

Amnesty International says it believes Chen's life is in danger and that his punishment was ordered by prison guards in response to his filing an appeal. Chen's wish to file an appeal has also been limited by the fact he is only permitted one 30-minute visit a month, said Amnesty.

Prison officials told Chen's wife that Chen himself began the fight by beating others.

Chen has been blind since childhood.[1254]

Fujian province, on China's eastern coast, tried to tackle gender imbalance more actively. It offered 200 million yuan (US$24million) insurance to be spread among 490,000 households as their daughters grow up, and exempted 100,000 girls from paying school fees each year.[1255]

The month before this, however, Henan, which is China's most populous province with 100 million citizens, passed laws banning gender-related abortion, stipulating fines of between 10,000 to 30,000 yuan (1,250 to 3,750 US dollars) for violation of the law.

The Henan laws also mandated close control of ultrasound techniques, chromosome technologies, abortion operations and drugs, and stated that fetal gender identification for medical reasons had to be approved by at least three doctors. Abortions would need to be approved by the population and family planning department of at least a county government. [1256]

But no amount of measures to redress the gender imbalance will work if China is not able to change the cultural attitude that males are superior to females.

According to Vice-Minister Pan Guiyu, in charge of the State Commission for Population and Family Planning, such thinking has dominated China for many centuries. Some rural people just dumped female infants outside orphanages, she said. Pan also said that 99% of Chinese children adopted by foreigners are girls, further widening the gender imbalance. [1257]

Indeed, if the government is successful in cracking down on fetal gender testing, it is arguable that the sum total of misery will increase as couples desperate for male children return to the old ways of female infanticide.

Female infanticide is a practice that has never gone away. According to China's last census, in 2000, the mortality rates for male newborns was 8.61% in the cities and 28.28% in the countryside. But the rate for female newborns in the cities was 10.69% and a truly shocking 41.6% in the countryside.

364

"The difference between male and female infant mortalities may be related to some people's preference of sons to daughters" explained Chinese media, with noticeable understatement.[1258]

A 2004 survey in the eastern province of Zhejiang found that 90% of migrant workers surveyed, all aged between 20 and 40, were lonely and 35% of them were unhappy with their love life.

"If not vented properly, their stress could lead to alcoholism, suicide, rape and even murder in the worst cases," Xinhua News Agency quoted an unnamed psychiatrist as saying.

Professor Yi Rong, a member of Zhejiang University, which ran the survey, said that this was because more men than women had come to work in cities. He also explained that among the rural women who did come to the cities, the prospect of marrying a city man was far more tempting than marrying a countryside man. And, he added, "City girls are not likely to marry men from the countryside."

Migrant workers, said the professor, "Often feel they are disadvantaged in the city. With a loved one and a cozy nest, they tend to feel secure and less hostile towards the city."[1259]

In response to the plight of single migrant workers, Tang Mian, who lives in the beautiful eastern city of Hangzhou, opened a free matchmaking club for migrant workers. "I just want them to have someone to talk to. Life is not easy for these young people" she said.

But of the club's 135 members, 120 were men.

Mao stated in one of his most famous quotations that "women hold up half the sky." Nowhere in his writings does he mention whether men are equal to their half of the task, no matter how many more of them there are than women.

The soldiers of the 5th Army of Instability will certainly not be up to the task, but will seek masculine forms of rebellion as retribution for government meddling in the laws of nature.

The Gamblers and the
Purpose of Unemployment

In China's rush to become an economic superpower, the nation's leaders have followed Deng Xiaoping's famous phrase – 'Let some become rich first' – by creating an increasingly wealthy and pampered upper class. Deng's phrase today is more appropriately stated as 'Let some become richer and richer.'

When Deng Xiaoping opened the doors to China in 1979, he was effectively opening the doors to the world's biggest casino, and formally declaring that its almost 1.3 billion citizens could step up to the tables and throw the dice.

Deng also said 'To become rich is glorious.' And China's middle classes are enjoying scooping up as much of this type of glory as they can possibly find. That's why China's booming cities are becoming temples to conspicuous consumerism. It is why, despite the easy access to fake goods such as Louis Vuitton handbags, many young and well-heeled Chinese prefer to pay for the real thing, at a price which may represent many months' salary for them and perhaps a whole year's salary for those in the rural areas. It is why, in 2006, Chinese people bought over 12% of all luxury goods worldwide. Luxury car maker Bentley, for example, has sold more units of its US$1.2 million Mulliner 728 model in Beijing than in any other city in the world.[1260] Yachts. Cars. Houses. Jewelry. International travel. They're all being sought and bought by China's new rich.

According to the China 'rich list,' compiled by researcher Rupert Hoogewerf, China has more than 150,000 people each worth more than US$5 million, 35,000 worth more than US$10 million and at least 50 billionaires.

Not bad for a country that continually claims it is 'poor,' often describing itself as a 'developing nation.'

This 'poor' country has a foreign currency reserve of almost US$2 trillion (by late-2008), the largest and fastest-growing reserve in the world. In 2006, the US imported almost US$290 billion worth of goods from China, but China imported just US$55 billion from the US. It is estimated that by 2010 China will be the world's second largest market (with the US remaining the leader), worth around five trillion dollars. By then, China will be importing around 1.2 trillion dollars of goods and a further 200 billion dollars of services.[1261]

But this middle class – and China's economic miracle itself -- exists by economically preying on the much larger group of China's generally poor and less well educated rural citizens. China's growing wealth, in other words, relies on a combination of low wages, high unemployment and foreign direct investment.

Yet the massive boom in China's GDP places enormous stress on this cozy arrangement. When GDP rises, workers seek corresponding wage increases, thus undercutting the very factor that makes business in China so profitable – cheap labor.

As salaries rise, manufacturers will begin to look for profit margins elsewhere – principally by cutting corners in the quality of production. Chinese firms, already with an increasingly worrying reputation for poor quality or outright dangerous goods, will 'economize' even further by using cheaper product components and unsafe chemical additives, unchallenged by restrictive quality control. Running production lines with fewer people will lead to a deadly increase in workplace accidents.

Trouble for China's labor market can already be seen, as state media reported at the end of 2006. "Despite government figures to indicate China still has a contingent of 150 million migrant workers awaiting to be transferred from rural to urban areas, signs have emerged to show that the country's labor resources [are] on a trend of shrinkage," said reports, noting that booming Guangdong Province was already experiencing an annual shortfall of two million laborers.

Reports also indicated that salaries for migrant workers in this region of China had risen from 600 yuan a month to 1000 yuan a month (US$125) in the last three years. [1262] This rise, though superficially impressive, tells only half the story. As other state media reports indicated, city dwellers in Guangdong are making far more money (around US$233 a month). Nationwide, in 2005, urban workers earned on average an annual 18,400 yuan (US$2,300) a rise from an average of 16,024 yuan the year before. And even this sizeable increase, at 14%, was outstripped by salary rises for workers in government-owned firms, who saw raises of up to 20%.[1263]

China, previously the factory of choice for world manufacturing, now may face competing against other 'developing' countries for market share.

One of the reasons behind this impending labor shortage is not, in fact, a lack of people to do the work – it is instead a lack of decent wages on offer. With no meaningful way to protest exploitation and with labor unions firmly in the pocket of government, migrant workers are faced with a 'take it or leave it' choice. In the coming years, many will simply choose to leave it, a social trend which can already be observed.

Professor Wen Tiejun, who teaches at the Renmin University in Beijing, says that "For the sake of their survival, some factories kept the salary at a low level for the workers without buying their social insurance. Poor salary and welfare system cooled the migrant workers' zeal for working in cities." Additionally, noted media, "some rural labor began returning home because of poor welfare system for migrant workers in cities." [1264]

Nor is this just an internal problem for China. With the nation's boom fueled by vast amounts of foreign direct investment, Chinese firms and international firms work hand in hand to keep prices low – and to keep migrant workers exploited. The demand for low prices that international firms make and insist be written in blood into contracts, along with the desire to make profit at the expense of any other consideration, means that China's tens of millions of poor are not just exploited by the country's middle classes, but by the whole world as well.

Pressed relentlessly by major foreign firms to reduce prices in a market that is intensely competitive, and assailed by rising costs of raw materials, it is little wonder that Chinese manufacturers often cut corners. Working in a competitive environment where just a fraction of a cent can make the difference between winning a contract and losing it (a situation that can lead to bankruptcy) the 'survival' option is to cheat, to use low-quality materials and then simply present the buyer with a fake certificate of quality – something that is easy to fabricate in China.

If you think fake or pirate goods are produced with high quality in China, you should see the kind of counterfeit certificates of authenticity that go along with the products.

It is China's self-indulgent middle classes who are most directly stuck with this conundrum. The prosperity that they enjoy is based on exploitation of their own poor countrymen, yet the only way to enjoy that prosperity countrywide is to begin to allow the poor to work their way out of poverty – in other words, to join the exclusive middle-class club. But that very process, if it happens, will require China's factories to be even more competitive, innovative, and profitable.

China certainly is facing a shortage of cheap labor. "The country's abundant supply of low-cost labor, seen as a backbone of its remarkable economic expansion, could stop growing in one or two years and start dropping in eight to 10 years," noted Chinese media in 2008.[1265] But it is not facing a shortage of labor itself. What China is really facing is its own unwillingness to pay its poorer citizens a just and equitable wage.

But the disadvantaged, in China, can never be allowed to earn a fair wage. The much trusted American concept of 'A fair day's pay for a fair day's work' has no place in the casino that is China. China's government in fact needs unemployment to remain high and wages to remain low, and the continuation of China's economic success is based on the dangerous gamble that the millions of poor will continue to bear this rapacious exploitation in silence.

But this is not the only high-stakes gamble that China is playing. China's current stock market boom is one of the most frenzied, greedy and dangerous social phenomena in the nation today. China offers few options for those who wish to invest their money. Bank interest rates are negligible, gold purchases are restricted, and controls on currency conversion make it hard for the average citizen to put money to work outside China.

China's government has offered a more exclusive casino field for speculation to its citizens; the China A-share index, both in Shenzhen and Shanghai. Within this domestic stock exchange shares can only be traded by Chinese citizens and qualified institutions. Since it is almost the only legal get-rich-quick way people have to try to increase their wealth, it is astonishingly popular. Chinese history has shown the people that their money can disappear overnight, along with governments, and thus it runs in their blood to increase their wealth while they can.

In 2006, the Chinese stock market's value increased by 150%. Between January and May 2007 it rose another 50%. The amount of money being poured in is almost beyond conception – is this China, the 'poor' developing nation? In April 2007 alone, 250 billion yuan was invested in the market – and around 170 billion yuan of that sum came from individual investors rather than financial institutions.

Noted media, "It only took eighteen months for the Shanghai Stock Index to hit 2000 points, from 1000 points; from 3000 points to 4000 points, it took just forty-eight trading days."[1266] Between January and April of 2007, 70 billion yuan (US$9.1 billion) was transferred into stock markets just from saving accounts in Shanghai. When markets re-opened after the annual May Day holidays in 2007, investors were so desperate to resume playing that 421,831 new stock accounts were registered – in one single day. [1267]

A survey by the Securities Fund of China, released in August 2007, said that 70% of these individual investors were putting up to a third of their family savings into the stock market, and more than 13% had invested their *entire* life savings. A further 11% were using borrowed money to speculate.[1268] A lot of this borrowed money entering the stock market comes from semi-legal and thus unreported sources, such as black-market loan sharks. Usury is also a boom industry.

Some people even pawn their apartments to raise money to gamble on the stock market. According to Yan Xingnong, general manager of a large pawnshop in Beijing, around ten stock investors pawn their apartments in his shop every month. The China Securities Journal reported that in Beijing alone 1.5 billion yuan (almost US$200 million) was raised on pawned apartments, nearly all of the money going into the stock market.

Chinese media did the sums, and concluded that since the pawnshops give only 70% of the market value of whatever item is pawned, and moreover charge a monthly interest rate of 3.2%, "If an investor pawns an apartment worth one million yuan and his stocks yield a 50% profit, then he or she will still only earn 81,200 yuan (US$10,600) a year."[1269]

The global economic crash of 2008 did not leave China unaffected. From its peak of October 2007, the Shanghai Composite Index ended 2008 about 65% lower. Yet by 2009 the exuberance was

370

coming back - "An unprecedented $1.3 trillion of loans this year and a $586 billion stimulus package pushed China's economy to record 8.9 percent growth in the third quarter, the fastest expansion in a year. The credit boom helped the Shanghai Composite Index rally 79 percent this year and Hong Kong's H-share index surge 70 percent. Home prices in 70 major cities in the mainland climbed at the fastest pace in the 14 months to October, the government reported on Nov 10" said media.[1270]

Gambling fever dictates that you play the game. Fever does not allow much consideration for rationale. To lose face with your friends and neighbors by 'foolishly' not playing the stock market is a worse fate than gambling your own home for questionable earnings ratios.

The stock market is the only game in town, and this means everyone wants to play it – even if they know little about stock and shares. Even a professional would find this market hard to play, given the opaque financial reporting of most Chinese companies combined with the widespread practice of simply making up the numbers. It is said in China that companies keep several sets of account books – one for the taxman, one for investors, and one for the company. Each tells a different story, and only the latter approximates to the truth. The entire sector is riddled with corruption, with many unlisted firms making public share issues without any official approval, and with numerous illegal brokerages selling shares issued by unlisted companies.[1271]

But perhaps that does not matter. For most Chinese people, the stock market is an emotional investment, not a business investment. Indeed, it may be an expression of freedom. It is driven by gossip and speculation. And when all your neighbors, your friends and your colleagues are talking about their stock investments, it is hard to resist the temptation to get involved. The fear of missing out on big rewards and subsequent loss of face overwhelms the fear of losing all your money.

Even the simplest rumor or most idle speculation can affect the markets. For example, when China put its first man in space, tech firms, even those only tangentially related to space research, surged. Insider trading? In China, it's *all* insider trading.

Just like it manipulates the poor to stay poor, China's government also manipulates the middle classes. It is well aware that the Chinese stock market is a pure emotional gamble. Several measures intended to cool the markets (such as tax increases) had little noticeable effect, and the government plays on citizens' emotion to keep the market active by suggesting institutional purchases or releasing formerly government-held stocks.

But this is a two-way street. The people of China also know that the government simply cannot afford to let the stock market crash, especially given the massive psychological investment the nation had in the 2008 Olympics. That's why, according to the pre-Olympics survey by the Securities Fund of China, 60% of investors "said they expected the rally to continue until 2008, when the Olympic Games are held in Beijing." Their faith that the government, the 'house' in this giant economic casino, could miraculously allow every player to win, stopped the stock market crashing and was a public relations coup that even Las Vegas would find impossible to produce.

There are millions of Chinese citizens who, though invited to play, are unable to based on meager yearly incomes scratched from ground they do not own. Deng Xiaoping never indicated when the rich should stop seeking riches, turn around, and extend a hand down to those less fortunate.

Meanwhile, the gamblers line up, cash in hand, ready to fulfill Deng's offer, without a similarly insightful government leader now available to say 'enough.'

It did not have to be this way but China's leaders have lined up with the rest of the Western lemmings enroute to the cliffs.

A depression, with Chinese Characteristics of course, will allow everyone in China economic democracy at least.

Reason 45

The Generals Theory

At the end of 2006, China released a White Paper, "China's National Defense in 2006" which stated that the army was directly run by the Party via the Central Military Commission. "The National People's Congress (NPC) elects the chairman of the CMC. The NPC decides on war and peace and exercises other functions and powers relating to national defense as prescribed by the Constitution" said the paper.[1272]

The governments of developed nations have a clear divide between military and political power. Military control most usually remains beholden to leaders directly chosen by the people.

This is not the case in China, where a number of senior military leaders are members of the government. Cao Gangchuan, for example, China's Defense Minister, is also the vice-chairman of the nation's Central Military Commission. He joined the People's Liberation Army in 1954 and has steadily risen in its ranks, becoming a general and director of the PLA's General Armaments Department in 1998. [1273]

Cao frequently speaks of the PLA's loyalty to the Communist Party of China. In summer 2007 he said "PLA officers and soldiers would carry on the tradition of following the CPC leadership, serving the people, and doing their duty with courage." He then called for "all PLA officers and enlisted ranks [to] unite around the CPC leadership to push forward national defense and military development."[1274]

"Troops obeying the command of the Party Central Committee is the principle of the PLA's establishment and the greatest political demand of the military put forward by the Party and the Chinese people," Cao has said

Cao does show us his political side by also saying "Some hostile forces have made it their policy to Westernize the Chinese military and have preached the non-politicization and nationalization of the military in an attempt to separate the military from the Party leadership."[1275]

Another PLA general, Guo Boxiong, said "We must unswervingly adhere to the fundamental principle and system of the Party's absolute leadership over the military, and make sure that the troops will obey the command of the Party Central Committee, the Central Military Commission and (CMC) Chairman Hu Jintao at any time and under any circumstances."[1276]

Guo is also a senior politician, and currently is a member of the Politburo, one of the very highest political bodies in China. In his words, Guo again demonstrates the People's Liberation Army is the Party's army and not in fact the People's Army at all.

Politicians with extensive careers in the PLA serve in many of China's highest political levels. Both Cao Gangchuan and Guo Boxiong joined the PLA before they joined the CPC, a pattern that is quite typical among army careerists serving in the government.

Xu Caihou, for example, is a member of the Secretariat of the CPC Central Committee, which helps to manage the Politburo and make political appointments. He joined the PLA in 1963, but did not join the CPC until 1971.

Army personnel hold positions in all senior areas of government. The Vice Chairman of the Law Committee of the NPC is Zhou Kunren. He has been a PLA general since 2000. Army members also hold positions in provincial governments all across China. They are active in academia, as well. Li Shenming, a vice-president of the Chinese Academy of Social Sciences, one of the country's most prestigious academic bodies, has been a major-general in the PLA since 1997.

Generals are asked by non-military CPC leaders to demonstrate the PLA's loyalty to the Party at every opportunity. Giving a speech to commemorate the 80th anniversary of the founding of the PLA, President Hu Jintao said "To follow the CPC's command is the overriding political requirement that the Party and Chinese people have placed on the PLA and is the unshakable and fundamental principle for the PLA."

"The noble spirit that the PLA has nurtured over the years is to adhere to the absolute leadership of the Party" said Hu. "Only by putting itself under the CPC leadership has the PLA been able to stay on the right course politically and maintained its strong cohesion and combat effectiveness and well as its vigor and vitality."[1277]

Presumably, an army with Chinese characteristics would not be able to fight for the people or the state. According to Hu, combat effectiveness can only be demonstrated by Party loyalty, as indicated again when he also urged the PLA to be "loyal to the Party, socialism, the motherland and the people, for ever" earlier in 2007.[1278]

The theory that the PLA has no backbone but the Party is not new. Back in 2001, for example, Fu Quanyou, then Chief of Staff of the PLA, "urged military institutions of all levels to increase their sense of political responsibility and historic mission. The PLA should be constantly armed with Marxism-Leninism, Mao Zedong Thought, Deng Xiaoping Theory and a series of important instructions by Jiang Zemin," reported Chinese media.[1279]

In 2005, during the PLA's 78th anniversary, the Liberation Army Daily, the PLA's newspaper, wrote criticizing "the hostile forces that want to change the nature of the [PLA] by attempting to turn it into a non-Party and non-political army." Non-Party and non-political is rhetoric for a national army directed by the people, something democracies insist on.

The article "attributes the success of the PLA to the adamant leadership of the Party, which has ensured the army to grow up from small to large and from weak to strong and win victory after victory" said media. "The history of our army is a history of adherence to the Party's leadership over the Army."[1280]

Even so, the Party's increased stress on the loyalty of the PLA rose to a noticeable crescendo in 2007. Why? Perhaps it is because the Party feels losing its grip on the PLA would lessen its ability to control the people.

The Party's traditional use of the army to maintain its lock on power has resulted in high-ranking generals now permeating every sector of Chinese political life. Under leaders such as Mao Zedong and Deng Xiaoping, there was no need to make overt public statements of PLA loyalty, since PLA loyalty was an unquestionable given. Deng and Mao's close personal links to the army through military leadership meant that they enjoyed the direct loyalty of the soldiers.

But today there is no such close link between soldiers and leaders, with most of the classroom-indoctrinated political leaders today seen as paper-pushing bureaucrats. As in any army, there is a much closer bond between soldiers and the generals they have served with than there is between soldiers and the distant, faceless and pampered political elite in Beijing.

In previous outbreaks of social unrest in China – most notably the Tiananmen Square Massacre in 1989 – the Party was able to rely on the loyalty of the PLA to comply in murdering the innocent citizens of China. A military takeover at that time was simply unthinkable. Not only did the PLA have personal, direct loyalty to Deng Xiaoping, but Deng also enjoyed the active support of the population.

But today things are very different. Today's political leaders have only managed to acquire the passive and acquiescent support of the people, not the active worship that Deng and Mao enjoyed – however dogmatic that worship was. China's current leaders inspire no affection and no loyalty, either among the soldiers of the PLA or the ordinary people of China.

At the 2007 anniversary celebrations of the PLA, Hu Jintao said "In these 80 years, the PLA has fostered its fine revolutionary traditions. The traditions, in essence, mean that the PLA is forever at the CPC's command."

This is not essentially true, which is why there are so many public calls for PLA loyalty. The Party can no longer rely on the PLA to offer its unquestioning obedience. Corruption at the provincial level, nepotism among key political leaders, and procrastination over regaining Taiwan has caused the PLA to pause and reflect.

Should China experience profound social turmoil in the coming years – unavoidable in the opinion of the authors – then something very different will happen.

'Isms' are politically popular in China. Marxism. Leninism. Communism. Socialism. The advent of 'Napoleonism' in China's political landscape may allow a Chinese Napoleon, a PLA general, backed by the total personal loyalty of the men under his command, to effortlessly take power.

The generals, who may well one day run China, are already in positions of political power, and it is very hard to remove them. A politician who is only a member of the Party loses all his power when dismissed from his position. But a politician who is also a general can easily retain the military allegiance of his troops if he must step down from his government position.

And because the generals already have their fingers wrapped around the levers of power at all levels in China, Napoleonism will not be a bloody revolution. There will be little overt violence. All that will happen is a smooth, efficient takeover at the top. The country will not suffer revolution, merely replacement.

The Chinese Napoleon, backed by his own men and then the wider forces of the PLA, will quickly assume complete control of the nation, perhaps after snuffing out those elements of the armed forces remaining foolishly loyal to the CPC.

There will be bland, anodyne press announcements that the current crop of political leaders is stepping down or has been removed from power. Those leaders without military connections will disappear, silently, quickly, to be replaced by a military junta that will ask the people to remain calm, expressing their desire to initiate stability and harmony, themes they have been so well indoctrinated in previously.

The Party knows this and fears this, hence all the demanding rhetoric about PLA loyalty. This, in the end, will count for nothing against the personal charisma of one single man, regardless of the vaunted Chinese theory of rule by consensus.

This man, this Chinese Napoleon, is today just one more PLA general. But a time is coming when not just China, but the whole world, will know his name.

There are 167 generals in the PLA today. Choose one.

Reason 46

Meet the New 'Ugly American'

China today continually espouses a victim mentality, and it is with this mentality that it bases some of its actions in other 'victim' countries around the world.

Indeed, if there was a victim society, a club for countries that felt previously oppressed and dominated by others, China would wish to be its president.

But is China a true victim nation when compared with the entire continent of Africa, where each and every nation has suffered unparalleled misery?

In early 2007, China was remarkably keen to remind the world who to blame when it came to the exploitation of Africa.

After blaming companies such as Shell and Chevron for transforming Nigeria's wetlands into 'an industrial wilderness' Chinese media noted that "The situation in Nigeria is widespread across the African continent, only serving to remind people of the days of the European empires, when they came here with guns and left with treasure. In return for plundering the continent of ivory, cocoa, diamonds and slaves, they left an underdeveloped, volatile and ravaged land."[1281]

China also implicitly links its history with that of Africa, suggesting the two countries share a common experience. According to Chinese State Councilor Tang Jiaxuan, China "stood firmly with the African people and provided them with moral support and material assistance in their strenuous struggle to overthrow colonial rule and gain national liberation."[1282]

And opening a major diplomatic conference with Africa in late 2006, Chinese president Hu Jintao said "In the long course of history, the Chinese and African peoples, with an unyielding and tenacious spirit, created splendid and distinctive ancient civilizations. In the modern era, our peoples launched unremitting and heroic struggle against subjugation, and have written a glorious chapter in the course of pursuing freedom and liberation, upholding human dignity, and striving for economic development and national rejuvenation." [1283]

In explaining China's policies towards Africa, the state-controlled Xinhua news agency said that "Sharing similar historical experience, China and Africa have all along sympathized with and supported each other in the struggle for national liberation and forged a profound friendship."[1284]

It is our view that the above comments are profound nonsense. The experience of China, for fewer than one hundred years subjugated to the economic whims of Western and Eastern colonial powers, simply cannot be compared to the centuries that Africa, as an entire continent, suffered of slavery, one of the gravest sins committed in world history,

377

exploitation by white colonialists, and the continuation today of a lack of positive investment from developed countries. China's suggestion that its own history mirrors that of Africa is every bit as offensive as its claim that the Nanjing Massacre was equivalent to the Holocaust.

With this claimed 'similar historical' experience, China alleges it offers a relationship with Africa that is not only different to the Western model but much better. 'Victim' helping 'victim' is nothing more than wolfish exploitation dressed in sheep's clothing.

The truth of the matter is that China's behavior in Africa is greedy, rapacious and cruel. Under a mantle of 'mutual benefit' China is exploiting Africa at a colossal rate, buying up vast amounts of mineral resources from the continent and offering little but window-dressing such as stadiums, bridges and other infrastructure in return.

Chinese investment in Africa rose from US$17 billion in 2004 to US$31 billion in 2005. It hit over US$50 billion in 2006, and China intends to increase that sum to US$100 billion by 2010.[1285] All of China's direct economic investment is calculated to return energy resources to the rapacious Chinese economy.

According to Chinese premier Wen Jiabao, who when speaking at the African Development Bank's 2007 meeting said, "We are truly sincere in helping Africa speed up economic and social development for the benefit of the African people and its nations."[1286]

But Amnesty International's 2007 Report says "Africa has long been the victim of the greed of Western governments and companies. Now, it faces a new challenge from China. The Chinese government and Chinese companies have shown little regard for their "human rights footprint" on the continent."

"The deference to national sovereignty, antipathy to human rights in foreign policy, and readiness to engage with abusive regimes, are all endearing China to African governments [often undemocratic]. But for those same reasons, African civil society has been less welcoming. The health and safety standards and treatment of workers by Chinese companies have fallen short of international standards," says Amnesty.

Far from wanting to help Africa, the record shows that China has explicitly hurt the continent, by using its membership of the UN Security Council to veto action aimed at stopping genocide in Sudan. Though in 2007, under international pressure and the threat of an Olympic boycott, China began to make limited moves to allow international action in the country, it is clear that China is perfectly willing to tolerate any level of abuse in its quest for resources. And not only did China veto UN action in Sudan – it also sold the Sudanese government weapons with which it committed crimes against humanity.

China dismissed global concern of its indifference to suffering in Sudan as "foul water" and "filthy phrases." And China's deputy Foreign Minister, Zhai Jun, incredibly said that those who were pressuring China to allow action to stop the genocide were "ignorant," had "hidden motives," and knew "little about Darfur or China's position and role over the crisis."[1287]

"Isn't it obvious that a tribal conflict to vie for cropland, pastures and water sources was said to be a genocide, and isn't it obvious that a situation turning stable gradually was said to be a war turmoil, and even casualties and the number of refugees exaggerated up to a dozen-fold" [sic] asked Chinese media adding, with astonishing hypocrisy, "Speaking truth does indeed require courage."[1288]

China is very quick to downplay suffering in other countries, claiming the death toll in Sudan (around 200,000) was greatly exaggerated. Yet when anyone has the temerity to suggest that the China's figure of 300,000 victims in the Nanjing massacre is exaggerated (for example pointing out that many estimates place the death toll between 150,000 and 300,000) Beijing reacts with apoplectic fury.[1289]

When Wen Jiabao visited Africa in 2006, he said that "China has been developing relations with Africa under principles of 'mutual benefit' and 'non-interference in Africa's internal affairs.'"[1290] China frequently repeats this stance of non-interference, as well as requiring African countries to follow its one-China policy, basically externalizing its internal affairs.

Much of the rhetoric coming out of China about its activities in Africa is simply a misrepresentation of official Chinese policy. China's involvement with politics, assistance and investment in Africa is not in fact one of non-interference, but can be viewed as arm-twisting of disadvantaged post-colonial African governments.

"The one-China principle is the political foundation for the establishment and development of China's relations with African countries and regional organizations. The Chinese Government appreciates the fact that the overwhelming majority of African countries abide by the one China principle, refuse to have official relations and contacts with Taiwan and support China's great cause of reunification," says state media.

"China stands ready to establish and develop state-to-state relations with countries that have not yet established diplomatic ties with China on the basis of the one-China principle."[1291]

In other words – no investment from China to any country that does not perform the Taiwan kowtow. China, which when defending its support of crimes against humanity in Sudan said "An issue of internal Sudanese affairs [has been] internationalized" seems to have no qualms about externalizing its internal affairs when it comes to stifling Taiwan's claims to freedom.

"For not recognizing Taiwan, African countries can get government-supported foreign direct investment, aid and military assistance with 'no strings attached'" wrote Africa analyst Mark Sorbara in The Nation, a Kenyan newspaper. "In the end…China's Africa policy today is largely driven by self-interest, mainly access to resources."[1292]

"China's great cause of reunification" takes precedence over the restoration of dignity to all African peoples in the eyes of the Chinese government.

It was not until 2006 that China re-established diplomatic relations with Chad after breaking them off in 1997 when Chad officially recognized Taiwan. But once Chad, poverty stricken and unable to resist the lure of money held out by Beijing, had agreed to turn its back on Taiwan, Chinese Vice President Zeng Qinghong said that his government "attaches importance to Sino-Chadian relations and is willing to work with Chad to strengthen political mutual trust, friendship and cooperation."[1293]

For China, the Taiwan kowtow was far more important than the fact that in Chad, says Amnesty International, "civilians continued to suffer human rights abuses, and the most affected were women, children and the elderly." Five months after re-establishing diplomatic ties China began to give financial aid to support Chad's abusive government, announcing a series of loans, debt relief and economic cooperation agreements worth $81 million.[1294]

China also made its presence felt in Zimbabwe. In April 2007 China said it would "work with Zimbabwe to deepen bilateral reciprocal cooperation in economy, trade and other fields." Chinese media ran photos of Jia Qinglin, one of China's most senior politicians, shaking hands with Robert Mugabe, one of Africa's most despotic leaders. Naturally, there was no mention of the extensive human rights abuses perpetrated by Mugabe's government against the Zimbabwean people.[1295]

Nor was there any mention of the fact that China threatened to use its UN veto to stop international sanctions against Zimbabwe.

China is now the biggest investor in Zimbabwe, pouring money into the country just as other nations are pulling out in protest at human rights violations. In April 2007 China agreed a US$58 million loan to Zimbabwe, to purchase farming equipment – bought from Chinese manufacturers. In return, Zimbabwe agreed to deliver 11,000 tons of tobacco to China in the following two years.[1296] Perhaps it's a win-win situation for China and the Zimbabwean government, but not such good news for the long suffering population of the country.

China is developing increasingly close ties with Eritrea. Hu Jintao said that "China will take measures to expand Eritrean imports and encourage domestic companies to invest in the country" in 2005.[1297] According to Amnesty International, "In Eritrea, members of minority evangelical churches were imprisoned because of their faith, and former government leaders, members of parliament and journalists continued to be held without trial, many of them feared dead."

Even in African countries that are relatively peaceful, China is making few friends. In Zambia, for example, China has been developing extensive mining interests. But, reported the Guardian newspaper, when Hu Jintao visited the country in 2006 he had to cancel attending the planned opening of a smelter at a Chinese-owned copper mine due to local protests about working conditions in the mine. The Guardian said resentment against the sheer size of Chinese interests and growing number of Chinese workers in the country was stoking local resentment.

"If you go to a market you find Chinese selling beansprouts and cabbages. What is the point of letting them do that? There's a lot of Chinese doing construction. Zambians can do that. The Chinese building firms are undercutting Zambian firms" the paper quoted Guy Scott, a Zambian member of parliament, as saying. "Our textile factories can't compete with cheap Chinese imports subsidized by a foreign government. People are saying 'We've had bad people before. The whites were bad, the Indians were worse, but the Chinese are worst of all.'"

The Guardian also quoted Zambia's former Trade and Industry Minister as saying "We have a lot of Chinese traders selling in the market and displacing local people and causing a lot of friction. You have Chinese laborers here moving wheelbarrows. That's not the kind of investment we need... The government needs to be very careful about what kind of investment it wants. If it's just shipping out resources and shipping in cheap goods and people, that's not to our benefit. We in Zambia need to be very careful of this new scramble for Africa. What's happening is the Chinese are very aggressive. They have a strategic plan."

China accused one political group in Zambia, the Patriotic Front, of racism. Prior to elections in Zambia, Beijing warned that it would end its construction projects in the nation if the Patriotic Front won.[1298] Such statements belittle China's claims of 'non-interference.'

In January 2007, China and Russia vetoed a UN resolution calling for the restoration of democracy in Myanmar, a conflicted south-east Asian country. While most of the Security Council supported the motion, amazingly South Africa rejected it. Bishop Desmond Tutu told the Associated Press that "I am deeply disappointed by our vote. It is a betrayal of our own noble past. Many in the international community can hardly believe it. It is inexplicable."[1299]

But perhaps it was not so inexplicable in the light of the major investment China is pouring into South Africa. Visiting South Africa just weeks after this vote, Hu Jintao said that "strong China-South Africa relations of all-around cooperation serve the fundamental interests of both countries and peoples."

"The Chinese government and people will work closely with the South African side to enhance mutual political trust and practical cooperation, as well as to steadily strengthen the bilateral strategic partnership to benefit both peoples," he said.[1300] Each word of President Hu's statement seems carefully calculated to invoke a brotherhood of trust. Yet South Africa's history is dominated by the white Western racial apartheid towards African native peoples. China's long history effectively demonstrates the Chinese government's desire to dominate and oppress its own people. It is this basic historical difference that means there can be no brotherhood that will "benefit both peoples."

China caused anger in Namibia in 2009 when it was revealed that scholarships it had granted were all given to the children of top officials. "In a country where five in six high school graduates do not go on to college" wrote the New York Times, "many find it unconscionable for well-paid government leaders to accept overseas study scholarships for their children."[1301]

China is also a major force in the Democratic Republic of Congo's mining sector, which is creating resentment in the country. Moise Katumbi, the governor of mineral-rich Katanga Province, brought in new regulations to ensure more of the mined ore was processed in the country. He said that the mining companies "are keeping the money and sending it overseas," and decried how little improvement this activity had brought to his country. "Show me even one toilet that has been built with that money."

Not everyone resents China, reported Reuters. One African miner said that "The other buyers will give you 100 francs (about US$0.18) per kilogram, and you have to wait a day. With the Chinese you're ok. They pay 500 francs. You come, they weigh it, and you get your money right away." But according to legitimate miners in the area, the informal purchase of ores is technically theft "and the ore bought by the Chinese firms constitutes stolen goods," said Reuters.[1302]

Beijing ensures it does not interfere with how African national governments use the money it gives them, caring little whether they buy butter or guns. Both the World Bank and the International Monetary Fund say that China's unrestricted lending undermines their efforts to make sure aid money is spent wisely. Most big banks lending to Africa have signed up to the Equator Accords, a set of principles that guides ethical investment. The Accords help "to ensure that the projects we finance are developed in a manner that is socially responsible and reflect sound environmental management practices."[1303]

Paul Wolfowitz, when head of the World Bank, said "We don't think that … a bank should lend to a project that involves large scale resettlement without the people being resettled being taken care of properly. I can't tell you that Chinese banks support such projects, but I can tell you they haven't yet signed up to the Equator Principles [Accords]. I hope they would."[1304]

It is precisely because Chinese banks have not agreed to the Equator Accords that it is "Easier for Chinese banks to do business with corrupt government officials."[1305] It is also easier for them to finance engineering projects that come at a steep human cost – for example, the Merowe Dam in Sudan, the construction of which is forcing 70,000 people to move from their homes. "China should consult African civil society groups and affected communities in the projects it finances," said Ali Askouri, a representative of dam protestors, to the Associated Press.[1306]

China's Industrial Bank did subsequently sign up to the Equator Principles, and in 2009 the Fujian Bank followed suit. But despite China's government's decision to "encourage more banks to adopt the principles," take-up of the accords seemed to draw no further interest.[1307]

For the Chinese government, the sole dictator of infrastructure projects within the nation that involve the forced relocation of millions of people, the moving of 70,000 people, African people, pales in scope.

China, with no interest in its own citizens' representations, is therefore not interested in listening to the voice of the African people.

Yang Wenchang, president of the Chinese People's Institute of Foreign Affairs, says that "Some European scholars have made irresponsible comments on China-Africa relations. In those people's minds, China would be responsible only when it dealt with its relations with Africa in line with Western values, and non-interference in Africa's internal affairs would be equal to irresponsibility."

"China is not against development of democracy in African countries. However, more important than the specific forms of democracy is whether real benefits can be brought to 800 million people in Africa as a result. Once Africa attains fast development, democracy on that continent will be greatly promoted," says Yang.[1308]

China's insouciance about its activities in Africa was still showing clearly in November 2009. Writing for China Daily, commentator He Wenping made a virtue out of China's willingness to work with even the most corrupt and abusive governments. "Western countries have never relented on demands that African nations push for so-called 'good governance' and improve human rights conditions in the process of offering economic assistance," he wrote. "In contrast, China's aid to Africa is free of any 'ideological element.' It is China's consistent stance that aid is based on non-intervention in African countries' internal affairs and its respect for the recipients' choice of their own development paths. China has never attached any preconditions for its aid." He also sounded the tired cliché that "The Chinese share with African people painful memories of their colonial and semi-colonial past" to justify this laissez-faire attitude.[1309]

Just as in China itself, for the Communist Party personal freedom takes second place to business. China's demand for natural resources cannot be postponed while the African people develop democracy that will hopefully control corruption in their governments.

Even the concept of democracy for Africa is viewed as something foreign and certainly something troublesome. According to Li Baoping, a professor of International Relations at Peking University, "Because Africa has many different cultures and history, Western-style democracy has a lot of negative impact on their national unity."[1310]

China's willingness to work with any regime was again demonstrated in 2009. The EU suspended aid to Niger based on the fact that its then president, Mamadou Tandja, had dissolved the country's Constitutional Court after it ruled against his bid to change the constitution to allow him to retain power. But China continued to pour money into the nation, allowing Tandja to continue in his quest to dismantle democracy.

In February 2009, a military junta, led by Salou Djibo, deposed Tandja. The junta, calling itself 'Supreme Council for the Restoration of Democracy' said it would undo Tandja's changes. China barely batted an eyelid and was just as happy to work with Djibo as it had been with Tandja. A local politician, Mohamed Bazoum, said that the Chinese could not care less who ran the country. "The Chinese, they were about to destroy democracy. They were playing a very negative game," he said.[1311]

China seems to have no interest in exerting any sort of positive impact on the African nations it is so keen to exploit. Its only interaction with the continent is commercial, not cultural.

"The Chinese simply do not care about us" Martin Buywomo, the mayor of Paloich, a large oil-producing town in Sudan, told the Christian Science Monitor. "They have no contact. They never even come to my tent to pay respects. They think we are lesser people. We see them in their trucks but they overlook us. If they saw us dying on the road, they would overlook us."

"This is colonialism all over again" he says.[1312]

In November 2009, Chinese Prime Minister Wen Jiabao announced a plan to offer US$10 billion in preferential loans at a conference in Sharm el-Sheikh, Egypt. Good news? Well, Libyan Foreign Minister Musa Kusa, addressing the same conference, echoed Buywomo's words, speaking of the Chinese presence in Africa as a 'new form of colonialism.'

Explaining his remarks to media after the speech, Kusa said, "We have a positive opinion of the Chinese because they aided the liberation movement in Africa .. We are also aware of the importance of China as a strong country contributing to international balance."

But he went on to say, "When we look at the reality on the ground we find that there is something akin to a Chinese invasion of the African continent. This is something that brings to mind the effects that colonialism had on the African continent [in the past] from the creation of settlements to the dispersal of African communities. Therefore we advise our Chinese friends not to follow in this direction i.e. bringing thousands of Chinese workers to Africa under the pretext of employment, for at the same time as this Africa is suffering from unemployment. Therefore we invite the Chinese to contribute to solving the problem of unemployment in Africa. And so perhaps the Chinese can train the African workforce, thereby creating a labor market that could include thousands of African workers, rather than bringing in Chinese workers who are provided with farms and homes in Africa, for this is something that we consider to be re-settlement."[1313]

Also talking of Wen's US$10 billion offer, Dr. Pradeep Taneja, a political economist and lecturer in Chinese politics at the University of Melbourne, said in a radio interview with Radio Australia, "If you look at the ruling elite in Africa, certainly they seem quite comfortable in dealing with China and particularly those leaders who are facing sanctions from Western governments, they feel quite pleased with China's efforts in Africa...the concern on the side of the trade union, are that many of these companies from China are bringing workers with them, Chinese workers, and we're not talking here only about skilled workers, we're talking about unskilled workers also, who are being brought in from China. Many of the trade unionists in Africa are concerned that Chinese aid is not contributing to creating employment in Africa."[1314]

For China, Africa is just a continent to be exploited – a source of raw materials and a destination for goods produced so cheaply that they drive African firms out of business. While China is happy to build extensive infrastructure which will let it more efficiently plunder the continent, purely altruistic investment, such as in schools and hospitals, is almost unheard of.

China's behavior in Africa is currently endearing it to the governments of that nation, both despotic and democratic. But the murmurs of discontent, already rising among the people of Africa themselves, will only grow louder. 'China go home' will undoubtedly be the cry of the future.

Reason 47
Micro-Faults

More than any other country, China seems to be able to produce dozens of problems, unnecessarily created by inattention, greed and a lack of care, problems that perhaps would overwhelm other smaller countries.

1. Nature bites

China's massive civil engineering projects have had some unforeseen side effects. While the reservoir created by the construction of the massive Three Gorges dam drowned thousands of years of cultural and historical relics, and required the forced relocation of hundreds of thousands of people, it also had some more curious side effects.

In summer 2007, 22 counties circling Dongting Lake in central China's Hunan Province were over-run by a plague of two *billion* rats and mice. Shi Dazhao, director of the rodent control lab at the Chinese Agricultural University, placed the blame on the Three Gorges Dam combined with global warming. The vast amount of water stored in its reservoir had caused the water table for hundreds of miles around to drop. This meant large tracts of land dried out and became ideal areas for rodents to live. The population of rats and mice thus boomed, exacerbated by extensive reed-growing around the lake, which is China's second-largest freshwater lake. Though the reeds were grown to make paper, they also provided an ideal food source for the rats and mice.[1315]

When the River Yangtze flooded in 2007, it caused the water level in Dongting Lake to rise, thus flooding the rat and mouse holes and driving the rodents out. In one county, "a ditch along the lake shore was filled with mice. Residents were using clubs and shovels to beat them to death," media reported, adding that 2.3 million rodents, weighing a combined total of 90 tons, had been killed. There is of course no way to prove the accuracy of these figures.

Truckloads of mice were allegedly also being delivered to Guangdong Province, where they are considered a culinary delicacy – even though eating them was banned back in 2003 as a measure to prevent the SARS epidemic spreading. Though this ban was still enforced, the chance for quick profit led to trucks arriving covertly late at night in Guangdong markets, one Chinese paper reported. Authorities were quick to deny this, however.

Qi Genxian, a professor at Guangdong Provincial Insect Research Institute, said "it is very difficult to catch live field mice in great numbers. How can you have truckloads of live mice from Hunan?" Newspaper reports asked "But what if dead mice were being supplied from Hunan?," going on to answer the question by saying "That is impossible. 'How can you have truckloads of dead rats?' says a Hunan official. People around the Dongting Lake will be relieved to know that."[1316]

Authorities were also quick to reassure people there was no danger of disease. "It's not possible for rodent-borne diseases to break out in the lake area," said Chen Xiaochun, vice director of Hunan's provincial health department – without explaining how he was able to make such a bold prediction, nor perhaps including the possibility of bites from live rats prior to the killing of the rodents.[1317]

Dam building "violates the laws of ecology" says Deng Zhi, a researcher at the Academy of Military Medical Sciences. "It not only facilitates floods, but also creates an ideal condition for rodent reproduction."[1318]

Given China's fondness for massive civil engineering projects just like the Three Gorges Dam, plus the huge changes occurring in every area of the country's environment, such plagues may likely become more common in the future.

2. What's the Chinese expression for Aviation Chaos?

The rapidly rising standard of living in China's eastern areas and big cities has caused a boom in the nation's aviation industry, leading to congestion "that threatens safety standards," China's air regulator said in 2007. In the last decade, China's aircraft fleet has doubled. In the first half of 2007 alone, China's passenger and cargo traffic grew by nearly 20%.

"Our human resources and facilities can't support such fast growth" Yang Yuanyuan, head of China's General Administration of Civil Aviation, told Bloomberg News Agency. And Ma Ying, an analyst in Shanghai, also said the country's aviation infrastructure and staff training could not keep up with the fast growth.[1319]

Most of the Chinese media, however, downplays such news, instead focusing on 'positive' stories, such as a cut in aviation fuel surcharges and the fact that airports will "guarantee safe, sound and comfortable air transport during the [then-forthcoming] 2008 Beijing Olympic Games," and only briefly alludes to looming problems in the country's aviation market.

But some are less silent. "Beijing's capacity of handling flights has reached the maximum level," said Professor Zhao Yibing, with China's Civil Aviation University. "In addition, the airport has to deal with the shortage of air traffic control staff and communications facilities and natural emergencies such as rainstorms."[1320]

While China's aviation accident rate is currently lower than international levels (0.29 accidents per million flying hours as opposed to a global average of 0.70), the nation seems remarkably complacent about the situation. It was not until 2006 that China set up the China Civil Aviation Safety Academy, said media quoting Yang Yuanyuan as saying "safety is an important criteria in judging a country's aviation development."

Wang Changshun, president of the academy, said it would endeavor to set up a complete series of courses on aviation safety in *five years*, and aimed to offer up to 8,000 training courses for aviation staff annually.[1321] How financing for these courses would be provided, the kind of courses they would be, and what kind of expert staff would teach the courses was not disclosed.

Given China's extraordinary expansion plans for its aviation industry, it seems unlikely that the Safety Academy will be able to keep up. In 2007, China planned to add 155 aircraft to its fleets, but retire just 25. In 2006, five airports were opened, bringing the (civilian) total to 147. And, based on China's 11th Five-Year Plan, which runs from 2006 to 2010, the nation will build or expand *sixty* airports. Projections suggested that in 2007 the sector would carry 187 million passengers and 3.85 million tons of cargo.[1322]

While it is dangerous to increase the stress on infrastructure and machinery, it can be fatal to increase stresses on air traffic controllers, pilots, mechanics and ground service crew, all turning around aircraft at an ever-faster rate. And, naturally, as seems constant within China, the problems don't stop there.

China has more than 7,000 airline pilots who do not meet language standards for international flights. Currently, China uses dedicated in-flight translators to relay English-language communication to the pilots, but all these communicators will retire in the next two to three years (due to aircraft equipment changes), says Air China pilot Liang Peng. And Chen Guangcheng, a senior official at China's General Administration of Civil Aviation, says that there simply are not enough qualified interviewers to test the pilots.[1323]

3. Official Fortune

In 2007, nearly 60 years after 'New China' was founded, theoretically ending feudalism and superstition, more than half of government officials still believed in "reading faces and stars, predicting dreams and 'qiu qian' – casting lots at a temple to tell their fortune."

Cheng Ping, a researcher who investigated the subject, said that "When officials face great pressure at work, but cannot find a way to let it out and have nothing to turn to, they turn to superstition." Cheng also said that corrupt officials' fear of being caught, resulting in the subsequent loss of jobs and power, also led to a surge in superstitious beliefs.

Superstition may be more understandable among less well-educated communities. Many rural farmers, for example, are often reluctant to pay into heath care plans because they believe that since they have to be sick to see any benefit from their investment, they are inviting bad luck.[1324]

When leaders are guided by superstition – such as the official who moved his ancestral family tombs thousands of miles to the foot of the famed and spiritually positive Tianshan Mountain in northwestern

Xinjiang Province to boost his career prospects – then China's prospects of becoming a well-run and developed country may be questioned.[1325]

While Western voters are familiar with leaders seemingly having vested interests with the powers above, non-voting citizens of China may find democracy a better option than 'qiu qian' in removing the 'medicine men' of the party.

4.   Tourist Guerrillas

"Uncivilized behavior is becoming a real embarrassment for China as tourism continues to increase rapidly" noted Chinese media in late 2006. "Some experts attribute the uncouth behavior to Chinese people's lack of awareness of public property and selfishness.

Zhang Peng, who works at Beijing's historically famous Yuanmingyuan, or Summer Palace, told media that tourists often defaced relics in the park with graffiti. This, said Zheng, was hard to clean up without causing yet more damage. Surprising, since the tourists are Chinese, effectively insulting and degrading the motherland

During the 'Mid-Autumn Festival' on October 6th 2006, many tourists headed to Hainan Island, a beach resort in southern China to partake in the traditional habit of enjoying the beauty of the full moon. While they may have enjoyed the beauty above, they were creating ugliness below, and it took sanitation workers the whole of the next day to pick up all the litter left on the beach.

On China's National Day, which falls on October 1st, a visit to Tiananmen Square is a popular choice. On that single day in 2006, 600 sanitation workers cleared almost forty tons of rubbish from the square, dumped by masses of Chinese tourists.[1326] So much for national pride.

"Decent behavior is a reflection of a country's character," said Robert Lao, a retired senior Chinese-Canadian official who frequently arranges overseas trips for Chinese officials. "Travelers should also learn social conventions, table manners and etiquette in different countries," said Lao, now resident in Beijing after more than thirty years of service to the Canadian Government.

State media offered tips to its citizens. "Don't spit, litter or be loud. Don't yell into [your] mobile phone, and wash your hands before and after eating" it said, adding that "These are not rules for kindergarten kids .... [but are] basic do's and don'ts."[1327]

In August 2007 China's Foreign Ministry attempted once more to improve the manners of some of its citizens, by publishing new guidelines for would-be Chinese international tourists. These rules advised travelers not to talk loudly or shout, not to get into fights and, if they should get involved in trouble with the authorities, not attempt to bribe their way out of the situation – as might be an option for Chinese nationals traveling within China.[1328]

Outbound tourist numbers are rocketing, expected to hit 100 million by 2020, a fantastic number. Imagine 100 million Chinese tourists

390

just throwing away just one piece of litter, or each of them spitting in the street just once. The sheer volume of those minor mistakes is where China's reputation and the problem lies.

It's not the people, it's the numbers.

5. Shrinking China

China has tens of thousands of islands and islets along its coastline. And they're disappearing fast, scraped clean above the water line of whatever particular asset nature bestowed each one with.

"Construction-oriented land reclamation has caused some precious islands to disappear" said China's State Oceanic Administration in 2007. [1329] "Rampant stone quarrying and rubbish dumping have accelerated the deterioration of island ecosystems" it said. "The situation is getting worse, especially because even a single project has the potential of destroying up to a dozen such islets" reported media.

Media announced new laws to protect the nation's 16,500 plus islands, but said they would not be ready for two years. That makes two more years in which accelerated destruction of the islands will occur, and the time taken to initiate enforcement of the law, plus the time taken to catch and prosecute violators, means that cartographers will be busy redrawing maps and deleting islands well into the future.

And media also hinted the real reason for China's sudden concern for its islands. It is not environmental, but territorial. "Seventy-five of the 77 territorial base points that China has declared are islands." That is, the nation defines its borders (and thus its maritime claims, which are of vital importance to its future strategic needs) via these islands. "But the general lack of protection for these islands means there could be hidden dangers for China's security and sovereignty." [1330]

In a related situation in 2007, Vice Minister of Water Resources, E Jingping, said that China could lose more than 60,000 square kilometers of land by 2010 due to erosion. [1331] That's more than the entire area of Switzerland (41,284 square kilometers) and with Kuwait (17,818 square kilometers) thrown in as well.

The key causes of erosion were "overgrazing, deforestation, hillside faming, mining and road construction" said media. There was an 11.5% increase in the amount of land lost between 2001 and 2005, E said. Annually, said E, China as a whole loses about 4.5 *billion* tons of soil. That's more than three tons of soil for each man, woman and child in the nation, every single year. [1332]

The motherland should expect more protection from the government, and from the children she has nurtured for thousands of years.

6. Copper Robbers

Soaring global copper prices, fuelled by China's demand for the metal, have led to a surge in theft of copper cables. While no national figures are available for this type of crime, its extent is shown by China Netcom, a major telecommunications firm, saying that in one province alone, Henan, it recorded 20,491 thefts of copper in the first ten months of 2006, or an average of 67 thefts a day.

In 2005, the figure was just 16 cases a day. But even thieves know a booming market when they see it. "Some thieves think stealing wire is like withdrawing money from a bank" said Yuan Xinfeng, a China Netcom official. "Whenever they lack money, they just cut a few meters." Yuan gave no indication how many meters it would take to buy a house.

Thefts of cabling affect the entire nation's networks, said the Ministry of Public Security. "Electricity, telecommunication and broadcasting faculties are vital components of the country's infrastructure and public services" said Vice-Minister of Public Security Liu Jinguo. "However, they are currently being threatened by people driven by the prospect of higher economic returns.[1333] Without realizing it, Liu has condemned the economic purpose of telecommunication and broadcast facilities.

Of course, the stolen cable is sold for just a fraction of its true value, but the companies involved have to replace it at market prices – thus driving global costs of copper even higher, and giving thieves yet more incentives to carry on stealing.

One wonders, once the stolen copper has been refined and made back into wire, just how many more times it will be stolen, refined, and stolen again, basically guaranteeing that recycling will ensure the 'prospect(s) of higher economic returns.'

7.   What Weather?

In late 2006, China's government announced it was banning "foreign-related meteorological exploration stations from military areas and regions that are either closed or crucial to national security," from January 1st 2007. 'Crucial to national security' can of course mean anywhere in China.

According to Zheng Guoguang, deputy director of the China Meteorological Administration, more international organizations and individuals were entering China for meteorological exploration. "Some of them are illegal, which not only infringes on China's sovereignty, but also poses a menace to national security," said Zheng.

He did not explain how a weather forecast could be "a menace to national security."[1334]

China also announced that it was banning "individuals and organizations from providing meteorological survey venues and information to overseas services without approval" – thereby formalizing that weather was a national secret.

One of the reasons for this new law is, of course, that the Chinese government wishes to downplay the extent of natural disasters.

392

Up until 2005, natural disasters were classified as state secrets, and reporting them could lead to severe jail sentences.

"Declassification of these figures and materials will facilitate our disaster relief work and also ensure the people's right to know," said Shen Yongshe, spokesman for the National Administration for the Protection of State Secrets in 2005. "Declassification of such information is conducive to boosting our disaster prevention and relief work," he said then, perhaps too hopefully.[1335]

But now it seems the government is thinking again. While it can always stop Chinese media reporting natural disasters, no matter what the law says, it has less control over international media. Thus reporting the weather in the first instance – just like conducting hydrological surveys -- has now become strictly controlled.

In China, if you can't prevent bad weather, it's best to deny it exists at all.

8. Good, Poor Quality Service

State media recently reported that passengers on China's airlines have unrealistic expectations. The increase in consumer complaints about China's domestic air service reached such a point that recently the China Civil Aviation Authority issued a pleading request for long-suffering travelers to stop complaining so much. Thus China's solution to passenger dissatisfaction with poor-quality service provided by its airlines is simple but revolutionary – lower your expectations.

Less-than-friendly cabin crew, non-functioning in-flight entertainment systems and unexpected delays of fully-boarded aircraft sitting on tarmac have caused a flood of complaints even to the point of physical violence. But in fact, say the airlines, it just the passengers' lack of education about flying that has caused the dissatisfaction.

"We hope to increase consumers' understanding about the special nature of the civil aviation industry, so that together we can create a cozier, more harmonious travel environment," said China's General Administration of Civil Aviation. "Safety is at the root of airline travel, and on-board service revolves around this. This is what restricts the type of food carried, as well as the fact that on-board food is frozen first for freshness, and then reheated, so naturally the flavor suffers."[1336] At last, the reason behind the lousy food on airlines is revealed.

China Southern Airlines had another piece of 'useful' advice for its customers – that they should use toilet facilities in airports rather than on board the plane. Doing so would save money, said the airline, which planned to save 47 million yuan (US$6.2 million) a year by filling toilet water tanks 60% full.[1337]

China's aviation industry made a profit of 4.62 billion yuan in the first half of 2007, and the industry is growing fast.[1338] Yet instead of focusing on using these profits to help improve services, the Chinese solution is to encourage passengers to lower their expectations. Or, in effect, it is better to reduce the customer's unhappiness quotient rather than increase the customer's satisfaction level.

Poor quality service as a virtuous tenet has been achieved.

9. The Lovers of Rumor

In a nation like China where the news is directly controlled by the government, people have learned not to place much trust in the media. They rely on word of mouth and gossip, and due to the prevalence of mobile phones with text messaging and the internet with email sometimes a groundswell of dubious or fallacious information is created.

One such rumor that did the rounds in 2007 was 'SARS in bananas.'

SARS, or Severe Acute Respiratory Syndrome, broke out in China in 2003. News of it was suppressed, resulting in the disease being transmitted around the world. Now, in China, even the slightest hint of disease causes 'message-itis,' with the citizens eager to spread the secret that seemingly everybody knows.

In early 2007 a mobile-phone SMS message spread across China saying that bananas in the nation's southern island of Hainan had been found to contain a virus similar to SARS.

Zhang Xingwang, deputy director of China's Ministry of Agriculture's market department, said "It is utterly a rumor. There has not been a case in the world in which humans have contracted a plant virus, and there is not any scientific evidence." And Li Huaifang, a professor at the China Agricultural University, said "no scientists have found even one virus that humans can contract from plants."

But this had no effect. Prices for the fruit immediately plunged as credulous customers shunned it.

Chinese media described a Hainan farmer, a woman surnamed Zhang, as saying that in 2006 she got two yuan (25 US cents) per kilogram for her bananas. But after the SARS rumor, the price plunged to 0.2 yuan per kilo.

Zhang Xiyan, secretary general of the Hainan Bananas Association, said that the losses from the rumor amounted to as much as 20 million yuan (US$2.6 million) per day, exerting a profound impact on the island, which grows a sixth of all China's bananas.[1339]

In a country where few people believe the official news, such rumors become part of life. But the 'SARS in bananas' rumor was particularly effective since the government had created a climate of fear surrounding the disease by covering it up in 2003.

10. Earth, the City Planet

Between 1995 and 2004 China's urbanization rate – the amount of people living in cities rather than the countryside – shot up from 29.04% to 41.76%. Between 2000 and 2005, the total amount of land given over to urban construction rose from 22,439 square kilometers to 32,521 square kilometers, a difference of over 10,000 square kilometers.

To put that in context, it is more than the urban areas of London (1,623 sq. km.), Washington (2,996 sq. km.), Paris (2,723 sq. km.), Bangkok (1,010 sq. km.), Rome (842 sq. km) and Copenhagen (816 sq. km) combined – in just *five* short years.[1340]

In the same period China's housing stock (in square meters) rose from 4.41 billion to 10.77 billion, while the urban population density rose from 442 people per square kilometer to 870 people per square kilometer.[1341]

China's urban population, said media in 2007, was 562 million, but was growing fast as the economic boom in China required a change from rural dwelling to urban dwelling in order to maintain its rapid development.

In one province alone, Liaoning in northeast China, planners who drew up the 2006-2010 'five year plan' for the province specified that "Ten medium cities with a population of 200,000 to 500,000 each and 10 small cities with a population of 100,000 to 200,000 each will come into being... All the new cities will grow from small cities and towns, and most of them are in coastal areas."[1342]

In 2005, Chen Xiaoli, chief planner with the Ministry of Construction, said that "We have to change our traditional mode of economic growth and urban development, boost recycling-based economy and protect our ecological environment in order to build resource-saving and environment-friendly cities."

"In a country with 1.3 billion people, every 10% rise in urbanization rate moves 130 million people from the countryside to cities -- about the entire population of Japan. If China's urbanization drive advances by 20%, the number of migrants is close to the population of the United States," she said.[1343]

China was quick to demonstrate how 'green' much of this expansion had been, noting in 2004 that Shanghai had been given 'National Garden City' status, and that "the city's green coverage and per capita green area have reached 35.78% and 9.2 square meters respectively."[1344]

Yet other reports in 2007 questioned this news. Residents of "the urban jungles of Beijing and Shanghai live in grey neighborhoods proliferated by massive apartment buildings, busy roads and bright neon lights that lack greenery and open recreation space" wrote Wang Shanshan in China Daily. "The fact that many ordinary people fail to benefit from the expansion of their cities casts doubt on the supposed benefit of China's rapid urbanization" wrote Wang.

Lu Dadao, an academic with the Chinese Academy of Sciences, said that "People all want some public space that is within five minutes' walk for the old and the children, where there are several chairs and trees.

But there is often not such a space because some officials think that it cannot impress their superiors."

Rapid urbanization, said media, "has led to the growing number of urban poor, the loss of farmland and the existence of 50 million farmers who have been deprived of their land." Many of these farmers got very low compensation for the appropriation of the land. In Beijing, for example, land on the outskirts of the city was purchased by government officials for around 100,000 yuan ($12,821) per mu from some 'lucky' farmers (a mu is equal to one-sixth of an acre, a standard unit of measurement in China). The same land was then resold to developers for several million yuan per mu. Some 'unlucky' farmers only got 3,000 yuan per mu.[1345]

China is still calling for more urbanization. In 2005 state media said "The only way to eventually solve China's problems in agriculture and rural areas is to reduce the farming population by getting them to move into the cities," citing the annual Strategic Report on China's Sustainable Development, drawn up by the Chinese Academy of Sciences.

This report said that by 2050 China's urban population would reach 1.1 billion, and that the cost of urbanization would be 15 to 16 trillion yuan (US$1.8 to 1.9 trillion.) This would mean 75% of China's population would be city-based, the same as in an average developed country. China would thus create a social change in mere decades that took centuries everywhere else.[1346]

In 2006, Guo Shuqing, chairman of China Construction Bank and a member of the Chinese People's Political Consultative Conference said "The pace of urbanization must be accelerated."[1347]

But what will be the cost of this 'acceleration'? Trillions of dollars, vast utilization of resources, despoliation of natural land, the erosion of centuries-old rural traditions, and a rural-urban migration unlike anything the world has ever seen.

In the face of such profound changes, perhaps 'stability' and 'harmony' will be the first victims, followed by the citizens.

Reason 48
Red Medicine

You are waiting for a train at the local railway station. You are carrying a large amount of cash with you – more than you should for practical purposes. You notice several young men watching you, talking about you. They come very close to you, and suddenly your face is struck by what appears to be a club. You begin to flee.

You break away from the robbers, and as you are running away your luck is good. You see a police car. It stops, and the officers assist you.

A 37-year-old farmer, Ye Zhengsheng, had sought police help because he felt robbers were trying to steal the 10,000 yuan he was carrying. As he was running away, a police car had driven by. Ye attracted their attention and was finally taken with the officers to the police station. In his report, he indicated he was still scared he would be robbed. He did not want to leave police protection, and clung desperately to one particular officer.

In response they took him to a local mental health hospital, leaving him there without giving doctors any contact number. He was swiftly diagnosed by the hospital president as mentally ill. Ye refused to take medication – or food. He held out for ten days, and after that time, whenever he got angry at his predicament, he was drugged unconscious.

After more than 40 days of 'treatment' he begged a nurse to call his relatives, offering a reward of 1,000 yuan. The nurse agreed, and two of Ye's relatives arrived the same day. Yet hospital authorities refused to discharge Ye until his relatives sought police help.[1348]

Wang Wanxing was even more unfortunate, being locked up in a psychiatric hospital for 13 years due to allegedly suffering "delusions of grandeur, litigation mania and conspicuously enhanced pathological will" according to Chinese authorities. But when he was tested by Dutch psychiatrists after being released in 2005, their verdict was that "he was not suffering from any mental disorder that could justify admission."

Mr. Wang was originally detained for criticizing the Communist Party. According to Brad Adams, director of the Asia division of Human Rights Watch, "The conclusion of the expert team confirms our long-held suspicions. China has been repeatedly accused of using psychiatry as a tool of political repression, but until Wang left China, it was impossible to verify the accusations."

"This independent assessment confirms, finally, what Wang himself has been arguing for 13 years: that he was detained not because he was 'dangerously mentally ill,' as claimed by the Chinese authorities, but solely on account of his peacefully held dissident viewpoints," said Robert van Voren, secretary-general of the Global Initiative on Psychiatry (GIP).[1349]

While in the hospital, Wang said he was forced to take medication to keep him docile and that staff members used electrified needles to punish patients.

Robin Munro, another Human Rights Watch official, said that Chinese doctors "clearly got a failing mark. The Chinese diagnosis of Mr. Wang was based on disreputable theories inherited from the Soviet Union that certain types of dissident thinking and behavior can be attributed to severe mental pathology. This is completely at variance with international standards today."[1350]

But while Mr. Wang and some others get too much treatment from mental health authorities, most patients get too little.

China announced the results of its *first* national survey of mental illness in 2007. This survey found the country had nearly eight million people suffering from schizophrenia, and that 30% of them do not take drugs for the problem, either because it is 'too troublesome' or they fear side-effects. Doctors said the number of patients with mental health problems was on the rise.[1351]

Additionally, China has at least 26 million sufferers from depression, with many more undiagnosed. Ten percent to 15% of those attempting suicide, and 50% to 70% of all people who commit or attempt suicide, suffer from depression. But 90% of sufferers get no treatment, and most clinically depressed people fear being stigmatized for their illness, because, say doctors, Chinese society simply does not understand depression and tends to blame the individual.[1352]

Poverty, not depression, drove a couple in central Hunan Province to suicide in 2007. The husband, 38-year-old Chen Zhengxian, suffered from hepatitis-B and kidney stones, among other ailments, but could not afford medical care. Chen and his wife tied themselves together with a rope and leapt into the River Yangtze, leaving behind a 12-year-old son and Chen's mother.

They had spent their life savings in 2005 on medical treatment for the son, and still owed more than 8,000 yuan from that time. They could not even afford to pay the 60 yuan fee for the family of four that would have given them basic medical insurance.

After their death local villagers raised 11,000 yuan for their funeral and to look after their son.

Perhaps too little, and certainly far too late.

Chinese Minister of Health Gao Qiang was quoted by media as vaguely saying the country would improve its medical care system by extending access to fairly-priced treatment and better insurance, without offering when or how.[1353]

China's elderly also face extremely limited medical care. According to a 2007 survey by the country's Ministry of Health, 98.4% of people between 65 and 74 suffer from tooth decay. More than 90% of them receive no treatment. On average, people over 65 have lost 11 teeth said the report, and seven percent of them are toothless.

China suffers a shortage of 70,000 dentists, said media, and 97.6% of the population suffers dental problems such as tooth decay or gum disease.[1354]

More worrying, 10% of all families in China have children with birth defects. Nationwide, 30 million households are raising children with birth defects, and each year nearly a million babies are born with defects such as cleft palate, neural problems, excessive fingers or toes, heart problems and water on the brain. Of these children, 70% get absolutely no treatment other than parental care. Forty percent suffer lifelong deformities and another 30% die at or around birth.[1355]

Even for those lucky enough to be able to afford medical care, there are still many hazards awaiting them.

Fake medicine is widespread in China. In addition to the numerous cases of fake drugs in 2007, there was yet another widespread scandal, this time involving fake blood protein. More than 2000 bottles of this were found in 18 hospitals and 39 drug outlets in China's northern Jilin Province alone. Fake blood products were also found across many other provinces, though Chinese authorities did not give precise figures.[1356]

Though the fake packaging had been produced to look like the real thing, the medicine itself had less viscosity and was less cloudy than the genuine product. Even so, it was still administered leading to at least one death. State media said the fake product cost around US$1.30 to make, but was sold profitably for up to US$38.

The State Food and Drug Administration said at the time they had no spokesman available to answer questions.[1357]

The horrors of totally fake drugs aside, there is still widespread risk from drugs that have simply been poorly-produced.

For example, in 2006 several people died from rabies after being treated with substandard vaccines. "Vaccines with quality problems will be sealed where found and seriously dealt with according to the law" said China's State Food and Drug Administration, responding once again with too little, too late.[1358]

Low quality vaccines were also blamed for a number of children becoming paralyzed after receiving injections against Japanese encephalitis. The father of one such child, Liang Yongli, said he cycled from his home in southern China to Beijing, a very long distance, to seek help. "I filled out many forms but there has been no reply even though they promised me one in two months. An official said it was my bad luck and that this is my destiny" Liang told Reuters news agency.[1359]

Other dangers abound. In 2004, State media announced that 390,000 people had died prematurely from unsafe injections, without giving a time-frame. Three hundred and ninety *thousand* people!

Thirty percent of immune injections and 50% of therapeutic injections were unsafe, said the report, adding that in China's poor western rural areas, more than 70% of 'disposable' syringes intended for single use were in fact *reused* without effective disinfection measures.

Though disposable syringes cost just 1 US cent more than a reusable needle, they are seldom used. While China has the manufacturing capacity to make 1.7 billion disposable needles a year, sales are stuck at only 100 million a year.[1360]

Another 200,000 people die a year just using drugs improperly.

"People should be told that they can't consume drugs any way they want. There is no drug that has no side effects, they must not take drugs like they eat rice," said Professor Jin Shiming of the Guangdong Provincial Science and Technological Association, speaking at conference on drug safety in 2007. "For example, some people don't know that they can't mix certain drugs with alcohol, so they die," Jin said.[1361]

Corrupt medical staff poses another problem for patients.

Profiteering is a major problem in Chinese hospitals, most commonly through the sale of drugs, often prescribed wholly unnecessarily – and at greatly inflated prices. Prices of drugs are high even before they get to the hospital pharmacy, since they are sold via a long chain of wholesale and retail agents.

When China's National Development and Reform Commission cut the retail prices of thousands of common drugs, many manufacturers simply stopped making them, replacing them with 'new' medicines containing similar ingredients with different packaging at a higher price.

In May 2007, China's Office for Rectifying Malpractice said that profiteering and malpractice should be 'checked' and education of nurses and doctors should be 'strengthened' to prevent such abuses, as well as to stop them taking bribes in return for good treatment, another common industry abuse.

The Office for Rectifying Malpractice did *not* say such behavior should be outlawed.[1362]

A lack of well-trained medical staff is a huge problem, and China currently faces a shortfall of around five million health care workers.

At the end of 2005, there were approximately 1.35 million nurses in China, or approximately one nurse to every 1,000 people. The World Health Organization standard is one nurse per 500 people.[1363] This is why over 95% of patients rely on relatives, who provide more nutritious food and the kind of 24-hour attentive care Western patients expect from professional medical staff, during their stay in hospital.[1364]

In May 2007, Ministry of Health spokesman Mao Qun'an gave different figures, saying that "In most countries, the ratio of the number of nurses to the total population is about 0.5%, but in China is only 0.1%."

One reason for the shortage, said Mao, was that some hospitals have cut their nurses' salaries by reclassifying them as 'temporary workers,' driving many to leave the profession.[1365] Another reason is that hospital managers prefer to hire more doctors instead, in the belief that doctors can attract more patients, and thus generate higher profits.[1366]

400

This lack of nursing staff means many hospitals take on unqualified workers to fill the gap.

In response to this, Shanghai, which has an annual shortage of around 1,000 nursing staff, first introduced qualification tests in 2007. The test would focus on workers' basic nursing knowledge, administration of injection procedures and caregiving skills, and would be overseen by experienced nursing staff.

In 2006 China's Ministry of Health said that all nurses 'should' (should!) hold a license. But according to Zhang Yaqing, vice-president of the Shanghai Institute of Health Sciences, the lack of staff means many unlicensed workers take on important tasks.[1367]

China's nurses are overwhelmingly female, with just one percent male. In 2005, Shanghai had just 36 male nurses out of 40,000 in total – that's 0.0009%.[1368]

An important feature in the future of Chinese healthcare will be social workers, of which China also faces a critical shortage. "Social work in China is in its infancy" said Xu Ruixin, director of the China Association of Social Workers. China has a shortfall of three million social workers, and "It will take years to reach this goal," says Xu. Though more than 10,000 students graduate in social work each year, the underdeveloped nature of the social work industry makes it hard for them to find work, he said.[1369]

The government's lack of organization of public health administration means that there is quite literally no infrastructure offering graduates an opportunity to exercise their skills.

Unqualified 'doctors' are another problem in China. Brothers Sui Guorong and Sui Guiliang were given jobs at Suzhou People's Hospital, despite the fact they were not doctors. In December 2005, they performed eye surgery on 10 cataract patients. Nine of those victimized subsequently had to have one eye surgically removed due to infection caused in the procedure. Sui Guorong was fined 300,000 yuan (US$37,500) and jailed for six years, and his brother was fined 200,000 yuan and jailed for five years.[1370]

Xu Qing, a genuine ophthalmologist involved in the case who had been working alongside the brothers, had his license revoked.

The brothers and Dr. Xu had traveled from the nearby city of Shanghai to perform these operations on a commercial basis in conjunction with Suzhou People's Hospital. Such practices are banned in Chinese law, as are doctors from traveling to a new city to work without re-registering.[1371]

The Ministry of Health announced in early 2007 that in the two years preceding it had dealt with 174,000 cases of unlicensed medical practice. The Ministry penalized 58,000 medical institutions for employing unqualified doctors, confiscated 80 million yuan (US$10.2 million) of illegal income, and imposed total fines of 280 million yuan.

It did not indicate if this money gained by financial penalties was reassigned to medical care.

The Ministry also said it had *suspended* two doctors of a five-member team in eastern Anhui Province for *six months* because they allowed unlicensed medical personnel to treat a baby girl who died after a misdiagnosis. The other three team members treating the girl had no practitioner's license.[1372]

In 2006 Chinese media reported that Shanghai was China's only city that required its doctors to demonstrate understanding of clinical trials, systematic reviews and meta-analysis (that is, an overall analysis of many individual analyses) when being considered for promotion.[1373]

Also in 2006 China Central TV broadcast a program about medical corruption which revealed how in one hospital in China's southern Hainan Island, doctors' salaries were tied to the amount of medicine they prescribed, with 50% of their income coming from drug royalties. Fifteen percent of the profit made on the medicine went to the doctor, with the rest going to the hospital and its various departments.

One insider said the hospital touted him as a doctor even though he was not one. They said he was a respected urologist, and he would 'analyze' patients' urine and falsely claim they suffered from a sexual disease. They would then be prescribed unnecessary and expensive drugs.[1374]

Figures released by the Ministry of Health in 2007 said that average in-patient costs rose to 4,669 (US$548) yuan in 2006, an increase of 44% from 2001.[1375]

The rampant pursuit of profit means that patients who are ill are simply turned away if they cannot afford to pay – even if they need emergency treatment. This led China's government to make a requirement that hospitals should offer emergency treatment irrespective of the person's ability to pay.

Only 6% of doctors supported the new requirement, with 18% against it. The remainder were less than positive, asking who would pay the extra costs.

The government offered no financial support for this, leading hospitals to wonder how they would cover these costs, given that they already face hundreds of thousands of yuan in unpaid bills every year. While the Health Ministry acknowledged these losses, Vice-Minister of Health Ma Xiaowei said that "Hospitals should not use this as an excuse for refusing to give patients treatment."

One doctor who refused to be named said that "My hospital stipulates that doctors who offer emergency treatment must pay the bill themselves if their patient cannot afford it. This is a blow to my commitment, and it has hurt my commitment to save lives."

The above quote is a stunning indictment of the present-day Chinese medical profession, and undoubtedly is felt by a large number of medical professionals within the system today.

Chinese media noted the 'unsatisfactory situation' was a threat to 'social stability,' but had nothing to say about the humanitarian aspects of the problem.[1376]

The utter lack of health care for those without money led one young farmer, suffering from bone marrow disease, to commit armed robbery because being sentenced to prison was the only way he could get free medical treatment. Chinese media reported in November 2008 that his plan had been successful and he was receiving the life-saving treatment he needed under police supervision.[1377]

Hospitals profit from lucrative areas such as plastic surgery, catering to the boom for surgical intervention among China's growing middle class. Shanghai, which had almost no specialized plastic surgery hospitals in 1999, had nearly 100 of them by 2007. Face lifts and weight reduction are popular, as are operations to enlarge breasts and widen the eyes, made popular in response to notions of perceived Western-style beauty.[1378]

Maternity is also big business. The Xiyue Postnatal Hospital opened in Shanghai at the end of 2006. It was dubbed China's first 'five star' hospital. Its cheapest room cost 40,000 yuan a month (US$5,000) while its most expensive, a two-floor luxury suite with kitchen and karaoke bar, costs 10,000 yuan a day.

The hospital defended these prices as 'reasonable,' and said it was expecting to do good business, partly because 2007, a 'Pig' year based on the traditional Chinese lunar calendar, was deemed to be a good time to give birth, and partly because traditional Chinese belief suggests women should stay confined for a month after giving birth lest they fall prey to 'evil spirits.' Such beliefs are fostered even by modern hospitals to increase revenue from extended stays.[1379]

Not only are the hospitals chasing the cash. Because many medical specialists only see patients once or twice a week, hospitals have set up a numbered queuing system via which patients buy a ticket to see the doctor. But 'fake patients' queue up early in the morning to buy the limited numbers of tickets and then sell (scalp) them on to genuine patients at around double the legitimate price - and sometimes far more. Media reported in 2009 that scalpers were charging 3,000 yuan (US$440) for tickets at several Beijing hospitals. They were able to ask such a high price because the tickets were for appointments with specialist doctors who only see a handful of patients a week.[1380]

Some scalpers try to make money in other ways, by luring patients from major hospitals to smaller ones – or even to unlicensed facilities.[1381]

Even the press has difficulty making the public aware of the inadequacies of the Chinese medical care system.

One group of Chinese reporters tried to expose some of the failings of local hospitals in 2007 by submitting 'urine' samples to ten hospitals in the southern city of Hangzhou. The samples were in fact tea.

Six of the hospitals 'diagnosed' urinary tract infections, and five of them prescribed medicine costing up to 400 yuan (US$50). One 'patient' diagnosed as having an 'inflammation' was billed 1300 yuan (US$168) for medical treatment.

The journalists were later criticized by Ministry of Health spokesman Mao Qun'an. "If people keep bringing liquids like beers and sauce as urine specimens for medical tests, hospitals must add a new procedure to test whether the specimen is actually urine" he said. Doctors and other medical experts, however, were scathing about this suggestion.[1382]

Mao also said the media should learn more about science and medical services before trying to uncover problems because medical technologies are complicated, reported Shanghai Daily.[1383]

China's Health Minister, Gao Qiang, faced a rare moment of genuine questioning in early 2007 after nine senior medical experts said China's Ministry of Health was inefficient and losing authority, Hong Kong media reported.

The experts called for the creation of a commission to oversee public health, but when reporters asked the Minister his response to this he avoided giving a direct reply. The experts also questioned why government spending on health was just 2.6% of GDP, or a total of 690 billion yuan, especially when China's soaring tax revenues *increased* by 800 billion yuan in 2006.[1384]

Healthcare, of course, should extend to all members of society, whether emergency care or extended therapeutic care.

Disabled people, for example, face widespread discrimination in China, and most are not financially independent. According to the Second China National Sample Survey on Disability, China has around 83 million disabled people, but only 22.66 million of them are employed.[1385]

In 2007 China implemented legislation to try to address this problem, stipulating that handicapped people should make up no less than 1.5% of the workforce in government-run enterprises and departments. A more natural figure, reflecting the actual number of disabled people relative to the population base, would be a little over 6%.

Only 5.1% of disabled citizens in rural areas receive government benefits, rising to 13.3% in urban areas, said the survey, which interviewed more than 2.5 million people across the whole of China.

In 1987, 59% of disabled people above the age of 15 were illiterate. That figure had dropped to just over 43% by 2006 – a decrease, but not a very large one given China's economic success in that period.[1386]

The rapidly-growing level of pollution in China is having a profoundly negative effect on the health of the nation. According to health experts, air and water pollution along with heavy use of pesticides and food additives were behind cancer becoming the top killer in China in 2006.

The next nine major killers were cerebrovascular diseases, respiratory diseases, heart diseases, injuries and poisoning, diseases of the digestive system, endocrine nutritional and metabolic disturbance, diseases of the urinary and urogenital system, diseases of the nervous system and mental disorder.[1387]

"The main reason behind the rising number of cancer cases is that pollution of the environment, water and air is getting worse day by day," said Chen Zhizhou, a health expert with the Cancer Research Institute affiliated to the Chinese Academy of Medical Sciences.

A Ministry of Health survey across 30 cities found that the cancer rate had risen by 19% in cities and 23% in rural areas in recent years, though media did not give precise dates.[1388]

More bad news came from a different survey in 2006. This survey, carried out by the Party School of the Communist Party of China's Central Committee, which interviewed more than 3,000 officials, found that more than 60% of them had little awareness of AIDS prevention and control. Astonishingly, 38% of them believed China had already developed an AIDS vaccine.[1389]

This lack of awareness of health issues among China's government officials perhaps explains why even when China does try to address the situation, it does so in a flawed and uniformed manner, fostered by a high degree of ignorance.

New regulations issued in spring 2007 were designed to stop the growing trade in human organs for transplant. But, admitted vice-minister of health Huang Jiefu, the legal framework was incomplete, since the legislation did not specify how death was to be defined. This is important because, if organs are to be used for transplant, they must be removed from the donor body within 15 minutes of the heart stopping, or they are unusable.

This is why most countries use brain death rather than the heart stopping as the measure of when life ends, since it enables the organs to be removed earlier, thus maximizing benefit to others.

In China, where 1.5 million people need transplants every year but only 10,000 organs are available, it is surely critical to do anything possible to make donation easier.

But in Chinese culture it is believed that life goes on until the heart stops, and it is currently illegal to remove organs at brain death alone. Yet even though academics have been pressing for legislation to address this point since the 1980s, nothing has been done.

Legislation on brain death would be completed in three to five years, said vice-minister Huang.[1390]

The official government response to so many of China's medical problems is to make vague pronouncements along the lines of 'something must be done' – but very rarely to specify what, if any, measures are being taken.

For example, China's rural areas suffer an acute shortage of doctors. Eighty percent of China's two million registered doctors work in the country's cities, and 80% of those work in major hospitals. At present, there is no logistical program requiring doctors to first practice the early stages of their career in rural areas.

"It's the government's duty to keep improving community-based medical services, which offer those who cannot afford expensive hospital bills convenient access to healthcare" said Chinese Vice-Premier Wu Yi. She urged local governments to improve their community health services.

She did not make any mention of funding from central government, nor did she offer any specific targets.[1391]

While matters of finance and economics receive lightning response from government officials in the way of new policies and directives, medical and social care receive only vague pronouncements of future efforts intended to improve situations that are current today. In fact, the lack of immediacy in solving these problems allows them to escalate in size and seriousness beyond the ability of even the vague pronouncements to control them.

You are a father. You take your sick daughter, suffering from leukemia into the hospital. The hospital charges are prohibitive. She needs a bone marrow transplant. You don't have the money. What do you do?

In China, you just walk away and leave her there.

In November 2006 a farmer from China's central Henan Province was forced to abandon his 18-year-old daughter when he ran out of money to pay for her leukemia treatment. He had taken her to a Beijing hospital but the 80,000 yuan the family had borrowed had been used up. Leaving a deposit of 5,000 yuan, the farmer left his daughter, Zhou Huan, in the care of the hospital explaining he would return home to borrow more money.

Three days later he telephoned to say he had been unable to raise more cash and was leaving his daughter in the hospital's care.

Doctors said that surgery for her leukemia, assuming a suitable bone marrow donor could be found, would cost 200,000 yuan. Authorities in the family's hometown said that the family could not apply for charity until their financial status had been checked.[1392]

For those who do not walk away, there are no alternatives to the medical care the Chinese government offers its people.

There are no airplane rides to overseas countries for specialized treatment, no foreign medicines and international doctors. There is only the suffering, and finally the horror, as you watch your loved ones cling to life knowing that there is an answer, if only you had the money.

If only you had the care a great nation should offer its citizens.

Reason 49
Daughters, Wives, & Mothers in Fear

Confucius said in effect that a 'good' woman should first obey her father, then her husband and, when widowed, her son -- though the truly virtuous woman would kill herself when her husband died.

While virtually every society in the world has discriminated against women in some capacity, few countries have formalized their discrimination as much as China. Based on centuries of Confucian heritage, the place of Chinese women comes at the bottom of a deeply patriarchal and hierarchical structure. Confucian beliefs expressed the idea women were to be bought and sold as wives or concubines and expected to offer unquestioning obedience and servitude.

Also well-known is the Chinese practice of foot-binding, introduced during the Tang Dynasty (618-907AD), perhaps the ultimate disfiguration of a species just for the pleasure of man. The purpose of this brutal practice was to ensure women had what were known as 'golden lotus' feet, just three inches long.

When a girl was just five or six years old her feet would be bound in bandages to restrict normal development. Sometimes mothers would even break the toes or arch bones of their daughter's feet as part of this brutal process. As the child grew the flesh of the feet would often suppurate and rot, dripping blood and pus. Because of this the bandages wrapping the foot were soaked in perfume. When they were changed and washed the smell was intense.

But in the eyes of Chinese men, tiny feet were deemed desirable, as was the slow, shuffling walk that resulted from them. This walk also, men believed, gave the woman a tight vagina, thus enhancing her sexual value. Tiny feet became sexualized, even fetishized, but the foot itself would always be hidden from male view inside an elaborately-embroidered slipper (even in bed), hiding the rotting flesh and broken bones from sight.

It was impossible for a woman from the upper classes to marry if she had normal feet. At first the practice was restricted to the aristocracy, where, since a woman with bound feet was unable to work, it was also a sign of wealth. Bound feet also made it impossible for a woman to walk far, thus, in the eyes of men, helping to enforce her chastity. Over the centuries it became widespread. But throughout its history foot-binding remained an exclusively Han custom, and indeed was used to demonstrate Han 'superiority' and distance from other races. The rulers of the Qing Dynasty (1644-1911AD), who were Manchu nationality, not Han, did not practice foot-binding and indeed tried to ban it, without any success. Foot binding only began to be eradicated when the Qing Dynasty fell.

The Communist Party attempted to rectify centuries of imperial dynastic oppression with the very first law passed after the People's

Republic of China was founded in 1949. The 1950 marriage law sought to legalize and enforce the rights of women.

The changes brought about by the Communist Party were undoubtedly a significant advance for women's rights, providing a sharp break from the traditional view and treatment of women in society. In the early days of Mao Zedong, women were favored with conditions of equality beyond that which they had ever experienced previously in the history of China.

Though jobs demanding heavy physical labor, such as mining, remain the preserve of men, women take an active part in what today are still largely male-dominated professions, such as engineering.

Strangely, with the passing of Mao, there seems to be also a reduction in the social and political fortunes of the women of China.

One of the key problems holding back women is their under-representation in politics and business. Though China does have some prominent women, such as China's Vice-Premier Wu Yi (cited as the third most powerful woman in the world by Forbes in 2006) Xie Qihua, chairwoman of China's biggest steelmaker, Baosteel, and Ma Xuezheng, a senior vice president of computer manufacturer Lenovo, (named by Forbes as one of the world's most powerful women in business in 2006) these cases are very much the exception.

Xie Qihua was the only female boss in her industry until her retirement in 2007. Wu Yi also retired, in early 2008. She was replaced by a man, and, at the time of writing (mid 2010) there are virtually no women at all in the highest levels of the Chinese government. All China's vice premier's are men, and among the five state councilors (the next highest political level) there is just one woman, Liu Yangdong.

Ma Xuezheng also retired in 2007 for 'personal reasons' though Forbes hinted this was to do with problems in Lenovo's takeover of IBM's global PC business.[1393]

China's political and business culture is a world of men. Only 20% of members of China's National People's Congress are women, and only about 16% of the Chinese People's Political Consultative Conference.[1394] China did not get its first female governor, Gu Xiulian, until 1983. Nationwide, there are 15 million female officials, accounting for 38% of the total number of officials. But most of these 15 million serve at a low level. Only 9.9% serve at provincial or ministerial level.[1395] And at the highest level of government, just 2% are female said media in 2005.[1396]

In business, only 20% of the 'entrepreneurial class' is female, but in many of those businesses run by women, female employees make up more than half the total, compared to around 40% nationwide, a case of female bosses opening the doors for female workers.[1397]

While the position of women today in China is clearly vastly better than it was a century ago, the change has not been as dramatic as

China's government likes to suggest. And most statistics suggest the situation is getting worse, not better.

In early 2005, a nationwide survey revealed that 71% of Chinese women had been sexually harassed. Other surveys resulted in similar findings. Later in 2005 a survey of more than 8,000 Chinese people found that 78% of men said they had never experienced sexual harassment. Just 21% of women said the same.

A different survey, by the Chinese Academy of Social Sciences, stated that nearly 40% of women in private and foreign-funded businesses had suffered sexual harassment. And in 2005, a survey of nearly 3,000 women found that 60% experienced sexual harassment occasionally, and 17% experienced it frequently.[1398]

Another 2005 survey found that 600,000 people in Beijing suffered from depression, and that the key cause of this was unhappy marriages and domestic violence, with an additional survey in the same year putting the proportion of women suffering sexual harassment in the workplace and elsewhere at 86%.[1399]

In 2002, Wu Changzhen, a member of the Chinese People's Political Consultative Conference, China's rubber-stamp parliament, announced she was "considering" putting forward a proposal for a national law on domestic violence.

She said "spreading family violence is posing an increasingly serious threat on social stability in China. Children, the elderly, especially women, are major victims of family violence," reported Chinese media, noting that cases of domestic violence rose by 25.4% in China between the 1980s and 1990s.[1400]

But in 2008 Mo Wenxiu, Vice-Chair of the All-China Women's Federation was still calling for "incorporating a domestic violence prevention law into the country's legislation plan for the next five years" said Chinese media. The All-China Women's Federation also reported that between 2005 and 2007 reports of domestic violence had doubled. [1401]

It is true that China has some laws that at least address domestic violence. Yet these laws are both weak and unclear. China's revised Marriage Law of 2002 does outlaw marital violence. But it does not say how violence is to be defined, leaving victims in a legal grey area. China's previous marriage law, drawn up in 1980, did not mention domestic violence at all.[1402]

China's Law on the Protection of Women's Rights and Interests (1992) prohibits violence against women, but does not offer any preventative measures. It does not even say which government bodies are responsible for dealing with domestic violence.[1403] And all this law is aimed at married couples only -- cohabiting couples are not covered.

"It's a long way to go for Chinese women to realize equality de facto from equality in law," says Wu Changzhen, who is also on the Executive Committee of the All-China Women's Federation and a professor of marriage law with the China University of Political Science and Law.[1404]

It was only in 2005, when the 1992 Law on the Protection of Women's Rights and Interests was revised, that the equality of men and women was explicitly announced as state policy.[1405]

Yet one must ask just how much effect this law has had, since it was only in July 2008 that China used the law to impose the first *ever* jail sentence for sexual harassment. The malefactor in this case was Liu Lun, a personnel manager in the city of Chengdu. He had forcibly tried to kiss a female employee, Chen Dan. Liu was sentenced to five months in prison.[1406]

In fact, the law on the protection of women's rights does *not* even state that sexual harassment is against the law. It merely suggests such behavior is morally questionable. It was only in October 2009 that legislators began to mull amending the law so that it would contain the phrase "Sexual harassment against women is forbidden." Proposed updates would also make it easier for women to sue perpetrators or get the police involved. However, lawmakers in the central government proposed it should be up to each province individually to decide exactly what constituted sexual harassment - thus effectively guaranteeing women would not gain any meaningful, settled code to offer them protection.[1407]

A survey conducted by the Domestic Violence Network in nine cities of three provinces between 2000 and 2001 found that 34.7% families suffer from domestic violence.[1408] Though Chinese media in 2006 cited these figures as the latest available, another survey released by the All-China Women's Federation in 2004 gave the same overall picture, saying a third of all China's married women experience domestic violence. Domestic violence occurs in three out of every 10 families, said the Federation, and is a factor in three-fifths of the country's divorce cases.[1409]

According to Xie Lihua, director of the Cultural Development Centre for Rural Women, 66% of the roughly 170,000 annual cases of suicide among women in China's countryside were the result of domestic violence. Xie said that more than a third of rural women suffer from physical violence *every few months.*

Li Ying, with the Centre for Women's Law Studies and Legal Services at Peking University Law School, said in 2006 that current legislation was too general and could not properly protect victims. And according to Mao Yu'e, another member of the National People's Congress and also a judge, abusers often escaped punishment due to the absence of an explicit definition of domestic violence and penalties in the legal code.[1410]

The All-China Women's Federation says it has seen a big spike in the number of cries for help it has received about domestic violence, dealing with more than 45,000 cases in 2003, double the number it had handled in 2000. Of the 2003 cases, 263 involved violence that led to death. Deng Li, a senior official with the Federation, says "domestic

410

violence has become a pervasive social problem in recent years, seriously endangering women's psychological and physical security and health," reported Chinese media.[1411]

In a women's prison in northern Shandong Province, half the inmates in recent years have been jailed for violent crimes such as murder, said Chinese media in 2004. Most of them committed their crimes fighting their abusing husbands. It seems the police were on hand to punish women when domestic abuse pushed them too far, but not available to stop it in the first place.[1412]

A survey of 4,000 urban citizens across China in the year 2000 found that there were six main types of harassment -- inappropriate sexual advances by male superiors in offices, harassment by ex-husbands, groping on buses, cat-calls on the street, and sexual misconduct by doctors to women patients and teachers to students. Also, the survey found, women regarded murder, kidnapping, rape, spousal abuse and marital rape as common forms of violence inflicted upon women.[1413]

According to Ge Shannan, an attorney in Shanghai who specializes in representing women, she has never had the chance to fight a sexual harassment case in court because women are unwilling to talk about the abuse.[1414]

Seeking to define the circumstances surrounding sexual harassment, the Chinese government promulgated a revision of the 1992 law, trying to update sexual harassment parameters in 2005.

Between 2001 and 2005, just 10 sexual harassment cases were heard by China's courts. Of these, just one plaintiff won. One![1415]

While the need to give women the power to fight abuse was totally clear, even this law, like so many other laws designed to help women, was flawed. It failed to define what sexual harassment was, and so gave women almost no power to take abusers to court.

Even Beijing, the center of law making, did not hear its first sexual harassment case until 2003. The woman in that case, Lei Man, lost because she was unable to provide proof of her claim, and because medical authorities for the defense diagnosed her as "suffering from paranoia."[1416]

Again in 2003 a teacher in the central China city of Wuhan took a work superior to court, claiming he had harassed her. She won her case, and the defendant was ordered to make a public apology and pay her 2000 yuan (US$242.) Later, a higher court quashed this verdict, since it felt the harassment did not have any serious effect on the woman.[1417]

Zhou Meizhen, an expert on the issue at a Shanghai-based hotline for women and children experiencing psychological problems, said that "Almost every woman has been harassed at least once on a bus. We suggest women learn to protect themselves and gather the courage to fight against offenders, rather than keeping silent."

Zhou explained that many who called the line did not tell family members when they experienced harassment because, said media, "they were afraid that people would think it was their own frivolous behavior that had caused men to begin harassing them."

According to Xiong Lei, a journalist who has covered women's rights issues for many years, the widespread abuse of women is relatively new. Xiong refers to a story she published in 1992 about a researcher with the Chinese Academy of Social Sciences who pioneered study of the issue of sexual harassment in China. That researcher, Tang Can, interviewed 30 women over the age of 40, and found that few of them could recall even a single instance of sexual harassment 20 years before. "We Chinese, men in particular, behave much less decently now than we used to" concludes Xiong.

Or perhaps it is only that today's modern Chinese woman feels the need and compulsion to speak out. Along with a sense of sexual freedom enjoyed by today's less traditional young Chinese people also comes the freedom to express sexual outrage.

"What is missing in our society are some ideals we used to treasure" says Xiong. In earlier decades, she writes, "People truly believed men and women were equal and should respect each other. Society was not free from residues of feudal ideas and discrimination against women, but the overwhelming ideology held those ideas to be wrong, and people would be ashamed to be identified as chauvinist." [1418]

As Xiong's comments seem to indicate, even her memories of the freedoms enjoyed by women are full of mythology and wishful thinking.

In traditional China it was common – even desirable – that women remained uneducated. "It is a virtue in a woman to be without talent" said Confucius. And, according to China's 'Book of Songs' written around 1000BC, "When a son is born, let him sleep on the bed, clothe him with fine clothes, and give him jade to play with. When a daughter is born, let her sleep on the ground, wrap her in common wrappings, and give her broken tiles to play with."

These were the attitudes that shaped China for thousands of years, and are still part of the male cultural psyche today.

The weakness of the national law on sexual harassment has led many regional governments to write their own laws. The western city of Xi'an, for example, enacted a sexual harassment law at the beginning of 2007. A local woman, Liu Li, used this to sue her boss, Zhang Feng who, she said, forced her to "kiss and stroke him" in 2004 and had made further sexual advances in 2005. She sued for damages of US$12,500. [1419]

Later on in 2007, Shanghai also passed a sexual harassment law, which stated that "sexual harassment includes verbal abuse, written text, pictures, text messaging and physical contact." The law also gave victims the right to lodge complaints with the employer, relevant departments and public security organizations. [1420]

A 2006 survey of 4,000 white-collar workers found that 90% "thought that women who dress in a provocative manner were inviting harassment." [1421]

Sexual harassment is also a problem in China due to the cultural reticence to talk about sex. This reticence means children are very rarely taught about the dangers of sexual abuse. "People in China have read of cases of sexual abuse in other countries, but many do not seem to realize that it's a problem here as well. Many children and parents simply ignore it and know little about it" said Chinese media in 2004. The sexual abuse of children was not made a criminal offence in China until 1991.

A survey of more than 6,000 primary and middle school students found that only half had the vaguest knowledge of what sexual abuse was and one third had "seriously misguided ideas about it." Zhong Yinping, chief editor of the magazine which ran the survey, said "If children do not know what sexual abuse really means, of course they won't know their rights or how to protect themselves consciously when they find themselves in a dangerous situation."

An earlier survey in 2003 interviewed 10,000 primary and middle school students and 17,000 parents. When asked to name the key dangers facing children, the top answers were traffic accidents (chosen by 57% of children and 58% of parents) and robbery on the way to and from school (18% of students and 25% of parents.) Sexual assault came last in the list.[1422]

As too often in China, the relevant laws hinder rather than help the situation. Zhang Wenjuan, vice-director of the Beijing Youth Legal Aid and Research Center, said that "According to the current law, abused minors must collect evidence themselves to sue their parents. This is ridiculous."

Zhang also said that molestation cases by teachers were a nationwide problem, and that these teachers took advantage of their privileged status to abuse minors. She added that reports of sexual abuse in Beijing increased 50% in 2009 compared to 2008. "In Beijing, child trafficking is not a serious problem, but domestic and sexual abuses are quite prominent," she said.[1423]

It was not until 2007 that China's Ministry of Education released a guide, to be taught in schools, telling minors of the dangers of sexual abuse.[1424] The concept of 'street proofing' children appears to be unheard of in China. Chinese children seem to be completely approachable, by themselves or with parents, by strangers. In many ways this hearkens back to an older era in Western culture, when a child's life seemed full of innocence.

For women, sexual abuse is simply a part of life in China. The practice of kidnapping women, either to sell as brides or force into prostitution, is rampant in the country.

According to Khalid Malik, a U.N. resident coordinator in China in 2004, "In eight to 10 years, we will have something like 40 to 60 million missing women." Forty to sixty million missing women! One of the reasons behind this vast pool of human misery is that China's growing gender imbalance will leave many millions of men with no way to find a wife or even to experience the sexuality of women – except through the criminal acts of prostitution and rape.[1425]

On Beijing's understaffed and underfinanced hotline to help victims of domestic violence, 96% of callers are women. One caller to the line was a woman in her early forties living in eastern China's Fujian Province. She told hotline staff she had been kidnapped from her home in southwestern Sichuan Province when she was 20 years old and sold to the man who was now her husband. He had constantly beaten her throughout the marriage.

Although she had complained to government organizations many times, they had not helped her. The woman explained that wife-beating was common in her village, and no one was willing to get involved in what were regarded as other people's private family affairs.[1426]

Another caller to the line, the mother of an eight-year old girl, said she "could no longer bear her husband's 10 years of sexual abuse, which caused her to fall prey to serious physical suffering and serious gynecological diseases. Sometimes her husband forced her to have sex even as their relatives and children were present," reported media. She had even considered suicide as well as murdering her abusive spouse as her only options.

Awareness that such a crime as marital rape even exists is very low. Between 1994 and 2000, for example, only around 20 cases of marital rape were heard by courts in the whole of China. [1427] Male awareness of safe sex practices is also very low, because of which an astonishing 80% to 90% of women in rural areas suffer from some form of genital infection, according to media reports in early 2007. Efforts to treat these women have not been successful because, says Xiao Yang, director of Woman's Studies Institute of China, men are not sufficiently aware of the importance of safe and hygienic sex, and reject mutual treatment.[1428]

Against this background of overt sexual harassment and physical violence, low-level discrimination against women is woven into the very fabric of contemporary Chinese society, often handed down from father to son.

The authors met one young father giving baijiu, a highly potent alcoholic beverage, to his two-year-old son. "It will make him grow up into a real man" said the father.

A 2007 survey by the Shanghai Women's Association revealed that women were finding it hard to meet an ideal spouse. In a society that is already experiencing a severe 'shortage' of women due to the growing gender imbalance, this seems to be counter-intuitive. But the reason women find it hard to meet a good husband in fact grows out of China's cultural attitudes combined with its policies of population control.

414

Discrimination against women also exists in other areas of Chinese life. A law passed in 1978 sets the retirement age for professional women working for government institutions and companies at 55, but for men at 60. Blue-collar female workers leave work at 50.[1429]

"Chinese lawmakers formulated well-intentioned stipulations allowing women to retire five years ahead of their male colleagues out of concern for women's health," said China's media in 2005. "They could not in their wildest dreams have imagined that their goodwill would be interpreted as gender discrimination decades later." In December 2008 Chinese media announced that the retirement age in Beijing would be equalized for government officials at county level and above. This law, if approved, would make Beijing China's only city to have equalized the retirement age.[1430]

Mature women in China often find themselves alone, either from divorce, death of a spouse or separation, and completely unsupported by the former husband or his relatives. Unable to work in the chosen profession, such women must often take employment beneath their educational level and a former position obtained through years of work experience. For the millions of women who have had no education, such as factory or textile workers, the opportunities for work in their retirement include street-sweeping, operating elevators, and kitchen help, where pay scales are often below legal limits.

Many Chinese men do not like independent women. As the Shanghai Women's Association survey found, "men's preference to marry women who are comparatively weaker in every aspect makes the search [for a husband] even more difficult."[1431] In China there is a common saying – "There are three genders – men, women, and women with PhDs." This saying refers to the fact that a woman with a doctoral degree finds it particularly hard to get married.

At present, women are trapped in a triangle of power, each point equidistant from the other. The first angle for women to be concerned with is the long tradition of a patriarchal society dominating every aspect of their life. The second angle is the current gender imbalance, ironically enforced by men themselves, that is slowly and indirectly leveraging their sense of control over their own destiny. The final and most important angle at this juncture in Chinese history is that the women of one-child only families are receiving extremely high levels of education. The women of China, in fact, over the next two or three decades, will become more highly educated than at any time in the history of China.

Will the Chinese Communist Party play a part in this triangle of power? We think not. The Party has already failed in over 60 years to bring equality to women through legislative reform and law enforcement. As the number of single, well-educated and independent-minded women increases in China, changes in the traditional patriarchal society will come from within. Accepted norms of treatment of women will change.

Lawyers, judges, and finally politically motivated women will exercise their voice and turn the present chauvinistic society of China inside out.

Across almost all of Chinese history, the most important single thing that has changed for women has been, simply, the one-child policy. The women educated through this quirk of birth control will grow in stature, as will grow the admiration from the younger women wishing to emulate their older 'sisters' not only for equality and freedom for themselves individually but also political liberty for their gender.

Reason 50
The Long March of Truth

Three versions of China's history of the 20th century are being written today. The first is written by historians vetted by the Communist Party, for whom the history of China's growth into a modern society is a specialty. The second rendition of Chinese modern history is written by dissidents or Chinese expatriates living in relative freedom overseas. The third is written by Western historians and fact finders - some of whom have been armchair theorists their whole academic lives.

In our many interviews we found that the Chinese people do not entirely believe the Communist version of their history, yet they allow their children to be taught the glories bestowed upon the people by the Party as truth. Mainlanders have no easy access to the dissident or expatriate versions, but even if they did, words from 'traitors' would be suspect. And out of pure nationalist impulse they deny the Western versions of China's history as being designed to hold back the peaceful rise of the Motherland.

This leaves the average citizen bereft of any solid understanding of the truth, certainly since 1949, of how today's China came into being. The Chinese people have no basis of belief, no solid footing of who they really are. This is a paradox, because they maintain a very solid belief that 'I am a traditional Chinese' – without being able to define what that means beyond the use of language, the preparation of food and a reference to Chinese Opera, an art form currently dying from lack of interest.

The single greatest victim of this predicament is, of course, the truth, and the standards by which truth can be tested.

Truth in China today suffers from several debilitating conditions. In most democratic societies truth is sought, analyzed and studied for its heritage and veracity. The Communist Party seeks only to manipulate facts in order to serve up truth like a drug to be injected into the public body to pacify and calm.

Holding truth to be self-evident is designed to allow the individuals of a country to seek their own version of the truth. The party designs truth to fit (or fool) all the people all of the time. What is truth can be as individualistic as what beauty is, or love. China wishes only to find the Chinese truth - or more correctly the Party's truth - then profess that truth is pure.

Truth can lead a society safely into the future, as a beacon that guides and directs. Today there are over 1.2 billion Chinese who are stumbling blindly about the planet, dangerous to themselves, and even more dangerous to other societies.

The greatest amount of truth in any society is held by the elderly. In China, so is the greatest amount of fear. Thousands of elderly Chinese are dying every day, each a vast reservoir of truth, or a personal version of truth gained from genuine experience, not CPC fabrications designed to smooth over the rough realities of life under the party.

If you had actually been on the Long March (1934-36) in person, a wide-eyed youth of 20 years of age, you would now be 96.

If you had suffered the Great Leap Forward (1958-61) at the age of 20, you would now be 72 years old and remember horrors created by economic policies, still untaught in China's schools.

If you had been a Red Guard at the beginning of the Cultural Revolution (1966-76) at the age of 20, you would now be 64 years old, perhaps hiding your feelings of guilt with government approval.

If you had survived the massacre at Tiananmen Square in 1989 at the age of 20, you would now be 41 years old. Perhaps you were a soldier at that time and have visions of students mowed down by the bullets fired from the automatic weapon held in your hands.

The passing of time means the passing of truth - or at least the experiences, views and feelings behind the truth. China's political system prevents those Chinese from speaking out freely and also prevents younger people from questioning parents and grandparents freely. And yet, even if they could question freely, with the expectation of getting some kind of response, what would they do with it? How would they apply the information into their life and their understanding of the truth of China?

The death of an old person is the death of an encyclopedia of personal truths about China. The graying of any nation should increase its wealth of knowledge of itself. As in most free societies, those with knowledge are revered. But in China today, the elderly are only revered for their age in a kind of false traditional respect and meaningless social worship. Those elderly citizens who dictate memoirs of even the slightest contentious nature must first pass rigorous government intervention to get their truth published.

The value of speaking out can clearly be shown best from examples. In May 2009, Du Daozheng, an 86-year-old committed communist who publishes a small journal in Beijing, revealed that he had helped record the volatile personal history of Zhao Ziyang, the reformist Party Secretary who opposed the use of force in Tiananmen Square in 1989. Published in English as 'Prisoner of the State: The Secret Journal of Premier Zhao Ziyang,' the book is an open view of the Party. Mr. Du's dances with the authorities keep his journal just a few steps away from being shut down.[1432]

Woeser, 42, is a poet whose Tibetan heritage reverberates within her poetry and her blog, 'Invisible Tibet.' Her books and of course her blog are both banned in China because she attempts to counter the Party's view that they brought freedom and prosperity to backward Tibet.[1433]

Two brothers, Gao Qiang, 47, and Gao Zhen, 53, both of whom are sculptors, tell the truth guardedly. They have created a brilliant, life-

418

sized statue of a seemingly remorseful Mao, kneeling and, dependent on where their work is displayed, headless. By design they have approached the limitations of China's art scene with a statue that has a 'portable' head, which rejoins the body when the work is displayed in more liberal environments.[1434]

These four people are a few examples of people who do not seek democracy and are perfectly content to try to fashion from their skills a sense of what the truth means to them.

Often Western political theorists view democracy as the first step towards freedom of a country. However, it is our contention that for a country so mired in totalitarian politics, the exercise of truth must be the first step towards freedom.

Ask a 15-year-old schoolgirl or schoolboy in China what happened in 1989, and they will first have a blank look. If you are a Western person and tell them what happened, they will deny it as lies. If you are Chinese person telling them about it, they may think about it and even Google it. But as Google colludes with the CPC to censor information, they will only have access to the sanitized non-history provided by the CPC.

That 15-year-old child will one day be an adult, fully functioning in the political system of China. What future political decisions can they make based on truth, on actual events, on actual policy?

Even China's economists must lean towards 'good news' before releasing year-end reports.

If there was a stack of 100 fifty yuan notes to be counted, but it better suited policy that the count should be less than 100 then certainly the count would be 99 notes. If it suits that more is needed for rosier reports, then 101 notes will be reported.

Every Chinese citizen is enamored by the idea of China's past being a strategic element for its future. Yet if the past is wearing a mask, hiding itself behind a sanitized, manipulated version of reality, how can the Chinese have power over the direction of their future?

We believe that democracy in China lies farther ahead in the historical perspective, certainly farther away than most Western governments would wish to believe. The search for truth should be an everyday occurrence. Every society needs to be involved in truth in order to progress toward democracy. Long before democracy comes to China, truth must be a standard by which all citizens live.

Today's digital technology enables the truth to be subverted, manipulated and concocted to a fine degree. Photographs can be doctored, documentary films can be altered, and computerized documents fashioned at the whim of those in power.

Most Western commentators feel IT will bring China freedom, that the internet will contribute as the great liberator. We contend it will not. Technology is simply a more powerful chain with which the Communist Party binds the people of China.

The Party expresses positivity from the use of hi-tech for its citizens, knowing full well that the end product can be fully controlled to a point where a search for truth becomes impossible. The layers of falsehood are so thick that the pearl of truth is obliterated.

In China, you are not required to convince someone you are telling the truth – merely to convince them that everyone else is lying - Western media lies, democratic activists lie, dissidents lie. The net result of this is that there is only one voice telling the truth – the Party. In China the truth requires constant government inspection. The government of China cleans the truth, presses it, and then tells the people how to wear it.

Citizens of China forget that if the Party provides everything, it can also take away everything, selectively. And the truth is the first thing to be taken away. As Western writers in China, we found people willing to speak to us more freely because they had little to fear from us.

We were not their neighbors; we would not report them to the police. We were not their teachers or professors; we would not restrict their education. We were not their leaders; we would not imprison them.

We have heard stories, we have seen things, we know things – perhaps far greater in sum total than most Chinese may wish to accept. However, because our faces are Western, white, and in particular non-Han, we seem doomed to be excluded from the Chinese (non-party) search for truth. The fear that only Chinese people can know the truth as it should apply to Chinese people is holding back the nation. In fact the only people who threaten the rise of China are the very Chinese who fear others are preventing the natural rise of the Motherland.

As we mentioned in Reason 23, China is a graying society. It has a vast wealth of its own recent history waiting to be exposed and examined as a conduit to the past. The question as to why young people don't open this great resource of knowledge for themselves is a puzzling one. Most young people know that the Party hides, diverts and manipulates the truth. But then why do the young citizens of China not actually speak to people who know the truth – their fathers, mothers, grandparents, and in some cases great-grandparents?

What forces are present in young people's minds today that disavow a sense of responsibility to the future? Why are they so adverse to personal fact-finding – facts that can be close at hand on a daily basis and that will disappear or fade from memory as their own relatives age?

Most single children today are filled with the agony of supporting their parents economically, yet they fail to realize that later in life they will suffer the greater agony of not knowing their country's history.

Our final question in this book must be to ask what element of nature will change the direction of China's truth? We say 'element of nature' because there is no clear indication that the people wish to change the truth. In other words – what divine wind will blow down the Communist house of cards?

420

The energy of the country, held primarily within its young people, is so devoid of any search for truth that reform must come from some other source, some national cataclysm.

Hence our comments in the introduction of this book – that China may be the harbinger of the next Armageddon.

The greatest long march in China's history will be the one of truth. A national reckoning for the truth, real facts, a deep search into the consciousness of the Chinese people, must come before China can ever be called great.

ENDNOTES

Reason Number 1. The Domestic Imperialists

[1] Details concerning the destruction of Tibet's culture can be found in 'Religion and national identity,' by the Government of Tibet in Exile, on www.tibet.com. Personal reminiscences by Tibetan monks of these events can be found in 'The Lamas of Sera Je Monastery' on the same site.

[2] 'China says state owns Tibetan religious relics.' Reuters, 29th May, 2007. For age restrictions on becoming a monk, see 'Question of the violation of human rights and fundamental freedoms in any part of the world,' www.savetibet.org.

[3] 'Violence in Tibet as Monks Clash with the Police.' By Jim Yardley, the New York Times, 15th March 2008.

[4] 'Call on China to release Tibetan film-maker.' Amnesty International, 30th April 2010.

[5] See, for example, 'From whence cometh my help,' The Economist, 29th April 2010, and 'Tibetan writer Zhogs Dung held for organizing Yushu quake donations,' by Jane Macartney, The Independent, 26th April 2010.

[6] 'Beijing Sidelines Tibetan Monks' Heroism.' Chen Pokong, The Epoch Times, 24th April 2010.

[7] Details concerning the Gulja/Yining massacre can be found in 'China: Remembering the victims of police brutality in Gulja, Xinjiang on 5-6 February 1997' at web.amnesty.org. For a very detailed and balanced look at the wider issues in Xinjiang, see 'The Xinjiang Problem,' by Graham E. Fuller and S. Frederick Starr, Central Asia-Caucus Institute, The Johns Hopkins University, 2003.

[8] A full list of the minorities can be found at www.c-c-c.org/chineseculture/minority/minority.html#table

[9] See J. A. G. Roberts: A History of China, Palgrave Macmillan, 2006, p.xiv

[10] 'Full text of history and development of Xinjiang.' China Daily, 26th May 2003.

[11] See 'Internal Colonialism and the Uyghur Nationality: Chinese Nationalism and its Subaltern Subjects,' by Dru C. Gladney, Cahiers d'etudes sur la Mediterranee Orientale et le monde Turco-Iranien, www.cemoti.revues.org

[12] '2nd highway built in Xinjiang deserts.' Xinhua, 14th May 2006

[13] http://en.wikipedia.org/wiki/Xinjiang

[14] 'Xinjiang: An Integral Part of China.' White Paper, Information Office of China's State Council, People's Daily, 28th May 2003.

[15] Country Reports on Human Rights Practices, 2006. Released by the Bureau of Democracy, Human Rights, and Labor, U.S. Department of State.

[16] 'The Great Leap west.' The Economist, 26th August 2004.

[17] 'Remember the Gulja massacre? China's crackdown on peaceful protesters.' www.asiapacific.amnesty.org

[18] 'China opposes U.S.'s interference in internal affairs.' Xinhua, 7th June 2007.

[19] 'Rebiya 'an insult to Peace Nobel,'' China Daily, 9th January 2007. The 2007 Nobel Peace Prize was awarded to Al Gore and the Intergovernmental Panel on Climate Change jointly.

[20] 'Rumormonger held over south China toy factory brawl.' Xinhua, 28th June 2009.

[21] 'Trials due over Xinjiang riots.' BBC News, 24th August 2009.

[22] 'Family's open letter to Rebiya.' China Daily, 6th August 2009.

[23] Uighur businesswoman Rebiya Kadeer's Trade Centre to be demolished.' By Jane Macartney, The Times (UK), 9th September 2009.

[24] 'US Urges China fair trial after executions,' AFP, 10th November 2009 and

[25] 'China sentences 4 more to death over ethnic riots.' The Guardian / AP, 27th January 2010.

[26] See 'China replaces party chief of riot-hit Xinjiang,' The Washington Post / Reuters, 24th April 2010, and 'China Sentences 5 More To Death Over Xinjiang Riots,' AFP / Xinhua, 3rd May 2010.

[27] 'Muslim executed for trying to 'split' China.' By Benjamin Kang Lim, Reuters, 9th February 2007.

[28] 'China warns Canada to stay out of Xinjiang terrorism case.' AFP, 19th April 2007.

[29] 'Ethnic Uighur's life sentence blow to Sino-Canadian relations.' By Michel Comte, AFP, 20th April 2007.

[30] 16 cops die in Kashgar terror strike.' China Daily, 5th August 2008.

[31] 'Doubt Arises in Account of an Attack in China.' By Edward Wong, The New York Times, 28th September 2008.

[32] 'Kublai Khan: The Mongol King who Remade China.' John Man, Bantam Press, 2006, pp4-5, p.345.

[33] http://en.wikipedia.org/wiki/Mausoleum_of_Genghis_Khan

[34] 'Battle for Mongolia's soul.' The Economist, 19th December 2006.

[35] 'Progress in China's Human Rights Cause in 2003.' Information Office of the State Council of the People's Republic of China, March 2004, Beijing

[36] 'China invests 300 million yuan a year to develop 22 ethnic minorities.' Xinhua, 3rd April 2007.

[37] 'Deep in China, a poor and pious Muslim enclave.' By Jim Yardley, The New York Times, 19th March 2006.

Reason Number 2. The Five Armies of Instability

[38] 'President stresses social harmony in New Year Address.' Xinhua, 1st January 2007.

[39] 'CPPCC calls for social harmony.' By Xie Chuanjiao, China Daily, 16th March 2007.

[3] 'From poor areas to poor people: China's evolving poverty reduction agenda. *An assessment of poverty and inequality in China.*' The World Bank, March 2009.

Reason Number 3. Children, The Endangered Species

[41] For the figure of 70,000 per year, see 'Roads unsafe for kids.' By Cai Wenjun, Shanghai Daily, April 27th 2007. For the 2003 figure of 100,000, see 'Accidents top killer for children,' China Daily, November 19th 2003. For the 200,000 figure, see 'Accidents top killer for kids under 14,' China Daily, May 31st 2004.

[42] 'Teach them young.' by Liu Fangfang, China Daily, June 2nd 2008.

[43] 'Accidents top killer for children.' China Daily, November 19th 2003.

[44] 'Traffic accidents take high toll of kids.' People's Daily Online, 28th April 2007.

[45] 'Six students killed in Jiangxi school stampede.' People's Daily Online, November 20th 2006.

[46] '8 students die, 26 injured in stampede.' By Yan Jie and Feng Zhiwei, China Daily, 12th December 2009.

[47] '200 kids abducted in Yunnan,' Xinhua, 27th April 2004.

[48] 'It's a long way home for abducted children.' By Joy Lu, China Daily, 20th June 2006.

[49] 'China executes 3 baby traffickers.' China Daily, via agencies, 11th December 2004.

[50] 'Rural Chinese kids face trafficking risk.' By Alexa Olsen, AP, 4th April 2007.

[51] 'Baby traffickers get death in Guizhou.' Shanghai Daily, 20th October 2005.

[52] 'China's left-behind kids struggle as parents migrate.' By Lindsay Beck, Reuters, 7th February 2007.

[53] 'China to step up fight against trafficking in women, children.' By Wang Zhuoqiong, China Daily, 30th September 2009.

[54] 'A league of their own out to trace missing children.' By Zhang Yuchen, China Daily, 28th April 2010.

[55] See 'DNA databank to trace kidnapped kids,' by Cao Li, China Daily, 2nd May 2009, and 'Grassroots website tightens on kidnappers,' Wang Ru, China Daily, 5th June 2009.

[56] 'In China, Children of Inmates Face Hard Time Themselves.' By Maureen Fan. The Washington Post, October 13th 2006.

[57] See 'Dalian Children's Village Charity Target of Criticism.' ChinaCSR.com, October 12th 2007.

[58] 'Suicide top killer of young Chinese: newspaper.' Reuters, 27th March 2007.

[59] 'Teens' situation cause for concern.' China Daily, 11th October 2008

[60] 'In China: young people most prone to suicide.' China Daily, September 11th 2008

Reason Number 4. Degrees of Unhappiness

[61] 'Teacher jailed for raping girl.' Shanghai Daily, 22nd December 2006.

[62] 'Web of moral corruption under fire.' By Vince Lee and Jo Jiang. Shanghai Star, 9th August 2004.

[63] 'Sexual abuse in minors is 'prominent': Expert.' China Daily, 20th November 2009.

[64] 'Youth sex abuse must be tackled.' Beijing Today, April 12th 2004.

[65] 'Clinic: Abortion patients younger.' Shanghai Daily, April 28th 2007.

[66] 'Two girls plied with liquor as punishment.' Reuters, 23rd October 2006.

[67] 'Dance school probed for sending students to bars.' Shanghai Daily, 30th November 2006.

[68] 'Educators suspended over freezing death of student.' By Wang Yan, China Daily, 25th December 2009.

[69] 'Chinese teacher jailed for needle assault on preschoolers' Xinhua, 24th March 2010.

[70] 'Teacher convicted of murder free from punishment.' By Guo Qiang. China Daily. 9th October 2006.

[71] 'Schoolyard stabbing kills child, injures 18.' By Qin Jize. China Daily, August 5th 2004.

[72] '28 children injured in day-care center attack.' Xinhua, September 11th 2004

[73] 'Man arrested for stabbing 25 pupils.' Xinhua, September 21st 2004.

[74] 'Kindergarten murder suspect arrested in Beijing.' Xinhua, 23rd October 2004, and 'Beijing kindergarten murderer executed,' Xinhua, 21st December 2005.

[75] 'Eight students slain; attacker arrested.' By Qin Yuding, China Daily, 26th November 2004, and 'Killer of nine students in central China executed,' People's Daily Online, January 20th 2005.

[76] 'Jealous man shoots students; injures 16.' By Wu Chong, China Daily, October 14th 2005.

[77] 'Kindergarten arson kills 3 kids.' China Daily, 9th May 2006.

[78] 'Man kidnaps 19 pupils, subdued by police.' Shanghai Daily, May 26th 2006.

[79] 'Pupils knifed to death in attack near school.' Shanghai Daily, December 21st 2006.

[80] ''Desperate' man drives truck into student crowd, killing 5.' By Chen Hong and Hu Yinan, China Daily, 7th November 2008.

[81] 'School stabbing killer executed in E China.' Xinhua, 28th April 2010.

[82] 'School knife attack suspect undergoing psychiatric check.' Xinhua, 29th April 2010

[83] 'Second school stabbing this week raises security concerns.' By Ding Congrong and Tong Hao, China Daily, 30th April 2010.

[84] 'School security a 'major political task.'' Xinhua, 4th May 2010.

[85] See 'Man kills eight at Chinese nursery,' by Tania Branigan / Agencies, 12th May 2010 and 'Property dispute drove Wu Huanming to kill seven Chinese children,' by Tania Branigan and Kuang Ling, 13th May 2010.

[86] See 'China censors attack news to calm panic after ninth child stabbing in weeks.' By Malcolm Moore, The Daily Telegraph, 12th May 2010.

[87] See '36 million students admitted into college in three decades,' People's Daily Online, 15th May 2007, and 'Job-hunting may be tougher for graduates,' by Wang Ying, China Daily, 11th July 2008.

[88] 'Campus employment: More recruitment, stricter selection.' China Daily, 9th November 2009.

[89] 'Students suffer for 'low quality' education. China Daily,11th November 2009.

[90] 'Chinese graduates not well enough prepared for work: survey.' Xinhua,5th April 2010.

[91] 'Significant Problems in China's Existing Education System.' The Epoch Times, 6th June 2006.

[92] 'Innovation the next challenge.' By Yan Zhen, Shanghai Daily, 18th June 2006.

[93] 'Shame of fake TCM research.' China Daily, 4th February 2009.

[94] 'Professor sacked for academic plagiarism.' By Chen Jia, China Daily, 22nd March 2010.

[95] 'Unwritten rules rampant on campus.' By Wang Wei, China Daily, 11th November 2009.

[96] 'Cold response to heat request.' By Yan Zhen, Shanghai Daily, 24th December 2005.

[97] 'Over 9,000 University Students Demand Electricity to Watch World Cup.' The Epoch Times, 21st June 2006.

[98] See 'Rioting in China Over Label on College Diplomas,' by Joseph Kahn, The New York Times, 22nd June 2006; 'Campus riot rocks central China university,' Reuters, 20th June 2006; and 'Security tight at China university, students wary,' AFP, 21st June 2006.

[99] 'Expulsion controversy.' By Rachel Yan, Shanghai Daily, 2nd August 2005.

[100] 'Condoms on campus? Some are delighted, some frown.' People's Daily Online, 16th March 2004.

[101] 'Elite universities drop plan to hand out condoms.' Xinhua/AP, 25th November 2004.

[102] 'Asian students care more about their looks: survey.' Xinhua, 31st December 2006.

[103] 'Graduates struggling with slim job market.' Xinhua, 17th March 2007.

[104] 'Survey: Hike in university tuition fees dramatic.' By Guo Qiang, China Daily, 16th January 2007.

[105] 'Help rural students get education.' By Liu Shinan, China Daily, 19th June 2006.

[106] 'Arbitrary fees total US$2.82m.' By Zhu Zhe, China Daily, 21st February 2006.

[107] 'Significant Problems in China's Existing Education System.' The Epoch Times, 6th June 2006.

[108] 'China to double its financial aid fund for students next year.' Xinhua, 22nd May 2007.

[109] 'Gorgeous mooncake boxes.' By Liu Shinan, China Daily, 28th September 2005.

[110] 'Commission gives nod for more bonds.' China Daily, 16th September 2003.

[111] 'Gov't employees may lose car privileges.' By Ma Chenguang, China Daily, 9th November 2005.

Reason Number 5. There Are No Bill Clintons In China

[112] 'Postgraduates lose free tuition.' By Wang Wei, China Daily, 30th September 2009.

[113] 'Upward with the 'Four Steadfasts.' By Tim Johnson, McClatchy, 17th July 2007.

[114] Hu Jintao: Reformer or Conformist?: A Report by Free Tibet Campaign into Hu Jintao's relationship with Tibet. The Free Tibet Campaign, 1st November 1992. See www.freetibet.org

[115] 'Non-Communist member appointed new minister in China's cabinet.' Xinhua, 27th April 2007.

[116] 'Profiles of New CPPCC Leadership.' People's Daily, 14th March 2003.

[117] 'Teacher turned politician.' By Yao Lan, Shanghai Star, 5th July 2007.

[118] 'A Big City Mayor for China's Future.' By Tom Plate, Contra Costa Times, 22nd February 1998.

[119] 'Factional intrigue hots up in China.' By Willy Wo-Lap Lam, CNN, 11th December 2001.

[120] Mao: The Unknown Story. Jung Chang and Jon Halliday, Jonathan Cape Ltd., 2005. p 509-510.

[121] 'The making of a hero.' China Daily, 11th April 2006.

[122] 'Lei Feng Remains National Icon Despite Social Changes.' People's Daily, 4th March 2003.

[123] 'Unselfish spirit is still alive.' Shanghai City News, www.shanghai.gov.cn, 6th March 2006.

[124] 'Book casts 1960s idol in true light.' China Daily, 11th April 2006.

[125] 'Lei Feng becomes online game hero.' Shanghai Daily, 15th March 2006.

[126] 'Protection laws proposed for Chinese heroes.' China Radio International / China Daily, 20th May 2007.

[127] 'Helping hand.' By Cui Xiaohuo, China Daily, September 30th 2009.

[128] 'Bribe-hungry officials can no longer hide behind mistresses, says new judicial interpretation.' Xinhua, 27th July 2007.

Reason Number 6. Dry Cleaning the News

[129] 'China newspaper editors sacked over Tiananmen ad.' Reuters, 7th June 2007.

[130] See 'Nearly 10,000 magazines get published in China,' People's Daily, 9th May 2007, and 'Report: China's copyright trade deficit still significant,' 28th June 2007.

[131] 'China closes 677 state newspapers, saving 1.8bln yuan' People's Daily, 15th March 2004.

[132] 'Chinese Press Begins Catering to Readers' Needs.' 2nd September 2003.

[133] '14 Shanghai publications shut down.' People's Daily, 2nd December 2003.

[134] 'Print media reform stops mandatory subscription.' People's Daily, 28th November 2003.

[135] 'China: keep government, Party organs away from press distribution.' People's Daily, 15th February 2004.

[136] 'Freezing Point' Journalists Hit Out at Chinese Government Over Press Freedom.' Radio Free Asia, 17th February 2006, www.rfa.org.

[137] 'Attacks on the Press in 2006.' www.cpj.org.

[138] 'Family of killed reporter gets compensation.' By Guo Qiang, China Daily, 28th June 2007.

428

[139] 'Police chief sacked for revenge on newsman.' Xinhua, 30th October 2005.

[140] 'Former Chinese reporter Zhao Yan sentenced to three years in prison.' Xinhua, 25th August 2005.

[141] 'New York Times researcher Zhao Yan freed on completing jail term.' Reporters without Borders, 15th September 2007. See www.rsf.org.

[142] 'China reporter jailed for spying.' BBC News, 31st August 2006.

[143] 'Hong Kong reporter freed early from China jail.' AFP, 5th February 2008.

[144] 'China - Annual report 2007.' www.rsf.org.

[145] See 'Censorship and attacks on journalists in run-up to 1 October anniversary.' Reporters without Borders, 29th September 2009.

[146] 'Rules on news release by Foreign News Agencies issued.' Xinhua, 10th September 2006.

[147] 'New regulations on foreign media do not affect foreign journalists' reporting during Olympics.' Xinhua, 13th September 2006.

[148] 'China: Challenge to World Bank Pollution Claim.' By Howard W. French, The New York Times, 18th July 2007.

[149] 'China Reportedly Urged Omitting Pollution-Death Estimates.' By David Barboza, The New York Times, 5th July 2007.

[150] 'China bans books in crackdown: report.' AFP, 19th January 2007.

[151] 'Media Investigation of Milk Powder Suppressed.' By Cao Guoxing, Radio Free Asia, 22nd September 2008.

[152] 'Chinese Dairy Exports in Decline.' By Chris Hogg, BBC News, 2nd December 2008.

[153] 'Bush's words on communism draw fire.' China Daily via Agencies, 14th June 2007.

Reason Number 7. Better Than Cheap – It's Fake

[154] 'Date Cheats.' Shanghai Daily, May 1st 2007.

[155] '"Pirated" English town in China amuses and riles.' Reuters, 6th November 2006.

[156] 'China deals with 200,000 counterfeit cases in 2009.' Xinhua, 6th January 2010

[157] 'China cracks down on bogus military vehicles, plates.' Xinhua, 26th September 2006.

[158] 'China drivers vent road rage.' China Daily via Reuters, 4th August 2006.

[159] 'Army license plates misused.' By Dong Zhen, Shanghai Daily, 26th May 2007.

[160] 'Crackdown launched after dangerous tires uncovered.' By Zhou Kuanwei and Chen Qian, Shanghai Daily, 21st April 2007.

[161] 'Official arrested in lard scandal.' By Zhang Lihao, Shanghai Daily, 4th December 2006.

[162] China seizes 2.4b counterfeit cigarettes.' Xinhua, 18th July 2009.

[163] 'Food safety concerns disturb dinners.' By Pan Haixia, Shanghai Star. 22nd June 2004.

[164] 'Food safety spawns public concern.' By Bai Xu, China Daily, 26th March 2005.

[165] See 'Most cooked food not hygienic in Guangzhou,' by Zheng Caixiong, China Daily, 9th October 2009, and 'Half of Liaoning's bottled water 'unhygienic,'' by Wang Qian, China Daily, 8th October 2009.

[166] '22 detained for fake milk products.' By Li Jing, China Daily, 26th April 2004 and '47 detained for selling baby-killer milk.' China Daily via agencies, 10th May 2004.

[167] 'Light Industry: Reprocessing mooncakes banned.' Shanghai Daily, 19th October 2006.

[168] 'Can Harry Potter battle the fakes?' People's Daily Online, 23rd September 2003 and 'Fake Harry Potter novel hits China,' BBC News, 4th July, 2002.

[169] http://en.wikipedia.org/wiki/Harry_Potter_and_Leopard-Walk-Up-to-Dragon

[170] 'China cracks down on fake books.' China Daily, 14th March 2005.

[171] 'China confiscates 49 million illegal publications in first four months.' Xinhua, 22nd May 2007.

[172] See 'Shanghai Expo organizers ripped off theme tune from 1997 Japanese hit, say critics,' by Leo Lewis, The Times, 28th April 2010; 'Chinese pavilion rekindles debate over copycat reputation,' by Aileen McCabe, Canwest News Service / Vancouver Sun, 25th April 2010; and 'Has Gumby Been Robbed in Shanghai?' by Jonathan Adams, Aol News, 30th April 2010.

[173] 'Nation's youngest tycoon behind bars.' China Daily, 2nd December 2006.

[174] 'Fraud seen in fake uni notice.' Shanghai Daily, 7th December 2006.

[175] 'Free rides costing Shanghai bus firms.' China Daily via Eastday.com, 5th February 2004.

[176] 'New workers given forged notes on payday.' By Kang Yi, China Daily, 10th May 2007.

[177] 'Counterfeit cash machine screens wedding gifts.' China Daily, 4th February 2006.

[178] 'China seized $100M of fake banknotes.' Xinhua, 9th October 2009

[179] '17-year-old rice hits market as new in China.' Reuters, 16th November 2006.

[180] 'China seizes 1 million toxic towels.' Reuters, 3rd April 2006.

[181] 'Pigs regularly fed illegal chemical.' By Hu Yan, China Daily, 19th September 2006.

[182] '$29m fake agricultural materials found,' by Lan Tian, China Daily, 7th January 2009.

[183] 'More than 60 pct of Chinese consider food safety a concern: survey.' Xinhua, 16th February 2007 and 'Eight-five percent of rural Chinese concerns food safety.' Xinhua, 23rd January 2007.

[184] 'Police release theft figures.' Shanghai Daily, 25th May 2007.

[185] 'Biggest ticket racket busted.' By Zheng Caixiong, China Daily, 1st February 2007.

[186] 'Reward offered for tip-off on scalpers,' by Tan Yingzi and Zheng Caixiong, China Daily, 20th January 2009.

[187] 'Quality of sex products sparks concern.' By Li Jian, Shanghai Star, 25th July 2004.

[188] 'Drug pirates leave death in their wake.' By Jonathan Watts, The Guardian, 4th December 2006.

[189] 'Ex-SFDA chief goes on trial for graft.' By Wu Jiao, China Daily, 17th May 2007.

[190] 'Pirating of drugs 'a joke' that must be stamped out.' By Minnie Chan, South China Morning Post, 16th March 2007.

[191] 'China checks safety of 170,000 medicines after graft case.' AFP, 9th February 2007.

[192] 'Prescription to become a must for antibiotics.' China Daily, 3rd June 2004.

[193] 'Ensuring food safety must be a priority.' China Daily, 24th May 2004.

[194] 'Former drug watchdog head to go on trial.' By Wu Jiao, China Daily, 9th May 2007.

[195] 'Effective supervision will cure China's corruption woes.' Xinhua, 9th February 2007.

[196] 'Fake Band-Aid factory raided, bacteria feared.' Shanghai Daily, 21st October 2005.

[197] '17 nabbed for fake rabies vaccine.' By Hu Yinan, China Daily, 3rd August 2007.

[198] 'Largest fake medicine gang in Beijing court.' By Zhang Yan, China Daily, 31st December 2009.

[199] 'Fake Viagra maker given 10-year prison term.' By Shao Xiaoyi, China Daily, 10th May 2006.

[200] 'Drug pirates leave death in their wake.' By Jonathan Watts, The Guardian, 4th December 2006.

[201] 'Fake Viagra ring facing prosecution.' By Liu Li, China Daily, 13th December 2005.

[202] See 'Authorities: Viagra patent found invalid,' by Guo Nei, China Daily, 9th July 2004, and 'Pfizer wins patent protection for Viagra in China,' China Daily via The Wall Street Journal, 6th June 2006.

[203] 'Pfizer plea against Viagra court ruling.' By Li Fangchao, China Daily, 8th February 2007.

[204] 'Bogus drug kills 11th victim in China.' Xinhua, 25th June 2006.

[205] 'China denies cover-up of problematic antibiotic.' Reuters, 9th August 2006.

[206] 'PLA names bogus military medical bodies selling fake drugs.' Xinhua, 28th July 2006.

[207] 'Regulators struggle to tame fake medicine market.' China Daily, 25th May 2009.

[208] 'More poisoned products may have originated in China.' By Walt Bogdanich and Renwick McLean, The International Herald Tribune, 19th May 2007.

[209] 'China says fatal drug outside scope of regulators.' Reuters, 8th May 2007.

[210] 'China calls for cooler heads over product safety.' China Daily via Reuters, 24th May 2007.

[211] 'Gov't probes 'tainted toothpaste' case.' By Xu Xiaomin and Wang Hongyi, China Daily, 24th May 2007.

[212] 'China Investigates Contaminated Toothpaste.' By David Barboza and Walt Bogdanich. The New York Times, 22nd May 2007.

[213] 'Another Chemical Emerges in Pet Food Case,' by David Barboza, The New York Times, 9th May 2007.

[214] See, for example, 'China Says More Dairy Makers Have Contaminated Milk' by Jian Jianguo and Theresa Tang, Bloomberg, 2nd October 2008.

[215] '60 arrested over melamine-tainted Sanlu milk powder.' Xinhua, 11th January 2009.

[216] 'Appeals sought in milk case.' By Hu Yinan and Cui Xiaohuo, China Daily, 25th June 2009.

[217] 'China officials shut legal aid centre.' By Tania Branigan / Agencies, The Guardian, 18th July 2009.

[218] 'Milk scam officials get fresh positions,' by Xie Chuanjiao, China Daily, April 10th 2009.

[219] 'Health jitters shortening China's menus,' China Daily via agencies, 24th January 2004, and 'S. Korea, China agree to cool off row,' China Daily via AP, 15th November 2005.

[220] 'Food safety tops the menu.' By Xie Chuanjiao and Wu Jiao, China Daily, 28th November 2006, and 'Chinese beer rumored containing carcinogen,' China Daily via agencies, 12th July 2005.

[221] 'Excuse for trade barriers.' China Daily, 13th June 2003.

[222] 'China asks U.S. to clarify food regulations after catfish ban.' AP, 26th May 2007.

[223] 'China's food safety woes expand overseas.' By Christopher Bodeen, AP, 13th April 2007.

[224] 'Food Imports Often Escape Scrutiny,' by Alexei Barrionuevo, The New York Times, 1st May 2007.

[225] The US Food and Drug Administration keeps an online record of rejected shipments at www.fda.gov

[226] 'China a top violator of US food standards: report.' AFP, 21st May 2007.

[227] 'China the main culprit in EU report on dangerous consumer goods.' AFP, 19th April 2007.

[228] 'Two-Thirds of Chinese Drug Stores Sell Counterfeit Medicine, Says Investigator.' By Qiao Qi, The Epoch Times, 29th September 2008.

[229] '9 hospitalized amid fake drug scandal in NW China.' Xinhua, 3rd February 2009.

[230] 'Woman blames clinic after suicide attempt fails,' China Daily, 30th May 2009.

[231] 'Drug pirates leave death in their wake.' Jonathan Watts, The Guardian, 4th December 2006.

[232] 'Authorities announce bust of fake Tamiflu network,' 30th August 2006, and 'US signals positives in IPR efforts,' China Daily/Xinhua, 15th November 2006.

[233] 'Hu emphasizes solidarity with African countries.' Xinhua, 2nd January 2007.

[234] 'Chinese President opens China-Africa summit.' Xinhua, 4th November 2006.

[235] 'China wants 'new partnership' with Africa.' AFP/China Daily, 22nd June 2006.

[236] See "China-made' fake drugs investigated,' by Shan Juan and Xie Chuanjiao, China Daily, 13th May 2009, and 'NAFDAC Arraigns Two for Importing Fake Malaria Drugs,' by Patience Akpuru, Daily Champion, Nigeria, 3rd November 2009.

[237] 'Fake malaria drugs threatening Africa: WHO expert.' By Tan Ee Lyn, Reuters, 25th July 2006.

Reason Number 8. The Godless

[238] 'Bible ministry exhibition tells China's Bible story.' People's Daily, 8th June 2007.

[239] 'Major religions co-exist in harmony in China.' People's Daily Online, 17th March 2007.

[240] Ministry of Reconstruction of Theological Thinking. Www.chineseprotestantchurch.org

[241] Annual Report of the United States Commission on International religious Freedom, May 2007. See www.uscirf.gov.

[242] See 'China jails 2 church leaders,' the Associated Press, 9th July 2007 and 'Arrest, jail terms, fines for 22 evangelical leaders,' www.asianews.it, 9th July 2007.

[243] White Paper: Human Rights in China -- 'Guarantee of Human Rights in China's Judicial Work.' See www.china.org.cn

[244] 'Closed Door Trial for Chinese Christian Pastor Zhang Zhongxin Scheduled for September 26.'By Daniel Burton, Christian News Wire, September 24th 2008.

[245] 'Catholics arrested after Vatican trip.' 12th October 2006, www.iol.co.za.

[246] 'China executes leader of Christian sect and 11 followers.' By Joseph Kahn, The New York Times, 29th November 2006.

[247] See 'Chinese reporter arrested for posting church expose,' The Taipei Times / Agencies, 13th August 2006 and 'Journalist freed after one week but fired from newspaper,' Reporters without Borders, 21st August 2006.

[248] 'China's Constitution: Guarantee for People's Rights.' By Xu Chongde, China Society for Human Rights Studies, www.humanrights.cn.

[249] World Report 2000: China and Tibet. See www.hrw.org.

[250] 'A Brief Biography of His Eminence Ignatius Cardinal Kung Pin-Mei.' See www.cardinalkungfoundation.org

[251] 'The Persecution of the Catholic Church in China.' Presented to the Congressional-Executive Commission on China at the Hearing: Religious Freedom in China. 18th November, 2004.

[252] 2005 Annual Report, Section III (d) and 2006 Annual Report, Section V(d). See www.cecc.gov

[253] 2007 Annual Report, Section II, 'Freedom of Religion.'

[254] 'China bans Western religious music.' By Richard Spencer, The Daily Telegraph, 30th September 2008.

[255] 'Tibet's missing spiritual guide.' BBC News, 16th May 2005.

[256] 'The crackdown on Falun Gong and other so-called 'heretical organizations.'' Amnesty International, 23rd March 2000.

[257] 'Urgent Action: China: Fear of torture or ill-treatment.' 20th March 2007. web.amnesty.org

[258] See 'Human Rights Lawyer Detained, Tortured: Wang Yonghang,' 28th July 2009 and 'Wang Yonghang jailed for defending human rights,' 7th December 2009, on www.amnesty.org,

[259] Amnesty International, 15th June 2009.

[260] See 'China dissident lawyer Gao Zhisheng ''missing again,' BBC News, 30th April 2010, and 'Chinese Dissident Disappears for Second Time,' Voice of America, 1st May 2010.

434

[261] 'China seethes over US report accusing it of persecuting Falungong' [sic]. People's Daily, 16th June 2007.

[262] 'China backs Pakistani crackdown on pro-Taliban mosque.' AFP, 6th June 2007.

[263] 'What is required of us as fathers today.' (1919) Lu Xun, Selected Works. Tr. Yang Xianyi and Gladys Yang, Foreign Languages Press, Beijing, 1985. Vol II, p.67.

[264] 'Confucius in modern China.' Op. cit. vol IV, p.188.

[265] 'The Chinese Character.' Lin Yutang, My Country and My People (1935). Foreign Languages Teaching and Research Press, 2000. P.48-49.

Reason Number 9. The Largest Box of Toy Soldiers in the World

[266] China's National Defense in 2006. Section III. China's Leadership and Administration System for National Defense.

[267] 'China promotes 3 generals.' Xinhua, 6th July 2007.

[268] China's National Defense in 2006. Section V. People's Armed Police Force.

[269] 'Along the border and in the kitchen: Chinese army goes digital.' Xinhua, 10th June 2007.

[270] 'Chinese army bolsters fighting capability by carrying on traditions.' Xinhua, 23rd July 2007.

[271] 'Foreign forces laud war games.' By Li Xiang, China Daily, 26th September 2008.

[272] 'Military personnel to undergo psychological tests.' Xinhua, 28th May 2007.

[273] 'PLA beefs up military training system.' By Qiang Pen, China Daily, 1st May 2007.

[274] 'Chinese Air Force recruits more than 1,400 pilot students in 2007.' Xinhua, 25th July 2007.

[275] 'PLA hires over 6,000 non-combat employees.' Shanghai Daily, 24th March 2007.

[276] 'China's armed forces begin to shed cloak of mystery.' Xinhua, 31st December 2006.

[277] 'PLA show impresses foreigners.' China Daily, 19th July 2007.

[278] 'China's armed forces go stylish.' Xinhua, 2nd July 2007.

[279] 'Chinese servicemen to wear new uniforms.' Xinhua, 2nd July 2007.

[280] 'China increases soldiers' food subsidy.' Xinhua, July 05, 2007.

[281] 'What are foreigners' major concerns about Chinese army?' People's Daily Online, 19th July 2007.

[282] 'China reopens memorial on uprising producing first Communist army.' Xinhua, 29th July 2007.

[283] 'China Unicom aims to profit from PLA anniversary through new military service.' Xinhua, 31st July 2007.

[284] '300,000 service people lose lives since 1949.' People's Daily, 19th July 2007.

[285] Mao: The Unknown Story. By Jung Chang and Jon Halliday, Jonathan Cape, 2005. P. 394, n.

Reason Number 10. The Builders of Myth, The Tellers of Tales

[286] 'Documents proving Japanese atrocities added to China's archives.' Xinhua, 23rd June 2007.

[287] 'Pentagon fears baseless.' China Daily, 1st June 2007.

[288] See 'China 'is no threat to anyone,'' China Daily, 1st August 2007 and 'China tells Paulson it's poor and poses no threat,' by David Lawder, Reuters, 31st July 2007.

[289] 'China unlikely to rescue Wall Street.' By Paul Wiseman and Calum MacLeod, USA Today, 2nd October 2008.

[290] 'Chen's UN bid 'threatens peace, stability.'' China Daily, 25th July 2007.

[291] 'Facts & Figures: Human Rights Record in the United States in 2006.' People's Daily, 8th March 2007.

[292] 'China issues human rights record of the United States.' Xinhua, 8th March 2007.

[293] 'Chinese Human Rights delegation visits New York.' Xinhua, 20th June 2007.

[294] 'Chinese vice premier urges religious group to play 'active role' in social harmony.' Xinhua, 26th July 2007.

[295] 'Social harmony and stability constitute China's leading characteristics.' People's Daily Online, 27th December 2006.

[296] 'CPC promotes democracy by open elections.' Xinhua, 18th July 2007.

[297] 'Authenticity reiterated after cardboard bun saga.' People's Daily, 24th July 2007.

[298] 'Per capita GDP in Tibet reaches 10,000 yuan.' People's Daily Online, 23rd June 2007.

[299] 'China lauds minority rights on key anniversary.' By Ben Blanchard, Reuters, 8th August 2007.

[300] 'China-Japan talks on East China Sea 'conducive.'' Xinhua, 25th May 2007.

[301] 'East China Sea talks test warming China-Japan ties.' By Feng Zhikai, China Daily, 25th May 2007.

[302] 'China, Japan tackle East China Sea issue.' China Daily, 26th May 2007.

[303] 'Commentary: Chinese officials taking on public apology, and should mean it.' Xinhua, 6th April 2007.

[304] 'Nearly 2,000 Chinese officials confess wrongdoings.' Xinhua, 2nd August 2007.

[305] 'Wild animal trade still alive and well.' China Daily, 30th May 2007.

[306] 'Two girls drown in 'honor' suicide.' Xinhua, 4th June 2007.

[307] 'Poverty-hiding 'Loincloth.'' By Li Qian, China Daily, 18th April 2007.

[308] 'Chinese do craniotomy 5,000 years ago.' People's Daily Online, 19th June 2007.

[309] 'Architect likens one-year celebration to a 'fake smile.'' Reuters, 11th August 2007.

[310] 'Ai Weiwei Undergoes Brain Surgery After Beating.' Www.artinfo.com, 16th September 2009.

[311] 'S. China judge not beaten to death while in detention.' Xinhua, 30th April 2007.

Reason Number 11. Crossing the Line for a Penny

[312] 'Poverty line to be raised to international standard.' China Daily/Agencies, 14th April 2008.

[313] '10% of Chinese live in poverty.' China Daily, 1st November 2006.

[314] 'Up from poverty' China Daily, 15th April 2008.

[315] 'From poor areas to poor people: China's evolving poverty reduction agenda. An assessment of poverty and inequality in China.' The World Bank, March 2009.

[316] 'China quick facts.' Web.worldbank.org.

[317] 'China's economy – What's in store for 2007?' Xinhua, 15th December 2006.

[318] 'China makes strides in poverty alleviation in rural areas.' Xinhua, 6th October 2006.

[319] 'China aims to rid dire poverty by 2010.' China Daily, 7th March 2007.

[320] 'Developing world should hold on to its advantage.' By Ma Chao, China Daily, 18th December 2009.

[321] 'Poverty alleviation in China: Commitment, policies and expenditures.' By Zhang Amei, UNDP, http://hdr.undp.org/

[322] 'Country Evaluation: Assessment of Development Results – China.' www.undp.org

[323] 'Loopholes undermine unemployment insurance system.' Xinhua, 6th December 2006.

[324] 'China beefs up efforts in rural poverty reduction.' Xinhua, 6th October 2006.

[325] See 'China's defense budget to exceed 280b yuan,' Xinhua, 5th March 2006, and 'Rand study predicts China's defense spending is lower than previous outside estimates,' www.rand.org, 19th May 2005.

[326] 'Promising future for west despite economic woes.' China Daily, 8th October 2006.

[327] 'Almost half poverty-stricken villagers live in ethnic regions.' Xinhua, 28th December 2006.

[328] 'China's poor getting poorer and more dispersed: World Bank.' By Peter Harmsen, AFP, 1st December 2006.

[329] 'China quick facts.' Web.worldbank.org.

[330] 'China suffers widening income gap: report.' Xinhua, 8th January 2007.

[331] 'Media's bias on economics shows.' By David Su, The Taipei Times, 21st March 2006.

[332] 'CPC to change lives of low-income citizens, poor population: experts.' People's Daily, 8th October 2006.

[333] 'China orders boost in minimum wages as food prices soar.' China Daily/AP, 29th June 2007.

[334] See 'Lowest earners get 14% rise,' by Cao Li, China Daily, 26th March 2008, and 'Minimum wage hike planned to plug labor shortage,' by Liang Qiwen, China Daily, 21st June 2008.

[335] 'Time not ripe to leave all to market.' By Hong Liang, China Daily, 24th June 2008.

[336] 'Low income residents face growing difficulties.' China Daily, 16th May 2006.

[337] 'Experts: China's urban poverty worsens.' Xinhua, 13th February 2006.

[338] '"Slums" sting Chinese cities, hamper building of harmonious society.' Xinhua, 9th September 2005.

[339] 'China's poor getting poorer and more dispersed: WB.' By Peter Harmsen, AFP, 1st December 2006.

Reason Number 12. The Conformists

[340] 'Workloads prove deadly for police.' China Daily, 5th April 2007.

[341] 'China Bars Doctor From Travel.' Voice of America, 26th July 2007.

[342] See 'Eco-warrior Wu Lihong charged for blackmail,' Xinhua, 6th June 2007, 'Chinese 'environment activist' sentenced to 3 years,' Xinhua, 11th August 2007, and 'China environmental activist imprisoned,' by Christopher Bodeen, The Associated Press, 10th August 2007.

[343] 'Lawyer for detained Chinese quake dissident granted access.' AFP, 24th September 2008.

[344] 'China detains teacher for earthquake photos.' By Tania Branigan, The Guardian, 31st July 2008.

[345] 'Wife of Chinese green activist targets watchdog.' Reuters, 5th June 2007.

[346] 'China bans AIDS rights meeting, group says.' Reuters, 29th July 2007.

[347] 'In China, bribers get off easy.' By Mark Magnier, The Los Angeles Times, 10th August 2007.

[348] 'Farmers stay homeless while land sits idle.' By Zhang Lihua, Shanghai Daily, 1st November 2006.

[349] 'Ire Over Shanghai Rail Line May Signal Turning Point.' By Howard W. French, The New York Times, 10th August 2007.

[350] 'Chinese corruption watchdog orders checkup on luxurious gov't buildings following latest scandal.' Xinhua, 4th June 2007.

[351] 'China warns against cover-up of government extravagance.' Xinhua, 18th June 2007.

[352] 'Online 'arrest orders' boom in China, arousing controversy.' Xinhua, 25th May 2007.

Reason Number 13. Culture's Price Point

[353] 'I did not see the Great Wall from space: Yang Liwei,' People's Daily, 17th October 2003.

[354] See www.wildwall.com and 'The times they are a-changin,'' by Lydia Holden, City Weekend Magazine (Shanghai and Beijing), 3rd January 2007.

[355] 'China's Great Wall future more secure –campaigner.' By Ben Blanchard, Reuters, 15th December 2006.

[356] 'Wall on the wildside,' by William Lindesay, Conde Nast Traveler, UK Edition, December 1999. Article available on www.wildwall.com.

[357] 'Great Wall suffers from excessive tourism and neglect.' People's Daily, 27th January 2004.

[358] 'Great efforts needed for Great Wall.' People's Daily, 6th June 2006.

[359] 'Toll-dodging truckers breach China's Great Wall.' Reuters, 2nd June 2007.

[360] 'Sandstorms devouring Great Wall in NW China.' Xinhua, 29th August 2007.

[361] 'Three people detained for damaging Great Wall in N. China.' Xinhua, 28th November 2006.

[362] 'China's first regulation protecting the Great Wall goes into effect.' Xinhua, 1st December 2006.

[363] 'Should Yuanmingyuan be rebuilt?' People's Daily, 21st May 2005.

[364] See "Yuanmingyuan official opposes replica proposal," China Daily, 28th February 2008, and "Project to re-create imperial garden opposed," China Daily, 29th February 2008.

[365] 'Nearly 70 pct Beijing hutongs destroyed: survey.' Xinhua, 19th December 2006.

[366] 'A wrecking ball for Beijing's history.' By Peter Ford, The Christian Science Monitor, 25th May 2007.

[367] 'Ancient opera theater will be demolished.' Xinhua, 24th April 2007.

[368] See 'Calls for halt to demolition of hutong,' China Daily, 15th May 2007, and 'Demolition suspended of Beijing ancient hutong,' Xinhua, 28th May 2007.

[369] 'Developer calling for halt to urban renovation in Shanghai.' Shanghai Daily, 4th February 2004.

[370] See 'Shanghai has a glorious past – let's not erase it,' China Daily, 2nd July 2006 and 'Shanghai revises law to better protect historic buildings,' Xinhua, 26th April 2006.

[371] 'Heritage hero fights long to save Shanghai.' By Nancy Zhang, Shanghai Daily, 19th July 2009.

[372] See 'Historic Jewish Haven In Shanghai Faces Demolition,' by Louisa Lim, NPR, May 6th 2010, and '5 historic Shanghai buildings we lost in 2009,' by Paul French, www.shanghaiist.com, 22nd December 2009.

[373] 'Developer's IPO price at top of indicative range.' China Daily, 28th September 2006.

[374] 'Historical sites ruined in renovations.' By Li Fangchao, China Daily, 11th June 2007.

[375] 'Fears grow for China's relics.' By Wang Zhuoqiong and Hu Yinan, China Daily. 21st December 2007.

[376] 'Fears over culture survey.' By Yan Zhen, Shanghai Daily, 16th January 2007.

[377] 'Petition stirs online vote to boycott Christmas.' By Zhang Liuhao, Shanghai Daily, 23rd November 2006.

[378] See 'Starbucks should be verboten in Forbidden City, say netizens,' by Wang Shanshan, China Daily, 18th January 2007, and 'Starbucks closes Chinese palace outlet,' AP, 14th July 2007.

Reason Number 14. The Glass Children

[379] 'Single-child population tops 100 million in China.' Xinhua, 7th July 2008.

[380] 'Educating China's "little emperors."' China Daily, via agencies, 5th November 2003.

[381] ''One child' generation grows up to face strained family ties.' Xinhua, 13th April 2004.

440

[382] 'Dad, where's the silver spoon?' China Daily, 29th November 2001.

[383] 'Psychological Problems Affect One Third of Children in Tianjin.' People's Daily, 18th September 2000.

[384] 'China's school children suffering from lack of sleep.' Xinhua, 20th March 2007.

[385] 'One child generation grows up to face 'strained family ties.'' Xinhua, 13th April 2004.

[386] 'Growing up hard for single child generation.' China Daily, 24th August 2005.

[387] 'Marriage and the 'me' generation.' Xinhua, 25th November 2004.

[388] 'Post-80s feel the pressure.' By Yu Tianyu, China Daily, 19th April 2010.

[389] 'Experts Warn of Psychological Problems.' Xinhua, 13th February 2001.

[390] 'Dangerous Minds.' By He Na, China Daily, 27th February 2009.

[391] '90% of depression sufferers fail to get proper treatment.' Xinhua, 18th May 2007.

[392] 'Experts Warn of Psychological Problems.' Xinhua, 13th February 2001.

[393] '30 million Chinese suffering from depression.' By Zhang Kun, China Daily, 18th May 2007.

[394] 'China's only children at risk of divorce.' Xinhua, 7th December 2006.

[395] 'Three misunderstandings in marriage today: expert.' China Daily, 19th August 2003.

[396] 'Marriage and the 'me' generation.' Xinhua, 25th November 2004.

[397] 'Only children face employment discrimination.' By Guo Qiang, China Daily, 30th November 2006.

[398] 'One-child generation faces loneliness.' By Sun Xiaohua, China Daily, 14th May 2005.

[399] 'Tough for one-child generation.' Xinhua, 29th November 2004.

[400] An Intellectual History of China. He Zhaowu, Tang Yuyuan and Sun Kaitai. Institute of History, Chinese Academy of Sciences. Foreign Languages Press, Beijing, 1998. pp72-86.

[401] A History of China. J.A.G Roberts, Palgrave Macmillan, 2006. P. 288.

[402] 'Minister: One-child policy to remain.' By Zhang Feng, China Daily, 7th January 2006.

[403] 'Thousands at risk of forced sterilization in China.' Amnesty International, 22nd April 2010.

[404] 'Couple fined $94,000 for one-child policy lapse.' China Daily, via agencies, 21st September 2004.

[405] 'Widening wealth gap challenges China's family planning efforts.' Xinhua, 8th March 2007.

[406] 'China to name those who skirt child policy.' AP, 8th February 2007.

[407] 'Retirees to get childless subsidy.' By Steffie Lu, Shanghai Daily, 13th December 2006.

[408] 'Second child to be encouraged in Shanghai.' China Daily, 23rd October 2009.

[409] 'Family policy cuts poverty.' Shanghai Daily, 29th October 2005.

[410] 'New policy will offer cash instead of kids.' By Zhang Feng, China Daily, 16th October 2006.

[411] 'Local official expelled from CPC, government job for having extra kids' Xinhua, 9th April 2007.

[412] 'Birth Control Measures Prompt Riots in China.' By Joseph Kahn, The New York Times, 21st May 2007.

[413] 'China arrests 28 as tensions runs high after family planning riots.' By Robert J. Segal, 23rd May 2007.

[414] 'Riots against gov't in China.' By Anita Chang, AP, 21st May 2007.

[415] 'Villagers riot in China, attack officials, burn cars.' Reuters, 21st May 2007.

[416] 'Expectant mothers take big risks.' China Daily, 8th May 2007.

[417] 'Ministry announces major gap in rural, urban maternal morality rates.' Xinhua, 26th November 2004.

[418] Form 'Child Health USA 2003.' Available from the US Health Resources and Services Administration, http://mchb.hrsa.gov/

[419] See 'Universal healthcare reform offers hope for rural poor,' by Shan Juan, China Daily, 9th April 2009, and 'Maternal deaths drop by 59%,' by Wang Zhuoqiong, China Daily, 13th March 2009.

[420] 'Kidding the System.' By Didi Kirsten Tatler, South China Morning Post, 9th July 2006.

[421] 'A brother for her.' The Economist, 18th December 2004.

[422] 'The rich 'have to follow' family planning.' China Daily, 24th January 2007.

[423] 'Money can't justify having more kids.' People's Daily Online, 24th March 2007.

[424] 'Population faces risk of rebound.' China Daily/Agencies, 8th May 2007.

[425] 'Nation's one-child policy 'will not change.'' China Daily, 30th September 2006.

[426] The figure is given as 300 million in 2004 (see 'Family planning sparks population imbalances,' Xinhua, 24th May 2004) but 400 million by 2007 (see 'Expectant mothers take big risks,' China Daily, 8th May 2007).

Reason Number 15. The Value of our Death

442

[427] 'Migrant workers are dying to work.' By Xu Qin. Shanghai Daily, 30th October 2005.

[428] 'China must do more to prevent occupational diseases.' Xinhua, 5th April 2007.

[429] 'Diseases at work haunt migrant workers.' By Cao Desheng, China Daily, 17th January 2006.

[430] 'Workplace diseases in spotlight.' By Zhang Feng, China Daily. 25th April 2006.

[431] 'Expert worries about coal mine working safety.' Xinhua, 7th October 2004.

[432] 'Lung disease proves to be the top occupational killer.' Shanghai Daily, 1st May 2007.

[433] 'Black lung tops occupational diseases list.' By Xie Yu, China Daily, 31st October 2009.

[434] See 'After long struggle, 'black lung' diagnosis was welcome news,' by Shan Juan, China Daily, 31st July 2009, and 'Sick worker finally gets compensation,' by Lan Tian and Qin Zhongwei, China Daily, 18th September 2009.

[435] 'Hospital punished for aiding lung patient.' By Qin Zhongwei and Lan Tian, China Daily, 14th August 2009.

[436] 'Occupational Disease.' China Daily, 10th December 2009.

[437] 'Accidents kill over 100,000 in 2007, down 10%.' Xinhua, 11th January 2008.

[438] See 'Coal mine deaths fall to 14-yr low,' by Cui Xiaohuo, China Daily, 17th January 2009, and 'China work safety accidents death toll down 15.2% in Jan.-Feb. period,' Xinhua, 19th March 2009.

[439] See 'Coal mine deaths drop amid safety drive,' China Daily, 14th January 2008, 'Coal mine deaths drop 15% in 2008,' Xinhua, 28th January 2009 and 'China's coal mine accidents, fatalities drop in 2009,' Xinhua, 20th January 2010.

[440] '320 Chinese die on job daily, report says.' Shanghai Daily, 22nd December, 2006.

[441] 'China enslaved by rising demand for coal.' By Francois Bougon, AFP, 14th December 2006.

[442] 'Flood in Shanxi coal mine traps 44 miners.' AP, May 21st 2006.

[443] 'Miners: Accident was preventable.' Xinhua, 5th May 2006.

[444] 'Profit undermines safety.' China Daily, 29th May 2006.

[445] 'Officials handed tougher sentences in coal mine disaster retrial.' 13th February 2007.

[446] '7,000 coal mines to close in crackdown.' By Fu Jing, China Daily, 31st August 2005.

[447] 'China enslaved by rising demand for coal.' By Francois Bougon, AFP, 14th December 2006. Also in the Chongqing area, only 33 of the 175 mines that the government ordered to close did so. See 'Many

mines flouting crackdown,' by Li Fangchao, China Daily, 16th February 2006.

[448] 'China to shut 4,000 more small coal mines by 2010.' Xinhua, July 10th 2008.

[449] 'Coal resources blatantly wasted.' Xinhua, 2nd May 2007.

[450] 'Coal mine blast kills 24, eight missing.' Reuters, 30th April 2006.

[451] 'Li: corruption hides behind man-eating mines.' Shanghai Daily, 21st December 2006.

[452] 'Officials blamed for accidents.' By Wu Jiao, China Daily. 11th May 2007.

[453] 'Mine blast kills 20, another 10 missing.' Reuters, 6th May 2007.

[454] '183 punished in five major accidents that killed 189.' Xinhua, 23rd January 2008.

[455] 'Chinese colliery boss gets life for cover-up.' By Jonathan Watts, The Guardian, 1st May 2007.

[456] See '35 killed in concealed July mine accident,' Xinhua, 24th October 2008; '113 punished for landslide that kills 277,' Xinhua, 18th April 2009; 'Colliery blast kills 18 in Hunan,' Xinhua, 18th April 2009; 'Coal mine officials sacked after deadly explosion in NE China', Xinhua, 28th November 2009, and 'Scribe gets 16 years in mine accident coverup,' by Wang Qian, China Daily, 6th January 2010.

[457] See '22 probed in mine blast cover-up,' by Xie Chuanjiao, China Daily, 9th October 2008; '37 dead in Central China coal mine gas outburst,' Xinhua, 21st September 2008; 'Final body recovered from flooded north China colliery,' Xinhua, 26th April 2010; and 'All ten miners found dead after Xinjiang coal mine collapse,' Xinhua, 14th April 2010.

[458] 'Cover-up may have delayed rescuers,' Shanghai Daily, 2nd April 2007, and 'Subway contractor faces stiff penalty over collapse,' China Daily, 10th May 2007.

[459] 'Exposing the cover-up.' China Daily, 11th January 2010.

[460] 'Molten metal kills 32 in steel plant.' Xinhua, 19th April 2007.

[461] '2nd molten steel spill kills workshop head.' Shanghai Daily, 27th April 2007.

[462] 'Six injured.' Shanghai Daily, 26th April 2007.

[463] See 'Six injured,' Shanghai Daily, 26th April 2007; 'Molten iron kills 4, injures 14 in China,' Xinhua, 26th December 2008; and 'Molten steel spill kills four in E China,' Xinhua, 17th January 2009.

[464] 'Poison report reveals high cost of calling.' Shanghai Daily, 13th December 2006.

[465] 'Cadmium poisoning spurs compensation saga.' By Zhan Lisheng, China Daily, 20th December 2006.

[466] 'Huizhou Battery Workers Fight for Compensation.' The International Hong Kong Liaison Office of the international trade union movement. See www.ihlo.org

[467] Wikipedia.org/wiki/All-China_Federation_of_Trade_Unions

[468] 'China to criminalize accident cover-ups.' Reuters, 27th April 2006.

[469] 'New regulation seeks to guarantee fair death trials.' China Daily, 1st March, 2007.

[470] 'China details penalties for industrial accidents.' By Gu Jia, Shanghai Daily, 20th April 2007.

[471] 'Companies now required to monitor workplace hazards.' China Daily, 14th August 2009.

[472] 'China calls on Italy for fair treatment.' By Le Tian, China Daily. 14th April 2007.

[473] 'Envoy: Milan clashes 'unfortunate.'' China Daily, 16th April 2007.

[474] 'Chinese FM urges US to punish officer for beating.' China Daily, 26th July 2004.

[475] 'US brutality violates human rights.' People's Daily, 30th July 2004.

[476] 'US regrets for beating of Chinese woman.' Xinhua, 30th July 2004.

[477] 'Chinese-American trade group lodges protest against beating of business woman.' Xinhua, 26th July 2004.

[478] 'Officer acquitted in beating of Chinese tourist.' AP, 9th September 2005.

Reason Number 16. Mount Rubbish

[479] 'Nation Set to Concentrate on Rubbish Problem.' China Daily, 22nd May 2001.

[480] 'Country Faces Great Wall of Waste.' China Daily, 9th January 2007.

[481] 'Paying for waste.' By Pan Haixia, Shanghai Star, 22nd July 2004.

[482] 'Beijing to Clean up its Garbage Dumps.' Xinhua, 26th July 2006.

[483] 'Waste Management in China: Issues and Recommendations.' Urban Development Working Papers, East Asia Infrastructure Department, World Bank. Working Paper No. 9, May 2005.

[484] 'Landfill sites fail green screen.' By Wang Qian, China Daily, July 6th 2009.

[485] 'Waste Fees on the Way.' China Daily, 4th April 2007.

[486] 'Need for education in garbage disposal.' By Huang Qing, China Daily, 2nd January 2008.

[487] 'China to charge urban dwellers for sewage and garbage disposal.' Xinhua, 3rd April 2007.

[488] 'Waste Management in China,' p.29.

[489] 'China sees severe waste of mobile phones.' People's Daily Online, 15th November 2006.

[490] '120 million mobile phones sold in 2006.' Xinhua, 4th February 2007.

[491] 'Cakes take the bite of packaging.' By Qin Jize, China Daily, 28th September 2004.

[492] 'Stop excessive packaging.' China Daily, 15th June 2005.

[493] ''Green packaging' demand to help environment.' By Le Tian, China Daily, 20th April 2006.

[494] 'Support green packaging.' China Daily, 21st April 2006.

[495] 'Trade: Draft rule set to limit packaging.' By Zhu Zhe and Diao Ying, China Daily, 10th September 2008.

[496] 'Shanghai Promotes 'Green Sale.'' People's Daily, 6th May 2000.

[497] See www.polystyrene.org/environment/environment.html

[498] 'Finding solutions to 'white pollution.'' By Chen Zhiyong, China Daily, 21st January 2006.

[499] See 'Residents reluctant to separate waste,' by Yang Wanli, China Daily, 20th March 2010, and 'Beijing plans waste separation in 3,000 areas,' by Quan Li, China Daily, 13th April 2010.

[500] 'Let the law bite.' China Daily, 30th June 2008.

[501] 'Hand-torn plastic bags favored.' Xinhua, 2nd July 2008.

[502] 'Plastic bag ban ignored at open food markets.' By Liu Shanshan, 10th June 2009.

[503] 'Shoppers reject 'green' plastic bags.' By Cai Wenjun, Shanghai Daily, 3rd September 2008.

[504] 'Millions of China's junk collectors to be licensed.' Xinhua, 7th May 2007.

[505] 'China risks becoming world hi-tech waste bin.' China Daily/Agencies, 24th May 2005.

[506] 'China set to curb foreign waste imports.' Xinhua, 24th January 2007.

Reason Number 17. Faux Pop-Culture

[507] 'First movie co-produced by Disney, Chinese film makers to be shown next year.' Xinhua, 15th December 2005.

[508] 'Superman returns to Chinese screens but fails to compete with big earners.' Xinhua, 14th July 2006.

[509] 'China's Film Industry Rankles as Spiderman's Web Snares Cinemas.' Xinhua, 16th May 2007.

[510] 'From Beijing With Love - 007 Hits China in 07.' By Zhang Rui and Chris Dolby, China.org.cn, 30th January 2007.

[511] 'Disney's 'Pirates 3' slashed in China.' People's Daily, 15th June 2007.

[512] 'China Film says no release for 'Rush Hour 3.'' By Clifford Coonan, 2nd August 2007, www.varietyasiaonline.com.

[513] 'Ang Lee's Oscar honor brings joy to Chinese.' By Raymond Zhou, China Daily, 7th March 2006.

[514] 'Zhang Ziyi says Chinese should be proud of her for role in 'Memoirs of a Geisha.'' Xinhua, 3rd April 2007.

[515] See 'Dark Knight won't be on big screen in China,' CBC News, 26th December 2008, and 'No Dark Knight for China,' Jacques Steinberg, The New York Times, 25th December 2008.

[516] 'China drops curtain on 'The Da Vinci Code.'' By Joseph Kahn, The New York Times, 9th June 2006.

[517] See 'Confucius Says: Ouch,' by Melinda Liu, Newsweek, 4th February 2010, and 'China Bans Screenings Of 'Too Popular' Avatar,' by Izzy Broughton, Sky News, 20th January 2010.

[518] 'Top leaders hail centennial anniversary of Chinese movie industry.' Xinhua, 29th December, 2005.

[519] 'Only 10% of films attract audiences.' Xinhua, 23rd April, 2006.

[520] 'Strict rules set to rein in reality TV show.' Xinhua, 6th April 2007.

[521] 'Bones, skeletons buried in Chinese version of fantasy game.' China Daily/Xinhua, 12th July 2007.

[522] 'Swedish game banned for harming China.' Xinhua, 31st May 2004.

[523] 'One third of Chinese recreation, sports stars have health problems, survey.' Xinhua, 2nd July 2007.

Reason Number 18. The Mirror of Japan – The War of Apology

[524] 'Joint Communiqué of the Government of Japan and the Government of the People's Republic of China.' 29th September 1972.

[525] 'U.S. sounds alarm bell for Japan.' People's Daily, 28th June 2007.

[526] 'Speech at a Meeting Marking the 60th Anniversary of the Victory of the Chinese People's War of Resistance Against Japanese Aggression and the World Anti-Fascist War.' www.mfa.gov.cn, 3rd September 2005.

[527] 'Speech at a Meeting Marking the 60th Anniversary of the Victory of the Chinese People's War of Resistance Against Japanese Aggression and the World Anti-Fascist War.' See www.mfa.gov.cn

[528] See www.hawaii.edu/powerkills.

[529] 'Japan rejects China WWII slavery suit.' The Associated Press, 17th July 2007.

[530] 'Survivors may take Japan's shame to world.' Xinhua, 22nd May 2006.

[531] 'Japan rejects China WWII slavery suit.' The Associated Press, 17th July 2007.

[532] 'Japanese orgy in Zhuhai hotel sparks Chinese fury.' 27th September 2003.

[533] 'Japanese company name delays IPO.' By Ren Wei, China International Business, November 2003.

[534] 'More Japanese chemical weapons found.' China Daily, 31st May 2004.

[535] 'Civility and reason: excitement likely for Chinese fans.' People's Daily Online, 6th August 2004.

[536] 'China lodges complaint over Japanese Taiwan error.' People's Daily, 5th August 2004.

[537] 'Japan sink China in heated Asia Cup final.' Reuters, 8th August 2005.

[538] 'China regrets for foreign reporter's injury after Asian Cup final.' People's Daily, 7th September 2004.

[539] 'China's reputation takes beating in soccer tourney.' AFP, 26th February 2008.

[540] 'Millions click 'no' to Japan's UNSC bid.' People's Daily, 30th March 2005.

[541] 'Japan to deploy 'expo diplomacy' for UNSC seat.' People's Daily, 23rd March 2005.

[542] 'Chinese protest against move on islands,' China Daily via agencies, 16th February 2005.

[543] 'Bird choice sparks anti-Japan sentiments.' By Guo Qiang, China Daily, 24th May 2007.

[544] 'Koizumi urged not to visit war shrine.' AFP, 11th August 2006.

[545] 'China Hails a Good Nazi and Makes Japan Take Notice.' By Howard W. French, the New York Times, 15th March 2006.

[546] 'Statement by Prime Minister Junichiro Koizumi.' 15th August 2005. See www.kantei.go.jp

[547] 'Patriotism and self-examination.' People's Daily Online, 29th January 2007.

[548] 'Hu Jintao hails CPC's leading role in Anti-Japanese War.' Xinhua, 27th August 2005.

[549] 'Speech at a Meeting Marking the 60th Anniversary of the Victory of the Chinese People's War of Resistance Against Japanese Aggression and the World Anti-Fascist War.' www.mfa.gov.cn, 3rd September 2005.

[550] The Generalissimo: Chiang Kai-Shek and the Struggle for Modern China. By Jay Taylor, Belknap Harvard, 2009. Page 169.

[551] 'Decades don't dim memory of Sino-Japan war.' Reuters, 7th July 2006.

[552] 'Japan's wartime deeds not easily forgotten in China.' By Ben Blanchard, Reuters, 7th April 2007.

Reason Number 19. Hegemony with Chinese Characteristics

[553] See www.chinesefolkculture.com

[554] J. A. G. Roberts, A History of China: Palgrave Macmillan, 2006, p160-161.

[555] Bamber Gascoigne, The Dynasties of China: Robinson, 2003, p188.

[556] 'China, Australia's top legislators satisfied with bilateral ties.' Xinhua, 30th May, 2007.

[557] 'Australian PM: China's development good news to world.' Xinhua, 23rd March 2007.

[558] 'Clark: NZ glad to promote FTA agreement with China.' Xinhua, 27th March 2007.

[559] 'Chinese, Vanuatuan premiers exchange congratulations on anniversary of diplomatic ties.' Xinhua, March 26th 2007.

[560] 'PNG PM welcomes China's role in South Pacific.' Xinhua, 30th March 2007.

[561] 'China, New Zealand vow to boost bilateral ties.' People's Daily, 24th May 2007.

[562] 'Chinese FM meets senior EU officials on ties.' 29th May 2007.

[563] 'Chinese vice president meets German DM.' Xinhua, 18th April 2007.

[564] 'Chinese vice premier meets Dutch FM.' Xinhua, 11th April 2007.

[565] 'China, Poland vow to boost co-operation.' Xinhua, 25th May 2007.

[566] 'Chinese, Canadian FMs hold talks on bilateral ties, int'l issues.' Xinhua, 1st May 2007.

[567] 'Chinese FM meets Azerbaijani Counterpart.' Xinhua, 1st June 2007.

[568] 'Chinese, French presidents hold telephone talks.' Xinhua, 24th May 2007.

[569] 'China satisfied about ties with Madagascar: Premier.' Xinhua, 16th May 2007.

[570] 'Chinese, Barbados PMs exchange greetings on anniversary of diplomatic ties.' Xinhua, 30th May 2007.

[571] 'China, Slovakia Vow to Enhance All-round Cooperation.' Beijing Review, 6th February 2007.

[572] 'Chinese State Councilor meets Maltese FM.' Xinhua, 26th May 2007.

[573] 'China, Greece vow to strengthen relations in various fields.' Xinhua, 31st January 2007.

[574] 'Sri Lankans consider China's development as theirs: president.' Xinhua, 27th February 2007.

[575] 'China, Cote d'Ivoire pledge to strengthen bilateral ties.' Xinhua, 11th May 2007. As of late 2009, Taiwan is recognized by Belize; Burkina Faso; the Dominican Republic; El Salvador; Gambia; Guatemala; Haiti; Honduras; Kiribati; the Marshall Islands; Nauru; Nicaragua; Palau; Panama; Paraguay; Saint Kitts and Nevis; Saint

Lucia; Saint Vincent and the Grenadines; São Tomé and Príncipe; the Solomon Islands; Swaziland; Tuvalu; and the Vatican City

[576] 'China, Zambia vow to strengthen cooperation.' Xinhua, 4th February 2007.

[577] 'China, Suriname vow to advance bilateral ties.' Xinhua, 28th March 2007.

[578] 'See 'New EU chief good for ties with China,' by Wu Jiao, Li Xiaokun and Cheng Guangjin, China Daily, 21st November 2009, and 'Many good tidings from Obama's visit,' by Jin Canrong, China Daily, 20th November 2009.

[579] 'Hu meets with Obama in Washington on China-US ties.' Xinhua, 13th April 2010.

[580] 'Chinese, Sudanese senior military leaders hold talks on closer ties.' Xinhua, 4th April 2007.

[581] 'Taiwan accuses China of buying former ally Senegal.' AFP, 13th May 2007.

[582] This is a number that fluctuates - generally downwards - in response to Beijing's maneuvering.

[583] 'Beijing, Taipei vie for Caribbean support.' By Carol Williams, The Los Angeles Times, 30th April 2007.

[584] 'China vetoes U.N. resolution on Guatemala.' CNN, 10th January 1997

[585] 'China vetoes renewing U.N. force in Macedonia.' CNN, 25th February 1999.

[586] 'China says OIE's resolution shows int'l support of one-China policy.' Xinhua, 29th May 2007.

[587] 'Overseas Chinese urged to stand against 'Taiwan secessionists.'' Xinhua, 25th May 2007.

[588] 'Report on the Work of the Government [full text].' China Daily, 17th March 2007.

[589] 'Chinese state councilor urges overseas Chinese to stand against Taiwan secessionists.' Xinhua, 1st June 2007.

[590] 'Overseas Chinese hold photo show in Taiwan issue.' Xinhua, 20th May 2007.

[591] 'Overseas Chinese to promote peaceful reunification.' Xinhua, 21st May 2007.

[592] 'Crackdown on illegal mapping websites.' Xinhua, 27th March 2008.

[593] Roberts, op. cit., p.152.

[594] 'China's outrage at island links.' Shanghai Daily via Xinhua, 2nd May 2007.

[595] 'Diplomatic ties with St. Lucia cut.' Xinhua, 5th May 2007.

Reason Number 20. Suicide China

[596] 'Centre offers mental aid to prevent suicide.' By Li Jing, China Daily, 5th December 2004.

[597] 'Suicide the major cause of death among young people.' By Wang Shanshan, China Daily, 27th March 2007.

[598] 'Man stabs eight people to death in China: state media.' The China Post, 10th May 2010.

[599] See 'Urban affliction rates 'worrying,'' by Wang Hongyi, China Daily, 11th October 2008 and 'Suicide attempts on the rise in China,' Xinhua, 31st March 2004.

[600] 'Changing needs and new perspectives for psychiatry and mental health services in China.' By Professor Zou Yizhuang, M.D. Ph.D., Scientific Secretary of Chinese Society of Psychiatry (CSP).

[601] 'Killings highlight mental health challenges.' By Wang Jinqiong, China Daily, 2nd December 2009.

[602] 'General Hospital Psychiatry in China.' By Wu Wenyuan, MD. See www.21jk.com.

[603] 'Psychology service for the rich.' By Wu Chong, China Daily. 29th January 2005.

[604] 'Rise in suicide sounds campus alarm.' By Kang Yi, China Daily, 21st May 2007.

[605] 'Too much pressure.' By He Na, China Daily, 26th May 2009.

[606] See 'Suicide top cause of death among 15-34 years old,' China Daily, 4th April 2009 and 'Suicide tops student-killer list,' by Wang Hongyi, China Daily, 23rd April 2009.

[607] 'Suicide a selfish act for 'Me Generation.'' By Qin Zhongwei, China Daily, 1st April 2010.

[608] 'Doctor in life-and-death struggle.' By Wu Chong, China Daily, 31st October 2004.

[609] 'Prevention project offers an outlet.' China Daily, 1st November 2005.

[610] 'In rural China, a bitter way out.' The Washington Post, 15th May 2007.

[611] 'Suicide rate called crisis for rural, young people.' People's Daily, 20th November 2003.

[612] 'Traditions weigh on China's women.' By Christopher Allen, BBC News, 19th June 2006.

[613] 'Centre offers mental aid to prevent suicide.' By Li Jing, China Daily, 5th December 2004.

[614] 'China's first group of qualified hotline counselors take post in Beijing.' Xinhua, 26th July 2005.

[615] 'Calming voices from the loneliness of the night.' By Zhao Yangrong, China Daily, 5th May 2010.

[616] 'Action at last to tackle suicide rate.' By Wang Yanlin, Shanghai Daily, 12th October 2005.

[617] 'Self-Identity and the Problematic of Chinese Modernity,' The Humanities Bulletin, Vol 4, 1995.

[618] 'We still need sense of right and wrong.' By Raymond Zhou, China Daily. 6th January 2007.

[619] 'Would-be jumper gets 'helping' hand.' By Qiu Quanlin, China Daily, 23rd May 2009. Chen was not killed, landing on a partially-inflated police pontoon and injuring his spine.

Reason Number 21. Boxing in Ideas for Mr. Marx

[620] 'China aims to tame internet and spread party line.' Reuters, 23rd April 2007.

[621] '84.5m Chinese use mobile phones to surf Internet.' Xinhua, 15th October 2008.

[622] 'A web on the Internet.' China Daily, 3rd May 2010.

[623] 'Rural Chinese children still in world without Internet.' Xinhua, 10th November 2009.

[624] 'Over 70% of Chinese netizens sub-healthy.' Xinhua, 15th September 2007.

[625] 'Parents of Net addict get 1m-yuan compensation over beating death.' China Daily, 28th August 2009.

[626] See 'Teen beaten in Net boot camp in critical condition,' by Hu Yongqi and Zhang Ao, China Daily, 19th August 2009 and 'China bans physical punishment for Internet addicts,' China Daily / Agencies, 5th November 2009.

[627] 'Blog real name system not yet officially decided.' People's Daily Online, October 23rd 2006.

[628] 'Government crusade against online anonymity.' Reporters without Borders, 7th May 2010.

[629] www.wikipedia.org\shi_tao.

[630] 'WAN Welcomes Release of Golden Pen of Freedom Laureate.' World Association of Newspapers, 5th February 2008. See www.wan-press.org.

[631] 'Cyber-dissident Guo Feixiong given electric shock torture in Shenyang prison.' Reporters without Borders, 29th May 2007.

[632] 'Time China burnishes its image globally.' By Frank Ching, The New Straits Times, 7th February 2008.

[633] 'Reporters without borders urges internet users to join in 24-hour online demo against internet censorship.' www.rsf.org, 26th October 2006. The figure of 52 imprisoned in China comes from Reporters without Borders' 2007 China Report.

[634] 'Blogger Hao Wu freed after being held for five months.' www.rsf.org, 11th July 2006.

[635] 2007 Annual Report, Reporters without Borders, available from www.rsf.org.

[636] 2008 Annual Report, Reporters without Borders, available from www.rsf.org.

[637] Reporters without Borders, 5th January 2010.

[638] 'Mobile phone users will have to provide ID information.' By Wang Xing and Xie Yu, China Daily, 4th February 2010.

[639] See 'Chinese Student in U.S. Is Caught in Confrontation,' by Shaila Dewan, The New York Times, 17th April 2008 and 'Nationalism is Beijing's brainchild,' by Paul Lim, The Taipei Times, 25th April 2008.

[640] Transcript: 'Duke Student Targeted for Mediating Tibet Protest.' NPR, April 21st 2008.

[641] See 'Online Throngs Impose a Stern Morality in China.' By Howard W. French, The New York Times, 3rd June 2006, and 'Should Google stay in China?,' MIT News, 30th April 2010.

[642] Zhang wrote in Chinese. A translation of the article is available at www.zonaeuropa.com

[643] 'Taiwan actress' remarks spark anger.' By Li Qian, China Daily, 7th September 2006.

[644] 'Meng Guangmei and Toiletgate: The latest Chinese Internet swarm.' By Jeremy Goldkorn, www.danwei.org.

[645] 'Basic information of 1.25 bln Chinese recorded in police data bank.' Xinhua, 7th April 2006.

[646] 'Virtual cops to weed out Internet gambling, porn.' By Li Fangchao, China Daily, 14th April 2007.

[647] 'China targets campus porn sites.' Agencies/China Daily, 29th May 2007.

[648] 'China shuts down media freedom site 'within hours.'' AFP, 30th May 2007.

[649] The minutes of this meeting, held on 31st October 2006, can be read at www.intgovforum.org

[650] 'China Again Censoring Web After Summit, Blocking of Foreign Sites Resumes.' By Clay Chandler, The Washington Post, 23rd October 2001.

[651] 'As Chinese Students Go Online, Little Sister Is Watching.' By Howard W. French, The New York Times, May 8th 2006.

[652] 'People's war against porn websites shows results.' People's Daily Online/China Daily, 29th May 2007.

[653] 'China nabs 5,400 people for online porn in 2009.' China Daily / Agencies, 3rd January 2010.

[654] 'China official blames internet for youth crime.' Reuters, April 19th 2007.

[655] 'China launches campaign to crack down on Web porn.' People's Daily, 13th April 2007.

453

[656] 'Gambling and porn targeted.' People's Daily, April 16th 2007. Other lengthy jail sentences have been handed down since then; for example a student identified only as Chen received an 11-year sentence for distributing cell phone porn in 2010, and a man named Huang Yizhong was sentenced to 13 years, also in 2010, for running a porn website - even though the server was based in the US. See 'College student phone porn peddler gets 11 years in jail,' by Xu Shenglan, the Global Times, 22nd February 2010, and 'China Jails Man 13 Years for Running Porn Web Site,' ABC News / The Associated Press, 6th February 2010.

Reason Number 22. Once the Masters of Invention

[657] Kublai Khan: The Mongol King Who Remade China. John Man, Bantam Press, 2006. p.73.

[658] Cultural Flow Between China and Outside World Throughout History. By Shen Fuwei, Foreign Language Press, Beijing, 1997. p 188-192.

[659] See 'Awards highlight innovation capacity,' By Jia Hepeng, China Daily, 28th February 2007 and 'Sixth Successive Vacancy for China's Top Sci-tech Award,' by Liu Heng, People's Daily, 2nd September 2003.

[660] 'Sixth Successive Vacancy for China's Top Sci-tech Award.' People's Daily, 2nd September 2003.

[661] 'What are China's new 'four great inventions?'' People's Daily Online, 14th February 2006.

[662] 'China's Four Great Modern Inventions Selected.' Xinhua, 10th February 2007.

[663] See 'China's self-made EVD enters market,' Agencies/Xinhua, 21st November 2003, 'EVD players not selling as expected in China,' People's Daily, 10th January 2004, 'Chinese manufacturers aim to replace DVDs with homegrown EVD standard,' Xinhua, 1st December 2006, and 'China Firms Unveil New Players,' by Joe McDonald, The Associated Press, 6th December 2006.

[664] 'Despite shelving WAPI, China stands firm on chip tax.' By Sumner Lemon, IDG News Service, 22nd April, 2004.

[665] 'China appeals to ISO against Intel-dominated wireless encryption standard.' Xinhua, 29th May 2006.

[666] 'Chinese WAPI delegation calls for diplomatic support after 'unfair treatment.'' Xinhua, 9th June 2006.

[667] 'Cell phone puzzle: Imitation, innovation, irritation.' By Peng Yining, China Daily, 23rd February 2010.

[668] 'Manned moon mission expected in 10 to 15 years.' Xinhua, 27th November 2005.

[669] 'Space heroes get a rapturous welcome.' By Hu Yinan, China Daily, 30th September 2008.

[670] 'Junk from China missile test raises fear of satellite collision.' By Dan Glaister, The Guardian, 7th February 2007.

[671] 'Orbital debris threatens future space journeys: Chinese experts.' People's Daily, 26th November 2003.

[672] Daily Press Briefing. Tom Casey, Deputy Spokesman, Washington, DC. 19th January, 2007. See www.state.gov

[673] 'Concern grows over China's satellite-killing missile test.' By Chris Buckley, Reuters, 19th January 2007.

[674] 'Outer space not let to overcast with 'war clouds''[sic]. By Wang Baofu, People's Daily, 3rd April 2007.

Reason Number 23. Graying Reds

[675] China's State Council's White Paper, 'The Development of China's Undertakings for the Aged.' Published in China Daily, 13th December 2006.

[676] See '100-plus club enjoys great old fun.' China Daily, 8th March 2004, and 'Care for the elderly,' China Daily, 8th October 2008.

[677] 'China faces challenges with doubling elders.' By Winnie Wang, Shanghai Daily, 12th December 2006.

[678] 'Aging population a major challenge.' By Xie Chuanjiao, China Daily, 12th March 2007.

[679] 'China faces elderly dilemma.' China Daily, 21st August 2004.

[680] 'The Most Populous Nation Faces a Population Crisis.' By Joseph Kahn, The New York Times, 30th May, 2004.

[681] 'China faces elderly dilemma.' China Daily, 21st August 2004.

[682] See 'Case Study: China' by Fu Hua and Xue Di. World Health Organization, www.who.int

[683] 'Shanghai seniors generally happy: Survey.' By Wang Hongyi, China Daily, 8th October 2008.

[684] 'Shanghai committed to its aging population.' By Cao Li, China Daily, 17th May 2007.

[685] 'Elderly must contribute in ageing society.' By Li Xing, China Daily, 2nd March 2006.

[686] 'China faces challenges with doubling elders.' By Winnie Wang, Shanghai Daily, 12th December 2006.

[687] 'China goes from red to gray.' By Robert C. Pozen, Fortune Magazine, 14th June 2006.

[688] China International Business, March 2007.

[689] 'China faces elderly dilemma.' China Daily, 21st August 2004.

[690] 'As China ages, a shortage of cheap labor looms.' By Howard W. French, The New York Times, 30th June 2006.

[691] 'Elderly must contribute in ageing society.' By Li Xing, China Daily, 2nd March 2006.

[692] 'Graying Shanghai.' By Wu Jun, Scene Magazine, May 2005.

[693] 'China frets at pensions for aging population.' Reuters, 25th February 2006.

[694] 'Rural elders forgotten as youth rush to cities.' By Zhou Yan and Hu Tao, Shanghai Daily, 6th December 2006.

[695] 'Poor rural elderly deserve attention.' Xinhua, 3rd December 2006.

[696] 'Rural elders forgotten as youth rush to cities.' By Zhou Yan and Hu Tao, Shanghai Daily, 6th December 2006.

[697] 'In China, aging in the care of strangers.' By Maureen Fan, The Washington Post, 22nd December 2006.

[698] 'China goes from red to gray.' By Robert C. Pozen. Fortune Magazine, 14th June 2006.

[699] 'China scrambles for stability as its workers age.' By Howard W. French, The New York Times, 22nd March 2007.

[700] 'Welfare for elderly a priority.' Shanghai Daily, 13th December 2006.

[701] 'Ageing population cannot be ignored.' By Guo Zhe, China Daily, 19th December 2006.

[702] 'Chinese auditors say 30.8 billion yuan in social security funds misused.' People's Daily Online, 16th March 2007, and 'US$900m misused from pension fund,' China Daily, 24th November 2006.

[703] 'Rest homes leave poor out in the cold.' By Ji Mi, Shanghai Daily, 1st December 2006.

[704] The Development of China's Undertakings for the Aged. White Paper, the Information Office of China's State Council, December 12th 2006.

[705] 'AXA Retirement Scope 2007.' Available at www.retirement-scope.axa.com

[706] 'Survey finds future finances a major concern.' China Daily, 13th January 2007.

[707] 'Adjust retirement policy.' China Daily, 11th July 2006.

[708] 'Weighing up social costs of raising pension age.' By Xie Hu, China Daily, 10th September 2004.

[709] 'China may raise retirement age to ease pension shortage.' AFP, 28th November 2006.

[710] 'Court upholds female retirement age.' Shanghai Daily, 19th October 2005.

[711] 'Service targets lonely elderly people.' China Daily, 1st March 2006.

[712] 'Beating the empty-nester blues.' By Raymond Zhou, China Daily, 16th April 2004.

[713] 'Empty-nesters flock to each other.' China Daily, 20th April 2006.

[714] 'Rush for Wealth in China's Cities Shatters the Ancient Assurance of Care in Old Age.' By Howard W. French, The New York Times, 3rd November 2006.

[715] 'Grave matters - remembering the deceased.' By Qiu Lin, China Daily. 5th April 2007.

[716] 'Chinese 'Can't afford to die' as funeral costs soar.' Reuters, 6th April 2007.

[717] 'Tomb prices up and up: Let's squeeze the dead.' By Xu Xiaomin, Shanghai Star, 5th April 2004.

[718] 'China to rein in graveyard speculators.' AFP, 15th May 2007.

[719] 'The deceased find eternal peace at sea.' By Wang Zhuoqiong, China Daily, 5th May 2006.

Reason Number 24. Why Am I Speaking English?

[720] 'Appeal of overseas studies grows in China.' By Wang Ying, China Daily, 17th October 2008.

[721] '25.77 percent overseas students return home after studies.' People's Daily Online, 12th June 2006.

[722] 'How foreign countries attract Chinese students?' People's Daily Online, 30th May 2007.

[723] 'Returned overseas students privileged in China.' Xinhua, 30th March 2007.

[724] 'Chinese University Students Pursue Materialism Over Communism.' The Epoch Times, 20th June 2006.

[725] 'Graduates struggling with slim job market.' Xinhua, 17th March 2007.

[726] 'Parents stress education.' By Angela Xu, Shanghai Daily, 24th May 2005.

[727] 'Cultural Transfer: The Impact of Direct Experience on Evaluations of British and Chinese Societies.' By Professor Greg Philo, Glasgow University Media Group. See www.gla.ac.uk/centres/mediagroup

[728] 'How foreign countries attract Chinese students?' People's Daily Online, 30th May 2007.

[729] ''Sea turtles' losing the job race.' China Daily, 25th June 2004.

[730] 'Parents stress education.' By Angela Xu, Shanghai Daily, 24th May 2005.

[731] 'English in Shanghai.' By Mao Xing, China International Business Magazine, March 2007.

[732] 'English craze is baffling.' China Daily, 31st March 2006.

Reason Number 25. The Silence of Chinese Conservation

[733] 'Yellow River in crisis as pollution takes hold.' Xinhua, December 14th 2006.

[734] http://en.wikipedia.org/wiki/Wuhai

[735] 'Joint Efforts to Clean up Yellow River.' China Daily, March 30th 2006.

[736] '30% of Yellow river fish species extinct.' By Jonathan Watts, The Guardian, January 18th 2007.

[737] 'Yellow River's health continues to decline.' Xinhua, November 6th 2006.

[738] 'Tibetan glacier melt leading to sandstorms.' AFP, 2nd May 2006.

[739] 'Glacier study reveals chilling prediction.' China Daily, September 23rd 2004.

[740] 'Yellow River source faces ecological woes.' By Sun Xiaohua, China Daily, 11th October 2005.

[741] Discharge figure from www.china.org.cn/english/travel/40876.htm. Science magazine reports a slightly lower figure of 960,000 million cubic meters – 'Going Against the Flow' by Richard Stone and Hawk Jia, 25th August 2006.

[742] 'China's Yangtze river in peril.' AFP, 15th April 2007.

[743] 'Yangtze drought triggers debate over China's Three Gorges Dam.' AFP, March 22nd 2007.

[744] For example, August Pfluger, who runs a conservation program aimed at the white-flag dolphin, says it is 'functionally extinct.' This "is a tragedy, a loss not only for China, but for the entire world" says Pfluger. See www.baiji.org. 'Baiji' is the Chinese name for the dolphin.

[745] 'Vigilance against the Potential Loss of Finless Porpoise Warned by WWF.' 14th December 2006, Worldwide Fund for Nature. See www.wwfchina.org.

[746] 'Pollution takes toll on Yangtze.' By Sun Xiaohua, China Daily. 16th April 2007.

[747] 'Yangtze river 'cancerous' with pollution.' Reuters/Xinhua, 30th May 2006

[748] 'Top official tough on polluters.' China Daily, 7th October 2006.

[749] For example, more than US$50 million was embezzled in 2000 alone. See, for example, 'Three Gorges corruption scandal,' BBC News, 21st July 2000.

[750] 'The Rising Dragon's Environmental Disaster.' By Jasper Becker, from The Asia Sentinel, 22nd November 2006.

[751] 'China urgently needs to protect wetlands.' Xinhua, April 20th 2007.

[752] 'Polluting paper mills shut down.' Shanghai Daily, April 4th 2007.

[753] 'Excessive lead has water for thousands cut off.' China Daily, April 6th 2007.

[754] '80,000 villagers without safe water for a month' South China Morning Post, March 14th 2007.

[755] 'Dirty tap water.' Shanghai Daily, November 9th 2006.

[756] '17m people in Sichuan live without safe water.' By Huang Zhiling and Wang Wei, China Daily, 25th January 2008.

[757] 'Massive fish kill confirmed.' By Legolas Zhang. Shanghai Daily, 6th December 2006.

[758] 'Top official tough on polluters.' China Daily, 7th October 2007.

[759] This was one of the rare cases where China apologized to another nation – in this case, Russia. This scandal was widely reported at the time. See, for example, The Christian Science Monitor for 28th November 2005, available online.

[760] 'Chemical firm gets fine for polluting Yangtze tributary.' Xinhua, 10th October 2008.

[761] 'Dongting Lake in severe danger.' Shanghai Daily, 17th April 2007.

[762] 'A modest proposal.' The Economist, October 26th 2006.

[763] '30% of Yellow River fish species extinct.' By Jonathan Watts, The Guardian, 18th January 2007.

[764] 'Drip technology helps save water.' Shanghai Daily, 2nd April 2007.

[765] 'Oceanic environment deteriorating.' By Zhang Liuhao. Shanghai Daily, September 14th, 2006.

[766] Footnote 18, op. cit.

[767] 'Marine environment rings alarm.' China Daily, 30th November 2009.

[768] 'Pollution 'likely to peak at earlier stage of growth,'' by Li Jing, China Daily, 10th February 2010.

[769] 'Estuaries of China's greatest rivers declared "dead zones."' AFP, October 20th 2006.

[770] 'Yellow River estuary 'cleanest in years,'' Reuters, June 9th 2006.

[771] 'City governments fined for Yellow River pollution.' Xinhua, 11th March 2010.

[772] 'China says water pollution double official figure.' China Daily / Agencies, 10th February 2010.

[773] 'New concept applied in Yellow River management.' Xinhua, 23rd October 2003.

[774] 'Artificial forests 'root of eco-crisis,'' South China Morning Post, 14th March 2007. Also see www.fon.org.cn

[775] 'China has 104 plant species in danger of extinction.' By Winny Wang. Shanghai Daily, 17th April 2007.

[776] 'Accelerated ban on refrigerant sought.' By Keith Bradsher. International Herald Tribune, 15th March 2007.

[777] 'China asks construction industry to go green.' International Herald Tribune, January 18th 2007.

[778] 'Chinese bureaucrats blasted for energy-wasting office buildings.' AFP, 28th March 2007.

[779] 'Protected trees cut for villas.' Shanghai Daily, March 28th 2007. The report also says local police had no records of relevant ownership documents, meaning the owners must have obtained the certificates by illicit means.

[780] 'The Greening of China.' The Economist, October 22nd 2005.

[781] 'Industrialization on track: report.' China Daily, 29th January 2007.

[782] 'China admits it failed to meet environmental goals.' AP, 13th February 2007.

[783] 'Industrial parks protect polluters.' Shanghai Daily, 28th November 2006.

[784] 'Some regions fake reports on emissions.' Xinhua, 29th December 2006.

[785] 'CCTV says blind eye turned to pollution.' Shanghai Daily, April 16th 2007.

[786] 'China tightens control over foreigners' hydrological activities.' People's Daily Online, 8th May 2007.

[787] 'Four Japanese citizens fined for illegal surveying in China.' Xinhua, 27th April 2007.

[788] See 'China in an energy quandary,' by Jasper Becker, August 28th 2003 (at www.atimes.com) and 'The Great Pall of China,' Michael McCarthy and Clifford Coonan, The Independent, 25th April 2007 respectively.

[789] 'Coal resources blatantly wasted.' Xinhua, May 2nd 2007.

[790] Figures from the International Energy Agency.

[791] 'Coal burning having a devastating impact on rural Chinese.' By Benjamin Morgan, AFP, 16th April 2007.

[792] 'China's Power Capacity Soars.' By Richard McGregor, Financial Times, February 6th 2007.

[793] 'China's coal addiction causing environmental disaster.' By Robert J. Saigal, AFP, 5th November 2006.

[794] For example, in 2004, half the power stations built had not been approved by the central government. They were put into service anyway. See, for example, 'Power plant construction boom worries experts,' People's Daily, December 10th 2004.

[795] 'The Great Pall of China.' By Michael McCarthy and Clifford Coonan, The Independent, 25th April 2007.

[796] See 'Market forces crucial to low-carbon economy,' by Song Ping, China Daily, 30th April 2010, and 'China makes rapid new energy strides.' By Xiao Wan, China Daily, 7th May 2010.

[797] 'The Xinfeng Power Plant Incident and Challenges for China's Electric Power Industry.' By Chen Chun-ni, Electric Power & Gas Industry Group, Strategy and Industry Research Unit, The Institute of Energy Economics, Japan. Available at eneken.ieej.or.jp

[798] 'China's coal addiction causing environmental disaster.' By Robert J. Saiget, AFP, November 5th 2006.

[799] 'China about to become biggest CO2 emitter: IEA.' By Barbara Lewis, Reuters, 18th April 2007.

[800] Saiget, op. cit.

[801] The Intergovernmental Panel on Climate Change, 30th April-4th May 2007. See www.ipcc.ch and also, for example, 'China, India, Brazil hold up climate change talks,' AFP. By Emmanuel Angleys, May 2nd 2007.

[802] 'Question marks over China's climate commitment.' By Karl Malakunas. APF, 6th May 2007.

[803] See, for example, 'China is No. 1 again, this time in CO2 emissions,' CNET News, June 19th 2007.

[804] 'China seen topping U.S. carbon emissions in 2007.' By Emma Graham-Harrison and Gerard Wynn, Reuters, 23rd March 2007.

[805] 'New analysis finds alarming increase in expected growth of China CO2 emissions.' By Sarah Yang, Media Relations, UC Berkeley, 10th March 2008.

[806] See, for example, 'China denies report of green house gases emissions,' Li Xinran, Shanghai Daily, 25th April 2007 and 'China won't be top CO2 emitter this year – official,' Reuters, 25th April 2007.

[807] 'China's economy reaching environmental limits.' Robert J. Saiget, AFP, April 4th 2007. Xu was speaking at an MIT energy forum in Shanghai.

[808] 'Is China turning green?' By Daniel Esty, Fortune, May 4th 2007.

[809] '1st national pollution census starts.' By Sun Xiaohua, China Daily, 5th January 2008.

[810] ''Iron hand' to help realize green goals.' By Li Jing, China Daily, 6th May 2010.

[811] 'China fails to meet environmental targets.' By Robert J. Saiget, AFP, 10th January 2007.

[812] 'Nuclear power not the solution for China: official.' AFP, 23rd April 2007.

[813] 'Power troubles may soon be solved.' By Guan Xiaofeng, China Daily, August 1st 2006.

[814] 'China finds large oil deposits in Bohai Bay.' AFP, 4th May 2007.

[815] 'Vast metal reserves on 'roof of world.'' By Li Fangchao, China Daily, 13th February 2007.

[816] 'Hydropower mania poses challenges.' China Daily, 27th July 2005.

[817] 'Winter blues for Beijing as pollution worsens.' AFP, December 12th 2006.

[818] Ibid.

[819] 'Ambitious 'blue sky' target for Beijing.' Xinhua, 2nd January 2007

461

[820] 'IOC boss demands cleaner Beijing air.' AFP, South China Morning Post, March 16th 2007.

[821] 'China to force rain ahead of the Olympics.' AP, 25th April 2007.

[822] 'US cyclists provoke Beijing smog row.' The Daily Telegraph, 6th August 2008.

[823] 'U.S. Olympic Officials Call Beijing Pollution Levels 'Awful.'' By Stephanie Sy and Beth Loyd, ABC News, 15th February 2008.

[824] 'Beijing weighs added pollution plans for Olympics.' By Jim Yardley, The New York Times, 29th July 2008.

[825] 'Beijing Olympics: China declared safe from pollution for opening ceremony.' By Bonnie Malkin, The Daily Telegraph, 7th August 2008.

[826] See 'Beijing Olympics Air Pollution: Worse Than L.A.,' by Robin Lloyd, www.livescience.com, 22nd June 2009, and 'Athletes, spectators faced unprecedented air pollution at 2008 Olympic Games,' www.scienceblog.com.

[827] 'Beijing ends its Olympics' pollution curbs.' By Tini Tran, Associated Press / USA Today, 21st September 2009.

[828] 'China by numbers.' China Economic Review, December 2005.

[829] 'China finds large oil deposits in Bohai Bay.' AFP, 4th May 2007.

Reason Number 26. The Migrant School of Revolution

[830] 'Chinese lawmaker calls for more political rights for migrant workers.' Xinhua, 4th March 2007

[831] 'CPPCC Members Call for Protecting Migrant Workers' Rights.' People's Daily, 7th March 2002.

[832] 'China to End Inequities to Rural Migrant Workers.' People's Daily, 8th August 2002.

[833] 'Zeng: Pay all owed wages to migrant workers.' By Fu Jing, China Daily, 24th August 2004.

[834] 'Full Text: Report on the Work of the Government.' People's Daily, 14th March 2005.

[835] Article 50 of the Labor Law of the People's Republic of China

[836] 'Zeng: Pay all owed wages to migrant workers.' By Fu Jing, China Daily, 24th August 2004.

[837] 'State Council Vows Rural Laborers to Be Paid on Time.' Xinhua, 10th July 2006.

[838] 'Wage rage: Grassroots fight for equal playing field.' China Daily, 5th March 2007.

[839] 'Rise of wages for migrant workers a must.' By Liu Shinan, China Daily, 24th February 2010.

[840] 'Migrants face loneliness and depression.' China Daily, 16th August 2004.

[841] 'Zeng: Pay all owed wages to migrant workers.' By Fu Jing, China Daily, 24th August 2004.

[842] 'Unions Help Migrants Chase Wages.' Xinhua, 28th December 2006.

[843] 'No Delay of Payment to Workers Allowed.' Xinhua, 29th December 2005.

[844] 'News Feature: Migrant worker's suggestions appear in Premier's work report.' Xinhua, 6th March 2007.

[845] See 'Back-pay a major worry for migrants,' by Li Fangchao, China Daily, 7th February 2007, and 'Rural Migrant Workers Still Make Low Income,' Chinanews.cn, 7th February 2007.

[846] 'Number of cases involving delays in migrant workers' wages down in 2006.' Xinhua, 18th February 2007.

[847] 'Wage rage: Grassroots fight for equal playing field.' China Daily, 5th March 2007.

[848] 'Gov't move to ensure migrants get paid.' China Daily, 5th February 2007.

[849] See 'Pay dispute man critical,' China Daily/Xinhua, 3rd July 2007 and 'Worker beaten in wage dispute dies,' China Daily/Xinhua, 5th July 2007.

[850] 'Chongqing wants 'fair treatment' for assaulted workers.' 4th July 2007.

[851] 'Migrants frustrated over unpaid wages.' Xinhua, 31st December 2006.

[852] 'Chinese lawmaker calls for more political rights for migrant workers.' Xinhua, 4th March 2007.

[853] 'Construction workers alienated.' By Wang Zhuoqiong, China Daily, 9th July 2007.

[854] 'Chinese employees' legal rights need more protection.' Xinhua, 3rd July 2007.

[855] 'China brickwork slave children may number 1,000.' Reuters / China Daily, 15th June 2007.

[856] 'Farmers' living standards lag 7 years behind urban residents.' 25th April 2007.

[857] 'Migrant workers' income rises in 2007.' Xinhua, 11th January 2008.

[858] 'Migrant workers feel the pinch amid crisis.' Xinhua, March 2nd 2009.

[859] 'Pearl River Delta cracks down on fugitive bosses.' Xinhua, March 7th 2009.

[860] 'Workers stranded waiting for unpaid wages.' By Wang Huazhong, China Daily, 10th December 2010.

[861] 'Labor pains: Stabbing highlights need to protect migrant workers.' By Hu Yongqi and Peng Yining, China Daily, 20th January 2010.

[862] 'Illegal schools for migrant workers' kids await government approval.' Xinhua, 19th February 2004.

[863] 'Millions of migrant children can't afford education.' People's Daily, 17th February 2004.

[864] 'Henan natives battle against hometown notoriety.' Shanghai Star, 25th May 2005.

[865] 'Police apologize for discriminatory banners.' By Chen Hong, China Daily, 10th February 2006.

[866] 'More than half migrant workers hope to settle in cities: survey.' Xinhua. 26th October 2006.

[867] 'Political consultation: China's unique instrument for social consensus and harmony.' Xinhua, 12th March 2007.

Reason Number 27. The Chinese 'Gold' Push

[868] 'China gets 'battle orders' for 2008 preparations.' Reuters via China Daily, 19th January 2007

[869] 'China puts glory before honor at National Games.' Reuters via China Daily, 25th October 2005

[870] 'Athletes banned from 'social activities.'' China Daily, 10th November 2006.

[871] 'Marathon runner running short of money sells medals.' By Coldness Kwan, Chinadaily.com.cn, 10th April 2007.

[872] 'Popular Books Follow Trends.' Xinhua, 20th November 2001.

Reason Number 28. A Traditional Feast of Cruelty

[873] 'Blood stains cruel nation.' By James Rose, The Standard (Hong Kong), 28th June 2007.

[874] 'Why the ducks dance.' Shanghai Star, 12th December 2002.

[875] 'New Campaign Hunts Down Illegal Wildlife Traders.' People's Daily, April 29th 2003.

[876] '13 jailed in China's largest illegal wild animal trade case.' Xinhua, 16th February 2007.

[877] 'Hey, poachers! Leave those beasts alone.' By Chen Jia, China Daily, 3rd July 2008

[878] 'Wildlife on menu spurs smuggling.' By Wang Zhuoqiong, China Daily, 24th June 2009.

[879] 'Administration denies China's tiger bone trade ban has been eased.' Xinhua, 11th January 2007.

[880] See 'More animals reported dead in Shenyang zoo,' 14th March 2010, 'Source: Zoo starved tigers to ransom govt,' by Zuo Likun, China Daily, 15th March 2010, '13 tigers die in 3 months,' by Wu Yong and Liu Ce, China Daily, 15th March 2010, 'Tiger-bone liquor 'open secret' in zoo, by Zhang Jiawei, China Daily, 17th March 2010, and 'A dark pall over the zoo,' China Daily, 18th March 2010.

[881] 'Bears on farms face 'thrilling cruelty.'' China Daily/Agencies, 22nd February 2005.

[882] See www.animalasia.org

[883] 'Extraction of bear bile 'is painless, necessary.'' China Daily, 13th January, 2006.

[884] 'Animal Olympics under way.' www.chinanews.cn, 30th September 2006.

[885] See China Daily, 7th September 2006.

[886] 'China sees rising calls for legislation against animal abuse.' Xinhua, 5th April 2006.

[887] 'Draft law to punish animal cruelty.' By Wang Qian, China Daily. May 19th 2009.

[888] 'Draft law highlights ban on cruelty to animals.' By Wang Jingqiong, China Daily, 19th March 2010.

Reason Number 29. Blue China Crime

[889] 'Shanghai Sets New Population Goal Under 19 Mln.' Shanghai Daily, 8th March 2007.

[890] 'Chinese police crack nearly two million criminal cases in 2006,' Xinhua, 17th January 2007; 'Chinese police detect 18,000 homicide cases in 2006,' Xinhua, 7th February 2007; 'Facts and figures: China's judicial work in 2006,' People's Daily, 13th March 2007.

[891] 'China police complain of manpower shortage in countryside despite crime rate falling.' Xinhua, 14th November 2006.

[892] 'Chinese police detect 18,000 homicide cases in 2006,' Xinhua, 7th February 2007

[893] 'Underage crime on the rise in China: procuratorate.' Xinhua, 31st May 2007.

[894] 'Robbery, rape top crime list by minor criminals.' Xinhua, 9th December 2006.

[895] 'Law stresses ban on underage booze, cigarettes sales.' By Cao Li, China Daily, 8th November 2004.

[896] 'Muddled murder mystery in coal-rich Guizhou raises doubts.' By Wang Yong, Shanghai Daily, 11th December 2006.

[897] See 'Police probe Foshan family slaying,' by Qiu Quanlin, China Daily, 30th December 2006, and 'Official confesses to murder,' by Qiu Quanlin, China Daily, 5th January 2007.

[898] 'NW China court judge found murdered with family and housemaid.' Xinhua, December 14th 2006.

[899] 'Police arrest two for killing family of six.' By Kat Jiang, Shanghai Daily, 7th May 2007.

[900] 'Serial rapist, killer confesses after arrest in NE China.' Xinhua, 22nd July 2008

[901] 'Man stands trial for killing six police in Shanghai.' Xinhua, 26th August 2008

[902] See 'Five die in south China killing spree,' Xinhua, 15th November, 2009 'Spree killing suspect caught in S. China,' Xinhua, 30th November 2009, 'Man who kills 13 captured in Hunan,' by Uking Sun, China Daily, 13th December 2009, 'Police offer reward for spree murder suspect,' China Daily, 4th August 2009, and 'Killing spree leaves four dead in C. China,' by Wang Jingqiong and Shan Juan, China Daily, 1st July 2009.

[903] See 'Man who killed 7 of own family surrenders,' By Wang Jingqiong, China Daily, 5th February 2010, 'Tianjin road rampage kills 9,' by Wang Yu and Lan Tian, China Daily,' 2nd February 2010, and 'Eight killed in stabbing spree,' China Daily, 10th May 2010.

[904] 'Mass murders are 'not on the rise.'' China Daily, 7th February 2007.

Reason Number 30. The Fallibility of Chinese Characters

[905] 'China's Illiterates: 50% in the West, Female 70%.' 4th March 2002.

[906] 'China Sets Target for Illiteracy Elimination.' People's Daily, 4th March 2002.

[907] 'Youth illiteracy rate in W. China to be under 5% by end of 2007: official.' People's Daily, 25th March 2004.

[908] 'Premier Wen pledges to eliminate illiteracy in five years.' Xinhua, 8th September 2004.

[909] 'China committed to fighting illiteracy.' China Daily, 5th April 2007.

[910] 'Illiteracy returns to haunt country.' By Wang Zhuoqiong, China Daily, 2nd April 2007.

[911] 'UN to award Confucius prize for elite educational efforts.' Xinhua, 24th July 2006.

[912] 'Nation committed to fighting illiteracy.' China Daily, 5th April 2007.

[913] 'Illiteracy returns to haunt country.' By Wang Zhuoqiong, China Daily, 2nd April 2007.

[914] '40% Chinese cannot speak Putonghua.' 5th September 2006.

Reason Number 31. Taiwan – The Poison Pill of Democracy

[915] 'Taiwan looks askance at Hong Kong's handover formula.' By Ralph Jennings, Reuters, 24th June 2007.

[916] 'China's PLA Daily Criticizes Lee Tung-hui's Divisiveness.' People's Daily Online, 20th August 1999.

[917] See 'China anger over Taiwan Lee's shrine visit,' CNN, 7th July 2007, and 'Taiwan separatist Lee Teng-hui visits Tokyo's Yasukuni war shrine.' Xinhua, 7th July 2007.

[918] "Green' Taiwan businessmen not welcomed: official.' People's Daily Online, 3rd June 2004.

[919] 'Beijing: Chen Shui-bian is a 'troublemaker, saboteur.'' Xinhua, 8th February 2006 and 'Beijing reaffirms stand against independence,' By Xing Zhigang, China Daily, 12th April 2006.

[920] 'Taiwan takes another broadside from the mainland.' The Economist, 13th April 2000.

[921] 'PLA: Chen is to blame if war breaks out.' China Daily, 3rd December 2003.

[922] 'Anti-Secession Law adopted by NPC (full text).' Xinhua, 14th March 2005.

[923] Annual Report to Congress: Military Power of the People's Republic of China 2006, p11, p28.

[924] Annual Report to Congress: Military Power of the People's Republic of China 2007, p5, p33.

[925] 'US report 'interfering' in China's internal affairs – FM.' China Daily via Reuters, 28th May 2007.

[926] 'Delegates back new defense budget increase.' Xinhua, 7th March 2009.

[927] Annual Report to Congress: Military Power of the People's Republic of China, 2009. Executive summary and p.31

[928] 'Defense budget to see 'modest rise.'' China Daily, 5th March 2008.

[929] 'No threat from military development.' By Wu Jiao and Peng Kuang, China Daily, 16th January 2009.

[930] 'Thousands of Taiwanese hold anti-China rally.' AFP, 18th March 2006.

[931] 'Taiwan looks askance at Hong Kong's handover formula.' By Ralph Jennings, Reuters, 24th June 2007.

[932] See, for example, 'Resisting China's charm offensive.' The Economist, 6th November 2008.

[933] 'China should use Hong Kong as democracy test: Chan.' By Stephanie Wong, AFP, 25th June 2007.

[934] Sino-British Joint Declaration on the Question of Hong Kong, Annex I, Section XIII. Full text available at www.cab.gov.hk

[935] See, for example, 'Standing up for Hong Kong,' Time, 14th July 2003.

[936] 'No More Concessions On Hong Kong Anti-Subversion Law, says Official.' By Kurt Achin, 28th June 2003.

[937] 'Chinese Premier Warns Against 'Taiwan Independence.'' People's Daily, 16th March 2000.

[938] 'Hong Kong's freedom remains under basic law: former secretary for justice.' Xinhua, 15th June 2007.

Reason Number 32. China Fat

[939] 'China: From diseases of poverty to diseases of affluence. Policy implications of the epidemiological transition.' T. Colin Campell, Chen Junshi, Thierry Brun, Banoo Parpia, Qu Yinsheng, Chen Chunming, and Catherine Geissler.

[940] 'Children suffer from deteriorating health condition.' People's Daily, 21st August 2006.

[941] 'All that rich food is leading to poor health.' By Wang Shanshan, China Daily, 16th May 2006.

[942] 'Obesity bane of pupils.' By Yu Ping, China Daily, 30th January 2007.

[943] 'China renews call to tackle young people's health problems.' Xinhua, 17th September 2008.

[944] 'It is possible to prevent cancer, says experts' report.' By Ye Jun, China Daily, 22nd October 2008.

[945] 'Health experts call for action to curb China's youth obesity crisis.' People's Daily, 22nd August 2006.

[946] 'Youngsters getting fatter, not fitter, survey says.' People's Daily, 9th May 2007.

[947] Figures from the University of Illinois at Urbana-Champaign. See http://van.physics.uiuc.edu.

[948] 'Obesity of China's kids stuns officials.' By Calum McLeod, USA Today, 9th January 2007.

[949] 'Fighting the battle of the bulge.' By Zou Hanru, China Daily. 2nd March 2007.

[950] 'Chinese children's play sites shrinking: survey.' People's Daily, 8th May 2007.

[951] 'Health experts call for action to curb China's obesity crisis.' People's Daily, 22nd August 2006.

[952] 'Chinese children's play sites shrinking: survey.' People's Daily, 8th May 2007.

[953] 'Obesity bane of pupils.' By Yu Ping, China Daily, 30th January 2007.

[954] 'Youngsters getting fatter, not fitter, survey says.' People's Daily, 9th May 2007.

[955] 'China's children too busy for playtime.' People's Daily, 13th May 2007.

[956] 'Chinese people's need to succeed draining children's energy and parents' money.' People's Daily, 8th March 2007.

[957] 'Youngsters getting fatter, not fitter, survey says.' People's Daily, 9th May 2007.

[958] 'Survey puts student short-sightedness in focus.' By Zhou Zuyi, Shanghai Daily, 16th December 2006.

[959] 'Children suffer from deteriorating health condition.' People's Daily, 21st August 2006.

[960] 'Health experts call for action to curb China's youth obesity crisis.' People's Daily, 22nd August 2006.

[961] 'Nutritionists sought to fix poor diets.' China Daily,

[962] 'U.S. fast food giant KFC plans to lower threshold for franchise.' People's Daily, 15th November 2006.

[963] 'Beijing's homeless 'living' in McDonalds 24-hour restaurants.' Xinhua, 16th December 2006 and 'Drive-thru restaurants speeding ahead in China,' Xinhua, 14th August 2006.

[964] 'Chinese among world's top-five fast food fans.' People's Daily, 26th January 2005.

[965] 'Obesity levels in China rising fast – study.' China Daily via agencies, 9th July 2008.

[966] 'All that rich food is leading to poor health.' By Wang Shanshan, China Daily, 16th May 2006.

[967] 'Time to kick the nation's smoking habit.' By Chen Weihua, China Daily, 29th April 2006.

[968] 'China facing health disaster due to smoking.' AFP, 9th November 2006.

[969] 'It is possible to prevent cancer, says experts' report.' By Ye Jun, China Daily, 22nd October 2008.

[970] See 'More children taking up cigarettes in Beijing,' by Lan Tian, China Daily, 29th July 2009, and 'Smoking kills - but few aware,' by Xin Dingding, 1st June 2009.

[971] See 'Time to kick the nation's smoking habit,' by Chen Weihua, China Daily, 29th April 2006, and 'Tax hike has little effect on smokers,' by Lan Tian, China Daily, 28th July 2009.

[972] 'Smoking curbs could 'upset China's stability.'' China Daily, 13th March 2007.

[973] 'Foreign enterprises banned from selling tobacco.' By Kat Jiang, Shanghai Daily, 21st March 2007.

Reason Number 33. Marching On

[974] See 'National Flag, National Emblem and National Anthem' on www.china.org.cn

[975] See 'About China: Tian Han' on www.english.cri.cn

[976] 'China military commander advocates offensive strength.' Reuters, 14th June 2007.

[977] 'Military urged to contribute more to social harmony.' Xinhua, 29th December 2006.

[978] 'China issues white paper on national defense.' People's Daily, 29th December 2005.

[979] 'White paper: China's national defense policy purely defensive in nature.' People's Daily, 29th December 2005.

[980] 'National security hinges on strengthened internal, external harmony.' People's Daily, 30th December 2006.

[981] 'From peasant guerrillas to high-tech troops: 80 years of the PLA.' People's Daily, 14th July 2007.

[982] 'China's army declares zero tolerance of 'Taiwan independence.'' Xinhua, 1st August 2007.

[983] Anti-Secession Law, adopted at the Third Session of the Tenth National People's Congress, 14th March 2005, Article 8.

[984] See 'Top Chinese general warns US over attack,' by Alexandra Harney, Demetri Sevastopulo and Edward Alden, Financial Times, 14th July 2005 and 'Chinese general warns of nuclear risk to US,' by Jonathan Watts, The Guardian, 16th July 2005.

[985] 'Aid From China Builds An Ally in East Timor.' By Seth Mydans, The New York Times, 26th July 2007.

Reason Number 34. White China Crime

[986] 'Bank of China targets Hong Kong IPO in May.' China Daily / Agencies, 8th February 2006.

[987] 'Bank officials flee after US$120m go missing' [sic]. China Daily / Agencies 24th January 2005.

[988] 'Risk controls urged for Bank of China.' China Daily via agencies, 1st February 2005.

[989] 'Bank chief arrested.' China Daily, 23rd February 2007.

[990] 'Former CCB head jailed for 15 years.' Reuters, 3rd November 2006.

[991] 'US$35.8 billion of funds abused this year.' By Liu Weiling, China Daily, 27th December 2005.

[992] 'Housing loan fraud may involve 400m yuan.' Shanghai Daily, 7th June 2006.

[993] 'BoCom unveils financial fraud of 200m yuan.' Xinhua, 11th June 2006.

[994] 'Auditors uncover 20 fraud cases.' By Yang Zhen, China Daily, 20th February 2009.

[995] 'Bank official detained in private lending scam probe.' Xinhua, 22nd May 2009.

[996] 'Foreign banks to report suspicious transactions.' By Zhu Zhe, China Daily, 20th December 2006.

[997] 'China shuts down seven illegal underground banks.' AFP, 19th December 2006.

[998] 'Money laundering rampant in China with more underground banks reported.' Xinhua, 19th December 2006.

470

[999] 'Bank thief suspect: We spent 43m on lottery tickets.' By Hou Jinchun, Shanghai Daily, April 20th 2007.

[1000] See 'PriceSmart shuts shop after suppliers demand payment,' by Liu Chang, China Daily, 10th January 2005, and 'Supermarket chain boss gets life in prison for fraud.' China Daily, 21st March 2007.

[1001] 'Chinese police ferret out 58,000 economic cases in the first 11 months.' People's Daily, 28th December 2006.

[1002] 'Key figure in fund scandal gets 19 yrs.' China Daily, 8th April 2008.

[1003] See 'High court upholds jail term for tycoon,' by Cao Li, China Daily, 22nd January 2008, and 'Shanghai Tycoon Falls From Grace,' by Jim Yardley, the New York Times, 1st December 2007.

[1004] See 'China's Sprint to the Top,' by David Barboza, The New York Times, 21st November 2009, and 'Original Sin,' The Economist, 5th September 2009.

[1005] 'Counterfeit coins found on sale in 8 major cities.' China Daily, 6th July 2007.

[1006] 'Justice totally blind when cops allowed judge to operate a casino.' By Wang Yong, Shanghai Daily, 28th March 2007.

[1007] 'Chief judge pledges to fight judicial corruption.' By Xie Chuanjiao, China Daily, 24th March 2007.

[1008] 'Officials break graft records.' China Daily, 10th November 2008.

[1009] 'Former Chongqing official arrested.' China Daily, 28th October 2009.

[1010] 'Corrupt police officers racked up fortune.' By Wang Huazhong and Ma Wei, China Daily, 29th September 2009.

Reason Number 35. Looking for Mr. Anuode Shiwaxinge

[1011] 'Purity of Chinese language debated.' By Xing Zhigang, China Daily, 13th September 2004

[1012] 'Climb mountain of language to see more.' By Wang Shuda, China Daily, 25th August 2006.

[1013] See 'The Language Log' at www.itre.cis.upenn.edu/

[1014] 'Chinese characters, beauty or burden?' Jacob von Bisterfield, Shanghai Star, 23-29 October 2003.

[1015] See www.fas.harvard.edu

[1016] See www.pinyin.info for a list of these sounds.

[1017] See 'About Ikea: Timeline' on www.ikea.com

[1018] See 'Brand History' on www.haagen-dazs.com

[1019] 'Chinese language a 'spectator' in scientific fields – report.' By Xiao Guo, China Daily, 5th July 2007.

[1020] 'Internet 'codewords' give rise to digital gap.' China Daily, 13th September 2004.

[1021] 'Name for baby? Check out national database.' By Zhu Zhe, China Daily, 17th March 2006.

[1022] 'NPC deputy calls for promoting Chinese.' By Xing Zhigang, China Daily, 10th March 2006.

[1023] 'SARS: Unmasking Censorship in China.' By Zhang Erping, www.asianresearch.org, 8th November 2003.

[1024] See 'Institutes not 'increasing too rapidly,'' by Wang Shanshan, China Daily, 12th May 2007 and 'Cultural Interaction,' China Daily, 29th April 2009.

[1025] 'Confucius can survive in this modern world.' By Qin Xiaoying, China Daily, 16th May 2006.

[1026] 'Confucius institutes help spread Mandarin.' Shanghai Daily, 4th January 2007.

Reason Number 36. Hot Borders

[1027] A History of China. J.A.G. Roberts, Palgrave Macmillan 2006, p183, p.205.

[1028] Russia has 12 direct land borders. It has two further borders, with Lithuania and Poland, but these borders are with the Russian enclave of Kaliningrad, which itself lies outside Russia's main border.

[1029] See 'Indian PM keen on building strong ties with China,' People's Daily via agencies, 4th April 2005 and 'Premier Wen's India trip to discuss border disputes,' People's Daily Online, 2nd April 2005.

[1030] 'Arunachal Pradesh is ours, not China's, Pradesh.' Press Trust of India, 14th November 2006.

[1031] 'China raises tension in India Dispute.' By Jo Johnson and Richard McGregor, the Financial Times, 10th June 2007.

[1032] 'India can't part with territory, Pranab tells China.' The Hindu, 17th June 2007.

[1033] 'China reaffirms sovereignty over Diaoyu Islands.' By Gang Bian, China Daily, 24th June 2003.

[1034] See 'The truth of Diaoyu's ownership,' by Tong Shen, China Daily, 1st September 2004 and 'China rejects joint gas development with Japan,' The Associated Press, 3rd September 2006.

[1035] 'Diaoyu Islands, adjacent islets belong to China.' Xinhua, 17th July 2008

[1036] 'Book shows Diaoyu Island was China's 200 years ago.' By Zhao Chunzhe, China Daily, 3rd December 2009.

[1037] See 'China's energy and territorial concerns,' by John C. K. Daly, The Jamestown Foundation, 20th December 2004 and 'Border issue solved with Kyrgyzstan,' by Meng Yan, China Daily, 22nd September 2004.

[1038] 'Vietnam's actions on Nansha Islands infringe on China's sovereignty, FM spokesman.' Xinhua, 10th April 2007.

[1039] 'Peaceful Way Urged to Resolve Nansha Dispute.' People's Daily, 10th June 2000.

[1040] 'Security of Bhutan: Walking Between the Giants' by Dorji Penjore, Researcher, The Centre for Bhutan Studies. Paper written for Asia Pacific Center for Security Studies (APCSS), Honolulu, Hawaii. See www.bhutanstudies.org.bt

[1041] 'China pledges to strengthen cooperation with Bhutan, Brunei.' Xinhua, 5th June 2007.

[1042] 'US, Myanmar hold rare talks in China over Aung San Suu Kyi,' by P. Parameswaran, AFP, 28th June 2007.

[1043] 'Kazakhstan-China Border Trade Thrives After Demarcation Treaty.' By Claes Levinsson and Ingvar Svanberg, Central Asia – Caucasus Institute, 16th February 2000. Www.cacianalyst.org

[1044] 'Environmentalists say China misusing cross-border rivers.' By Gulnoza Saidazimova, Radio Free Europe, 18th July 2006.

[1045] 'S. Korea-China history dispute over ancient kingdoms.' Yonhap News Agency, 6th September 2006.

[1046] 'Dispute over China-Kyrgyz border demarcation pits president vs. parliament.' By Alisher Khamidov, Director, Osh Media Resource Center, Kyrgyzstan, 28th June 2001.

[1047] 'China's energy and territorial concerns,' by John C. K. Daly, The Jamestown Foundation, 20th December 2004 and 'Border issue solved with Kyrgyzstan,' by Meng Yan, China Daily, 22nd September 2004.

[1048] 'Sino-Laotian bilateral ties.' People's Daily, `16th November 2005, via Foreign Ministry of the People's Republic of China.

[1049] 'Reaching for a renaissance.' The Economist, 29th March 2007.

[1050] 'Battle for Mongolia's soul.' The Economist, 19th December 2006.

[1051] See http://bordernepal.wordpress.com/2007/01/

[1052] 'China, Russia solve all disputes along shared border.' 3rd June 2005, Embassy of the People's Republic of China, www.chinaembassy.org.cn.

[1053] See 'China's energy and territorial concerns,' by John C. K. Daly, The Jamestown Foundation, 20th December 2004 and 'Border issue solved with Kyrgyzstan,' by Meng Yan, China Daily, 22nd September 2004.

[1054] 'China-Vietnam Border Enters New Era: Vietnamese Official.' People's Daily, 16th September 2002.

Reason Number 37. Brand China

[1055] 'Chinese Premier calls on firms to secure reputation of 'Made in China' label.' Xinhua, 28th July 2007.

[1056] 'Chinese businesses lag behind in global skills.' China Daily, 25th May 2007.

[1057] 'Three steps for Chinese companies to go global, interview.' People's Daily Online, 25th May 2007.

[1058] See 'An importer's worse nightmare,' by David Welch, Business Week, 23rd July 2007, 'Chinese Company Denies Tire Defect,' by David Barboza and Andrew Martin, The New York Times, 27th June 2007, 'China says alleged faulty tires up to U.S. standards, blames misuse for fatal accident,' People's Daily, 18th July 2007, and 'Great Leap Forward?,' by Jim Smith, The Tire Review, 1st August 2007.

[1059] See 'Trial starts for China's once-richest man.' By Wang Huazhong, China Daily, 23rd April 2010 and 'Ex-Gome Chairman Sentenced to 14 Years in Prison,' by Jason Dean, The Wall Street Journal, 17th May 2010.

[1060] 'Brilliance unveils 'excellent' auto plan. China Daily, 21st August 2002.

[1061] 'International auto giants cast shadow over Chinese auto manufacturers' growth.' Xinhua, 25th April 2005.

[1062] 'Chinese automakers pop tops.' China Daily, 30th November 2006.

[1063] 'Brilliance Auto to enter US market.' Xinhua, 9th March 2007.

[1064] 'Brilliance plans US sales as early as 2007.' Reuters, 24th April 2007.

[1065] 'Chinese fail new crash tests.' 3rd July 2007, www.newcarnet.co.uk

[1066] 'Brilliance Auto Shifting Gears.' China Daily, 16th July 2007.

[1067] 'Crash Course in Quality for Chinese Car.' By Andrew Osborn, The Wall Street Journal, 8th August 2007.

[1068] 'China warns U.S. against 'smear attacks' on imports.' Reuters, 20th July 2007.

[1069] 'China says Panamanian merchants responsible for deadly cough medicine.' Xinhua, 1st June 2007.

[1070] 'China says no to 'Toxic Chinese Toothpaste Incident.'' People's Daily Online, 20th June 2007.

[1071] 'Eligibility rate of China's food exports to the US hits 99%.' People's Daily Online, 6th June 2007.

[1072] 'Fifth of China goods substandard.' China Daily / Reuters, 4th July 2007.

[1073] 'China source of 80 percent of suspected fakes seized.' Reuters, 15th May 2007.

[1074] 'BW's 20 Best Chinese Brands.' By Brian Bremner, Business Week, 17th June 2007.

[1075] 'Court supports airliner's refusal to carry injured girl.' By Winny Wang, Shanghai Daily, 27th June 2007.

Reason Number 38. The 'Big' Factor

474

[1076] 'CPC members hit 70 million.' Xinhua, 20th June 2006.

[1077] 'Snapshots at the 16th CCYL National Congress.' Xinhua, 13th June 2008.

[1078] 'China's Communist Youth League has 73.496 million members.' Xinhua, 5th May 2007.

[1079] See 'China's budding food industry faces scrutiny,' by Elizabeth Weise, USA Today, 22nd May 2007, 'Insatiable China,' by Cinthia Murphy, China Economic Review, June 2004, and 'Carlsberg adds new brewery in west China,' by Dominique Patton, 5th August 2005.

[1080] 'China Develops Improved Varieties of Rape.' People's Daily, 8th January 2002.

[1081] 'Cotton Rises to 5-Week High as Drought in India May Curb Output.' Bloomberg, 20th June 2005.

[1082] 'Selling butter and cheese to the Chinese palate,' By Clifford Coonan, The Irish Times, 11th September 2006.

[1083] 'Project to help prepare for flu pandemics.' China Daily, 27th April 2007.

[1084] Statistics from the Food and Agriculture Organization of the United Nations, www.fao.org.

[1085] 'Pesticides next frontier in China food safety.' Reuters, 13th May 2007.

[1086] 'A China Environmental Health Project Factsheet: Pesticides and Environmental Health Trends in China.' By Yang Yang, 28th February 2007, www.wilsoncenter.org

[1087] See 'Arable land shrinks to 121.8 million hectares,' Xinhua, 13th April 2007 and 'Preserving arable land.' China Daily, 26th June 2007.

[1088] 'China's cement output ranks first in world.' People's Daily, 4th October 2003.

[1089] 'Review: 2006's cement industry.' By Lu Guixin and Zhuang Chunlai, 22nd January, 2007. Chinese Ministry of Commerce, www.fec2.mofcom.gov.cn

[1090] 'China now no. 1 in CO_2 emissions; USA in second position.' See www.mnp.nl

[1091] 'China to see worsening mineral shortage in next 15 years: expert.' Xinhua, 5th May 2007.

[1092] 'Metal sector set for bumper year.' China Daily, 27th March 2007.

[1093] See www.steelonthenet.com

[1094] See www.world-aluminium.org

[1095] See 'Country's copper imports grow for 2nd time in 3 years,' China Daily, 26th January 2006 and 'Copper climbs to record high in Shanghai,' China Daily, January 18th 2006.

[1096] 'China's 2006 crude oil imports 145 mln tons, up 14.5 pct – customs,' Forbes via AFX News, 11th January 2007.

[1097] 'Hungry China gorges on Asia's scrap metal.' By James Brook, The International Herald Tribune, 12-13th June 2004.

[1098] 'China overtakes Germany as world's biggest electrical producer.' Xinhua, 18th January 2007.

[1099] 'Patent fees drag down DVD player exports.' China Daily, 3rd August 2004.

[1100] 'Chinese expected to get back on their bikes.' China Daily, 16th May 2006.

[1101] 'Chaozhou: World's Biggest Wedding Gown, Evening Dress Producer.' People's Daily, 6th May 2001.

[1102] 'Red light on.' Shanghai Star, 7th March 2003.

[1103] 'Adult sex toy expo touches sensitive area.' By Vince Lee, Shanghai Star, 8th August 2004.

[1104] 'NDRC: Energy-efficiency could save China 300 mln tons coal annually.' Xinhua, 4th August 2006.

[1105] 'China's economy reaching environmental limits.' By Robert J. Saiget, AFP, 15th April 2007.

[1106] 'China's energy dilemma.' China Economic Review, September 2005.

[1107] 'Worsening drought leaves more Chinese short of water,' Xinhua, 26th July 2007 and '22.72 million people nationwide affected by floods,' Xinhua, 27th July 2007.

[1108] 'Report: Farmland is polluted.' China Daily, 1st November 2006.

[1109] 'Seawater quality deteriorates.' China Daily, 18th May 2007.

[1110] 'Report finds 20% of Guangdong shore polluted by sewage.' Xinhua, 26th September 2008.

[1111] 'Ambitious plan to save reserve.' China Daily, 9th May 2007.

[1112] 'Painted mountain sparks controversy.' China Daily, 14th March 2007.

[1113] 'Officials asked to drink 2-million-yuan alcohol.' By Zhong Bei, Shanghai Daily, 6th April 2007.

Reason Number 39. Red China Crime

[1114] 'China punishes 67,505 crooked officials in less than 4 years.' Xinhua, 24th October 2006.

[1115] 'Sacked party official expelled from CPC.' Xinhua, 26th April 2007.

[1116] 'Year of tough lessons for corrupt businesspeople, officials.' China Daily, 9th January 2008

[1117] 'Corruption top issue for public.' By Cui Xiaohuo, China Daily, 27th February 2009.

[1118] '9,000 officials guilty of graft: SPP.' By Xie Chuanjiao, China Daily, 17th July 2009.

[1119] 'Love-corrupted cadres targeted.' Shanghai Daily, 30th June 2007.

[1120] See '4,000 corrupt officials fleed with US$50 billion' [sic], Xinhua, 11th August 2005 and 'MOC denies releasing data on fleeing corrupt officials,' Xinhua, 25th April 2010.

[1121] 'Corruption trial begins for former Chinese Communist official.' Xinhua, 12th April 2007.

[1122] 'Power corrupts. In some places, almost everyone.' by Zong He, China Daily, 24th October 2006.

[1123] See 'Three officials sentenced to death, life in prison,' Xinhua, 20th November 2008, and 'Court confirms death decisions on 2 officials,' by Chen Qian, Shanghai Daily, 15th August 2009.

[1124] 'CPC official sacked for breach of discipline.' Xinhua, 3rd May 2007.

[1125] 'Party expels ex-discipline czar.' By Zhang Liuhao, Shanghai Daily, 13th April 2007.

[1126] 'Cadres who buy posts seen as major problem.' Shanghai Daily, 14th November 2006.

[1127] 'Sacked former top statistician Qiu Xiaohua expelled from Party.' Xinhua, 23rd January 2007.

[1128] 'Former sports lottery boss faces trial.' By Li Xinran, Shanghai Daily, 2nd April 2007.

[1129] 'Sacked party official expelled from CPC.' Xinhua, 26th April 2007.

[1130] 'Shanghai leader stripped of power.' China Daily, 26th September 2006.

[1131] 'Corrupt mayor gets maximum penalty.' By Wang Zhenghua, China Daily, 24th October 2008.

[1132] See 'Collecting cash was his 'labor of love,'' by Zhan Lisheng, China Daily, 21st May 2009 and 'Shanghai official given life imprisonment for corruption,' Xinhua, 3rd February 2009.

[1133] 'Vice-chairman in Ningxia investigated for corruption.' China Daily, 16th October 2009.

[1134] 'Most corrupt ex-county leader gets 18 years,' by Zhang Jiawei, China Daily, 19th April 2010.

[1135] 'Officials protected 'majority of gangs.'' By Wang Yan, China Daily. 24th April 2010.

[1136] 'Que Jingde: Just the first of many.' By Chen Weihua, China Daily, 7th July 2009.

[1137] 'CPC recruits 12M members in five years. Xinhua, 16th July 2007.

Reason Number 40. Party Capital and Sino-Cash

[1138] 'CPC Congress Meets with Positive Response Nationwide.' Xinhua, 9th November 2002.

[1139] 'Private entrepreneurs gain political status.' China Daily, 3rd December 2003.

[1140] 'Entrepreneurs energize the economy.' China Daily, 29th November 2003.

[1141] 'CPC expert: Party, gov't officials in corruption ties with business.' Xinhua, 16th March 2007.

[1142] 'Confess now, corrupt officials urged.' Xinhua / China Daily, 8th June 2007.

[1143] 'Chinese official orders a 'push' on fight against commercial bribery.' Xinhua, 18th May 2007.

[1144] 'Do students need golf? Speech tees off debate.' By Xie Chuanjiao, China Daily, 17th October 2006.

[1145] 'Shanghai University introduces golf course.' China Radio International, 19th September 2006.

[1146] 'Millions may become tax-filing delinquents.' By Zhang Fengming, Shanghai Daily, 30th March 2007.

[1147] '99% of Chinese firms never donate to charity.' Xinhua, 22nd November 2005.

Reason Number 41. A Nation of Health Terrorists

[1148] 'Global flu pandemic would probably kill 62m, study says.' By Sarah Boseley, The Guardian, 22nd December 2006.

[1149] 'Avian Flu 'Supermap' Yields New Info On Source/Spread.' Www.medicalnewstoday.com, 5th May 2007

[1150] 'Lawmakers warn of animal disease epidemic in China.' Xinhua, 25th August 2009.

[1151] 'China is source of bird flu virus, study shows.' By Maggie Fox. Reuters, 5th March 2007

[1152] 'China finally admits to first case of bird flu.' By Jonathan Watts. The Guardian. 9th August 2006.

[1153] See 'China suspected of covering up bird flu outbreak,' by Malcolm Moore, The Daily Telegraph, 4th February 2009, and 'Deadly tide of birds fuels fears of bird flu cover-up,' by Hazel Parry, monstersandcritics.com, 6th February 2009.

[1154] 'So who's really to blame for bird flu?' By Joanna Blythman. The Guardian, 7th June 2006.

[1155] 'Bird Flu Drug Rendered Useless.' By Alan Sipress. The Washington Post. 18th June 2005.

[1156] 'China Denies Promoting Use of Drug on Chickens.' By Alan Sipress. The Washington Post. 22nd June, 2005.

[1157] 'So who's really to blame for bird flu?' By Joanna Blythman. The Guardian, 7th June 2006.

[1158] 'WHO requesting human bird flu samples from China, none shared since last year' AP, 18th April 2007

478

[1159] 'China to send WHO H5N1 virus samples.' By Shan Juan. China Daily, 20th April 2007.

[1160] The FAO media release can be found on www.fao.org.

[1161] 'China's SARS Problem, and Ours: How China's totalitarian government put the rest of the world at risk to the new virus.' By Ellen Bork, The Weekly Standard, 4th April 2003.

[1162] 'Whatever happened to ... the Sars pandemic?' By Iain Hollingshead. The Guardian, 25th February, 2006.

[1163] 'China slams Taiwan's WHO membership hopes.' China Economic Review, 26th April 2007.

[1164] 'China says Taiwan not eligible for WHO membership.' Reuters, 16th June 2007.

[1165] 'China says needs more funds, aid in bird flu fight.' By Ben Blanchard, Scientific American, 26th April 2007.

[1166] 'Shanghai taxis to be equipped with spit sacks.' By Yin Ping, China Daily, 23rd January 2007.

[1167] 'China targets bad tourist behavior ahead of Olympics.' Reuters, May 8th 2007.

[1168] 'China wants Olympians to see its best behavior.' By Calum MacLeod, USA Today, 8th February 2006.

[1169] 'Campaign doomed if AIDS ignorance starts at the top.' By Ashley Tian, Shanghai Daily, 31st October 2005.

[1170] 'Rising HIV infections tied to poor awareness.' Shanghai Daily, 23rd October 2006.

[1171] 'History of Chinese homosexuality.' Shanghai Star, 1st April 2004.

[1172] 'China issues guidelines on tackling HIV/AIDS.' AFP, 12th February 2006.

[1173] 'Beijing to build 110 star hotels.' Xinhua, 21st May 2006.

[1174] 'AIDS expected to spread faster.' Shanghai Daily, 21st April 2007.

[1175] 'Marriage boom expected.' China Daily, 15th September 2003.

[1176] 'Blood Debts.' The Economist, 18th January 2007.

[1177] 'Blood station chiefs quizzed over sales scandal.' By Winnie Wang. Shanghai Daily, 12th April 2007.

[1178] 'China closes almost 5,000 illegal blood banks.' Xinhua, 28th March 2008.

[1179] See www.globalhealth.org

[1180] See http://www.rmaf.org.ph/

[1181] 'Chinese AIDS Activist Defies Police.' Radio Free Asia, 5th April 2007.

[1182] 'China bars AIDS doctor from U.S. for award: activist.' Reuters, 2nd March 2007.

[1183] 'Aids activist 'harassed' in China. By Chris Xia. BBC News, 20th April 2007.

[1184] 'China detains green activist once hailed hero.' Reuters, 23rd April 2007.

[1185] See 'Chinese Aids activist Dr Gao 'in exile in United States.'' By Malcolm Moore, The Daily Telegraph, 2nd December 2009, and 'Gao Yaojie, anti-AIDS activist: 'If I go back to China I risk my life,'' www.asianews.it , 3rd December 2009.

[1186] 'Group: China AIDS activist missing.' AP, 25th November 2006.

[1187] See www.en.wikipedia.org/wiki/Wan_Yanhai

[1188] 'HIV/Aids activist flees China for US.' By Tania Branigan, The Guardian, 10th May 2010.

[1189] 'Chinese AIDS Activist Defies Police.' Radio Free Asia, 5th April 2007.

[1190] See 'Outcry as Chinese activist Hu Jia jailed,' by Richard Spencer, The Daily Telegraph, 3rd April 2008, 'Hu Jia spends his 35th birthday alone in prison,' Reporters without Borders, 25th July 2008, 'Chinese Dissident Is Gravely Ill, Wife Says,' by Michael Wines and Jonathan Ansfield, The New York Times, 8th April 2010, and 'China: Health Professional Action: Hu Jia,' www.amnesty.org,17th April 2010.

[1191] 'China not investing enough to fight AIDS: experts.' Reuters, 6th April 2007.

[1192] 'Chinese HIV cases jump 30 percent in 2006.' 21st November 2006.

[1193] 'Latest AIDS victims put at 650,000, down 20%.' By Sun Xiaohua, China Daily, 26th January 2006.

[1194] 'Syphilis back with a vengeance in China, report says.' Reuters, 12th January 2007.

[1195] 'One baby with syphilis born each hour in China.' The China Post, May 7th 2010.

[1196] 'New regulation restricts sex info on Internet.' By Shan Juan, June 26th 2010.

[1197] 'Health ministry gets tough on hepatitis B.' Shanghai Daily, 6th April 2007.

[1198] ''Bare-foot docs' bring gift of life to child vaccination.' Xinhua, 20th November 2009.

[1199] 'Doctors not up to scratch on hepatitis.' By Chen Zhiyong, China Daily. 2nd September 2005.

[1200] Viral Hepatitis B FAQ. US Centers for Disease Control and Prevention. www.cdc.gov

[1201] 'Hepatitis B virus carriers abandoned by society.' Shanghai Star, November 13th 2003.

[1202] 'HIV stigma rife in China.' Www.iafrica.com, 14th May 2007.

[1203] '41m Chinese believed to have hepatitis C virus.' Xinhua, 27th June 2004.

[1204] 'Expert calls for more hepatitis awareness in China.' People's Daily, 26th October 2006.

[1205] 'Former drug head faces graft probe.' China Daily, 25th January 2007.

[1206] 'Guangdong reports increased rabies deaths.' Xinhua, 8th June 2006.

[1207] 'Campaign to take bite out of rabies.' China Daily, 24th October 2006.

[1208] 'Animal cruelty law not acceptable.' By Chen Weihua, China Daily, August 11th 2009

[1209] 'Rabies under control in Beijing but rising dramatically in other areas.' Xinhua, 24th August 2006.

[1210] 'Shanghai in hot debate over pets.' People's Daily, 20th March 2007.

[1211] 'Campaign: Barking up wrong tree?' People's Daily, 16th August 2006.

[1212] 'Rabies under control in Beijing but rising dramatically in other areas.' Xinhua. 24th August 2006.

[1213] 'Tuberculosis remains top epidemic killer.' China Daily, 15th February 2007.

[1214] 'Rabies kills 61 in C. China province leading to a dog cull.' Xinhua, 5th March 2007.

[1215] 'Dogs bite over 50,000 people in Shanghai, resulting in 3 deaths.' People's Daily, 16th September 2006.

[1216] 'Rabies under control in Beijing but rising dramatically in other areas.' Xinhua, 24th August 2006.

[1217] 'Man's best friend must be friendly, and short.' By Wang Qian, China Daily. 11th September 2009. However, it should be pointed out - in what is another example of the mixed messages the Chinese government sends - that a draft law was mooted in June 2009 to make such culls illegal. No word was given on when the draft might become law. See 'Draft law to make dog cull illegal,' China Daily, 16th June 2009.

[1218] 'Six million Chinese suffer active pulmonary tuberculosis.' Xinhua, 6th September, 2004.

[1219] http://en.wikipedia.org/wiki/Tuberculosis.

[1220] 'Tuberculosis remains top epidemic killer.' China Daily, 15th February 2007.

[1221] See 'Mega-trends of tourism in Asia-Pacific.' The United Nations World Tourism Organization, www.unwto.org.

[1222] 'Behavior of tourists has no quick fix.' By Liu Shinan, China Daily, 11th October 2006 and 'Tourists urged to get rid of bad habits,' Xinhua, 5th May 2005.

Reason Number 42. Sino-Spite

[1223] 'Japanese comment on China's nationalism 'illogical.'' Xinhua, 26th July 2007.

[1224] ''Not made in China' trade mark application is a disgrace to China.' People's Daily Online, 22nd February 2006.

[1225] 'China accuses media of hyping toy safety problems.' AFP, 17th August 2007.

[1226] 'Mattel apologizes over toys recall.' Xinhua, 21st September 2007.

[1227] 'China quality boss says problems sapping trade strength.' Reuters, 18th August 2007.

[1228] 'US criticized for WTO complaints over piracy.' Xinhua, 11th April 2007.

[1229] 'Safety watchdog rejects US FDA's toothpaste warning.' China Daily, 4th June 2007.

[1230] 'Beijing food, drug safety drive 'complete success.'' By Zhu Zhe, China Daily, January 17th 2008.

[1231] 'China willing to boost NATO ties.' China Daily, 25th May 2007.

[1232] 'No one in China would like to pick up such 'filthy' coins!' People's Daily Online, 4th August 2006.

[1233] See 'Taking a stand against forced labour,' Corporate Social Responsibility Asia, www.csr-asia.com, 18th May 2007, and 'Taking a Stand Against Forced Labor: German Parliament Condemns China's 'Laogai' Camp,' Der Speigel, 14th May 2007.

[1234] 'China firmly opposes to German parliament's resolution attacking China's reeducation through labor system.' Xinhua, 16th May 2007.

[1235] 'Foreign Ministry Spokesperson Jiang Yu's Regular Press Conference on 8 May 2007.' Chinese Foreign Ministry, www.fmprc.gov.cn.

[1236] 'Foreign Ministry Spokesperson Qin Gang's remarks on the Pope's letter to Chinese Catholics.' 30th June 2007. www.fmprc.gov.cn.

[1237] 'Foreign Ministry Spokesperson Qin Gang's Remarks on Australian Prime Minister's Meeting with Dalai Lama.' 18th June 2007. www.fmprc.gov.cn

[1238] 'Foreign Ministry Spokesperson Jiang Yu's Remarks on the 2007 Annual Report Released by the US Commission on International Religious Freedom.' 11th May 2007. Www.fmprc.gov.cn

Reason Number 43. Can You Trust Men to Hold up Half the Sky?

[1239] 'Lonely path to abortion for women.' Shanghai Daily, 18th June 2007.

[1240] 'Fighting to save, respect the girl child.' By Li Xing, China Daily, 24th October 2008.

[1241] See 'China will have 30 million more men than women of marriageable age in 2020: report,' Xinhua, 12th January 2007, 'China to Usher in Major Changes in Population Policies,' People's Daily, August

20 2003, and 'China's most populous province legislates to curb gender imbalance.' Xinhua, 30th September 2006.

[1242] 'Mao's War Against Nature: Politics and the Environment in Revolutionary China.' Judith Shapiro, Cambridge: Cambridge University Press, 2001. See online review by Gregory A. Ruf, Associate Professor, Chinese Studies and Anthropology, Stony Brook State University of New York at jpe.library.arizona.edu

[1243] China Economic Review, September 2005.

[1244] A History of China. JAG. Roberts, Palgrave Macmillan 2006, p288.

[1245] 'Reining in world's largest population.' By Chen Zhiyong, China Daily, 6th January 2005.

[1246] 'China vows to half growing sex ratio imbalance.' Xinhua, 22nd January 2007.

[1247] 'China's gender imbalance 'likely to get worse.'' By Tania Branigan, The Guardian, 19th May 2009. An abstract of the relevant research paper - 'China's excess males, sex selective abortion, and one child policy: analysis of data from 2005 national intercensus survey' - can be found on www.bmj.com

[1248] See 'China will have 30 million more men than women of marriageable age in 2020: report,' Xinhua, 12th January 2007, 'Serious birth gender imbalance inflicts 9 Chinese regions,' People's Daily Online, 25th August 2004.

[1249] From 'Gong Cheng's Teapot.' The Blue House, by Cheng Naishan. Foreign Languages Press, Beijing, 2005. Page 243, p. 262

[1250] 'Legislation urged to ban gender selection.' China Daily, 3rd October 2006.

[1251] 'China vows to halt growing sex ratio imbalance.' Xinhua, 22nd January 2007.

[1252] 'Gender Imbalance Becomes Serious Problem in China.' People's Daily, August 25th 2003.

[1253] 'China's excess males, sex selective abortion, and one child policy: analysis of data from 2005 national intercensus survey.' April 2009, abstract available on www.bmj.com.

[1254] See 'Blind Chinese activist beaten, wife says,' by Anita Chang, The Associated Press, 22nd June 2007, and 'China: Torture/Medical concern/Prisoner of conscience, Chen Guangcheng (m),' Amnesty International Online Documentation Archive, 21st June 2007.

[1255] 'Incentives offered to families with girls.' China Daily, 12th August 2004.

[1256] 'China's most populous province legislates to curb gender imbalance.' Xinhua, 30th September 2006.

[1257] 'Gender Imbalance Becomes Serious Problem in China.' People's Daily, August 25th 2003.

[1258] 'Serious birth gender imbalance inflicts 9 Chinese regions,' People's Daily Online, 25th August 2004.

[1259] 'Transient workers quest for love in cities.' Xinhua, 22nd March 2004.

Reason Number 44. The Gamblers and the Purpose of Unemployment

[1260] 'China's hunger for luxury goods grows.' By Jehangir S. Pocha, The Boston Globe, 21st March 2006.

[1261] 'China never purposely pursues trade surpluses: vice premier.' Xinhua, 25th May 2007.

[1262] 'China under threat of labor shortage.' Xinhua, 28th May 2006.

[1263] 'Worker shortage drives salary rise.' By Fu Jing, China Daily, 27th May 2006.

[1264] 'China under threat of labor shortage.' Xinhua, 28th May 2006.

[1265] 'Drop in low-cost labor forecast.' By Wang Zhenghua, China Daily, 12th March 2008.

[1266] 'Who moved China's huge savings?' People's Daily Online, 21st June 2007.

[1267] 'Chinese pour savings deposits into stock market.' Xinhua, 13th May 2007.

[1268] 'Family funds go to market.' China Daily, 6th August 2007.

[1269] 'Beijingers pawn apartments in pursuit of stock market profits.' Xinhua, 26th January 2007.

[1270] 'Fund winds blowing eastward.' China Daily/Agencies, 4th December 2009.

[1271] 'China tackles illegal share activity.' Reuters / China Daily, 25th February 2007.

Reason Number 45. The Generals Theory

[1272] China's National Defense in 2006. Section III. China's Leadership and Administration System for National Defense.

[1273] Biographical details drawn from Chinese media and www.chinavitae.com

[1274] 'China's army declares zero tolerance of 'Taiwan independence.'' Xinhua, 1st August 2007.

[1275] 'Chinese DM reiterates army loyalty to Party leadership.' Xinhua, 17th July 2007.

[1276] 'PLA generals swear loyalty to Party leadership.' Xinhua, 6th March 2007.

[1277] 'Chinese President stresses PLA's loyalty to the CPC.' Xinhua, 1st August 2007.

[1278] 'Hu Jintao hails army's role, contribution to nation.' Xinhua, 27th July 2007.

[1279] 'Generals Pledge Loyalty to Communist Party.' People's Daily, 8th March 2001.

[1280] 'Army's newspaper calls on enhancing Party's leadership over PLA.' Xinhua, 1st August 2005.

Reason Number 46. Meet the New 'Ugly American'

[1281] 'Plundered or breaking away from exploitation?' Xinhua, 15th March 2007.

[1282] 'China considers boosting China-Africa friendship a strategic decision.' Xinhua, 24th October 2006.

[1283] 'Chinese President opens China-Africa summit.' Xinhua, 4th November 2006.

[1284] 'China's African Policy.' Xinhua, 2nd November 2006.

[1285] See 'Package gives Chinese, African entrepreneurs impetus,' Xinhua, 5th November 2005 and 'China's FDI in Africa on the rise.' China Daily, 15th May 2007.

[1286] 'China sincere in helping Africa – Wen.' Agencies / Xinhua, 16th May 2007.

[1287] 'Olympic boycotters over Darfur are 'ignorant.'' By Gu Jia, Shanghai Daily, 12th April 2007.

[1288] 'Whom can lies cheat?' People's Daily Online, 29th April 2007.

[1289] For example, 'Timeline of the Asia–Pacific War' at the Center for Excellence on the Study of the Holocaust, Genocide, Human Rights and Tolerance, www.csuchico.edu

[1290] 'China has 'no selfish interests' in Africa.' China Daily, 21st June 2006.

[1291] 'One China principle serves as political foundation for Sino-African relations.' Xinhua, 12th January 2006.

[1292] 'Analysis.' By Mark Sorbara. The Nation, Nairobi, 13th April 2006.

[1293] 'China is keen to develop Sino-Chadian ties.' Xinhua, 21st October 2006.

[1294] 'Chad gets loans and debt relief.' By Le Tian, China Daily, 1st June 2007.

[1295] 'China to deepen reciprocal cooperation with Zimbabwe.' Xinhua, 22nd April 2007.

[1296] 'China biggest investor in Zimbabwe: official.' AFP, 23rd April 2007.

[1297] 'China, Eritrean presidents call for more trade collaboration.' Xinhua, 7th November 2006.

[1298] 'Thanks China, now go home: buy-up of Zambia revives old colonial fears.' By Chris McGreal, The Guardian, 5th February 2007.

[1299] 'Desmond Tutu 'deeply disappointed' with South Africa's vote against U.N Security Council resolution on Myanmar.' The Associated Press, 21st January 2007.

[1300] 'Chinese president continues Africa tour, communiqué signed with Mozambique.' Xinhua, 9th February 2007.

[1301] 'Favoritism of Chinese Angers Namibians.' By Sharon LaFraniere, The New York Times, 28th November 2009.

[1302] 'Chinese firms face reality of Congo mining.' By Joe Bavier, Reuters, 14th May 2007.

[1303] See /www.equator-principles.com/principles.shtml.

[1304] 'World Bank - Press Briefing: Mr. Wolfowitz in The Hague' Www.econ.worldbank.org, 28th February 2006.

[1305] 'China: oil at any cost.' The Los Angeles Times, 27th October 2006.

[1306] 'Warnings on China's Africa Projects.' The Associated Press, 14th May 2007.

[1307] See 'China's Industrial Bank adopts Equator Principles.' People's Daily, 2nd November 2008, 'Banks to adopt new lending rules,' by Xin Zhiming, China Daily, 1st November 2008, and 'Green rules eye Chinese firms abroad,' by Liu Jing, China Daily, 29th May 2009.

[1308] 'Time to correct those Western misconceptions.' By Yang Wenchang, China Daily, 9th July 2007.

[1309] 'China offers new growth pattern.' By He Wenping, China Daily, 19th November 2009.

[1310] 'China and the promising Africa.' People's Daily Online, 18th May 2007.

[1311] See 'Military junta seizes power in Niger coup,' by David Smith / Agencies, The Guardian, 19th February 2010, and 'After a Coup, Niger Resumes Business as Usual With China,' The New York Times, 24th April 2010.

[1312] 'In Sudan, China focuses on oil wells, not local needs.' By Danna Harman, The Christian Science Monitor, 25th June 2007.

[1313] Q & A with Libyan Foreign Minister Musa Kusa, by Sawsan Abu-Husain, Asharq Alawsat Newspaper, 10th November 2009.

[1314] A transcript of Dr. Taneja's interview can be found at www.radioaustralia.net.au

Reason Number 47. Micro-Faults

[1315] '2 billion Chinese mice overrun lake area.' The Associated Press, 9th July 2007.

[1316] 'Rats on menus or a bagful of lies from the media?' China Daily, 20th July 2007.

[1317] 'Rats in central China lake areas to cause no epidemic.' Xinhua, 19th July 2007.

[1318] 'Experts analyze cause of rat scourge.' China Daily, 16th July 2007.

[1319] 'China Aviation Regulator Says Growth Is Too Fast.' By Tian Ying, Bloomberg, 25th July 2007.

[1320] 'Getting airport ready for the Games.' China Daily, 23rd January 2007.

[1321] 'China sets up aviation safety academy.' Xinhua, 25th May 2006.

[1322] 'Airlines add 155 aircraft in fleet expansion.' By Xin Dingding, China Daily, 27th December 2006.

[1323] 'Tough English test could ground Chinese pilots.' Xinhua, 24th June 2007.

[1324] 'China facing huge task to promote rural co-op health system.' Xinhua, 8th March 2007.

[1325] 'Half of China's local officials superstitious.' Reuters, 12th July 2007.

[1326] 'Chinese tourists urged to behave.' Xinhua, 9th October 2006.

[1327] 'Don't disgrace your country.' China Daily, 17th August 2006.

[1328] 'China tells its tourists no shouting.' The Associated Press, 21st August 2007.

[1329] 'Islands disappearing under rubble.' The Standard (Hong Kong) / AFP, 30th June 2007.

[1330] 'Islands to receive strategic protection.' China Daily, 29th June 2006.

[1331] 'China may lose 60,000 sq km to man-made soil erosion by 2010.' Xinhua, 30th June 2007.

[1332] 'China's hillside farmland loses 1.5 billion tons of soil annually.' Xinhua, 30th June 2007.

[1333] 'Cables disappear as copper price soars.' China Daily, 14th June 2007.

[1334] 'China bans unapproved foreign-related meteorological exploration.' Xinhua, 23rd December 2006.

[1335] 'Natural disaster toll no longer state secret.' Xinhua, 12th September 2005.

[1336] 'Lower your expectations, fliers told.' Agencies / Shanghai Daily, 23rd December 2006.

[1337] 'To flush or not to flush - the price of mid-air convenience.' Xinhua, 30th November 2006.

[1338] 'China's civil aviation industry reports profit of 4.62 bln yuan in first half.' Xinhua, 14th July 2007.

[1339] See 'China dismisses banana virus rumor,' Xinhua, 25th May 2007, and 'Banana conspiracy revealed,' by Zhang Liuhao, Shanghai Daily, 4th June 2007.

[1340] Figures taken from www.citymayors.com

[1341] 'China's urban area reaches 32,251 kilometers.' People's Daily Online, 14th May 2007.

[1342] 'NE China province to have 20 medium & small cities.' Xinhua, 23rd January 2007.

[1343] 'Resources, environment top concern in China's urbanization drive, expert says.' Xinhua, 9th November 2005.

[1344] 'Shanghai honored Garden City status.' Shanghai Daily, 15th January 2004.

[1345] 'Rapid urbanization 'too much, too quickly.'' By Wang Shanshan, China Daily, 23rd May 2007.

[1346] 'China to spend 15 trillion yuan for urbanization in 50 years.' Xinhua, 4th March 2005.

[1347] 'Faster urbanization 'is needed.'' China Daily, 6th March 2006.

Reason Number 48. Red Medicine

[1348] 'Frightened man thrown in asylum.' Shanghai Daily, 16th January 2007.

[1349] 'China: No Medical Reason to Hold Dissident.' 17th March 2006, www.hrw.org.

[1350] 'Sane Chinese Put in Asylum, Doctors Find.' By Joseph Kahn, the New York Times, 17th March 2006.

[1351] 'More than 7.8 million Chinese suffer from schizophrenia.' Xinhua, 19th June 2007.

[1352] 'Depression demands our compassion and treatment.' By Cai Wenjun, Shanghai Daily, 10th October 2005.

[1353] 'Couple suicide over medical costs.' By Winnie Wang, Shanghai Daily, 5th April 2007.

[1354] 'Average Chinese elderly lose 11 teeth: survey.' Xinhua, 14th June 2007.

[1355] 'Birth defects in 10% of families.' Xinhua, 26th September 2006.

[1356] 'Fake blood protein found.' China Daily / Xinhua, 12th June 2007.

[1357] 'China investigates fake blood protein.' Reuters, 14th June 2007.

[1358] 'China to crack down on fake rabies vaccines.' Reuters, 14th December 2006.

[1359] 'Parents press China for answer to fake, bad drugs.' Reuters, 25th July 2006.

[1360] 'Unsafe injections kill 390,000 prematurely.' Xinhua, 5th August 2004.

[1361] 'Drug misuse kills 200,000 Chinese a year – doctors.' China Daily via Reuters, 21st May 2007.

[1362] 'Government to decide prescription drug prices.' Shanghai Daily, 11th April 2007.

[1363] 'Ministry warns of nurse shortage.' China Daily, 11th May, 2006.

[1364] 'China short of nurses with nurse to patient ratio at 1:3.' Xinhua, 2nd August 2005.

[1365] 'China facing nursing shortage as hospitals underpay staff.' Xinhua, 12th May 2007.

[1366] 'Ministry warns of nurse shortage.' China Daily, 11th May, 2006.

[1367] 'Nurses to face test on ability.' By Yan Zhen, Shanghai Daily, 14th April 2007.

[1368] 'Who says a man should not be a nurse?' China Daily, 16th May 2005.

[1369] '3m social workers needed: Expert.' China Daily, 18th June 2007.

[1370] 'Botched eye surgeries lead to jail.' Shanghai Daily, 1st December 2006.

[1371] 'Sentence Upheld for Bogus Cataract Surgeons.' Xinhua, 20th March 2007.

[1372] 'Crackdown hits unlicensed docs.' Shanghai Daily via Xinhua, 23rd March 2007.

[1373] 'Medicine promotion.' Shanghai Daily, 20th June 2006.

[1374] 'Doctors' ethics in a critical condition.' By Wu Jiayin, Shanghai Daily, 27th October 2005.

[1375] 'Chinese medical costs on the rise.' Xinhua, 9th May 2007.

[1376] 'Doctors feel pain at new regulation.' Shanghai Daily, 7th April 2007.

[1377] 'Desperate farmer stoops to robbery to get free medical treatment.' China Daily, 28th November 2008.

[1378] 'Curse of Golden Scalpel enriches plastic surgeons.' By Wang Yanlin, Shanghai Daily, 5th January 2007.

[1379] 'Five-star' hospital set to open its wards,' Xinhua, 17th December 2006 and 'Quite a price, Mom,' Shanghai Daily, 18th December 2006.

[1380] 'Scalpers sell appointments for 3,000 yuan.' By Yang Wanli, China Daily, 24th December 2009.

[1381] 'Hospital scalpers a major headache, special city police to be deployed.' By Cai Wenjun, 12th October 2005.

[1382] 'Chinese reporter rebuked for hospital urine expose.' AFP, 12th April 2007.

[1383] 'Wrong results on 'urine tests' not hospitals' fault.' By Winny Wang, Shanghai Daily, 11th April 2007.

[1384] 'Health Minister rejects experts' accusations.' By Josephine Ma, the South China Morning Post, 16th March 2007.

[1385] 'New regulations banning trade of human organs go into effect.' Xinhua, 2nd May 2007.

[1386] 'Most of China's disabled not financially independent: survey.' Xinhua, 29th May 2007.

[1387] 'Health Ministry: malignant tumor No. 1 killer for urban, rural residents.' People's Daily Online, 9th May 2007.

[1388] 'Pollution makes cancer the top killer.' China Daily, 21st May 2007.

[1389] 'Survey reveals AIDS ignorance.' Shanghai Daily, 13th October 2006.

[1390] 'Recognition of brain death will aid organ transplants: Chinese health official.' Xinhua, 3rd May 2007.

[1391] 'Chinese Vice-Premier calls for improvements to community medical services.' Xinhua, 1st May 2007.

[1392] 'Lacking money, father leaves girl in hospital.' Shanghai Daily, 25th-26th November 2006.

Reason Number 49. Daughters, Wives and Mothers in Fear

[1393] 'Public Face Of Lenovo Retires.' By Shu-Ching Jean Chen, Forbes, 28th May 2007.

[1394] 'Women's Participation in Politics.' All China Women's Federation, 28th September 2006. See www.womenofchina.cn

[1395] 'Over 670 women mayors in China.' People's Daily Online, 22nd August 2006.

[1396] 'Open debate on women's rights.' By Louisa Winkler, China Daily, 20th July 2005.

[1397] 'Women's Employment.' All China Women's Federation, 28th September 2006. See www.womenofchina.cn.

[1398] 'A lack of morals leads to sexual harassment.' By Xiong Lei, China Daily, 8th March 2006.

[1399] See '600,000 Beijingers suffer depression,' Xinhua, 5th September 2005 and 'The yin and yang of a harmonious society,' China Daily, 8th March 2005.

[1400] 'CPPCC Member Calls for Law to Curb Family Violence.' People's Daily, 4th March 2002.

[1401] 'Pulling no punches against domestic abuse.' By Wang Ying, China Daily, 25th November 2008.

[1402] 'Bigamy, Domestic Violence Should Be Punished: Survey.' People's Daily, 3rd August 2000.

[1403] 'Anti-domestic violence drive needs legal support.' China Daily, 23rd August 2005.

[1404] 'Woman Lawmaker Condemns Family Violence, Extramarital Affairs.' People's Daily, 8th March 2001.

[1405] 'Law Revised to Protect Women's Rights.' By Rong Jiaojiao 20th September 2005. See www.chinese-embassy.org.uk

[1406] 'First sexual harassment case gets 5 months' jail.' China Daily, 24th July 2008.

[1407] 'Welcome draft law on an important subject.' By Li Xing, China Daily, 14th October 2009.

[1408] 'Action demanded to stop violence against women.' China Daily, 28th November 2006.

490

[1409] See 'Chinese lawmaker calls for legislation against domestic violence,' People's Daily, 6th March 2006, and 'Marriage Law to Better Protect Women, Children' People's Daily, 1st May 2001.

[1410] 'Chinese lawmaker calls for legislation against domestic violence.' Xinhua, 6th March 2006.

[1411] 'Marital Problems, Domestic Abuse Plague China's Women.' People's Daily, 9th March 2003.

[1412] 'Chinese women: no longer silenced lambs of domestic violence.' Xinhua, 10th August 2004.

[1413] 'Sexual Harassment Needs More Attention in China.' People's Daily, 25th July 2000.

[1414] '71% of Chinese women sexually harassed?' Shanghai Star, 31st March 2005.

[1415] 'Sexual harassment against women outlawed.' Xinhua, 29th August 2005.

[1416] 'City's 1st sex harassment case heard.' People's Daily, 7th November 2003.

[1417] 'Protect women from sexual harassment.' China Daily, Hong Kong edition, 11th November 2003.

[1418] 'A lack of morals leads to sexual harassment.' By Xiong Lei, China Daily, 8th March 2006.

[1419] 'Xi'an worker files first sexual harassment suit.' China Daily, 31st January 2007.

[1420] 'Shanghai defines sexual harassment, offers protection.' Xinhua, 27th April 2007.

[1421] 'Sexy clothes blamed for sexual harassment.' By Miao Qing, China Daily, 7th September 2006.

[1422] 'Youth sex abuse must be tackled.' Beijing Today / China Daily, 12th April 2004.

[1423] 'Sexual abuse in minors is 'prominent': Expert.' By Zhang Yan, China Daily, 20th November 2009.

[1424] 'Juveniles taught how to fend off sexual harassment.' Xinhua, 8th March 2007.

[1425] 'China grapples with legacy of its missing girls.' China Daily via agencies, 15th September 2004.

[1426] 'Anti-domestic violence drive needs legal support.' China Daily, 23rd August 2005.

[1427] 'More and more women saying no to abusers.' By Wang Ying, China Daily, 3rd March 2004.

[1428] 'Ten best men as seen by women.' China Daily, 19th January 2007.

[1429] 'China won't change retirement age.' Xinhua, 16th December 2005.

[1430] 'Retirement age to rise for women.' By Xie Chuanjiao, China Daily, 4th December 2008.

[1431] 'White-collar women keep marriage on top of mind.' China Daily, 5th March 2007.

Reason Number 50. The Long March of Truth

[1432] 'Saturday Profile: Party Elder Still Jousts with China's Censors.' By Sharon LaFraniere and Jonathan Ansfield. The New York Times, 16th October 2009.
[1433] Her full name is Tsering Woeser, but she uses the single name Woeser. The Chinese version of her name is Cheng Wensa. Her blog, in Chinese, is at http://woeser.middle-way.net/
[1434] 'In China, a Headless Mao is a Game of Cat and Mouse.' By Jimmy Wang, The New York Times, October 6th 2009.

David Marriott

After studying literature to graduate level in the UK, David Marriott decided to strike out in a new direction - China. In 1999, he began to work with Shanghai Daily, a newspaper that was then in the process of being launched.

Marriott attempted to inject the traditions of the Western press into the fledgling journal. But working with young Chinese journalists, he observed a pattern that he was to see repeated many times, and one that continues today – the potential of the younger generation's talent being squandered and belittled by the intransigence and inflexibility of the older generation.

Marriott spent two and a half years at Shanghai Daily before moving on to a career in teaching and writing, bringing him into further contact with a wide cross-section of Chinese people.

In 2006, he began to write the 'ChinaBounder' blog, which drew blistering attacks from Chinese nationalists, and then gained international attention.

Using the desire of the Chinese media to pursue salacious stories, Marriott's use of disinformation and half-truths allowed him to avoid being unmasked and possibly physically attacked.

In 2008, as a result of his political writing activities, he was arrested by Shanghai police, questioned for 24 hours, and then given an hour to pack a bag before being deported to Hong Kong.

He hopes to be able to return to China one day, but given the communist regime's inability to accept any form of criticism, Marriott does not expect this to happen any time soon.

In addition to a continuing interest in Chinese literature, Marriott is a keen student of the Chinese language and the nation's history, and enjoys collecting Chinese antiques. His penchant for a glass of fine wine keeps at least one foot in Europe.

"China's young generation need to find their voice and raise it loud" he says. "They need to understand that criticizing their own country is the truest form of patriotism. Only when this happens will China ever be able to meaningfully change."

David Marriott dedicates this book to his father, a man who understands the value of truthful words in today's overly commercial media, and to his mother, who taught him the importance of following his own path.

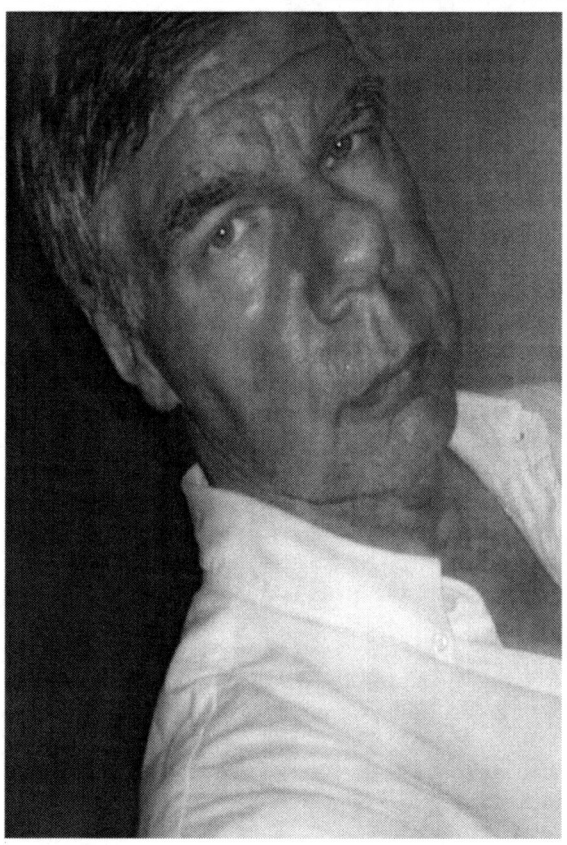

Karl Lacroix

Karl Lacroix's arrival in China in the summer of 1992 was for him a dream come true. Initiated as a young boy with the spirit of travel adventure, Karl found the warm and muggy August night air of Shanghai intoxicating. At first breath he hoped China would fulfill his need for a 'new' land and the element of philosophical promise.

Karl's father, serving in the Canadian army, moved his family across oceans and continents as his soldier's duty called, instilling Karl's youth with wanderlust that only Asia has really satiated. An English-born mother and an American-born father gave birth to a sense of bicultural internationalism that formed Karl's character and directed his future lifestyle.

495

Writing came to Karl at an early age, as a cub reporter for a local city newspaper in Ontario, Canada. Words became important, not because they were rewarded, but because they could receive a profound reaction if written well and boldly.

In the early nineties, China indeed was the new 'promised land' for many Western adventurers. For Karl, the search for that special but elusive promise lasted from 1992 until 2008.

Now in his early 60s, Karl's powers of observation, combined with a liberal viewpoint, have directed him to voice his 'protest' over China's failure to seek a higher calling than that of just being the largest consumer market in the history of the world. The reality that there never was the kind of promise within China that great countries exude has long left its mark on many truth seekers.

"China needs to envision the world's benefit from a free and democratic Chinese people. Great countries have a duty to the world to do great things. China should be no less than the greatest democracy, the greatest country, with the greatest future for the benefit of all mankind."

"The blockades to China's greatness have been fashioned first by blindness, then by the Party. This book deals with the blindness. It's the Chinese people who must deal with the Communist Party."

He dedicates this book to his son, Conor (born of two worlds) in the hope that one day he will understand.

CPSIA information can be obtained at www.ICGtesting.com
Printed in the USA
LVOW011808080112

262908LV00020B/237/P